A Cognitive Psychology of Mass Communication

In a constantly changing media landscape, *A Cognitive Psychology of Mass Communication* is the go-to text for any course that examines mass communication from a psychological perspective.

Now in its seventh edition, the book continues its exploration of how our experiences with media affect the way we acquire and process knowledge about the world and how this knowledge influences our attitudes and behavior. Updates include end-of-chapter suggestions for further reading, new research and examples for a more global perspective, as well as an added emphasis on the power of social media in affecting our perceptions of reality and ourselves.

While including real-world examples, the book also integrates psychology and communication theory along with reviews of the most up-to-date research. The text covers a diversity of media forms and issues, ranging from commonly discussed topics such as politics, sex, and violence, to lesser-studied topics, such as emotions and prosocial media.

The accompanying companion website also includes resources for both instructors and students.

For students:

● Chapter outlines, summaries, and review questions
● Useful links

For instructors:

● Guidelines for in-class discussions
● Sample syllabus

Readers will be challenged to become more sensitized and to think more deeply about their own media use as they explore research on behavior and media effects. Written in an engaging, readable style, the text is appropriate for graduate or undergraduate audiences.

Fred W. Sanborn is Professor of Psychology at North Carolina Wesleyan College, where he teaches a wide range of psychology courses. He is also the founding director of the NCWC's Teaching and Learning Center and the assistant director of the Honors Program.

Richard Jackson Harris is Professor Emeritus of Psychological Sciences at Kansas State University in Manhattan, KS, where he worked from 1974 until his retirement in 2016.

A Cognitive Psychology of Mass Communication

Seventh Edition

**Fred W. Sanborn and
Richard Jackson Harris**

Routledge
Taylor & Francis Group

NEW YORK AND LONDON

Seventh edition published 2019
by Routledge
52 Vanderbilt Avenue, New York, NY 10017

and by Routledge
2 Park Square, Milton Park, Abingdon, Oxon, OX14 4RN

Routledge is an imprint of the Taylor & Francis Group, an informa business

First edition published by Lawrence Erlbaum Associates Inc 1989
Sixth edition published by Routledge 2014

British Library Cataloguing-in-Publication Data
A catalogue record for this book is available from the British Library

Library of Congress Cataloging-in-Publication Data
A catalog record has been requested for this book

ISBN: 978-1-138-04626-9 (hbk)
ISBN: 978-1-138-04627-6 (pbk)
ISBN: 978-1-315-17149-4 (ebk)

Typeset in Minion-Regular
by Out of House Publishing

Visit the companion website: www.routledge.com/cw/harris

(Fred) To my husband and partner, Tony Hefner, who is also my favorite media consumption partner. Thank you for listening, advising, and calming through all aspects of writing this book—and through all aspects of life.

(Richard) To my wife Caprice Becker and children: Clint (born 1989), Natalie (born 1991), and Grady (born 1991), who have taught me so much about what is really important in life. Watching them grow up in a world of rapidly changing media has provided much food for thought which has affected the words on these pages in so many ways.

Contents

List of Illustrations   viii

Preface   ix

A Note from Fred W. Sanborn   xii

A Note from Richard Jackson Harris   xiii

About the Authors   xv

1   Mass Communication in Our Digital Society: The Changing Media Landscape   1

2   Research and Theory in Mass Communication: How Are Media Studied Scientifically?   24

3   The Psychology of Mass Communication: Thinking about Our Media Use   45

4   Emotions and Media: Music and Sports as Exemplars   62

5   Media Portrayals of Groups: Distorted Social Mirrors   92

6   Advertising: Baiting, Catching, and Reeling Us In   142

7   News: Setting an Agenda about the World   184

8   Politics: Using News and Advertising to Win Elections   231

9   Violence: Media Mayhem Matters   268

10 Sex: Is Tuning In Turning Us On? Sexuality through a Media Lens   306

11 Socially Positive Media: Teaching Good Things to Children (and the Rest of Us)   339

Note   374

References   375

Index   473

Illustrations

Table

5.1   Percentage of ethnic group members in U.S. population and as represented
      in TV and film   116

Figure

9.1   Desensitization as classical conditioning   281

Preface

Today's traditional college-age students, born in the 1990s or 2000s, have no memory of life before the Internet. In their minds there has always been the capability to post videos online or keep track of their favorite celebrity on social media. Photographs, videos, or information about almost anything have always been instantly available. They can't remember arranging social gatherings without Facebook or text messages. E-mail is so last generation, and calling on a phone tethered by a cord when you can't even text is almost unimaginable. They are as likely to watch a TV show on their computer, phone, or tablet as on a TV set. The world of media, and by extension entertainment and popular culture, has changed immensely in the last few decades.

Yet, in a broader perspective, such a communications revolution is not entirely unprecedented. Still photography and telegraphy were transformative in the 1840s, telephones a few decades later, and cinema starting around 1896 radically transformed the way people saw the world and communicated with each other. In the last hundred years or so, radio in the decade of the 1920s, television in the 1950s, video technology in the 1980s, the Internet in the 1990s, and social media in the 2000s also transformed our lives within a mere decade in each case.

A popular movie some years ago, *The Truman Show*, featured Jim Carrey as a man whose entire life had been a television show, filmed nonstop under a huge bubble that was his whole world. His eventual discovery of this situation is personally devastating, and Truman knows he can never be the same again. In a sense he is an exaggerated but apt metaphor for this entire book. Our lives, and all that we know, are far more heavily influenced by the media than most of us realize, even if our whole lives are not completely reducible to a reality TV show. Although by reading this book you will not, like Truman, find out that you have no identity except as an entertainment figure, you may discover that a surprising amount of what you know and how you behave is a direct product of your interaction with television, radio, print, and computer-mediated communications. In any event, you will probably never look at media the same way again! At least that is our hope.

Some real people are almost as much media creations as Carrey's Truman. In recent years there have been certain individuals who have received extensive media coverage more because they were celebrities than because of any artistic, athletic, or other accomplishments. Think of the Kardashians or the latest "social media influencer." Maybe even think of President Donald Trump. Well-known people become part of our consciousness, even if we never meet them in person. People around the world cried over the deaths of Britain's Princess Diana in 1997, Michael Jackson in 2009, and Prince in 2016. Those were not fake tears; the loss was real. These deaths were a true personal loss for millions of people who had only known them as friends through the media.

Sometimes the media and reality become intertwined in odd ways. A few years back the Westport Dry Cleaners in Manhattan, Kansas, was suddenly inundated with calls asking for "God" and delivering prayer requests. Why? The business happened to have the same phone number as the "God" character in the recently released movie *Bruce Almighty*. Similar telephone encounters were reported in Florida, South Carolina, Colorado, and Arkansas. Didn't those callers know that it wasn't really God's telephone number? Maybe, but if they only meant to harass or play a joke, why not call any number and ask for God? Why this particular number? And why leave prayer requests?

This is the seventh edition of this text and much has necessarily changed since its inception. Seldom does the content of a textbook become obsolete so fast as when it deals with the media.

Probably the major change overall in this edition has been the addition of much new material on computer-mediated communication, especially social media and the Internet. This has also necessitated an extensive discussion of fake news, which is intricately linked with social media. As recently as 2003, Facebook, YouTube, and cell phones with Internet capabilities did not even exist. Indeed, the whole media landscape has radically changed in the last ten years. We always shudder to think how much it will change in the next five and how obsolete and inadequate the words we have just written will be by the time you read this book.

Although we have updated examples and research throughout, we have also consciously tried to avoid the pitfall of creating an entirely ahistorical work. We are firm believers that we can only understand the present and the future by understanding the past, so we have retained some particularly cogent and informative historical examples. If you don't understand some of these, ask your parents, grandparents, or professors for more information. They will remember and will be glad to tell you about them.

Beyond the obvious updating, we have reorganized some material within this edition. Instead of the 12 chapters in the last edition, we now have 11. In addition, at the end of each chapter there is a now a section of very applied information specific to that chapter's topic, some of which you may be able to use in your own everyday approach to media. We are calling the new sections Media Applications. There is also a new chapter (Chapter 4, replacing the previous Chapter 6) specifically devoted to our emotional experiences as they relate to media. We use media coverage of sports and music as exemplars of how emotion and mass communication are intertwined.

Some chapters have some extensive new sections. Chapter 3 has added information about cognitive processes we use when consuming media (especially social media) such as multitasking, change blindness, and inattentional blindness. Chapter 4 has an additional discussion of media depictions of people of faith. Perhaps the biggest change from the previous edition to this one appears in Chapter 7, where there is an extensive new section on fake news. We discuss why fake news emerged, how it is created, who is attracted to fake news, and what can be done about it. As with many of the updates of this edition, there is also discussion of how social media are intertwined with media news. Social media are also discussed in the chapter on politics (Chapter 8) as are the associated effects on the 2016 U.S. presidential election and the media challenges associated with covering an unconventional politician like President Trump. Chapter 9 has increased coverage of video game violence. Chapter 10 has added information about sexting. Finally, Chapter 11 has an additional section on newer research investigating the positive psychological meaning behind consuming some forms of media.

A large percentage of the references in this edition are from the second decade of the twenty-first century, a strong testimony to the impressive volume of quality research currently being done on media issues. In this process we have to continually remind ourselves that we cannot read and include everything that has been written on the subject of media. If we have omitted some of your favorites, forgive us; the amount of research and scholarly literature on the media is staggering.

Although overall the book has a cognitive perspective, we think you will find the book quite eclectic theoretically, as we believe it needs to be. Chapter 2 reviews the major theories that have been used to study mass communication, and these are all referred to throughout the text. We believe that each has something of value to offer, most of them being more useful in some areas than others. We would also argue that most theories of media effects have a strong cognitive component, which we have tried to highlight on these pages.

Our hope is that you enjoy reading this book as much as we have enjoyed writing it. We hope it will be a source of both great pleasure and much learning. It will amuse you in places and probably disturb you in others, but we hope it will always be interesting and relevant to your life. Students and teachers, please send us your comments. You can reach us by e-mail at rjharris@k-state.edu or fwsanborn@ncwc.edu. Your reactions are always helpful in improving the book in future editions. Also, please feel free to send us interesting examples to illustrate the principles discussed; maybe we can use them in the next edition.

A Note from Fred W. Sanborn

I must admit that I didn't know much about the study of mass communication and psychology until I was assigned to be Richard Harris's teaching assistant early in my graduate school career. I had signed on to graduate school at Kansas State University to study Social and Developmental Psychology, which I loved and still do. However, when I learned that I could also study psychology in relation to media, which had fascinated, provoked, and entertained me my entire life, I was smitten. Like many others, media have been a large part of my life since I was very young. As a child, television in particular was a window on the world for me, allowing for "encounters" beyond my own narrow set of experiences. Even now, when seeing something new in person, I sometimes catch myself thinking, "It's just like on TV!" Somewhere along the line in my experience with mass communication, I realized that media were indeed creating a reality for me and others. Understanding this "reality" is the focus of this book and the work that Richard Harris and I have done in writing it.

I moved on from being Richard's teaching assistant to eventually conducting research in the area of psychology and mass communication and teaching my own classes on the topic. When I received an appointment at North Carolina Wesleyan College in 2004, I found that Psychology of Mass Communication blended beautifully with the Psychology Department's senior capstone course because it integrated many areas of psychology (cognitive, social, developmental, among others) and had the added benefit of engaging students in a topic that affected their lives every day. I now teach a standalone course in media psychology, which necessarily changes each time it is taught.

I thank especially Richard Harris who has nurtured my scholarship in so many ways. Through the years, he has provided me with an excellent model of a teacher, researcher, writer, colleague, and friend. I also am tremendously grateful for him allowing me to contribute to his many years of work on this book with this latest edition. I have tried not to disappoint him or the readers. I also thank my parents, John and Lyna Sanborn, for being my first media teachers. Thanks also go to my husband, Tony Hefner, for his support and encouragement as I worked on this book. Finally, I would like to thank all of the many students who have taken my Psychology of Mass Communication or Senior Seminar in Psychology/Media Psychology course since 1999. You have contributed in countless ways to my passion for this topic and desire to better understand it. A special thanks goes to Joseph Lloyd, who helped tremendously with the reference section of this edition.

A Note from Richard Jackson Harris

The first edition of this book appeared in 1989 and initially evolved from my development of the course "The Psychology of Mass Communication" at Kansas State University in the early 1980s. I am grateful to the students in this class over the years for their enthusiasm, inspiration, and challenge; their ideas and dialogue with the material have constructively affected each edition of the book. More and more I have become convinced that the area of mass communication is a wonderful area in which to apply theory and research methodology from experimental psychology. Media research deals with some of the major activities that occupy our time and addresses problems that people are vitally interested in, such as sex and violence, values in media, and images of different groups. Trained in the 1970s at the University of Illinois at Urbana-Champaign as a rigorous experimental psychologist with an emphasis in studying language, I became interested in applying what I knew about text processing to study the sort of language that people encounter every day. Some research I conducted on the cognition of deceptive advertising starting in the late 1970s first challenged me to start thinking seriously and more broadly about mass media consumption as information processing. Through this work the cognitive perspectives on the media came to influence my thinking.

When it became time to add a co-author for this current edition, Fred Sanborn was a natural choice. Fred, Professor of Psychology at North Carolina Wesleyan College in Rocky Mount, NC, earned his Ph.D. in Social and Developmental Psychology from Kansas State University in 2004. During this time he assisted me with the Psychology of Mass Communication course, first as a TA and later teaching the class on his own, something he has continued to do at NCWC. From his first assignment as a TA for the course, Fred showed an amazing love both for the material and for the process of effectively teaching it to students. He has gone on to have a distinguished career as a teacher and is the founding director of the Teaching and Learning Center at NCWC.

The support of the Psychology Department at Kansas State University and the editors, first at Lawrence Erlbaum Associates and later at Routledge Taylor and Francis during the writing of all seven editions has been tremendous. I also greatly appreciate the Fulbright Visiting Lectureships I held in Belo Horizonte, Brazil in 1982 and Montevideo, Uruguay in 1994, and the Visiting Scholar position at Massey University in Palmerston North, New Zealand in 2005; these experiences gave me an internationalist perspective for which I am immensely grateful and that I have tried to bring to each edition of this book. Contemporary media are part of an international culture. Although this book disproportionately relies on U.S. media, since that is what we know best and that is what has been studied the most, the principles are equally applicable elsewhere, as we try to suggest with frequent examples from other nations' media.

Although countless present and former students have influenced the ideas on these pages, particular thanks are due to Steven Hoekstra, Jennifer Bonds-Raacke, Elizabeth

Cady, John Raacke, Christy Scott, Jason Brandenburg, J. Andrew Karafa, Christopher Barlett, John Berger, Rebecca Schlegel, Lindsay Firebaugh, J. Bret Knappenberger, Sherry Wright, Christopher Rodeheffer, John Smyers, Jeff Hyder, Jorge Piocuda, Tuan Tran, Lindsay Cook, Natalie Barlett, Brynne Glynn, Kyle Bures, Michael Hinkin, Andrew Fiori, Abby Werth, Chelsea Bartel, Sawyer Borror, Kelsey Koblitz, Cindy Cook, Sara Smith, Maureen Pierce, Kristin Bruno, Morgan Pearn, Julia Pounds, Tony Dubitsky, Michael Klassen, John Bechtold, Ruth Sturm, and Rachel Peeples for their helpful reactions and conversations over the years about this material.

Also, I would like to thank my parents the late Dick and Helen Harris for modeling incredibly effective media use in my home of origin long before people were talking much about media literacy. For a long time I used to assume everyone grew up with the kind of positive media environment I knew. Our family media use was often quality family time. My own media literacy training started early with my parents questioning what they saw on television and encouraging me to do the same. Many conversations around the television or the evening newspaper provided some intellectual seeds that bear some fruit in this book. I remember them commenting on negative values, unfair stereotyping, and excessive violence from my earliest days of watching TV. Although TV was a part of our household, so were print media, whose use my parents faithfully modeled.

About the Authors

Fred W. Sanborn is Professor of Psychology at North Carolina Wesleyan College, where he teaches a wide range of psychology courses. He is also the founding director of the NCWC's Teaching and Learning Center and the assistant director of the Honors Program. Fred received his B.A. in Psychology and Psychological Service at Kansas Wesleyan University in 1996. He also earned an M.S. (2000), and a Ph.D. (2004) in Social and Developmental Psychology from Kansas State University. Like you, Fred consumes media every day!

Richard Jackson Harris is Professor Emeritus of Psychological Sciences at Kansas State University in Manhattan KS, where he worked from 1974 until his retirement in 2016. Growing up in suburban Pittsburgh, PA, he earned a B.A. at the College of Wooster in Wooster, OH and an M.A. and Ph.D. in Cognitive Psychology at the University of Illinois at Urbana-Champaign IL. He is the author of over 100 published research articles on memory and comprehension of verbal material in media and elsewhere, as well as a textbook *Learning and Cognition* (with Thomas Leahey) and some edited volumes of research papers.

Chapter 1

Mass Communication in Our Digital Society

The Changing Media Landscape

Q: Why did TV viewers in 2013 see images of the White House surrounded by terrorists accompanied by emergency alert audio stating, "this is not a test"?

A: Viewers were seeing a commercial for the film *Olympus has Fallen*. The ad was so similar to a real Emergency Alert System warning that the Federal Communications Commission leveled millions of dollars' worth of fines against broadcasters such as NBCUniversal, Viacom, and ESPN who aired the ad (Wyatt, 2014).

Q: How much material is on the World Wide Web?

A: No one quite knows for sure. One 2017 estimate indicated that there were at least 4.8 billion indexed web pages, a number which excludes much of the activity on social media apps such as Twitter and Facebook ("The Size," 2017). In fact, the growth of the web has been so rapid that the number of available web addresses dwindled from more than one billion in 2006 to 117 million in 2010, forcing a new Internet protocol addressing system to be developed (Worthen & Tuna, 2011).

Q: How have mobile phones revolutionized developing countries?

A: Developing countries with poor infrastructure have found mobile phones much more reliable and attractive than traditional, wired phones and Internet service. In numerous countries like Botswana, Rwanda, Ivory Coast, Paraguay, and Venezuela, mobile phone users outnumbered conventional phone users by 2000 (Romero, 2000). In 2016, one study (Manyika, Lund, Singer, White, & Berry, 2016) estimated that 80% of people in developing countries had access to mobile phones, and many of them were using apps on those devices as a means to pay for goods and services. One such app, M-Pesa, has taken the place of cash and traditional banking services for many in the developing world.

In 1969, a young news reporter from the British Broadcasting Corporation (BBC) was sent to cover the Vietnam War. Not being very experienced or knowledgeable about what he was observing, he led off his first televised report of an American attack on a Vietcong stronghold with, "My God! It's just like watching television" (Bogart, 1980).

In 2001, 13-year-old Jason Lind of Torrington, CT, was hospitalized with second- and third-degree burns after he and a friend poured gasoline on his feet and legs and set him on fire, in imitation of a stunt seen on MTV's popular show *Jackass*.

In the wake of the 2016 U.S. presidential election, Edgar M. Welch of Salisbury, NC, drove 350 miles to a pizza restaurant in Washington, DC. Once there, he fired an assault rifle. Although he didn't hit anyone, Welch said he was taking it upon himself to investigate a child sex-slave ring allegedly connected to Hillary Clinton. Welch believed this false conspiracy as a result of fake news stories that were circulating on social media sites like Facebook, Twitter, and Instagram. "I just wanted to do some good and went about it the wrong way," Welch later said (Goldman, 2016, ¶2).

In different ways, these examples suggest the main theme of this book: that our experience with media is a major way that we acquire knowledge about the world. How we act on this knowledge then has consequences in terms of attitudes and behavior. We may call this a cognitive approach to mass communication because the emphasis is on the way that our minds create knowledge, a mental reality, about the world constructed from our experience with the media. This mental reality then becomes the basis for developing our attitudes and motivating our behaviors and thus has a great impact on our lives. Instead of the media being a more or less accurate reflection of some external reality, it has become the reality against which the real world is compared. The media view of the world has become, in many cases, more real than the real world itself!

Prevalence of Mass Communication

Mass communication in the form of print media has been with us almost since Gutenberg's invention of movable type and the printing press in 1456. However, the nature of mass communication, indeed of life in general, was radically changed in the twentieth century by the rapid penetration of electronic media, starting with radio in the 1920s, followed by television in the 1950s, video and cable technology in the 1980s, the Internet in the 1990s, and social media since 2000. Television in particular has transformed the day-to-day life of more people in the last 60 or 70 years than has perhaps any invention in human history. Radio and print media have been greatly changed, though by no means replaced, by TV as well. Computer-mediated communications are well on their way (if not already there) in eclipsing television in transforming society.

Americans spend more time watching television than doing anything else except working and sleeping, though Internet use is catching up fast, especially among youth (Bureau of Labor Statistics, 2015; Kaiser Family Foundation, 2010; Nielsen Company, 2016). The lines between Internet and television are also increasingly blurred, with many receiving a large portion of their television content via online streaming services. Nevertheless, every week residents of the United States spend about 15–30 of their average 39 hours of free time in front of a screen watching television content, making TV by far the most popular leisure activity (Bureau of Labor Statistics, 2015; Nielsen Company, 2016; Roberts, 2000). All other sources of leisure, such as spending time with friends, helping others, reading books, playing sports, and taking vacations, lag far behind. Besides changing the way we spend our time, media have also revolutionized the way we think and the way we view the world. The Internet and its various computer-mediated communication modes are currently revolutionizing our lives. The many effects of media on our perception and our cognition are particular emphases of this book. The media are not only the magic windows through which we view the world, but also the doors through which ideas enter our minds as we interact with them.

Media are far more than mere conduits of knowledge, although that role is not a trivial one. We have come a long way from Gutenberg to the millions of newspapers, magazines, television channels, radio stations, and websites in the world today. To prepare to look at the effects of all of this, in this chapter we introduce the concept of mass communication and look at our use of the media from a cognitive psychological perspective.

Today no place on earth is beyond the reach of mass media. For political reasons South Africa was for a long time the last large nation without TV, holding out until 1976 (Mutz, Roberts, & van Vuuren, 1993). The remote island nations of Cook Islands (1989), Fiji (1995), and St. Helena (1995) were among the last nations to welcome TV and the Internet (Wheeler, 2001), and the isolated mountainous Himalayan kingdom of Bhutan may have been the very last to receive television and the Internet, finally becoming wired to both in 1999.

In the 1970s, a unique study was done in Canada to assess the effects of the introduction of television. Three towns in interior eastern British Columbia were very similar except for the fact that one ("Multitel") received several Canadian and U.S. TV channels, another ("Unitel") received only one channel, and the third, because of its particular isolated valley location, received no television signals ("Notel"). This study compared children and adults in the three towns before and after television was finally introduced to Notel. For example, children's creativity scores were higher before TV in Notel than in either (1) the other towns before TV or (2) any of the three towns after TV. See Macbeth (1996) for a summary of the findings and Williams (1986) for a collection of papers reporting the results of this research in more detail. For a similar though more recent examination in a smaller place, see Charlton, Gunter, and Hannan (2002) for a study of the effects of the introduction of television to the remote South Atlantic island of St. Helena in 1995. These will probably be the last studies of that sort which can ever be done because no such TV-less (or Internet-less) places still exist.

What Is Mass Communication?

What makes mass communication "mass"? First, unlike interpersonal communication, the audience of mass communication is large and anonymous, and often very heterogeneous (Wright, 1986). Groups of individuals can be targeted, but only with limited precision. Second, large audiences are pursued using a linear process by which communication sources (like a TV network) originate a message that is then communicated to masses of people (like a TV audience) (DeFleur, 2010). Third, communication sources are institutional and organizational (Wright, 1986). Some communication sources such as television networks, movie studios, newspaper chains, wire services, or the conglomerates that own such businesses (and their accompanying websites), are among the largest and wealthiest private corporations. Fourth, and perhaps most importantly, the basic economic function of most media in most nations is to attract and hold as large an audience as possible for the advertisers (Wright, 1986). In one way or another, advertising pays a very high percentage of the costs of newspapers, magazines, local TV and radio stations, television networks and cable channels, and the

Internet. Even public television and government-subsidized networks like the Public Broadcasting Service (PBS), Canadian Broadcasting Corporation (CBC), or the British Broadcasting Corporation (BBC) are increasingly dependent on commercial revenues. For a discussion of the differences between interpersonal communication, mass communication, and mediated communication, see Close-up 1.1.

❖ CLOSE-UP 1.1 THE BLURRY LINES OF MODERN COMMUNICATION: INTERPERSONAL, MASS, OR MEDIATED MESSAGES?

As discussed elsewhere in this chapter, one of the goals of mass communication is to reach a large audience. In contrast, interpersonal communication has traditionally been thought of as communication between two people, like friends having a conversation (Perloff, 2015a), or sometimes as between one person communicating to a group, like a professor delivering an interactive lecture to a class; the key to interpersonal communication seems to be interaction. In addition, interpersonal communication has been customarily thought of as taking place face-to-face. But what about celebrities who have huge social media followings like Katy Perry with almost 100 million Twitter followers in 2017 (Twitter, 2017)? Or politicians like Barack Obama and Donald Trump, who also have tens of millions who follow their every tweet? Such individuals frequently use their social media platforms to reach a vast audience. In fact, that is often the point, as when Beyoncé chose Instagram to announce her new album in 2013 (Sisario, 2013) and her pregnancy in 2017 (Coscarelli, 2017), knowing that the messages would get lots of buzz, including coverage by more traditional media outlets.

In a thoughtful examination of the intersection of old and new media forms, Perloff (2015a) argues that interpersonal communication *now may include one person using social media to deliver a message to others, if there is some interaction among individuals*. Mass communication, then, can be thought of as when messages emanate from traditional organizations (such as cable news channels) that have established avenues for reaching a large audience. Finally, mediated communication involves "...any social or technological procedure or device that is used for the selection, transmission, and reception of information" (Altheide, 2013, as cited in Perloff, 2015a). This kind of communication would include most, if not all, forms of social media (which might also be considered interpersonal mediated communication if social interaction occurs). Confused? So are some scholars. Perloff also points out that not all communication researchers agree on such distinctions and that things get increasingly cloudy when one considers that a great deal of mediated communication (i.e., social media) includes information that originates with mass communication outlets (i.e., reports from traditional sources such as newspapers, cable news channels, and TV networks).

Despite some within the industry espousing high-sounding rhetoric about serving the public, the bottom line of commercial mass media is money, which comes from advertisers at rates directly determined by the audience size and composition. The size of the audience in turn determines the content. Thus, there is tremendous pressure for media to be as entertaining as possible to as many people as possible. This imperative to entertain also holds for non-entertainment content like news, sports, or advertising. All of this is not to say that editors and programmers are not concerned about responsibly meeting the needs of the public. In many cases, they are, but such needs must necessarily be considered within the constraints of the economic realities of the media industry. If there is no audience, there is no money to support even the best programming. This is true at both the national and local levels, with local media outlets often as concerned as, or more so than, national sources about ratings, circulation, and the number of Internet "hits."

Often, economic pressures, and sometimes political and ideological ones as well, influence the content of media. For example, magazines that accept tobacco advertisements print fewer stories about the health risks of smoking than those that have no cigarette ads (Lee & Solomon, 1991; Strasburger & Wilson, 2002). Similarly, the ABC television network, which is owned by Disney, has killed news stories reflecting negatively on Disney theme parks (Steyer, 2002). Indeed, with more and more media mergers (as when cable company Comcast purchased broadcast company NBC, which had previously purchased movie company Universal Studios), it has become increasingly difficult for media consumers to know how the corporate sources of their media may (or may not) be influencing media content.

Incidentally, media content standards change: 60 years ago we did not hear the words "damn," "hell," or even "pregnant," although we might have heard "nigger," "wetback," "jap," and other highly inflammatory ethnic slurs in the early days of radio or TV. Real or feared reaction from advertisers is another subtle source of self-censorship. Television networks and stations are loath to risk offending those who pay the bills for their livelihood. Advertisers occasionally threaten to withdraw their ads in protest. In 1979 General Electric was unhappy with ABC's Barbara Walters's plans to interview Jane Fonda about her antinuclear activism and pulled their ads in protest. However, ABC still aired the interview. Advertisers with many products to sell (and accompanying ad budgets) may hold influence that many of us don't realize. According to Gloria Steinem, co-founder of *Ms.* magazine, Procter and Gamble (maker of many, many familiar household consumer products) even issued an edict to publishers of women's magazines that "its products were not to be placed in any issue that included any material on gun control, abortion, the occult, cults, or the disparagement of religion" (Steinem, 1990, p. 26).

Concern over public reaction may be another source of self-censorship. All but one U.S. commercial network once refused to run an anti-smoking public service announcement (PSA) that showed a fetus smoking a cigarette in the womb. In 2005 all U.S. networks but the History Channel refused to run a PSA by the United Nations Mine Agency, which showed suburban school girls playing soccer when a landmine suddenly blows up, followed by screaming and a man carrying his daughter's lifeless body, and then a dark screen with the words "If there were land mines here, would you stand for them anywhere?" (Huus, 2005).

In addition to its mass nature, there is also "communication" in mass communication. In all communication there is a reciprocity that necessitates some kind of response from the audience. Even though the media user, especially the TV viewer, is often characterized as extremely passive, mindlessly absorbing the program content, such a picture is far from accurate. Although the meaning of a particular program certainly depends on the content of that program, it also depends on what is in the mind and experience of the viewer. A TV movie dealing with rape will have a very different effect on, indeed, a different meaning for, a viewer who has herself been a rape victim than for someone else with no such personal experience. A violent pornographic website may incite one man to sexual violence because of the way his mind interprets and interacts with the content of the video, whereas another man who sees the same video may be repulsed by it, showing no sexual arousal or antisocial behavioral response (see Close-up 1.2 for a discussion of movie ratings related to sex and violence).

❖ CLOSE-UP 1.2 THE MPAA RATINGS: DOES SEX OR VIOLENCE CARRY MORE WEIGHT?

Ever since their introduction in 1968, the Motion Picture Association of America's (MPAA) ratings for movies have been controversial. The ratings have usually been made by 10 to 13 people on a board called the Classification and Ratings Administration. Although the raters are said to be parents, their identities are typically kept secret. The chair is the only publicly known member, and he or she hires all the others (Dick, 2006). Over time, there have been some adjustments to the ratings categories, most notably the addition of the PG-13 category in 1984 and the replacement of the pornography-tainted label of X by NC-17 (no one under 17 admitted) in 1990. The ratings are made based on violence, sex, nudity, language, and thematic content, although the specific rating criteria have never been made public and are not always applied consistently. By 2000, over 60% of films submitted were rated R, almost none NC-17, and very few G. Sometimes a rating is negotiable; a studio will appeal an R rating or remove or edit an offending scene to obtain the PG-13 rating. The latter rating is often considered the commercially most desirable, since it neither excludes anyone nor has the "kiddie movie" stigma of G and even PG movies. There is widespread belief than many films that previously would have been R are now PG-13 and many PG films would have been PG-13 some years ago.

One specific continuing controversy concerns the relative weighting of the different factors, particularly sex and violence. Although the MPAA denies it, there is good reason to believe that sexual content and language carry greater weight than violence. Indeed, many PG and even G movies contain considerable amounts of violence, though a partial nudity scene may earn a film a PG-13 rating. Leone (2002) provided some empirical support for this by finding that scenes present in an NC-17 or unrated versions of a film but removed from the commercially released R-rated version were more sexually explicit and graphic than they were violently explicit and graphic. Four times as many films are rated NC-17 for sex than for violence (Dick, 2006) and the amount of violent content allowed in PG-13 rated movies appears to have grown over the past 15 years (Romer, Jamieson, & Jamieson, 2017).

In the final analysis, however, parents must use the movie ratings as part of their own parental mediation. It is important to look at not just the rating but what it is for (most DVD boxes, parental websites, and some film reviews give this information). There may be an occasional R-rated movie you would want your 12-year-old to see and some PG-13 movies you wouldn't want your older child to see.

For additional discussion of MPAA ratings related to sex and violence, see Chapters 9 and 10, *including a discussion of the era before these ratings in Close-up 10.1.*

The nature of the media consumption experience must also be considered. Watching television, going to the movies, or listening to the radio may be done alone or in small groups. Using the Internet or reading a magazine are typically, though not always, solo activities. The social situation of who else is watching, listening, or reading and how they react greatly affects the media consumption experience. Consider the difference between watching an exciting ball game alone, with a group of friends, or with a group rooting for the other team. Your enjoyment and the level of fear you feel while watching a horror film can be affected by whether someone who is watching with you shrieks in fun, cries in severe distress, laughs, or makes no obvious reaction at all (Zillmann & Weaver, 1996). In one study looking at anticipated enjoyment of watching different types of movies with different viewers, college students found watching a sexual R-rated movie with their parents was by far the most uncomfortable combination (Harris & Cook, 2011). Similarly, within families, television may either promote family harmony and interaction or be a divisive force, depending on how it is used (Bryant & Bryant, 2001).

The Media of Mass Communication

Through the years, various forms of media have emerged as technology has advanced in delivering mass communication. One distinction that is often made is print media (newspapers and magazines) versus electronic media (film, radio, television, Internet). Another classification is traditional (or "old," or "legacy") media such as newspapers, magazines, radio, and television versus "new media," which is online, on-demand, and interactive (Giobbi, 2014). Of course, these days such distinctions have become increasingly blurred, as when readers view a newspaper online and comment on an article or when television viewers live stream a show and comment on that program via Twitter.

Now let us turn to how various forms of media have been used for the purposes of mass communication and how we tend to use those media.

Newspapers

Arguably the earliest form of mass communication, newspapers, at least in a primitive form, began soon after the introduction of the printing press around 1450 (Giobbi, 2014). In the United States, the heyday of newspapers (in terms of prestige and revenue) was the mid to late twentieth century. However, the circulation of daily newspapers in the United States has been falling for many years, down from 62.3 million in 1990 to 46.2 million in 2010 (Pew Research Center, 2011). Since then, circulation has continued to drop on average 2–3% per year (Pew Research Center, 2016). However, newspapers have seen growth in online readership, particularly with those who read content on mobile devices (Pew Research Center, 2016). Still, newspapers have also taken a hit in the past decade with decreased advertising revenue. This is especially true of the once-lucrative classified advertising market, which has largely moved online with free website services such as Craigslist. This decreased revenue has resulted in fewer and fewer newspaper employees industry-wide (Pew Research Center, 2016).

More than television or magazines, newspapers have a local identity and are the preeminent source for local news, advertising, and sports. In fact, sports sections tend to be the most read parts of newspapers. Even as the number of dailies continues to fall, the number of weekly newspapers keeps growing. Indeed, the largest decreases in circulation in the past few years have been primarily in big city daily papers (Pew Research Center, 2011, 2016), some of which (e.g., *Detroit Free Press*, *New Orleans Times-Picayune*) began curtailing their print editions. In the United States, newspapers are almost totally regional, with the important exceptions of *The New York Times*, *The Wall Street Journal*, and *USA Today*, although large national papers are the rule in many nations (e.g., *Guardian* or *The Times* in the United Kingdom, *Le Monde* in France). In spite of their regional nature, newspapers are becoming increasingly similar, a trend attributable to a consolidation of media ownership to fewer and fewer sources and especially to an increasing reliance by most newspapers on a few international wire services like Associated Press (AP), Reuters, and Agence France Presse (AFP) as news sources.

Demographically, groups who read more newspapers are generally those who watch the least TV: those who are older, White, better educated, and of a higher socioeconomic status. Newspaper readers like to keep up on the news. They are more likely than nonreaders to also view TV and Internet news. Those who consume news usually use multiple sources; alternatively, those who do not read newspapers usually do not watch TV news either (Pew Research Center, 2011, 2016).

Magazines

Print magazines are the most narrowly targeted of the traditional media, having become increasingly so after an earlier period of popular general-interest magazines (e.g., *Life*, *Look*, *Collier's*, *Saturday Evening Post*) ended in the 1960s. An estimated 11,000 magazines were published in the United States in the mid-1990s (Wilson & Wilson, 1998), mostly devoted to special interests. However, traditional national weekly news magazines were suffering; by 2011 *U.S. News and World Report* had abandoned its print version, and *Newsweek* was sold by The Washington Post Company for $1 and the assumption of its debt (Pew Research Center, 2011).

Magazines combine newspapers' permanence and opportunity for greater in-depth coverage with television's photographic appeal. Reading magazines is primarily an adult activity, although there are children's magazines such as *Boys' Life*, *Sports Illustrated for Kids*, *Teen Vogue*, and *National Geographic Kids* that are useful in developing children's reading and print media habits. For girls, certain magazines such as *Seventeen* and, later, *Glamour*, *Vogue*, and *Cosmopolitan* are an important part of the female adolescent experience and are major contributors to the socialization of girls as women in Western society (see Chapter 5). The emphasis in these kinds of magazines tends to be on fashion, attractiveness, romance, and sex. There really are no comparable gender-role socializing magazines for boys, although many of them read *Sports Illustrated* and *Sports Illustrated for Kids*.

Radio

One of the first electronic forms of media, radio, rapidly permeated society in the 1920s, much as television would do 30 years later. The current network TV format of prime-time entertainment programming was borrowed from radio, which later reorganized into a primarily music-and-news format in the 1950s after TV co-opted its programming agenda. More than television, radio is highly age- and interest-segmented (e.g., top 40, classical, country & western, Christian, oldies rock, easy listening, news and talk). Increasingly, the lines between online and terrestrial radio are another area of media that are blurred. One 2017 U.S. study reported that 53% of respondents listen to online or streaming radio programming (such as Pandora and iHeartRadio) at least once a week. However, traditional AM/FM radio was still the most widely used audio medium (Infinite Dial, 2017).

Worldwide, radio is the most available mass communication medium. It is crucially important in isolated societies because it depends neither on literacy nor electricity nor the purchase of a relatively expensive television set, computer, or mobile phone. Although there are premium satellite and streaming Internet radio services available, most radio receivers are cheap and run well on batteries. Compared to television or print media, programming is very inexpensive to produce, especially talk and music formats. Talk radio, of course, can be anything from ennobling to dangerous. One of the most shocking abuses of radio was the Rwandan station that broadcast calls for genocide and fomented hysteria, culminating in the disastrous Hutu–Tutsi civil war and genocide of 1994 to 1995, chillingly recreated in the 2004 film *Hotel Rwanda*. However, more often radio serves as an important part of the social fabric, tying diverse constituencies together; even that infamous Rwandan radio station later starting broadcasting a soap opera designed to encourage dialogue between Hutu and Tutsi (Phillips, Urbany, & Reynolds, 2008). See Close-up 1.3 for an example of the role of radio in a country sorely lacking in modern infrastructure.

❖ CLOSE-UP 1.3 RADIO IN NAMIBIA

Sparsely populated and largely undeveloped, the southern African nation of Namibia was plundered under German and, later, South African colonial rule before its independence in 1990. Its only large city is its capital, Windhoek (pop. 150,000). According to Wresch (1996), Namibia radio had a call-in talk show, The Chat Show, *from 9 to 10 a.m., in which listeners called in with specific complaints about treatment from a business, the government, or the police. The announcer played a humanistic therapist kind of role, listening to and summarizing the caller's concerns. After the show ended, station personnel would call the government agencies or businesses who received complaints. They recorded the officials' responses to the complaints and played those back, along with the original complaint, when the second installment of the show aired three hours later. However, in 2009, the state-run Namibian Broadcasting Corporation decided to pull the plug on* The Chat Show, *a move that was panned by several human rights groups.*

In rural Namibia, radio serves an even broader communicative function. In areas with virtually no phones or mail service, one can relay messages through the local radio station, which will broadcast (free of charge) that a particular listener should, for example, call his grandmother or pick up the textbook for his correspondence course. Even if the intended recipient is not listening, someone who knows him or her usually is and the message is delivered (Wresch, 1996).

Television

Although experimental sets appeared in the late 1930s, television was essentially unknown by the general public at the end of World War II. Whereas only 0.02% of U.S. homes had TV in 1946, that figure rose to 9% by 1950 and 23.5% by 1951. By 1962, TV ownership had exploded, with 90% of U.S. homes having a set. By 1980, televisions were found in about 98% of U.S. homes, a figure that has remained constant since then; today, there are an average of 2.3 TV sets in each American home, a number that has declined slightly in recent years, most likely due to the ability to view TV programming on devices other than televisions (Andreasen, 1994; Nielsen Company, 2016; U.S. Energy Information Administration, 2017).

Although most of the television programming in the early years was by networks or local stations, the rapid growth of cable and satellite technology in the 1980s and 1990s greatly expanded the offerings, with a corresponding decline in the broadcast network market share. Associated with television sets were video cassette recorders (VCRs), which were in 98% of U.S. households of families with children by 1999 (Jordan, 2001). However, in the new millennium, an increasingly popular technology, the digital video recorder (DVR), was present in 50% of households by 2016 (Nielsen Company, 2016). Also by 2016, Americans were increasingly "time shifting" their television viewing by accessing TV content online via the Internet or through cable video-on-demand services (Nielsen Company, 2016). This has led some viewers to engage in "binge viewing," watching entire seasons of some shows in one sitting (Jurgensen, 2012). It has also led to some measurement challenges for companies like Nielsen that track TV viewership (Steel, 2016).

Although access to computers and mobile devices is high even among young children, a 2013 U.S. study found that TV is still a dominant medium in that age group, with 58% of children under 8 watching television at least once a day, most for around an hour a day (Common Sense Media, 2013). By 2008, 60% of U.S. adolescents and 30% of preschoolers (26% of those under 2) had television sets in their bedrooms, and 76% of American households paid for a television subscription through cable, satellite, or telephone companies (Carlsson-Paige, 2008; Horrigan & Duggan, 2015; Kotler, Wright, & Huston, 2001; Nielsen Company, 2016). Figures for European children and families tend to be slightly lower overall but vary greatly by country (Austin, Barnard, & Hutcheon, 2015; d'Haenens, 2001).

The television phenomenon is almost as pervasive in developing countries as it is in the Western world. Even the worst urban slums in developing countries sprout a myriad of television antennas and satellite dishes. The number of TV sets per 1,000 people worldwide doubled from 117 to 234 between 1981 and 1997 ("The Faustian Bargain," 1997), although they are hardly distributed evenly across the globe. For example, in 1996 there were 906 TVs per 1,000 people in the Netherlands and 850 per 1,000 in the United States, but only 5 per 1,000 in Bangladesh and 9 in Kenya (Wresch, 1996). Time spent viewing television also varies by region, with North Americans watching the most, and African and Asian countries watching the least (Austin, Barnard, & Hutcheon, 2015). Nevertheless, this worldwide television reach has led to a global audience for some events. For instance, audiences as large as three billion people tune in for sporting events such as the Olympic Games and World Cup soccer finals on TV. See Close-up 1.4 for a look at an anthropologist's views of the stages of a society's acceptance of TV.

❖ CLOSE-UP 1.4 STAGES OF TELEVISION IMPACT

Drawing on his studies of television use in several Brazilian communities with varying lengths of exposure to television, cultural anthropologist Kottak (2009) identified five stages of societal interaction with television. In Stage 1 the medium is new and strange and attracts people with glued gazes—no matter what the content is. "The medium rather than the message is the mesmerizer" (Kottak, 2009, p. 139). Stage 2 is usually the next 10 to 15 years, when people begin to interpret TV's messages and selectively accept or reject them. Due to its high status, television ownership displays conspicuous consumption and becomes a source of privileged information. In Stage 3, the community is saturated with television, and the length of exposure increases. By Stage 4, adults have spent their whole lives in a culture permeated by television, whose lifelong impact on members of society is taken for granted. Finally, Stage 5 occurs with the widespread appearance of cable TV and video capability. At this stage, there is much more individual control of TV, in terms of both time shifting and abundant selection of programming. Marketing is increasingly directed at homogeneous segments, not to the mass audience.

The bulk of mass communication research has studied television, because we spend so much time watching it. Adults in the United States watch about five hours of television per day (not counting the TV content they may be accessing via mobile devices) (Nielsen Company, 2016). A TV set is turned on in the average U.S. household between 7 and 8 hours each day, with the typical child age 8 to 18 watching over 2.5 hours per day. Throughout childhood, it is estimated that the average U.S. child sees nearly 15,000 sexual references, innuendoes, and jokes per year, with only 1.1% of those dealing with abstinence, birth control, pregnancy, or sexually transmitted diseases (Kaiser Family Foundation, 2010; Strasburger & Donnerstein, 1999). By the time a child reaches the age of 18, he or she has seen an estimated 200,000 televised acts of violence (Huston, Wright, Rice, Kerkman, & St. Peters, 1990).

Group Differences
The amount of television viewing changes through the lifespan. It rises sharply between ages 2 and 4. It then levels off until about age 8, rising again by age 12. It then starts to fall during the high school and college years and young adulthood, when people are busy with romance, studying, working, listening to music, and parenting young children. There is another rise, however, in the older adult years after one's children are grown. In fact, seniors watch more television than most groups. Other groups who watch television more than average are women, poor people, and ethnic minorities (Nielsen Company, 2016; Roberts, 2000). It is interesting that many of the groups who watch the most television are the same groups that are the most underrepresented in TV programming, where characters are disproportionately middle class, White, male, professional, and affluent. We return to this issue in Chapter 5.

Time-of-Day Differences
Television viewing also changes sharply throughout the day. Typically the largest network TV audience is during "prime time"—8 to 11 p.m. Eastern and Pacific times in

North America (7 to 10 p.m. Central and Mountain). These are the hours that earn the highest advertising charges and the greatest investment and innovation in programming. The most obvious pinnacle of such efforts may be seen in the prime-time "sweeps weeks" in February, May, July, and November, in which Nielsen audience size over a four-week span is used to calculate advertising charges for the next several months. These are the weeks when the networks outdo themselves presenting blockbuster movies, specials, and landmark episodes of top-rated series.

Video

Starting from Sony's slow introduction of $2,000-plus Betamax machines into the U.S. market in 1975 (five years later, less than 1% of U.S. homes owned a VCR), growth took off in the early 1980s until, by 1995, 85% of U.S. homes owned a VCR (Hull, 1995). These days, the presence of VCRs has dropped greatly, most likely having been replaced with DVD players, DVRs, and streaming Internet television and movie viewing (Nielsen Company, 2010a, 2016).

Although bitterly opposed to videotape at first, Hollywood studios later forged a very symbiotic and lucrative relationship between theater movies and home video. VHS and, more recently, DVD and streaming rentals and sales have brought huge additional income and interest to the film industry. The widespread renting of movies has raised some new issues, however. Although the U.S. film rating system (G, PG, PG-13, R, NC-17) can have some effect in theaters, it has had very little impact at DVD rental kiosks, or online, where 13-year-olds generally have no trouble accessing an R-rated movie. More recently, increasing numbers of films have been produced solely for DVD or online distribution, or released in "unrated" or "director's cut" versions, bypassing both theaters and the need to have any rating at all. Such distribution channels have been an additional boon to home movie viewing, since they are generally marketed with additional "special features," such as deleted scenes, interviews with stars and directors, and background information on filming. A growing trend is the tendency to view movies via cable on-demand and online streaming services. Indeed, this trend has largely been responsible for the weakened presence or demise of brick-and-mortar video rental stores such as Blockbuster (Kehr, 2011).

One segment of television still distressed by video technology is advertising. Time shifting, which enables viewers to record TV shows and watch them later while fast-forwarding through the ads, has spurred new creativity in the ad industry in an attempt to produce ads that viewers will be reluctant to fast-forward through. There are also increasing attempts to create commercials whose highlights can be noticed while fast-forwarding. It is no accident that the ads have come to look more like the programming, using artsy montage and cinema vérité techniques. In addition, on-demand services often prevent skipping ads or require an extra fee for doing so.

Some television markets have grown exponentially in recent years. China is now by far the largest TV market, with well over 350 million homes having access (174 million having cable), reaching most of its 1.3 billion population. China moved from only 18 million people having access to TV in 1975 to 1 billion 20 years later, putting it first in the world in the number of TV viewers. In contrast, the United States had only 98 million homes with TV, and third-place India 79 million (Madden, 2010; Thomas, 2003). The rapid growth of markets in developing countries will have far-reaching advertising implications in future decades.

An important emphasis in future media research, as indeed in all social science research, will be on cross-cultural dimensions. Virtually every society in the world is becoming more multicultural, in part due to the increased ease of access to online information. We are all exposed to media from many different national and cultural sources, and it is necessary to understand how different cultures perceive the same message differently. Useful collections of papers on comparative and cross-cultural media research include: Esser, Bernal-Marino, and Smith (2016), Kamalipour (1999), Korzenny and Ting-Toomey (1992), and Kottak (2009). It is a common experience in much of the world to be able to watch a foreign language television program or film that has been dubbed or subtitled in the local language. For a discussion of how people process subtitles, see Close-up 1.5.

❖ CLOSE-UP 1.5 READING, IGNORING, OR NOT HAVING TO DEAL WITH SUBTITLES

In much of the world a considerable amount of television originates in a place where a different language is spoken. Thus, the program is either dubbed or subtitled in the local language. Dubbing allows one to hear one's own language, though it may not match the lips of the characters on the screen. However, reading subtitles, while simultaneously processing the visual content and ignoring the sound track in an unfamiliar language, involves a set of cognitive skills that requires some practice to do effectively (Harris, Borror, Koblitz, Pearn, & Rohrer, 2017; Perego, del Missier, Porta, & Mosconi, 2010). Belgian psychologist d'Ydewalle and his colleagues (e.g., de Bruycker & d'Ydewalle, 2003; d'Ydewalle & de Bruycker, 2007; d'Ydewalle, Praet, Verfaillie, & Van Rensbergen, 1991) have measured eye movements as indicators of people's relative attention to subtitles and visual content. They found that people look at subtitles in their own language and may find them distracting in cases in which they know both the languages involved (Lavaur & Bairstow, 2011). Belgians are very familiar with reading subtitles; most of their movies and much television is foreign and subtitled, sometimes bilingually in two subtitled parallel lines in French and Dutch (the country's two languages).

Movies and TV shows with subtitles can even be used to learn a language (d'Ydewalle & Van de Poel, 1999; Koolstra & Beentjes, 1999). For example, the Italian newsmagazine L'Espresso promoted itself by giving away "MovieTalk" CD-ROMs of old Beverly Hills 90210 and Columbo episodes to use for English lessons. In addition to the original voicing, users had the option of pressing another button to hear a slower, less slurred, and more precise voiceover (Stanley, 2000).

The United States is unusual among nations in having virtually no subtitled television available. Presumably because so much domestic programming, almost all in English, is available, U.S. audiences have never had to become used to reading subtitles. Subtitled foreign films are shown, but with rare exceptions only as art films to highly specialized audiences. The conventional industry wisdom, accurate or not, is that American audiences will not watch foreign language subtitled films or television. This largely untested assumption may exclude much high-quality and potentially popular television from American viewers.

Changing technology is accelerating fundamental structural changes in television. Broadcast network TV (e.g., ABC, CBS, Fox, NBC, in the United States), which accounted for over 90% of the audience as recently as 1978, has slowly but surely seen its audience decline as proliferating cable and online channels have vastly increased the number of offerings available. The psychological impact of all these choices is less clear; it is not obvious how receiving 500 channels will change one's TV viewing. VCRs, DVRs, on-demand cable services, and the Internet have greatly increased audience control in program selection and timing, as well as introducing the option of at least partially avoiding commercials. Although the days of the mass audience are not over (top-rated broadcast network TV shows, especially live sports such as NFL football, remain a very widely shared experience), the movement in the direction of more precisely targeted audiences is probably unstoppable.

Other changes in television can be expected to grow. It is common now for TV viewers to watch their favorite shows across various platforms (televisions, smartphones, tablets), sometimes pausing programming on one device and resuming it later on another. Interactive TV projects allow viewers, for example, to press one button to see the original live feed and another to call up additional background information during newscasts or sports events. Pressing yet another button can bring up a close-up shot of an athlete during a ball game, whereas another can provide an instant replay or start the game over. Increased opportunities for connecting one's computer, television, mobile phone, tablet, and music system together will continue to change the face of mass communication and further blur its distinctions from social media and entertainment.

Computer-Mediated Communication

The origins of what we think of today as "the Internet" can be traced to the Cold War. Concerned that a nuclear attack by the Soviet Union would cripple U.S. communications capabilities, computer scientists in the government and universities in the 1960s began working on a way for computers to communicate across distances (Hafner & Lyon, 2006). When e-mail and the World Wide Web became available to average citizens in the 1990s, an information revolution began, and we are still seeing that revolution unfold before our eyes. Indeed, it is progressively more difficult to draw clear boundaries of what is included in mass communication when it comes to computer-mediated communication (CMC). Many varieties of CMC, such as the Internet, World Wide Web, instant messaging, e-mail, streaming content, social networks, and blogs, have characteristics of both traditional print and broadcast media. The boundaries between mass and personal media are also growing increasingly fuzzy (see Close-up 1.1). Personal messages or videos may be sent to mass audiences or posted on the Internet. Movies may be viewed on television and, increasingly, be sent like a message to others. With the advent of online media, entertainment, most notably film, is looking like and is handled more like mass communication.

The capacity for very wide circulation of material on the Internet allows it to share many characteristics with traditional print and electronic media. When large documents are released to the public, they are routinely posted first on the Internet. A major gaffe on camera by a politician or movie star is watched and re-watched on YouTube for the next several days. Whenever people want more information about anything, they go online and Google the topic or check Wikipedia.

Another capability which computers bring to mass communication is the ability to digitally alter photographs. With modern technology, photographs can be so totally changed as to be completely unrecognizable. They can also become associated online with an article or story unrelated to their original context, a common technique of fake news (see Chapter 7). The ethical boundaries are blurry here. Although few would have problems with digitally cropping a photo to remove irrelevant background, how about digitally composing a photo to put people together who never were in that particular place at the same time? No doubt a national leader would object to an altered photo that showed her shaking hands with a terrorist, but what about altering a student group shot for a university recruiting brochure to make it more ethnically diverse than the original photo was? This actually was an issue at the University of Wisconsin-Madison, where an African American student was digitally pasted into a photo of a football crowd scene to make it more ethnically diverse (Boese, 2006; Jacobson, 2001). Is this misrepresentation in a recruiting brochure? The student was in fact a UWM student and could have been at that football game, although in fact he wasn't (see Wheeler, 2002, for a careful discussion of this issue).

Do such alterations matter? Yes, they do. Experimental participants acting as newspaper editors reviewing a story about a hurricane saw a picture of either a village before the hurricane hit or the same devastated village after. Although there was no mention of personal injuries or death in the story, about a third of those who had seen the "after" picture falsely remembered the story as having mentioned injury or death, compared to only 9% of those seeing the "before" photo (Garry, Strange, Bernstein, & Kinzett, 2007). Doctored photos can also affect one's memory for public events widely covered in the news. Sacchi, Agnoli, and Loftus (2007) showed Italians either the original photo of a lone protester facing a line of tanks in the 1989 Tiananmen Square protest in Beijing or a doctored photo of the same with masses of spectators watching. Participants in the study were also shown one of a comparable pair of photos of a 2003 Rome protest of the Iraq War. People who saw the doctored photos remembered the events as involving more people with more confrontation and damage to persons and property.

As with print and broadcast media, the theories and research methodologies of mass communication (see Chapter 2) have increasingly been used to study CMC (Mundorf & Laird, 2002). However, because boundaries between traditional and online media are now blurred, media scholars are working to adapt. Specifically, Perloff (2015a) points out that in many instances interpersonal communication is now also mass communication. For example, it is common for viewers, watching a live broadcast of a television show, to tweet their reactions to friends and followers while also monitoring the reactions of others. More importantly, platforms such as Facebook and Twitter sometimes have become news sources when users post videos detailing newsworthy incidents such as police brutality (Victor & McPhate, 2016). Indeed, "in an age of citizen journalism and Twitter, receivers have become senders" (Perloff, 2015a, p. 532).

Walther, Gay, and Hancock (2005) discuss five qualities of the Internet that are particularly worthy of study and theory. The *multimedia aspect* of the Internet is not unique to CMC but is a central part of it. CMC stimuli may contain any or all of the following: written words, spoken words, pictures, sounds, video, and social interaction of the user with other users. How these various channels are processed in parallel, or as task-switching, offers a major research challenge, made all the more daunting by the fact that users often are doing other, non-CMC activities at the same time!

Hypertextuality is perhaps the most unique characteristic of the Internet. The availability of multiple links to many other sites and stimulus sources makes the Internet perhaps the most profoundly nonlinear of the mass media. How people choose to navigate through the various links, how websites can be designed to facilitate navigation in the most efficient way, and how people mentally combine information from the various sources are all hugely important topics that need much further study. It is not clear how the nonlinear nature of most websites either facilitates or inhibits learning. Some research has suggested that print format or linear web designs lead to better factual learning but nonlinear web formats contribute to a better understanding of connections among facts (Eveland, Cortese, Park, & Dunwoody, 2004; Eveland & Dunwoody, 2001, 2002).

Interactivity also is not unique to the Internet but is a major attribute of many of its uses. Whether it is talking to friends through instant messaging, mobile phone texting, Facebook postings, or shopping online, interaction with the media is far more fundamental in CMC than with the traditional print or broadcast media. How do electronic conversations differ from face-to-face or written ones? How are experiences like shopping, information seeking, auctioning, or even visiting, different, perhaps even fundamentally so, on the Internet?

A fourth characteristic, *packet switching*, has received the least behavioral research attention, according to Walther and colleagues (2005). This has to do with the fact that the Internet sends digital bits, encoded with identity and routing information, as well as content, over multiple paths, such that it can be retrieved in multiple ways through multiple links. This is useful, for example, in keeping access open in the face of hardware or infrastructure crashes or in subverting authoritarian attempts to block Internet access. However, it poses challenges in other ways, such as making it difficult to block child pornography, online predation, cyber-bullying, fake news, and electronic piracy. Generally the packet switching technology is well ahead of the regulatory process and often far ahead of the behavioral research in understanding how such processes work.

Finally, the characteristic of *synchronicity* is important. Four types of CMC synchronicity (Strasburger & Wilson, 2002) are a part of the world all children grow up with now, though only a short time ago none of them even existed. *One-to-one asynchronous communication* includes traditional e-mail. Improved technology now allows the sending of visual, voice, video, and all sorts of written material via e-mail. *Many-to-many asynchronous communication* involves electronic bulletin boards and distribution lists, in which a receiver signs up for a service or logs on to a program to access messages from a particular group, usually focused on some specific topic. If a user must seek out a site in order to asynchronously access information, it may involve one-to-one, *many-to-one*, or *one-to-many* source–receiver relationships, most often involving visiting a website. Also, synchronous communication includes texting, instant messaging, and the use of video services like Skype. These are very popular forms of communication among preteens and teens but are also increasingly used by most segments of society. However, even the line between synchronous and asynchronous communication is blurry now, in that social media platforms like Twitter and Facebook allow users to either follow posts in real time or catch up later. Whether one is communicating by CMC in a synchronous or asynchronous manner can affect the way people process information and perform a cognitive problem-solving task (Münzer & Borg, 2008).

There are interesting age differences in the use of CMC. Although the stereotypes of the adolescent computer geek and the technologically clueless older adult still exist, increasing numbers of older adults are effectively using the Internet. One survey found that 67% of those in the United States over 65 used the Internet (compared with 90% overall). However, most of those seniors indicated that they were not that confident in using technology, particularly newer devices (Anderson & Perrin, 2017). Older adults are more likely to use the Internet for information seeking on topics of interest to them, as well as frequent use for shopping and auctions (Hilt & Lipschultz, 2004). They are less likely than younger groups to use CMC for social media purposes (Anderson & Perrin, 2017).

Not surprisingly, the young are especially frequent users of CMC, with 99% of those 18–29 saying that they use the Internet (Pew Research Center, 2017). Among teens 13–17, 92% said they go online every day, 24% of whom indicated they do so "almost constantly," many with the aid of smartphones (Pew Research Center, 2015). The most common uses of the Internet among teens are for texting, social networking, and gaming (Pew Research Center, 2015). By 2003, teens aged 13 to 14 reported spending more time per week online (16.7 hours) than watching television (13.6 hours) (Weaver, 2003b). Often the Internet becomes the primary media source of information.

Teens and young adults also make huge use of social networking sites such as Facebook, Twitter, Instagram, and Snapchat. According to Facebook's own statistics, as of 2017, there were over 1 billion daily users and almost 2 billion monthly users of the site worldwide (Facebook, 2017). Another survey found that 76% of Americans (65% of those over 18) reported using at least one social networking website (Perrin, 2015). In fact, according to at least one estimate, by 2010, Americans spent more time on social networking sites than in any other online activity (Nielsen Company, 2010b). Interestingly, implicit rules have evolved for behavior on these sites (Walther & Bunz, 2005). There is also a correlation between the amount of time adolescents spend on these sites and the likelihood that their social well-being will be affected by information received from the site (Valkenburg, Peter, & Schouten, 2006). On sites like Facebook, there are multiple cues (photos, wall postings, profile, etc.) to give information about a user, and we are only beginning to understand how people combine that information to form impressions of others in the absence of traditional interpersonal face-to-face cues (Anderson, Fagan, Woodnutt, & Chamorro-Premuzic, 2012; Lee, 2007; Walther, Van de Heide, Kim, Westerman, & Tong 2008). The ways that one's personality affects one's level and quality of self-disclosure on social networking sites has also received some preliminary study (Schouten, Valkenburg, & Peter, 2007). Still, the psychological ramifications of social networking sites, including cyber-bullying (Barlett & Gentile, 2012), are only beginning to be understood.

There is disagreement in the literature about whether Internet use is associated with social isolation or loneliness (Cole, 2000; Kraut et al., 1998; McKenna & Bargh, 1999; McKenna & Seidman, 2005; Sheldon, Abad, & Hinsch, 2011). Overall, Internet use is typically more social than television viewing, in part due to social options like instant messaging and Facebook. At least one study found that young adults were happier following instant messaging communication than following comparable face-to-face interaction (Green et al., 2005). There is also evidence that attempting to present oneself as extraverted on a blog, compared to writing private text documents, leads people to actually see themselves as more extraverted (Gonzales & Hancock, 2008). Compared to face-to-face (FTF) interactions of two people, those who instant messaged each other drew interpersonal perceptions about the other person equally well, and even clearer social roles of dominant and submissive emerged in the CMC condition. These findings suggest that CMC is neither totally lacking in social cues, nor is it the "great equalizer" in terms of status (Boucher, Hancock, & Dunham, 2008). The strongest evidence for social isolation comes in the minority of the population who spend a very large number of hours online, perhaps due to a preference for online interaction fostering compulsive Internet use, which in turn results in negative social outcomes (Caplan, 2005). Effects of Internet use on social isolation are much weaker or nonexistent for moderate users. See Close-up 1.6 for more about the issues of making friends online.

❖ CLOSE-UP 1.6 MAKING PERSONAL CONNECTIONS ONLINE

Are relationships that are formed online, through e-mail, chat rooms, or social networking sites, inherently shallow, impersonal, and even hostile and dangerous? Or, do they allow a liberation from the confines of physical locality and superficial aspects like physical appearance? In an early survey study of online relationships of people in a variety of newsgroups and Usenet hierarchies, 60% of respondents reported making some sort of personal relationship online (Parks, 1996). Women were somewhat more likely than men to have such electronic friends, though age and marital status did not matter. Almost all had corresponded with their friend via e-mail and about a third each had used phone, letter, or face-to-face contact as well. These relationships developed in many of the same ways that traditional relationships do.

In the realm of romantic relationships, a 2016 survey revealed that 15% of adults reported having used online dating sites, while 41% of adults in the United States indicated that they knew someone who had used an online dating website. About 29% said that they knew someone who was in a long-term relationship that started on such a website, a figure that had doubled since 2006 (Smith, 2016).

In a study comparing self-disclosure online and face-to-face, McKenna and Seidman (2005) found that people shared more of their true selves online than face-to-face and liked an Internet partner more than a face-to-face partner. Of course, individual differences are important. People more strongly prefer online relationships if they are socially anxious or lonely or if their circumstances of current roles or relationships constrain face-to-face encounters. Far from keeping people from interacting personally, computers may thus sometimes enhance the development of friendships, free of the usual constraints of the first reactions to physical appearance and personal mannerisms.

Numerous questions about CMC remain. Why do people e-mail, text, or use Facebook, and how do these newer media complement or replace traditional communication means like the telephone and writing (Dimmick, 2003; Ramirez, Dimmick, Feaster, & Lin, 2008)? What is gained psychologically from instant messaging, texting, blogging, tweeting, and using Facebook? How do people search websites and evaluate the worth of the information they find? How do they make friends online?

Media Applications, Chapter 1: Media Literacy as a Compass for the Media Landscape

When considering all that has been discussed in this chapter regarding the prevalence and power of media, additional questions may arise. For example, how do we navigate the increasingly complex world of mass communication? How can we discern real news from fake news? How do we arm children with the tools they need to deal with violent or sexual media they may encounter? One well-known movie mogul may have the answer. In a 2004 interview, *Star Wars* filmmaker George Lucas aptly suggested the great need for media education:

> When people talk to me about the digital divide, I think of it not being so much about who has access to what technology as who knows how to create and express themselves in this new language of the screen. If students aren't taught the language of sound and images, shouldn't they be considered as illiterate as if they left college without being able to read or write? Unfortunately, most learning institutions find that idea very difficult to swallow. They consider the various forms of non-written communication as some type of therapy or art.
>
> (Media deconstruction, 2012, p. 2)

There is a critical need for greater media literacy in modern society. *Media literacy* may be defined as a set of critical thinking skills involving the "ability to access, analyze, evaluate, and process media" (Steyer, 2002, p. 195). Its goals are to teach people to use media consciously and selectively and to think critically about media messages and images. Media literacy may be conceptualized in different ways, including as a public policy issue, an educational curriculum issue, a responsible parenting issue, or as an area of scholarly inquiry from a variety of disciplinary perspectives (Christ & Potter, 1998). See Potter (2001) for a comprehensive formulation of media literacy, Potter (2004) for a more theoretical approach, and Jeong, Cho, and Hwang (2012) for a meta-analysis of media literacy intervention programs.

Consistent with recent theory and research on mass communication, the contemporary emphasis in media literacy is more on the empowerment of consumers rather than on protection from some monolithic, pernicious influence. Realistically, no one can be completely shielded from media and popular culture, nor should we want to be; media are omnipresent, enduring, and often very useful and rewarding parts of our lives. Rather, we must learn to live not only with traditional print and electronic media, but also with all the rapidly evolving new technologies of mass, personal, and computer-mediated communication, especially the Internet, social media, and other aspects of cyberspace. In all of this, the purpose of media literacy is to give us more control over our interpretations of media (Potter, 2001).

Scholars identify different types of media literacy. Meyrowitz (1998), for example, suggests three. *Media content literacy* focuses on characters, themes, information, behaviors, and so on. *Media grammar literacy* looks at learning the features of each particular medium. For example, as children mature and experience more TV, they acquire the knowledge of how to interpret the cuts, fades, dissolves, and general montage techniques used in the editing of film or TV. Very young children may misinterpret things that they see on television because they fail to understand these techniques. The third type of literacy, *medium literacy*, involves learning the specific conventions, modalities, and processing requirements for using each particular medium. Different media require the use of different sensory modalities and parts of the brain. Specific conventions of visual literacy require different skills and understanding than what is required for understanding purely verbal media (Messaris, 1994, 1997, 1998). For example, television to some extent and especially some computer-mediated communications like hypertext on the Internet are notoriously nonlinear in character, in contrast to radio and print.

Media literacy interventions can have two broad categories of intended outcomes: media-relevant outcomes and behavior-relevant outcomes (Jeong, Cho, & Hwang, 2012). *Media-relevant outcomes* focus on knowledge, particularly on understanding that there are often motives behind media. One example of media-relevant outcomes is knowing the persuasive intent of ads and the techniques that advertising uses to persuade (Austin, Pinkleton, Hust, & Cohen, 2005; Buijzen, 2007). Another media-relevant outcome is influence, understanding that media affect audiences in a variety of ways, from cultivating world beliefs to changing attitudes to teaching behaviors (Duran, Yousman, Walsh, & Longshore, 2008). The final media-relevant outcome is the outcome of realism, referring to the understanding that media represent, to varying degrees, factual and/or social reality (Austin, Pinkleton, & Funabiki, 2007).

Behavior-relevant outcomes include understanding the consequences of performing a behavior or holding particular attitudes about it, for example, knowing that accepting the assumptions of a certain type of political ad could lead to voting against one's own interest (Banerjee & Greene, 2006, 2007). These types of outcomes also include perceptions of one's own self-efficacy (perceived ability to perform some behavior) and the perception of the behaviors of others in regard to media (Austin *et al.*, 2005).

Overall, media literacy interventions have been quite successful in a number of areas such as teaching about topics of violence (Cantor & Wilson, 2003; Scharrer, 2006; Webb, Martin, Afifi, & Kraus, 2010), body image and sexuality (Allen, d'Alessio, Emmers, & Gebhardt, 1996; Richardson, Paxton, & Thomson, 2009; Wilksch & Wade, 2009; Yamamiya, Cash, Melnyk, Posavec, & Posavec, 2005), advertising (Livingstone & Helsper, 2006), news (Loth, 2012), and health promotion (Bergsma & Carney, 2008). Of course, the effectiveness of media literacy interventions is also affected by several moderating variables (Jeong, Cho, & Hwang, 2012). For example, the agent or source of the teaching and the setting in which it occurs may be factors. The source may be a teacher, a parent, a peer, or an author of a curriculum (Webel, Okonsky, Trompeta, & Holzemer, 2010). Also, the audience is important. A program for children of a certain age will be more effective if it deeply understands the cognitive processing skills and psychological needs of children of that age.

One of our hopes is that this book will help arm you with tools that will provide you with a greater media literacy. The words "arm" and "tools" in this section of the chapter may seem extreme, but the power of the media is immense. However, our ability to understand and effectively deal with the media is even more powerful. This book invites you to fully equip your media literacy toolbox.

Overview of the Book

This chapter has introduced mass communication from a psychological perspective. The next chapter explores, in some depth, the types of research methodologies that have been used to study media. It also looks at the various theoretical bases of research on mass communication, drawing on models from the different disciplines of communication, psychology, and other fields. The general, though not exclusive, emphasis is on a cognitive perspective. Chapter 3 then examines several psychological constructs important in understanding our interaction with media. The overarching theme of how we construct meaning from media and how that constructed meaning becomes our perceived reality is introduced. Chapter 4 takes an in-depth look at how our emotions interact with media. Two particular areas of media are explored as they relate to emotion: sports and music. Media coverage can encourage competition, cooperation, gender-role development, hero worship, and the enjoyment of sports violence. The second area—music—is a very important medium, especially for teens and young adults. The uses and gratifications of music consumption are examined, as well as specific issues like the nature of content in lyrics and how popular music has (and has not) changed over the years.

Chapters 5 to 11 are topically organized to explore several specific content areas. Chapter 5 explores the issue of group portrayals in the media. The emphasis here is on how media portray various groups of people and what the effects of such presentations are. We will see how media stereotypes may become a perceived reality in the minds of the public, especially in cases when the viewer has limited life experience with members of a particular group. Are men and women portrayed in stereotyped fashion? What about families? What are the effects of such portrayals on the socialization process of children? Also examined are African Americans, whose depictions have been more carefully studied than any other group in the history of TV. The portrayals of Latinos, Native Americans, Asian Americans, Arabs, older adults, sexual minorities, people with physical and psychological disabilities, and those in various professions are also examined. What are the effects of unrealistic or even nonexistent portrayals on the public's perception of these groups?

Chapter 6 examines the world as created by advertising. Advertising is a type of information to be processed—one very important way we learn about the world as well as its products. Techniques of persuasion are examined, focusing on various types of psychological appeals, especially as they involve persuasion through the creation of a new reality which then becomes real for the consumer (e.g., a reality full of danger in which one needs to buy locks and weapons, a reality in which most people are very thin and suntanned, a reality of status-conscious people that one has to continually impress with one's dress and possessions). We particularly examine the cognitive view of advertising, with a focus on the psychology of deceptive advertising. The issue of advertising to children is treated in some depth, identifying some surprising and disturbing trends and connections. Next, the issue of subliminal advertising is discussed to see if it is possible to persuade viewers at subconscious levels through subtle messages or embedded sexual figures in art work. Finally, we look at the emergence of advertising in new places, such as classrooms, product placements, the Internet, and prescription drug advertising.

Chapter 7 examines how the media's coverage of news affects our understanding and attitudes about events in the world. News is perhaps the area in which people are most likely to believe that media merely reflect and report the reality that is out there. Drawing especially on agenda-setting theory, we make the argument that such is not the case, that in fact news reporting is by no means such a reality transmission, but is necessarily a constructed interpretation of reality, often based more on what is newsworthy than on what is really important. Even by choosing what to cover and what not to cover, media are setting an agenda. This necessarily involves only a partial presentation of reality, but this partial reality becomes the basis of our knowledge about the world, even affecting foreign policy.

Chapter 8 continues to examine news by looking at how politicians manipulate media coverage to convey their own intended reality. As practically all of our information about political candidates and officeholders comes through the media, the importance of mass communication in this area can hardly be overstated. Such issues as image building and the construction of an electronic personality are discussed. The impact of televised candidate debates is examined. A final topic in politics and media concerns the appeals and effects of political advertising, including the controversial negative or attack advertising. Types of appeals in political advertising and their effects on attitudes and voting behavior are examined.

In Chapter 9 we look at media violence, the most heavily researched issue in mass communication. Different effects of television, movie, and video game violence are examined, including induced fear, modeling, catharsis, desensitization, and the cultivation of fear. In addition, we explore what types of people are drawn to enjoy violent media and what different factors may interact with media violence to enhance or lessen its impact. Long-term effects of watching television violence and recent research on the effects of playing violent video games are also examined. The question of the effects on children of viewing violence turns out to be more complex than is frequently admitted by partisans on either side of this controversial issue, although the weight of the total body of research comes down strongly on the side of demonstrating negative effects. These effects are substantial but usually in interaction with each other, suggesting a perspective looking at multiple risk and protective factors to predict negative effects of watching violence.

Chapter 10 examines the history, character, and effects of sexual content in media, looking at both mainstream and sexually explicit media. The creation and transmission of sexual values through media, as well as the socialization in regard to sexuality and the behavioral effects of media sex, are addressed. Research on the effects of sexual violence, both in pornography and in mainstream movies, is considered in some detail, pointing toward the conclusion that viewing sexual violence may be more damaging than viewing either sex or violence alone.

Turning in a more positive direction, the final chapter, Chapter 11, examines the media's prosocial uses, beginning with children's prosocial television. We start with a detailed look at *Sesame Street*, one of the longest-running and most evaluated TV shows in history. Other specifically prosocial TV shows are examined more briefly. The second part of the chapter deals with explicit attempts to use media to teach skills or persuade people to change their attitudes or behaviors in a more health- or safety-oriented direction. One section discusses principles of social, as opposed to product, marketing. The media's role in public health marketing campaigns to increase prosocial behaviors like stopping smoking, increasing exercise, or wearing seatbelts is also considered. Public service announcements (PSAs) and other social marketing uses of media face greater obstacles in many ways than does commercial advertising. A second part of this section looks at the use of mainstream entertainment media for explicitly prosocial ends (entertainment education), a format very common in developing countries and increasingly so, albeit in more subtle ways, in Western countries.

Further Reading

Calvert, S. L., & Wilson, B. J. (Eds.). (2011). *The handbook of children, media, and development.* Malden, MA: Wiley-Blackwell.

Carlsson-Paige, N. (2008). *Taking back childhood: Helping your kids thrive in a fast-paced, media-saturated, violence-filled world.* New York: Hudson Street Press.

Dill, K. (Ed.). (2013). *The Oxford handbook of media psychology.* New York: Oxford University Press.

Jeong, S.-H., Cho, H., & Hwang, Y. (2012). Media literacy interventions: A meta-analytic review. *Journal of Communication, 62,* 454–472.

Potter, W. J. (2004). *Theory of media literacy: A cognitive approach.* Thousand Oaks, CA: Sage.

Reineke, L., & Oliver, M. B. (Eds.). (2017). *The Routledge handbook of media use and well-being.* New York: Routledge.

Strasburger, V. C., Wilson, B. J., & Jordan, A. B. (2014). Children, adolescents, and the media. 3rd ed. Thousand Oaks, CA: Sage.

Useful Links

Center for Media Literacy:
www.medialit.org/

Common Sense Media:
www.commonsensemedia.org/

Federal Communications Commission:
www.fcc.gov/

Motion Picture Association of America:
www.mpaa.org/

National Association of Broadcasters:
www.nab.org/

Pew Internet and American Life Project:
www.pewinternet.org/

For more resources, please visit the companion website:
www.routledge.com/cw/harris

Chapter 2

Research and Theory in Mass Communication

How Are Media Studied Scientifically?

Q: What is the gender breakdown of TV and movie characters that children see?

A: According to a study of almost 20,000 children's TV programs worldwide, 32% of the main human characters were female, while only 13% of the nonhuman characters like animals, monsters, and robots were female. Of speaking characters in G-rated movies from 1990 to 2005, less than one-third were female (Fine, 2010). A more recent study found that among the top-grossing films in 11 countries, only 31% of characters were female (Smith, Choueiti, & Pieper, 2014).

Q: What does body weight have to do with adolescents' favorite TV characters?

A: When middle and high school age students were asked to name their favorite same-sex TV character, they consistently chose thin characters over heavier ones. In fact, the thinner the characters were, the more the adolescents compared the characters to themselves (Te'eni-Harari & Eyal, 2015).

Q: Does watching reality TV turn female college students into "mean girls"?

A: One study discovered that young women who saw conflict-oriented "docusoaps" like *Keeping Up with the Kardashians* as realistic perceived women in general to be socially aggressive, which was also viewed as a valuable characteristic to have (Behm-Morawitz, Lewallen, & Miller, 2016).

In some sense everyone is a media critic. Few, however, have real answers to the questions and concerns that are so easy to raise. The most reliable and useful answers come from scientific research like the studies cited above. The results from such research are cited throughout this book, but in this chapter we look at what it means to do research on media, and we also examine the theoretical frameworks that guide this research. For example, it is easy to raise concerns about violence in the media but more difficult to precisely measure the effects of viewing that violence. It is easy to bemoan the lack of positive values on TV but more difficult to identify exactly what values television does communicate. In terms of the sheer amount of social science research on media, there has been far more study of television than of radio, print, or CMC. This is important because although many of the psychological questions discussed in this book apply equally well to all media, some studies have been examined primarily in regard to television. We begin by looking at some general approaches to studying media scientifically and examine the types of answers we can find. Then we move on to examine specific theories about media, drawn primarily from the disciplines of psychology and communication.

Media Research Frameworks

In addition to being of great concern to the general public, the media are also of considerable interest to the worlds of both commerce and science, both of which engage in research using various perspectives to study media. Much research has been done by or for TV networks, publishers, corporations, or ad agencies for commercial purposes; this is known as *administrative research*. For example, the Nielsen ratings of the television audience (see Close-up 2.1) or marketing research studying the public's taste in colas is done for the purpose of increasing the profits of a corporation. Since most administrative research is not published in peer-reviewed journals, it is typically not even available to scientists or the public. The second general type of scientific study is usually performed by independent scientists, most often professors at colleges and universities, with the goal of understanding and explaining the effects of media and studying their role in society and in people's lives; this is called *critical research*. For example, studies of the effects of media violence or content analyses of sexist content in ads are generally done with no commercial motivation. It is this noncommercial critical research that is primarily cited in this book. When we study media, we can examine the content itself, our exposure to this content, or the effects of that exposure. We begin by examining these three general ways of looking at media and then move on to specific theories.

❖ CLOSE-UP 2.1 THOSE ALL-IMPORTANT RATINGS

The Nielsen ratings are the measures used to track audience size for television programming in the United States. It is on these ratings that programs, careers, and even broad social trends rise and fall. The A. C. Nielsen Company selects thousands of American homes as a sample. In many of these homes "people meter" machines are hooked up to people's TVs, DVRs, cable boxes, or satellite dishes to measure when the set is on, who is watching, and what is being viewed. The Nielsen ratings provide two types of information. The rating itself is the percentage of the potential audience that is viewing a program (e.g., a rating of 30 means that 30% of the homes with TVs have that program on). The share compares that program's performance with the competition on at the same time. Network advertising charges are usually based primarily on the Nielsen ratings and shares measured during the four four-week sweeps periods in February, May, July, and November. Advertising charges are based primarily on the number of homes reached by an ad, adjusted for demographics. For example, a higher proportion of 18- to 49-year-olds (a much sought-after marketing demographic) in the audience can translate into higher ad charges. The cost for a 30-second spot on the Super Bowl rose from $125,000 in 1975 to around $5 million by 2017. The even more lucrative 15-second spot typically sells for 55–60% of the 30-second price. Charges per minute are typically much lower for the non-prime-time slots and cable channels with smaller audiences.

Looking at Content

One very straightforward way to study media is to study its content. Such *content analysis* is often an important precursor to research on exposure or effects. For example, some studies count the number of characters of different racial, ethnic, or gender groups in TV shows. If we want to argue, for example, that television ads or shows are sexist, we must carefully define what we mean by sexist and then study the ads or shows to see what percentage of those fit those criteria. Studies of the effects of sex or violence make use of content analysis studies to provide data on the prevalence of such themes and changing trends over time. In such research, *operational definitions* of important constructs are crucial. For example, if I am interested in studying how much violence is on television, I must carefully define what I mean by a "violent act." Without that, I do not know what acts to count. Without knowing other scientists' operational definitions, I am not able to interpret their research. That is why it is so important to include such definitions in published reports of research. We may not always agree with others' operational definitions, but knowing what they are allows us to interpret their results.

There are several important methodological issues involved in content analysis research, one of the major ones being *interrater reliability* or agreement (Lombard, Snyder-Duch, & Bracken, 2002; Tinsley & Weiss, 2000). For example, a researcher may have several different raters independently count the number of violent acts in a movie scene. For the analysis to have much meaning, the raters need to be in general agreement about what they have seen. For extensive discussions of content analysis as a methodology, see Neuendorf (2002), Riffe and Freitag (1997), and Riffe, Lacy, and Fico (1998).

Looking at Exposure

A second general way to study media is to study the amount of exposure people have to them. Who reads which newspapers or watches how much TV and when? How much do people use Facebook? Demographic information about different groups of people watching different shows comes from this type of study. This type of information does not always adequately assess real exposure, however. Just because the radio or television is on or someone is surfing the Internet is no assurance that he or she is devoting much attention to it, nor can we conclude that, merely because people are not paying full conscious attention to the source, that they are unaffected by it. Often people are simultaneously doing something else besides listening to the radio or checking Facebook. Sometimes they leave the room altogether for some period of time, especially during TV commercials or while waiting for a friend to come online. To understand the cognitive processes involved in experiencing media, it is crucial to take seriously the amount and nature of attention devoted to the medium; we return to this issue in Chapter 3.

Looking at Effects

Probably the most common general perspective in studying media is to study the effects of exposure to mass communication. To the general public, most major concerns about the media probably center on their effects. The nature of these effects can take different forms. Specifically, these effects can be direct, conditional, or cumulative (Perse, 2001; Perse & Lambe, 2017).

With the *direct effects model*, effects appear quickly and are relatively similar across all audience members. The crudest version of a direct effects model is the *theory of uniform effects.* This model argues that most individuals in a mass society perceive messages from media in the same fashion and react to them strongly and very similarly. Media messages are thus "magic bullets" piercing the mind of the populace. Such a view had some influence in studies of propaganda popular in the so-called "hypodermic needle" model of the 1920s and 1930s, whereby media were thought to "inject us with their venom." See Close-up 2.2 for an interesting example from this period. The assumption that media producers are evil thought controllers who manipulate everyone in a passive and helpless population in a uniform way has not been a serious theoretical position among communications researchers for many decades but is still implicitly assumed by some strident popular media-bashing critics, who blame the media for most social ills (e.g., Key, 1976, 1981, 1989; Winn, 2002). Indeed, a direct effects model is often implicitly held by members of the public critiquing media. An example of this is the belief of many regarding "subliminal" messages in advertising or music, which is discussed in Chapter 6.

❖ CLOSE-UP 2.2 REEFER MADNESS: MARIJUANA'S HYPODERMIC NEEDLE?

An interesting study in the direct effects or hypodermic model is the 1936 film Reefer Madness. *Originally released under the title* Tell Your Children, *the movie depicted frightening (if unrealistic) consequences of marijuana use. The storyline has several clean-cut youths falling in with shady characters who persuade them to use marijuana. As the film progresses, characters resort to prostitution, rape, suicide, and murder as a result of their marijuana use. One character is even locked away in a mental asylum for the rest of his life, apparently the result of a mental breakdown after using too much reefer.*

Despite this over-the-top portrayal, Reefer Madness *was not unique in its style. Similar films of the era included* Narcotic, Cocaine Fiends, *and* Sex Madness. *This movie genre has sometimes been labeled "cautionary film," the notion being that the producers' main goal was to warn viewers of the dangers of drugs, sexually transmitted infections, and the like. Such thinking reflects the direct effects/hypodermic model in the belief that audience members would be uniformly "immunized" by viewing the effects of others' sins. However, some see this view as naïve, calling movies like* Reefer Madness *"exploitation films," meaning that filmmakers, seeking profit, intentionally played upon moviegoers' curiosity about lurid and taboo topics. Summing up this notion, Feaster and Wood (1999, p. 18) say, "Just as the exploiter's primary concern was not liberating his customers from the catacombs of ignorance, moviegoers also turned to exploitation for something beyond moral betterment. The explorations of vice promised vivid displays of human shame and debauchery, and it was for this dramatization that tickets were purchased."*

Reefer Madness *has lived well beyond the 1930s. In the 1970s, the movie became a cult favorite among many, with at least one pro-marijuana advocacy group screening it as a campy protest to governmental restrictions of the drug (Feaster & Wood, 1999). That cult popularity eventually led to a satirical* Reefer Madness *musical in the 1990s and, later, a cable TV movie version of the musical. Whatever its original motivation,* Reefer Madness *has been fascinating audiences for decades.*

With the *conditional effects model*, the media can still have substantial effects, but only under certain conditions or for certain audience members, often in less dramatic form than suggested by the most vocal critics. This is a model of limited or selective effects based on individual differences (Bryant, Thompson, & Finklea, 2013; Krakowiak & Oliver, 2012). Different people perceive the same message differently and respond to it in different ways. For example, a violent TV program probably will not incite all of its viewers to go out and commit mayhem, but it may reinforce the already existing violent tendencies of a small sample of the viewers and slightly dull the sensitivities of many others. Similarly, certain positive or negative aspects of media may affect exceptional children more than average children (Abelman, Atkin, & Lin, 2007; Grimes, Anderson, & Bergen, 2008; Sprafkin, Gadow, & Abelman, 1992). A major effort of this type of research has been to discover other interactive variables that mediate or moderate the effects of consuming media. Such interactive variables include demographics of the media consumer (e.g., gender, ethnicity, age), properties of the message (e.g., in a violent scene, who commits the violence and whether it is reinforced), and the context of the message's reception (e.g., children watching television with their parents or alone). Taken together, these interactive variables may be considered risk factors; the effects will be stronger in relation to the greater number of risk factors present in a particular person (Kirsh, 2006). The fact that effects may be conditional and not uniform does not denigrate their importance. For example, even if a given effect occurs in only 0.01% of the viewers of a certain TV program, that still has an impact on 4,000 people out of an audience of 40 million!

The third model, *cumulative effects*, emphasizes the importance of repeated exposure to media stimuli and suggests that effects are due not so much to a single exposure as to the additive effects of many instances of exposures. For example, a single instance of viewing a *Seventeen* supermodel is unlikely to trigger an eating disorder, but repeated exposures to ultra-thin, large-breasted women may cumulatively encourage a young woman to push her body in that direction, especially if she likes and identifies with the media models (Harrison, 1997). In looking for any effects of media, we must always keep in mind the importance of cumulative exposure. Most media messages or images are encountered dozens, if not hundreds or thousands, of times. Although such massive exposure is difficult to fully simulate in a laboratory setting and difficult to control in a field study, there are ways it can be studied. For a conceptual paper on defining what an "effect" of media is, see Potter (2011).

Behavioral Effects

Beyond the theories of media effects, there are four general classes of measurable effects of media. Probably the type most people think of first are *behavioral effects*, in which somebody performs some behavior after seeing a media model do it; for example, acting violently, buying a product, voting for a candidate, or laughing or crying. This is the particular emphasis among proponents of social cognitive theory (Bandura, 2009), which is discussed later in this chapter. Although behavior may be conceptually the most obvious type of media effect, it is often very difficult to measure and even harder to definitively attribute a causal role to media. For example, we can know if somebody sees a certain toothpaste commercial and we can check to see if that person buys that brand, but knowing for sure that he or she bought that product because of seeing the particular ad and not for other, unrelated reasons is very difficult to demonstrate. Even in tragic cases like a school shooting by a teen who had recently seen a similar scene in a movie, it is very difficult, in either a legal or scientific sense, to demonstrate a cause-and-effect relationship between the teen seeing the movie and pulling the trigger himself.

Attitudinal Effects

Attitudinal effects make up a second general class of media effects. For example, an ad might make you think more highly of some product or candidate; whether this attitude would be followed up in actual buying or voting behavior is another question. For example, U.S. and Japanese moviegoers viewing the anti-General Motors documentary *Roger and Me* showed a more negative attitude toward GM in particular and U.S. business in general (Bateman, Sakano, & Fujita, 1992), but effects on car-buying behavior were less clear. Conversely, children who watched clips of the movie *Alvin and the Chipmunks* that prominently featured Utz Cheese Balls were more likely than other kids to eat Cheese Balls after viewing, but the exposure didn't seem to affect their attitudes toward the product (Matthes & Naderer, 2015).

Although attitudes consist of an intellectual component (e.g., reasons that you favor one political candidate's position over another's), much of the psychological dynamic in attitudes is emotional (e.g., liking one candidate more than another). Sometimes the intellectual and emotional components may be inconsistent with each other, as when many U.S. voters in 1984 disagreed with President Ronald Reagan's positions on issues but re-elected him in a landslide because they liked him and trusted him. Holding such inconsistent attitudes simultaneously is labeled by social psychologists as *cognitive dissonance* (Festinger, 1957).

Positive feelings about products or candidates may be taught through the process of *classical conditioning*, whereby a conditioned stimulus (a product) is associated with an unconditioned stimulus that naturally elicits some positive response. For example, an attractive model paired with some product may engender positive attitudes, especially positive feelings, through the association of the product with the sexy model, who naturally elicits that positive response. The precise processes by which classical conditioning occurs in advertising are discussed in more detail in Chapter 6.

Media may induce many sorts of attitudes on a given subject. For example, a dramatic TV movie or documentary on human trafficking may sensitize people to this problem and make them more sympathetic to its victims. Stereotyped portrayals of social groups may contribute to prejudice in viewers. Seeing horror movies in which women appear sexually aroused by being raped or assaulted may teach viewers that women derive some secret pleasure out of being victims of sexual violence. Attitudes are much easier to measure than behaviors and often are of great importance, for they influence behaviors and affect the way we cognitively process future information. However, we can't always assume that a given attitude is always followed by a corresponding behavior.

Attitudes may have influence beyond one's opinion about a particular subject. Sets of attitudes may form a sort of mindset through which we view the world. These attitudes color our selection of what we perceive in the world and how we interpret it. The interaction of this knowledge gained from media with our experience in the world can lead to what is called *cultivation* (Bryant *et al.*, 2013; Morgan, Shanahan, & Signorielli, 2009). For example, if we accept the cop-show image of large cities being very dangerous places, that knowledge colors our attitudes about cities but also can affect cognitions and behaviors indirectly in ways that can be measured experimentally. Cultivation theory is discussed later in this chapter.

Cognitive Effects

The third class of media effects is *cognitive effects*, which alter what we know or think. When we are watching TV, on social media, or flipping through a magazine, we are continually processing, comprehending, and remembering the information we are exposed to (Harris, Cady, & Tran, 2006). The most straightforward type of example would be learning new information from media (e.g., facts about chimpanzees from a Discovery Channel documentary). There are also more subtle kinds of cognitive effects. Simply by choosing what news stories to cover, for example, media set an agenda. By covering American presidential primary campaigns much more thoroughly than complex but abstract economic issues like the world debt crisis or the shift from domestic to export agriculture, the media are telling us that the political details of all those primaries are very important, whereas the other issues are relatively less so. Agenda setting is discussed in more detail later in this chapter.

Although cognitive effects are most often measured by testing the information acquired, other types of methods are also useful. For example, attention to TV may be studied by measuring the time the eyes are focused on the screen (Anderson & Kerkorian, 2006). Similarly, the amount of cognitive effort required may be assessed indirectly by measuring the reaction time to remember some information and respond (Cameron & Frieske, 1994) or to do some secondary task (Basil, 1994). Chapter 3 deals with the cognitive effects of consuming media in detail.

Physiological Effects

The fourth class of media effects involves the *physiological effects* or the physical changes in our bodies resulting from exposure to media. For example, increases in breathing and heart rate result from watching a scary movie or an exciting ball game. Sexual arousal from viewing pornography may be measured by sensors on the penis or vagina (Lohr, Adams, & Davis, 1997). Even such mundane material as television or radio commercials can induce changes in the heart rate and orienting reflex (Lang, 1990, 1994b), skin responses (Hopkins & Fletcher, 1994), facial activity (Bolls, Lang, & Potter, 2001; Hazlett & Hazlett, 1999), and changes in alpha waves given off by the brain (Reeves *et al.*, 1985; Simons, Detenber, Cuthbert, Schwartz, & Reiss, 2003; M. E. Smith & Gevins, 2004). See Lang, Potter, and Bolls (2009) for a review of physiological measures of media effects and Ravaja (2004) for a review of research using the measures of heart rate, facial movement, and skin response to study attention and emotional reactions to media.

One of the newest and most exciting physiological measures of media effects comes from functional magnetic resonance imaging (fMRI) scans of the brain. For example, Anderson and colleagues (Anderson, Fite, Petrovich, & Hirsh, 2006) found complex patterns of multiple brain areas which were characteristically activated by watching video action sequences. When the action contains violence, other consistent areas are activated (Murray *et al.*, 2006). Playing violent video games activates brain areas similar to those triggered during actual violent behavior (Weber, Ritterfeld, & Mathiak, 2006) and may change, at least temporarily, the neural structure of the prefrontal cortex (Wang *et al.*, 2009). There has even been success with fMRI scans predicting the effectiveness of anti-smoking messages, similar to those contained in public service announcements (Falk *et al.*, 2016). As studies using fMRI techniques become more common, there will no doubt be additional findings regarding how media consumption affects the brain.

Caveat: The Third-Person Effect

One general principle from social psychology, the *third-person effect*, is very important to consider when looking at media effects. As applied to media, this principle is the notion that people tend to believe that (1) persuasive messages and other media influences can affect behavior, and (2) other people are more vulnerable than we are ourselves to such media influence. This principle, soundly supported by research, suggests that people think other people are more influenced by ads, more distressed about their own bodies relative to supermodels, more corrupted by negative media values, or more likely to emulate violent media models than they themselves are. This effect has been shown in a wide variety of areas, including Internet use (Li, 2008), video game playing and influence (Cruea & Park, 2012), Internet pornography (Lee & Tamborini, 2005), political attack ads (Wei & Lo, 2007), tabloid newspapers and TV sitcoms (Reid & Hogg, 2005), and even things like reality television shows (Leone, Peek & Bissell, 2006) and responding to the H1N1 swine flu pandemic (Lee & Park, 2016; Liu & Lo, 2014). There is even evidence that the third-person effect is particularly large when dealing with seriously antisocial behaviors, such as violence (Hoffner & Buchanan, 2002; Hoffner *et al.*, 2001). A variety of explanations for this robust finding have been offered, as well as delineation of conditions affecting it (see Perloff, 2009, for a review; for meta-analyses see Feng & Guo, 2012; Paul, Salwen, & Dupagne, 2007; Sun, Pan, & Shen, 2008). Being one of several self-serving biases used to maintain a positive self-image (Tal-Or & Tsfati, 2007), the third-person effect leads people to consistently underestimate the media's influence on their own lives, even as they loudly decry its corrupting manipulation on others.

A more general model derived from the third-person effect is the *influence of presumed influence model* (Gunther & Storey, 2003). This model postulates that individuals perceive that some particular media message will have an effect on others. In turn, the individuals who hold this perception change their attitudes or behavior toward the "others." For example, Gunther and Storey evaluated the effect of a radio health campaign in Nepal targeted at health clinic workers. The broader population expected the campaign to affect health care workers, and this, in turn, raised their expectations about their own interactions with those workers, with the result that they held more positive attitudes toward those professionals and the quality of their interaction improved. Thus, the message directly affected the perceptions of people other than its target audience, and those perceptions in turn affected the behavior of the target persons.

The Strength of Effects

Although calculating the precise strength of media effects is a very difficult task, there have been some attempts to do so, using statistical techniques like meta-analysis and computation of effect sizes (Perse, 2007; Perse & Lambe, 2017). For example, such strength measures have been developed for effects of media violence (Christensen & Wood, 2007), gender-role perceptions (Herrett-Skjellum & Allen, 1996), ads targeted to children (Desmond & Carveth, 2007), and pornography (Allen, Emmers, Gebhardt, & Giery, 1995). Perhaps it will be surprising to you, but such studies generally show small to modest (though statistically significant) effect sizes. As would be expected, these effect sizes are almost always larger in laboratory studies than in field studies or surveys, due to the greater degree of experimental control that reduces random error.

Why aren't the effects of media greater than they are? The major reason is that there simply are so many other influences, including some that most everyone would expect to be stronger. For example, parents' behavior and the level of community violence have greater effects on children's level of violent behavior than violent media do. Personal experience with a particular product has more effect on purchasing behavior than advertising does. Whether one's peers and parents smoke is a better predictor of whether a teen will start smoking than is exposure to cigarette advertising or anti-smoking campaigns. None of this is surprising, however. Personal long-term influence has long been known to be highly influential on all sorts of behavior. A good way to look at this is through the idea of risk and protective factors (Kirsh, 2006). A child who will behave in extremely violent ways probably will not do so solely in response to watching a violent movie, being a product of parental neglect, living in a violent community, or getting involved with drugs or gangs, but the more of these risk factors he or she has, the greater the likelihood of violent behavior. In this sense exposure to violent media is one of numerous risk factors. Similarly, the more protective factors a child has (e.g., safe community, strong schools, supportive parents, good friends, high level of empathy), the less likely he or she will be to engage in violent behavior after watching violent media or playing first-person-shooter video games.

Just because media are not the strongest influence, however, does not mean their effects are trivial. In fact, there is good reason to believe that scientific studies may underestimate media effects, especially for very dramatic types of media. For example, studies of sex and violence, especially with children, do not show extremely graphic violence or pornography for ethical reasons. Would you give permission for your 5-year-old to see *Kill Bill*, *Saw*, or child pornography? Although we do not know for sure, it is quite possible that effects of highly graphic stimuli (that many children do, in fact, see in their everyday lives) are greater than those already documented in the research with milder stimuli.

Also, effects may not always be linear, although such linearity is often implicitly assumed by researchers and the public. For example, it is probably not the case that advertising effects gradually increase the more times one sees a particular ad. There is evidence that this is true up to a point, but after that point people seem to grow tired of and even annoyed with the ad, and its impact actually starts to decrease. Sometimes a particular media stimulus contains two different influences which have an opposite impact and thus cancel each other out. For example, watching violence may cause viewers to believe the world is a more violent place, but this fearfulness may also cause them to stay inside more and thus avoid situations where they may be likely to behave violently.

Another issue is the direction of causal influence (Tal-Or, Cohen, Tsfati, & Gunther, 2010). For example, does watching pornography have a causative effect on one's attitude toward censorship, or are they merely correlated? Do seeing and remembering ads for a certain political candidate cause one to vote for that candidate? It is a challenging task for researchers to test and establish such causative relationships, especially in an environment in which many antecedents may have causal impact on a complex behavior.

Finally, because media affect different people so differently, it may be the case that a disproportionate amount of media effects occur with the relatively small number of audience members who experience a very large effect, while most others experience little effect. Thus, group analyses may show overall small effects, but that may not be the whole story. For thorough discussions of these issues in more detail, see Perse (2001, 2007) and Perse and Lambe (2017). For a history of media effects research, see Sparks (2016).

Theories of Mass Communication

Now that we have looked at different media research frameworks and types of effects measured, let us turn to some specific theories that have guided mass communication research over the years. In their current versions, most contemporary theories are heavily cognitive in nature. By this we mean that they view perception and information processing of media messages as constructive; that is, people do not literally encode and retrieve information that they read or hear in the media (or anywhere else). Rather, as they perceive and comprehend media, they interpret in accordance with their prior knowledge and beliefs and the context in which the message is received. Comprehension of a TV program, for example, emerges through a continual interaction between the content of the program and the knowledge already in our minds. The mind is continually and actively thinking about what we see or hear and those thoughts become an important part of the constructive process of comprehension. Now we will examine some of the major theoretical frameworks that have been used to study media.

Social Cognitive Theory (Social Learning, Observational Learning, Modeling)

The social cognitive approach originally grew out of stimulus-response (S-R or behaviorist) psychology as "social learning theory," first developed by social psychologist Albert Bandura and his associates in the 1960s (Bandura, 1977; Bandura, Ross, & Ross, 1961, 1963; Bandura & Walters, 1963). The basic premise of this theory is a simple one: we learn behaviors by observing others performing those behaviors and subsequently imitating them ourselves. The relevance to media occurs when a media actor becomes the model of observational learning. Over its years of development the social cognitive model has increasingly stressed cognitive processes and personal agency or choice.

There are four subfunctions of observational learning from media, according to Bandura (2001, 2002, 2009). The first is obvious. For modeling to occur, a person must be exposed to the media example and pay attention to it. Second, he or she must be capable of symbolically encoding and remembering the observed events, including both constructing the representation and cognitively rehearsing it when the media example is no longer present. Third, the person must be able to translate the symbolic conceptions into appropriate action. Finally, motivations must somehow develop through internal or external reinforcement (reward) in order to energize the performance of the behavior. For example, a girl may see a character being verbally aggressive in a movie when frustrated; later, when frustrated herself, the girl may mimic the behavior in her own life, yelling at her brother. In behaving this way, the girl might think of how the movie character's verbal aggression was reinforced when that character elicited praise from others in the film. As a result, she may expect praise from her friends or some other form of satisfaction for performing the aggression against her brother.

Social cognitive theory was initially applied to media in the context of studying the effects of violent media models on behavior (see Chapter 9). Although that is still the most studied application, the model has many other applications as well, as in the modeling of sexual, prosocial, purchasing, or risky behaviors. For example, children randomly assigned to view high-risk behaviors on TV were more likely to later self-report their own tendency to engage in risk-taking behaviors (Potts, Doppler, &

Hernandez, 1994). Such reported risk-taking was reduced by viewing a safety educational videotape showing high-risk behavior and its negative consequences (Potts & Swisher, 1998). The amount of social aggression (e.g., spreading rumors, social ostracism) that girls aged 5–10 watched predicted increased socially aggressive behavior at school (Martins & Wilson, 2012). Similarly, young women exposed to media portrayals of promiscuous sexual behavior (like one-night stands) were more likely than those not seeing the media models to anticipate doing such behaviors themselves if they did not already have such life experience, regardless of whether the consequences were portrayed as positive or negative in the media portrayal (Nabi & Clark, 2008). See Bandura (2009) for a detailed formulation of the social cognitive model as applied to mass communication.

Cultivation Theory

The *cultivation* approach draws on a cumulative effects model to look at the way that extensive, repeated exposure to media over time gradually shapes our view of the world and our social reality. The more media we are exposed to, the more our views of the world will come to resemble the media worldview. According to this theory, the media shape, nurture, indeed cultivate and grow our worldview. Cultivation theory was initially developed by Gerbner and his colleagues in the Cultural Indicators research project studying television at the University of Pennsylvania. See Gerbner, Gross, Morgan, Signorielli, and Shanahan (2002) and Morgan *et al.* (2009) for overviews of the theory, and Bilandzic (2006) for an integrated theoretical perspective.

One of the major constructs of cultivation theory is *mainstreaming*, the gradual homogenization of people's divergent perceptions of social reality into a convergent belief. This apparently happens through a process of *construction*, whereby viewers learn about the real world from observing the world of media. Because memory traces from media experiences are stored relatively automatically (Shapiro, 1991), we use this stored information to formulate beliefs about the real world (Hawkins & Pingree, 1990; Hawkins, Pingree, & Adler, 1987; Potter, 1989, 1991a, 1991b; Shrum & Bischak, 2001). When this constructed world and the real world of one's experience have a high degree of consistency, *resonance* occurs, and the cultivation effect is even stronger. For example, a woman who has never been to New York City may hold a perception that it is a high-crime area due to portrayals in police dramas or news coverage (mainstreaming). If, upon visiting New York, she frequently sees police cars with lights flashing, her media-spawned idea of a crime-ridden city may be reinforced.

In terms of methodology, cultivation research usually compares frequent ("heavy") and infrequent ("light") viewers of television, researchers' usual medium of study. A typical study finds that the worldview of heavy viewers is more like the world on television. For example, people who watch a lot of violent TV believe the world to be a more violent place than it really is, the so-called "mean world syndrome" (Signorielli, 1990). There is also a greater variance of views among light viewers, suggesting that one effect of watching a lot of mainstream TV is to inculcate a sort of middle-of-the-road view. For example, people who watch a lot of mainstream TV shows are less likely to be either extremely liberal or extremely conservative politically, whereas the political views of light viewers run the entire ideological spectrum, and those who watch mostly polarizing cable news channels become more extreme in their views. Mainstreaming pulls deviants from both directions back toward the middle.

The domains of social reality cultivated through mainstreaming take many forms, including gender roles (Barret & Levin, 2015; Morgan, 1982; Preston, 1990); estimations of crime risk (Parrott & Parrott, 2015b; Shrum, 2001; Shrum & Bischak, 2001); science and scientists (Dudo *et al.*, 2011; Potts & Martinez, 1994); health beliefs and practices (Gerbner, Gross, Morgan, & Signorielli, 1981; Lee & Niederdeppe, 2011); materialism and life satisfaction (Shrum, Lee, Burroughs, & Rindfleisch, 2011); and attitudes about the elderly (Hetsroni & Tukachinsky, 2006) and ethnic groups (Gross, 1984; Vergeer, Lubbers, & Scheepers, 2000).

Cultivation theory has also been applied cross-culturally (e.g., Appel, 2008; Morgan, 1990; Morgan & Shanahan, 1991, 1992, 1995). For an example of how reality shows may cultivate a belief that one is living in such a show, see Close-up 2.3.

Drawing upon the ideas of cultivation theory, Meyrowitz (1985) and Postman (1982, 1985) have argued that children are socialized into the role of adults far earlier since the advent of television than had been the case for the previous several hundred years. Television is the window through which children learn about the world of adults, which is no longer kept secret from them. The effect of television thus is a cultivation and homogenization of developmental stages: children become more like adults, and adults become more like children. This has numerous social implications beyond the world of media. For example, children and adults dress more alike, talk more alike, and go to more of the same places than in the past. No longer do only children wear T-shirts or use slang and only adults wear designer clothes and swear. Similar blurring of the dichotomies of masculinity–femininity and politician–citizen are also posited and attributed to electronic media, increasing androgynous (gender-nonspecific) behavior and holding political candidates to personal standards. Whether such changes are positive or negative socially is probably a matter of personal opinion.

❖ CLOSE-UP 2.3 REALITY SHOWS AS FEEDING DELUSION

Psychiatry professors and brothers Joel Gold and Ian Gold (2012) report several patients whose delusional beliefs took the form of believing they were characters in a reality television show, much like the 1998 movie The Truman Show, *in which Jim Carrey plays a man whose whole life, unbeknownst to him, is a contrived reality show for the entertainment of others and where all his associates, even his wife, are hired actors playing parts. For example, one of the Golds' patients began his first session with his psychiatrist by demanding to speak with the "director" of the reality show he was starring in. Another believed that his life was being continually taped for broadcast as part of a TV show. The Golds argue, not that reality TV has caused these delusions, but rather that existing illnesses such as schizophrenia, in which delusions are a common symptom, interact with major cultural events such as reality shows to give specific content to the delusions. They argue that cultural and media studies are an important component of understanding the cognitive aspects of delusions.*

Although cultivation theory generally focuses on the cumulative effect of many repeated images, some images may be far more influential than others. Greenberg's (1988) *drench hypothesis* says that a highly respected and popular TV character can have far more impact than a dozen other characters seen and identified with by far fewer viewers. Following this argument, Will and Jack, from the sitcom *Will and Grace*, or gay dads Mitchell and Cameron from *Modern Family*, may help improve people's attitudes toward gay men far more than numerous characters on less often seen shows (Bonds-Raacke, Cady, Schlegel, Harris, & Firebaugh, 2007).

In spite of being very influential, cultivation theory is not without its critics. Potter (1991b) has argued that the cultivation effect really involves several components, some of which operate independently. Several studies show that careful controls of certain sociodemographic and personality variables tend to reduce or eliminate cultivation effects (Doob & Macdonald, 1979; Hawkins & Pingree, 1981; Potter, 1986; Wober, 1986). Cultivation studies have also been criticized on conceptual and methodological grounds, including concerns about response biases and problems with the measuring instruments (Hirsch, 1980; Perse, 1986; Potter, 1986, 1993; J. A. Schneider, 1987). There have also been criticisms of some of the assumptions underlying cultivation theory. For example, it seems to assume that the messages of TV are essentially uniform (Hawkins & Pingree, 1981) and that viewers accept what they see as perceived reality (D. Slater & Elliott, 1982). This seems less likely with the advent of hundreds of cable TV channels and streaming services like Netflix. Tamborini and Choi (1990) pointed out the frequent failure of non-U.S. data to strongly support cultivation theory and suggested some reasons for this. See Rubin, Perse, and Taylor (1988) for a review of the methodological critiques of cultivation theory, see Potter (1993, 2014) for a review of conceptual critiques, and see Morgan, Shanahan, and Signorelli (2015) for a discussion of how cultivation theory relates to the modern landscape of television.

Another adaptation of cultivation theory has been to add more cognitive variables, especially the encoding and storage of media messages in memory, in an attempt to increase the rigor and predictability of the theory (Shrum, 2002, 2009; Tapper, 1995). Some have reinterpreted cultivation theory in line with a uses and gratifications approach (see below), stressing the active mental activity of the viewer while watching TV (Levy & Windahl, 1984; Weaver & Wakshlag, 1986). Cultivation then grows out of the viewer's active processing of information and construction of reality. Finally, taking into account cultural differences in media and societal factors and the degree of congruity between the two can help to predict why cultivation occurs in some areas but not in others (e.g., Morgan & Shanahan, 1995).

Uses and Gratifications Theory

The *uses and gratifications* perspective places much emphasis on the active role of the audience in making choices and being goal-directed in its media-use behavior (Oliver & Bartsch, 2010; Palmgreen, 1984; Rosengren, Wenner, & Palmgreen, 1985; Rubin, 2009). The experience and effects of media depend, in part, on the uses one is putting those media to and the gratifications one is receiving from them. For example, the experience of watching a horror film will be very different for someone who is experiencing a good deal of empathy with the victim than for someone who is being only superficially entertained by the suspense of the plot. Watching CNN or surfing Internet news sites may be a very different experience for someone trying to kill time than for someone trying to be seriously informed on the details of a political candidate's positions.

Even the idea of entertainment is more complex than it first appears. Although much of the public (and many researchers) assume that the wish to be entertained is *hedonic*, or pleasure-seeking, often it may be seen as non-hedonic, or *eudaimonic*, involving personal expressiveness, competence, autonomy, and self-development. In fact there is evidence that both hedonic and non-hedonic factors are important components of entertainment (Tamborini *et al.*, 2011). For example, we may enjoy playing a video game in part because of the sense of mastery or competence achieved. Similarly, we can be entertained by a sad film, which gives us some understanding of the human condition, although watching it may not exactly be an immediately pleasurable experience (Oliver & Raney, 2011). What we find the most entertaining may also change over the lifespan. Bartsch (2012) found that young adults aged 18–25 were more interested than adults over 50 in emotionally intense entertainment, such as thrills from horror or adventure films and tear-jerking sadness from dramas. Older adults, on the other hand, preferred more contemplative entertainment experiences. This goes a long way to explaining why young people like horror and action films and their parents prefer quieter, more thoughtful dramas.

We may use media for many other reasons besides basic entertainment or information-seeking. Perhaps it is to avoid studying. Maybe it is to escape into a fantasy world or be turned on by a particularly sexy star. Perhaps it is to find out what everybody's talking about in regard to some popular show or to be more like our friends who are watching. Sometimes we watch a program we strongly dislike simply to make ourselves feel less alone or to be emotionally stimulated. For many solo drivers, the radio or podcasts are a constant traveling companion. What draws different people to consume different types of media may be a critical issue; for example, it is very helpful to know the factors that cause some people to seek out and watch violent pornography. See Rubin (2002) and Conway and Rubin (1991) for discussions of psychological motives in uses and gratifications research.

Rubin (2009) identified several research directions for uses and gratifications research. One is to develop taxonomies of communication motives. This might be a particularly important area of research with regard to newer computer-mediated technologies, especially social media (Quan-Haase & Young, 2010). An additional approach to uses and gratifications theory has looked at different social and psychological circumstances of media use, including co-viewers, personality, lifestyle, or religiosity (Harris & Cook, 2011). Yet another direction has examined the role of individual differences in experiences, motives, and exposure on the media experience. For example, one intriguing behavior genetics study comparing identical and fraternal twins concluded that up to one-third of the differences in media use habits and behaviors across people may be due to genetic influences (Kirzinger, Weber, & Johnson, 2012).

Agenda Setting Theory

This theory, which initially grew out of communications research on political socialization (Dearing & Rogers, 1996), defines *agenda setting* as the "creation of public awareness and concern of salient issues by the news media" (Heath & Bryant, 1992, p. 279). The idea here is that the media do not necessarily tell us what to think, but rather what to *think about*. Note that there is a distinction between agenda setting theory (media tell us what issues are most important for our consideration) and cultivation theory (media shape and form our thoughts on issues). For example, through heavy coverage of such issues as Hillary Clinton's misuse of an e-mail server, the news media may tell us that this is an important issue on which to base our vote. Other issues covered in less depth, such as a candidate's positions on taxation or foreign policy, are thus positioned as less important. See Chapters 7 and 8 for further discussion of agenda setting in regard to news, and Kosicki (1993), McCombs and Reynolds (2002), Tai (2009), and Wanta (1997) for theoretical conceptualizations.

Although it has been explored most fully in regard to news and politics, agenda setting is also relevant to other media issues as well. DeFleur (2010, p. 160) calls this "collateral instruction." For example, in their basic ignoring of religion, mainstream entertainment media in the United States are sending a message that spiritual issues are not important factors in people's lives. Soap operas and movies that continually show characters engaging in seemingly unprotected casual sex with no apparent concern for consequences like HIV infection or pregnancy are subtly telling us that those concerns are not important. Likewise, characters' incessant preoccupation with body image tells viewers they should be concerned about that.

One way that an agenda can be set is through the use of *framing* (Borah, 2011; Entman, 1993; McCombs & Ghanem, 2001; Scheufele & Tewksbury, 2007; Tewksbury & Scheufele, 2009; Wicks, 2001). The way a problem is described selects or highlights certain aspects of its reality and neglects or downplays others. This framing will affect how people respond to it. For example, is some indiscretion described as a "caper," an "affair," or a "scandal"? Jamieson and Waldman (2003) argued that press coverage of the U.S. presidential election campaign of 2000 framed the candidates as the "lying panderer" (Al Gore) and the "ineffective bumbler" (George W. Bush) and that media and the public noticed details consistent with the frames and neglected details that were inconsistent (see Chapter 8 for further discussion of the framing of the candidates in the 2000 and other elections). Framing effects can be quite persistent, particularly if media consumers have moderate, rather than high or low, levels of political knowledge about the issue (Lecheler & de Vreese, 2011).

There have been some attempts to integrate agenda setting with other theoretical approaches. For example, Wanta (1997) draws on the cognitive and uses and gratifications perspectives to develop a model of agenda setting that focuses more on the individual, rather than the issue, as the unit of measurement. Wanta tested this model and concluded that those most susceptible to agenda-setting effects are those who more actively process information from news media. McCombs, Shaw, and Weaver (1997) extended agenda setting to some new areas, including political advertising, economic news, and comparative effectiveness of television and print media in setting agendas. Wanta and Ghanem (2007) offer a meta-analysis showing agenda-setting effects of news across a wide variety of studies.

Schema (Script) Theory

Part of what guides the perception, comprehension, and later memories of information from media are *schemas* (Brewer & Nakamura, 1984; Rumelhart, 1980). The construct of schema refers to knowledge structures or frameworks that organize an individual's memory for people and events. A schema is a general mental construct or model about some knowledge domain. A person holds mental schemas based on past experiences; for example, our schemas about Latinos, schizophrenics, or psychologists are connected to our memories and personal experiences. One consequence of holding these schemas for information processing is that the individual is likely to go beyond the information actually presented to draw inferences about people or events that are congruent with previously formed schemas (Harris, 1981; Rojahn & Pettigrew, 1992). For example, someone with a very negative schema about Mexican Americans might notice and remember all sorts of negative things about Latinos in response to watching a TV show set in Latino East Los Angeles, whereas someone with a more positive schema would notice and remember different, and more favorable, information from the same show. Typically, much of the content in schemas is culture-specific. The schema that members of one culture may hold may cause them to interpret the same story very differently than members of a different culture (Harris, Schoen, & Hensley, 1992; Lasisi & Onyehalu, 1992). Cultural differences must be carefully considered by TV producers in international programming sales (see Close-up 2.4).

❖ CLOSE-UP 2.4 THE INTERNATIONALIZATION OF POPULAR CULTURE

Although the United States is a major exporter of television programming and movies, no country is able to totally dominate media today, if indeed this was ever possible (Chung, 2011; Straubhaar, 2007; Tunstall, 2007). What is actually happening is a globalization of all cultures (Legrain, 2003). McDonald's is becoming more popular worldwide, but so are Indian curry, Japanese sushi, and Greek or Arab hummus. Hollywood studios dominate world movie distribution, but film productions are multinational efforts. For example, many top "American" entertainment figures are not really American at all: Salma Hayek and Gael Garcia are Mexican; Nicole Kidman, Hugh Jackman, Cate Blanchett, Chris and Liam Hemsworth, and Russell Crowe are all Australian; Christian Bale, Kate Winslet, Ewan McGregor, and virtually the entire cast of the Harry Potter films are British; Ryan Gosling, Seth Rogen, and Ryan Reynolds are Canadian; Antonio Banderas, Penélope Cruz, and Javier Bardem are Spanish; and Colin Farrell is Irish. Many top Hollywood directors similarly are from elsewhere than the United States: Peter Weir and Baz Luhrmann (Australia), Stanley Kubrick and Ridley Scott (Britain), Pedro Almodovar (Spain), and Peter Jackson and Jane Campion (New Zealand). In terms of music, despite the pressure to record in English, many of international music's biggest sellers are not Americans. A few of these include the Beatles and the Rolling Stones (UK), Marc Anthony and Shakira (Colombia), U2 (Ireland), Bjork (Iceland), Justin Bieber and Drake (Canada), Abba (Sweden), and Julio and Enrique Iglesias (Spain).

The United States itself is a market as well as a producer. Many broadcast and cable markets now carry Univision and/or Telemundo, both Spanish-language channels headquartered in the United States. Mexico's Televisa earns millions exporting its soap operas, with some of those sales going to the United States. The British BBC and ITV have exported programs to America's PBS for years. With the improvement in cable and satellite technology, there are now specialized American and/or international versions of some channels such as BBC America. In addition, many American cable and satellite systems offer international channel packages with foreign stations available from around the world.

In mass media, activation of a schema in the mind of the audience member may be triggered by some particular information in the TV program, magazine article, or website. It may also be triggered by the content of certain *formal features* of the particular medium, such as flashbacks, montage, or instant replays in television or film. Young children do not understand these conventions and will interpret the input literally (e.g., thinking that a flashback or instant replay is continuing new action). Part of the socialization to the use of a medium like television is to learn about these formal features and how to interpret them (Bickham, Wright, & Huston, 2001; Calvert, 1988; Kraft, Cantor, & Gottdiener, 1991; Lang, Geiger, Strickwerda, & Sumner, 1993; Rice, Huston, & Wright, 1986; Wilson, 1991).

One place we learn schemas and scripts about our world and how to live in it is from media (Luke, 1987). *Script* here refers to a schema about an activity and is not the same meaning as "pages of dialogue." For example, when we watch a TV drama about a woman who discovers she has breast cancer, we may acquire a mental script for dealing with that particular situation. The viewer may learn specific activities like breast self-examination, how to tell her husband about her illness, how to seek out information about possible treatments, and how to cope with a mastectomy and chemotherapy in terms of her own self-image and sexuality. Through exposure to samples of activities following a particular script, that abstract script is inferred and gradually becomes a part of our permanent memory (Ahn, Brewer, & Mooney, 1992). This skeleton structure of an activity is then used to interpret future instances of that activity. For instance, listeners of a British radio soap opera, *The Archers*, used knowledge of a general familiar script from that show to help them remember specific details from individual episodes (Reeve & Aggleton, 1998).

The potential consequences of learning scripts from media become especially clear when we consider a situation for which readers or viewers have little prior knowledge or scripts from their own life experience. For example, suppose a child's knowledge of dealing with muggers has resulted from watching TV adventure heroes trick and overpower the robber. If that child were to try that script on a real mugger by attempting the same moves as seen on TV, the consequences might be disastrous. As another example, consider a TV movie dealing with incest. A preteen in the story is being sexually molested by her uncle and is sufficiently troubled to mention this to a school counselor, a revelation that sets in motion a sequence of events that eventually, but inevitably, brings this event out in the open. Because incest was not discussed for so many years, many viewers, including some current or former victims, may have had no mental script for how to handle it. In this sense, such a movie, if done sensitively yet realistically, could help victims to come forth and seek help. It could provide information on how one may expect to feel about that experience and where to seek help, and, through the context of the drama, could offer a scenario of what the effects of such a revelation might be.

In a more general sense, media fiction sometimes draws on very abstract scripts such as "overcoming adversity." This implicit theme may be reflected in a story about a slave escaping from forced servitude in the antebellum South, a child learning to cope with alcoholic parents, or a burned-out police officer coming to terms with a vicious crime syndicate. Such a script is also used in many human interest news stories.

There is a very general script for stories in Western culture (Kintsch, 1977). This *narrative script* is learned implicitly from the earliest days of young children hearing stories from their parents. Such stories are composed of episodes, each of which contains an exposition, complication, and resolution. That is, the characters and setting are introduced (*exposition*), some problem or obstacle develops (*complication*), and that problem or obstacle is somehow overcome (*resolution*). We grow up expecting stories to follow this general script. Children's stories such as fairy tales do so very explicitly ("Once upon a time there was a ..."). Adult stories also follow the same script but often in a more complex fashion. For example, some of the complication may be introduced before all of the exposition is finished or there may be two sub-episodes embedded in the resolution of a larger episode.

Entertainment media, like television or film, also draw on the narrative script to make their stories more readily understandable. Children's cartoons follow the script very explicitly. Most TV sitcoms and action-adventure shows also do, although perhaps in a somewhat more complicated fashion; for example, there may be two interwoven episodes (subplots), each with its own narrative structure. The use of schemas enhances our information-processing capabilities. Meadowcroft and Reeves (1989) found that children had well-developed story schema skills by age 7, and such skills led to better memory for the central story content, a reduction in processing effort, and a greater flexibility of attention-allocation strategies. Soap operas traditionally hold an audience by concluding each day's story just before the resolution. Because we have this sense of our narrative script being incomplete, we are motivated to return the next day or the next week to complete it. This principle of the cliffhanger has been used in some prime-time season finales to ensure the interest and return of viewers for the first show of the next season so that they can learn the resolution of the story.

Even many ads draw upon the narrative script. For example, a nice young fellow is ready to go out on a hot date (exposition), but alas, he notices his teeth are yellowed (complication). But his mom and her amazing dental whitening strips come to the rescue to brighten his teeth just in time (resolution). Because of our familiarity with the narrative script, we are able to comprehend such a commercial very easily, which is of course to the advertiser's advantage. Also, because it fits the story structure of many programs, it seems more entertaining and is thus more likely than a traditional sales pitch to hold viewers' attention. The narrative script is a deeply ingrained knowledge structure; Esslin (1982) went so far as to argue that the 30-second story of an unhappy hemorrhoid sufferer has the same dramatic structure as a classic Greek tragedy!

Limited Capacity Model

Another heavily cognitive model is Lang's (2000) *limited capacity model* (sometimes called the Limited Capacity Model of Motivated Mediated Message Processing or *LC4MP*). Drawing on basic cognitive psychology, Lang makes two basic assumptions: (1) people are information processors, and (2) the ability to process information is limited. These information processes are sometimes automatic and sometimes controlled, that is, involving conscious choice. Information processing involves three major sub-processes: *encoding* (understanding and putting information in), *storage* (hanging onto information for possible later use), and *retrieval* (being able to recall information later). These may be done partially in parallel, but the processing resources are limited, and heavy allocation to one may result in superficial allocation to another.

One of the automatic selection mechanisms steering the encoding of information is the orienting response. When this occurs, as in our attention being captured by a jolting message on TV, more cognitive resources are allocated to encoding the information from that source. Encoding of that information is enhanced, provided that the cognitive load is low. For example, if we're watching a relatively boring TV show and a loud, jarring commercial suddenly appears, we're likely to pay attention to it. Similarly, if we're not distracted (by say, a side conversation or our smartphone), we're more likely to process the information in the commercial.

If, however, the cognitive load is high, the limited resources will be overwhelmed, and less encoding will occur. For example, if we're watching a politician on TV discuss numerous issues with which we have limited knowledge (like the intricacies of budgets and legislative procedural rules), we may struggle, spending so much energy trying to understand basics of the message that we miss the larger points being made. As a result, we may later have difficulty recalling what was said at all.

Conclusion

The theoretical frameworks discussed above have all been influential in guiding the research on mass communication. Some have been particularly useful in certain content areas or with certain types of research designs. All are at least somewhat cognitive in nature, as they deal with the knowledge representation of information from the media and the processing of that knowledge through attention, perception, comprehension, and memory. The theories are not necessarily mutually exclusive, either. In fact, in many cases they are quite complementary, as they emphasize different aspects of our interaction with media. For example, social cognitive theory focuses on the modeling of behavior, while cultivation looks more at attitudinal effects, and schema theory and limited capacity say more about the information processing dimension.

Now we have some idea of what research in mass communication is all about and what sort of answers it seeks. There are different types of research and different theories to guide this research. In the next chapter we turn to look at various psychological constructs and topics which are important in understanding media.

Media Applications, Chapter 2: Using Media Research to Influence School Curriculum

As discussed at the end of Chapter 1, media literacy involves critically thinking about media as a way to effectively deal with it. There is great opportunity for teachers at all levels of education to use the lessons from research in media and psychology to help their students successfully navigate the media world.

Numerous attempts have been made to develop curricula for use in schools to help children become more critical viewers of television. These programs have been more widespread in places like Australia, Canada, and the United Kingdom than they have in the United States, where media literacy has sadly often been seen as a "frill" and one of the first programs to be cut in times of budget problems and "back-to-basics" movements in education. For reviews and evaluation of some of these projects, see Brown (1991), Buckingham (1993, 1998, 2003), Hoechsmann and Poyntz (2012), and Potter (2016). Such curricula have been developed by school districts, universities, religious organizations (e.g., U.S. Catholic Conference, Media Action Research Center), private companies (e.g., The Learning Seed Co., Television Learning Ltd.), United Nations/UNESCO, and other governmental or nongovernmental organizations (e.g., Scottish Film Council, Western Australia Ministry of Education, National Congress of Parents and Teachers).

An example of an early program was developed by Dorothy and Jerome Singer and their colleagues at Yale University starting in the late 1970s. They offered 8 lessons to be taught twice a week over a 4-week period to third-, fourth-, and fifth-grade children. Topics included reality and fantasy on TV, camera effects, commercials, stereotypes, identification with TV characters, and violence and aggression. Evaluation studies showed sizable increases in knowledge in the experimental group, particularly at immediate testing. The program was then extended to kindergarten and first- and second-grade children; extensive pilot testing suggested that such children could be taught considerable amounts about the nature of television through such a curriculum (Singer & Singer, 1981, 1983; Singer, Singer, & Zuckerman, 1981; Singer, Zuckerman, & Singer, 1980).

Another example is an 18-lesson, 6-month classroom intervention for third and fourth graders (Robinson, Saphir, Kraemer, Varady, & Haydel, 2001). This program was designed to reduce television, videotape, and video game use, which would thus lead to fewer effects of those media on the children. It succeeded in doing so, and also in reducing the number of children's reports of requests to parents to purchase advertised toys, especially in the children who reduced their TV and video use more. However, it did not affect the parental reports of toy purchase requests, compared to a control group. Still, this suggests that it is possible to reduce television and video consumption and such reductions can have other positive effects.

These projects, as well as most others that have been developed, have focused primarily on television. A meta-analysis (Jeong, Cho, & Hwang, 2012) looked at 51 evaluative media literacy studies and concluded that they were generally effective, especially those which did not try to evaluate too many components in one project. A review of the research on media literacy programs designed to reduce stereotypes (Scharrer & Ramasubramanian, 2015) found the programs to be effective, although more research still needs to be done. How might your experience with media have been different if you had had a media literacy course in school as a child? What might you be able to do to influence how your children (and others) learn about media in school?

Further Reading

Bryant, J., & Oliver, M. B. (Eds.). (2009). *Media effects: Advances in theory and research.* 3rd ed. New York: Taylor & Francis.

Feaster, F., & Wood, B. (1999). *Forbidden fruit: The golden age of the exploitation film.* Baltimore: Midnight Marquee Press.

Perse, E. M. (2001). *Media effects and society.* Mahwah, NJ: Erlbaum.

Potter, W. J. (2011). Conceptualizing mass media effect. *Journal of Communication, 61,* 896–915.

Potter, W. J. (2014). A critical analysis of cultivation theory: Cultivation. *Journal of Communication, 64*(6), 1015–1036. doi: 10.1111/jcom.12128

Tai, Z. (2009). The structure of knowledge and dynamic of scholarly communication in agenda setting research, 1996–2005. *Journal of Communication, 59,* 481–513.

Useful Links

Cognitive Dissonance:
www.simplypsychology.org/cognitive-dissonance.html

Geena Davis Institute on Gender in Media:
https://seejane.org/

The Nielsen Company:
www.nielsen.com/us/en.html

Reefer Madness (full movie):
www.youtube.com/watch?v=yEx0Hvojwm4

Social Cognitive Theory:
www.simplypsychology.org/bandura.html

For more resources, please visit the companion website:
www.routledge.com/cw/harris

Chapter 3

The Psychology of Mass Communication

Thinking about Our Media Use

Q: In the classic 1939 film *The Wizard of Oz*, what's wrong with Dorothy's shoes when she and the Scarecrow fight off angry apples trees?

A: At first, Dorothy is wearing the famed ruby slippers. In the next scene, she is wearing black shoes. The film cuts again to Dorothy in the ruby slippers. Although this information is taken in by viewers' eyes every time they view the movie, most never register the discrepancy unless it is pointed out to them.

Q: When Disney's Animal Kingdom opened in Orlando, what was the major complaint about the live animals there from its first visitors?

A: That they were not "realistic" enough, that is, not like the active robotic animals elsewhere in Disney World or in depictions seen on TV (Turkle, 2011).

Q: During the 1980 U.S. presidential election campaign, candidate and former movie star Ronald Reagan liked to tell of a World War II pilot who stayed with an injured gunner rather than bail out after his plane was hit. When did this event occur?

A: Never in real life. Reagan was remembering a scene from the 1944 war movie *Wing and Prayer* (Schacter, 1996).

In the last chapter we looked at how scientists study media and what theories they use to guide them in that endeavor. We continue in this chapter by examining the psychology of using media. There are numerous psychological processes operating as we interact with media. We start out by looking at children in particular and some of the developmental issues they bring to media use. Then we look at several cognitive processes we use in understanding media. Finally, we conclude the chapter with a more in-depth look at the overall theme of this book, namely, the perceived reality created by media.

Children's Distinctive Use of Media

Although young children regularly encounter fiction in both book and television format, because TV looks more like "real life," children recognize at an earlier age when books, as opposed to television, are representing fiction rather than fact (Kelly, 1981). Thus, the world of television is more easily confused with reality than is the printed equivalent.

Mental Effort and Social Interaction

The nature of specific media affects how the child can extract information from that medium and represent it in memory. In general, television involves less mental effort than print media, although this varies somewhat with age and type of program (Bordeaux & Lange, 1991). Historically, when the invention of print came along several centuries ago, it permitted the widespread physical storage of information (Greenfield, 1984). People who had acquired the skill of literacy thus had access to vast amounts of information previously unavailable except through oral transmission. Literacy also had social implications, in that it was the first medium of communication that required solitude for its effective practice (Olson, 1994). Critics of television who fear that its advent has isolated children from social interaction are in fact concerned about a far earlier effect of the onset of print media; television only continued the requirement of physical isolation, but it did not initiate it. In fact, research has shown no relationship between the amount of television watched and time spent in interpersonal activity.

Of course, recent concerns have focused particularly on children's use of the Internet and social media. The fears expressed that web surfers are becoming socially isolated, perhaps even socially inept, sound amazingly like concerns expressed in the early days of print and later in the early days of television. In a very provocative book, Reeves and Nass (1996) argued that our interactions with computers, televisions, and other media are much more similar to the way that we interact with other people than most of us realize. For example, at times we treat computers with emotion (politeness, anger) and even perceive them as having personalities; this may be especially true of "virtual assistants" like Apple's Siri and Amazon's Alexa. See Turkle (2011) for a provocative look at how Internet technology has changed (and not changed) social interactions.

The Medium and Imagination

Although media, especially television, have the potential to either stimulate or reduce children's creativity and imaginative play, overall there is much more evidence for some type of reduction effect (Calvert & Valkenburg, 2013; Valkenburg, 2001). Certainly creative play can be stimulated by watching certain TV shows, especially educational TV, but facilitated creativity does not appear to be a widespread effect. It has long been known that *Sesame Street* and especially the slower-paced shows like *Mister Rogers' Neighborhood* have been shown to stimulate imaginative play (Singer & Singer, 1976; Tower, Singer, & Singer, 1979), whereas action-adventure shows are associated with the lowest imaginative play scores (Singer & Singer, 1981).

Reductions in creativity or imaginative play could occur for several reasons. First of all, there is some evidence that television watching displaces more creative play and interferes simply by replacing that activity. Other possible explanations remain possibilities but have as yet garnered less overall support (Calvert & Valkenburg, 2013; Valkenburg, 2001; Valkenburg & Peter, 2006). TV may induce passivity, which is inconsistent with imagination and creativity, and the rapid pacing of children's programs does not allow time for reflection and imagination. Finally, the highly visual nature of television could be so salient that it may distract from processing ideas creatively, a type of thinking that may be easier with print or radio presentation. For instance, pre-school children who watched more TV were less likely to have an imaginary playmate and showed lower scores on imaginative play (Singer & Singer, 1981). Does watching television interfere with the development of reading skills or fantasy play? It probably depends on what activity television is replacing.

Information Extraction and Memory in Children and Adults

Different forms of media may stimulate different types of cognitive processing. Older media like radio and print are largely verbal, whereas the Internet and television, of course, involve the visual dimension as well. There is much similarity in the way that a story is comprehended from a book and from the radio, but less similarity between a story read and one seen on television (Pezdek, Lehrer, & Simon, 1984). In early studies comparing cognitive effects of radio versus television in telling stories, children produced more original endings for incomplete stories heard on the radio than they did for stories seen and heard on television (Valkenburg & Beentjes, 1997). This offers some research support for the intuitive claim that radio activates the imagination more than TV does. However, children tend to remember visual, action, and overall infor-mation better from television than from verbal media like radio (Gunter, Furnham, & Griffiths, 2000). In addition, materials with previews and/or summaries or visual scene repetition, that is, some redundancies, were better remembered by 6- to 8-year-old children than the same material that was not repeated (Michel & Roebers, 2008). Thus, television, being both visual and repetitive, is a very efficient way to transmit informa-tion to children, suggesting both greater potential and greater concern regarding this medium.

Internet use is different than all other modalities in that it is visual, frequently auditory, and often interactive. Further, different uses of the Internet (i.e., gaming vs. communication vs. surfing the web) demand differing cognitive tasks (Johnson, 2006). One interesting study examined cross-media advertising (i.e., advertising a product on TV as well as the Internet) with adult participants. Compared to single modal ads, those that were presented in both formats were better recalled. However, this effect disappeared when implicit memory for the products was tested (e.g., completing word fragment tests that could spell a brand name) (Vandeberg, Murre, Voorveld, & Smit, 2015). Effects of medium were also shown in memory for news from the 2000 U.S. pol-itical campaign (Eveland, Seo, & Marton, 2002). People gained more political know-ledge when they accessed media information from varying media modalities (e.g., print news combined with Internet news) than from one modality alone (Shen & Eveland, 2010). In a related study that foreshadowed the 2016 U.S. presidential election, Lee and Shin (2014) compared perceptions of a political candidate based on Twitter posts or a newspaper story. In contrast to those who read the newspaper article only, participants who gleaned information about the politician via Twitter had a more favorable impres-sion and said they were more likely to vote for the candidate.

Cognitive Components of the Media Experience

We now turn our attention to different cognitive processes involved in experiencing media. By "cognitive," we mean the thought processes involved in attending, perceiving, comprehending, interpreting, and remembering the material that we encounter through media. The stimuli that we cognitively process may be in the form of language (written or spoken) or pictorial (filmed still or moving pictures), or some combination of the two. Often, as in the case with television and film, language and pictorial stimuli occur in parallel together, though sometimes they occur separately. There also may be multiple levels of pictorial stimuli; for example, the viewer may encounter cues about character movement and action but also background lighting, shadows, and other aspects of the visual stimulus, as well as nonlinguistic auditory stimuli like background music or sound effects. The way that a TV show's sets are laid out and the how the scenes are filmed can affect the difficulty of the viewing process as well. Shows with traditional set layouts (like the typical sitcom house with a missing "fourth wall") are easier for people to imagine than a complicated set (like a hospital) (Levin, 2010).

Now let us look at several different aspects of media cognition, starting with attention.

Attention

As a prerequisite to any comprehension of media, we must first select some information to attend to and process further; this necessarily entails neglecting other information. For example, while viewing television, children initially allocate considerable attention to difficult TV segments but quickly reduce that attention if the material is beyond their level of comprehensibility (Hawkins, Kim, & Pingree, 1991). Overall, children also spend more time attending to "child content" than to "adult content" (Schmitt, Anderson, & Collins, 1999).

Although there are many ways, some very sophisticated, of measuring exposure to filmed media (Simons *et al.*, 2003; Smith, Levin, & Cutting, 2012), it is naïve to assume either that viewers are fully processing everything that they encounter in media or conversely that it is not affecting them at all unless they are paying full conscious attention. The issue is also relevant across media. For example, how much do we process the typical magazine or Internet ad as we flip through a publication or scan a web page with little if any conscious attention to the ad?

Multitasking

Merely measuring when a television is on or how much time we allow a certain web page to remain before we click on another link does not give us complete information about how much is being understood or what influence it is having. A big question, particularly in the study of television, film, or the Internet, is how much attention viewers are paying to the screen while it is on. For example, we know that when the TV is on, it is often receiving less than total undivided attention from viewers. Research studying people watching television has found that the typical adult or child over age 5 attends to the TV between 55% and 70% of the time it is on (Anderson & Burns, 1991; Anderson & Field, 1991; Anderson & Kerkorian, 2006; Schmitt, Woolf, & Anderson, 2003), varying some depending on the time of day and the type of program being watched. For example, morning and afternoon TV shows seem to receive less attention (and more multitasking) than do evening shows. Comedies receive a little more attention than dramas or news and much more attention than commercials (Hawkins et al., 2005; Voorveld & Viswanathan, 2015). In addition, more attention is given to moving images than to static ones (Simons et al., 2003), and we seem to cognitively process information at a lower, more concrete and superficial level while multitasking with TV than while processing information separately (Kazakova, Cauberghe, Pandelaere & De Pelsmacker, 2015).

Overall, both structure and content factors help determine the amount of attention allocated (Geiger & Reeves, 1993a, 1993b), and familiar content may partially compensate for structural confusion (Schwan & Ildirar, 2010). Sometimes we may not be looking at the screen very much but may nonetheless be monitoring the sound for items of interest so we can redirect our vision toward the screen, if necessary. Even very young children are quite skilled at doing this (Rolandelli, Wright, Huston, & Eakins, 1991). Children are regular multitaskers well before adolescence, with greater multitasking for those high in sensation seeking and those with televisions and computers in their own rooms (Jeong & Fishbein, 2007).

These days, much of our attention while watching TV is drawn to our smartphones, tablets, or computers. Sometimes called two-screen viewing, studies have shown that when this happens, our attention tends to focus more on the computer or phone screen than on the television (Brasel & Gips, 2011; Jago, Sebire, Gorely, Cillero, & Biddle, 2011). Interestingly, however, people may often be using their electronic devices to engage others online about what is airing on TV (Shim, Oh, Song, & Lee, 2015).

Multitasking of media may be particularly appealing because of our desire to meet multiple needs and achieve multiple gratifications (Wang & Tchernev, 2012). There are even a few people with exceptional multitasking ability that goes beyond what most of us are capable of (Watson & Strayer, 2010). At some point, however, our attention becomes overloaded. Despite the increasing popularity of multichannel information sources, such as cable news networks, which often have multiple screens of different information and unrelated news crawls at the bottom of the screen, there is evidence that viewers are unable to grasp all of that information and actually acquire less information than they do from a less cluttered format (Bergen, Grimes, & Potter, 2005).

Attending to Changes

One fascinating aspect of attending to film is how much we do not see. The well-documented phenomenon of *change blindness* (Simons & Ambinder, 2005; Simons & Levin, 1997, 1998) refers to the fact we do not notice changes in a continuous visual scene as we watch it. In one famous experiment (Simons & Levin, 1998), the unwitting experimental participant was talking to someone else on campus when two workers carrying a door "rudely" walked between them. Unknown to the participant, one of those men switched places with the man who had been in the conversation. After the door passed, the conversation continued with the new speaker. Although the two men did not look particularly similar, about half the participants never noticed that their conversation partner had changed! Such effects are even more dramatic when considering *inattentional blindness*, or the inability to see something because our focus is drawn elsewhere. For instance, in one famous example, while watching a video of a group playing a basketball-like game, people do not notice a gorilla walk through the middle of the visual field because they are occupied counting the number of ball tosses (Simons & Chabris, 1999).

In terms of filmed entertainment, change or inattentional blindness is a very good thing. Movie scenes are not filmed in the final order they appear on film. Multiple takes, often filmed at different times, are edited together much later to make what is hopefully a coherent story. Often, editors rely on devices such as audio cues or quick cuts to action to distract us from the fact that something has changed (Smith & Martin-Portugues Santacreu, 2017). Virtually every film ever released has multiple continuity errors, which, fortunately for our movie enjoyment, most of us never notice. For example, someone is eating a sandwich and later in the scene there is more sandwich on the plate than there was earlier, or early in the scene a woman is wearing a necklace and a minute later in the same scene she is not. Although we seldom see these discontinuities unless they are pointed out, descriptions (and sometimes clips) of many are readily available online.

Why don't we notice such "obvious" changes when we are attending to the screen? As we attend, our minds are constructing an interpretation of what we are seeing, with a focus on the action and characters. We do not notice changes in the background unless they are quite blatant. This constructive nature of film comprehension is a major reason that we can enjoy film and perceive it so continuously.

Although it has been so far studied primarily with regard to television and filmed media, attention is also an important issue with newer computer-based technologies. With its numerous links that can be clicked, the Internet offers the chance to make many more choices than television does. One study found that allowing women to choose the type of ad they watched increased the attention subsequently devoted to that ad, although the effect was not obtained in men (Nettelhorst & Brannon, 2012). One of the most controversial issues in attention has been the mobile phone, especially the possible distraction effects of using mobile phones while driving. In recent years many jurisdictions have passed laws forbidding talking or texting on handheld phones while driving. There is reason to be concerned, and not only for handheld devices. See Close-up 3.1 for some troubling results from some well-controlled experimental research on the effects of talking on the phone while driving.

❖ CLOSE-UP 3.1 WHICH IS WORSE: DRIVING DRUNK OR WHILE TALKING ON A CELL PHONE? (THE ANSWER MAY SURPRISE YOU)

Some of the most popular driving activities in recent years seem to be talking or texting on a cell phone. Is this harmless multitasking or a dangerous distraction? University of Utah psychologist Strayer and his colleagues (Strayer, Drews, Crouch, & Johnston, 2005) used a high-fidelity driving simulator to answer this question, and their findings are sobering. Compared to those in a control group devoting full attention to driving, those talking on a cell phone missed twice as many red lights, recognized fewer billboards they had driven by, took longer to hit the brake to stop while following another car, took longer to recover speed after passing the car, and had more accidents, in spite of leaving more distance between themselves and the next car.

Some additional conditions helped to better understand what was happening. Talking on a hands-free phone was just as bad as on a hand-held phone, so it is the cognitive distraction of the conversation, not the motor skill requirement of holding the phone that is the major problem. Also, drivers who were listening to the radio or a recorded book or talking to a passenger in the car did not differ from the control group, so these conditions do not place strong demands on attention. One does not have to respond to the radio or talking book, and when the other conversant is in the car with the driver, he or she can also see the driving conditions and make adjustments in the conversation as conditions warrant, such as keeping quiet for a while. In one study, Strayer got his participants drunk to the minimum blood alcohol level for legal intoxication after they had driven in the control and cell-phone conditions. In the car-following task, students who were legally drunk actually stopped and later regained speed faster than those talking on the cell phone, though they were slower in doing so than the controls. Thus, talking on a cell phone actually impaired driving more than being legally drunk!

This research used the experimental design of cognitive psychology to address a question of vital social importance. The results support recent legislation in many places to ban cell phone use while driving, although limiting the ban to hand-held units may not completely do the job. Even though perceptions of driving after drinking have shifted over the years, many of us still excuse mobile phone use behind the wheel. Terry and Terry (2016) found that although college students thought drunk driving and cell phone use while driving were both dangerous, they were far more likely to admit to using their phones when driving.

Suspending Disbelief

Like movies or theater, television entertainment involves the social convention of the "willing suspension of disbelief," in which we, for a brief time, agree to accept the characters portrayed on screen as real human beings so that we can identify with them to experience their joys and sorrows (Cohen, 2006; Esslin, 1982). We know that two actors are not really married to each other, but we agree to suspend our disbelief and accept them as a married couple when we watch them in a weekly sitcom. Because of the continuing nature of a television series (often several years to a decade for a successful show), this suspension of disbelief for television is a far more enduring fantasy than it is for a two-hour movie or play. Producers in the early days of television may have doubted the ability of the public to suspend that much disbelief. Many of the earliest TV series featured real-life spouses playing TV partners (e.g., Lucille Ball and Desi Arnaz, George Burns and Gracie Allen, Jack Benny and Mary Livingstone, Ozzie and Harriet Nelson). Apparently the public could handle this suspension of disbelief just fine; however, this phenomenon of married actors playing spouses on the screen has been rare since the 1950s.

Sometimes disbelief is suspended so long that the distinction between fantasy and reality becomes blurred. Although young children have difficulty understanding the difference between actors and the characters they portray (Fitch, Huston, & Wright, 1993), this problem is not limited to children. As any series actor knows, adult fans frequently ask an actor playing a doctor for medical advice or hurl epithets at an actress playing a villain in a soap opera. Such fantasies are covertly encouraged even more by spinoff series, in which the same character moves from one series to another (e.g., Dr. Frasier Crane of *Frasier* was originally a supporting character on *Cheers*; actor Kelsey Grammer ended up playing the same character for nearly 20 years!). Children's cartoon or puppet characters like Mickey Mouse, Big Bird, Dora the Explorer, or Spongebob Squarepants may reappear in commercials, toys, and kids' menus at restaurants, all of which support a belief in their reality apart from the show.

Sometimes television may provide such a salient exemplar of an extremely unpleasant reality once the disbelief is suspended. Close-up 3.2 explores the feared and actual effects of a much-hyped TV movie on nuclear war.

❖ CLOSE-UP 3.2 THE 1980S NUCLEAR WAR ON TV

One of the most hyped television entertainment events of all time was the 1983 ABC TV movie The Day After (TDA), a drama depicting the aftermath of a nuclear attack on the American Midwest, aired at the height of the Cold War. Its anticipation became such a media event in itself that 60 Minutes on the competing network CBS took the unprecedented step of covering TDA hype as one of its feature stories 1 hour before the movie's airing. It also became a political event. Antinuclear groups encouraged people to watch it, whereas conservatives decried it as an unfair move in the battle to mold public opinion on arms control issues. Mental health professionals worried over its impact on impressionable young minds and warned people to watch it only in groups and to not allow young children to see it at all. All of this heavy media coverage, of course, ensured a large audience, which numbered over 100 million viewers, the largest audience to date for a TV movie.

Psychologists Scholfield and Pavelchak (1985) studied exactly what impact this controversial film's airing actually had. Contrary to some fears or hopes, the movie actually did little to change attitudes about arms control and related issues. Arguments such as the possible failure of a deterrence-through-strength policy had been widely discussed in the media and were not really new ideas to most viewers. Many viewers felt that, horrible as it was, TDA's portrayal of the effects of a nuclear attack was actually milder than hype-weary viewers had expected and in fact was somewhat akin to many disaster and horror movies. The movie did have its effects, however. Viewers were more likely to seek information about nuclear issues and become involved in disarmament activities, and they reported thinking about nuclear war twice as often after seeing the film as they had before.

Transportation

Part of what happens when we willingly suspend disbelief is that we allow ourselves to be *transported* into a narrative world, drawn into a story (Green & Brock, 2000, 2002; Green, Brock, & Kaufman, 2004). Any good narrative media transports us into the world of the story. This state of high engagement includes four dimensions: *narrative understanding* (following and making sense of the story), *attentional focus* (paying attention to the story and characters), *emotional engagement* (experiencing feeling for and with the characters), and *narrative presence* (losing track, for a time, of the real world as we are drawn into the story) (Busselle & Bilandzic, 2009).

Transportation involves both cognitive (e.g., attention, imagery) and emotional (e.g., empathy, suspense) activation. Someone who is more strongly transported into the world of the narrative enjoys the experience more (Krakowiak & Oliver, 2012) and is more likely to be persuaded by it (Appel & Richter, 2010; Zwarun & Hall, 2012).

Although the content and emotion are often positive, they need not be. People also enjoy being transported into the scary world of a horror film or a war movie, for example. In fact, we achieve especially high levels of transportation when there are heightened moments of drama and suspense (Bezdek & Gerrig, 2017). In the case of video games and some CMC, we are also physically interacting with the medium, which cannot help but enhance the degree of narrative transportation (Barlett, Rodeheffer, Baldassaro, Hinkin, & Harris, 2008). Research has also shown that reading a book can enhance the degree of transportation later experienced upon seeing the movie based on the book (Green *et al.*, 2008).

Identification

The amount of transportation that we experience while watching a filmed drama also depends on how much we identify with the character; that is, mentally compare ourselves to and imagine ourselves like that character (Cohen, 2001, 2006; Tian & Hoffner, 2010). It is easier to identify with characters with whom we have more experiences in common or like (Tian & Hoffner, 2010), although that is not a prerequisite for identification. Though both men and women identify more with same-sex characters who are successful and intelligent, women also identified with those who were attractive and admired, while men identified with media males who were violent (Hoffner & Buchanan, 2005). There is a certain universality in most good drama, however. The basic humanity of characters in very different historical circumstances may be portrayed so well that viewers can identify emotionally with them at some level without having experienced similar situations themselves. In fact, fictional portrayals often evoke stronger emotions and better memory than do documentaries on the same subject (Pouliot & Cowen, 2007). Perhaps the ultimate case of identification would be an actor's identification with the character he or she is portraying on screen. See Close-up 3.3 for discussion of some cognitive research on how actors learn lines and construct a character.

> ### ❖ CLOSE-UP 3.3 USING COGNITIVE PSYCHOLOGY TO HELP ACTORS LEARN LINES
>
> *Cognitive psychologist Helga Noice and her actor and theater professor husband Tony Noice have collaborated for years on a fascinating research program studying how actors learn lines and develop characters in preparing a role for the stage. Surprisingly, most professional actors told the Noices they do not focus on explicitly memorizing lines but rather work hard to understand the character and be able to respond to the situation on stage as that character would. Many of the techniques they report using successfully are exactly those strategies suggested to students for learning material in an academic situation. For example, they elaborate the ideas, that is, think about what the character would be thinking as they speak those lines. Some directors even have their actors write a background biography of their character before they start rehearsal. Actors also report strongly taking the perspective of their character, trying to match their mood to the character, and trying to understand the motivation for every single line of dialogue and every blocking movement. In their research, the Noices found that both professional actors and students using these*

techniques had better verbatim memory for lines than did those who tried explicitly to memorize the words. They coined the term active experiencing *to refer to the process in which an actor uses physical, mental, and emotional means to communicate to another. For example, a line of dialogue is intrinsically associated with the movement the actor makes while speaking it and the feeling he or she has at the time (Noice & Noice, 1997, 2006).*

Media as Perceived Reality

Now that we have examined some of the psychological constructs involved in our enjoyment of media, let us return for a more careful look at the theme briefly introduced in Chapter 1: the reality created by the media.

The Reflection Myth

A common and popular view of media is that they merely reflect the world around them. News stories report what happened in the world that day. Sitcoms reflect the values, lifestyles, and habits of society. Movies reflect the concerns and issues that viewers struggle to face. Facebook feeds represent the views of those in our communities. The presence of violence, pornography, Internet predators, and offensive stereotypes merely reflects the ugly reality of an imperfect world. Advertising reflects the needs and wants that we really have. Media, in this view, are a sort of window on reality.

This view of media is used in authoritarian societies which attempt to control media and thus control their people's view of reality; see Close-up 3.4 for what may be the most extreme modern example of such control.

❖ CLOSE-UP 3.4 THE "REALITY" OF NORTH KOREAN CINEMA

Perhaps the most rigidly controlled authoritarian society in the modern world is the North Korean police state, ruled by Kim Jong-un since 2011 and by his father Kim Jong-il before that. As well as being a ruthless dictator, Kim Jong-il was also a film fanatic, particularly enjoying American and Hong Kong action and horror films, which he saw at private screenings, although they were not available to his fellow citizens. He was thought to particularly enjoy the Friday the Thirteenth *films and gangster movies like* Scarface *and* The Godfather. *All North Korean films are made according to Kim's 1973 book,* The Art of Cinema, *and are overtly for propaganda purposes. They show only a positive image of North Korea, which is in fact one of the most desperately poor, repressive, and backward countries in the world. The soldiers are usually the heroes who come to rescue the people. For example, in one film, soldiers carried buckets of water for miles and joined hands to form a human dam to hold back a flood. Help comes from the army and from working harder, never from foreign nations, the UN, or nongovernmental organizations.*

Kim also had a film made to model another favorite movie, Titanic. *Kim's film told of the sinking of a North Korean ship in 1945 and even had a love story modeled on the Rose and Jack romance in the 1997 Hollywood film. Perhaps Kim's most outrageous act was to kidnap an admired South Korean movie star, Choi Eun-hee, and force her to act in North Korean films. Later, Kim also captured Choi's ex-husband and noted South Korean film director*

Shin Sang-ok. In addition to convincing the movie star and director to remarry, Kim put them to work making North Korean films. Among those movies was Pulgasari, *an imitation of the Japanese Godzilla, transformed into an iron-eating lizard who fights with the peasants against their feudal overlords (North Korean movies' propaganda role, 2003).*

Would anybody believe such heavy-handed messages so far removed from reality? Probably so. North Koreans are not allowed to leave their country or have any exposure to foreigners or foreign media, and they have heard this heavy propaganda all their lives. Even the auto-cratic ruler Kim Jong-il hardly ever left his country; he may very well have believed that his beloved American horror and gangster movies actually portrayed typical American life.

In addition to becoming a dictator in his father's mold, Kim Jong-un also has a strange rela-tionship with Hollywood movies. Before the 2014 Seth Rogen comedy movie The Interview *was to be released, the younger Kim got wind that the plot of the movie involved an assas-sination attempt on himself. Enraged, Kim and the North Korean government threatened Sony Pictures that if the movie was released, it would be considered "an act of war" and "a resolute and merciless response" would follow. It did. North Korean cyber attackers hacked into Sony's computer system, leaking personal e-mails and even some upcoming movies online (Fackler, Barnes & Sanger, 2014).*

The reflection view is not the only way to view mass communication, however. It may be that we think certain events and issues are important because the news tells us they are. Sitcoms may portray certain values, lifestyles, and habits which are then adopted by society. Dramas deal with certain issues that are then considered by the viewers. Media stereotypes implicitly teach young viewers what different groups of people are like, and the presence of media violence teaches that the world is a violent place. Advertising convinces us that we have certain needs and wants that we did not know we had before. In this view, media are not merely reflecting what is out there in the world. Rather, they are constructing a world that then becomes reality for the consumer. This world may be accepted by heavy media users, who are often unaware that such a process is happening, as they believe they are only being entertained. Soon the world as constructed by media may become so implanted in our minds that we cannot distinguish it from reality.

So, do the media reflect the world as it is or create a new reality? Certainly media do in many ways reflect what is out there in the world. However, they also choose what to tell us about what is out there in the world (agenda setting), and we then accept that inter-pretation, which then becomes part of our memory and our experience (cultivation). In this book, we will continually examine how media create a world which then becomes our reality. This cognitive perspective focuses on the mental construction of reality that we form as a result of our contact with media. An individual's constructed reality often differs substantially from objective reality in ways not always open to our conscious awareness, such as when we inadvertently consume fake news (discussed further in Chapter 7).

The Study of Perceived Reality

Each of the theoretical approaches discussed in Chapter 2 has something to say about studying the perceived reality that we cognitively construct through our interactions with media. For example, agenda setting (McCombs & Reynolds, 2009) tells us what is important to think about. Social cognitive theory (Bandura, 2009) examines how we learn the behavioral component of this reality. Cultivation theory (Morgan *et al.*, 2009) focuses on the construction of a worldview. Uses and gratifications theory (Rubin, 2009) looks at the uses we make of media and the gratifications they give us, increasingly connecting this research to an examination of the effects of media. Schema/script theory and the limited capacity model (Lang, 2000) both look at the knowledge structures that we create from exposure to the media.

When we speak of the reality constructed from the media, this is actually a more complex idea than it may first appear. At least two different components are involved (Fitch *et al.*, 1993; Potter, 1988). The first component in perceived reality is *factuality*. This is the belief in the literal reality of media messages. This reality can be conveyed at the level of either style or content. The style of news reporting, for example, may convey a message of factual correctness more strongly than would the style of an entertainment program (although the lines between real and fake news have become harder to distinguish; see Chapter 7). The content of action-adventure shows, presenting a world that is very dangerous, may cultivate a view that the real world is also like that (Morgan *et al.*, 2009; Signorielli, 1990).

The understanding of factuality develops gradually (Chandler, 1997; Davies, 1997; Wright, Huston, Reitz, & Piemyat, 1994). Two-year-olds do not understand the representational nature of filmed images at all and will try to answer a TV personality who talks to them. By around age 10, children's factuality judgments are essentially equivalent to those of adults. During the transition period, as they learn to "read" TV programs, their emotional experience may be affected by the complexity of the plot and also by how realistic they perceive the program to be. For example, Weiss and Wilson (1998) found that the higher the degree of realism attributed to a sitcom episode, the more concerned elementary school children were about similar negative emotional events in their own lives. Even seemingly mundane factors can affect perceived reality. For example, a larger screen size can lead to greater arousal and involvement of the viewer (Detenber & Reeves, 1996; Grabe, Lombard, Reich, Bracken, & Ditton, 1999; Lombard, Reich, Grabe, Bracken, & Ditton, 2000).

As human information processors, we are always monitoring the sources of what we know and judging whether those sources are reliable or not (Johnson, 2007). However, much of this reality monitoring process fails to accurately remember the source and thus may assign far too much credibility to some memories. When our media sources fail to exercise reasonable reality monitoring, there are significant consequences. This happens, for example, when a news writer is caught fabricating a story or when a website intentionally posts fake news. The proliferation of unreliable news sources such as tabloid journalism and fake news sites may tend to lower these expectations overall, contributing to a greater mistrust of media in general (see Chapter 7).

Viewers do not have to believe in the literal reality of media to have it become real for them, however. The second component of perceived reality is *social realism*, which refers to the perceived similarity or usefulness of the media representation to one's own life, even while recognizing its fictional nature. For example, a viewer with a strong belief that soap operas present real-life situations would expect more application to her own life than another viewer who feels that soap operas present wildly unrealistic and purely escapist content (Rubin & Perse, 1988). Stories in which events happen as we would predict them are seen as more realistic (Shapiro, Barriga, & Beren, 2010), as are those which adhere more strongly to familiar narrative structures such as following a familiar narrative script of exposition + complication + resolution discussed in

Chapter 2 (Igartua & Barrios, 2012; Kintsch, 1977). Viewers rely heavily on typicality to judge the social reality of television; the more typical a situation seems, the more real it is judged to be (Shapiro & Chock, 2003). Because of their shorter life experience, young children often see greater social realism in television content than adults do, in that they have less experience with which to compare the media representation to assess its reality. In general, media have greater effects on people who attribute a higher degree of social realism to them. This has important consequences whether we are talking about violence, sex, advertising, news, or prosocial media.

When we make assessments of the degree of social realism, those judgments may differ depending on whether the particular relevance is at the personal or social level (Chock, 2011). For example, a high degree of identification with a character may lead us to judge that show as relatively more realistic for ourselves, while identification would be less important in judging the perceived realism for others. Also, different shows, or even commercials, contain cues to the degree of realism (Shapiro & Kim, 2012). With the increase in reality TV shows, we may also have the odd situation of objective factuality without much social realism. Even though the people on *Jersey Shore*, *Survivor*, or *The Bachelor* are acting as themselves and unscripted, the application to a viewer's reality may be quite limited (Skeggs & Wood, 2012).

Parasocial Media Relationships

Social realism can be enhanced by the degree to which viewers believe that a character is important in their own lives. One interesting issue to come out of the uses and gratifications perspective concerns the relationships we have with media figures we have never met in person, that is, *parasocial* relationships or interactions (Klimmt, Hartmann, & Schramm, 2006; A. M. Rubin, Perse, & Powell, 1985; R. B. Rubin & McHugh, 1987; Tsay & Bodine, 2012). We may think of morning show hosts more as our breakfast companions than as news sources. Radio DJs are regular commuting partners, not merely people we hear through the car speakers as we drive to work. This feeling of connectedness with public figures is sometimes dramatically illustrated, such as in the intense worldwide outpouring of grief following the sudden death of Britain's young Princess Diana in a car crash in 1997 (Brown, Basil, & Bocarnea, 2003). Her loss was a genuinely personal one to millions who knew her only through media. There were similar large-scale displays of public affection and mourning when Michael Jackson died in 2009 and Prince in 2016.

Parasocial interactions and relationships are not limited to real people. For instance, actors who portray villains in ongoing television series have been known to receive hate mail from viewers. One can even develop parasocial relationships with video game characters (Coulson, Barnett, Ferguson, & Gould, 2012). When decades-old soap operas have been canceled, faithful viewers feel a genuine sense of loss at the demise of beloved characters. One study that examined viewers' experiences with the last episode of *Friends* in 2004 found that there can be similarities in the distress of a "parasocial breakup" with a media "friend" when a long-running show ends and ending a relationship with a real person (Eyal & Cohen, 2006). Similar results were discovered in a study of Israeli television viewers and the potential loss of their favorite TV characters or personalities (Cohen, 2004). Interestingly, however, there are no social conventions or social support for parasocial grieving, which in fact often is met by others with outright ridicule.

Parasocial feelings have many of the same characteristics of real interpersonal interactions (Perse & Rubin, 1989) and are strong predictors of television viewing motivation and behavior (Conway & Rubin, 1991; see Schiappa, Allen, & Gregg, 2007 for a meta-analysis of effects of parasocial interactions). People who form parasocial relationships tend to be especially high in the personality dimensions of agreeableness and neuroticism (Tsay & Bodine, 2012). These one-sided relationships can even lead to romantic feelings for celebrities whom fans have never met. McCutcheon and colleagues (McCutcheon, Ashe, Houran, & Maltby, 2003) draw parallels between this kind of celebrity worship and erotomania, a psychological disorder in which a person has delusions of a romantic relationship with another. Such parasocial connections can be carried to extremes; see Close-up 3.5 for some examples.

❖ CLOSE-UP 3.5 WHEN PARASOCIAL MEDIA RELATIONSHIPS TURN DEADLY

At times, parasocial media relationships take an especially dark and tragic turn. For example, John Hinckley, Jr., a sometimes musician and college student, attempted to assassinate President Ronald Reagan in 1981. Hinckley's delusional motivation was a belief that killing the president would win the heart of actress Jodie Foster, with whom he had become obsessed after watching her over and over again in the film Taxi Driver. *Hinckley was later diagnosed with a number of psychotic and personality disorders ("Excerpts," 1982; Haynes & Rich, 2002).*

In a couple of other tragic cases that same decade, two celebrities were actually murdered. In 1989, obsessed fan and stalker Robert John Bardo shot and killed actress Rebecca Schaeffer, star of the then-popular sitcom My Sister Sam *after he had become obsessed with her on television and in movies. After his arrest for the homicide, Bardo was diagnosed as schizophrenic (Axthelm, 1989). By 1980, fellow schizophrenic Mark David Chapman had become obsessed with former Beatle John Lennon and the novel* The Catcher in the Rye. *In Chapman's warped way of thinking, he identified with Holden Caulfield, the teenage protagonist in the book, who railed against phonies. Although he loved and admired Lennon's music, Chapman saw Lennon as the ultimate hypocrite who sang about the virtues of having "no possessions" but also owned an extravagant New York apartment. To protest this phoniness, Chapman gunned down Lennon outside that apartment in December of 1980. When he was arrested, authorities learned that Chapman had other "phony" celebrities on his hit list, including David Bowie, Elizabeth Taylor, and Paul McCartney (Holden, 2008).*

Although it is rare for deranged fans to murder celebrities, it is quite common for stars to be stalked, harassed, and threatened by those who claim to "love" them. As was the case with the assassins discussed above, mental illness is often a factor. But star worship, fan culture, and constant celebrity media exposure also fuel such dangerous and unhealthy parasocial relationships.

Nevertheless, parasocial media relationships may have somewhat of a beneficial "social surrogacy" mental health effect. Derrick, Gabriel, and Hugenberg (2009), found that watching favorite TV shows provides a sense of belonging, particularly for those who are lonely. They even discovered that merely thinking about favorite TV shows while recalling a fight with a close other can help protect against drops in self-esteem. Interestingly, however, these sorts of effects only seemed to be present with favored TV shows, leading the authors to conclude that the effects were not due to mindless escapism from watching just any show. The intensity of a parasocial relationship can be affected by many factors. For example, attractive personalities engender more intense parasocial interactions, as do characters who directly address the audiences. Those higher in the individual difference factor of perspective-taking ability are also more likely to develop more intense parasocial relationships. More intense parasocial interaction is also associated with greater enjoyment of the media experience (Hartmann & Goldhoorn, 2011).

As we have seen, whether positive or negative, parasocial media relationships can become passionate. However, we have all probably felt some emotional connection to figures we know only through the TV, movie, or computer screen. See Giles (2002) for a literature review and proposed model for parasocial interaction. He argues for the importance of specifying the continuum of the relationship between social and parasocial relationships and for identifying the stages in the development of parasocial relationships. Tsay and Bodine (2012) argue that we should consider parasocial interaction as a multidimensional construct that affects our perceptions of reality.

Conclusion

The rest of this book draws on various cognitive approaches, drawing on various theoretical perspectives, as appropriate, to approach the study of how media construct reality. In fact, the different theories are not necessarily mutually exclusive in all ways and may in fact be quite complementary. The meaning of something in the media, at either a cognitive or an emotional level, depends on how that information is processed during our experience of interacting with the medium. Elements of the different theories and psychological processes are brought in as appropriate in discussion of the topics in the rest of the book.

The media create a reality for us in many different areas, drawing on different psychological processes as they do so. In the next chapter, let us turn to how our emotions interact with media to create a perceived reality.

Media Applications, Chapter 3: Using Cognitive and Developmental Psychology to Discuss TV with Children

One theme of this chapter (and, indeed, this entire book) is that media, particularly television, have the power to influence our ideas about reality. This effect can be especially strong with children. With regard to children and TV, authors have labeled television "the stranger in the house" (Chen, 1994) and "the other parent" (Steyer, 2002) because of its potential to influence children and their sense of the world.

When parents think about their children's TV consumption, the developmental needs and abilities of their kids should be considered. For example, one of the greatest lessons from the area of developmental psychology is that young children don't tend to think about things in the same ways that adults do. Legendary cognitive developmental psychologist Piaget noted that young children can be thought of as egocentric in their thought. By this, he meant that children are cognitively unable to think about the world in any perspective other than their own. Carlsson-Paige applies this notion to media, saying "I often wish I could impress this upon adults: children do not see what we see when they watch movies or TV. When adults hear news of a stabbing or a car bomb, we can think logically about the likelihood of these things happening to us. Children, in contrast, can easily imagine that these scary and dangerous events are imminently threatening to them" (2008, p. 18).

In addition to understanding how children think about television, parents should also realize the profound effect they can have on their children's perceptions of TV. Austin, Roberts, and Nass (1990; see also Desmond, Singer, & Singer, 1990; Nathanson, 1999) developed and tested a model of how parent–child communication about TV and its portrayals can affect children's construction of reality. In studying children and their parents' reactions to TV sitcom families, Austin and colleagues determined that children evaluate the realism of TV content (i.e., how closely what they see on television relates to how they imagine the world to be). In addition, children think about the similarity of what they are seeing to their own lives as well as how much they identify with content (i.e., the extent to which a child would like to emulate what is viewed). Interestingly, the research revealed that these factors are significantly influenced by parental communication. In other words, parents in the study who discussed TV content with their kids had a strong impact on their children's perceptions of how television depictions related to the real world. Summing up, Austin and colleagues said, "Direct parental mediation, the discussion of the parent's views of the television content with the child, appears most successful in shaping the child's perceptions of television's match to the real world close to home" (1990, p. 561).

It may sound simplistic to merely discuss television (and other media) with children, but the effects can be powerful, particularly if the discussion takes place as the children are consuming the media. For example, if a particularly violent cartoon comes on, a parent could ask the child, "What do you think would happen to you if you acted like that when you are angry? Can you think of a better way that character could have handled it?" Or, if a child spots an ultra-thin model on TV, her parent might probe: "Do you know any women in your life who look like that? What do you think that model has to do in order to look that way?"

Television may also be used as a catalyst for discussion of important issues within the family. Although it is frequently difficult for parents and children to discuss topics like sex or drugs, it may be easier in the context of discussing a TV program on such a theme. Even if the program is not particularly well done or consistent with the family's values, it still may serve as a relatively nonthreatening catalyst for discussion. Parents should take advantage of such opportunities. Television need not be an antisocial medium that isolates one family member from another (a "shut-up-so-I-can-listen" model). It can also be an activity that brings them together to watch as a family, but also to talk about the content and other topics that it leads to (a "hey-look-at-this" model). Discussion of TV programming can help family members to understand each other's reactions to many topics and situations. It can be a stimulus to cognitive, emotional, and personal growth. All of this is not to say that television always will be such a positive influence, just that it can be. The more carefully programs are selected and the more intentional the parent is about discussing the content, the better the outcome. Social, cultural, and family structure variables also have a role in determining the effect of family interactions on the impact of TV on children (Greenberg, Ku, & Li, 1992; Wright, St. Peters, & Huston, 1990).

One last thing to keep in mind is the third-person effect. Remember from Chapter 2 that this is the notion, when applied to media, that others are more affected by media content than we are ourselves. With parents and their children, it may be tempting to believe that other people's kids might be negatively affected, but "not my kids!" Resist the lure of this kind of thinking. For excellent general books to help parents guide their children through the decisions and challenges of television, see Chen (1994) or Steyer (2002). For help with the specific issue of dealing with fear induced in children by violent media, see Cantor (1998b). See Levin and Kilbourne (2009) for help in dealing with the overly sexualized popular culture or Lindstrom (2011) for dealing with advertising. For a broader approach helping parents to deal not only with media but also with other potentially toxic aspects of popular culture, see the excellent book by Carlsson-Paige (2008).

Further Reading

Carlsson-Paige, N. (2008). *Taking back childhood: Helping your kids thrive in a fast-paced, media-saturated, violence-filled world*. New York: Hudson Street Press.
Chen, M. (1994). *The smart parent's guide to kids' TV*. San Francisco: KQED Books.
Eyal, K., & Cohen, J. (2006). When good Friends say goodbye: A parasocial breakup study. *Journal of Broadcasting and Electronic Media*, 50, 502–523.
Steyer, J. P. (2002). *The other parent: The inside story of media's effect on our children*. New York: Atria Books.
Turkle, S. (2011). *Alone together: Why we expect more from technology and less from each other*. New York: Basic Books.

Useful Links

Change blindness example:
www.youtube.com/watch?v=VkrrVozZR2c

Inattentional blindness articles:
www.apa.org/monitor/apr01/blindness.aspx
www.smithsonianmag.com/science-nature/but-did-you-see-the-gorilla-the-problem-with-inattentional-blindness-17339778/

Inattentional blindness example:
www.youtube.com/watch?v=z-Dg-06nrnc

The Lovers and the Despot movie site:
www.magpictures.com/theloversandthedespot/

Movie continuity errors:
www.moviemistakes.com/

For more resources, please visit the companion website:
www.routledge.com/cw/harris

Chapter 4

Emotions and Media

Music and Sports as Exemplars

Q: What is the most uncomfortable combination of audience and movie type for college students to consider watching?

A: Watching an explicit R-rated sexual movie with your parents is thought to be much more uncomfortable a situation than watching a sexual movie with anyone else or watching a graphically violent movie with anyone, or any one of several other combinations of audience and movie (Harris & Cook, 2011).

Q: When pop songs mention drug and alcohol use, what is the most common associated impetus for the use?

A: Sex. Celebrating/partying and mood management are other typical motivations (Cougar Hall, West & Neeley, 2013).

Q: As of 2017, what was the most watched television event in U.S. TV history?

A: Super Bowl XLIX in 2015 between the New England Patriots and the Seattle Seahawks, which attracted over 114 million viewers (Collins, 2015). Of the 20 most watched U.S. telecasts of all time, 19 have been Super Bowls.

Think for a moment about some of your favorite movies, TV shows, and websites. Why is it that you enjoy them? Chances are that one of the main reasons why you like these media is because they provoke some sort of emotional experience in you such as feelings of humor/laughter, poignancy, romance, or joy. Indeed, feeling emotions is a key element to enjoying media. Although emotion is a major component of many, if not most, types of media use, there are some domains in which both what we feel in response to consuming the media and how we express those feelings are particularly central to the experience. This chapter looks at two of those content areas: music and sports. These would seem to be hugely diverse areas of media, but both centrally involve emotion, although in very different ways. To get started, let's look a little at the psychology of emotion.

The Emotional Side of Experiencing Media

What Is Emotion?

Something that makes the study of emotion difficult is that we cannot directly observe it. We do not see anger or hear happiness. We see violent behavior and feel angry; we hear laughter and feel happy. Emotions themselves are internal states and must be inferred from behavior. This can be tricky because sometimes the obvious inference is not the correct one. We may see someone crying over a TV movie and infer that she feels sad, when in fact she might be crying for joy or in anger, or for that matter, she might have an allergic condition in which the crying does not reflect emotion at all. The behavior we observe is not the emotion felt inside by the person behaving, and it is not always even a good clue to that emotion. To further complicate matters, the terms we use for emotions can sometimes be confusing; see Close-up 4.1.

❖ CLOSE-UP 4.1 AFFECT, MOOD, OR EMOTION?

As often happens with the English language and the field of psychology, terminology surrounding a particular topic can become conflated, with psychology scholars and the general public using the same word to mean similar, but different things. This is especially true when it comes to the study of emotion.

In popular culture, we might talk about a "moody" song or an "emotional" movie, meaning essentially the same thing—that these media are attempting to provoke the media consumer's feelings in some way. However, when psychologists discuss the term emotion, they usually define it as a feeling with a direct object (Konijn, 2013; Russell & Barrett, 1999). For example, a mother may love her daughter, a student may be angry with his professor, or a TV viewer may feel sad that a beloved character was killed off in a favorite television series. Thus, emotions also tend to touch on very personal feelings.

Psychologists often differentiate emotion from a related term, affect (rhymes with "laugheckt"). Unlike emotion, affect does not have a direct object, instead it ebbs and flows over time. Affect also tends to be either positive or negative (Russell & Barrett, 1999). For example, you may experience an affective state of frustration when stuck in heavy traffic. Or, you might have the affect of disgust when seeing a disliked celebrity saying something you perceive as stupid in a TV interview. Affect does not feel especially deep or personal and tends to disappear once the stimulus provoking it goes away.

Mood, on the other hand, is long-lasting and can be thought of as a prolonged affective state, "characterized by being global and not clearly elicited by an external event" (Konijn, 2013, p. 190). For instance, someone may feel anxious for a few days but cannot pinpoint a specific stimulus that is making him feel this way. The feelings of anxiety, while they last, may also seem overwhelming. Sometimes, moods persist for even longer. Major depressive disorder (a mood disorder) includes symptoms such as feeling down/depressed for a period of weeks, often without a clear stimulus for the depression.

To confuse things further, psychologists and researchers themselves don't always draw clear distinctions between these terms. "The boundaries to the domain of emotion are so blurry that it sometimes seems that everything is an emotion" (Russell & Barrett, 1999,

p. 805]. "Clearly, the concepts of emotion, mood, and affect are not often used in the strict senses as defined but rather are used interchangeably" (Konijn, 2013, p. 191). Because most of the research on media does not distinguish between mood, affect, and emotion (usually labeling it all as "emotion"), this chapter will also not make this distinction. Hopefully, this will not complicate (or simplify) things too much for our readers!

Emotions are an integral part of the appreciation of media, especially radio, television, and film. Perhaps no kind of programming hooks into emotions more strongly than music and sports, but many other genres do so as well, including action-adventure, soap operas, game shows, reality shows, and comedies. What we feel while watching or listening is a central part of the whole psychological experience. If the emotional aspect is absent, we miss an important dimension of the media consumption. Consider the unsatisfying experience of watching a ball game between two teams when you have little knowledge of the teams and no interest in who wins. It's not very exciting, is it?

There are two components of emotion: the physiological and the cognitive. When we are aroused, certain changes occur in our bodies, such as increased heart rate, respiration, sweating, and changes in electrodermal (skin) measures. We also think about our feelings and attribute causes and interpretations to them. For example, at some moment your body may be very hyped up, but you would have a different interpretation of the state of bodily arousal if you had just consumed ten cups of coffee or if you had just escaped from the clutches of a crazed killer. Thus, the emotions we feel are a product of both our aroused bodily state and our cognitive appraisal of that state (Schachter & Singer, 1962; Zillmann, 2006b).

Media as Vicarious Emotional Experience

Watching a crime show on TV allows us to experience some of the emotion felt by the characters without ourselves being in any physical danger. Thus we can become aroused safely and vicariously; that is, we experience the emotion through someone else's experience. This indirectness allows us to focus on the excitement of a movie car chase or to enjoy the humor of a sitcom. If we actually experienced those situations in real life, the danger or embarrassment might overpower the positive aspects, and they would not be nearly as much fun as they are on TV. Many emotions are more enjoyable to experience vicariously. Often, comedies show people in embarrassing situations that are more humorous when happening to someone else. TV characters may do things we would like to do but have moral or ethical proscriptions against. We can, however, with a clear conscience, watch others have extramarital affairs, verbally insult their boss, drive recklessly, or drop bags of groceries all over their floor.

Game and reality shows are representative of programming genres in which participants are particularly encouraged to be highly expressive emotionally. In fact, a major screening characteristic for participants is high emotional expressiveness. The producers want bubbly, emotive, expressive people who yell, scream, cry, and hug. Such "reality" shows are far from a representative sample of real people; in fact, the participants have been highly selected to be very expressive emotionally.

Occasionally, a particular live media event is so emotionally compelling as to make a lasting impact, for example, the collapse of the twin towers of the World Trade Center after the September 11, 2001, terrorist attacks. When the U.S. space shuttle *Challenger* exploded in January 1986, this event was seen live at the time on TV or later that day by 95% of the population of the country (Wright, Kunkel, Pinon, & Huston, 1989). In a study of the reactions of school children to the event, Wright and colleagues found evidence of strong emotion evoked by the tragedy, especially among girls, though that may reflect in part the gender stereotyping of girls being willing to admit to feeling more emotion.

Emotional Expression and Media

Mainstream North American and Northern European societies often discourage direct expression of intense emotions. Media popular culture, however, sets some new rules that are more flexible. It is more acceptable to yell and shake your fist at a referee in a ball game on TV than to do the same at your boss. Sports is one of the very few arenas in some societies where heterosexual adult men may show physical affection toward other men without intimations of same-sex attraction, and some of the same license is transferred to viewing sports on television. Thus, two men may playfully slap each other or even embrace or cry after watching a spectacular play in a televised ball game. To some extent listening to music also allows masculine expression of emotion. Interestingly, such behavior would he highly unlikely from the same men watching a movie, however.

The social situation of watching TV also makes a difference in our experienced emotion. Watching a ball game or scary movie might be very different if one were alone versus at a party with friends. There is often more overt expression of emotion when in a group. A cheesy horror movie might be scary to watch alone but funny with a group. Even though the stimulus is the same in both cases, the experience, especially the emotional experience, may be quite different. The social experience of teenagers going to a horror film together is often very different from what one might predict purely from considering the content of the film; for example, they may laugh at graphic horror (Zillmann & Weaver, 1996; Zillmann, Weaver, Mundorf, & Aust, 1986). Another study (Ahn, Jin, & Ritterfeld, 2012) indicated that viewing a very sad movie also resulted in high levels of enjoyment for those who were emotionally and cognitively involved with the film.

Social cognitive theory (discussed in Chapter 2) tells us that we learn by watching others. Thus, children may learn from media, helpfully or otherwise, how to deal with and express emotions they feel in various situations. When dramas and comedies regularly show smoking and alcohol consumption as common ways of dealing with stress, children and teens will learn that as a coping strategy. Some years ago, young children learning to play tennis cursed and threw their racquets in imitation of tennis great John McEnroe, whose angry antics on the court became a model for dealing with frustration in sports. More seriously, if media regularly portray men who feel frustrated with women as expressing such feelings through violence (battering or rape), children may learn that these antisocial ways of dealing with those feelings are acceptable. An interesting longitudinal study on adolescents found that high levels of media violence (TV and video games) were related to lower levels of trait empathy and sympathy (Vossen, Piotrowski, & Valkenburg, 2017). There is also ample evidence of emotional contagion, whereby we unconsciously mimic and synchronize our language and behavior to those around us (Hatfield, Cacioppo, & Rapson, 1992, 1993). This mimicking and synchronicity then lead to an emotional convergence with the person being mimicked. Such persons may be from the media as well as in real life. Sometimes, TV and radio take advantage of this process by intentionally eliciting and manipulating negative emotions for their own ends of entertaining and promoting a particular agenda. See Close-up 4.2 for some particularly egregious and outrageous examples of this emotional manipulation.

❖ CLOSE-UP 4.2 TALK SHOWS THAT ELICIT AND MANIPULATE NEGATIVE EMOTIONS FOR ENTERTAINMENT

Popular radio talk show host Rush Limbaugh calls feminists "feminazis who look like rhinoceroses" and called a Georgetown University law student a "slut," after she testified before Congress in 2012 about the need for health care to cover birth control. He also has said that the NFL and NBA look like gangs and thugs and made fun of former first lady Michelle Obama's body. Limbaugh's radio show became nationally syndicated in 1988 and still garners high ratings.

The Jerry Springer Show (on the air since 1991) allegedly encourages yelling, screaming, crying, and even hitting among its guests. Nikki and her new husband Chico once appeared on the show without being told what the producers really had in mind. During the taping it was revealed that Chico was still seeing his old girlfriend Mindy and also had a male lover, Rick. Both of them were on the show with the couple, and Mindy even assaulted Nikki. The audience was encouraged to show contempt for them. "It's white trailer trash! I love it!" said an 81-year-old farmer from Oregon (Collins, 1998). The height of the show's popularity in the late 1990s was also the height of its violence. In one week in 1998, every day's Jerry Springer contained physical brawls. At the same time, Springer had overcome the dominant Oprah Winfrey Show in the ratings (St. John Kelly, 1998). The show offers to pay for counseling for guests afterward, but few accept the offer.

In one of the most notorious cases of reality talk shows gone wild, The Jenny Jones Show guest Jonathan Schmitz was told he would soon meet his secret admirer who had a crush on him. The mystery person turned out to be another man, Scott Amedure, who spoke of fantasies of tying Schmitz in a hammock and spraying him with whipped cream and champagne. Schmitz was very agitated at this revelation and three days later was arrested for killing Amedure. He told the police that the embarrassment from the program had eaten away at him (Gamson, 1995). Are such programs freak shows that exploit guests and bring out the worst in the audience, or are they legitimate formats to hear people's stories that we would otherwise not hear (but perhaps should)?

Media and a Few Specific Emotions

As we have seen, media and emotion are intimately connected. For almost every emotion that humans can experience, there is probably a corresponding media stimulus that can evoke those emotions. In the next section of this chapter, we take a closer look at how media relates to three specific emotional experiences: empathy, suspense, and humor.

Empathy

Empathy, the ability to understand and feel what someone else is feeling, may also be thought of as a form of identification (see Chapter 3). More specifically, empathy is also *emotional identification*, and it is a very important factor in the enjoyment of media. Empathy is a trait, with some people naturally more empathic than others. However, most everyone shows some level of empathy in media situations, and that empathy enhances our enjoyment. We enjoy a comedy more if we can feel something of what the characters feel. We enjoy watching baseball more if we have played the game ourselves and can relate to the tense feelings of being at bat with two outs in the bottom of the ninth, with our team down by one run. We especially enjoy a tragic movie if we can easily empathize with the suffering of the characters (Mills, 1993). In fact, fMRI studies have shown that some "pain areas" of the brain, notably the anterior cingulate cortex and the anterior insula, respond similarly to physical pain and watching a movie character be embarrassed (Dahl, 2011).

In the case of media, empathy is diminished somewhat by the relatively omniscient position we occupy relative to the characters (Zillmann, 2006a). We generally know more of what is going on than they do, as when we know that the bad guy is just around the bend waiting to ambush our unsuspecting hero. If we know the final outcome, it is often difficult to become as emotionally involved as we could if we knew as little as the character did. Such enjoyment varies greatly depending on the genre, however. Audiences for reruns of sporting events are almost nonexistent, whereas audiences for reruns of comedies hold up quite well. Apparently, loyalty to the characters and show and the empathy and degree of parasocial interaction with those characters are crucial factors.

Empathy is composed of both cognitive and emotional components. *Cognitive empathy* involves the ability to readily take the perspective of another, whereas *emotional empathy* involves readily responding at a purely emotional level. Davis and colleagues (Davis, Hull, Young, & Warren, 1987) showed that the level of both of these types of empathy influenced emotional reactions to viewing the films *Brian's Song* (a sentimental fact-based drama about a football player dying of cancer) and *Who's Afraid of Virginia Woolf?* (a wrenching psychological drama about a vindictive and destructive marital relationship), but each type of empathy influenced reactions in different ways. In another study that measured empathy in fictional contexts (sometimes called *trait fantasy empathy*), participants scoring relatively high in this attribute were better able to remember emotional content from two movies than were those scoring lower in the trait (Harris *et al.*, 2017).

Empathy has also been conceptualized as a three-factor construct (Zillmann, 2006a), being *dispositional* (a built-in feature of humans), *excitatory* (a reflexive response to a stimulus), and *experiential* (a conscious monitoring of stimuli that sometimes results in a reaction). One factor may override another that initially dominated. For example, a normal, dispositional empathic response to an injured athlete may be overridden if one has a negative experiential disposition toward that athlete (e.g., he's on the hated opposing team), and one may respond with cheers. A dispositional empathic response may also be overridden by an abrupt, excitatory change to material of a different mood, such as the shift from an intense TV drama to an upbeat commercial. Thus, what might otherwise elicit considerable empathy may not do so, in part due to the sound-bite nature of the medium of television. This could explain why it is much more difficult to become caught up emotionally in a TV movie broken up by multiple commercials than it is seeing a film uninterrupted in a theater.

Another approach, not yet extensively examined in the research, is the extent to which media, especially television, teach empathy to children or could potentially do so, if more sensitivity were given to such issues by writers, directors, and networks (Feshbach, 1988; Feshbach & Feshbach, 1997). Interestingly, however, one study (Mar, Oatley, Hirsh, dela Paz, & Peterson, 2006) has indicated that frequent readers of fiction score higher in self-reported empathy than do frequent readers of nonfiction.

Suspense

Suspense is usually characterized as an experience of uncertainty whose properties can vary from noxious to pleasant (Vorderer & Knobloch, 2000). The suspense that we feel as we anticipate the outcome of an adventure show or drama is maximal if some negative outcome (hero is about to die) appears highly likely but is not absolutely certain; for example, everything points to disaster with just a slight hope of escape. If the negative outcome either is not very likely or is absolutely certain, there is not much suspense. We experience a high level of suspense, for example, if our hero appears about to be blown up by a bomb, with just a slight chance to escape. Suspense is also heightened by the omniscient status of the viewer; we know something about the imminent danger that the character does not know, and that knowledge heightens the suspense we feel. The physiological excitation of suspense is relatively slow to decay and may be transferred to subsequent activities (Wang & Lang, 2012; Zillmann, 1996). Much of the positive experience of suspense is mediated by the presence of the pleasant relief that we feel after our hero has averted the imminent danger (Madrigal, Bee, Chen, & LaBarge, 2011).

Suspense may be studied through either an examination of the program script (*text*) or an analysis of the audience activities, expectations, emotions, and relationships with the characters (*reception*) (Vorderer, Wulff, & Friedrichsen, 1996). The text-oriented approach examines such factors as outcome uncertainty, delay factors, and threats to the character. The reception approach studies the audience's identification with the character, their expectations and curiosity, their emotions, and their concurrent activities and social situation, which may enhance or detract from the experience of suspense. The fact that both text and audience aspects of suspense are important confirms how the experiencing of suspense emerges as the person interacts with the text of the medium to create the emotional experience of suspense.

Sometimes conventional wisdom about suspense does not hold up against hard scrutiny. See Close-up 4.3 about how so-called spoilers do not necessarily spoil the suspense.

❖ CLOSE-UP 4.3 DO SPOILERS REALLY SPOIL ENJOYMENT OF A STORY?

Does knowing the end of a story remove the enjoyment from reading or watching it? Many people apparently believe so, as seen by the irate responses to movie reviewers who reveal the ending of a film or people who tell their friends how a story ends before the friends see it. Jonathan Leavitt and Nicholas Christenfeld (2011) decided to test to see if it was in fact true that people hate spoilers. In three experiments they asked college students to read three short stories each, some literary, some mystery, and many with an ironic twist at the end. After reading them, students rated how much they had enjoyed the story. Some had an opening paragraph with a "spoiler," that is, telling how the story ended, and some did not. Surprisingly, readers actually preferred the stories that included the spoiler. Why would readers actually prefer to know the surprise ending at the beginning? The authors suggest that this knowledge allowed them to organize the information in the story somewhat differently as they read it. This more omniscient perspective, although very different from that of the character in the story, may actually heighten pleasure, perhaps by allowing them to anticipate events and think more deeply about them. Many movie viewers enjoy watching a film for a second or third time for the same reason.

Apparently NBC was confident enough of the lack of a spoiler reaction when broadcasting the 2012 Summer Olympics. Although previous Olympics had held off broadcasting events until the edited evening presentations, in 2012 NBC showed live coverage on its various cable channels hours ahead of its edited evening summary broadcasts. Evening attendance did not suffer. This was also true of the 2016 Summer Olympics in Rio de Janeiro. However, NBC was criticized for not showing more events live, considering that Rio was only one hour ahead of Eastern Time (D'Addario, 2016).

Humor

One very common emotional component of consuming media is the enjoyment that comes from experiencing something funny (D. Brown & Bryant, 1983; Zillmann, 2000). But what makes something funny? Why is one line of comedy so hilarious and a very similar one not at all funny, perhaps even offensive? Most comedy involves some sort of incongruity, inconsistency, or contradiction, which is then subsequently resolved, as in the punch line of a joke (Attardo, 1997; Perlmutter, 2000; Vaid, 1999; Wyer & Collins, 1992). For example, Attardo (1997) offers a three-stage model of humor, beginning with the *setup*, followed by some *incongruity*, and finally a *resolution* of that incongruity. Neither the incongruity nor the resolution by itself is necessarily very funny, however. Although the joke, "Two elephants got off the bus and left their luggage by the tree" is highly incongruous, it is not particularly funny because there is no resolution. On the other hand, "Two soldiers got off the bus and left their trunks by the tree" has a resolution, but it is not very funny either, because there is no incongruity. Only "Two elephants got off the bus and left their trunks by the tree" has both incongruity and resolution (and, perhaps, humor!).

The best jokes offer some intellectual challenge, but not so much that we cannot "get it." Some of the most satisfying jokes are very esoteric, as in jokes involving knowledge from a particular group, such as a profession. What presents an adequate challenge for one person may not do so for another. For example, many children find certain very predictable, even dumb, jokes funny, whereas adults do not. They are simply not novel or challenging enough for adults. Sometimes the relevant in-group may be the viewers of the show themselves; some jokes on *The Big Bang Theory* may be funny only to regular viewers of the show, especially as they experience solidarity with others as they watch the show together.

Another important concept in understanding media humor is the psychodynamic notion of *catharsis*, the emotional release of tension we feel from expressing some repressed or unacknowledged feelings. For example, if you are very worried about some problem but talk to a friend and feel better just for having "gotten it off your chest," what you are experiencing is catharsis. Humor is often seen as a healthy and socially acceptable outlet for dealing with some of our darker feelings. For example, we might be able to deal with some of our own hidden sexual or hostile impulses by listening to a caustic stand-up comedian insult people. Although we might never say such things ourselves, though we might secretly want to, hearing someone else do it partially fulfills our need to do so. Catharsis is often invoked to explain why people appreciate racist, ethnic, sexist, or sexual jokes (Scheele & DuBois, 2006). It is also frequently put forth as a socially beneficial outcome of consuming sexual or violent media, although research has failed to confirm such a conclusion (see Chapters 9 and 10).

Social factors can make a lot of difference in the experience of humor, too (Apter, 1982; Vaid, 1999). Sometimes the presence of others watching with us enhances our enjoyment, particularly for broader, more raucous humor. The presence of others may genuinely enhance our enjoyment, or we may only outwardly pretend to enjoy it, due to peer pressure to conform to our co-viewers. If we are in a room full of people laughing uproariously at a movie, it is hard to avoid at least a few smiles, even if we are not particularly amused. This is the principle behind the inclusion of a laugh track on some sitcoms. The person who tells the joke is also an important factor. It is often perceived as acceptable for a member of a particular group to make fun of that group. A joke poking fun at Mexican Americans may be very funny if told by a Latino but highly offensive if told by an Anglo or an African American.

There are also individual and cultural differences associated with the appreciation of humor. Some people prefer puns, others prefer physical humor or practical jokes, still others prefer sexual or ethnic jokes. Also, societal standards change over time. In the very early days of television (early 1950s), *Amos 'n' Andy* could make fun of African Americans as dim-witted (see Close-up 5.5); a few years later Ralph Kramden could playfully threaten his wife with physical violence on *The Honeymooners* ("One of these days, Alice, pow, right in the kisser!"), and the audience roared with laughter. Now we have the chance to laugh at more sexual innuendo on TV than we could then, but Andy and Ralph's actions do not seem quite so funny anymore.

All of these factors affect the dispositional consequences of *moral assessment*, as theorized by Zillmann (2000). According to this view, the recipient of the humor is a "moral monitor" who either applauds or condemns the intentions of the other character(s). A lot depends on whether that response is positive or negative. For example, a sitcom character who responds to a witty putdown from another character with a retort in kind is implicitly offering approval, and the viewers experience humor and liking for both characters. On the other hand, if the recipient character is offended and lashes back at the first character, it sets the stage for an antagonistic relationship, where viewers' emotional support goes to the "good guy" (usually the unfairly wounded party) and roots for the discomfort of the "bad guy." Both types of responses are common in comedy, but the dynamics are different and the experience of viewing is different.

Different ages find different things humorous as well. For example, in an analysis of humor in Dutch television commercials, Buijzen and Valkenburg (2004) found that slapstick, clownish humor, and misunderstanding were common in commercials aimed at young children, while ads aimed at adolescents tended to use satire, parody, and surprise. Commercials aimed at a broad audience often used slapstick, irony, surprise, and occasionally sexual or hostile humor. Ads targeted to men and boys used relatively more irony, satire, and slapstick, while those aimed at girls and women used more clownish humor. Sometimes a TV show or movie has multiple aspects of humor to appeal to a broader audience. For example, young children's TV shows like *Sesame Street* or *Spongebob Squarepants* contain numerous witty retorts and popular culture allusions designed to appeal to teens and adults as well as kids. Many animated movies like the *Shrek, Incredibles, Cars*, and *Toy Story* series are filled with double entendres and pop culture references and parodies to appeal to older audiences without making it inappropriate or uninteresting to the youngest viewers.

Different cultures find different themes and approaches funny. In North American society, for example, certain topics are off limits or very touchy, at least for prime-time humor (late night TV and some cable programs are more permissive). Jokes on U.S. TV about racism, feminism, violence against women, or mainstream religion are risky; such humor does exist, but people are likely to take offense and thus producers and comedians are very cautious. On the other hand, a Brazilian TV commercial for a department store chain during one Christmas season showed the Three Wise Men walking to Bethlehem. Suddenly, to a rock beat, they throw open their robes and start dancing in their pastel underwear, featured on sale at the store. It seems unlikely that such an ad would be aired in the United States. See Close-up 4.4 for some examples of humor that ran up against powers who were not amused.

❖ CLOSE-UP 4.4 HUMOR IN UNFRIENDLY POLITICAL CONTEXTS

Sometimes political realities conspire against humor. When the producers of Sesame Street *tried to launch an Israeli version designed to promote harmony between Israelis and Palestinians, they ran into difficulty. Palestinians did not want their Muppets living on the same street as the Israeli Muppets. A later proposal to have the show set in a neutral park foundered on the problem of which side owned the park. In another example, a former president of Zimbabwe, Canaan Banana, banned all jokes about himself after he tired of banana jokes. Perhaps the most extreme case is North Korea, where all satire is banned because "everything is perfect in the people's paradise" (also see Close-up 3.4). There are those who resist even draconian restrictions, as in the case of one enterprising Chinese wit who created a computer virus in the 1990s that destroyed the hard drive of anyone who answered "no" to the question, "Do you think that Prime Minister Li Peng is an idiot?" (What's so funny? 1997). The polarized political scene in the United States has also become a minefield for comedians recently. While comics like Stephen Colbert and Samantha Bee have routinely criticized President Donald Trump and his policies, comedian Kathy Griffin apparently went a step too far in 2017 when she published online satire photos showing a mock beheading of Trump. Heavily criticized by Republicans and Democrats alike (as well as many fellow comedians), Griffin's stunt resulted in an investigation by the Secret Service (Deb, 2017).*

One function of media humor is as a sort of leavening in the context of a more serious offering. A little so-called "comic relief" in the midst of a serious drama can be much appreciated, although if done badly, it runs the risk of offending people and being considered as being in poor taste. If done well, it can increase motivation and interest and make the characters seem more human. If the humor is too funny, of course, it may distract from the major content.

Effects of humor in serious drama are complex and depend on many other factors, including viewer gender, character status (hero vs. villain), and context (King, 2000). This is particularly a concern with commercials. Some of the funniest and more creatively successful TV commercials have not been very effective at selling because the humor overshadowed the commercial message. People remember the gag but forget the product, not a situation that advertisers want (see Chapter 6)!

Humor, suspense, and empathy are only three emotional experiences that relate to media. Another very important media emotion, fear, is covered in detail in Chapter 9, which discusses fear as it relates to violent media.

Mood Management

Besides appealing to specific emotions, another important emotional function of media use, especially entertainment media, is to maintain good moods and alleviate bad ones. This relates directly to uses and gratifications theory (discussed in detail in Chapter 2). People in good moods will often seek the least engaging stimulation in order to perpetuate their current state, while people in negative moods may seek stimulation to alter that bad mood (Knobloch-Westerwick, 2006; Knobloch-Westerwick & Alter, 2006; Potts & Sanchez, 1994). This could help explain why happy people frequently turn on some mindless sitcom rerun or unhappy people watch an outrageous comedy that could distract them from their negative mood.

This kind of mood repair can occur through satisfaction of psychological needs (Reinecke et al., 2012). High sensation seekers, who are more easily bored than others, may seek highly arousing fare in order to achieve and maintain a high arousal level (Zuckerman, 1994, 2006). Severely depressed people may not take full advantage of this mood-altering function of media and might helpfully learn to do so (Dillman Carpentier et al., 2008). Media may also helpfully direct attention away from ourselves and our failings to meet our ideal standards (Moskalenko & Heine, 2003). Indeed, we have all probably had the experience of turning to media, such as a favorite song, movie, or TV series, in order to temporarily feel better about a distressing situation in our real lives.

Although emotion is present in, and evoked by, most types of media, we turn in the rest of this chapter to examining in more detail two domains of media where the emotional response is absolutely central, namely music and sports.

Emotional Exemplar 1: Music

Listening to popular music is one of the most preferred leisure activities worldwide by adolescents and young adults, occupying between 2 and 3 hours per day for the average teen (Rideout, Foehr, & Roberts, 2010; Strasburger, Wilson, & Jordan, 2014). Since the advent of rock and roll in the 1950s, the latest artists, whether it be Elvis Presley, the Beatles, Metallica, Michael Jackson, Lady Gaga, or Justin Bieber, have been immensely popular with teens but thought scandalous by their parents.

Popular music has also always been associated with dancing, going back in recent history at least to the Charleston in the 1920s, which raised parents' eyebrows in its time. Indeed, rock music has always been connected with movement, particularly dancing but also screaming, clapping, stomping, and what some concerned onlookers have even called "rioting." Sexually suggestive movements associated with music have been particularly threatening to some. When Elvis appeared on *The Ed Sullivan Show* in the 1950s, he was only photographed from the chest up, so that his gyrating hips would not unduly arouse teens beyond their control. Later, "dirty dancing" and "twerking" would become scandalous. Taking a broad historical perspective, Ehrenreich (2006) argues that this strong association of movement and music actually has been much more the rule than the exception throughout history. In fact she notes that the sedentary custom of sitting quietly and listening to music, with parallel sedentary behaviors for theater and worship, only began in Europe in the early nineteenth century. Rock music's debt to various African American musical traditions like blues, jazz, gospel, and hip hop is also seen in its emphasis on movement, always stronger in African musical and worship traditions than in European cultures.

Pop musicians have also often been at the forefront of fashion. When the Beatles came on the pop music scene in 1963, their "Beatle boots" and "long hair" created an immense stir, but within a few years much of the male population was wearing their hair at least that long, with the Beatles themselves sporting much longer hair. Punk and heavy metal rockers may have scandalized people in the early 1980s by wearing earrings, but 15 to 20 years later body piercings in all sorts of places were widespread. Music performances and award ceremonies are common venues for everything from fashions that are merely avant-garde to those which are truly outrageous, such as Lady Gaga's appearance at the 2011 Grammy awards wearing a dress made of meat.

Beginning in the early 1980s, recorded music developed a visual component. Music Television (MTV) began in 1981 (MTV Europe in 1987) by playing promotional videos produced by record companies. Discovering that these video ads had very wide appeal, the cable channel played more and more music videos and grew until it became a youth icon. MTV grew to be both a barometer and a leading trend-setter of the youth culture market. Some have argued that the demand for access to international popular culture was a major impetus for the democratic revolutions in Eastern Europe between 1989 and 1991, that it was not so much the failure of the Marxist systems but rather the inability of these systems to deliver Big Macs, Levis, and rock music. Karl Marx in his political theory never anticipated the problem that "I want my MTV" could create for decision makers in socialist countries (Orman, 1992).

In later years MTV has evolved to include other kinds of teen and young-adult oriented programming, such as the stunt program *Jackass* and its annual spring break marathon. Other music-video-oriented channels, notably VH-1 and Black Entertainment Television (BET), arose to provide more music video programming (although in recent years, as with MTV, these networks devote little of their schedules to music videos, which are now more commonly available online).

The heavy influence of American and British bands and soloists has been a major factor in the ascendance of English as the worldwide language of popular culture. However, there is also much rock music in numerous other languages. It is a fact, however, that international stars need to record in English to break into the U.S. market. Whereas South Americans, Europeans, or Africans will listen to music sung in languages they don't understand, it is commonly believed that North Americans will not do so.

There are also increasing cross-national and cross-genre influences as almost every musical style has become more international (Hutcheon, 2002). With the availability of the Internet, formerly very local music now has found international audiences: Indian sitar music, Jamaican reggae, Brazilian samba, Irish Celtic ballads, Louisiana Cajun and zydeco, and Caribbean salsa have worldwide audiences. New hybrid styles are continually emerging and finding new listeners, too. For example, Afro-Colombian cumbia blends African percussion, European melodies, and Andean flutes and accordions. Nigerian Afrobeat combines traditional African beats with American funk. There even are several Islamic heavy metal bands in Morocco, Egypt, Pakistan, Lebanon, and other Muslim countries (LeVine, 2008). See Close-up 4.5 for examples of how music has political power in Africa.

❖ CLOSE-UP 4.5 AFRICAN POP MUSIC AND DEMOCRACY

Pop music from Africa's Ivory Coast has long been quite political. When a 1999 coup by General Robert Gueï took over, it announced the overthrow of the Ivorian president with reggae superstar Alpha Blondy performing a song and then introducing the new president. In 2010, Blondy gave a free concert honoring the next president, Laurent Gbagbo, who was later overthrown in 2011 (Ford, 2015). Singer Tiken Jah Fakoly was even more identified with the 1999 revolution, having been an advisor to Gueï's forces. The singers also frequently acted as liaisons between media and law enforcement agencies (Lee, 2000). Ivorian anthems have been used by political forces elsewhere. For example, Fakoly's "We've Had It" was taken up by protesters in Madagascar and his "The Country's in Trouble" became the opposition anthem in Chad's 2000 election (Médioni, 2002). Nigerian singer Fela Anikulapo-Kuti, founder of the Afro-beat style, found an international audience before his death in 1997. His son Fema Kuti founded a movement against corruption and regularly writes editorials in song, most of which are censored in his native Nigeria. Afro-funk singer Angélique Kidjo emerged as the most popular person in her native Benin in a poll asking who they would prefer as president. Not interested in politics, she nonetheless has integrated Afro-Brazilian and African traditions to support democracy in Africa, as well as entertaining large international audiences (Médioni, 2002).

The advent of the Internet has also opened up new possibilities for preserving, sharing, archiving, and commenting on music. Music from earlier analog formats has been converted to digital files and made available on the Internet, along with ample opportunity for commenting in blogs. For example, Brazilian music alone has numerous websites and YouTube channels, including Sabadabada for popular music of the 1960s and 1970s, Loronix to preserve "forgotten music" and offer a chance for comment, and Toque Musical (Musical Touch) to offer a chance to hear and comment on rare or forgotten albums (Fullerton & Rarey, 2012).

The Emotional Uses and Gratifications of Popular Music

Popular music, indeed all music, centrally appeals to the emotions in many different ways (Strasburger & Wilson, 2002). There are numerous uses and gratifications that we receive from music. For one thing, music is physiologically arousing. The body is "pumped up" in response to many kinds of music, although individual tastes vary greatly. Music can induce pleasant mood states of different sorts, and it can reduce feelings of anxiety and generally lift the spirits. Indeed, music is frequently used as a tool for mood management and mood repair (Chen, Zhou, & Bryant, 2007; Knobloch, 2003; Knobloch & Zillmann, 2002).

Music is also used to fill silence and supply background noise, either at home or while driving a car. Thus, it can relieve boredom. It also has a social function, being a natural background or a part of talking with friends, partying, or other recreation. Sometimes it is difficult to definitively separate social and solitary uses of music (Roberts & Christenson, 2001). Teens may often listen to music by themselves but for reasons that serve social relationships ("quasi-social" uses). For example, music may remind one of an absent friend and relieve loneliness or serve to strengthen one's social identification with others who like that music.

Music can also help define one's self-identity and facilitate one's entry into groups. Within a high school, for example, one group listens to hip hop, one to heavy metal, another to country music, and so on. The music can be an agent of socialization to bring the teen into the subculture by influencing how he/she dresses and acts. This musical culture is not necessarily restricted to one's culture of origin. Many popular American musical genres (e.g., jazz, blues, rock, gospel, rap, hip hop) had their origin in the African American community but have wide appeal beyond that subculture. Many continue to be amazed at the current popularity of rap, given its urban Black origins, with affluent White suburban teens. Sometimes even the same genre of music has different divisions within it; for example, "redneck" and "blueneck" political partisans within country music (Willman, 2005) or Christian punk and secular punk.

Finally, music in adolescence, along with its accompanying dancing and other movement, serves as a marker of separation from adults. Part of its appeal is frankly that adults dislike it and don't understand it. This phenomenon repeats itself with rap and heavy metal today as it has in the past with rock and roll in the 1950s or the Charleston in the 1920s. Even something as simple as a teen turning on the radio or streaming music in the car or house serves as a separation from parents. If the music is on, she doesn't have to talk to her parents.

Music is powerful material, and anything powerful can potentially be threatening. See Close-up 4.6 for some examples of how music has threatened the status quo throughout history and Close-up 4.7 for how music has even been used to torture.

❖ CLOSE-UP 4.6 MUSIC AS A THREAT

Music has often been a threatening force and sometimes can produce a violent reaction. Perhaps the most extreme example of a backlash against music was seen in the brutal Taliban regime in Afghanistan, which sought out musical instruments, cassette tapes and videos, and cassette players and burned them in public pyres. Musicians caught playing were beaten with their instruments and then imprisoned. Other puritanical authoritarian regimes have also opposed music. Believing it had hypnotic or addictive effects, theocratic ruler Ayatollah Khomeini banned music from TV and radio in Iran after the Islamic Revolution of 1979 (Taruskin, 2001).

Such extremes have also been seen in Western church and secular traditions as well, however. Plato's Republic *was highly suspicious of music as taking hold of the soul. In the history of Christianity, there have been many religious leaders and traditions suspicious of music, including such diverse company as St. Augustine, St. John Chrysostom, the Massachusetts Puritans, and various conservative Protestant groups.*

Music also derives power and threat from its culture of associations. For many years the music of German nationalist composer Richard Wagner was not performed in Israel (by custom, not by law). When composer Daniel Barenboim broke this taboo in 2001, the decision was very controversial and many Israelis found his choice insensitive (Taruskin, 2001).

❖ CLOSE-UP 4.7 MUSIC AS TORTURE

Although music has long been used in warfare to rally troops and distract the enemy, sometimes it goes beyond that to become a weapon of torture. In the U.S. invasion of Panama in 1989, forces helped drive dictator Manuel Noriega out of hiding in the Vatican embassy by blasting Van Halen and Metallica at high volumes from multiple boom boxes. In the early days of the Iraq War in 2003, U.S. forces exposed captives to prolonged loud music, including Metallica's "Enter Sandman" and Barney the Dinosaur's theme song "I Love You." The next year in the second battle of Fallujah, AC/DC's "Shoot to Thrill" was used to flush out insurgents. Even long before the age of electronic media, the Mexican army band played loud music the night before their attack on the Alamo in 1836. In recent years several professional music research and musicology societies have passed resolutions condemning the use of music as torture (Pellegrinelli, 2009; Ross, 2016).

Content

Though it probably will not surprise you, the most common theme in music lyrics over the last 70 years is being in love, although the lyrics are more sexually explicit than they used to be; for example, expressing love as lust (Hansen & Hansen, 2000). There was an increase of violent and misogynistic themes starting in the 1990s, especially in rap, punk, and heavy metal. Increasingly these themes became more mainstream. The advent of music videos in the early 1980s offered a new outlet for women to be presented as sex objects and ornamental decorations, much as they had long been portrayed in many other entertainment genres and advertising. Music videos also provided more opportunities for the intertwining of sexual and violent themes.

One content concern with popular music has been the promotion of drug use. Roberts, Henriksen, and Christenson (1999) analyzed the lyrics from the 1,000 most popular songs in 1996 and 1997. They found that 17% of the songs overall had reference to alcohol and 18% to illicit drugs. With rap, however, figures were much higher (47% for alcohol and 63% for illicit drugs). More importantly, any mention of negative consequences of drug use was rare; only 9% of songs mentioning alcohol mentioned any negative consequences of its use. Tobacco was rarely mentioned, although more often in rap and hip hop than other genres. There were similar findings in analyses of popular songs in 2005, with rap and country songs being most likely to reference drugs (Primack, Dalton, Carroll, Agarwal, & Fine, 2008).

These antisocial themes were generally more prevalent in music videos than in the lyrics themselves, especially in rap videos (DuRant *et al.* 1997). For example, Jones (1997) found the following percentages of themes in rap videos: profanity (73%), grabbing (69%), guns (59%), drug use (49%), alcohol use (42%), and explicit violence (36%). In another interesting study that looked at the most popular songs in the United States between 1959 and 2009, it became clear that references to drugs became much more common toward the end of that time frame (Cougar Hall *et al.*, 2013). The authors attribute this partially to the advent of Parental Advisory labels that began appearing on music with explicit lyrics in 1985; ironically these labels may have given music artists more license to include racy content since they could argue that consumers were "warned."

Content analysis itself does not tell the whole story, however. The interpretation of that content is important, and different ages do not always interpret lyrics in the same way (Hansen & Hansen, 2000). For example, in response to lyrics which are quite sexually explicit, teens perceive less sex and more love where adults see only sex (Rosenbaum & Prinsky, 1987). Girls often perceive a sexy woman as a powerful figure, whereas boys see her as an erotic plaything. Children will interpret a video more literally than a teen or adult will. Often teens do not fully understand the lyrics anyway (Desmond, 1987; Greenfield *et al.*, 1987; Strasburger & Wilson, 2002). Lyrics may also mean different things in different times. For example, a popular mainstream hit "Young Girl" in 1968 by Gary Puckett and the Union Gap today sounds like a creepy pedophile anthem ("Young girl, get outta my mind, my love for you is way outta line, better run girl").

There may also be a socially positive side to even fairly extreme lyrics. For example, some have argued that rap music has a positive social role, being a voice for very marginalized and disenfranchised groups, at the same time empowering young Black males and drawing the broader society's attention to their plight (Krohn & Suazo, 1995; McDonnell, 1992).

At the same time, these lyrics or videos probably serve to prime ideas and serve as cues to retrieve related knowledge. If a teen watches lots of videos that portray women as sexual playthings, for instance, that will prime gender-role memories and attitudes consistent with that type of schema. This in turn will guide future attention and information processing, directing attention toward exemplars that confirm such beliefs and away from those which are inconsistent with it. For example, Gan, Zillmann, and Mitrook (1997) found that sexually enticing rap videos primed a negative stereotype for African American women in White viewers, and that this negative schema was subsequently used to evaluate other Black women in more negative ways. Clearly, the content of music programming is important to consider. See Close-up 4.8 for an example of the use of music in attempts to gain international influence.

❖ CLOSE-UP 4.8 POP MUSIC IN THE SERVICE OF DIPLOMACY

Who is the largest distributor of Arabic-language popular music in the Middle East? It is Radio Sawa ("Together"), and it will probably surprise you to know that Radio Sawa is funded by the U.S. government in its efforts to woo the hearts and minds of young adult Arabs. Radio Sawa is the successor to the Voice of America Arabic service, a 7-hour-daily news service on shortwave radio that was little more than U.S. political propaganda without much popular appeal, even for those few who could receive it. Designed by Norman Pattiz after intense local market research, Radio Sawa broadcasts on FM and sometimes AM with a 24-hour format of eclectic popular music from the Arab world, the United States, and elsewhere. There are also two hourly news segments (a 10-minute segment with correspondent reports and a 5-minute headline segment), as well as PSAs on topics like drugs, drunk driving, and AIDS. In an attempt to win local appeal, announcers use local Arab dialects and broadcast local news, weather, and traffic reports. Of course, the most controversial aspect is the news, this being a part of the world with a high level of distrust and dislike of the U.S. government. Radio Sawa, with headquarters in Dubai, is broadcast to Jordan, Qatar, the United Arab Emirates, Kuwait, Bahrain, Djibouti, and Cyprus, with access from these places to Iraq, Egypt, Palestine, and elsewhere (Gubash, 2002). What do you think of Beyoncé and Kanye West being an integral part of the U.S. diplomatic message to the Arab world?

Effects

Parallel to popular judgments about media violence (see Chapter 9), people often take an extreme position on popular music, either damning it as the cause of all moral decline in society or dismissing the criticisms as "no big deal." People also frequently experience a third-person effect (see Chapter 2) when considering how music may affect them personally. Although it is difficult to do well-controlled research on causative effects of music consumption, we do know something about its effects (see Levitin, 2006, for a fascinating look at how the brain processes music, and Allen, Herrett-Skjellum, *et al.*, 2007, for a meta-analysis on effects of music on behavior).

First of all, there is clear research support for arousal; that is, music does arouse us emotionally, even though specific tastes differ greatly and what is pleasant for one person may be highly aversive for another. The tempo of music differentially affects skin conductance, with fast-paced music consistently causing greater arousal than slower-paced music, which in turn arouses more than silence (Dillman Carpentier & Potter, 2007). Music also can clearly affect mood (Ballard & Coates, 1995). Although a possible causative role is not entirely clear, there is some evidence that a preference for heavy metal music, in particular, may be a marker for alienation, psychiatric disorders, risk-taking, or substance abuse in adolescence (Strasburger & Wilson, 2002), in that heavy metal is disproportionately preferred by teens with these conditions. In an interesting study looking at effects of listening to opera, Balteş and colleagues (Balteş, Avram, Miclea, & Miu, 2011) found that listening to an excerpt from Puccini's *Tosca* elicited positive emotion and arousal, as measured by heart rate, respiration rate, and skin conductance. Following that, reading a synopsis of the opera's sad plot before listening to the music a second time led to decreased positive emotion but continued high arousal. This was moderated somewhat by listening to the excerpt a third time while watching a subtitled film of the segment.

Different music lyrics can elicit different sorts of behaviors. Listening to music with aggressive lyrics can lead to more aggressive cognitions, emotions, and behaviors (Anderson, Carnagey, & Eubanks, 2003). On the other hand, people listening to music with prosocial lyrics leave larger tips in restaurants and donate more to a charitable organization (Greitemeyer, 2009a, 2009b, 2011a; Jacob, Guéguen, & Boulbry, 2010). Listening to prosocial lyrics also was associated with a decrease in state hostility, which led to reduced aggression (Greitemeyer, 2011b). Such findings suggest great untapped potential for music having positive effects on society.

Reactions to music can also depend on one's prior knowledge, experiences, and prejudices. Fried (1996, 1999) conducted a couple of very interesting experiments on reactions of adults of various ages to music lyrics. The lyrics to an obscure 1960s Kingston Trio folksong "Bad Man's Blunder" were pretested and shown to be not recognized as a folk song and to be equally credible as country or rap music. The lyrics, very similar to the controversial Ice T "Cop Killer" rap of 1992, tell of a young man who intentionally shoots and kills a police officer and shows no remorse for it. The written lyrics were identified as being from an artist named "D. J. Jones" and were then shown to White and Latino adults in public places like malls and coffee shops. The key manipulation was that half were told it was a country music song and half that it was a rap song, two genres identified as surprisingly similar by some text analyses (Armstrong, 1993; Noe, 1995). Participants were then asked to rate the lyrics on seven attitude scales like "I find these lyrics offensive" and "This song promotes violence, riots, and civil unrest," from which a composite score was created.

Results showed that adults over 40 rated the lyrics much more negatively when they were identified as rap than when the same lyrics were identified as country. Adults under 40, however, showed no difference as a function of the genre attribution and produced much more positive ratings overall. A second analysis, partitioned by whether the participants had children instead of by age, showed that adults with children rated the allegedly rap lyrics more negatively than the allegedly country lyrics, but that adults without children showed no difference. Clearly the reactions are not only to the presented lyrics but also to prior knowledge and attitudes about the musical genre. In the case of older adults and adults who are parents, rap was far more negative. Fried (1999) offers several possible explanations for these findings. One invokes a subtle racism, in which the rap music is associated with the urban Black culture, which has negative associations, especially with violence, for White and Latino parents. Another factor is familiarity, in which the less familiar is more threatening. The older adults were probably less familiar with rap as a genre than with country. In any case, these studies show that we bring considerable cognitive and emotional baggage when we respond to music.

There is also evidence of desensitization effects of music. For example, exposure to violent rap videos can lead to greater acceptance of violence in dating situations and lower academic aspirations of young African American teens and college students (Johnson, Adams, Ashburn, & Reed, 1995; Johnson, Jackson, & Gatto, 1995). Watching rock videos with antisocial themes led to greater liking of antisocial behavior (Hansen & Hansen, 1990b). See Chapter 9 for a discussion of desensitization of other kinds of violent media.

Music as a Memory Cue

Music turns out to be an excellent cue to memory, with melody providing an additional possible retrieval route beyond the words themselves. In many societies, extensive oral traditions have been handed down for generations through music, with the melodies serving to help encode the verbal information and preserve it in the collective memory (D. C. Rubin, 1995). Marketers have long known that musical jingles can aid memory for products advertised (Yalch, 1991). Songs can also be powerful cues for remembering the events of one's life (Cady, Harris, & Knappenberger, 2008; Schulkind, Hennis, & Rubin, 1999). People strongly associate certain songs with experiences like their senior year in high school, a long road trip with friends, or driving to work at a certain job. The popularity of oldies radio stations and classic rock in general is no doubt due to the highly effective triggering of personal memories by these songs. Cady and colleagues (2008) found that, when college students were presented with a list of songs popular during certain eras of their lives (e.g., preschool, middle school, high school), most could easily recall a personal memory associated with that song. For the most part these were very emotionally pleasant memories, with the earliest ones being the most pleasant and the more recent ones being more vivid.

Sometimes music memories enter our consciousness without being invited or perhaps even wanted. These melodic memories of a song "stuck in our head" are called *Involuntary Musical Imagery* (IAMs) or, more informally, *"earworms"* (Bailes, 2007; Beaman & Williams, 2010; Liikkanen, 2008; Williamson *et al.*, 2011). Earworms occur spontaneously and are hard to control, occurring most often in times of low alertness and low demands on our attention. Sometimes a very long-forgotten earworm may emerge into consciousness, such as when someone remembers an advertising jingle from decades earlier. Earworms are very common; 92% reported experiencing them at least weekly and 26% "several times a day" (Liikkanen, 2008). They are most often some very familiar song, often triggered by some cue that elicits that melody. Interestingly, women and younger people report earworms more often than men and older people. They are often experienced as pleasant but at times may be annoying and elicit emotions like irritation or anger.

Thus, as we have seen, music is intricately connected to our emotional experiences. Now let us turn to a second media domain which plugs in very centrally to our emotions, namely, the world of sports.

Emotional Exemplar 2: Sports

Media sports are a part of most everyone's consciousness today, even those who have no great interest in sports. Events like the Super Bowl, World Cup, and the Olympics have become emotional and cultural phenomena that touch the lives of many people, not only regular sports fans. Over one-third of all network programming on broadcast television involves sporting events (Bryant & Raney, 2000). The media, particularly television, are the way many of us learn about sports. Our perceived reality about particular sports is largely a media creation. In the case of sports not played locally, media may be the only source of information. The marriage of sports and television is so accepted and taken for granted today that it is easy to overlook the enormous influence that television and other media have had on the games themselves.

Audiences for major sporting events are among the largest for any programming, and television has become an integral part of the financing of most professional sports, as well as nominally amateur sports such as the Olympics and NCAA college football. Initially broadcast on weekend afternoons in the late 1950s, sports offered TV a chance to greatly increase the audience at traditionally low-viewing times. However, the immense popularity of sports soon led to prime-time broadcasting of games as well, such as ABC's (later ESPN's) *Monday Night Football*, evening baseball games, and the Olympics. The advent of popular all-sports cable channels like ESPN has tremendously increased the amount of TV sports available. Over the years, the television audience has become considerably more important than the stadium spectators, and sports have changed much more to adapt to the needs and desires of TV and its viewers than to the fans in the stadium. Even with the advent of Internet and smartphones, ESPN is still among the most popular outlets for live sports and sports information; it also commands some of the highest fees for transmission on cable systems. For economic reasons, the perceived reality of the TV audience has come to be more important than the reality of the fans in the stadium. As we will see, TV has also increased expectations that sports should involve emotions.

How TV Changed Sports

Television has changed sports in a myriad of ways (Sullivan, 2006). There is much more color in sports than there used to be. Before TV, tennis balls and players' outfits were always white. Pre-television football stadiums also had less colorful end zones. Uniforms became more colorful, with players' names written on the backs for TV audiences to read. Increasing numbers of domed and retractable roofed stadiums have lessened the number of boring rain delays that play havoc with TV schedules.

Continuing technical advances in broadcasting have also affected sports. One of the most dramatic is the instant replay, first seen in 1963. The same play can be seen over and over at different speeds, from different camera angles. Newer technology treats viewers to computer graphics indicating the line of scrimmage and the path of the fast-moving hockey puck.

The Telegenic Factor

Some sports are more naturally suited to the format of commercial television than others. Baseball, with its many half-inning divisions, is a natural for commercial breaks. Football and basketball have fewer structured breaks, but do have frequent time-outs. The continuous action and low scoring of hockey and soccer make them relatively poor TV sports. Some have suggested this to be why professional soccer, by far the most popular spectator sport worldwide, has never caught on to a large degree in the United States. However, this lack of TV friendliness is not an entirely satisfactory explanation, because soccer (usually called football outside North America) draws huge TV audiences in many countries. The quadrennial World Cup series is the most-watched professional sporting event worldwide, with an estimated viewership of over 3 billion.

In spite of what one might think, some of the most popular sports in terms of fan attendance are not particularly popular on television. Two of the top American sports in gate receipts are NASCAR auto racing and horse racing, yet, until quite recently, they have been seen by large TV audiences only in the very top contests like the Indianapolis 500 or the Big 3 of thoroughbred racing (Kentucky Derby, Preakness, and Belmont Stakes).

Institutional Changes

In additional to visual considerations, there have also been some dramatic structural changes in the institutions of sport due to television. For example, the 59 baseball minor leagues in the late 1940s were down to about 15 leagues 30 years later. The chance to see major league baseball on television from all over the country largely eroded the appeal and financial viability of the minor leagues. However, there may be a limit to growth of the TV audience. The formation of the United States Football League in the early 1980s and the XFL 20 years later were colossal failures. There are also signs of tedium and lower than expected ratings as division playoffs and tournaments extend the seasons of different sports longer and longer. People often tire of baseball by late October or NBA basketball and Stanley Cup hockey playoffs in June.

The large-scale reshuffling of NCAA athletic conferences in the early twenty-first century is largely due to the desire for television revenue. The postseason college football bowl games sold TV rights for multimillion-dollar deals as early as the 1960s, and the larger conferences depend on bowl appearances to recruit strong talent and bowl receipts to finance their programs. The proliferation of postseason bowl games and their corporate sponsorship (e.g., TaxSlayer Bowl, PlayStation Fiesta Bowl, GoDaddy. com Bowl) has opened new advertising and revenue opportunities. By the early twenty-first century, interest and attendance at some bowl games had declined, amid growing controversy about bowl-team selection processes. Although TV has brought big-time college football into the lives of many who never would have attended a game, it has been at the cost of heavily commercializing the football programs of the major schools and depleting the audience for small college football, whose supporters often prefer to watch top-rated teams on TV instead of attending a local game in person (Sperber, 2001).

Although college football had been popular since the nineteenth century, pro football was more of an athletic footnote on the U.S. sports scene before the age of television. Pro football learned how to deal with television more adeptly and in a more unified fashion than did baseball. Television close-ups and cogent interpretation by the sportscaster made a previously opaque and uninteresting game fascinating to large numbers of new fans, who now were able to follow what was happening.

One of the most brilliantly marketed events in media history has been the Super Bowl, which began in January 1967. By the early 1970s, the Super Bowl had overtaken the baseball World Series and the Kentucky Derby in TV audience size in the United States. Unlike other major sporting events, the Super Bowl was a creation of television, not a preexisting institution adapted to the medium. Now, each year's game is frequently watched in over half of U.S. households. The broadcast in itself has become the event; what happens in the game is almost irrelevant. By the 1980s, major advertisers, paying top dollar for ad time, launched new ad campaigns with commercials presented for the first time during the game. Many of these ads appeal to emotions discussed earlier in this chapter such as humor and suspense (also see Chapter 6). This annual advertising debut also has become a significant spinoff media event. A whole series of tangential events have emerged, such as numerous televised parties and pre- and postgame specials. Now, Super Bowl Sunday is practically an annual holiday, complete with ebullient media hoopla starting weeks in advance. In many Americans' minds, the Super Bowl is closely associated with the emotions of fun and togetherness because there is a mandate (from football, TV networks, and advertisers) that the Super Bowl is a major, national event that should be shared with friends and family. This large audience is sometimes even used for other purposes, such as collecting "Souper Bowl" food donations for food banks and consciousness raising about the problem of wife-battering that takes place during and after the Super Bowl (Gantz, Wang, & Bradley, 2006).

The Olympics and TV

Some immensely important sporting events, in terms of their TV impact, are the quadrennial summer and winter Olympics. Although they have been held in modern times since 1896, interest has soared exponentially since television debuted. In turn, the Olympics have become totally financially dependent on television. In the United States, NBC has exclusive broadcast rights to the games. The network paid $1.23 billion for all broadcast and Internet rights to the 2016 summer games in Rio de Janeiro, up from the $1.18 billion it paid for the 2012 London Summer Olympics (Dawson, 2016). Due to the traditionally amateur status of the Olympics, TV has popularized sports that have not otherwise been sources of large revenues. Most notable have been women's sports, which have received a tremendous boost from Olympic coverage. Certain sports that have little audience elsewhere are very popular in the Olympics (e.g., gymnastics and figure skating). In such sports, television serves an important educational function: people learn about new sports from watching the Olympics, which sometimes translates into their own participation in these activities.

TV Reveals (or Creates?) an Emotional Side to the Olympics
As with sport in general, emotional aspects of Olympic athletes are often highlighted, leading to some criticisms that broadcasting the sport itself has taken a back seat to tear-jerker side stories. This trend may reflect attempts to increase the numbers of female viewers. Competition between athletes is emphasized, even if somewhat artificially, as with the heavily hyped rivalry between American swimmers Michael Phelps and Ryan Lochte in 2012 or gymnasts Simone Biles and Gabby Douglas at the 2016 summer games. Probably the most dramatic such competition was the Nancy Kerrigan–Tonya Harding feud ("Dueling Figure Skaters") of the 1994 winter games. Harding and her boyfriend were implicated in a knee-bashing sabotage attempt against Kerrigan. This nasty side issue almost eclipsed the actual skating competition, although it ironically delivered a record boost to the figure skating audience.

A more common melodramatic theme is that of the triumph of the human spirit over adversity. Whether it be an athlete's cancer-stricken father watching his daughter earn her final gold medal or the first Olympic runner competing with two prosthetic legs, the emotional drama is framed as prominently as the athletic competition. When the expected heroic attempts do not actually occur, there is shame and derision, as in the 2012 summer games when several badminton players were disqualified for throwing matches to try to earn an easier later competitor in a round robin tournament. At the 2016 Summer Olympics, sports met news met tabloid scandal when Ryan Lochte was caught in a lie about being robbed at gunpoint at a Rio gas station.

A related theme (at least on U.S. television) is the domination of American athletes at the Olympics. Although Americans obviously do not win every competition, NBC frequently cuts together highlights that show the prowess and spirit of U.S. Olympians. NBC has been heavily criticized for this kind of coverage (D'Addario, 2016), especially when it comes at the cost of missing a prime opportunity to inform U.S. viewers about other countries, athletes, and cultures.

Occasionally, more light-hearted treatments can raise some eyebrows. In the 2012 games, American gymnast Gabby Douglas was hailed for winning medals but also criticized for her unkempt hairdo, a journalistic detail many found inappropriate. During the baseball games at the 2000 Summer Olympics in Sydney, every foul ball (even the grounders) was accompanied by sound effects of breaking glass. Beach volleyball had its own comic host, "Lifeguard Dave," who worked the crowd like a stand-up comedian. Roy Slaven and H. G. Nelson, Australian late night comedians, ran

Greco-Roman Olympic wrestling coverage to a sound track of Barry White love songs and commentary pondering why large men would try to grope and mount each other. Their show's mascot "Fatso the Fat-Arsed Wombat" became so popular that Olympic athletes all wanted to pose with it, until the International Olympics Committee (IOC) requested that they stop doing so (Luscombe, 2000). Do you think such coverage enhances or detracts from the Olympics?

The Psychology and Emotion Underlying Sports Media Consumption

Whether we're watching the Olympics, football, or some other televised sport, why do we seek out sports media, and what is the nature of that experience psychologically? On TV, only sports (and in a very different way, news) is live and unrehearsed with the outcome unknown. This is very different from the rather predictable, formulaic nature of most entertainment programming and advertising. Motivations for watching sports are many, including emotional (entertainment, arousal, self-esteem, escape), cognitive (learning, aesthetic), and social (release, companionship, group affiliation) (Raney, 2006). In this final section relating to sports, we examine several aspects of the sports media consumption experience, with the major focus being on emotion and the medium of television.

Sports Media Consumption as a Social Event

More often than for other TV programming, part of the reality of the experience of sports media consumption involves the presence of others (Wann, Melnick, Russell, & Pease, 2001). Friends gather at someone's home or patrons congregate in a sports bar to watch a big game. Often the game seems more enjoyable in a group than it would be watching alone, with the presence of others rooting for the same team somehow seeming more important than co-viewers when watching a movie, a sitcom, or the news (Wenner & Gantz, 1998). The expression of emotion, discussed later, may be part of the reason. Also, watching with a group partially recreates the stadium situation of watching the event in a crowd.

Even with the proliferation of smartphones and the Internet, most people still prefer to watch sports on TV. Furthermore, sports is the type of television most often consumed in a social context. Who one watches sports with and how much one enjoys the game help determine the nature of the viewing experience. For example, if one watches a sporting event alone, with a group, or with one's family or significant other, different uses and gratifications will be involved in each instance (Bonds-Raacke & Harris, 2006). Wenner and Gantz (1998) identified five levels of motivation for watching sports, in decreasing amounts of emotional involvement. First is the *fanship* dimension, focusing on the thrill of victory and identifying strongly with the players. Second, the *learning* dimension involves acquiring information about the game and the players. Third, the *release* dimension involves "letting off steam," relaxing, and eating and drinking, much like the catharsis discussed earlier in this chapter. Fourth, *companionship* involves watching in order to be in the company of others who are watching; such motivations are especially important in the case of family or significant others. Finally, the fifth dimension, which is the least emotionally involving, involves watching to *pass the time* or because one is bored.

Sports Violence

Although the appeal of violent sports goes back to ancient times (Guttmann, 1998), one recent concern is how the media, especially television, tend to focus heavily on, even glorify, the occasional brawl or fight on the field. In a sense, this is a secondary competition to the primary one being played. Although no sportscaster celebrates or even condones serious tragedies like player or fan deaths, camera and media attention immediately shift routinely to any fight that breaks out either in the stands or on the field. When results of the game are reported later on TV or Internet news, it is more likely the brawl, not a play from the game, which is chosen as the sound bite of the story. Even if fighting is clearly condemned by the sportscaster, which is often not the case, the heavy coverage given to the fight conveys a subtle agenda setting. The perceived reality to the viewer, especially a young one, may be that the winner of the brawl is to be admired as much as the winner of the game itself, because temper tantrums, rudeness, and racket-hurling are more photogenic and newsworthy than self-control and playing by the rules.

Do people really enjoy watching sports violence? Avid sports fans do enjoy watching rough and even violent sporting events, especially under certain conditions (Gunter, 2006). Inherently more violent people enjoy sports violence more than mild-mannered people. The more one dislikes the victim of the violence, the more that violence is enjoyed. Violence that is morally sanctioned, that is, presented as acceptable or even necessary, is enjoyed more and seen as more acceptable than violence presented as unfair or out of line (Beentjes, van Oordt, & van der Voort, 2002). Such moral sanctioning may come from several sources, including the rules and customs of the game, the tone of the commentary of the sportscaster or sportswriter, and even the reactions of other fans. The more of these conditions that are present, the more the sports viewer enjoys the violence. Overall, however, the higher the level of violence is in a game, the greater the fan enjoyment, especially so for men (Bryant, Zillmann, & Raney, 1998).

Hero Worship

Media coverage of sports has enhanced, or at least altered, the perceived reality of the hero. Sports stars have long been heroes emulated by youth, but the age of television, and to a lesser extent other media, has changed this role somewhat. On the one hand, LeBron James is seen by many more people on television than in person at games. On the other hand, the close scrutiny of television shows the faults as well as the nobler aspects of a potential hero. Tiger Woods is a prime example, his media portrayal shifting from a golfing wunderkind to a dejected, middle-aged man with marital and substance abuse problems.

Children emulate their TV sports heroes in all sorts of ways. A child may imitate not only his hero's great shooting but also his temper tantrums or drug use. Such emulation of athletes is not limited to children. Long-time golfers reported that play on golf courses slowed noticeably after major golf tournaments began to be televised in the 1960s. This occurred primarily because amateur golfers started bending down to line up their putts and imitating other behaviors they saw the pros do on TV, no matter that the amateurs may not have understood what they were looking for when lining up that putt. They'd just seen Jack Nicklaus do it.

Fans develop significant parasocial relationships (see Chapter 3) with sports figures. Sometimes this can be very traumatic, as seen in the outpouring of grief following the crash death of NASCAR driver Dale Earnhardt, Sr. in 2001. Rapidly expanding from its Southeastern U.S. base to become one of the fastest growing North American sports, NASCAR adherents are very loyal, especially to their favorite drivers. Earnhardt was a true hero to many, and his death was a troubling loss to countless fans.

One particular area of concern in regard to hero worship has been the use of drugs by sports stars and the resulting effects on youth (Donohew, Helm, & Haas, 1989). The widespread cocaine use by baseball and basketball stars in the 1980s seemed somehow worse than such use by other citizens, even by other public figures, because sports figures are heroes to youth. This has caused persons and institutions like the commissioner of baseball, the NCAA, the NBA, or the Tour de France to be tougher on drug users among their athletes than they might otherwise be. However, "doping" scandals in which athletes are caught using performance-enhancing drugs continue. Probably the most notorious case of this is one-time cycling hero Lance Armstrong, who was forced to relinquish seven Tour de France titles and a bronze Olympic medal (Wilson, 2013).

A substantial benefit of hero status is lucrative product endorsement contracts for the major stars. For Olympic athletes this is often a critical part of their financial support, allowing them to pursue an amateur career. For wealthy professional athletes it is more like the icing on the already rich cake. These endorsement campaigns lead to an even greater media presence because that person becomes familiar as a spokesperson in advertising for that product. Sometimes a single individual may endorse several different products in different classes. A certain wholesome and unblemished status is required, however. When basketball star Latrell Sprewell assaulted and threatened his coach in December 1997, he was immediately dropped from his Converse shoe endorsement contract. After former Romanian Olympic gymnast hero Nadia Comaneci emigrated to the United States, the fact that she was openly and unapologetically living with a man married to someone else apparently rendered her worthless to advertisers for endorsements. When his doping scandal broke in 2012, Lance Armstrong lost eight corporate sponsors in a single day, the largest of which was Nike (Rotunno, 2012).

In spite of television's enhancement of sports heroes, some (e.g., Rader, 1984) have argued that modern sports heroes can never be on the same pedestal as past stars like Willie Mays, Johnny Unitas, Jesse Owens, or Stan Musial. The huge salaries and fast-track living now seem to separate star athletes from the rest of us and encourage their narcissistic and hedonistic tendencies rather than the righteous and humble characteristics that we at least used to think our heroes possessed. The intrusive eye of television focuses on a ballplayer not only when he makes that glorious play, but also when he is petulantly fuming on the sidelines or selfishly proclaiming that he cannot make ends meet on a mere $2 million a year. No matter that all of us have our selfish and petulant moments; we like to think that true heroes do not, and the age of television makes it harder to maintain that fiction.

Emotional Benefits

Although there are clear health benefits from participating in sports, benefits from consuming sports through media are somewhat less clear. Obviously, physical health and fitness are not enhanced by watching ball games on TV and may even be hindered if watching takes up time that the viewers might otherwise spend exercising. Emotionally, the picture is a little less clear. Tension reduction or emotional release—catharsis—may result from physical exercise, where we release stress through muscular and aerobic exercise. Some psychologists in the psychodynamic tradition dating back to Sigmund Freud argue that catharsis may also be achieved through substitute activities. Although research has not supported the value of a cathartic release of aggressive feeling through watching sports, there is still widespread belief among the general public that such a process exists (Scheele & DuBois, 2006). See Chapter 9 for further discussion of catharsis via media consumption.

There clearly is often a lot of emotion felt while consuming media sports (David, Horton, & German, 2008). Zillmann, Bryant, and Sapolsky (1979) proposed a disposition theory of sportsfanship to describe such feelings. The enjoyment we experience emotionally from witnessing the success or victory of a competing individual or team increases with the degree of positive sentiments and decreases with the degree of negative sentiments we feel toward that party. The reverse is true for what we experience when we witness a failure or defeat. The more we care about a team's success, the more emotional satisfaction we feel when they do well and the worse we feel when they do badly. Thus, it is hard to become emotionally involved, or sometimes stay interested at all, in watching a game between two teams that we know or care little about.

There are also physical changes associated with these emotions. In a study of Spanish fans watching their national team in the World Cup final in 2010, van der Meij and colleagues (2012) found that both testosterone and cortisol (a stress hormone) were higher while viewing the match than in the same people on a control day, although neither level increased after the final victory by the Spaniards. Cortisol secretion during the match was higher among men than women and younger fans than older ones, although some of these differences were apparently explained by different levels of fan enthusiasm, suggesting the need to look at individual differences in responses to sports viewing.

Still, feelings about the competitors are not the only determinants of the emotional response to sports. As with any drama, the degree of perceived conflict is crucial in the experiencing of suspense. A game that is close in score and hard-fought in character evokes both more positive and more negative emotion, regardless of team loyalty, than one where the final victor is never in doubt or one where the participants appear not to be trying very hard (Knobloch-Westerwick, David, Eastin, Tamborini, & Greenwood, 2009). A strong emotional predisposition toward one team or the other is necessary in order to experience much suspense. A close basketball game between arch-rivals settled at the final buzzer carries the viewer along emotionally throughout its course. A game whose outcome is already known is less likely to be of interest to watch in its entirety. How many ball games are ever rerun on television? How many people watch a prerecorded game for which they already know the final score?

Conclusion

The emotions triggered by media can be very powerful, and they are a fundamental part of the media experience. These emotions can be wide and varied, but often include those discussed in this chapter: empathy, suspense, and humor (also see Döveling, von Scheve, and Konijn, E., 2015, for a thoughtful collection of writings on other emotional issues relating to media). Music and sports are two forms of media intricately connected to emotion. Indeed, for most people, few events elicit more emotion than listening to a song that they really love or hate or watching an exciting ball game between two teams they care about.

Music certainly has the power to stir many feelings within us. It can arouse us, relax us, or distract us. As we have seen, music also has the ability to boost our mood and improve our memory. In interesting ways, popular music has had tremendous influence on culture and politics, often being intimately involved in the changing of an entire civilization. There are also important social aspects to music consumption, including how we perceive ourselves and others.

Like music, sports are also inherently social and one of the most popular forms of media. When media report sporting events, they are doing more than reflecting the reality of that game. Television in particular has changed the very sports themselves. Television has also changed the way that our minds consider these sports and the way our hearts react to them. TV sports is a world all its own, a world often only imperfectly related to the sports in the field. When people think of sports, they are most likely to first think of watching television. The perceived reality of sports acquired through television is thus what sports become for most people. Just as media are our knowledge source about groups of people, social values, or products for sale, so do they tell us about sports, how to play them, how to watch them, and how to feel about them. The very high level of coverage also sets a clear agenda that sports are important. Sports fans consider what the sportscaster says, not what they observe with their own senses, as authoritative; this is why people take their radios and even their small televisions to the stadium, so they can know what is "really happening." See Billings (2011) for a series of papers on thinking about sports media.

As we have done in previous chapters, we devote the last section of this chapter on emotion to a specific, related issue of concern. More specifically, we take a close look at one particularly disturbing aspect of media sports: possible biased coverage.

Media Applications, Chapter 4: Bias in Sports Coverage

Gender Roles and Bias

Throughout the history of media sports, male sports have received much more coverage than female sports, which received only 5% of all local sports coverage in 1989 and only 8.7% by 1999; ESPN SportsCenter was even worse, with 2.2% of its coverage on women's sports (Duncan, 2006). Televised women's sport coverage has dropped to about 3% in recent years and tends to be blander than coverage of men's sports (Musto, Cooky, & Messner, 2017). A content analysis of *Sports Illustrated* covers from 2000 to 2011 found that only about 5% of covers featured female athletes, which was a similar coverage to that in the 1980s (Weber & Carini, 2013). Also, attendance at men's events is higher than at women's events. The nature of the relationship between coverage and fan interest is complex, however. Does the heavier media coverage of male sports merely reflect the reality of greater fan interest in men's sports, for whatever reason, or is the greater media coverage a cause of greater fan interest in men's sports?

Some major media sports such as American football and baseball are essentially male only, without parallel female teams for the media to cover. In other sports, such as pro golf, tennis, soccer, and basketball, there are parallel women's leagues and competition. Only in professional tennis and the Olympics does the media coverage of women's competition even approach what is given to the men, however, and both of these cases are fairly unusual, in that competition for both sexes occurs in the same structured event. The Olympics and Wimbledon or the Davis Cup include both men's and women's matches, whereas the PGA and LPGA or NBA and WNBA are separate and unequal events. In the reporting about female athletes that does occur, the coverage is asymmetrical, with women being described in less powerful and success-oriented language (Duncan, 2006; Eastman & Billings, 2000). They are more likely than men to be called by their first names and have their strengths described ambivalently; for example, "small but so effective," "big girl," "favorite girl next door," "her little jump hook." They are also more likely to be described in terms of their attractiveness and sexuality, while male athletes are described primarily in terms of their strength and athleticism (Baroffio-Bota & Banet-Weiser, 2006; Kane, 1996).

Curiously, the increase in sports participation by girls and the modest increase in broadcasting of women's sports have not translated into comparably larger audiences for professional women's sports. The male model of boys participating in sports and through that developing interest in watching sports has not been replicated for girls. Girls and women are watching more sports on television but much of what they watch is men's sports. Whiteside and Hardin (2011) noted this phenomenon and studied it. They concluded that women's sports viewing patterns were more a function of a woman's role in the family. For example, if one's husband or children are watching football, that is likely to capture Mom's interest as well.

The Olympics are an instructive and somewhat atypical instance. Both the summer and winter games are heavily covered by television, often with both live coverage and extended edited excerpts broadcast a few hours later at more convenient local times. Women's events receive nearly as much coverage as men's events, though overall numbers of minutes and quality of coverage still favor the men (Billings & Eastman, 2003). Interest in women's Olympic sports has been high for many years, and women superstar athletes such as Wilma Rudolph, Jackie Joyner-Kersee, Simone Biles, Mia Hamm, Bonnie Blair, Kristi Yamaguchi, Mary Lou Retton, and Dorothy Hamill have become genuine heroes and every bit as popular as the men.

Sportscasting and sports reporting is probably the last and most stubborn bastion of male supremacy in the journalism industry. Although female news anchors and reporters, meteorologists, and even editors are increasingly common and accepted, the female sportscaster or sports reporter (covering men's sports) is still highly exceptional. Not until 1993 was the first woman pro baseball announcer hired (Sherry Davis by the San Francisco Giants). It is unclear whether this absence reflects a true public dislike or distrust of women reporting men's sports or is merely an unfounded industry fear they will alienate viewers. It seems the problem is deeper than highly publicized but bogus pseudo-issues such as the awkwardness of sending female sportscasters into men's locker rooms for postgame interviews. (No reporters of either gender are allowed into women's locker rooms after the games; couldn't that model work for the men as well?)

Although not nearly as dichotomous as in the past, greater encouragement is given to boys than to their sisters to participate in all kinds of sports. Less obviously, the same asymmetry applies to media consumption of sports. Boys are encouraged by their parents, particularly their fathers, to watch games on TV as well as to play catch and shoot baskets in the yard. Both playing sports and watching sports on TV have become part of the male gender socialization role. The boy who is not particularly interested in spending his time this way, but whose father is, often receives subtle or not-so-subtle messages that such lack of interest does not measure up, perhaps calling into question his masculinity. Consuming media sports together has become a part of the reality of many father–son relationships, and, increasingly, some father–daughter ones as well.

One advantage for men watching sports is that this is probably the one arena where they are most free to express positive emotion to each other. Men watching a ball game together, somewhat like the players themselves, may relatively freely express feelings and even touch one another. In mainstream Anglo North American society this is practically the only time when many men feel comfortable publicly embracing. Many heterosexual men may never in their lives hug another man outside their family (or perhaps inside it as well), except in the context of playing or watching sports. For this reason, if for no other, sports are important.

In the past, girls were often given messages, especially after reaching puberty, that participation in sports was tomboyish and unfeminine and could be a serious liability in attracting a man. In recent decades, however, this has changed considerably, and girls and women are increasingly allowed to be athletic and sexy at the same time. Less and less is it considered surprising or awkward for women to watch ball games or to know more about sports than their men, although TV audiences for most sporting events are still majority male. Another important variable in media coverage may be whether a sport is "lean" or "nonlean" (Harrison & Fredrickson, 2003). In lean sports such as gymnastics, diving, or cross-country, weight and appearance are more important for success, whereas in nonlean sports like basketball, tennis, golf, track and field, volleyball, or softball, they are less relevant (see Creedon, 1994, for a collection of readings about women, sports, and the media).

Racial Bias

Although a large majority of American players in the NFL and NBA, as well as lesser but substantial numbers in other sports and the Olympics, are African American, their numbers are far smaller among front office personnel and head coaches. A few content analysis studies of play-by-play broadcasting suggest that racial stereotypes are sometimes being at least subtly reinforced by sportscasting. For example, Jackson (1989), looking at NFL and NCAA men's college football commentary, found that 65% of comments about African American football players pertained to physical size or ability, compared to 17% for White players. On the other hand, 77% of comments about White football players stressed their intelligence, leadership, or motivation, and only 23% of comments about African American players did (63% vs. 15% for basketball players). Similar findings occur for European sports media, where athletes of African, Asian, or Latin American descent are often admired for their "natural athleticism" but more often than White Europeans are described in terms of group stereotypes, such as "Latin temperament," "Pakistani religious fanaticism," or "superior African muscularity" (Blain, Boyle, & O'Donnell, 1993). Sometimes the "myth of natural physicality" of the Black athlete subtly appears in sports reporting, as does the association of African American manhood with criminality and drugs or the commodification and marketing of the Black street hip hop world (Grainger, Newman, & Andrews, 2006).

Further Reading

Allen, M., Herrett-Skjellum, J., Jorgenson, J., Ryan, D. J., Kramer, M. R., & Timmerman, L. (2007). Effects of music. In R. W. Preiss, B. M. Gayle, N. Burrell, M. Allen, & J. Bryant (Eds.), *Mass media effects research: Advances through meta-analysis* (pp. 263–279). Mahwah, NJ: Erlbaum.

Billings, A. C. (Ed.). (2011). *Sports media: Transformation, integration, and consumption.* New York: Routledge.

Döveling, K., von Scheve, C., & Konijn, E. (Eds.). (2015). *The Routledge handbook of emotions and mass media.* London and New York: Routledge.

Konijn, E. A. (2013). The role of emotion in media use and effects. In K. Dill (Ed.), *The Oxford handbook of media psychology* (pp. 186–211). New York: Oxford University Press.

Levitin, D. J. (2006). *This is your brain on music: The science of a human obsession.* New York: Penguin.

Raney, A. A. (2006). Why we watch and enjoy mediated sports. In A. A. Raney & J. Bryant (Eds.), *Handbook of sports and media* (pp. 313–329). Mahwah, NJ: Erlbaum.

Ross, A. (2016, July 4). When music is violence. *The New Yorker*. Retrieved from www.newyorker.com/magazine/2016/07/04/when-music-is-violence

Useful Links

Radio Sawa streaming:
www.liveonlineradio.net/arabic/radio-sawa.htm

Timeline of Ivory Coast politics and music:
www.tiki-toki.com/timeline/entry/467423/Ivory-Coast-MusicPolitics/

For more resources, please visit the companion website:
www.routledge.com/cw/harris

Chapter 5

Media Portrayals of Groups

Distorted Social Mirrors

Q: What percentage of teenage girls from Fiji suffered from eating disorders in 1995, before the advent of television to the island nation, and how many after?

A: Three percent in 1995. Three years later, 15% did, with another 29% "at risk" for eating disorders. Seventy-four percent of the teens said they felt "too big and fat" (Becker, 2004; Goodman, 1999; Numbers, 1999).

Q: How do media stereotypes of repressive Muslim cultures match the reality of people's day-to-day lives?

A: Although Saudi Arabia puts many social restrictions on its citizens, it also has reliable, high-speed Internet, and its monarchical government does not censor most social and communication apps. As a result, many young Saudis use their smartphones to gain a sense of freedom. They flirt online (forbidden in public), use Uber to get rides (women were only recently allowed to drive), and employ Twitter and Facebook to debate social and political issues (discouraged in open community settings) (Hubbard, 2015).

Q: How are women who have abortions portrayed in modern TV dramas?

A: Always a controversial topic in politics and public discourse, abortion is a plotline many shows avoid altogether. However, several recent series (*Crazy Ex-Girlfriend*, *Jane the Virgin*, *Scandal*, *Halt and Catch Fire*) have depicted female characters having abortions without much equivocation. This is in stark contrast to years past, when, if portrayed at all, female characters considering abortion tearfully struggled with their decision, often deciding to not terminate the pregnancy (Blake, 2017).

What do you know about Mexican Americans? Arabs? Jews? Farmers? People with schizophrenia? One of the major perceived realities that media help create for us involves information about groups of people. Through media we are exposed to a much broader range of people than most of us would ever encounter in our own lives. Not only are media our introduction to many different kinds of people, but sometimes media are practically the only source of our information about them. Sometimes almost everything that we know about some groups of people comes from media.

Some rural White North Americans have never met any Arabs or Jews in person. Many urban dwellers have never met a real farmer. Most people of the world have never met someone from the United States. In such cases, the media portrayal of Americans, Arabs, Jews, or farmers is reality for them. In one of the earliest studies of this issue, children several decades ago reported that most of their information about people from different nationalities came from their parents and television, with TV becoming increasingly important as the child grew older (Lambert & Klineberg, 1967). In this chapter we examine the media image of different groups of people and look at the consequences of such portrayals. The concerns regarding some groups (e.g., women, African Americans) are widely known and investigated, while portrayals of other groups (e.g., the mentally ill) have received relatively little research attention. Although the issue is relevant to all media, television and movies are of particular concern, especially with regard to programming and advertising. For example, if the world of TV is presented in a positive multicultural fashion, that could have enormous socializing effects on children (Asamen & Berry, 2003). Although the focus of research has been on media, especially television in the United States, the same principles (if not all the same specifics) hold true for any nation's media. Of course, with the advent of the Internet, international boundaries for media are weaker than ever, and popular culture is increasingly international.

Most American producers of television and films themselves tend to be rather affluent, mostly from New York City or Southern California. The media grossly over-represent the world of those who produce the programming, which tacitly presents their world as far more typical of overall life than is really the case. Most American shows and films are set in Los Angeles or New York, few in Tennessee or South Dakota. Some research suggests that such exported programs of glitz and glamour may be cultivating negative images of Americans for viewers elsewhere (Bech Sillesen, 2014; Harris & Karafa, 1999; Kamalipour, 1999). News coverage also has an effect. Certainly, the Trump presidency and the news media coverage of the controversies surrounding it have negatively affected perceptions of the United States abroad (Wike, Stokes, Poushter, & Fetterolf, 2017).

Although concerns about stereotyped group portrayals in media have been widely discussed and some good content analyses have been performed, rigorous scientific research addressing the effects of group portrayals has been much less common. It is difficult to isolate media effects from other influences to establish firm causal relationships. All theoretical perspectives discussed in Chapter 2 have made their contributions to this area, and the prevailing portrayals of some groups of people will increasingly come to be the perceived reality in those who partake heavily of the media.

Portrayals of the Sexes

To begin with, let us examine gender portrayals. What do media say about what it means to be a woman or a man? Although this question will be addressed in the current chapter, for reviews, content analyses, and meta-analyses of research on gender portrayals, see Verhellen, Dens, and de Pelsmacker (2016), Matthes, Prieler, and Adam (2016), Gerbner (1997), Herrett-Skjellum and Allen (1996), Oppliger (2007), Signorielli (2001), and Sink and Mastro (2017).

The View of Women

We have heard a lot about stereotyping of women by the media, but what, exactly, does content analysis research tell us about the way women are portrayed? Some of these concerns may be very familiar, whereas others are more subtle.

Numbers

Perhaps the most basic gender asymmetry is that there are far fewer females than males represented throughout media. According to the 2010 U.S. Census (and a 2015 updated estimate), the nation's overall population consisted of 49.2% males and 50.8% females (Howden & Meyer, 2011; U.S. Census Bureau, 2017). This roughly 50–50 proportion has been in place for at least the past century. However, content analyses of characters in television shows in the 1970s through the 2010s showed about twice as many males as females in prime-time shows and up to three or four times as many in children's programming (Gerbner, 1997; Signorielli, 1993; Sink & Mastro, 2017; Smith, Choueiti, & Pieper, 2016a; Smith & Cook, 2008; Thompson & Zerbinos, 1995). On a wide variety of popular current and former ensemble shows including *CSI*, *Saturday Night Live*, *Seinfeld*, *South Park*, and *Sesame Street*, a large majority of the characters have been and continue to be male. In fact, fewer than 20% of TV casts are gender balanced (Smith *et al.*, 2016a). The percentage of female characters on U.S. TV only increased from 28% to 36% between 1975 and 1995, and only 20% of characters aged 45 to 64 were women; those figures are essentially unchanged today (Gerbner, 1997; Sink & Mastro, 2017; Smith *et al.*, 2016a). This is despite the assertion of some that streaming TV platforms have helped usher in a "golden age" of television for women actors and roles (Sink & Mastro, 2017).

Until the advent of such mid-1980s shows as *Cagney and Lacey*, *The Golden Girls*, and *Designing Women*, shows with all-female lead characters were largely nonexistent in the United States, with very infrequent exceptions like *One Day at a Time* and the arguably sexist *Charlie's Angels* and *Police Woman* of the 1970s. However, virtually all-male shows have been common through much of the history of television, including most Westerns and police shows, and many kids' shows like *Teenage Mutant Ninja Turtles*, *Power Rangers*, or even Mickey Mouse, Bugs Bunny, and Roadrunner cartoons. In fact, children's cartoon characters are male two to three times as often as they are female (Dobrow & Gidney, 1998; Smith & Cook, 2008; Thompson & Zerbinos, 1995), and are especially likely to be male in cartoons that focus on adventure or comedy (Leaper, Breed, Hoffman, & Perlman, 2002). However, some newer animated shows like *My Little Pony: Friendship is Magic* have a primarily female (and non-stereotypical) cast (Valiente & Rasmusson, 2015). When it comes to shows aimed at "tweens" (i.e., those aged 8–12 years), there tend to be more male than female characters in action-adventure shows like *Aaron Stone* and *The Troop*, but relatively similar proportions of male and female characters in "teen scene" shows like *Hannah Montana* and *The Wizards of Waverly Place* (Gerding & Signorielli, 2014).

The same general patterns have emerged in the realm of film. For example, one study found that among the top grossing movies of 2015, female characters received only about half of the screen time as male characters. This was true even when there were male and female co-leads in a movie. However, when a female character was a lead in a movie, women tended to receive about 50% of the screen time (Geena Davis Institute on Gender in Media, 2016). A similar study revealed that females only accounted for 33% of all characters among the top 100 U.S. domestic grossing films in 2011 (Center for the Study of Women in Television and Film, 2012). There are comparable disparities in the domestic movies in many other industrialized nations, including Australia, France, Japan, and the United Kingdom (Smith *et al.*, 2014). Disparity even exists with how much male and female characters in film speak. One content analysis was conducted that examined male and female characters in all G, PG, and PG-13 rated movies released in the United States between 2006 and 2009 (Smith & Choueiti, 2010). Results revealed that 71% of speaking characters in these "family films" were male, with only 29% being female. Further, female characters were more likely than male characters to be portrayed in "sexy, tight, or alluring attire" (Smith & Choueiti, 2010, p. 3). Another study examining top-rated G-rated films found that only 28% of speaking characters were female (Smith & Cook, 2008).

Although 46% of characters in television commercials were female by the late 1990s and around 50% by 2016, even today the voice-over announcer is male around 65% of the time (Bartsch, Burnett, Diller, & Rankin-Williams, 2000; Ganahl, Prinsen, & Netzley, 2003; Matthes *et al.*, 2016; Paek, Nelson, & Vilela, 2011; Women's Media Center, 2017), percentages virtually unchanged from the early 1970s (Dominick & Rauch, 1972). An interesting study that specifically examined 20 years' worth of Super Bowl commercials discovered that women were underrepresented there, too. However, over time, Super Bowl commercials have become less sex-stereotyped, particularly among female characters (Hatzithomas, Boutsouki, & Ziamou, 2016).

Most popular in the 1980s and 1990s, sex stereotyping is still strong in today's music videos. As with other forms of media, music videos show at least twice as many males as females. They have also been shown to reinforce traditional gender stereotypes (Rodgers & Hust, 2017; Sommers-Flanagan, Sommers-Flanagan, & Davis, 1993; Toney & Weaver, 1994; Took & Weiss, 1994; Vincent, Davis, & Boruszkowski, 1987; Wallis, 2011).

A substantial minority of TV news anchors and weathercasters are now women, although very few sportscasters are. Still, there does seem to be progress in this area. A 2016 report indicated that there are now more women in TV newsrooms than ever before, although men still outnumber women (Papper, 2016). Nevertheless, disparities remain. Even public radio network NPR has about twice as many male as female voices reporting the news (Women's Media Center, 2017).

The medium of video games also underrepresents females. Lynch and colleagues (Lynch, Tompkins, van Driel, & Fritz, 2016) conducted an interesting content analysis of video games released in the United States between 1983 and 2014 that included playable female protagonist characters. Although they discovered that there was an increase in the number of female video game characters during that time frame, there were more secondary than primary roles for female characters. Also, there was a tendency for sexualized female characters to have enhanced physical capability. Thus, the game makers seemed to equate sexual and physical prowess.

Thus, as we have seen across multiple media modalities, there are far fewer females than males present. What message are we getting when we grow up seeing fewer girls and women than boys and men? What does it mean that even the females that we do see often don't speak very much?

Physical Appearance

Besides underrepresentation, a second concern is that women are too often depicted in media portrayals as youthful beauties whose duty it is to stay young, skinny, and pretty in order to please their men. Once a woman is no longer so young and slender and is therefore considered less attractive, she becomes an object of ridicule. Support for this criticism comes especially from the messages that a woman must not allow herself to age or gain weight. These anti-aging, anti-fat themes appear especially, although not exclusively, in advertising, the media area with the most stereotyped gender portrayals.

Don't Look Old!

Advertising tells women that wrinkles and gray hair are to be avoided at all costs. At least until recently, women obviously over 30, and especially those over 50, have been grossly underrepresented on television and movies and in all sorts of advertising. When present, they were often seen as stereotyped "old ladies" whom no one would want to grow up and be like. Women in TV ads also tend to be younger than men, a misrepresentation unchanged since the early 1970s (Dominick & Rauch, 1972; Ferrante, Haynes, & Kingsley, 1988; Kay & Furnham, 2013; Matthes *et al.*, 2016; Stern & Mastro, 2004).

The obsession with youth is so strong in advertising that sometimes grown women are depicted as eroticized young girls. One example of this is an ad campaign by Calvin Klein in the 1990s that intentionally mimicked child pornography with photos of scantily clad and very young looking models. Conversely, there also seems to be a tendency among some marketers to sexualize young girls by equating them with sexually mature women. One example of this is the Bratz doll line marketed to young girls. Typically, these popular dolls feature short, tight-fitting clothing and heavy makeup, which most adults would find inappropriate on a child. There is also an interactive website in which girls can have their dolls shop for clothing, shoes, pet accessories, salon services, and even furniture. Not to be outdone, Mattel introduced a Bratz-like My Scene Barbie collection (with accompanying website) and even Lingerie Barbies, some of which had see-through underwear and bustiers (Levin & Kilbourne, 2009). By 2015, this kind of content had transitioned largely to smartphone apps, which also allow users to share "selfie" photos (Castillo, 2015). The trend of premature sexiness even extends to clothes designed to be worn on girls' own bodies. In a content analysis of popular clothing websites, it was discovered that about 30% of clothes marketed to girls had sexualizing characteristics (Goodin, Van Denburg, Murnen, & Smolak, 2011). Examples include girls' products like thong underwear and panties with statements printed on them such as, "Who needs credit cards?" Amazingly, these kinds of items have been sold at mainstream retailers, including Wal-Mart (Durham, 2009).

Don't Get Fat!

Women in media became slimmer during the twentieth century (Percy & Lautman, 1994), but the weight gap between models and real women widened. Long gone are the idealized, voluptuous beauties of the 1950s and 1960s like Marilyn Monroe. By the mid-1990s, models weighed 23% less than the average woman, a figure up from 8% less in 1975 (Kilbourne, 1995, 2010). The numbers are even more startling when comparing Body Mass Index (BMI), a measurement of weight to height ratio. According to one source, the average BMI of a runway fashion model is 16; the BMI of a typical adult American woman is 26.5. In an effort to combat this kind of disparity, French lawmakers passed a law making it illegal to employ models with BMIs lower than 18 (Firger, 2016). Still, even in a recent analysis of prime-time television shows, female actresses were noted to be significantly skinnier than their male counterparts (Sink & Mastro, 2017).

The idealized portrayal of feminine beauty, especially in advertising, is a highly unusual body type, namely very tall, very thin, and small-hipped. This combination of characteristics occurs in less than 5% of the adult female population, but models are usually of this type. The other common supermodel characteristic, large breasts, is an attribute so infrequent for this tall, thin body type that at least one leading scholar in the area concludes that, if present, they almost surely must be implants (Kilbourne, 2010). Computerized image construction of models and the use of body doubles, even for very attractive stars, are common. For example, in a prominent movie poster for *Pretty Woman*, what appeared to be actress Julia Roberts was, in fact, composite body parts selected from the best of several models, plus computer graphic enhancement. Some of her sex scenes in the film used body doubles with even more beautiful bodies or body parts (Kilbourne, 1995, 2010). Interestingly, one analysis even concluded that thin, small-waisted, large-chested female characters were more common in animated than in live-action movies (Smith & Cook, 2008). Perhaps such body types are easier to draw than to find in real life! Close-up 5.1 discusses the complex interaction of food, sex, and weight loss.

> ### ❖ CLOSE-UP 5.1 FOOD, SEX, AND WEIGHT LOSS IN THE IDEAL WOMAN
>
> *The next time you're in a supermarket checkout line, pay attention to the cover headlines of magazines geared toward women. According to Kilbourne (2010), two major themes of magazine articles and advertising aimed at women are food and weight loss. Food is often presented as a way to deal with emotional needs (e.g., break up with a guy and indulge in some ice cream) and is sometimes even presented as a substitute for sex, as when a woman comes close to having an orgasm from eating fine chocolate or when Oreos are described in ads as "the most seductive cookie ever." Metaphors of addiction and loss of control are commonplace (e.g., I can't control myself with this candy), sometimes even modeling binge eating (downing a whole quart of ice cream). At the same time, however, women (but not men) are made to feel ashamed or guilty for eating, with supermodel thinness presented as the moral equivalent of virginity, both resulting from keeping one's appetites under control. Never mind the fact that no amount of dieting could possibly turn most women's bodies into supermodel shapes. This fear of losing control and losing one's figure is a powerful appeal in the advertising of everything from diet programs to cigarettes. Do such appeals work? With half of teens and adult women on diets, most of which fail, and 75% of normal-weight women thinking they are fat, it would appear that they do.*

Although the emphasis on women's physical beauty is important in many cultures, it's important to note that there are some differences. For example, many African cultures see plump women as healthy and attractive and very thin women as emaciated and unattractive. In some parts of Nigeria, young women have been sent to "fattening farms" to be fed and massaged to gain weight to be more attractive for their future husbands. In parts of Niger, in a desperate attempt to gain weight, some women risk their health by taking steroids or food or vitamins designed for animals. A woman who is too thin is seen as not being well provided for by her husband (Onishi, 2001). Facial piercing has long been popular among South Asian women and large body tattoos and corpulent physique are popular among some Polynesians of both genders. One content analysis of fashion ads in the United States, Singapore, and Taiwan concluded that a pretty face was the central beauty focus in the two East Asian cultures, while a shapely body was more central in the American ads (Frith, Shaw, & Cheng, 2005).

Placement of Women's Bodies in Advertising
When delving a little deeper into advertising featuring women, some interesting trends have been noted. For example, when comparing how male and female bodies tend to be presented in ads, Kilbourne (2010) as well as Conley and Ramsey (2011) have demonstrated that female models are frequently placed in more passive poses than male models. For example, in print ads featuring both male and female models, it is common for the male to be placed in front of the female and/or at a higher position in the photo. Likewise, men are more likely than women to be featured in action poses. Compared to males, female models in ads also tend to be presented as flawless, with perfect skin and hair; in contrast, it's more common for a man to be presented with a more rumpled or windblown look. Disturbingly, it is also relatively common for women's bodies to be dismembered in ads. For example, an ad for women's jeans presented only a view of a model's backside—no face, no head, no back, no arms. Another example is an ad for Bacardi rum that featured only a female model's torso (large breasts, pierced navel bared) next to a mixed drink.

Body Image and Media
What might be the effects of such stereotypical images of women? A relatively recent line of study has begun exploring how media depictions of bodies, particularly female bodies, affect media consumers. Central to this research is *social comparison theory* (Tiggemann, 2014). Originally proposed decades ago by social psychologist Leon Festinger (1954), social comparison theory is the notion that we constantly compare ourselves to others, sometimes to those we consider to be doing better than us (*upward comparison*), and more often to those we think are not doing as well as we are (*downward social comparison*). The mental comparisons we make can be in regard to almost anything, including social status and physical appearance. Applied to media depictions of females, the thought is that when comparing themselves to thin media models, average-sized women experience upward social comparison and a resulting sense of body dissatisfaction (Tiggemann, 2014).

Comparing ourselves to media models no doubt begins early in life. Several studies have demonstrated that preadolescent girls (but not boys) and college women (though not men) watching more entertainment TV later showed more disordered eating (Bissell & Zhou, 2004; Moriarty & Harrison, 2008). In related research (Harrison & Hefner, 2014), high school students were asked to view photos of other adolescents of the same sex. Sometimes, the photos were altered to make the adolescent models appear slimmer and/or more muscular, and in one condition of the study, these photos were labeled as "retouched." Interestingly, compared to other adolescents, both boys and girls in this condition of the study scored higher on body consciousness measures and lower on physical self-esteem measures.

In another study, college-aged students watched an episode of *Extreme Makeover*, a reality show in which contestants undergo plastic surgery and intense exercise regimes in order to change their appearance (Markey & Markey, 2012). In the episode the students saw, a woman underwent 12 cosmetic surgeries in order to achieve her ideal appearance. According to the authors of the study, both males and females who viewed the episode generally agreed with the show's message of physical attractiveness being important and related to happiness. Further, young women who had a positive reaction to the program indicated a greater interest in obtaining plastic surgery themselves than did women who had a more negative view of the show.

Unfortunately, aging does not seem to insulate us from the effects of media images influencing our perceptions of our own bodies. Hefner and colleagues (2014) point out a trend that may have started with shows like *Desperate Housewives* and *Cougar Town*: namely, that TV and movie actresses in their 50s are now expected to have similar body shapes as those in their 20s and 30s. These expectations seem to be affecting women in midlife. In their research, Hefner and colleagues (2014) studied women over 40 who were frequent viewers of programming that featured actresses who were thinner than might be expected for their age. These women viewers had increased reports of disordered eating and body perceptions. Similarly, women seeing slides of slender models with diet- and exercise-related storylines later ate less in front of female peers (Harrison, Taylor, & Marske, 2006).

Obviously we cannot expect any given type of portrayal of the sexes to have a uniform effect on the public. For example, women with a relatively greater difference between their ideal and actual body self-perception may be affected more negatively by ads of thin women than are women with less discrepancy (Bessenoff, 2006). Likewise, dieting women may react differently to thin media images than non-dieting women (Mills, Polivy, Herman, & Tiggemann, 2002).

Concerns of Women

In addition to being portrayed as thin, women in the media are still disproportionately seen as homemakers and mothers, with their business, professional, and community roles downplayed or not represented at all. This is rather amazing in the twenty-first century (see Close-up 5.2 for a discussion of how advertisers have marketed motherhood). Advertising through the years has especially emphasized the woman-as-homemaker stereotype (a slogan from one 1970s print ad for dinnerware: "A chip on your dinnerware is like a spot on your dress!") (Knill, Pesch, Pursey, Gilpin, & Perloff, 1981; Stern & Mastro, 2004). However, the range of occupational roles for women in ads has increased (Ferrante *et al.*, 1988), and the stereotyping of women in advertisements is not limited to the United States but occurs in many societies such as Australia, Mexico (Gilly, 1988), and South Africa (Luyt, 2011). Women are often seen as dependent on men and needing their protection. Even relatively egalitarian TV families generally show the wife deferring to the husband more often than the reverse, although the behaviors showing this are much more subtle than those of 50 or 60 years ago. Women are not seen making important decisions or engaging in important activities as often as men. Advertising often portrays women as terribly perplexed, even obsessive, about such matters as dirty laundry or spotted glassware. Women squeezing toilet paper or berating others about stinky shoes or uneaten lunches also make this point. Early sitcoms such as *I Love Lucy* that showed women playing bridge or gossiping with neighbors all day were illustrations of this concern as well. Although we have come a long way from the *Father Knows Best* dad telling his daughter in 1959, "Be dependent, a little helpless now and then. The worst thing you can try to do is beat a man at his own game" (Douglas, 1997, p. 24), some of the most gender-stereotyped

TV shows are those aimed at children. Often the females in children's shows have been rather frilly and wimpy supporting characters like Smurfette, Baby Bop of *Barney and Friends*, and April O'Neill of *Teenage Mutant Ninja Turtles*, both of whom, even into the 1990s, seemed mainly to nurture and support their male colleagues (Douglas, 1994). Some shows beginning in the late 1990s and 2000s offered more complex and positive role models for girls (e.g., *Hannah Montana, Dora the Explorer, iCarly, Peg + Cat, WordGirl*), and there is some evidence that gender roles on recent children and teen shows are somewhat less stereotypical than in earlier decades (Aubrey & Harrison, 2004; Kaveney, 2006). However, one analysis of shows aimed at kids and tweens such as *Drake and Josh* and *Suite Life of Zack and Cody* discovered many examples of common stereotypical "heterosexual scripts" such as boys valuing girls mostly for their looks or girls stroking the egos of boys (Kirsch & Murnen, 2015).

❖ CLOSE-UP 5.2 MARKETING MOTHERHOOD

How many ads can you recall that depicted a mom taking care of her family? Over the years, many advertisers, marketers, and advertising agencies have tried to tap into the sentiment people often feel about mothers and motherhood. These "warm and fuzzy" feelings coupled with the fact that mothers often are the primary consumers in a household also mean that mothers are frequent targets of advertising. But how are mothers portrayed?

One analysis of Canadian TV commercials (de Laat & Baumann, 2016) found that the overriding depiction was of mothers as "caring consumers." In other words, moms were portrayed as buying products in order to care for their families and keep their households under control. Echoing the stereotype of mother as selfless caregiver, another study on over-the-counter drug commercials (Craig, 1992) found that women were significantly more likely than men to appear in such commercials. In addition, the women were frequently depicted as mothers who were experts on home medical care, often caring for sick children. Another study examining outdoor advertising in London and Shanghai found a similar theme in both cities of mothers depicted as responsible home managers (Orgad & Meng, 2017). In an interesting contrast effect, de Laat and Baumann (2016) noted that women in TV commercials who were not portrayed as mothers were depicted as consuming products for indulgent self-gratification. Apparently, the message is that non-moms don't take care of others, and moms selflessly consume for their families while deriving great pleasure from doing so!

A related study (Coulter & Pinto, 1995) found that guilt is another frequent theme of advertising that depicts mothers. Such guilt themes seem to be aimed particularly at working mothers. Such ads highlight that moms, even working moms, are primarily responsible for the care of their families. To test the effectiveness of such advertising, Coulter and Pinto devised some ads with varying levels of guilt appeals aimed at moms (e.g., the announcer in one bread commercial was heard saying, "Mothers who don't teach their children to eat good meals have children who won't always learn. You shape your child's eating habits, so don't let your family down"). Results indicated that such "moderate guilt" ads elicited more guilt in working mothers than ads with a low-guilt appeal. However, such ads also were likely to provoke feelings of anger and thoughts that the ads were attempting manipulation for monetary gain.

Another study looked specifically at ads in the Philippines (Soriano, Lim, & Rivera-Sanchez, 2015). Even more specifically, the research examined how mobile phones and mobile phone services are marketed using images of mothers. Pointing out that the Philippines is a majority Catholic nation (with heavy usage of mobile phone technology), the authors argue that the Virgin Mary is invoked in many TV commercials in that mothers are implored to be pious and self-sacrificial—with their cell phones. For example, some commercials depict the mobile phone as a critical link between children and mothers, who are the light and the center of the home. There are related commercials that show mothers using their smartphones to complete chores like online shopping and paying bills—all allowing the moms more time to self-sacrificially care for their families.

What might be the ultimate use of mothers for marketing purposes? Some (e.g., Grold, 1968) have argued that it's Mother's Day. The origin of Mother's Day is often attributed to American Anna Jarvis, who in the early twentieth century thought the holiday would be a nice way to honor unselfish mothers. As time went on, Mother's Day became a major money maker for flower merchants, restaurants, and greeting card companies like Hallmark. Although plenty of moms enjoy special treatment on Mother's Day today, there's no denying that the holiday is also profitable business. Having grown angry at the commercialization of Mother's Day, Jarvis later publicly denounced the profiteering that had become involved with the holiday she helped create.

Sometimes the power that women do exercise is used in very underhanded and conniving ways, often directly or indirectly involving sexuality. The ruthless businesswoman character who sleeps her way to the top is a classic example. There are subtle messages that it is not ladylike to confront men (or even other women) directly, but it is perfectly acceptable to behave deviously in order to trick them. Portraying sexuality as a weapon of power subtly deemphasizes and even degrades its tender and relational aspects. Even strong female characters like those in *Scandal* or *Desperate Housewives* are very interested in sex and do not hesitate to use it to further their interests.

A related media depiction of women is that they are mean, socially aggressive, backstabbing and frequently double crossing others (particularly women) in order to get ahead. Some reality shows like *Bad Girls Club*, *Keeping up with the Kardashians*, and the *Real Housewives* franchise feature women displaying such behavior. Cable network Bravo seems to have been especially successful at attracting viewers for such programming, particularly affluent, female viewers (Cox, 2015). In a study that examined young women's perceptions of these kinds of shows, it was discovered that those who view this kind of programming as realistic tend to hold stereotypical views of women in general. Further, such viewers also expressed interest in being like their reality show models in their own lives (Behm-Morawitz *et al.*, 2016).

Sometimes, the stereotype that females are socially and verbally aggressive may even influence news narratives. For example, in 2010, when 15-year-old Phoebe Prince committed suicide in her home in Massachusetts, local and national media framed the story as a case of "mean girl" verbal aggression, with female classmates bullying Phoebe to the point that she could no longer take it. Although female bullying did seem to be a contributing factor in Phoebe's suicide, news media tended to gloss over the role of Phoebe's ex-boyfriend's bullying behavior as well as her preexisting mental health struggles in favor of a mean girl explanation (Ryalls, 2012).

Women and Violence

A final concern is that women are subtly linked with violence, especially as victims of sexual violence. Some advertising or entertainment playing on the seductiveness of women (especially women of color) also suggests that they are animals to be tamed, something wild to be brought into line by men (Kilbourne, 2010). A high fashion ad selling negligees by showing a scantily clad woman being playfully attacked by several fully dressed men, or an auto magazine ad showing a woman in a bikini chained inside a giant shock absorber (perhaps not so subtly) link sexuality and violence. Perfume ads may stress the wildness, the toughness, and the challenge that women provide for men. "Blame it on (the perfume)" seems to justify an attack from a man in response to some irresistible fragrance on the woman.

Although we may not find Ralph Kramden's (from the 1950s TV show *The Honeymooners*) mock threat of his wife with violence ("One of these days, Alice, pow! Right in the kisser!") as amusing as we did in 1955, far more graphic instances of violence toward women are common, especially in the so-called "slasher" films popular since the 1970s (e.g., *The Texas Chainsaw Massacre*, *Friday the Thirteenth*, *Nightmare on Elm Street*, the *Halloween* series) aimed at teenagers, and in violent pornography sold to adults. The association of women with violence is a lesser concern on most network television series, although it does occur. When Luke and Laura on *General Hospital* fell in love and married after he raped her, a message was sent to men that, when a woman says "no," she may really mean "yes." In fact, this image of a woman resisting but secretly wanting a man to force himself on her has a long cinematic tradition, including such classics as *Gone With the Wind* and numerous John Wayne Westerns. Possible desensitization effects of such portrayals are examined in Chapter 10. Also see Chapter 10 for additional discussion of how news media tends to frame female victims of sexual violence as either "virgins" or "vamps."

Although we have so far focused on women, there are also some serious concerns about media portrayals of men. Although these have received less general attention and scientific research than portrayals of women, unrealistic stereotyping is also a problem here.

The View of Men

The predominant image of men in our media is as calm, cool, self-confident, decisive … and totally lacking in emotion. Although this may be positive in some ways, it sends the message to young boys that this is what men are supposed to be like, and if a man cannot deny his feelings or at least keep them all inside, he is not a real man.

Emotionless Beings

The Marlboro Man is the quintessential media man, but many classic TV fathers and detectives come in a close second. Who could imagine 1950s TV dad Ward Cleaver (*Leave It to Beaver*) or a classic TV cop (like *Dragnet*'s Joe Friday) shedding a tear? This picture has changed somewhat; modern TV dads like Homer (*The Simpsons*) or the male characters on *Friends*, *How I Met Your Mother*, and *Modern Family* have been allowed to cry occasionally, although even they are generally somewhat embarrassed and ashamed to do so. Most men and boys in advertising are looking blankly at no one with a vacant stare (often shielded by sunglasses), whereas women and girls in ads appear to be looking at someone and are often smiling or giving some other hint of what they are feeling.

Physical Appearance

Like women, men are portrayed as young and attractive, but the rules are a little different. Well-developed upper-body muscles are an important part of the ideal male beauty. A study of images of men and women in heterosexual erotic magazines found that photos of women were more sexualized and idealized than photos of men (Thomas, 1986). Also, it is not quite as bad for a man to age as it is for a woman. A little gray hair may make a man look "distinguished" or possibly even sexy, whereas it just makes a woman look old. Can you think of a female version of popular graying movie star George Clooney? It is not unusual to see a man with some gray hair reporting the news, sports, or weather, but seeing a woman with gray hair in these roles is far less common. Indeed, veteran TV news personality Barbara Walters reportedly said that women in TV news "don't get older, they get blonder" (Kiviat, 2005).

In spite of this, the message to stay young is still a strong one for men. For example, although many men begin losing hair in their 20s or 30s, few sympathetic leading male characters in TV series, movies, or advertising ever have even the slightest receding hairline. A bald character, when he does appear at all, is usually an object of at least subtle ridicule (e.g., the stupid husband who needs his wife to find him the right laxative), or at best a character like the eccentric guy who doesn't believe oatmeal really could have all that fiber. Even sympathetic middle-aged or older male characters usually have full heads of hair. The occasional man who openly wears a hairpiece is almost always the butt of tired old toupee jokes. However, bald (apparently shaved) heads are increasingly common among some aging male stars like Bruce Willis, Dwayne Johnson, and LL Cool J.

There is alarming evidence that men are becoming increasingly obsessed with their bodies and feeling ever more inadequate in comparison to the heavily muscled media models (Pope, Phillips, & Olivardia, 2000). Some (see Labre, 2005) have attributed this, at least in part, to the advent of magazines such as *Men's Health* and *Men's Fitness*, which became prevalent starting in the late 1980s. Indeed, one content analysis determined that *Men's Health* included just as many objectifying bodily descriptors on its covers as a comparable women's magazine, although the descriptors tended to center on muscularity (Bazzini, Pepper, Swofford, & Cochran, 2015). Just as so many women see an unrealistically thin body as normal, so many young men see a heavily muscled upper body as normal and readily attainable. In one study cited by Pope and colleagues (2000), over half of a sample of boys aged 11 to 17 chose as an ideal body build a type completely unattainable without steroids. Another study (Farquhar & Wasylkiw, 2007) looking at advertisements in *Sports Illustrated* pointed out that many ads in the magazine now emphasize the aesthetics of male models rather than their athleticism. This obsession to be bigger and more muscular was demonstrated in other research in which men seeing slides of muscular men ate more in front of male peers, compared to control groups seeing other images (Harrison *et al.*, 2006).

Male models of the twenty-first century have far more defined "six-packs" and chests than models of 20 or 30 years earlier. This trend has even been transferred to toys. Star Wars, Batman, and G.I. Joe action figures since 2000 are far broader in the shoulders, beefier in the chest, and smaller in the hips than their 1970s counterparts. For example, proportionally, the 1998 G.I. Joe Extreme had a 55-inch chest and 27-inch biceps, compared to the 44-inch chest and 12-inch biceps of the 1973 model (Pope, Olivardia, Gruber, & Borowiecki, 1999). This look would be all but unattainable by real men and certainly not without the use of dangerous anabolic steroids. To make matters worse, such ideals may even affect our problem-solving abilities. Men handling highly muscular action figures as part of a research study responded more slowly to positive emotion words on a lexical decision task than those playing with action figures that had more "normal" physiques (Barlett, Smith, & Harris, 2006).

Besides the need for bulging "pecs" and "delts," many young men are concerned with other shortcomings of their bodies, including hair (must have plenty of it on your head but not on your back or chest), height (must be taller than your woman), genital size (need enough bulge in your pants), and even breast size (can't be too large and thus look feminine). When these concerns become strong enough to be seriously maladaptive in one's life, one may suffer from body dysmorphic disorder (BDD), a body-image condition therapists report seeing increasingly often in males.

Male Friendships

Although media images of friendship are common for both men and women, the nature of those friendships is often different (Spangler, 1989, 1992). Women characters tend to show a greater degree of emotional intimacy in their friendships than men do. TV images of male bonding go back to the Westerns of the 1950s, in which a cowboy and his sidekick went everywhere together. Sitcom friends like Ralph and Ed in *The Honeymooners*, Hawkeye and B.J. in *M*A*S*H*, or the Chandler–Joey–Ross triad in *Friends* were clearly close emotionally, although that was seldom explicitly discussed, unlike the more overtly emotional women's friendships of Lucy and Ethel in *I Love Lucy*, Mary and Rhoda in *The Mary Tyler Moore Show*, or the women in *Sex and the City*. This gender difference may fairly accurately reflect real life in terms of different communication styles of the sexes (Tannen, 1990), though most scholars agree that the feminine model is the healthier one (see Close-up 11.5 for a discussion of teen cross-sex friendships in movies).

Domestic Roles

Although men in movies and on TV are generally portrayed as competent professionally, they are often seen as ignorant and bungling with regard to housework and childcare. TV fathers of year-old infants often do not know how to change a diaper; this is unlikely to be true in even the most traditional real families. Men in commercials often seem to know nothing about housekeeping, cooking, or household appliances, and have to be bailed out by their wives, who, in the domestic sphere, are portrayed as the knowledgeable experts. Even TV psychologist Dr. Phil was shown ineptly shopping, cleaning, and baking during a "role reversal" episode of his show (Henson & Parameswaran, 2008). Over the last few decades there have been periodic TV shows and movies portraying the ineptness of men dealing with children (*Full House, Mr. Mom, Three Men and a Baby, Home Improvement, Two and a Half Men, Everybody Loves Raymond*). Although the characters typically learned and grew as persons from the experience, these men's initial ineptitude would seem to suggest that childcare is not a part of the normal male role. Although this "dumb dad" stereotype remains quite prevalent (see the section on "Dad as Buffoon" below) there is some evidence it is changing. More recently, there has been an increase in advertising portrayals of men seen at home and in softer, more paternal roles (Fowler & Thomas, 2015; Grau & Zotos, 2016).

Still, men in the media are often portrayed as insensitive and interpersonally unskilled. For example, they are usually very awkward in not knowing how to talk to their children about sensitive personal issues. Seeing a father struggle to avoid talking to his daughter about menstruation sends the message that men do not do that and should not want to; how much better it would be to show him talking effectively to her, perhaps providing males in the audience with a cognitive script about how to have that conversation. In another example, a nice young man in a pharmaceutical ad talks about how he suffered from acid reflux for years and finally his mother sent him to the doctor's office, where he received a prescription for this miracle drug. Why was this grown man too dim-witted to manage his own health only to be bailed out by his mother?

Some Overall Effects of Media Gender Stereotyping

Before we leave the topic of how males and females tend to be portrayed in the media, let us look at what some of the research indicates are the larger effects of this stereotyping. Although it is relatively easy to critique gender role portrayals in media, empirically demonstrating their effects is a far more difficult research problem. Nevertheless, Oppliger (2007) concludes in a meta-analysis that increasing exposure to gender stereotyping in media is followed by increasing sex-typed behavior and stereotypical gender-role attitudes. Negative or narrow gender images become a serious concern if they are seen as representative of real life. Although no single exposure to a sexist commercial is likely to irreparably harm anyone, the huge number of commercials we see (100,000 or more ads by the time we graduate from high school) is likely to have an effect, given what we have learned from cultivation and modeling research. Also, frequent playing of video games with sexist content has been associated with holding sexist attitudes (Stermer & Burkley, 2015). In general, effects of repetition are often underestimated; if the same themes about how men and women are supposed to look, behave, and think keep recurring on show after show, in movie after movie, in ad after ad, and in game after game, that "reality" is more likely to be perceived as accurate. For example, women may expect men to dominate them and to be relatively insensitive, or men may expect women to be submissive to them and to be preoccupied with their appearance.

Not only may we take the media portrayals of the other sex as reality, but we may take the portrayals of our own gender as cues to the ways we should look and behave. When we fail to meet these standards, that failure sets us up to experience low self-esteem. For example, women who watch more entertainment TV have lower sexual self-concepts than women who watch less of this kind of media (Aubrey, 2007). A woman who feels frazzled meeting the demands of career, family, and homemaking may well feel very inadequate comparing herself to the media superwoman who does it all so well. Similarly, a man losing his hair or a woman losing her youthful figure may feel inadequate when using TV bodies as the standard (Myers & Biocca, 1992).

There is also empirical evidence of greater objectification of women compared to men. In one study, college students looked at upright or inverted photos of men and women in swimsuits or underwear. They later recognized the upright and inverted photos of the women equally well but found the inverted images of the men much more difficult to decipher. This was interpreted as reflecting the brain's perception of the men as uniquely human, whereas women were perceived objectively, without the usual human advantage of the upright orientation (Bernard, Gervais, Allen, Campomizzi, & Klein, 2012). How might our repeated exposure to media gender stereotypes relate to such an effect?

Such concerns are especially important when considering effects on children. Children tend to prefer to watch entertainment characters of their own gender and ethnicity (Knobloch, Callison, Chen, Fritzsche, & Zillmann, 2005). Further, children who are heavy viewers of TV also hold more traditional sex-role attitudes than children who don't watch much TV (Saito, 2007).

Families

Now that we have looked at the images of women and men, let us take a broader look at how women and men are portrayed as interacting in the media sphere of the home. Specifically, we next examine the images of families in media.

Family Composition and Portrayals

A content analysis of hundreds of U.S. network TV shows featuring families over 45 years from the 1950s to the 1990s showed that overall about 55% of the children were boys, and that families were almost exclusively White until the 1970s, with African Americans the only sizable ethnic minority (Robinson & Skill, 2001). Although there are now many additional outlets for TV programming compared to 10 or 20 years ago, multicultural character representation of families doesn't seem to have improved much (Tukachinsky, Mastro, & Yarchi, 2015). Interestingly, single-father families have typically outnumbered single-mother families on TV, but the reverse is true in real life (Robinson & Skill, 2001). Divorced major characters did not appear on U.S. TV until the debut in 1975 of *One Day at a Time* on CBS, featuring a divorced mother and her two teenage daughters, although divorced adults have been fairly common on TV since that time (see Close-up 5.3 for a discussion of an early "reality TV" depiction of divorce). In fact, *One Day at a Time* got a 2017 reboot on Netflix, this time with a single Latino mother.

❖ CLOSE-UP 5.3 TV'S FIRST "REALITY" FAMILY

A remarkable portrayal of American family life that reflected its times was the 1973 documentary series An American Family. *Airing in 12 one-hour episodes, the PBS show tracked the upper-middle-class Loud family of Santa Barbara, CA.*

The series was groundbreaking in many ways, most notably because the Louds allowed a film crew to record nearly every aspect of their lives for seven months, years before reality shows like Cops, The Real World, *and* Survivor *first started to become popular. At the time, even noted cultural anthropologist Margaret Mead wrote that the docu-series was, "as new and significant as the invention of drama or the novel—a new way in which people can learn to look at life, by seeing the real life of others interpreted on camera" (Mead, 1973, p. 21).*

Drawing relatively good ratings for the fledgling PBS network, An American Family *also dispelled many wholesome myths of family life common in sunny sitcoms of the day like* The Brady Bunch *and* The Partridge Family. *For example, viewers watched gay adult son Lance openly discuss his life with his parents, even taking his mother Pat to a New York drag show in one episode. Perhaps the most compelling aspect of the show, however, was when Pat asked her husband Bill to move out of the house after having enough of his alleged adultery. In later episodes, viewers saw Bill move into an apartment and the family try to make sense of separation and divorce. Fans of the show said it was an unblinkingly accurate depiction of what many families were experiencing, particularly in those turbulent times. Some critics argued that it was sensationalistic and exploitative. Interestingly, after the series aired, the Louds (like some of their later reality show counterparts) said that the show had been edited to primarily highlight the negative aspects of their lives (Ruoff, 2002). Reflecting a twenty-first century interest in "reality" families like the Kardashians, in 2011 HBO made a dramatized version of the Louds' story,* Cinema Verite, *that starred Diane Lane and Tim Robbins.*

How are families portrayed on television? For one thing, working-class families are far rarer on TV than upper-middle-class families, and they show more distressed and less happy relationships than the middle and upper classes do (Douglas, 2001, 2003). Also, sibling relationships are positive overall, though less deep and meaningful than in real life (Larson, 2001a). When conflict exists, most often between siblings, it is generally handled positively and resolved by the end of the half-hour episode.

In recent decades, most often both parents in TV families have had careers outside of the home, or one parent brings his or her career into the home. However, a major departure from reality is the way that modern TV families appear to manage career and family demands so successfully and effortlessly; indeed, the difficulties inherent in managing two-career families are glossed over, if not totally ignored (Heintz-Knowles, 2001).

Mom as Superwoman

One common television portrayal of mothers is as the unrealistic superwoman who can effortlessly "have it all." Such portrayals have appeared as media attempt to represent modern women more accurately and fairly. Although mother characters in TV series are often employed outside the home, this only occurs about half as often on TV as in real life; in general, female characters are also less likely to be shown having a career than are male characters in film and on television (Smith, Choueiti, Prescott, & Pieper, 2013). Those women who are depicted as employed are most often in professional or managerial positions, and many are also mothers. Although some of these characters are truly positive role models of professional women, they appear to handle the demands of career, wife, and parent with amazingly little stress and difficulty (Heintz-Knowles, 2001). Real women in two-career families need such positive role models, but they also need some acknowledgment that the great difficulties they experience balancing all of those responsibilities are not abnormal. The media supermoms make it look all too easy.

The superwoman myth is also reinforced by advertising. For example, one notorious perfume commercial that began airing during the Women's Movement of the 1970s (and probably designed to reflect the times) could be considered damaging. Specifically, the Enjoli ad said that a woman can "bring home the bacon, fry it up in a pan, but never let him forget he's a man." In other words, a woman can (or at least should) work outside the home all day, come home and cook dinner for her husband, and still have enough energy left to be sexy for him that evening! Another notable ad slogan from that era was, "You've come a long way, baby," used by Phillip Morris to advertise Virginia Slims, cigarettes marketed specifically to women. This message also played on feminist themes and seemed to suggest that unlike their grandmothers, modern women should have it all, including their own brand of smokes! Are these realistic messages to send to young girls about what it means to be a woman in today's society? Are these helpful expectations to send to young boys about what they can expect from the women they may eventually marry? Do advertisers place similar, multi-role expectations on males?

One area that seems to challenge this image of working mothers as superwomen is the news media. Motro and Vanneman (2015) analyzed 28 years' worth of *New York Times* stories about working mothers. They found that beginning in the mid-1990s, articles discussing the difficulties working moms face became more common. However, as time as gone on, the articles seem to have shifted their tone from focusing on the problems working mothers face at home to the problems they tend to face at work.

Dad as Buffoon

Although there are sensitive portrayals of fathers on TV, like Jack Pearson of *This is Us*, a more common source of humor is the characterization of dads as dumb. There are many examples of this in American sitcoms, from dads in *The Simpsons* to *Home Improvement* to *Family Guy*. Even lovable Phil Dunphy of *Modern Family* often seems bumbling. However, such depictions of TV dads were once very different. Going back to early shows like *Leave it to Beaver* and *Father Knows Best*, dads were typically shown to be wise, calm, and sensible. Indeed, in a content analysis examining 40 years' worth of family shows, Scharrer (2001) found that the "foolish dad" trope had increased over time.

The dad-as-buffoon character is especially prevalent in TV dads who are depicted as working class. Homer Simpson, Peter Griffin, Tim Taylor, and even Fred Flintstone were all working class—and not too bright. In an interesting study examining fathers in a variety of TV sitcoms, Troilo (2017) found that working-class dads were, in fact, portrayed as having more negative relationships with their kids than white-collar fathers. Specifically, compared to upper-class dads, blue-collar fathers were more likely to have "caustic and critical" interactions with their TV children (Troilo, 2017).

Despite these stereotypes, there are positive depictions of fathers, especially when moving beyond the realm of TV sitcoms. For example, in analyzing stories in parenting magazines like *Parents* and *American Baby*, Schmitz (2016) discovered an increasing emphasis on the nurturing and expressive aspects of fatherhood. However, many of the magazine articles focused on issues like traditional masculine identity and worries about being a breadwinner.

Family Solidarity

Perhaps the most pervasive family image in media is that of family solidarity (loyalty, support, and love for one's family). This is most clearly seen in the family sitcom. The basic message here, as true for *The Simpsons*, *Modern Family*, or *Family Guy* in the twenty-first century as it was for *The Brady Bunch* decades earlier, is that one's family is more important than money, power, greed, status, or career advancement. Even the most irreverent family shows teach a family cohesiveness that tends in the final analysis to strongly affirm traditional values; for example, when Homer Simpson lost his job, the whole family pitched in to help save money (see A. S. Brown & Logan, 2005, for a fascinating set of readings on the psychology in *The Simpsons*). Interestingly, some have even argued that family unity is also a driving theme in a show not typically identified with family: the zombie apocalypse thriller *The Walking Dead*. Specifically, Ambrosius and Valenzano (2016) contend that in the show's post-apocalyptic setting, family (not religion, science, or the state) is the key to survival.

One may ask if such family solidarity is a realistic reflection of our society. It clearly is for many families and just as clearly is not for many others, whose troubled family dynamics would more typically be characterized by vicious backstabbing, betrayal, and generally putting oneself above other family members. Still, even those families might agree that the family solidarity characterization is a worthy ideal to hold up as a model, even if it is not totally realistic. Maybe this is a socially helpful model to portray and can help offer some useful new cognitive scripts to viewers in dysfunctional families. It may be particularly helpful in showing positive relations with extended families and non-traditional families, such as the positive interaction of a gay couple and their children with traditional extended family in *Modern Family*.

Such solidarity may occur in groups other than biological families. Television shows that feature a group of friends (e.g., *Friends*, *Seinfeld*, *The Big Bang Theory*) basically uphold the friend group as the de facto family unit. Typically, the loyalty to this social family is even stronger than to one's biological family, which the featured group has apparently replaced. Another common setting for both sitcoms and dramatic shows is the workplace, which essentially becomes a surrogate family (e.g., *Grey's Anatomy*, *The Office*, *Parks and Recreation*, *The Mindy Project*). The strong message in these shows is always love your co-workers (even if you really don't) and put their needs above your own. This, far more than traditional family solidarity, is more tenuously tied to reality.

One aspect of workplace solidarity is probably a direct consequence of the TV series format. This is the way that characters are so intimately involved in the personal lives of fellow workers, employers, and employees. Although real-life co-workers may sometimes be close friends, such intimacy is not typical, and it is almost unheard of in the real world for all of the workers in a unit to be close personal friends. Yet this is typical in television land. For example, when one character delivers her baby, the entire crew from the office may be on hand for the delivery. In real life this would not only be unlikely, but probably obtrusively inappropriate and unappreciated, even if for some reason it did occur.

Perhaps even more of a deviation from reality is the way that this workplace solidarity is extended to the clients of a professional. For example, one of the doctors on *Grey's Anatomy* or *Chicago Med* might spend her day off to find a lost family member of a patient or to smooth out a domestic quarrel that she believed was interfering with the recovery of the patient. In real life, physicians seldom do this sort of thing and might be considered derelict in their duty at the hospital if they did. Still, such an image of a professional is appealing because that is what we want to think our doctor would be like. Even if I have never been a patient in a hospital, it comforts me to feel that a doctor I might have would be as caring as the doctors in *Grey's Anatomy*.

The Influence of Media on Family Life

Do media enhance or detract from the quality of family life? The conventional wisdom is that media have a negative influence, but that conclusion is by no means certain or simple. In some instances, family TV viewing can be a positive time of family discussion and interaction, including commenting on the programs or laughing and crying together. In other instances, it can be very negative; for example, if it induces conflict among family members over what program to watch or whether to turn off the set. Particular quarrels can occur around certain events like meals, bedtimes, or children's disagreement with parental prohibitions of certain programs.

A uses and gratifications approach to studying family TV use looks at motivations for watching, which may vary greatly depending on the program or the individuals' moods. For example, Kubey (1986) found that divorced and separated people watch TV more when they feel down and alone than married or other single people do, perhaps due to their use of TV for solace and comfort to replace a lost relationship. Also, people who have especially heavy diets of TV and movie romance programming (like *Grey's Anatomy* and *The Notebook*) also have relatively unrealistic expectations of marriage (Osborn, 2012).

Portrayals of Minorities

Other than gender, one of the most studied areas in media psychology is how minorities have been portrayed. As we will see, the portrayals, particularly in the early days of television and film, were neither accurate nor kind.

The Four Stages of Minority Portrayals

A still useful model presented many years ago by Clark (1969) identified four chronological stages of the portrayals of minorities on television, although the model can easily be extended to all media. The first stage is *non-recognition*, in which the minority group is simply excluded. It is not ridiculed; it is not caricatured; it is simply not present. Someone from an alien culture watching the media would never know that such people even existed in that society. For example, many early films and TV shows had no African American characters at all, even when it might have been logical for them to be present (one wonders, for instance, why there were no Blacks in the Southern town of Mayberry on the *Andy Griffith Show*). Until fairly recently, non-recognition was also largely the position of gay and lesbian people in U.S. media.

The second stage of minority portrayals is *ridicule*. Here the dominant group bolsters its own self-image by putting down and stereotyping the minority, presenting its members as incompetent, unintelligent buffoons. Very early television programs like *Amos 'n' Andy* and movie characters like Stepin Fetchit or Jack Benny's TV valet Rochester reflect this stage in terms of portrayals of African Americans. In current media, Arabs are a good example of a group at the stage of ridicule; we seldom see positive or likeable Arab or Arab-American characters in U.S. TV or film.

A third stage is *regulation*, in which minority group members appear as protectors of the existing order (e.g., police officers, detectives, spies). Such roles were typical of the first positive roles open to African Americans in the 1960s such as *Julia* (played by Diahann Carroll), who was a nurse. One often sees Latinos in the same types of roles today, including various law enforcement characters in the *Law and Order* franchise.

The final stage is *respect*. Here, the minority group appears in the same full range of roles, both good and bad, that the majority does. This is not to say that there is never a stereotyped character or that all the characters are sympathetic, but just that there is a wide variety: good and intelligent characters as well as evil and stupid ones. The 1980s sitcom *The Cosby Show* is often held up as an example of this stage.

Now let's turn to looking specifically at the media's portrayal of several particular ethnic minorities, starting with African Americans, the minority receiving the most public attention and scientific study for the longest time.

African Americans

Probably the most studied ethnic group portrayal anywhere has been the U.S. media image of African Americans. Although they comprised about 12–13% of the U.S. population in the 2010 census (and have comprised roughly similar percentages since 1900), until the 1960s there were almost no African Americans as models in mainstream U.S. advertising or television programming (Colfax & Steinberg, 1972; Kassarjian, 1969; see also Close-up 5.4 for an exception to the invisibility of Black models in ads).

❖ CLOSE-UP 5.4 HISTORICAL VIEW OF AFRICAN AMERICANS IN ADVERTISING

African Americans have been a part of advertising in America as far back as ads for the sale of slaves or return of runaways (Kern-Foxworth, 1994). In the late nineteenth and early twentieth centuries, Blacks became common in advertising targeted at European Americans, which in this era included all advertising except that in specifically Black publications. Often the portrayals were pictorially demeaning (huge lips, bulging eyes, characters portrayed as cannibals or as mammy figures like Aunt Jemima) and verbally insulting (brand names like Nigger Head canned vegetables and stove polish). Many of these figures thankfully disappeared quietly, but some of these symbols evolved in interesting ways. For example, Aunt Jemima was first developed in 1889 by Charles Rutt with his introduction of the first ready-mixed pancake flour. In the early years, Aunt Jemima in ads (and her spinoff dolls and personal appearances by various actresses) was right off the antebellum plantation, with her characteristic headdress, uneducated speech style, and subservient behavior. Aunt Jemima gradually became less slave-like over the next 80 years, though the greatest change came in 1968, when she wore more of a headband than a slave bandanna and also appeared younger and more intelligent. Only in 1989, in her 100th year, did Aunt Jemima lose the headgear altogether for the first time (Kern-Foxworth, 1994). There has been a similar (although less pronounced) evolution of the African American Uncle Ben (Rice) and Rastus (Cream of Wheat) characters.

Depictions of African Americans

The only African Americans in prime-time TV programming in the early days were limited to a few stereotyped and demeaning roles, such as the reliable maid *Beulah* and the affable but dim-witted African American friends on *Amos 'n' Andy* (see Close-up 5.5 for a discussion of the *Amos 'n' Andy* show).

> ### ❖ CLOSE-UP 5.5 THE AMOS 'N' ANDY PHENOMENON
>
> *The history of the show* Amos 'n' Andy *in many ways parallels the history of White social attitudes toward African Americans in the early to mid-twentieth century, being "partly a tale of White obtuseness" (Ely, 2001, p. xiv). Starting off as a radio show in the 1920s,* Amos 'n' Andy *employed two White actors using their interpretations of Black English to portray the title characters. The show became wildly popular on the radio, with reports of listeners speeding to get home and refusing to go to movies until after the program had ended. There was even one account of prisoners rioting when a warden refused to let them listen to the show (Shankman, 1978). As further evidence of this popularity, there were also* Amos 'n' Andy *candy bars, greeting cards, toys, and records (Ely, 2001).*
>
> *Movie producers tried to translate the radio success of* Amos 'n' Andy *to film in 1930 with the movie* Check and Double Check, *using the White radio actors as Amos and Andy in blackface (Shankman, 1978). With the advent of television, CBS decided to create an* Amos 'n' Andy *TV show in 1951. This time, however, Black actors were cast in the roles.*
>
> *As might be expected,* Amos 'n' Andy *was controversial in the African American community. Although many Black listeners of the early radio show were happy to hear some portrayal of African Americans, it was disheartening to many. One editor of a Black newspaper lamented that "the men playing the characters are White. The company employing* Amos 'n' Andy *is White. The people reaping the financial gain from the characterizations are all White" (Shankman, 1978, p. 239). The TV show was also disappointing to many, with the NAACP pressuring sponsors to withdraw support. Although it received fairly high ratings (and even an Emmy nomination in 1952), the show was canceled by CBS after two seasons, due (at least partially) to the controversy (Ely, 2001). Although some tried to forget that a show such as* Amos 'n' Andy *ever existed, the story behind it provides an interesting cultural history of early portrayals of African Americans in electronic media. See Ely (2001) for a very thoughtful and thorough examination of* Amos 'n' Andy.

In the United States, media reflected this prejudiced viewpoint before radio or television ever appeared. One of the earliest movies was *Uncle Tom's Cabin* in 1903. Based on the well-known book by the same name, the film highly stereotyped African Americans. The groundbreaking but intensely controversial 1915 Civil War epic film *Birth of a Nation* presented the Ku Klux Klan as heroic saviors of the Reconstruction era. Such treatment persisted in films for many years. In 1942 the NAACP convinced the Hollywood movie studio bosses to abandon the characteristic negative roles for African Americans and to try to integrate them into a variety of roles; this agreement did not produce overnight results, but change did come eventually (Bogle, 1973).

The American Civil Rights Movement of the 1960s ushered in significant changes in media (Berry, 1980). African American models began to be used in advertising, with none of the feared offense taken by Whites (Block, 1972; Soley, 1983). African Americans also appeared for the first time in leading roles in prime-time TV during this era, most notably *I Spy* with Bill Cosby, and *Julia*, the first African American family sitcom. In addition, there were African Americans as part of the starring ensemble on 1960s drama programs like *Mission Impossible*, *Peyton Place*, and *Mod Squad*. Although these were generally positive portrayals, many such shows have been criticized as having been out of touch with the civil rights struggles of those times. It is interesting to note, for example, that the title character in *Julia*, played by Diahann Carroll, was a widowed, single mother who worked for a White employer, had predominantly White neighbors, and seemed to only have White friends (Miller & Pearlstein, 2004).

In the 1970s and 1980s, there were usually some African American characters on TV, although they tended to be heavily concentrated in sitcoms and were largely absent from dramas, daytime soap operas, and children's programming. Some of these characters were more well-rounded than early TV African Americans but still retained some stereotypical characteristics, such as the buffoonery and posturing of J.J. in *Good Times*, George Jefferson in *The Jeffersons*, and Fred Sanford in *Sanford and Son*. In the 1970s, about 8% of prime-time TV characters were African American (Gerbner & Signorielli, 1979; Seggar, Hafen, & Hannonen-Gladden, 1981; Weigel, Loomis, & Soja, 1980), with less than 3% in daytime soaps (Greenberg, Neuendorf, Buerkel-Rothfuss, & Henderson, 1982).

A landmark event occurred with the phenomenal commercial success of the 1977 TV miniseries *Roots*, based on Alex Haley's multigenerational saga of his ancestors' forced journey from West Africa into American slavery and their later emancipation. Although widely praised for both its artistic and entertainment value, *Roots* was also controversial. Some called it biased for presenting few sympathetic European American characters, whereas others took it to task for transforming the horrors of slavery into an epic triumph of the American dream (Riggs, 1992). Nevertheless, *Roots* is considered by many to be monumental in that it was one of the first times that age-old race issues were confronted in an approachable yet powerful prime-time TV dramatization (Miller & Pearlstein, 2004). In 2016, *Roots* was remade into a four-part miniseries airing on cable networks A&E, Lifetime, and the History Channel. It was greeted with critical and ratings success, indicating that there was still strong interest in the story and issue of American slavery.

The current media situation is vastly improved from the *Amos 'n' Andy* days. For example, in 2018, the box office and critical success of the *Black Panther* superhero movie indicated to many that there was a strong market for powerful Black characters (Wallace, 2018). Nevertheless, some argue that there are still subtle indicators of racism on television (Edwards, 2016; Greenberg, Mastro, & Brand, 2002; Taylor, Lee, & Stern, 1995). For example, African Americans are still underrepresented in most TV genres and are largely absent in high-level creative and network ownership and administrative positions (Craig, 2014; Miller & Pearlstein, 2004; Smith *et al.*, 2016a).

Before the allegations of Bill Cosby's purported sexual assault on numerous women came to light in 2014, the phenomenal success of *The Cosby Show* (1984–1992) presumably laid to rest any commercial concerns about Whites not watching "Black" shows. However, that show's relevance to the experience of the large majority of less affluent African Americans was hotly debated. Cliff Huxtable and his family were clearly positive role models, but they also enjoyed a lifestyle that was beyond the reach of most African American families (and, for that matter, most of the rest of the population as well). Interestingly, one study (Matabane & Merritt, 2014) even suggested that watching *The Cosby Show* and its spinoff *A Different World* in earlier years influenced young African American women to become college students at historically Black colleges, just as some of the characters in the shows had done.

By the late 2000s, TV shows with predominantly African American casts were largely absent from U.S. broadcast networks, although such shows were common on cable networks such as BET (with shows like *The Game*) and TBS (*House of Payne*) (Armstrong, 2011). However, broadcast network shows with African American leads saw a resurgence in the 2010s with shows such as *black-ish*, *Scandal*, and *Empire*.

Animated Portrayals of African Americans
Some of the earliest animated portrayals of African Americans were used by advertisers (see Close-up 5.4). Although we seldom, if ever, see such racist ads or programming from the pre-civil rights era, some blatantly racist cartoons from as far back as the 1940s are still available in video anthologies; for instance, some villains have dark skin, big lips, and even exhibit cannibalistic behaviors. Disney's 1946 combined animated and live-action film *Song of the South* is rarely seen anymore because of its stereotyped characterizations. Barcus (1983) found cartoons to be the most ethnically stereotyped of all television genres. More recently, video game villains have tended to be darker skinned than the heroes (Carlsson-Paige, 2008). However, there are some signs that things may be changing for the better. For example, two very popular children's animated series feature minority female characters. *Doc McStuffins* stars Doc, an African American "doctor" who fixes toys, and *Dora the Explorer* is about Dora, a Latina adventurer. In contrast to racial and gender stereotypes, both girls are frequently shown as heroes and leaders (Keys, 2016).

News Portrayals of African Americans
There is a long history of prejudiced portrayals of African Americans in the news media (Entman, 1990, 1992, 1994a, 1994b; Heider, 2000). One misrepresentation is the over-emphasis of African Americans in news reports as criminals (with an accompanying overemphasis of Whites as victims and/or officers, see Dixon & Linz, 2000). However, more recent research (Dixon & Williams, 2015) discovered less emphasis on African Americans as criminals, but also less emphasis on Blacks as victims; thus, in contrast to actual violent crime statistics, African Americans in the news may have become some-what "invisible."

Several studies were also conducted regarding news coverage of African Americans in the aftermath of Hurricane Katrina in 2005. In one content analysis, it was discovered that although New Orleans contained a preponderance of Black residents after the hurricane, 87% of those who spoke in news reports at that time were White (Johnson, Dolan, & Sonnett, 2011). Other forms of implicit racism may have been present in the coverage of Katrina as well. For example, some reports juxtaposed visual images of Black males with voiceovers of discussions of violence, even though the males in the pictures were not necessarily behaving violently and in many cases may have had nothing to do with the violence being reported (Sonnett, Johnson, & Dolan, 2015).

Do these kinds of news stereotypes matter? One study found that exposure to a particular African American stereotype like a "mammy" or a "jezebel" later primed implicit prejudice responses toward an African American woman (Givens & Monahan, 2005). Hurley and colleagues (Hurley, Jensen, Weaver, & Dixon, 2015) conducted a study in which they exposed participants to TV newscasts that contained a majority of crime stories with African American suspects. Compared to participants in a control condition, those who saw these news reports were more likely to say that a different criminal suspect (race not specified) was unlikely to be reformed. Interestingly, this priming effect may work in the opposite direction, too. In another study, researchers had people read counter-stereotypical news articles about African American celebrities (e.g., a story about Morgan Freeman highlighting traits such as calmness). In contrast to those who read stereotypical news accounts (e.g., a story about Kanye West detailing an angry outburst), people who read the counter-stereotypical article showed reduced levels of stereotypes and racist beliefs (Ramasubramanian, 2015).

It will be interesting to see how future research explores depictions of African Americans in the news, especially in light of issues such as the Black Lives Matter movement. See Chapter 7 for additional discussion on how the news media and race sometimes interact.

Some Additional Effects of African American Portrayals

In addition to the research on news and African Americans, another focus of study has been on the comparative effects of African American TV portrayals on both White and Black Americans (Greenberg et al., 2002; Sanders & Ramasubramanian, 2012). Like everyone else, African Americans are more likely to identify with and emulate characters who exhibit personal warmth, high status, and power. Often these models have been White, yet African Americans will readily identify with media Blacks as role models, especially with the more positive ones (Ball & Bogatz, 1970, 1973; Jhally & Lewis, 1992; Matabane & Merritt, 2014). This effect has been shown to boost children's self-esteem, especially with regular viewing and when accompanied by appropriate parental communication and explanation (Atkin, Greenberg, & McDermott, 1983; McDermott & Greenberg, 1985; Vittrup & Holden, 2011). Sympathetic characters like *Doc McStuffins* or the children on *black-ish* thus become potentially very important models for young African Americans. Studies of White children have shown that prolonged exposure to television comedies or *Sesame Street* with regular African American and Latino cast members influences the attitudes of White kids in a more accepting, less racist direction (Bogatz & Ball, 1971; Gorn, Goldberg, & Kanungo, 1976; Vittrup & Holden, 2011).

Although everyone identifies more with characters who are perceived to be like themselves on whatever relevant dimensions (*identification theory*), being a member of a minority group makes certain attributes more salient (*distinctiveness theory*). Thus, one's race is a larger part of one's identity for a person of color in a largely White society than it is for the majority. Similarly, being left-handed, gay, red-headed, or six-foot-six is more salient than being right-handed, heterosexual, brown-haired, or five-foot-nine. As an illustration of this, one study asked Black and White people to recall media characters. African American viewers recalled Black characters better than White characters, while White viewers showed no difference in their recall of White vs. Black characters (Appiah, 2002). Thus, positive portrayals of African Americans in the media may have very real implications for real people.

Black Viewers

There is one last interesting area to discuss relating to African Americans and mass communication: actual media usage. African Americans of all ages watch more television than Whites, even when controlling for socioeconomic status (Graves, 1996; Kern-Foxworth, 1994; Nielsen Company, 2017). They especially watch more sports, action-adventure shows, and news. African Americans also tend to watch shows with Black characters and Black-oriented networks like BET in relatively greater numbers than White Americans do (Goldberg, 2002; Levin, 2017). As television has become more segmented, with different outlets like streaming services, African American viewers are also less likely to share favorite TV shows with other ethnic groups. For example, a recent analysis showed that among African American viewers, shows like *Empire* and *Love & Hip Hop Atlanta* were ratings winners. In contrast, the top shows for White viewers were *NCIS*, *This is Us*, and *The Big Bang Theory* (Levin, 2017).

Latinos

In contrast to the picture of considerable progress in media portrayals of African Americans over the years, the media image of another American minority of similar size is far less hopeful. Although Hispanics (those of Spanish-speaking origin), or Latinos (those who originate from Latin American countries), are growing very rapidly in numbers in the United States (15–17% of the population in the United States by 2010, collectively surpassing African Americans in number), they comprise only 5% of characters in TV and film (Mastro & Behm-Morawitz, 2005; Mastro & Greenberg, 2000; Monk-Turner, Heiserman, Johnson, Cotton, & Jackson, 2010; Smith *et al.*, 2016a; see Figure 5.1; also see Tukachinsky *et al.*, 2015, for trends over a 20-year period). Hispanics are, in fact, several very diverse groups of Americans with ethnic origins in Cuba, Puerto Rico, Dominican Republic, Mexico, Central America, South America, or Spain. Latinos are racially and culturally diverse. Although many Cubans, Puerto Ricans, and Dominicans have some African ancestry, most Mexican Americans are mestizos (mixed White and Indian/Native American) and seldom have African ancestry. Many Hispanic New Mexicans are purely of Spanish descent, whereas some recent Guatemalan refugees are pure indigenous peoples who speak Spanish as a second language, if at all.

The North American histories of various Hispanic groups are also very different. Although Spaniards have lived in New Mexico since before the Puritans settled in Massachusetts, some Mexicans and Central Americans are very recent immigrants. They are economically diverse, ranging from wealthy Cuban Americans of South Florida or the Spanish New Mexicans of Albuquerque and Santa Fe, to the poor

Table 5.1 Percentage of ethnic group members in U.S. population and as represented in TV and film (Humes, Jones, & Ramirez, 2011; Monk-Turner *et al.*, 2010; Smith *et al.*, 2016a)

	U.S. Census, 2010	Prime-time TV, 2009	TV & film, 2016
African American	12.6	16.0	12.2
Asian	4.8	<2.0	2.3
Latino	16.3	5.0	5.1
White	63.7	74.0	71.7

immigrant underclass of southern California and Texas. Latinos are also politically diverse, from the staunchly Republican and conservative Cuban Americans in Florida to the politically liberal Mexican Americans flexing their voting muscles in Texas and California. Since 2000, the greatest relative increases in Latina/o numbers in the United States have come in places which have historically been home to few of them, like South Dakota and Tennessee.

In spite of their growing importance in the United States, there are several pervasive stereotypes of Latinos in the media (Greenberg et al., 2002; Ramirez Berg, 1990, 2002; Rivadeneyra, Ward, & Gordon, 2007; Schmader, Block, & Lickel, 2015); portrayals and characters tend to be disproportionately lower class, criminal, inarticulate, and poor. The greasy, dirty Mexican bandit stereotype of the Westerns of the early to mid-twentieth century has been updated as the drug runner of more recent movies. It doesn't help when political candidates like Donald Trump characterize Mexican immigrants as criminals and rapists on TV. Variations of the bandit appeared in advertising with the heavily accented Frito bandito of the 1970s or the Taco Bell chihuahua of the 1990s. Other stereotypes include the harlot, the loose woman interested only in sex, and the buffoon or clown, such as Ricky Ricardo of I Love Lucy or Rosario of Will and Grace. Another stereotype is the sensual and musical, but slightly laughable, Latin lover of early films. On American television, characters who were criminals were one and a half times more likely to be Latino than European American. Latinos have been overrepresented in the criminal justice system of TV, both as police officers and as criminals (Dixon & Linz, 2000; Mastro & Behm-Morawitz, 2005; Mastro & Greenberg, 2000).

As early as the 1980s, a few signs suggested that movie studios and the TV networks were beginning to discover the largely untapped Latino market (Ramirez Berg, 2002). Spanish cable channels offered popular options to Spanish-speaking populations. In the mid-1980s, the unexpected commercial success of films like La Bamba allowed several new Latino films to be released shortly thereafter, although this trend did not continue. Even the modest success of the Spy Kids trilogy of the early 2000s, a sort of James Bond movie for kids in which the hero family just happens to be Latino, failed to give much boost to Latino movie fortunes.

U.S. television has been an even more dismal story. Following the commercial failure of several very short-lived Latino-oriented sitcoms in the 1970s and 1980s, the networks appeared to be wary about more such programs. Some shows have achieved limited success (e.g., George Lopez, Jane the Virgin, a One Day at a Time reboot), but a Latino Cosby Show has remained elusive. There are some signs of hope, as in the Nickelodeon bilingual preschool show Dora the Explorer (and a spinoff, Go, Diego, Go!), which has become very popular and profitable. There have also been several Latino breakout TV stars such as Mario Lopez (Saved by the Bell), Wilmer Valderrama (That '70s Show), America Ferrera (Superstore, Ugly Betty), and Sofia Vergara (Modern Family).

Still, overall Latinos in media are at a point somewhat similar to that of African Americans of 50 or 60 years ago (i.e., largely invisible or in negative or regulatory roles when they do occur). There are also documented negative effects of the stereotyped portrayals (Mastro, Behm-Morawitz, & Kopacz, 2008; Schmader et al., 2015). Heavy TV viewers see Latinos as more criminal-like and less intelligent and hardworking than do light TV viewers (Mastro, Behm-Morawitz, & Ortiz, 2007). Heavy TV-viewing Latino adolescents show lower self-esteem than their light viewing peers (Rivadeneyra *et al.*, 2007), thus supporting a cultivation effect. Greenberg and Brand (1994) as well as Smith, Choueiti, and Pieper (2016a) have attributed this at least in part to the low level of minority employment in the broadcast industry, due not necessarily to overt discrimination but more often to the low entry-level salaries that are not attractive enough to the relatively few qualified Latinos, who may have multiple job opportunities. Because decision makers and those at management level are mostly Anglo, it is their world that tends to appear on television.

Native Americans

Arguably the most mistreated group in the history of North America, Native Americans were the object of systematic extermination campaigns in the eighteenth and nineteenth centuries. Today their surviving descendants collectively comprise less than 2% of the U.S. population, with a large proportion living below the official poverty line. Stereotyped negative images have been pervasive in both news and entertainment media throughout U.S. history (Bird, 1996, 1999; Leavitt, Covarrubias, Perez & Fryberg, 2015; Merskin, 1998; Weston, 1996).

By far the best-known image is the bloodthirsty and savage Indian of old movies and early television. Westerns were one of the most popular genres of television and movies through the early 1960s. Indians were usually depicted as vicious killers or, at their very best, as lovable but dim-witted sidekicks to White men, such as *The Lone Ranger*'s Tonto (Tonto got a makeover in the 2013 Disney *Lone Ranger* movie—but this time was played by White actor Johnny Depp). Some of the stereotypical behaviors may actually have come from other groups; for example, some argue that historically, "scalping" was performed by European Americans on Native Americans before Native Americans ever began the practice. Later, slightly more serious portrayals of Indian men were most often the "doomed warrior" or "wise elder" characters (Bird, 1999). For the most part, when Westerns declined in popularity, Native Americans disappeared from the screen altogether. When Mastro and Greenberg (2000) did their content analysis of the 1996–1997 prime-time TV season, they found no examples of Native American characters at all! Representation has not improved much in the meantime (Leavett *et al.*, 2015; Tukachinsky *et al.*, 2015).

Although there are over 500 officially recognized Native American tribes today, those who have appeared in the media (usually in Westerns) have almost always been Plains Indians, and behaviors like living in teepees and hunting bison came to be identified with all Native Americans, although they were no more characteristic of the northeastern Iroquois, southwestern Navahos, or northwestern Tlingits than they were of the English or Africans. The overemphasis on Plains Indian peoples was still seen in a few 1990s films like *Dances with Wolves* (1990), *Thunderheart* (1992), and *Geronimo* (1993). Women seldom appeared, and when they did, they tended to be passive and rather dull background figures. The powerful women in matriarchal societies like the Navaho and Mohawk have never been seen on mainstream TV or in film. Most media Indians are seen in the historical setting of Westerns; the few modern characters are usually presented as militant activists, alcoholics, or casino owners. There is hardly any Native American news, and what does appear is usually about land claims litigation or controversies over Indian-run casinos or protests over pipelines. Without a large national constituency, substantial change may come only from Native American film and television production (Geiogamah & Pavel, 1993), which is largely nonexistent.

Asian Americans

Among the fastest growing minorities in the United States, Canada, Australia, and New Zealand in recent decades are Asians (Pew Research Center, 2013; Wu, 2002), although in the United States their immigration history goes back to the large numbers of Chinese brought over to build the railroads in the American West in the 1800s. Many Japanese emigrated to the United States, as well as to Brazil and elsewhere in large numbers, in the early twentieth century. Asian emigration in large numbers to Australia and New Zealand has only occurred since around 1970. Koreans and Filipinos came to America often as spouses of U.S. military personnel formerly stationed abroad. Vietnamese and other Southeast Asians came in large numbers as refugees following the end of the Vietnam War in 1975. There is also a substantial number of South Asian Americans, from India, Pakistan, Bangladesh, Sri Lanka, and Afghanistan, as well as large numbers of Iranian refugees to the West following the 1979 Islamic revolution.

As with Native Americans, there is a long history of media stereotyping of Asians in movies, such as the Fu Manchu and Charlie Chan characters, often played, incidentally, by White actors, sometimes well-known ones like Mickey Rooney, Marlon Brando, and even John Wayne (Iiyama & Kitano, 1982)! On television there have been few Asian Americans. The 1970s *Kung Fu* series had the Asian lead played by White David Carradine. Interestingly, Chinese American actor Bruce Lee was turned down for the same role (Miller & Pearlstein, 2004). The 1970s and 1980s saw some improvement, with the addition of some minor Asian American characters in shows like *Hawaii Five-O* and *M*A*S*H*, although they were often villains or in stereotyped occupations like Chinese running a laundry or restaurant (Mok, 1998). Representation has improved somewhat in the 2010s, with a reboot of *Hawaii Five-O* on CBS and *Fresh off the Boat* on ABC.

Asians have often been the villains of choice in movies and entertainment TV following news events. After World War II, the dastardly Japanese villain was common. Following the 1989 Tiananmen Square massacre, Chinese officials from the People's Republic of China (PRC) were frequent villains in action-adventure shows. During waves of U.S. concern about Japanese commercial power and ascendancy in the 1980s, Japanese businessmen were portrayed as buying up America in a sort of "yellow scare." There are similar portrayals today of the Chinese with the added twist of the Chinese (or generic Asian) gangster like Mr. Chow in the *Hangover* movies. As with African Americans, some very nasty old stereotypes live on in children's cartoons in video anthologies. For example, only in 1995 did MGM-UA Home Video pull a 1944 World War II-era Bugs Bunny cartoon in which Bugs hands out bombs concealed in ice cream cones to a crowd of Japanese people as he says, "Here you go Bowlegs, here you go Monkey-face, here you go, Slant Eyes, everybody gets one." Prior to the withdrawal, about 800 copies had been sold in the 1990s (What's up, doc?, 1995)!

Nevertheless, overall, Asian Americans are probably portrayed more positively than most other minorities in U.S. media. This follows a broader stereotype of Asian Americans as the *model minority*. This is an overgeneralized assumption that in comparison to other ethnic minorities, Asian Americans are better at adapting to mainstream (i.e., White) American culture and succeeding academically, commercially, and socially (Kiang, Huynh, Cheah, Wang, & Yoshikawa, 2017). Although this stereotype might be considered a positive one, it can put emotional pressure on Asian Americans to succeed (S. J. Lee, 1996; Thompson, Kiang, & Witkow, 2016). The model minority image may also be used to ignore problems that the group has or as an excuse to criticize other minorities for doing less well and thus seeming lazy.

Sometimes prejudice against different groups can interact in complex ways. For example, reading news stories about Asian Indians tended to increase hostility toward African Americans (Ramasubramanian & Oliver, 2007) or Mexican Americans (Ho, Sanbonmatsu, & Akimoto, 2002), perhaps due to valuing one group and subtly denigrating another for not being able to "make it."

Although like other ethnic minorities, Asians Americans are underrepresented in media (see Figure 5.1), Asian Americans from South Asian areas like India and Pakistan are increasingly present on mainstream American television. For instance, earlier relegated to supporting roles in *The Office* and *Parks and Recreation*, Indian American actors Mindy Kaling (*The Mindy Project*) and Aziz Ansari (*Master of None*), created their own successful shows on streaming platforms. In addition to starring in the shows, Kaling and Ansari are writers for the series. In general, such comedies depict the South Asian roles as complex and fully realized characters—professionally competent but unlucky in love (Moorti, 2017). Pakistani American comedian Kumail Nanjiani has also had television and movie success with hits like 2017's *The Big Sick*.

Arabs and Arab Americans

A much smaller American minority offers a look at a stereotype that is currently among the most unsympathetic and derogatory portrayals in U.S. media. There are an estimated 3–3.5 million Arab Americans (i.e., those whose heritage derives from Middle Eastern areas of Southwestern Asia or Northern Africa) (Arab American Institute, 2014). Stereotyping of this group, as well as Arabs in the Middle East and elsewhere, is widely seen in both news coverage and entertainment (Nacos & Torres-Reyna, 2007; Shaheen, 1984, 2008, 2014; Suleiman, 1988). There seems to be an implicit identification of Arabs with the Islamic religion, although Muslim Arabs worldwide represent only 20% of all the world's Muslims, who collectively represent about one-fifth of the planet's population (Shaheen, 2008, 2014). As for Arab Americans, a vast majority of them are Christian. In addition, Islam as a religion is often portrayed as cruel and vicious, in total contrast to the Judeo-Christian faith and civilization. Because most North Americans know very little about Islam except media reports of its extremist fringe, this may easily become their perceived reality about one of the world's major religions. Although many Americans have sufficient knowledge to recognize a Christian cult extremist on TV as very atypical of Christians, they may not have the necessary knowledge to so critically evaluate a media presentation of an Islamist suicide bomber, who is thus taken to be a typical Muslim.

According to Shaheen (2008, 2014), there have been over 1,000 films that denigrate or stereotype Arabs and only 29 (all post-2001) which present any positive image. Over the years, there have been several stereotypic ways that Arab men are portrayed, all very negative. One is as the terrorist. Although only a minuscule fraction of real Arabs are terrorists, there are many of these on television (on the series *Homeland* or *24*, for example), especially since September 2001. A second stereotype, common in some 1970s and 1980s movies, is of Arab men as wealthy oil sheiks, often greedy and morally dissolute. Their wealth, often suggested as being undeserved, is spent on frivolities like marble palaces, fleets of Rolls-Royce cars, and garishly kitschy homes in Beverly Hills. A third stereotype is that of a sexual pervert, often portrayed as selling

Europeans or Americans into slavery. This is an older stereotype seen in early movies, perhaps originally arising from medieval Christian Europe's enmity against the Muslim "infidels," who were, incidentally, primarily non-Arab Turks. Although probably less prevalent than the terrorist or oil sheik portrayal today, this image does appear occasionally. A fourth stereotype is the Bedouin desert rat, the unkempt ascetic wanderer far overrepresented on TV and in advertising, in relation to the approximately 5% of Arabs who are Bedouins. Visual images and jokes about camels, sand, and tents are frequent in connection with U.S.-media Arabs.

Arab men are generally seen as villains, a stereotype especially rampant in children's cartoons (e.g., Daffy Duck being chased by a crazed, sword-wielding Arab sheik or Heckle and Jeckle pulling the rug from under "Ali Boo-Boo, the Desert Rat"). More significantly, portrayals of these barbaric and uncultured villains are not usually balanced by those of Arab heroes or good guys. One of the very few positive media models was probably Lebanese American Corporal Max Klinger in *M*A*S*H*. He was a sympathetic and rounded character, yet (especially in early episodes) he dressed in drag and commented about his relatives having unnatural relations with camels. A more recent cable reality series, *The Shahs of Sunset*, profiled wealthy Iranian Americans living in Southern California. Some reviews said the show presented the castmates as likeable, but being a reality series, it also portrayed them at times as vain and shallow, focused on money and material objects. In an interesting article contrasting *Shahs of Sunset* with another reality show, *All American Muslim*, Alsultany (2016) noted that while *Shahs* has been a successful, multi-year series, *All American Muslim* was canceled after only one season amid low ratings. Alsultany argues that part of the reason for this is that *All American Muslim* addressed the issue of religion head on, while *Shahs* has focused more on affluent lifestyles and relationship conflict.

How about Arab women? They are seen far less often than Arab men on U.S. TV and in U.S. movies, but, when they are seen at all, it is usually as oppressed victims or in highly stereotyped roles such as that of a belly dancer or a member of a harem. The reality about harems, as Shaheen points out, is that they were never common and today are nonexistent in Arab countries. The public veiling of women is presented as the Arab norm, rather than as a characteristic of some, but not all, Islamic traditions. Arab children are practically nonexistent on U.S. television, even though the negative adult Arab stereotypes are perhaps more prevalent in children's cartoons than on any other type of programming. Even as we routinely see African American, Latino, and Asian faces on programs like *Sesame Street*, few if any Arabs appear.

Historically, Arabs may simply be the latest villains in a long list of many groups who have been maligned by the U.S. media. The vicious Arabs of contemporary entertainment were preceded by the wealthy but cruel Jews of the 1920s, the sinister Asian villains of the 1930s, and the Italian gangsters of the 1950s. Each of these stereotypes has been tempered and balanced following protests by the offended groups. Such media portrayals provide unwitting social support for racist and discriminatory policies and legislation, such as the network of Jim Crow laws and racist practices against African Americans in the century following the American Civil War.

Recent historical events have, at times, encouraged unflattering media portrayals of Arabs: the OPEC oil embargoes of the 1970s, various hostage-taking incidents, the Lebanese civil war, the Iran–Iraq War of 1980–1988, the Persian Gulf War of 1991, the 2003–2011 Iraq War, the continuing Israeli–Palestinian conflicts, and, most dramatically, the Al-Qaeda terrorist attacks of September 11, 2001, and the ensuing "War on Terror." The interpersonal and political mistrust against Arab Americans, particularly those believed to be Muslim, is real (Calfano, Djupe, Cox, & Jones, 2016). The consequences of this backlash since the 9/11 attacks stress the urgency to better understand this group. The concern is not that there are some negative portrayals of Arabs and Arab Americans. Rather, it is that such portrayals are not balanced by positive portrayals to feed into the perceived mental reality constructed by viewers. At the same time, network executives push for more dramas with terrorism storylines (Ryzik, 2016). Overall, there is very little programming on Arab culture or society. The Arab world was more intellectually and technically advanced than Europe in the Middle Ages and gave us many of the basics of modern science, mathematics, and music, but how many Americans know that? The close family values and other positive features of the Arab culture and Islamic faith also do not receive much play in U.S. media. Sometimes we do not even realize how mainstream a strongly negative portrayal has become. For example, the reality show *All American Muslim* (discussed briefly above), which profiled real Arab American families, was forced off the air in part when a major sponsor pulled its advertising in response to criticism that this realistic portrayal was unfair pro-Muslim propaganda!

Immediately after the Oklahoma City bombing in April 1995, investigating authorities and the general public immediately suspected Arab terrorists, although there was no evidence of such a link. When a pair of White Americans was arrested and later convicted of the crime, there were a lot of embarrassed faces. However, the stereotypes persist in entertainment TV and movies, and still there are almost no positive models. This is not without its consequences. For example, Arab nations have argued, sometimes rather convincingly, that Western coverage of the Israeli–Palestinian dispute over the West Bank is severely biased toward Israel due to anti-Arab prejudice.

The concern about stereotypical portrayals of groups is not limited to gender, race, and ethnicity. Let us look next at the media portrayal of a formerly invisible minority.

Sexual Minorities

Although there were some early film intimations of sexual minorities (lesbian, gay, bisexual, transgender individuals/LGBT), such as the effeminate "sissy" characters of some 1930s movies or the gender-ambiguous characters such as those played by Marlene Dietrich (Celluloid Closet, 1995), the Production Code of 1930 (see Close-up 10.1 for a further discussion) formalized the voluntary exclusion of all gay and lesbian portrayals from Hollywood films (V. Russo, 1981). Still, some negative stereotypes occurred, with just enough sexual ambiguity to elude the censors. These included lesbians as villains or prisoners and gay men as suicidal. *Victim* in Britain and *The Children's Hour* in the United States in the early 1960s were the first films with explicitly gay or lesbian heroes. *The Boys in the Band* (1970), a movie about a group of gay men, was a groundbreaker, followed two years later by the much more widely seen *Cabaret*. Several more films with gay characters followed, although the first with a major theme of a gay love affair was *Making Love* in 1982.

When television entered the picture, the code of silence regarding sexual minority characters was maintained, not to be broken until very occasional openings starting in the 1950s and 1960s (Capsuto, 2000). A televised version of the play *Lady in the Dark* on NBC in 1954 depicted the first clearly gay (and somewhat sympathetic) character on American TV (Paley Center for Media, 2010). A CBS documentary titled *The*

Homosexuals aired in 1967, with many of the film's subjects in disguise. Norman Lear's *All in the Family*, debuting on television in 1970, occasionally dealt with some gay and lesbian themes. A sympathetic dramatic TV movie, *That Certain Summer*, aired in 1972, followed by a gay character in the sitcom *Soap* in the late 1970s. Still, depictions of sexual minority characters were rare on TV throughout the 1970s. However, during that time there also may have been an interesting case of the viewing public not seeing what was in front of them. Specifically, two popular TV stars of the era (Paul Lynde of *Hollywood Squares*, Charles Nelson Reilly of *Match Game*) tended to be very flamboyant on game show celebrity panels. Although Lynde and Nelson Reilly were both later revealed to be gay, sexual orientation was never mentioned on the shows.

The advent of AIDS in the early 1980s greatly altered the media perception of sexual minorities, particularly gay men. Although neglected and marginalized at first as a problem of the gay and drug subcultures, the death from AIDS of romantic leading man Rock Hudson in 1985 helped bring AIDS coverage "out of the closet," although the media tended to redefine coverage of sexual minorities as "epidemic" coverage, with gay people cast in the role of villains carrying the dread disease or as victims of it, or both. There were some sympathetic portrayals of gay AIDS victims, though they were almost always male and upper-middle-class, as in the groundbreaking 1985 TV movie *An Early Frost*.

By the 1990s, greater numbers of gay men (and less often lesbian) characters began to appear in positive TV and film roles, some of them saintly, and most of them appearing rather mainstream and being well accepted by their straight friends. Physical contact was rare; a lesbian kiss on the sitcom *Roseanne* was almost vetoed by ABC in 1994, but Roseanne Barr insisted on it. The most publicized gay character in the history of TV was featured in the onscreen coming out of *Ellen*'s lead character Ellen Morgan in April 1997, which coincided with the offscreen coming out of the actress Ellen DeGeneres. Although the coming-out episode set ratings records and was itself the subject of many news stories at the time, the formerly high-rated sitcom was canceled at the end of the following season (Dow, 2001). Despite this setback, DeGeneres eventually found success and mainstream acceptance as a talk show host. Although the *Ellen* sitcom was canceled, another network comedy (*Will and Grace*), about a gay man living with a straight woman, became a mainstream hit (Battles & Hilton-Morrow, 2002) in the 1990s and 2000s and was revived in 2017. *Queer as Folk*, a British series adapted for premium cable in the United States, featured predominantly gay characters in the early 2000s and was followed by *The L Word*, about a group of lesbian friends. There was even a gay-themed basic cable channel (Logo) launched in 2005. Interestingly enough, however, some of the most daring programming with gay themes came on animated shows, such as *The Simpsons* and *South Park*.

By the late 2000s, two highly successful television shows were on the air, *Glee* and *Modern Family*, both of which featured main characters and storylines involving sexual minorities. In *Glee*, high school students Kurt and Santana dealt with romance, coming out to their families, and bullying by other students. *Modern Family* featured committed couple Cameron and Mitchell raising a young daughter together. In 2016, *The Real O'Neals* included an adolescent gay character as a main storyline.

Even though more gay characters appear on TV and in the movies all the time, representation of lesbian, gay, and bisexuals remains fairly low, at 2–5% of speaking roles in TV shows and movies (GLAAD, 2016; Smith *et al.*, 2016a). Also, some research has shown that even when they are shown, TV tends to depict gay and lesbian couples along stereotypically heterosexual gendered lines. In other words, plotlines will portray one partner as "passive" and the other as "dominant" (Holz Ivory, Gibson, & Ivory, 2009).

Although numerous films and even TV shows with gay and lesbian characters appeared in the 1990s, the topic continued to generate some controversy. The 2005 "gay cowboy" film *Brokeback Mountain* about two Wyoming cowboys falling in love in the 1960s poignantly dramatized the tragedy of such a union in a time and place that did not accept such love. The fact that it won several Oscar nominations brought unprecedented attention to the issue of gay media portrayals.

A few studies suggest that positive media portrayals such as Will Truman in *Will and Grace* can be instrumental in improving tolerance and acceptance of gays and lesbians by the broader society. Riggle, Ellis, and Crawford (1996) found that viewing a documentary film about a gay politician led to significantly more positive attitudes toward sexual minorities. Bonds-Raacke and colleagues (2007) found that just thinking for a few minutes about a positive media gay or lesbian character of one's choice led to improved attitudes toward gay men. Bond and Compton (2015) reported a relationship between exposure to gay characters on television and endorsement of gay equality issues. These results suggest a potentially important role for media entertainment in reducing prejudice in this area. However, mainstream media portrayals of LGBT characters have also been criticized as being "sanitized," with such characters being portrayed as uninterested in actual sexual relationships (Bond, 2015).

Transgender people have a shorter history of being portrayed in mainstream American media. Still, there were a couple of breakout movies. *Boys Don't Cry* won Hillary Swank an Academy Award for portraying real-life trans man Brandon Teena in 1999. *Transamerica* (2005) showed Felicity Huffman portraying a trans woman traveling across the country. Television came next. In 2011, for probably the first time, an openly transgender person, Chaz Bono, was featured on the highly rated reality series *Dancing with the Stars*. As transgender issues came more into American consciousness, Netflix viewers became familiar with Laverne Cox in 2013. Cox, a transgender woman, starred in *Orange is the New Black*, playing a transgender character. Trans issues also became a main focus of the Emmy-award winning *Transparent* in 2014, and Olympic medalist Bruce Jenner revealed in an ABC Diane Sawyer interview in 2015 that he would be transitioning to female. In addition, *Glee* and *Degrassi* featured adolescent transgender characters. However, in spite of growing awareness, according to a 2016 study (Smith *et al.*, 2016a), less than 1% of speaking parts in movies and TV shows depict transgender characters.

How LGBT rights and issues are communicated via news media is also an important consideration. Gays and lesbians have been treated qualitatively differently from ethnic, religious, or other social minorities. For example, Moritz (1995) points out that the Ku Klux Klan and neo-Nazis are not sought out for minority opinions for "journalistic balance" in coverage of issues concerning African Americans or Jews. However, spokespersons from the political right who would ban and suppress all expression, if not even all discussion, of LGBT issues are routinely sought out to present the "other side" in coverage of sexual minority issues. In a more recent commentary, Hancock and Haldeman (2017) took mainstream news media to task for its coverage of the 2016 Orlando nightclub mass shooting that resulted in the deaths of 49 people. Specifically, the authors argue that most media outlets focused on the death count while overlooking the homophobia and racism that motivated the killer.

Still, once limited to coverage of gay pride parades or protests, news coverage of gay issues has increased, along with public discussion of issues such as same-sex marriage. Although same-sex marriage doesn't receive as much news coverage since the 2015 U.S. Supreme Court decision legalizing it nationwide, several analyses of news reports are interesting. For example, a content analysis of U.S. newspaper stories on same-sex marriage revealed that reporting often focused on public opinion, particularly with regard to factors like generational effects and political beliefs (Vales *et al.*, 2014). Another study (Moscowitz, 2010) found that television news coverage of gay marriage tended to be dominated by a "straight perspective" that emphasized the traditional, heterosexual viewpoint. In fact, the study revealed that in many news stories, "gay and lesbian citizens were also given a shorter sound bite, speaking less than most other sources speaking on their behalf such as straight allies and gay rights activists" (Moscowitz, 2010, p. 36).

Older Adults

One of the most underrepresented demographic groups in U.S. media, especially television, has been the older adult (Dall, 1988; Davis & Davis, 1985). Although the percentage of the U.S. population over 65 has climbed from 4% in 1900 to about 13% in 2010 and is projected to be near 20% by 2100, only about 3% of characters on television and 11% in films are over 60 (Cassata & Irwin, 1997; Hajjar, 1997; Roy & Harwood, 1997; Smith, Choueiti, & Pieper, 2017; Smith, Pieper, & Choueiti, 2016). Even the relatively few older people who appear on TV are not particularly representative of the population. For example, 62–70% of the older adults in commercials were men, as compared with about 40% men in the over-65 age population (Hajjar, 1997; Roy & Harwood, 1997). A disproportionate number of TV seniors appear in sitcoms, with very few in action-adventure or children's shows. Often, the older adult is portrayed as more of a stereotype than a fully rounded character. These stereotypes take several forms.

Seniors have typically been portrayed as sexless. The major exception to this is the other extreme, the so-called dirty old man (or female "cougar"), who is preoccupied with sex and is usually a highly ludicrous character. The very active and healthy senior citizen may be an object of ridicule, such as the grandmother who rides a motorcycle or cruises bars to meet men. Narrow-minded older persons often complain, criticize, and generally make a pain of themselves for everyone else. As with the physically weak stereotype, the crotchety complainer is usually at best a laughable buffoon and at worst an object of scorn and derision. Older people tend to be seen doing relatively trivial things like playing bingo and sitting in rockers on the front porch. Such identifying symbols of aging are especially common in advertising. For example, a woman in a magazine ad for cookies is placed in a rocker to make sure we recognize that she is a grandmother.

In marked contrast to the unusually attractive young adults on TV, television's seniors are often stoop-shouldered, mousy-haired, badly wrinkled, and wearing out-of-style dowdy clothing. Such markers may be given to them so that we do not mistake them for younger people. Intentionally or not, it also contributes to their being perceived negatively. What's worse is that these stereotypical portrayals may influence people's perceptions about whether to hire an older worker (Kroon, van Selm, ter Hoeven, & Vliegenthart, 2016).

An interesting class of exceptions to these generalizations can be seen in TV commercials. Although older adults are as underrepresented there as in the programs, the characterization is a bit different. Seniors in ads often appear as the "young-old," with few of the stereotypic signs of aging except the gray hair, which is almost always there. Although they suffer more health problems than young people in ads, they retain their vigor. It is as if the producers give the character gray hair so we all realize that he or she is supposed to be older, but allow that person to show very few other signs of age that our society finds so distasteful. Baldness, wrinkles, and otherwise general dowdiness are unseemly. One content analysis of TV commercials in 1994 found the portrayals of older people to be largely positive (Roy & Harwood, 1997). Other research that focused specifically on Super Bowl ads between 2010 and 2014 reported that mature adults appeared in 32% of ads and were shown in a positive light 80% of the time (Brooks, Bichard, & Craig, 2016). Since the onset of prescription drug advertising in the United States in 1997, the largest number of older models have appeared in pharmaceutical ads, which are very prevalent on TV shows aimed at an older demographic. Similar TV commercials also target older adults with ads for reverse mortgages and medical devices. Because older adults hold the greatest amount of wealth among the U.S. population, such ads can be lucrative for advertisers (Reams, 2016).

Even in cases when seniors are portrayed very positively, they tend to be in rather a restricted and stereotyped range of roles. They are almost always in relation to family, very often as grandparents, but sometimes as the antagonist in a relationship with their adult child. We seldom see an older executive or professional. The older detectives of *Murder She Wrote*, *Matlock*, and *Diagnosis Murder* (all now off the air for quite a while) offer a few exceptions.

When NBC's sitcom *The Golden Girls* (1985–1992) featured four single women (three widowed, one divorced), aged about 50 to 80, sharing a house in Florida, what was new was the age of the stars. Never before had a sitcom, or perhaps any U.S. TV show, had its regular cast consisting entirely of older adults. There were no precocious children, no smart-mouthed teenagers, no hunks or supermodels, and no angst-ridden yuppie couples, yet the show had consistently high ratings. The characters were also not the stereotyped TV old ladies. Three of the four were working professionals, and all showed depth of character beyond the typical TV grandma. However, they were criticized for being excessively interested in sex, although that criticism may primarily reflect the critics' discomfort with sexual interest in the mature adult. Also, the humor of the show sometimes perpetuated stereotypes of aging by poking fun at counter-stereotypical portrayals (Harwood & Giles, 1992). In an interesting twist, *Golden Girls* star Betty White outlived her co-stars and saw a career resurgence in the 2010s when she was in her 90s. In spite of the success of *The Golden Girls*, it was not followed by other ensemble shows of older characters until *Grace and Frankie*, a Netflix series starring legendary septuagenarian actors Jane Fonda and Lily Tomlin, appeared in 2015. Perhaps reflecting a Hollywood interest in an aging population, *Grace and Frankie* depicts the title characters as interested in work, sex, and dating.

Despite these inadequacies in their portrayal on TV, older people are heavy users of television. Robinson (1989) offered a uses and gratifications interpretation of this. A reduction in the number of friends and family seen regularly, perhaps in part due to decreased mobility as a result of health limitations, leads to a proportionately greater reliance on media, especially television, with its high level of redundancy in the visual and auditory modalities. If one sense is impaired, the other may partially compensate.

In the case of the sound track, the volume may be turned up, so some older TV viewers may actually hear more of what is spoken on TV than what is spoken by other people around them.

Persons with Physical or Psychological Disabilities and Disorders

People with disabilities, either physical or mental, are also very concerned about their media image (Balter, 1999; Cumberbatch & Negrine, 1991). Unfortunately, in many ways, media portrayals of these groups have also not been kind.

Physical Disabilities

Disabilities only appear in less than 2% of series characters on TV, compared to 10–20% of the population having some sort of physical disability; movies are not much better, with only about 2% of characters depicted as having disabilities, most of them in minor or supporting roles (Balter, 1999; GLAAD, 2016; Smith, Choueiti, & Pieper, 2016b). To make matters worse, over 95% of disabled characters are played by non-disabled actors (Woodburn & Kopić, 2016). However, people with disabilities have occasionally appeared, often in the form of the "bitter crip" or "supercrip" stereotypes. In the former, the person with a disability is depressed and bitter due to the disability and other people's failure to accept him or her as a full person. Often such storylines revolve around someone (typically someone who is not disabled) challenging the character to accept him- or herself. The character with the disability then finds that this self-acceptance miraculously leads to a physical cure, perhaps subtly suggesting that happiness does in fact come only from being physically whole.

The supercrip image, on the other hand, is seen in characters like the superhuman and selfless paraplegic who wheels hundreds of miles to raise money for cancer research or the blind girl who solves the baffling crime by remembering a crucial sound or smell that sighted people had missed. Sometimes the two even coexist in the same person, as in *The Miracle Worker*'s Helen Keller, at first bitter and inept, almost animalistic, until she is "tamed" by the saintly teacher Annie Sullivan, after which she goes on to be almost superhuman. A covert message of both of these portrayals is that individual adjustment is the key to disabled people's lives; if they only have the right attitude, things will be just fine. Factors like prejudice and social and physical barriers of the broader society are underplayed (Longmore, 1985).

Positive images do count. The old TV show *Ironside* featured the lead detective who worked from a wheelchair. *Glee*'s Artie, who was in a wheelchair, generally went about the business of being a teenager as did Down syndrome character Becky (played by Down syndrome actress Lauren Potter). In 2016, *Speechless*, a sitcom about a family with a son/brother who has cerebral palsy, starred Micah Fowler, an actor who actually lives with cerebral palsy. Such portrayals can have substantial impact. One study revealed that exposure to a positive, short film about attitudes toward the disabled significantly changed participants' attitudes about employment for the disabled (Reinhardt, Pennycott, & Fellinghauer, 2014). In a less scientific example, when a popular Brazilian soap opera introduced a character who was ruggedly handsome and very sexy but also deaf, interest in learning sign language soared nationwide.

Psychological Disorders

The media image of psychological disorders (mental illness) is also an issue. One of the most common media stereotypes of those with psychological disorders is that they are violent. Indeed, a content analysis of week-long program samples from 1969 to 1985 showed that 72% of the prime-time adult characters who were portrayed as mentally ill actually injured or killed others, and 75% were victims of violence (Signorielli, 1989), whereas in reality about 11% of persons with psychological disorders are prone to violence, the same ratio as in the overall population (Teplin, 1985). A more recent study (Parrott & Parrott, 2015a) found that in TV shows, characters who were identified as having a mental illness were more likely to commit violence than other characters. In fact, those who are mentally ill are 12 times more likely to be victims of violence than those who are not mentally ill (Levin, 2011). A comparable bias exists in print media coverage of mentally ill persons (Day & Page, 1986; McGinty, Kennedy-Hendricks, Choksy, & Barry, 2016; McGinty, Webster, Jarlenski, & Barry, 2014; Matas, Guebaly, Harper, Green, & Peterkin, 1986; Shain & Phillips, 1991). It also doesn't help that many of the mass shooter killings in the United States and elsewhere have been perpetrated by people with serious mental illnesses, thus linking violence and mental illness in the minds of many.

In addition, those who are heavy media consumers have been shown to overestimate the prevalence of psychological disorders (Quintero Johnson & Riles, 2016). At the same time, one of the few truly violent disorders, antisocial personality disorder (sometimes labeled "psychopath" or "sociopath"), is greatly overrepresented among the media mentally ill (W. Wilson, 1999). The media image is but one reason for the stigmatization of mental illness, which becomes a major barrier to improving health care delivery (Hinshaw, 2007).

Besides the violent mentally ill person, another stereotype is the person with disorders as object of humor or ridicule (Wahl, 1995). Although mental illness is seldom ridiculed directly, there is frequent use of metaphors that many find demeaning and insulting. For example, in advertising, an ad portrays a straitjacket as appropriate for someone crazy enough to buy the competitor's product; a lawn mower is described as "schizophrenic"; a line of peanuts called Certifiably Nuts is sold by picturing cans of the product wearing straitjackets. Ads describe sunglasses as "psycho," and vicious criminals are labeled "psychotic killers" as if the two words were synonymous. These stereotypes even creep into political discourse.

A popular movie *Me, Myself, and Irene* poked fun at a character labeled as schizophrenic but having the symptoms of dissociative identity (formerly multiple personality) disorder, two completely different disorders frequently confused in the public mind. TV and movies also frequently give characters mental illness labels that don't exist in the real world of psychology like "extreme Internet addiction." People who have dealt with the tragedies of schizophrenia, depression, or other illnesses find such language and images very hurtful.

A third stereotype is that people with disorders are "a breed apart," that is, totally different from the rest of us (Wahl, 1995). People are presented as being obviously different, unmistakably symbolized by wild hair, disheveled clothing, bizarre behavior, and odd facial expressions. This encourages two inaccurate beliefs: (1) mental illness is immediately identifiable by one's appearance, and (2) people with an unusual appearance are obviously mentally ill and thus objects of suspicion and perhaps fear. Such attitudes support the stigmatization of mental illness that discourages people from disclosing their own disorders and perhaps even dissuades them from seeking much-needed treatment. Media discussion of this stigma is perhaps most clearly seen in its role as political poison (Rich, 1997). Traditionally, seekers of high political office admit their own use of counseling or psychiatric resources only at their peril. One of the most celebrated political casualties of such prejudice was probably U.S. Senator Thomas Eagleton, the original Democratic Party vice-presidential nominee in 1972. He was replaced on the ticket after "admitting" he had been hospitalized for depression some years before. Presidential candidate Michael Dukakis lost ground in 1988 after a rumor that he had sought therapy to deal with grief over his brother's suicide some years before. How sad when the desirable and healthy behavior of seeking help for problems is considered a moral failing or character flaw! Would someone make a better president if he or she ignored a problem and did not seek help?

Occasionally there are reassuringly helpful images. One of the most influential was the 2001 Oscar-winning film *A Beautiful Mind*, the true story of Nobel Prize-winning mathematician John Nash's descent into schizophrenia and largely successful treatment for it. In spite of some cinematic license (visual hallucinations instead of auditory ones, more successful treatment than is often the case), the illness and its treatment were presented realistically and sensitively. Important issues were dealt with, such as the gradual detachment from reality, the necessity of maintaining medication therapy, and the devastating impact on one's family. Someone watching this film will learn a lot about schizophrenia (though nothing about multiple personalities!), as well as being greatly entertained for two hours. With the proliferation of original cable and streaming shows, there has also been an increased opportunity for more sensitive and more realistic portrayals of mental illness. At the same time, some shows seem to be getting better at presenting mentally ill characters as likeable and well-rounded. Arguably, some of the best have been *Girls* (obsessive-compulsive disorder), *Atypical* and *The Good Doctor* (autistic spectrum disorder), *Homeland* (bipolar disorder), and *You're the Worst* (major depressive and post-traumatic stress disorders). See Close-up 5.6 for further discussion of stereotyping of mental illness in movies.

❖ CLOSE-UP 5.6 MENTAL ILLNESS IN THE MOVIES

According to Hyler, Gabbard, and Schneider (1991; see also Dine Young, 2012; Wedding & Niemiec, 2014), there are several common movie stereotypes of persons with mental illness. These include the rebellious free spirit (e.g., Randle McMurphy in One Flew Over the Cuckoo's Nest, *Joon Pearl in* Benny and Joon*); next is the homicidal maniac (e.g., Michael Myers in* Halloween, *Norman Bates in* Psycho, *the Joker in* The Dark Knight Rises*); third is the seductive woman (e.g., Alex Forrest in* Fatal Attraction, *Catherine Tramell in* Basic Instinct, *Amy Dunne in* Gone Girl*); fourth is the narcissistic parasite who sponges off society and gives nothing in return (e.g., several characters in* Annie Hall *and other Woody Allen films). Other characterizations include the zoo specimen, the curiosity whom others like to look at and feel glad they are not like themselves, and the enlightened member of society, whose greatness is unrecognized and whose creativity is mistakenly and cruelly labeled mental illness.*

Hyler (1988) suggested three common themes in movies that tend to establish and support these stereotypes. First of all, there is the "presumption of traumatic etiology," which seems to assume all mental illness has its origins in some traumatic event in childhood. Related to that is the "blame the parent" assumption, which assumes that the mental illness has its origin not only in childhood trauma but in one caused by a parent, perhaps through abuse, neglect, or even treating the child unfairly. Finally, and perhaps most perniciously, is the frequent theme that harmless eccentricity is labeled as mental illness and tragically treated as such, often with extreme measures like frontal lobotomies or mind-numbing drugs or shock treatments. Have you seen these themes in movies you remember?

Portrayals of People of Faith and Religion

Yet another group that is often misrepresented in media are people of faith. Throughout history, extremely positive actions have been done in the name of religion, such as the centuries of education and social services offered by church entities and church members. Sadly, strongly negative ones have been done as well, from the Crusades and the Inquisition down to the recent New York, London, Paris, Barcelona, and Madrid radical Islamist terrorist attacks.

Gallup polls consistently show the United States to be by far the most religious industrialized country in the world, with about 90% of Americans saying they believe in God and over 50% saying they belong to a church, synagogue, or mosque (Newport, 2016). However, religion is perhaps the most touchy and neglected area in American media, maybe because producers and journalists are afraid of the emotion associated with it. When Beatle John Lennon said offhandedly in 1966 that their group was more popular than Jesus, many were highly offended. Even subsequent clarifications of satirical intent and a sort of apology failed to mollify critics. Out of fear of controversy, religion often becomes invisible in mainstream media, especially in television and popular movies. Let us examine several aspects of religion in the media, including religion in entertainment and news, religious media, and effects of media on religion more broadly.

Religion in Entertainment

Generally speaking, religion plays almost no significant role in the lives of American entertainment TV series or movie characters. They hardly ever mention going to church or believing in God, nor do they mention that they do not go to church or do not believe in God. It appears that producers are loath to offend anyone either by identifying their favorite TV characters with a particular faith or by saying that they have no faith. Action-adventure shows have virtually no mention of religion either, with an occasional exception of having an extreme religious fanatic or terrorist as a villain. Nonetheless, one may derive religious moral lessons from just about any film or TV program (see Leonard, 2006, for a set of examples).

This absence of religious themes probably reflects (1) TV producers' and writers' relative lack of involvement with religion themselves, compared to most Americans, and, most importantly, (2) an implicit belief that religion is a very touchy subject and one where people are easily offended. Perhaps they fear that Protestants and Muslims will stop watching *Modern Family* if the Pritchetts and Dunphys were identified as Catholic or that atheists and agnostics would have lost interest in *I Love Lucy* if Lucy and Ricky became born-again Christians. Interestingly, however, we do know the religious backgrounds of the main characters on *The Big Bang Theory* (and its spinoff *Young Sheldon*), one of the most highly rated sitcoms of the past decade. Pointing to failed TV dramas with religion at their heart (like *Book of Daniel* and *Revelations*) Bird (2009) argues that that TV isn't anti-religion. Rather, TV executives tend to avoid religious storylines out of fear of offending someone, even if they try to present a positive portrayal. As Bird further points out, atheists and agnostics are also not identified among TV characters.

By most estimates, the prime-time show on American TV that takes religion the most seriously is the irreverent animated sitcom *The Simpsons* (Pinsky, 2007). Unlike almost any other TV family, the Simpsons attend church weekly, pray before meals, self-identify as Christians, and generally find spiritual issues important in their lives. To be sure, the sharp-edged show satirizes the foibles of religion, as it does just about everything else, but Homer and Marge and the kids return to God in prayer and trust time and again. They attend Springfield Community Church (no denomination specified). Neighbor Ned Flanders is a somewhat rigid evangelical Christian, but he is more rounded than the totally hypocritical caricature that many evangelical Christians in entertainment are reduced to. If Bart Simpson prays before dinner, "Rub-a-dub-dub, thanks for the grub," he is not unlike many of our own children. When Marge tells God she will be a better person and give the poor something they really like, not just old lima beans and canned pumpkin, it strikes a familiar chord.

Why do the producers of *The Simpsons* believe they can endow their sitcom family with a spiritual dimension while almost no other TV writers do? Is there something about the animated format that makes this less risky? Perhaps not coincidentally, two other fairly religious sitcoms are also animated, the edgy *South Park* and *Family Guy*, which both feature Jesus as an occasional character and have had plotlines dealing with Judaism, Scientology, Mormonism, and various other shades of Christianity.

Except for explicitly religious programming like Christian broadcasting, religious professionals are greatly underrepresented on U.S. television. When they are shown, they are often, at best, saintly but shallow characters, and, at worst, vicious hypocrites hiding behind their clerical collars. The fanatical cult preacher archetype is typically very extreme and very evil. Such characters have to be very perverted so as not to evoke any sympathy or any criticisms about the program saying negative things about a real man or woman of God. The unexpected success of the show *Touched by an Angel* in the mid-1990s caught the networks' notice of the public's interest in spiritual themes, even if in somewhat generic and non-specific form. Even so, similar shows have not followed, at least on mainstream broadcast networks.

Religion in the News

Although, in general, religious news has traditionally been underreported in the United States, relative to its importance, a look at what is reported reveals some interesting trends. Religious news that is centered on an individual person receives relatively heavier coverage, following the star model of political and entertainment news coverage (see Chapter 7). Most often the focus is either on Roman Catholicism, whose colorful pageantry and identifiable individual newsmakers (especially the Pope) make good photogenic copy, or on Protestant fundamentalist preachers, whose dogmatic theology and contentious political activism make good controversy-ridden stories, especially when centered on a charismatic individual. Groups of mainline Protestants politely discussing multiple points of view on social welfare, or Reform Jews examining different degrees of support for Israel may be just as important but are less photogenic and newsworthy. Media dealing with religious themes have considerable power to both promote peace and incite violence, and there is ample evidence of their having done both (Mitchell, 2012).

Why have mainstream media been so reluctant to cover religious news and religious dimensions of secular news? Hoover (1998, 2006) suggests six mistaken beliefs. First is the belief that as societies become more modern and advanced, they necessarily become more secular and less religious; this tenet seems to be widely believed in American intellectual life, in spite of poll numbers indicating that most Americans are still believers. Second is the notion that religion is fundamentally a private matter and thus largely outside the realm of public discourse, including the realm of journalism. Third, religion makes claims outside the empirical realm of what is knowable and concrete. Journalism is "all about verification and sources, but religion is fundamentally unverifiable" (Hoover, 1998, p. 29). Fourth, religion is thought to be complex and thus hard to cover in brief media sound bites. Fifth, religion is controversial and coverage, however careful and objective, is likely to offend someone. Finally, there is the misunderstanding that the First Amendment to the U.S. Constitution, forbidding the establishment of a state church, somehow mandates the complete separation of church and state in public discussion. It does not; it merely says that the state may not establish a state church.

Religious Programming

In the United States, although in few other places in the Western world, explicitly religious programming continues to be a thriving business (Bruce, 1990; Peck, 1992; Walton, 2009). Consistent with the separation of religion from other aspects of American life, it is produced and distributed totally separately from other television programming. Religious books are sold in separate bookstores from secular books, religious music is typically recorded by different artists and marketed separately from other music, and religious television is produced by religious networks. Although largely a U.S. phenomenon, there is some international growth of TV evangelism, especially in Latin America and most notably in Guatemala, the first majority Protestant country in Latin America. Increasingly, religious groups of all sorts are turning to the Internet as a domain for some of their more creative ministries (Campbell, 2010).

Although there was some Christian broadcasting in the early days of radio and television, the modern electronic church really began with Billy Graham's TV specials starting in 1957. These were later followed by televangelists Oral Roberts, Jerry Falwell, Jimmy Swaggart, Pat Robertson's *700 Club*, and Jim and Tammy Bakker's *PTL Club*. More recently, Joel Osteen and T. D. Jakes have had popular television ministries. These programs have had a variety of formats, and their emphases were also quite varied, including Robertson's talk show format, Falwell's emphasis on politics, and Roberts's focus on spiritual healing. All were theologically evangelical or fundamentalist, with a heavy emphasis on evangelism (Hoover, 1988). In spite of its evangelistic emphasis, however, Christian TV attracts few nonbelievers and, in fact, serves mainly to reinforce the existing beliefs of its viewers (Fore, 1987). Many of these kinds of television ministries have also been criticized as gaining tax advantages while imploring viewers for donations and at the same time preaching a "prosperity gospel," in which God blesses favored ones with money (Martin, 2015). To hammer home this point, comedian John Oliver created his own tongue-in-cheek TV church, "Our Lady of Perpetual Exemption."

Effects of Television on Religion

There are some who have argued that the mere presence of television as a medium has altered all religion in subtle but profound ways, so much so that the perceived reality about religion will never be the same again. In his now classic critique of popular culture, *Amusing Ourselves to Death*, Postman (1985) argued that television had radically reshaped practically everything about our lives. One domain that was greatly changed was religion, in ways that go far beyond the Sunday morning church broadcasts and TV evangelists. Postman argued that, because TV is, at heart, entertainment, the preacher is thus the star performer, and "God comes out as second banana" (p. 117). Although Christianity has always been "a demanding and serious religion," its TV version can acquire its needed share of the audience "only by offering people something they want" (p. 121), which is hardly historical biblical Christianity. Furthermore, Postman argues, TV is such a fundamentally secular medium that religious TV necessarily uses many of the same symbols and formats (e.g., *The 700 Club* was modeled after *Entertainment Tonight*).

Thus, TV preachers are stars who are attractive and affluent just like movie stars. Worship on TV is not participatory; the audience can sit at home and absorb, but does not have the communal worship experience of group singing, praying, or liturgy. Although a church may be considered holy ground where people act with reverence, there is no comparable sacred space when watching church on TV at home, where one can sit in dirty underwear drinking beer and eating pizza during the sermon without offending anyone.

In turn, some pastors have become concerned about providing the kind of worship conducive to television, even if the service is not being televised. Congregations expect to be entertained, even amused, as they might be while watching televangelists like Joel Osteen. As a result, it's now common for worship services to have rock music, rap liturgy, and computerized multimedia presentations. One church ran a full-page ad touting its contemporary Saturday evening service called "Church Lite" for college students who wanted to sleep in on Sunday. Other churches use Sunday school curricula like "The Gospel According to the Simpsons" or "The Gospel According to Harry Potter." Is this a creative reaching out to people in mission or selling one's soul on the altar of popular culture? The answer is not always obvious. For more texts on media and religion, see Stout (2012) and Winston (2009).

Portrayals of Occupations

Finally, in this look at portrayals of groups, our attention focuses briefly on another large area of group stereotyping on television, namely, various occupational groups. Many of us, including children and adolescents, use television and movies as a major source of information about careers and occupations (Gehrau, Brüggemann, & Handrup, 2016; Wright *et al.*, 1995; Wroblewski & Huston, 1987). However, such TV portrayals are often inaccurate.

Nevertheless, the presence of positive media models in certain occupations can greatly increase the numbers of those entering that profession. For example, the number of medical school applicants surged sharply from 1962 to 1963, apparently due to the debuts of the popular medical TV dramas *Dr. Kildare* and *Ben Casey* (Goldberg, 1988). The number of journalism students mushroomed after the Watergate scandal of the early 1970s, when investigative reporters had become heroes, especially with movie portrayals such as *All the President's Men* starring Robert Redford and Dustin Hoffman. More recently, the number of college students wanting to go into forensic science has skyrocketed with the advent of TV shows like the *CSI* series (see Close-up 5.7). Although the number of such actual jobs is minuscule, students often do not realize that. Effects of media portrayals of occupational groups are not always so dramatic, however. We examine a few especially interesting groups and see how the media present these professions.

> ### ❖ CLOSE-UP 5.7 THE CSI EFFECT: HAVE TV FORENSIC SHOWS AFFECTED JUROR VERDICTS?
>
> *One particularly interesting way that media may influence perceptions of reality concerns the area of forensic science in criminal investigations. Since 2000, several prime-time TV shows (at one point 8 out of the top 20 shows) have been police forensic science dramas, most notably the CSI franchise. Many prosecutors and judges are growing concerned that jurors are failing to convict defendants with strong evidence against them because of a lack of DNA evidence of the sort that exists in the TV shows but often is absent in real life. Has there been such a change in verdicts, or is this impression purely anecdotal? In spite of the widespread concern, controlled scientific studies have so far largely failed to confirm such an effect on juror verdicts, although work is continuing, even in countries like China, where such shows are popular (Hawkins & Scherr, 2017; Houck, 2006; Hui & Lo, 2017; Tyler, 2006).*
>
> *Even if the CSI shows are not directly affecting verdicts, they are clearly having huge effects in other ways. For one thing, police are gathering much more physical evidence than they used to, often hundreds of items, which are placing large burdens on the overworked minimal staff to analyze and store all this material. For example, the shows have higher tech equipment than the real world does, and jurors may not always understand that. One forensic scientist estimated that 40% of the forensic science on CSI does not exist in real life (Houck, 2006). Finally, enrollment in forensic science programs in universities has exploded since 2000. For example, the program at West Virginia University had four graduates in 2000 but six years later was the third largest major on campus, with over 500 students! Now, WVU offers Bachelor's, Master's, and Ph.D. degrees in forensic and investigative science. Criminal forensic science is an area most people have had little or no life experience in; these TV shows have stepped in to become the reality.*

Lawyers, Judges, and Courtroom Trials

Some controversy has arisen around realistic courtroom TV shows like *Divorce Court*, *Hot Bench*, and *The People's Court*. All of these present legal proceedings, either dramatizations of real cases (*Divorce Court*) or actual court proceedings (*The People's*

Court, Judge Judy). In shows like *The People's Court*, an actual judge presides over small claims court cases in which both parties agreed to have their case settled on the show in lieu of a more traditional setting. The cases are real, as are all parties in those cases. On the one hand, such shows have been praised for making the court system more available to the public, who now can better understand how this phase of our judicial system functions. In fact, the number of small claims cases rose considerably after the advent of *The People's Court* in the 1980s, although not necessarily because of that show. Speaking to this point, however, critics argue that many such cases are frivolous and that these shows trivialize the legal system by making impatient judges (and sometimes pseudo-judges) TV stars. Chief among these is Judith Sheindlin of the highly rated *Judge Judy*, who seems to delight in sassy one-liners such as, "You spent $72 getting your hair done? You wasted your money!" (IMDB, 2012). Some court personnel report that litigants in many courtrooms have become more contentious, dramatic, and emotional in court, apparently following the model of the parties on shows like *The People's Court*. Is the public well served by such shows? Do we have a more accurate perception of how courts function or is our reality colored by some "Hollywoodization" of the courtroom by the producers of these real-life judicial programs?

What is the effect of such shows on people's knowledge and beliefs about lawyers? Cultivation theory would predict that such knowledge in heavy TV viewers would come to approximate the image of occupations presented on TV. Using this framework, Pfau, Mullen, Deidrich, and Garrow (1995) examined prime-time portrayals of lawyers and the public perception about attorneys. They found that public perceptions were affected in the direction of the TV portrayal, which in this case, interestingly enough, was more positive than expected. More recently, Shniderman (2014) has argued that the long-running *Law and Order* franchise has skewed public opinion of lawyers, particularly defense attorneys, as "slick shysters" who battle against hard-working cops (rather than upholding defendants' constitutional rights). Others (e.g., Thaler, 1994) argue that television cameras in the courtroom are turning trials into entertainment, something they have never tried to be before.

Psychologists and Psychiatrists

Other highly stereotyped careers in entertainment media are the helping professions, including psychiatry, clinical psychology, marriage and family therapy, and counseling, which are generally not distinguished from each other in entertainment. As with other professions, viewers seem to get a good deal of their knowledge about psychologists from TV and movies (McDonald, Wantz, & Firmin, 2014). According to one study, 17% of Hollywood movies contained at least one helping professional (Young, Boester, Whitt, & Stevens, 2008). Sometimes the therapist is a source of humor (*Frasier*, *What About Bob?*, *The Bob Newhart Show*, various movies by director Woody Allen). Very often professional boundaries are violated, most blatantly by the therapist character having sex with his or her patients (*Prince of Tides*, *Basic Instinct*, *Eyes Wide Shut*). Other boundary violations include physically assaulting a patient (*Good Will Hunting*), making fun of patients (*Frasier*, *What About Bob?*), violating confidentiality (*Silver Linings Playbook*), being a socially repressive force (*One Flew Over the Cuckoo's Nest*), and perhaps most alarming of all, being severely disturbed oneself (*Silence of the Lambs*, *Anger Management*, *Web Therapy*) (Bischoff & Reiter, 1999; Dine Young, 2012; Gabbard & Gabbard, 1999; Young et al., 2008). Is it any wonder that many people who need help are reluctant to seek it if this is their image of those who provide it?

However, there are also some positive and realistic images scattered out there. The therapists portrayed in *The Sixth Sense* and *The Sopranos* have won high marks, and perhaps the all-time best cinematic portrayal was Judd Hirsch's Dr. Berger in the 1980 Oscar-winning film *Ordinary People*. Of even more concern than fictional portrayals, though, are media therapists like Dr. Phil (McGraw) and Dr. Drew (Pinsky) who actually do some semblance of psychotherapy on the air. Although sometimes the therapist is qualified (Dr. Phil has a Ph.D. in psychology, Dr. Drew has an MD), and the therapy is well-motivated (Dr. Phil has off-air follow-up therapy for his clients), television is at heart an entertainment medium with all the attendant pressures of ratings. Thus the "therapy" by these real "Frasier Cranes" must first and foremost be entertaining to the audience. This goal is utterly inconsistent with competent psychotherapy, which requires thoughtful reflection, privacy, and freedom from an audience. Amusing one-line zingers, dramatic on-air confrontations, and pat answers do not treat mental illness. If the public learns that this is what therapy is, that may be just as harmful as the distorted fictional portrayals. Indeed, such portrayals may have important consequences; Maier and colleagues (Maier, Gentile, Vogel, & Kaplan, 2014) found that people's experiences with media psychologists influenced their perceptions of real-world psychological professionals and those who seek therapy.

Farmers and Rural Life

As a rule, farmers and rural life in general are not highly visible in media, although the few rural TV shows have been among the most extremely stereotyped and unrealistic in the history of the airwaves. In earlier days, it was *The Beverly Hillbillies* and *Green Acres*, then *Hee Haw* and *The Dukes of Hazzard*. Today, we have the occasional view of Cameron's extended rural kin on *Modern Family*, complete with many pig jokes. All of these shows have portrayed rural people as uneducated, stupid rubes totally lacking in worldly experience and common sense. True, there was also *The Waltons*, perhaps the most popular rural show of all time, but its historical setting detracted from its use as a model of modern rural life. Many, if not most, of the farm shows have been set in rural Appalachia, one of the poorest and most atypical of rural regions nationwide.

This stereotype is not limited to television. Use of Grant Wood's American Gothic-type figures in advertising reflects an archaic stereotype. The popular comic strip Garfield occasionally features Jon Arbuckle's farming parents who come to visit him in the city wearing overalls and not knowing how to use indoor plumbing and other modern conveniences. Much humor is based on the fact that there is nothing to do on the farm except count the bricks in the silo. The relatively few films set in rural America often have people speaking in southern drawls, even if the setting is Montana or Michigan. Sometimes one sees rather silly rural symbols, such as a tractor driving down Main Street, used to remind us that we are not in a city.

Problems facing the profession of agriculture have typically been underreported in the news, probably because complex issues like the farm debt crisis of the 1980s or the worldwide food shortages of the 2000s are difficult to encapsulate into a brief TV or newspaper story. Also, the people involved with producing media are virtually 100% urban, usually from New York or Los Angeles or other large cities, with no roots or connections to any rural community.

College Students

Finally, let us consider the occupation of most of the readers of this book. According to movies, television shows, and advertising, how do college students spend their time? Perhaps foremost is drinking lots of beer and partying into the wee hours. Sometimes wildly excessive and destructive behaviors are presented as normal and amusing as in the movies *Animal House*, *Revenge of the Nerds*, and *Neighbors*. Advertising provides other examples. For instance, a phone company ad targeted at college students showed a fellow passed out on his bathroom floor after celebrating his 21st birthday by binge drinking. By presenting this sort of behavior as normal, such marketing could encourage binge drinking and all its serious consequences. Second, one would think from ads in university newspapers that almost everybody takes a spring break trip to some beach community where there is lots of fun, sex, and alcohol. Where is the studying or students' struggle to earn enough money for next month's rent? Where is the volunteer work? Where is the search for a job after graduation?

Does it matter? People in some communities have limited personal interaction with college students, and therefore, this media image becomes reality. One student reported that she had trouble finding a summer job back in her hometown because no one wanted to hire college students, thinking they would be constantly partying and would not be responsible workers. See Conklin (2008) for a thorough examination of the image of college students in American movies from the silent era through the new millennium.

Conclusion: So What If They're Stereotyped?

The concern about group portrayals may extend to any sort of group; the ones we have discussed are only some of the most maligned and most studied. Many other groups still struggle with achieving a balanced and realistic treatment from television and other media. We have talked a lot in this chapter about rather narrow and negative portrayals from media. But what is the impact? Many variables may moderate the effects of stereotyped portrayals. For example, it might be that comedy neutralizes some of the negative portrayals that would otherwise be considerably more offensive (Park, Gabbadon, & Chernin, 2006).

Although we have already discussed some effects of research in regard to gender and ethnic images, we close here with a few controlled experiments (Murphy, 1998; Slater, 1990). Murphy (1998) exposed people to either a gender-stereotypical or counter-stereotypical fictional or factual portrayal of a person. Subsequent (apparently unrelated) judgments about different people were affected by exposure to the previous portrayal. Particularly for men, exposure to the stereotypical portrayals led to less credibility given to different women in sexual harassment and acquaintance rape cases. It did not matter much whether the stereotype was a factual or fictitious person. Counter-stereotypical portrayals had the opposite effect, though it was not as strong. Slater (1990) presented people with information about some social group. The information was attributed to fiction (from a novel) or nonfiction (from a news magazine) and was about a group that was either familiar or unfamiliar to the participants. If the group was unfamiliar, the fictional portrayal actually was *more* influential in forming beliefs than was the nonfictional portrayal, whereas the reverse was true for the familiar group. This suggests the great power of fictional portrayals on knowledge and attitude formation, especially when life experience with the group in question is lacking. In a more applied study, Gillig and colleagues (Gillig, Rosenthal, Murphy, & Folb, 2018) demonstrated that regular viewers of a transgender storyline on the show *Royal Pains* had increased supportive attitudes toward transgender people. In fact, the more positive portrayals of transgender people that viewers saw, the more positive their opinions were; this effect held true even for socially conservative viewers.

For the groups described in this chapter, media are major, perhaps the predominant, sources of information for most of us. However, they are usually not the only source; there is often at least some reality to temper the media image. Thus, the perceived reality that our minds construct will not be totally taken from media, although it may be very heavily influenced by it. Occasionally, however, media may be the only source of information. Consider the example of prostitutes. Practically all adults know what prostitutes are and could give some basic facts about them (what they do, what they look like, why they are doing it). Few readers of this book, however, have probably ever known a real prostitute. Where does our perceived reality about prostitutes come from? In most cases it comes not mostly, or partly, but entirely, from television and movies. The garishly dressed TV hooker standing on the street corner in the short skirt, high heels, and too much makeup is the reality of prostitutes, as far as most of us know. We might describe someone we see dressed this way as "looking like a hooker." But is this what hookers really look like, or is it just the way media portray them? Even as the authors of this book, we honestly do not know the answer. All we know is what we see in movies. If we were to meet a woman tomorrow who was identified as a prostitute, the media stereotype (schema) would come to mind to guide the processing of information about this woman. It would not matter if that image was accurate or not. It would be the perceived reality. This is what is happening with children growing up learning from television about groups of people. Many children have had no more personal contact with Arabs, Jews, African Americans, Latinos, farmers, lesbians, or college students than their exposure in the media. This is why stereotypes matter.

Media Applications, Chapter 5: Responding to Media Stereotypes

As we have seen, many forms of media stereotype many different groups of people. As we also know, sometimes the media "reality" can also become our own reality. So what can be done? A few authors and researchers have some advice.

Dealing with Stereotypes in the Home

Durham (2009) argues that parents of children and adolescents, particularly daughters, should have ongoing discussions about how females are portrayed in media depictions. Specifically, she offers a number of strategies for steering conversations with children when they encounter "sexy" images of girls and women. For instance, it's a good idea to "look at the myth together," asking kids to think about whether they think the image is appealing and how/why the media producers are presenting it as attractive. It's also important for children to examine any accompanying text descriptors like "hot" or "sexy" and get them to think about what other areas of life are left out of these labels (such as school, athletics, art, family, friends, and spirituality). Durham also advises parents to direct children's analysis of these images to colors and how they may draw attention. It's also a good idea to talk to kids about how advertising and marketing often underlie these images—for example, when a fashion magazine presents features or articles that are really just ads. Finally, Durham suggests asking children about their emotional responses to the images. For example, how did it make them feel about women? How does it make them feel about themselves and their friends? One could imagine that Durham's strategies could also be applied to our interactions with media images of various other groups discussed in this chapter.

Some research studies also offer some insight. For example, Veldhuis, Konijn, and Seidell (2014) conducted an interesting study on adolescent girls' responses to very thin fashion models. When they showed some adolescent girls in the Netherlands images of thin models that included the informational label, "These models are underweight," those girls had lower levels of personal body dissatisfaction than girls who saw photos with no labels. This effect was especially strong with girls who had low self-esteem. Girls exposed to the informational labels also had fewer issues with body image than girls who were presented with photos of thin models that included warning labels like, "These models are underweight. Unconsciously, exposure to media models may negatively impact your self-image." This may have been due to a reactance effect, in which when told *how* they are going to react, people sometimes do the opposite. The implications from this study, combined with Durham's suggestions, indicate that pointing out and discussing stereotyped media images may have a strong, protective effect on how youth feel about themselves.

Influencing the Media

Beyond the powerful, interpersonal conversations that adults can have with children about media stereotypes, there are actions that can be taken to influence the media themselves. Very often, when we critically examine media, we are left with the feeling that there is much that we do not like, for whatever reason, but that there is little we can do about that state of affairs other than to choose not to use that medium. Just as we cognitively interact with the medium in understanding it, so can we behaviorally interact with it to help effect change in desired ways. Commercial and political interests have long been doing this, and it behooves concerned and interested individual media consumers to learn to do likewise.

Individual complaints can have disproportionate impact, in that those who receive them assume that each complaint represents a similar view of many others who did not comment. Certain types of letters, e-mails, online comments, or blog entries are more effective than others. A reasoned, logically argued case has a lot more impact than an angry tirade. For example, one brand of club cocktails once advertised in *Ms* magazine with the slogan "Hit me with a Club." The company received over 1,000 letters of protest, arguing that the ad implied acceptance of violence toward women. They responded that such a connection was never intended or imagined, yet editors were concerned enough by the letters to withdraw the ad (Will, 1987). Complaints do make a difference! Letters from a Michigan homemaker and her supporters concerned about negative family values once caused Kimberly-Clark, McDonald's, and other sponsors to pull their ads from the show *Married with Children*. Protests from some parents about the marketing of thong underwear printed with the words "eye candy" and "wink wink" to 10-year-old girls convinced Abercrombie and Fitch to stop selling these items

(Carlsson-Paige, 2008). See Close-up 5.8 for an example of a marketing campaign that offended people and was withdrawn due to their complaints.

❖ CLOSE-UP 5.8 CASE STUDY OF A MARKETING CAMPAIGN KILLED BY COMPLAINTS

In 2011 JC Penney and Forever 21 began marketing shirts to young girls featuring the slogans "I'm too pretty to do homework, so my brother has to do it for me" or "Allergic to Algebra." Various women's groups and the progressive Internet movement Credo Action mobilized a writing and petition-signing campaign against what it claimed were sexist messages. Their message was heard, when JC Penney CEO Myron Ullman responded to Credo, "JC Penney used this incident as a 'teachable moment' for our buying teams ... fully understand their responsibility in upholding the integrity of our company and share with you their commitment to ensuring better merchandise decisions in the future. We agree that the 'Too Pretty' T-shirt does not deliver an appropriate message, and we have immediately discontinued its sale ... We would like to apologize to our customers." Public complaints do make a difference.

This was not the first such sexist marketing gaffe. A 1992 talking Barbie doll whined "Math class is tough" before Mattel modified its message. Other questionable messages on girls' T-shirts have included "Future Trophy Wife" and "Who Needs Brains When You Have These?" both of which were killed by complaints from the public.

These days, some have harnessed the power of social media for positive benefit. These online "influencers," who have many followers, maximize their social media platforms to get people to think about, and perhaps change, their perceptions. For example, Em Ford, who has roughly one million Instagram and YouTube followers, frequently posts beauty tips. However, she also has posted many pictures of herself without makeup and has made a video challenging some of the negative comments she received. This turned into a larger online conversation on the unrealistic media expectations about beauty (Berg, 2017). However we respond to media, we certainly don't need to be a victim of it.

Further Reading

Douglas, W. (2003). *Television families: Is something wrong in suburbia?* New York: Routledge.

Durham, M. G. (2009). *The Lolita effect: The media sexualization of young girls and what we can do about it.* Woodstock, NY: Overlook Press.

Grau, S. L., & Zotos, Y. C. (2016). Gender stereotypes in advertising: A review of current research. *International Journal of Advertising*, 35(5), 761–770. doi: 10.1080/02650487.2016.1203556

Meyers, M. (2013). *African American women in the news: Gender, race, and class in journalism.* New York: Routledge.

Moseley, R., Wheatley, H., & Wood, H. (Eds.). (2017). *Television for women: New directions.* New York: Routledge.

Rodan, D., Ellis, K., & Lebek, P. (2014). *Disability, obesity, and ageing: Popular media identification.* Farnham: Ashgate Publishing.

Tukachinsky, R., Mastro, D., & Yarchi, M. (2015). Documenting portrayals of race/ethnicity on primetime television over a 20-year span and their association with national-level racial/ethnic attitudes: TV portrayals and national-level attitudes. *Journal of Social Issues*, 71(1), 17–38. doi: 10.1111/josi.12094

Wedding, D., & Niemiec, R. M. (2014). *Movies and mental illness: Using films to understand psychopathology*. 4th ed. Boston, MA: Hogrefe.

Winston, D. H. (Ed.). (2009). *Small screen, big picture: Television and lived religion*. Waco, TX: Baylor University Press.

Useful Links

Killing Us Softly 4 (advertising and women) trailer:
www.youtube.com/watch?annotation_id=annotation_493134379&feature=iv&src_vid=PTlmho_RovY&v=jWKXit_3rpQ

Resources for responding to media depictions of groups, especially women:
www.jeankilbourne.com/resources/

Some historical Aunt Jemima depictions:
http://gawker.com/397129/just-how-racist-was-aunt-jemima

TV tropes:
http://tvtropes.org/

For more resources, please visit the companion website:
www.routledge.com/cw/harris

Chapter 6

Advertising

Baiting, Catching, and Reeling Us In

Q: When did the first TV commercial air?

A: During a 1940 baseball game on WBNT-TV in New York. The ad was for Bulova watches (Sivulka, 1998).

Q: How many commercials do children see every year?

A: About 25,000–40,000 on television, a large majority of them for unhealthy food like candy and sugary cereals. Online, more than 80% of websites aimed at children contain advertising (Cai & Zhao, 2010; Common Sense Media, 2014; Kaiser Family Foundation, 2007).

Q: How much does advertising cost?

A: Corporate advertisers paid around $5 million for a 30-second spot during the 2018 Super Bowl. Regular season evening NFL games charge about $500,000 for a spot. In terms of a regular series, the highest-priced ad was $2 million for a 30-second spot on the final episode of the sitcom *Friends* in 2004. The finales of *Everybody Loves Raymond* in 2005 and *The Oprah Winfrey Show* in 2011 charged around $1 million per commercial (Goldberg, 2018; Steinberg, 2016).

Q: Did Elliott's use of Reese's Pieces candies to lure *E.T.* in the 1982 movie have any effect on candy sales?

A: The original plan was to feature M&Ms in the movie, but the Mars Company declined. Hershey's jumped at the chance, and sales of its Reese's Pieces rose 65% after their appearance in the movie (Rimmer, 2002).

The bottom line of media is advertising. With the exception of public television and radio and premium cable networks such as HBO, most television channels in the United States are almost 100% dependent on ad revenues for financial support. Newspapers have traditionally derived around 70% of their revenue from advertising, although as discussed in Chapter 1, this revenue source is declining. Magazines sometimes sell subscriptions below cost simply to raise the readership rate to allow them to charge higher advertising rates. The Internet is increasingly dependent on advertising revenue for support, particularly social media sites like Facebook and Twitter

(Swant, 2017). Everything in media except advertising costs money, whereas advertising brings in all the money. This simple fact explains much of the content of the media. Ultimately it is the advertiser, not the audience, who must be pleased, although when audiences become unhappy enough, they can definitely influence advertisers (see the Media Applications section at the end of this chapter as well as at the end of Chapter 5).

In spite of the tremendous costs of producing ads and buying time (or space) to broadcast (or print or post) them, advertising is still a remarkably efficient and inexpensive way to reach the buying public. Because of the huge size of the audience for highly rated TV shows, for example, the cost per viewer is often in the neighborhood of a quarter to a half a cent per ad. These, of course, only include the purchase of air time; production costs are extra. On a smaller scale, local newspaper and radio ads are far more reasonable in cost but still quite effectively reach the target area of interest to the advertiser. Perhaps the cheapest of all to produce and distribute are Internet ads, which can yield enormous profits. For example, Facebook reaped over $9 billion from ads in just one quarter in 2017 (Swant, 2017).

Advertising makes very heavy use of psychology, and the study of the psychology of advertising could easily fill an entire book. This chapter examines certain aspects of the perceived reality created by advertising but is by no means a comprehensive examination of its effects. After some initial introductory and historical material, we consider some psychological appeals in advertising, followed by a more specifically cognitive examination of ads, especially the issue of deceptive advertising, in which the perceived reality is at particular odds with objective reality. Next we examine how sexual appeals are used to build a reality of positive feelings and associations about a product. In this section we also consider the issue of subliminal advertising, which is claimed to affect us without our awareness. Then, we look specifically at advertising directed to children and adolescents, one of the fastest-growing demographic markets, in terms of amount of disposable income. Finally, we examine the many newer places where advertising appears, literally infiltrating all corners of our lives. It has become increasingly difficult to separate advertising from the more general category of marketing, because, while advertising traditionally has been restricted to mass media, it is increasingly appearing in different places which are not quite media, but are definitely marketing (Gibson, Redker, & Zimmerman, 2014; Stewart, Pavlou, & Ward, 2002).

One surprisingly difficult aspect of studying advertising is how to definitively answer the most important question about it, namely, does it work? Because there are so many other influences besides advertising that may affect a purchase decision, it is very difficult to design a critical experiment to test if an ad has the desired effect or not. Thus, surprisingly, actual purchase behavior is measured relatively infrequently. Rather, more indirect measures such as purchase intention, attitude toward the product or the ad, and belief about performance of the product are typically used. See Dillard, Weber, and Vail (2007) and Hornik, Ofir, and Rachamim (2016) for meta-analyses and discussion of the effectiveness of persuasive messages.

Historical Background

The earliest known written advertisement, from around 1000 BC in Thebes, Greece, offered a "whole gold coin" for the return of a runaway slave. Advertisements in mass communication did not really exist before Gutenberg's invention of movable type in the mid-fifteenth century, however. Newspapers started carrying ads regularly in the mid-1600s. The rapid commercial growth associated with the Industrial Revolution in the nineteenth century gave great impetus to advertising, as did the rise of magazines during this same period, when transportation infrastructure, especially railroads, allowed the distribution of national publications for the first time, particularly across a large country like the United States (see Close-up 6.1 for a brief account of the history of marketing personal hygiene products, which advertising helped establish as an everyday "necessity"). The rise of radio after 1920, television after 1945, cable TV in the 1970s and 1980s, the Internet in the 1990s, and social media in the 2000s provided expanding new outlets for advertising dollars and creativity.

❖ CLOSE-UP 6.1 PERSONAL HYGIENE PRODUCTS: A BASIC NECESSITY OR A MARKETING CREATION?

The history of personal hygiene products and how they have been marketed, particularly in the United States, is an interesting study in advertising and persuasion. Of course, if one goes back far enough in history, even the most basic hygiene product, soap, was non-existent. However, eventually the utility of cleaning agents became apparent, and home-grown recipes for soap developed. When soap first began to be sold in stores, it was usually broken off a large cake and sold by the pound. In the early days, there was no distinction between hand, laundry, dish, or body soaps (Sivulka, 2001). That all changed, however, when it was discovered that a market could be created for brand name soaps. "Along with patent medicine manufacturers, early soap makers pioneered the merchandising and packaging of brand-name goods ... Manufacturers also recognized that they could charge a higher price for goods with memorable brand names and attractive packaging" (Sivulka, 2001, p. 72). This led to soap being among the first nationally marketed products around 1900, with companies like Procter and Gamble and Palmolive devoting large advertising budgets to convince consumers, mostly women, to buy their products. Early ads ran in magazines such as Good Housekeeping and Ladies Home Journal (Sivulka, 2001) that targeted women. At the time, advertisers considered women easy targets whose "minds were vats of frothy pink irrationality" (Parkin, 2006, p. 15).

Over the years, advertising strategies for soap changed, from appeals to beauty and sex (beginning in the 1910s) to patriotism (around the time of World War I) to playing on health concerns and fear of germs (1920s–1940s) (Sivulka, 2001). Deodorant was first marketed to women in the 1920s as a way to protect against men perceiving them as smelly and unattractive. By 1935, advertisers realized that they could also market deodorant to men, playing on Great Depression era insecurities like fears of losing a job due to perspiration odors (Engber, 2014; Everts, 2012). Personal hygiene products were even marketed as an important marker of social status, with those who bought and used the products portrayed as being of a higher class. For example, a 1927 ad stated, "The Safe Solution of Women's Greatest Hygienic Problem, over 80% of the better class of women in America today employ Kotex" (Sivulka, 1998, p. 163).

Beginning in the 1920s, advertisers also focused consumers on making a good first impression by protecting against "halitosis" (bad breath) and "b.o." (body odor). Both of these *serious sounding afflictions were invented by manufacturers and advertisers (halitosis by Listerine and b.o. by Lifebuoy Soap) to help instill a sense of need for the products. It worked. Most Americans today would not dream of going on a first date, a job interview, or even leaving the house with conditions such as b.o. or halitosis. According to Sivulka, "Nationally advertised, brand-name soap, toiletries, and even bathrooms made their way from seldom-used luxuries to necessities of American life in a remarkably short period of time—less than 65 years spanning the period between 1875 and 1940" (2001, p. 291). By the 2010s, the deodorant industry alone was worth over $18 billion (Everts, 2012).*

Of course, because it was the first electronic medium, the first electronic ads appeared on radio. Although there were early experiments with radio by Marconi in Italy in the 1890s and DeForest in the United States in 1906, the first radio station was set up in 1919 in a Pittsburgh garage by some Westinghouse engineers. Station KDKA broadcast the 1920 presidential election results. There were 30 stations on the air by the end of 1920 and 400 by 1922. Ensuing concerns and debate about how to finance this new medium culminated in the Radio Act of 1927 for licensing and control of radio stations. This legislation established the free enterprise model to pay for radio; that is, total revenue would come from the sale of advertising time with no government subsidy. At about the same time, Great Britain made a very different decision in establishing the BBC, which is funded by television/radio license fees paid by consumers. Both of these economic models were carried over from radio to television in the late 1940s and still frame much broadcasting in their respective societies, although the United States now has some public broadcasting and Britain has had commercial television since the 1960s. One or the other of these two economic models of broadcasting has since been adopted by most of the countries of the world, although exceptions can be found online. Internet radio, with services like Pandora and Spotify, are increasingly popular. Many of these are supported with some combination of ad revenue and subscriptions.

Types of Ads

Advertising is the one type of communication most clearly designed to persuade (i.e., have some effect on the media consumer). This effect may be behavioral (buy the product), attitudinal (like the product), or cognitive (learn something about the product). Ads may be for particular categories of products (e.g., milk, cheese, beef, cotton), brands of products (e.g., Coca-Cola, Nike, Toyota), but also for services or businesses (e.g., banks, plumbers, dentists).

Frequently, the most direct purpose of an ad is not selling as such but rather *image building* or *good will*. For example, when a multinational corporation spends 30 seconds on TV telling us how it provides scholarships for underprivileged youth, it is trying to encourage viewers to think of it as a fine, upstanding corporate citizen. This is done by associating the company with very positive images. Image-building advertising is especially prevalent after a corporation or industry has received a public relations black eye, such as the 2010 BP oil spill in the Gulf of Mexico or when a passenger was dragged off a United Airlines plane in 2017. It also is common when a corporation tries to become involved in consciousness-raising on some issue of importance and public interest, such as when a distillery runs an ad encouraging people not to drive drunk. They believe that the good will they achieve by being perceived as taking a responsible public position will more than offset any decline in sales arising from people buying less of their product due to concern about driving under the influence.

A different kind of persuasive media message is the *public service announcement (PSA)*, usually sponsored by some government agency or nonprofit organization, or coordinated by the nonprofit Ad Council. Historically, the U.S. Federal Communications Commission (FCC) has mandated that radio and TV stations must offer free time for PSAs but does not usually specify when that time must be aired; thus PSAs frequently air heavily at off-peak hours like late at night, early in the morning or during weekday afternoons. With the deregulation and weakening of U.S. regulatory agencies starting in the 1980s, the placement and frequency of PSAs suffered even more.

A final kind of advertising is *political advertising*, usually designed to persuade viewers to support some candidate, party, or issue. In many ways political advertising is very similar to commercial advertising, although there are some important differences. Political advertising is considered in Chapter 8 and thus is not discussed further in this chapter.

All types of ads try to affect the reality perceived by the consumer (i.e., give us a new image of a product, candidate, or company or make us feel we have a need or desire for some product). Such processes involve attempts to change our behaviors by first changing our attitudes.

Our attitudes about products (or anything else, really) consist of three components. The *belief* or *cognition* is the informational content of the attitude. For example, Kyle prefers Toyota cars because of certain features they have. The *affective* (emotional) content of the attitude is the feeling toward that product. Kyle prefers Toyotas because he trusts them, likes them, and feels safe with them. Finally, the *action* is the attitude's translation into behavior. In the case of ads, the advertiser typically hopes the final step in the chain will be a purchase; in our example, Toyota hopes that its advertising has created the right beliefs and emotions in Kyle that will translate into him actually buying a Toyota himself. However, some ads are designed primarily to influence our beliefs, and others are designed to influence our emotions.

Psychological Appeals in Advertising

Any type of advertising uses a variety of psychological appeals to reach the viewer. In one way or another, ads attempt to tie the product or service to our deep and basic psychological needs. Implicitly, then, the message is that buying the product will do more than give us something useful or pleasant; it can help us be better people as well.

Informational Appeals

Although not the most common appeal, some ads primarily provide information in an attempt to influence the belief component of our attitudes. A good example of this type would be an ad for a new product; such an ad may explain in some detail what that product does, what its features are, and how those features differ from those of existing products. For instance, there was a strong push to advertise sanitizing cleaning wipes in the 2000s and explain how they were more convenient and hygienic than existing cleaners (Haruko Smith, 2012).

Some of the most common belief appeals are exhortations to save money or time, receive a superior product or service, and/or take advantage of sales. The feeling that we are getting a good bargain is a powerful motivator in deciding to purchase something. It is so powerful that often the official list prices are set artificially high so that products may be advertised as costing considerably less, when in fact they may have never been intended to sell at the full list price. *Framing* (Entman, 1993) is also very important. For instance, advertising a discount or offering a coupon for some amount off the price is more appealing than saying the price goes up after some time, even if the cost the consumer actually pays is the same. For example, most people prefer to receive a discount of $3 off the regular price of $30 for paying early than to pay a penalty of $3 on top of a regular price of $27 for being late, even though in both cases they are paying $27 on time or $30 if late (Kahneman, 2011). Cialdini (2006) has similarly proposed that believing that a product, especially at a particular price, is in scarce supply ("Hurry! This offer ends soon!") compels us to want that product all the more (see Cialdini, 2006, for other principles of influence).

Emotional Appeals

Frequently, ads appeal to the emotional component of our attitudes. Influencing emotions is often the best first step to influencing beliefs and, ultimately, behavior. For example, there are many ads that appeal to our love of friends, family, and good times and the good feelings that they bring us. We are asked to buy diamonds, flowers, and even cars to show how much we care, and drink certain beverages with friends as part of sharing a good time. Such classic slogans as, "Love. It's what makes a Subaru, a Subaru," or "Friends are worth Smirnoff" illustrate such appeals. The message is conveyed that products are an integral part of showing our love and caring for others. As with movies and TV shows, sometimes "moving music" can enhance this emotional effect (Strick, de Bruin, de Ruiter, & Jonkers, 2015). Emotional appeals have been especially targeted at women, who presumably can show love for their families by buying food products (e.g., "Put a little love in lunch with Skippy") (Parkin, 2006); also see Close-up 5.2 for a discussion of how motherhood has been marketed. The more closely the advertiser can link the product with the natural and positive emotions of love and interpersonal connection, the more successful the ad. A baby food company once advertised that it helped babies learn to chew. Such an appeal links the product with a very basic developmental event in the baby's life, thus giving it a much more central role in the child's growth than any mere product, even an excellent product, would have. Similarly, a car advertises itself as "part of the family," not merely offering something to the family but actually being a member of it.

Closely related to family and love appeals is the linking of the product with fun. This is especially clear in ads for soft drinks and beer and almost anything marketed directly to children. Photography and copy that link images of a product with people having a good time at the beach or the ski lodge, or just relaxing at home with friends, encourage people to think about that product whenever they have or anticipate having such times. For example, Corona has had an advertising campaign for years associating their beer with the beach, Adirondack chairs, and relaxing on vacation. The product becomes an integral part of that activity, and, more importantly, of the positive feelings associated with that activity. Watching a sports event on TV with friends may naturally cause us to seek that advertised product (such as beer), which has become part of the event.

Certain cultural symbols have also come to evoke warm feelings in viewers, which advertisers hope will transfer to warm feelings about the product. A boy and his dog, grandma baking a pie, the national flag, or a family homecoming are examples. For instance, for years Folgers coffee has run a series of commercials during the Christmas season depicting various family members (a college student son, a Peace Corps volunteer brother, a visiting grandmother) returning home for the holidays and waking their family with the fresh smell of brewing coffee. Such symbols appear frequently in advertising of all sorts. Connecting a product with the positive feelings that people have for such symbols can associate a lot of positive emotion with that product. Even the name of the product can evoke certain feelings, perhaps connected with a particular culture or country (see Close-up 6.2).

❖ CLOSE-UP 6.2 CHALLENGES AND PITFALLS IN CHOOSING INTERNATIONAL PRODUCT NAMES AND SLOGANS

Selecting the name for a new product or service may be more complicated than you realize. When a new cereal, car, or smartphone app comes on the market, companies often employ creative people to help them choose just the right name that will perfectly fit the product and stick in the minds of consumers. In fact, there are now companies that specialize in such services, running research studies and trademark searches to figure out which product names will be the best (Gabler, 2015). Things get more complicated for products that will be sold internationally. So, if you want to choose a foreign name for your product, how do you do that? The reality is more complicated than simply finding a real foreign word in some appropriate language (e.g., French for a perfume, Spanish for a tortilla, Norwegian for skis). It has to be a word that, for example, looks French to people who don't know any French. The American clothing brand Le Tigré, for instance, added the accent to the real French word for tiger ("tigre," with no accent). In doing so, they made the word less French in fact, but made it look more French to English speakers, who know that French uses accents and English doesn't. In another example, Häagen-Dazs ice cream has always been American but chose its unusual name "to convey an aura of old-world tradition and craftsmanship," according to the company's website. In reality, the words in the name don't mean anything in any language.

Reactions to foreign product names vary a lot depending on the product and the country (Chang, 2004; Harris, Garner-Earl, Sprick, & Carroll, 1994; Hong & Wyer, 1989, 1990). Perhaps the area of greatest danger comes in the chance that a brand name means something quite different in the language of a target market. When advertising its 1970s Pinto subcompact in Brazil, Ford discovered belatedly that pinto is a vulgar term for small penis in Brazilian Portuguese. Only after their introduction in Germany was it learned that the facial tissue brand name Puffs is slang for whorehouse. For a short time, the Japanese were puzzled why their popular soft drink Calpis (pronounced "cow-piss") did not sell well in a U.S. test market, where it was a vulgar expression for cattle urine. Similarly, brand name changes for the American market might be in order for the Iranian detergent Barf, the Mexican bread Bimbo, the Uruguayan real estate company Yucky, the Japanese drink Sweat, or Pee Cola from Ghana.

English advertising slogans are also sometimes lost in translation. For example, Perdue chicken's tagline, "It takes a tough man to make a tender chicken" ended up on Mexican billboards in Spanish as, "It takes a hard man to make a chicken aroused." For a time, Coors used the slogan, "Turn it loose." In Spanish, it came out as, "Suffer from diarrhea." In Chinese, Kentucky Fried Chicken's famous slogan "finger lickin' good" came out as "eat your fingers off" (James, 2014; Sivulka, 1998).

Occasionally, names of products can be changed in the short-term in response to political whims. For example, during the anti-German frenzy of World War I Americans took to calling sauerkraut "liberty cabbage," frankfurters and wieners "hot dogs," and hamburgers "liberty sandwiches." Such silliness is not purely a historical relic from the distant past. In 2003, after France refused to support President George W. Bush's invasion of Iraq, the U.S. House of Representatives cafeteria began serving "freedom fries" instead of French fries (Rawson, 2003).

Perhaps the most effective selling pitch focuses on how the product will affect one's individual psychological well-being and deep-seated personal needs. For example, a camera ad once said, "Look how good you can be" using the camera, not simply "Look what good pictures you can take." The product goes beyond merely providing the buyer with something worthwhile to purchase; the product actually makes the buyer a better person! Nike's well-known "Just do it" and Home Depot's "You can do it, we can help" slogans also appeal to this kind of sentiment. When the U.S. Army recruited with the slogan "Be all you can be" for over 20 years, it suggested the psychological appeal of self-actualization, whereby somebody is motivated to develop his or her fullest potential. Who knows what psychologist Abraham Maslow would make of advertisers appealing to this self-actualization top rung in his classic hierarchy of needs, a level Maslow believed was achieved by only the most psychologically well-adjusted and enlightened.

Sometimes the emotion elicited by an ad may change over time. For example, State Farm Insurance a few years ago considered retiring its longstanding "like a good neighbor" campaign, first introduced in 1971 (with a jingle written by pop star Barry Manilow). Although the company had an amazing 98% brand name recognition and nearly 70% of Americans could fill in the blank "Like a good neighbor, _____ is there," younger and more urban consumers increasingly saw a "good neighbor" in different terms. Apparently, to many contemporary young adults, a good neighbor is one who stays on his or her side of the fence and leaves you alone, not one who gets involved in your life and helps you, as State Farm was trying to suggest (Elliott, 2002a). In 2016, State Farm finally replaced the good neighbor marketing in favor of the slogan "Here to help life go right." Apparently, the company made the change because it wanted consumers to identify their products less with disasters and more with advanced planning (Channick, 2016).

Often an emotional appeal is centered on the uniqueness of the product or consumer. Interestingly enough, this type of appeal is especially common from the largest corporations, trying to fight an image of large, impersonal, and uncaring corporate institutions. For example, Burger King's "have it your way" and Wendy's ads against "assembly-line burgers" illustrate this approach, as does General Motors' "Can we build one for you?" and Microsoft's "Where do you want to go today?" campaigns. This theme was also apparent in advertising for the now-defunct Saturn automobile line, which stressed the importance of the individual consumer and, in fact, never even mentioned that Saturn was a General Motors product! Wal-Mart has used such appeals very effectively, with its mini-bios of happy families shopping at Wal-Mart and contented employee-models who love working there. For years, Delta Airlines has also run ads touting the happiness of its employees. Such marketing not only makes it seem that Delta and Wal-Mart are fun places to spend money, it also counteracts negative publicity about impersonal big box stores and unpleasant flying experiences. Personal attention to the individual is almost always appealing.

Different emotional appeals can work to varying degrees in different cultures, and sometimes a marketing appeal created in one culture does not translate well to another. This happened when Nissan developed magazine ads to introduce its luxury Infiniti auto line to the U.S. market. The ads featured several pages of nature scenes with the name of the car only at the end of the sequence. Research indicated that this did not especially appeal to American consumers. In the more holistic and collectivist Japan, people and nature are seen as having an inherent connectedness, but this was not appreciated in the West (Nisbett, 2003). Similarly, one study showed that American consumers responded more favorably to ads directly comparing two laptop computers than did Taiwanese consumers. The authors interpreted this finding as the Taiwanese not liking the "confrontational" aspect of two products being compared side by side (Muk, Chung, & Chang, 2017). A related content analysis of print ads in the most popular magazines in the United States and China demonstrated that when food was advertised in the United States, a common theme was independence. In contrast, Chinese food ads were more likely to stress community (Cheong, Kim, & Zheng, 2010). See Close-up 6.3 for a discussion of how some U.S. media outlets and brands are adapting to the growing Latino market.

❖ CLOSE-UP 6.3 MARKETING TO LATINOS

The largest (and quickly growing) ethnic minority group in the United States is Latinos, numbering over 56 million by 2015, about 17% of the population (Humes et al., 2011; U.S. Census Bureau, 2016). The billions Latinos spend annually on goods and services has started to attract major advertising attention recently and helped to integrate Latin American tastes and culture into the national mainstream. Seeing the demographic trend several years ago, NBC bought the second-largest Spanish-language network, Telemundo, for $2.7 billion in 2002. Similarly, many U.S. websites now have Spanish-language counterparts, as do magazines (e.g., People en Español), and Spanish-language TV is widely available in most U.S. markets. There are even Spanish versions of popular cable channels, including ESPN, CNN, and HBO. However, the Latino audience also watches much English-language programming, and a large percentage are bilingual and bicultural.

Marketing is also changing to attract the Latino consumer. Procter and Gamble aired a Crest Toothpaste commercial in Spanish during a recent Grammy Awards Ceremony. Likewise, many companies, including Pepsi and Nike, have used some Spanish in their mainstream TV ads. Kraft Foods now sells products geared toward Latinos such as a milk-based Jell-O (O Gelatina Para Leche), a Kool-Aid flavor (Aguas Frescas), and a lime-flavored mayonnaise. Pepsi and Nestlé sell fruit drinks with flavors like mango and tamarind, and Nabisco began selling Latin American cookie brands in the United States in 2003 (J. Weaver, 2003a). Colgate-Palmolive created the fabric softener brand Suavitel to appeal to Latinos, although it has become popular with other groups, too. Many mainstream U.S. supermarkets have also expanded their offerings to include large Latino sections. Indeed, American consumers are now becoming increasingly familiar with picking up items like Tecate beer, Marinela cookies, and Badia spices at the grocery store.

Patriotic Appeals

Appeals to consumers' national pride are common in ads. They are particularly abundant during the quadrennial Olympic and World Cup events, as well as during events like the U.S. Bicentennial (1976), the French Bicentennial (1989), or Queen Elizabeth II's diamond jubilee (2012). In 2016, apparently to celebrate the presidential election, Budweiser beer even temporarily rebranded itself as "America." Ironically, St. Louis-based Anheuser-Busch, maker of Budweiser, was bought by a Belgian company in 2008. Indeed, the nationality of the manufacturer is of minor importance when it comes to patriotic advertising. Toyota is just as likely as General Motors to use an American patriotic appeal to sell cars in the United States. Volkswagen advertises in New York by saluting U.S. Olympic victories; McDonald's in Dublin helps raise money for the Irish Olympic team. In terms of advertising themes, patriotism is where the market is, not where the home office is located.

How do people respond to patriotic messages? Generally, very positively; for example, in a post-9/11 study, Seiter and Gass (2005) had restaurant servers write various messages on the bottom of their customer checks. Customers who received "United We Stand" left significantly higher tips than those receiving "Have a Nice Day" or no message. However, another study discovered that these kinds of effects tended to be stronger among White Americans than among Asian Americans, although patriotic appeals to Asian Americans were more effective when they were reminded of a national American identity (Yoo & Lee, 2016).

Sometimes nationalism crosses the line to tasteless jingoism, as when a small-town U.S. restaurant published an "Iranian coupon—good for nothing," or when some advertisers took heavy-handed Japan-bashing approaches during times of intense feelings relating to Japanese trade practices. Public outcry against excessively mean-spirited patriotic appeals backfires on the advertiser in ways that tend to discourage such campaigns, at least in their most blatant forms. After the terrorist attacks of September 11, 2001, advertisers were extremely cautious about doing anything that might appear to be capitalizing on those events, but Americans still saw an increase in patriotic public symbols in advertising, whether it was the Statue of Liberty, the American flag, or heroes like firefighters and emergency personnel.

Fear Appeals

Advertising fear appeals involve some kind of threat relating to what may happen if one does not buy a particular product or service. For instance, an image in an ad scenario depicting children trying unsuccessfully to phone parents when in danger because their mobile phone service is unreliable. In the same way, selling home computers by asking parents, "You don't want your child to be left behind in math because you wouldn't buy him a computer, do you?" is a subtle but powerful emotional appeal to guilt and fear. Somewhat less subtle appeals involving the safety of one's children also occur, such as when one car manufacturer showed an apparent sonogram of a fetus in utero as the most important reason to buy its car. There may be a similar notion behind the well-known Michelin slogan "because so much is riding on your tires."

Psychological research on persuasion shows that fear appeals have varying effects. The conventional wisdom in both social psychology and advertising for many years has been that there is an optimal level of fear at which persuasion is the strongest. A weaker appeal will be less effective, but if the fear induced becomes too strong, the ad may turn people off and make them defensive, in which case they tune out the message. However, there has been some inconsistency in the research and theories regarding how fear appeals actually work (King & Reid, 1990; Maloney, Lapinski, & Witte, 2011; Mongeau, 2013; Rotfeld, 1988; Ruiter, Kessels, Peters, & Kok, 2014). Indeed, sometimes ads are viewed very differently by various segments of the audience, some of whom may be highly offended; see Close-up 6.4 for a few particularly controversial examples. Fear appeals in ads can be effective, but exactly which ones are most effective is not yet entirely clear.

❖ CLOSE-UP 6.4 BAD TASTE OR BRILLIANT MARKETING?

A Nike commercial that ran during the 2000 Summer Olympics became very controversial. The ad showed a horrified 1,500-meter Olympian Suzy Hamilton running from a masked pursuer wielding a chainsaw. She escaped him due to her superior running shoes and her own athletic ability. Nike defended the ad as one that empowered women and celebrated their strength. Critics assailed it as an insensitive "glorified rape fantasy" making light of violence toward women. NBC dropped the ad in response to complaints (Fussell, 2000).

Some other ads that have been pulled after consumer complaints include a pair of Bungee jumpers in which one survives because he is wearing Reeboks, a shoe store ad in which a barefoot African runner is tackled by White westerners who put shoes on his feet, and various Calvin Klein ads with apparent preadolescents in sexually suggestive positions that appeared to many to be uncomfortably close to child pornography.

A more recent commercial played more subtly on fear but was no less offensive. In 2017, Pepsi briefly ran an ad featuring celebrity Kendall Jenner. Jenner was shown handing a Pepsi to a police officer at a protest rally while the protesters cheered her on. The negative reaction to the ad was swift, especially online, as many accused Pepsi of appropriating imagery from the Black Lives Matter movement and trivializing police officer shootings of African Americans. It also stung that the commercial depicted Jenner, a privileged White woman, as defusing the tension at the protest (Victor, 2017a).

What do you think? Are these creative artistic endeavors or tasteless insensitive marketing? One thing that is not in dispute, however, is that all these ads were noticed.

Achievement, Success, and Power Appeals

Another popular theme in ads is striving to win, whether the prize is money, status, power, or simply having something before the neighbors do. A candy ad may blatantly say "Winning is everything," picturing a chocolate Olympic-style medal, or it may more subtly suggest that only the people who buy the decadent candy have really arrived. The idea that owning and using some product enables us to be winners is a powerful appeal, whatever the prize. Even a plea to altruism in a PSA can use an appeal to win, by calling on us to achieve a "moral victory" by helping to fund leukemia research.

Advertising appealing to success sometimes crosses a line into courting snobbery. This is sometimes the case in ads for expensive liquor, jewelry, clothing, and cars. The message seems to be that only the finest products will do. Occasionally, the snob appeal also becomes humorous. For example, in a classic Grey Poupon mustard commercial, two high-class gentlemen in Rolls-Royce sedans share their high quality mustard through their car windows. In another commercial, a rube at a fancy dinner party asks for "jelly" rather than "Polaner All Fruit," a faux pas causing one society woman at the table to faint in horror. Likewise, many items aimed at a middle-class, mainstream audience use this appeal, such as a cat food shown in a fancy crystal dish, or a clothing brand with models shown leaning on an expensive car.

Humorous Appeals

Humor is often used as an effective selling tool in ads; funny ads are often among the most popular and best remembered (see also the section on humor in Chapter 4). The audiovisual possibilities of television and Internet video offer a particularly rich set of possibilities for humor, although there is much humor in print and radio advertising as well. Indeed, some humorous ad campaigns have become classics of popular culture (e.g., Alka-Seltzer's "I can't believe I ate the whole thing" campaign of the 1960s, the Wendy's "Where's the beef?" of the 1980s, the Budweiser frogs of the 1990s, the quacking AFLAC ducks of the 2000s, or the Geico gecko of the 2010s). Radio's "see it on the radio" campaign drew on people's ability to use visual imagery to imagine a humorous situation described only through sound (Bolls & Lang, 2003). Overall, research seems to indicate that humorous ads help create positive consumer associations for products (Strick, Holland, van Baaren, van Knippenberg, & Dijksterhuis, 2013).

One caution regarding the use of humor concerns individual differences. Up to a point, humor clearly attracts attention and increases motivation and general positive feeling about the product or service. Sometimes humor in ads may lead to improved memory for the content (Krishnan & Chakravarti, 2003; Furnham, Gunter, & Walsh, 1998). However, memory may not work so well when the humor is expected or when the ad viewer does not find humor that appealing (Kellaris & Cline, 2007). For a meta-analysis on humor in advertising, see Eisend (2011).

Testimonials (Product Endorsements)

In the testimonial ad, some identified person, often a well-known entertainer or athlete, offers a personal pitch for some product or service. This person may clearly be an expert in the particular field or be no more informed than the average person (e.g., what does Michael Jordan know about underwear that you don't?). Social psychological research on persuasion indicates that we are more likely to be persuaded by a prestigious, attractive, and/or respected figure, even if that person has no particular expertise in the area of the product being sold (Heath, Mothersbaugh, & McCarthy, 1993; Kahle & Homer, 1985; Newton, Wong, & Newton, 2015). We tend to trust that person more due to our parasocial relationship (see Chapter 2) with him or her (Alperstein, 1991; Giles, 2002; Klimmt *et al.*, 2006), and the positive associations and feelings we have about the person may be transferred in part to the product, thus transforming that product's image (Walker, Langemeyer, & Langemeyer, 1992; Weisbuch & Mackie, 2009). For example, when 1996 presidential candidate Bob Dole later became a pitchman for Viagra, the hope was that the trust viewers felt for Dole and his long years of public service in the U.S. Senate would transfer to the medication.

Although typical spokespersons in testimonial ads are famous people, they can also be animated (*Family Guy*'s Stewie plugging Wheat Thins, Bart Simpson eating Butterfinger candy bars). Another variation on testimonials involves the "person-on-the-street" testimonial of some unknown person endorsing a product. Here, of course, the hope is that the viewers will identify with that everyday person and want to use the product like he or she does. One of the oddest types of testimonials is the posthumous plug. For example, Mahatma Gandhi has sold Visa cards and Apple Computers, Albert Einstein has sold Fuji film and Chryslers, and John Wayne has sold Coors beer. Although the companies don't have to worry about their deceased pitchman getting caught in some scandal that renders him worthless in testimonials (think O. J. Simpson, Bill Cosby, or Tiger Woods), they still have to pay royalties to the departed's estate. In 2004, Marilyn Monroe earned $7 million, Einstein $1 million, and most of all, Elvis Presley earned $40 million from advertising, all decades after their deaths (Taylor, 2005)!

One advantage of testimonials is that they often allow fairly precise age targeting. Betty White and Justin Bieber clearly reach different age demographics. Sometimes a product can be identified so strongly with a particular age group that others might be less interested. For example, Chrysler originally tried to market its 1930s-retro-look PT Cruiser to young adults. Although this appeal was not particularly successful, their baby boomer parents bought the car in droves, and it later became identified with that generation. Similarly, the small, economical Toyota Echo appealed not to its intended young buyers but to their parents. The same was true for the Saturn Vue SUV and the boxy Honda Element and Scion xB. In spite of these cars being pitched to them, the young adults instead preferred sportier cars (Fonda, 2003). An age-connected image can be hard to crack. High median ages of buyers for Buick (63) and Cadillac (55) make a strong youth appeal in marketing difficult. General Motors once tried to market against this image by advertising a certain model as "not your father's Oldsmobile" and even eliminating the Oldsmobile nameplate from some models. Young consumers didn't buy it; to them it was their father's Oldsmobile. GM stopped manufacturing Oldsmobiles altogether shortly afterward.

Can Appeals Be Unethical?

Just because an ad targets genuine human emotions does not mean that it is necessarily appropriate in a broader ethical sense. One of the most controversial international media campaigns in history centered on the selling of infant formula as an alternative to breast milk in poor countries. Although it was sold as being healthier than mother's milk, the fact that it was often mixed with unsafe water or in dirty containers actually led to a far greater danger of disease than using breast milk, to say nothing of the added expense for already desperately poor families. Concern over the alleged social irresponsibility of such media campaigns led to a worldwide boycott of Nestlé products (Fore, 1987).

The ubiquitous presence of television around the world has led to numerous advertising campaigns whose appeals have come under fire on grounds of social responsibility. Poor children often spend what little money they have on expensive junk food and soft drinks rather than on wholesome school lunches, thanks in part to the influence of advertising. For instance, even though 40% of Mexico's population has no access to milk, poor people are increasingly starting the day with a soft drink and a sort of Mexican Twinkie, in part due to massive TV ad campaigns of big companies like Coca-Cola and Pepsi. Faced with flat or declining sales in North America, tobacco companies have increasingly turned to developing countries as markets, finding less knowledge of health risks, fewer limits on smoking, and less draconian advertising regulation. The percentage of smokers in China, for example, has skyrocketed in recent decades (see the section on tobacco advertising later in this chapter). How the commercial demands of television and other media confront the real world of desperate poverty leads to many questions about media transmission of values. Is it the media's responsibility to promulgate a more culturally sensitive set of values?

A Theoretical Model

Although advertising may be studied from a variety of theoretical perspectives (see Chapter 2), one of the most useful in recent years has been the *elaboration likelihood model* (ELM; see Petty, Briñol, & Priester, 2009; Petty, Priester, & Briñol, 2002; Teeny, Briñol, & Petty, 2017). The ELM was initially developed to account for situations when full attention to processing was lacking but yet some influence might still be occurring; that is, exactly the situation with the typical exposure to advertising. Although there are some who question whether ELM applies to online advertising (Kitchen, Kerr, Schultz, McColl, & Pals, 2014), it is still a widely used and studied model across media modalities.

The central distinction in ELM is the postulation of two distinct routes to persuasion, the central and the peripheral. The *central route* involves effortful cognitive processing, in which we bring to bear our conscious thought processing and relevant information retrieved from long-term memory. Arguments of the persuader are thoughtfully evaluated to determine their merits, and a conclusion is rationally reached. The informational appeals discussed earlier in this chapter typically make use of the central route. Likewise, if a salesperson tries to convince you to purchase a car based on lots of information like safety ratings and price comparisons, she is using the central route.

In contrast to the central route is the *peripheral route*, which does not have to involve conscious, effortful processing. In fact, in the real world of responding to ads, it is neither possible nor desirable to bring the cognitive resources to perform central processing on every TV commercial or billboard. Peripheral processing tends to make an initial, often emotional, response to one salient aspect of the message. For example, we like a commercial because of the familiar rock music sound track or the cute animated tiger, or we dislike one because it features our most hated comedian. When the likelihood of active cognitive elaboration is high, the central route predominates; when it is low, the peripheral route does. When our psychological involvement with a product is low, the peripheral route tends to dominate. Emotional, patriotic, fear, power, and humorous advertising appeals (among others) make use of the peripheral route. Appeals to sex are perhaps the most blatant peripheral route technique and are discussed in their own section later in this chapter. Not surprisingly, peripheral route ads also predominate in comparison to those that appeal to the central route.

Thus far we have primarily focused on the general psychological appeals in ads. In any real ad, of course, there may be multiple appeals. Sometimes it is not entirely clear what appeal is being used (see Close-up 6.5). We now turn to look more closely at the cognitive aspects of advertising.

❖ CLOSE-UP 6.5 ADS AS SOCIAL STATEMENT: THE CASE OF UNITED COLORS OF BENETTON

One of the most controversial and longest running international ad campaigns of recent decades has been the United Colors of Benetton campaign by the trendy Italian clothing com-pany. Beginning in the 1980s and continuing into the 2010s, Benetton frequently features a variety of multicultural models in ads. However, instead of picturing their product, Benetton ads present powerful visual images of social issues. Some of these, such as the Hasidic Jew and the Palestinian embracing or world leaders (including President Obama) kissing, suggest uplifting possibilities. Others, such as real-life death row inmates, a burning car, or a guerrilla fighter holding a human leg bone, are more troubling. Still others, such as a Black woman nursing a White baby, Black and White hands shackled together, or a rack of vials of blood with names of world leaders on them, are very striking but vaguely disquieting.

Why such a campaign? In part, it seems to be a personal statement of company President Luciano Benetton and creative photographer Oliviero Toscani. Benetton has long been pol-itically active and was a member of the Italian Senate. Toscani has been a fierce critic of advertising and its promotion of consumerist values. United Colors is clearly a product of its leaders' social beliefs. Still, the ads have greatly increased attention to the company's products, there has been increased discussion of their ads, and this has probably helped lead to large increases in sales during this period. Critics, however, are troubled by the apparent exploitation of social problems to sell trendy clothing. The framing of social issues as products seems to demean or commodify them. Various United Colors ads were banned, or proposed for banning, in different North American and European countries (Tinic, 1997).

Cognition and Advertising: Ads as Information to Be Processed

The cognitive approach to advertising views an ad as information to be processed (Thorson, 1990). An ad is a complex stimulus, involving language (presented orally or in text) and often pictorial stimuli as well. Television and the Internet are particularly complex media, because they frequently contain both the visual and auditory modal-ities. Typically, there is a close relationship between the audio and video portion of a TV or Internet ad, but this is not always the case. For example, some online ads lack sound, and some TV commercials contain disclaimers in print across the bottom of the screen. The question of how the consumer processes and integrates information from the verbal and visual components of TV and Internet ads is a complex and important issue in itself (Cook, 1992; Gardner & Houston, 1986; Strick *et al.*, 2015; Wyer, Jiang, & Hung, 2008). What part of an ad a person looks at and for how long depends on both the content of the ad and the reason the viewer is looking at the ad (Rayner, Miller, & Rotello, 2008).

Stages of Processing

An older but still useful model (Shimp & Gresham, 1983; see also Wyer and Shrum, 2015, for a somewhat broader model) proposes that when we perceive and comprehend an ad, there are eight stages of processing involved in understanding and acting upon it. First of all, of course, we must be exposed to the ad (e.g., seeing an ad in a magazine or online, hearing a commercial on the radio). Second, we choose to attend to it, perhaps selectively perceiving some parts more than others. Peripheral cues such as humor or sex appeal that catch our attention may cause us to attend to some ads more than others. Third, we comprehend the message. This is usually a fairly straightforward process, but can be more difficult with strange or obtuse ads. Fourth, we evaluate the message in some way (e.g., agree or disagree with it based on our own thoughts, feelings, and experiences). Fifth, we try to encode the information into our long-term memory for future use (e.g., remembering the name of an intriguing new product for the next time we're at the store). Sixth, sometime later, we try to retrieve that information from memory (perhaps when we're ready to buy the product). Seventh, we try to decide among available options, such as which brand or model to purchase. Finally, we take action based on that decision (e.g., actually buying the product or not). If any one or more of the stages is disrupted in some way, overall comprehension or impact of the ad may suffer.

These eight stages are involved in our processing of every aspect of the ad. Even something as simple as the choice of a name or slogan for a product can have important ramifications for processing, depending on the nature of that name or slogan. For example, the memorability of a name may vary depending on various characteristics. A name that lends itself to a vivid logo or mental image may be especially likely to be remembered because it allows for a greater number of possible avenues of retrieval from long-term memory. For example, a waterproofing sealant named Thompson's Water Seal uses a logo of a seal (animal) splashing in water in the middle of a seal (emblem). This choice of a name allowed information about the product name (Water Seal), its use (sealing), and its sound (/sil/) to be unified into one visual image that is easy to remember. Characteristics of the ad may affect how many attentional resources are allocated to processing the ad. A major challenge to advertisers, especially in the age of multitasking, channel-surfing, and pop-up Internet ads, is to grab the attention of viewers. Some interesting brain research in this area is beginning to emerge. For example, Chang and colleagues (Chang, O'Boyle, Anderson, & Suttikun, 2016) used fMRI brain scans to demonstrate that ads using celebrities activated areas of the brain associated with perceptions and memories of attractiveness. In contrast, non-celebrity ads were more likely to activate areas of the brain responsible for self-reflection. At the same time, rational appeals (i.e., central route ads) were associated with logical decision making brain areas.

Sometimes the advertising stimulus may be altered in ways that do not substantially affect its processing. One interesting phenomenon than began in the 1980s is called *time compression*. This technique involves compressing a 36-second ad into 30 seconds by playing the ad at 120% of normal speed, an acceleration rate small enough that it is not readily detected and does not produce a higher pitch or other noticeable distortion. To allow time for additional commercials, some TV networks even speed up their shows, particularly re-runs (Hausknecht & Moore, 1986; Kirk & Wade, 2015; Moore, Hausknecht, & Thamodaran, 1986).

Memory for Ads

The memory recall stage of cognitive ad processing has been studied extensively. One of the most consistent findings is that the context in which an ad appears affects how well it is processed and remembered. For example, Furnham, Bergland, and Gunter (2002) tested students' memory for a beer commercial embedded in a popular prime-time British drama series *Coronation Street*. The target ad was remembered better if it appeared as the first ad in the commercial cluster than if it was shown later. They also found that similar program content (characters drinking in a pub) which appeared just after the break led to improved recall of the beer ad compared to a control group, but that the same content before the ad led to poorer recall of the ad. This may have been due to cognitive interference of the program content with the ad, although recall was also good when the program had characters drinking both before and after the commercial break.

There have also been a number of studies done on cognitive processing of advertising within the context of video games. Interestingly, a number (e.g., Peters & Leshner, 2013; Yeu, Yoon, Taylor, & Lee, 2013) have shown that there may not be *explicit memory* for these ads (i.e., the ability to recall the product names). However, *implicit memories* may be formed (i.e., familiarity with product names or logos after exposure to them, a fairly common effect of ads).

Violent Media, Advertising, and Memory

One of the most common themes in video games and television is violence (see Chapter 9). Violence also finds its way into advertising. It may surprise you, however, that violent TV programming actually reduces memory for the commercials in those shows and reduces the chance that people will intend to buy those products (Bushman, 1998, 2005; Lull & Bushman, 2015). In attempting to explain this finding, Bushman suggests one reason may be that watching violence raises people's physiological arousal by making them angry and putting them in a bad mood. An angry mood can prime aggressive thoughts, which in turn may interfere with retrieval of the ad content. Negative moods are also known to interfere with the brain's encoding of information. In addition, the effort taken to try to repair the bad mood may distract from attending to and processing the ad. Thus, it may be that advertisers are not getting as much "bang for their buck" with violent content as with nonviolent content. This suggests that other material being processed during violent entertainment might not be retained as well. Also, the use of such a context runs greater risks of substantial portions of the audience being offended by the material. Thus, in terms of memory, perhaps students shouldn't study while they also consume violent entertainment (see Bushman & Phillips, 2001, and Lull & Bushman, 2015, for meta-analyses on this topic)!

Whether or not the commercial itself contains violence may also make a difference in how well it is remembered. Gunter, Furnham, and Pappa (2005) found that a violent version of a commercial appearing in a violent film sequence was remembered much better than a nonviolent version of the same commercial in the same program. However, the nonviolent ad was remembered better in the context of a nonviolent program. Thus the congruence of the ad and program was important.

A Constructionist Framework for Understanding and Remembering Advertising

The cognitive principle known as *construction* argues that people do not literally store and retrieve information they read or hear, but rather modify it in accordance with their beliefs and the environment in which it is perceived. The encoding and later retrieval of information about the product is guided by knowledge structures called schemas (also see Chapter 2). A *schema* is a knowledge structure or framework that organizes an individual's memory of information about people and events. It accepts all forms of information, irrespective of the mode—visual or auditory, linguistic or nonlinguistic. The individual is likely to go beyond the information available to draw inferences about people or events that are congruent with previously formed schemas (Harris, 1981; Harris, Sturm, Klassen, & Bechtold, 1986; Stayman & Kardes, 1992; Sternberg & Sternberg, 2016).

For example, imagine a commercial for "Lucky Cola" with a group of happy young adults running on a beach and opening a cooler filled with soda. In bold letters at the bottom of the screen are the words "Get Lucky." The slogan and picture elicit a "beach party" schema from memory, which helps the viewer draw inferences about the scene, going beyond what is specified directly in the ad. The viewer uses the schema to infer information not specifically stated in the ad, such as (1) the people have been swimming; (2) the temperature is hot; (3) the people are thirsty; and, most importantly, (4) drinking Lucky makes the people happy and playful.

Deceptive Advertising

One issue of great concern to the general public is the issue of deceptive, or misleading, advertising. This relates directly to the theme of perceived reality and is at heart a cognitive question. The comprehension of an ad may be tested to determine whether the consumer constructs a meaning at variance with the facts; that is, whether the consumer is deceived (Harris, Dubitsky, & Bruno, 1983; Richards, 1990). Interestingly enough, research has also shown that there is a third-person effect for advertising that consumers consider highly deceptive; in other words, people have a tendency to believe that deceptive ads affect others more than themselves (Xie, 2016). Also, from a cognitive perspective, the question is more complex than merely determining the literal truth or falseness of the ad itself (Hastak & Mazis, 2011; Preston, 1994; Preston & Richards, 1986).

Advertising that directly states information which is not true is clearly both illegal and bad business and is thus fairly unusual, with the possible exception of ads for weight-loss and muscle-building products. A Federal Trade Commission (FTC) study of weight-loss advertising found that nearly 40% of the ads contained claims that were almost surely false, such as "You will lose 30 pounds of fat the first week" (Sommerfeld, 2002). Although there is no scientific evidence supporting over-the-counter supplements as leading to sustained weight loss, Americans spend billions of dollars each year on these products and services. People are so eager for a quick fix for losing weight that does not require them to decrease calorie intake or increase exercise that such outrageous claims continue to sell products.

Sometimes an ad may state a claim that is literally false, but we comprehend it in some non-literal way that is consistent with reality, and thus we are not deceived. For example, claims like "Our cookies are made by elves in a tree," "A green giant packs every can of our vegetables," or "At this price these cars will fly out the door" are unlikely to be understood literally; thus consumers are not deceived. Sometimes photographic conventions raise interesting issues as to whether a picture is deceptive (see Close-up 6.6).

❖ CLOSE-UP 6.6 THE CREATIVE WORK OF FOOD STYLISTS

Food stylists prepare food for photography and try to make it look as appealing as possible. Although there are many technical aspects, like lighting, that can make a difference (Dujardin, 2011), sometimes the realities of the studio conventions call for surrogate munchies, and what you see in the ad may not be the real thing. For instance, ice cream is likely mashed potatoes covered with chocolate sauce, because ice cream melts too fast under hot studio lights. In fact, mashed potatoes serve many purposes in food photography, like making up milk shakes and stuffing enchiladas. The head on beer is often shampoo or soap suds, because real beer bubbles do not last long enough for photography. White glue is added to milk to make it look whiter and creamier, and roasted chickens are spray-painted golden brown to look like they've been in the oven for hours—but aren't wrinkled (Chapin, 2016; Wilson & Wilson, 1998). Pancakes are sprayed with Scotchgard to keep the syrup from soaking in so you can see it run appetizingly down the sides of the pancake. Pieces of cereal may be glued into white cardboard in a bowl so they won't ever get soggy. These conventions have been justified on the grounds that the literal falseness actually presents the product less deceptively and more honestly than literal truth (e.g., real ice cream would look like creamed soup, not ice cream, whereas mashed potatoes look like ice cream). Some cases, however, have been more questionable and sometimes have been disallowed by the FTC or the courts. For example, how many marbles should be allowed in the bottom of a soup bowl to buoy up the solid ingredients before it should be considered deceptively suggesting more solid ingredients than are really there? How about the shaving cream commercial in which the sandpaper being shaved was actually loose sand grains on clear plastic? The razor would in fact shave sandpaper, but only fine grade sandpaper, not coarse. Because fine sandpaper looked like regular paper on TV, the advertiser used the sand grains on plastic. This particular case was argued in the courts for years (Preston, 1975).

Assuming that an ad does contain factual, rather than purely evaluative, information, determining whether or not an ad is deceptive is not the same as assessing its literal truth value. Truth may be considered a legal or linguistic question, which may be resolved by examining external reality. Deception, however, is a function of the understanding of the consumer and is thus a cognitive psychological question. It is covert and unobservable and must be inferred from an assessment of one's understanding of an ad. One may be deceived by an ad that is either true or false in some objective sense.

True-But-Deceptive Ads

The type of advertising claim that is potentially the most damaging is the statement that is literally true but deceives consumers by inducing them to construct a meaning of the ad that is inconsistent with reality. Psychologists have long recognized the inferential nature of information processing, and studies on inference strongly suggest that, in order to derive the meaning of a statement, people typically interpret beyond what is explicitly stated. When applied to advertising, the consumer may be led to believe things about a product that were never explicitly stated (e.g., an ad states that a mouthwash fights germs, and the reader infers that it destroys or eliminates germs).

There are several different types of linguistic constructions that may deceive the consumer without actually lying. All such claims invite the consumer to infer beyond the information stated and thus construct a stronger interpretation. This inference-drawing tendency plays on our knowledge in the form of mental schemas discussed earlier and is a natural component of our information-processing system.

One common class of claims that are true but potentially deceptive are *hedge words* or expressions (e.g., may, helps, could), which considerably weaken the force of a claim without totally denying it; for example, "Scrubble Shampoo helps get rid of dandruff symptoms"; "Rainbow Toothpaste fights plaque"; or "Although I can't promise to make you a millionaire by tomorrow, order my kit, and you too, may become rich."

Another common type of linguistic construction that may imply false information is the *elliptical comparative*; for example, "The Neptune Hatchback gives you more"; "Fibermunchies have more vitamin C"; or "PowderPower laundry detergent cleans better." Comparative adjectives or adverbs necessarily involve some sort of standard to which something is being compared. When a product merely says it gives "more," the statement is largely vacuous without knowing the basis of comparison ("more than *what*?"). As long as anything true could be used to complete the comparative, the statement cannot clearly be considered false. However, our brains tend to construct the most plausible basis of comparison, not necessarily the most accurate.

Often a causal relationship may be implied when no more than a correlational one in fact exists. Making further inferences beyond what is stated directly increases the active cognitive processing by the consumer, which in turn typically improves memory. One particular technique is the *juxtaposition of two imperatives*, as in, "Help your child excel in school. Buy an Apricot computer," or "Shed those extra pounds. Buy the Blubber-buster massage belt." In neither of these cases does the ad state that buying the product will have the stated effect, but the causal inference is very easy to draw.

Such a cause-and-effect relationship may also be implied in a more general sense. For example, consider a commercial for diet cola in which a young woman talks about using and liking the product. Then, at the end of the ad, an attractive man says, "And I like the way it looks on her, too." Listeners may infer that drinking that product will cause female listeners to be more attractive to men, although the ad never states that directly.

Sometimes something unfavorable may be implied about a competitor's products or services without stating that directly; this is sometimes known as an *implied slur*. For example, consumers may infer from some statements like, "We don't skimp on the quality of our ingredients," or "If we do your taxes and you are audited by the IRS, we will accompany you to the audit," that competing companies do not provide the same service or quality, whereas most in fact do so. The claim is true but not distinctive to that product.

Reporting of scientific evidence in incomplete fashion may also imply considerably more than what is stated. In reporting results of surveys, "Three out of four doctors recommended Zaier Aspirin" would not be false if only four people were questioned. Claiming that "2,000 dentists recommended brushing with Laser Fluoride," without reporting the dentist sample size or "In a survey of 10,000 car owners, most preferred the Venus Zip" without reporting the number responding is seriously incomplete and potentially misleading and can be labeled *pseudoscience*. Our minds tend to fill in the missing information in ways favorable to the advertiser.

Comparative advertising may employ very selective attribute comparisons to imply a much more global impression. For example the *piecemeal comparison*, "The Egret Pistol has more front-seat leg room than the Honda Accord, more rear-seat headroom than the Nissan Altima, and a larger trunk than the Toyota Camry" may imply that the car has a more spacious interior on most or all dimensions than any of the competitors, which is not necessarily a warranted inference from the given statements.

Studying Deception Scientifically

In experimental studies, people do in fact make the inferences as suggested and remember the inferred information as having been stated in the ad. For example, consumers may remember that a toothpaste prevents cavities when the ad only said it "fights" cavities. A related issue is *native advertising*, ads in a print or online publication that are made to look the same as the text of the publication (with subtle disclaimers like "sponsored news article") are perceived to be real news stories. Native advertising and inferences are both very strong and stable findings that have been shown to occur with a variety of dependent measures (Burke, DeSarbo, Oliver, & Robertson, 1988; Gardner & Leonard, 1990; Harris, Pounds, Maiorelle, & Mermis, 1993; Harris, Trusty, Bechtold, & Wasinger, 1989; Richards, 1990; Russo, Metcalf, & Stephens, 1981; Wojdynski, 2016).

Training people not to make such inferences is actually very difficult, because the tendency to infer beyond the given information is so strong. However, in a series of studies, a training session did have a significant effect in teaching people to put a brake on this natural inference-drawing activity. However, accomplishing this involved a multi-step process in which participants had to individually analyze ads, identify unwarranted inferences that could be drawn, and rewrite the ads to imply something more or less strongly (Bruno & Harris, 1980; Harris *et al.*, 1983). Also, mood has been shown to play a part, with consumers in a positive mood better able to detect false advertising than those in neutral or negative moods (LaTour & LaTour, 2009). In addition, once consumers have been shown that an ad's claims are false or misleading, they become distrustful of subsequent ads (Darke & Ritchie, 2007). Such research has direct application to the preparation of consumer-education materials, including some media literacy programs (see Chapter 1).

In addition, sometimes changing the wording of an ad (i.e., framing it in a different way) may induce highly different interpretations; for example, consider a meat advertised as "75% lean" versus one that is "25% fat." Consumers tend to evaluate the first example more favorably than the semantically identical second example (Levin & Gaeth, 1988; Sinha & Smith, 2000). The "positive frame" leads us to construct a more positive image of the product. One type of currently popular advertising, where one must carefully watch the wording, is ads that appeal to environmental or nutritional consciousness (see Close-up 6.7).

❖ **CLOSE-UP 6.7 GREEN ADVERTISING**

One of the most popular current kinds of social responsibility appeals in advertising capitalizes on consumer concern for the environment (Segev, Fernandes, & Hong, 2016). Being able to advertise one's product as being biodegradable, being organic, reducing the carbon footprint, or otherwise conserving the earth's resources is a popular concern and would seem initially to be a socially responsible position. In fact, the emphasis in green advertising is much more on the means of production and on the consumption process (Iyer & Banerjee, 1993), presumably because that is where the environmental impact is at issue. However, this may not be the best way to reach the consumer.

Green advertising has suffered from a problem of low credibility. Especially when they were new on the scene in the 1990s, consumers apparently did not believe many green ads' claims. Indeed, in what has been labeled "greenwashing," sometimes the scientific reality is more complex than what is presented in the ad (Fernando, Suganthi, & Sivakumaran, 2014; T. M. Smith, 1998). For example, one popular kind of trash bag advertised that it was made of biodegradable plastic. Although this sounds good, once a sealed bag of contaminants is in a landfill, it may actually be better for the environment if it is not biodegradable, rather than slowly decomposing over several years, gradually releasing toxic content into the groundwater system. Some such products rely on the sun to initiate the decomposition process, and it is questionable how much sun the typical bag buried deep in a landfill would receive.

Sometimes guidelines can be helpful to consumers. For example, in October 2002, the U.S. Department of Agriculture implemented legal definitions of "organic" foods. If a label says "100% Organic," that must mean that all the ingredients contain no synthetic pesticides, herbicides, chemical fertilizers, antibiotics, hormones, or artificial preservatives. These products actually contain a USDA seal. "Organic" means that at least 90% of the ingredients meet or exceed the USDA specifications, while "Made with Organic Ingredients" requires only 70%, and there are no specific guidelines for labels like "cage free" or "pasture raised" (Bjerklie, 2002; Carlson, 2018). Interestingly, a more recent content analysis (Segev et al., 2016) has indicated that as green advertising has become more common over the past 20 years, it has also become more acceptable to consumers and perceived as less deceptive than in the past.

Now we turn to some non-cognitive aspects of advertising, focusing on the use of sex to sell and more generally on the question of whether we can be persuaded by messages we are not even aware of, so-called subliminal advertising.

Sex and Subliminal Advertising

One of the most common types of appeals in advertising is sex. Although some products such as perfume and cologne are sold almost exclusively through sex appeals, practically any product can be marketed through associating it with a beautiful, sexy, or scantily-clad person. The sexual association and allure, and even more, the overall good feelings engendered then become a part of the perceived reality of that product for many consumers.

Classical Conditioning

A psychological process called classical conditioning sheds some light on how sex in advertising can affect us. Classical conditioning is the process discovered by the Russian physiologist Ivan Pavlov, who studied the physiology of hunger in dogs in the early years of the twentieth century. In his studies he noticed a curious fact: his dogs would often start to salivate merely at the sight of an empty food dish. Given that there is no natural connection between dishes and drooling, why did they do this? Pavlov eventually decided that they had been classically conditioned to associate the dishes with food. This process became one of the cornerstones of experimental (especially behaviorist) psychology and is as important for consumers of ads as it was for Pavlov's dogs.

An *unconditioned stimulus (UCS)* naturally, without learning, elicits an *unconditioned response (UCR)*. For example, meat (UCS) naturally produces salivation (UCR) in a dog. Similarly, the sight of a gorgeous woman (UCS) naturally elicits mild sexual arousal or at least some positive feelings (UCR) in most heterosexual males. At this point in the process, there is no conditioning. The conditioning occurs when the UCS is paired (associated) with the *conditioned stimulus (CS)*, which does not normally elicit the UCR. For example, Pavlov's dog dish (CS) was associated with meat (UCS), just as the attractive model (UCS) is associated with a product (CS) in a commercial. There may be some natural and obvious connection between the model and the product, such as a perfume ad that suggests a woman will attract sexy men if she wears that fragrance, or there may be no intrinsic connection at all, such as the beautiful woman who merely appears repeatedly next to the steel-belted radial tires.

After sufficient pairing of the UCS and the CS, the CS by itself comes to elicit the *conditioned response (CR)*, which in most cases is very similar to the UCR. Just as Pavlov's dogs eventually began to salivate (CR) to the empty food dish (CS), so may we continue to have positive feelings (CR) about the product (CS) when we see it without the gorgeous model. This basic classical conditioning paradigm is the psychological process being employed by most ads using sexual stimuli, for example associating a nonsexual product such as beer with a sexy model in a beer commercial. Ironically, sometimes advertisers themselves may be loath to be associated with certain stimuli that they feel evoke strong negative responses in a large segment of the population. For example, at one point condom manufacturers were wary of becoming too closely associated with the gay community for fear of alienating potential heterosexual customers.

Subliminal Advertising

Although we could look at classical conditioning as a subliminal effect in the broadest sense, people are more likely to worry about subliminal persuasion, especially as applied to advertising. In the late 1950s several popular press articles reported a study by advertising expert James Vicary wherein he reported increasing the sales of Coke and popcorn in a New Jersey movie theater by flashing the messages "Eat popcorn" and "Drink Coke" for a few milliseconds every 5 seconds during a film. Although the research was never published and in fact was admitted by Vicary in 1962 to have been a complete fabrication, intended only to increase his advertising agency's business (Pratkanis, 1992), the public became very alarmed, and the FCC and the National Association of Broadcasters (NAB) outlawed the practice. Excited about its prospects, however, a few radio stations threatened by the competition of television started broadcasting sub-audible messages like "Isn't TV dull?" and "TV's a bore" (Haberstroh, 1994).

Subliminal Existence vs. Behavioral Effect

Even today, large numbers of people continue to uncritically accept the existence of subliminal persuasion, in spite of there being no credible scientific evidence for its existence or effectiveness. *Subliminal* means below the threshold of conscious perception; by definition, if something is subliminal, we are not aware of it. Such stimuli may be a sub-audible sound message in a store ("Don't shoplift"), a very brief visual message in a movie or TV show ("Buy popcorn"), or a visual sexual stimulus airbrushed into an ad photograph (S-E-X spelled in the lines on crackers or sex organs drawn inside ice cubes). What are the alleged effects of such stimuli? Do they, in fact, work to sell products?

A helpful distinction to bear in mind in considering this question is the difference between establishing the *existence* of some subliminal stimulus and demonstrating that such a stimulus has some *effect*. Books like Key's *Subliminal Seduction* (1974), *Media Sexploitation* (1976), *The Clam-Plate Orgy* (1981), and *The Age of Manipulation* (1989) focus on demonstrating the existence of subliminal messages and embedded sexuality, but they give few arguments to demonstrate any effects that such stimuli have. Such authors often implicitly assume that showing the existence of subliminal media stimuli necessarily entails that it has some effect. This assumption is completely unwarranted, however. Although there is some older, reputed evidence of an effect (Cuperfain & Clarke, 1985; Kilbourne, Painton, & Ridley, 1985), much of the so-called evidence is anecdotal or open to other interpretations. Many examples, such as allegedly obscene images or messages in Disney animations like *The Lion King*, *Aladdin*, and *The Little Mermaid*, are mostly the result of big imaginations, rumors, free time, the Internet, and pause and rewind buttons (Bannon, 1995). In fact, there is little evidence that subliminal messages affect people very much (for reviews see Merikle & Cheesman, 1987; Newell & Shanks, 2014; T. E. Moore, 1988; Pratkanis, 1992; Pratkanis & Greenwald, 1988).

Moore (1982, 2008) identified three types of possible subliminal stimuli (subliminal visual perception, sub-audible speech, embedded sexual stimuli) and carefully examined research evidence on possible effects in each. The conclusion was that there is some evidence (although it is far from compelling and not directly related to advertising anyway) that subliminal stimuli may in some cases have a weak positive effect of a general affective nature (i.e., they make us feel a little better about the product, probably due to classical conditioning). However, there is no evidence for any effects of subliminal stimuli on behavior. The conclusion at this point seems to be that subliminal stimuli may exist on occasion but that their effects are minimal, fleeting, and/or nonexistent. Subliminal advertising seems to be a perceived reality in the mind of much of the public, but not an actual reality that stands up to scientific scrutiny. The same has been shown to be true for sub-audible recordings which, for example, purport to decrease smoking behavior (Greenwald, Spangenberg, Pratkanis, & Eskenazi, 1991; Merikle, 1988; Merikle & Skanes, 1992; T. E. Moore, 2008).

Similar issues are involved in heated controversies over subliminal messages in rock music. In 1990, the family of two teenage suicide victims in Nevada brought a suit against the group Judas Priest and CBS Records, on the grounds that subliminal and backmasked (recorded backwards) messages on the album *Stained Class* had directed the boys to take their own lives; the judge ruled against the family (Wilson & Wilson, 1998). Another concern has been allegedly satanic messages recorded backwards into certain rock music recordings. See Close-up 6.8 for details of a carefully designed research program to test for effects of such stimuli.

❖ CLOSE-UP 6.8 SATANIC MESSAGES IN ROCK MUSIC?

Periodically one hears the claim that some rock music contains embedded messages recorded backward. Although no one claims that these messages can be consciously perceived easily when the record is played forward, concern has been expressed that there may be some unconscious effect unbeknownst to the listener. Furthermore, some have even been concerned that such messages may be satanic, and they caused legislation to be introduced in several states in the 1980s that would call for warning labels about such messages to appear on album jackets.

Psychologists John Vokey and Don Read (1985) of the University of Lethbridge in Alberta conducted a careful series of studies designed to test the effects of such messages— assuming for the moment that they exist (an assumption that is not at all established, but we will leave that for now). When verbal messages on tape were played backwards, research participants showed no understanding of the meaning; identifying the sex or voice of the speaker was about all that they could perceive. Next, they tested for unconscious effects by giving a spelling test in which some of the words were homophones (e.g., read, reed). A biasing context sentence ("A saxophone is a reed instrument") was played backward, but listeners were no more likely than a control group to write "reed" instead of "read." When backward messages were played and subjects were merely asked to assign the statement to the category Christian, satanic, pornographic, or advertising, based on its content, they could not do so at greater than chance level. The only time that people ever perceived and reported anything at greater than chance level was in one study in which the experimenter picked out phrases in advance and asked the participants to listen for them. Only under conditions of such strong suggestibility could people comprehend anything from the backward messages.

Vokey and Read's studies clearly demonstrate that, even if backward messages do exist in music, it is highly unlikely that they could be having any effect on the hearers. This conclusion is all the more striking considering that in their studies there was no competing forward message as there is with real music CDs or MP3s. In at least a couple of cases, proposed record-labeling legislation was withdrawn based on results of this research. If you want to hear some backward speech and music with some alleged messages, see jeffmilner.com/backmasking.

Now let us turn to advertising aimed at the youngest segments of our population.

Advertising to Children

Children are an enormous and growing market for advertising. There actually are three distinct markets for children, the primary market, the influence market, and the future market (Valkenburg, 2004; Valkenburg & Piotrowski, 2017).

The *primary market*, in which children spend their own money, has exploded in recent years as parents have fewer children later in life with more money to spend on them. Children in the United States spent $27 billion of their own money in 2003, and advertisers spent $15 billion to influence that spending, up from only $100 million in 1983 (Carlsson-Paige, 2008). Those numbers have only continued to grow. Although most of these ad dollars were spent on television, substantial amounts also went to Internet and point-of-purchase advertising and product placements in children's programming (Common Sense Media, 2014; Speers, Harris, & Schwartz, 2011). As technology has increased, advertising campaigns to children have also become more sophisticated. For example, Coca-Cola ran advertising known as the "AHH effect" campaign. In addition to TV commercials, Coke advertised with dozens of websites aimed at children and teens, including YouTube videos starring teen idols. There were also online interactive games ("advergaming") and social media elements (Common Sense Media, 2014; Valkenburg & Piotrowski, 2017). This kind of integrated, cross-platform advertising may be especially effective (and ruthless) in marketing to kids because it tends to be interactive (i.e., playing a game) and immersive (i.e., the child is in a "fully branded" online environment). It also allows advertisers to collect tremendous amounts of data, such as viewer clicks, likes, and shares (Common Sense Media, 2014).

A meta-analysis (Desmond & Carveth, 2007) found that children's advertising exposure results in more positive associations with advertised brands and more likelihood of selecting those brands, although the effect sizes were small. Children at different ages are affected by different sorts of persuasive techniques because of their particular stage of cognitive development and level of media literacy (Livingstone & Helsper, 2006). For example, very young children are more persuaded by a lively visual appeal and older children by a social norms appeal.

The second child advertising market is the *influence market*, whereby children influence their parents' buying decisions either through direct request or demands or more indirectly by parents taking children's wishes into account when they make their purchases. Preschool children can readily identify corporate logos and characters they have seen in advertising (Fischer, Schwartz, Richards, Goldstein, & Rojas, 1991; Valkenburg & Buijzen, 2005). In addition, children by age 2 already request specific products when shopping with parents in stores. Such requests increase to a peak at around age 7 (Buijzen & Valkenburg, 2008; Valkenburg & Piotrowski, 2017). It has been estimated that the overall influence of children on family purchasing is around 28–30%, varying for different products from a high of 70–80% for toys and video games to a low of 10% for the family car (McNeal, 1999; Valkenburg, 2004). Children's influence no doubt also depends on the family's income and culture (Isin & Alkibay, 2011; Calderon *et al.*, 2017). However, as children grow older, they tend to exert more influence on family purchases, although that influence becomes increasingly indirect, and children seem to believe they have more influence than they actually do (Gram, 2007). The influence of children on parental spending is growing rapidly and tends to have a negative effect on the quality of parent–child relationships.

The third child advertising market is the *future market*, in which children are developing brand preferences that often carry over into adulthood. Children ages 3 to 6 already consistently ask for specific product or restaurant names. For example, McDonald's golden arches is a brand very familiar to children. Some of these restaurants and products will become lifelong favorites, so it's no wonder that advertisers work hard to establish brand loyalty early.

One of the most important media concerns in regard to children are television commercials aimed specifically at kids, such as those aired on weekend mornings, during after-school shows, and on child-oriented cable networks like the various Nickelodeon and Disney channels. Keep in mind, however, that children's programming constitutes only a minority of the hours of TV that children watch, although the percentage of that time filled with commercials has increased in the United States since the 1980s. The rest of the many thousands of commercials that a child sees every year are those appearing on general programming (i.e., prime-time and daytime offerings such as game shows, movies, dramas, reality shows, and syndicated sitcom reruns).

Turning now to "kidvid" ads specifically, about 80% of them advertise products in only four or five categories: toys and games, cereal, candy and snacks, sodas/soft drinks, and fast-food restaurants, figures essentially unchanged since the 1980s (Kaiser Family Foundation, 2007; Kunkel & Gantz, 1992; Kunkel & McIlrath, 2003; Young, 2011). Almost half of these ads are for food products, mostly high-calorie, low-nutrition foods (Stitt & Kunkel, 2008). In fact, only 3% of the ads are for healthy foods. In addition, almost half of the food ads are for breakfast cereals, and around 20% plug fast food restaurants (Bower, 2002). The toy ads are many but highly seasonal, being primarily concentrated during the pre-Christmas season, with numbers much lower during the rest of the year. This advertising creates strong demand. According to one economist, U.S. kids receive 45% of the toys manufactured worldwide, averaging 70 new toys a year per child (Carlsson-Paige, 2008)!

Children's ads are technical marvels, full of color, movement, and animation, with most of them emphasizing how much fun children can have with the product. Special visual and sound effects are common and captivating. The pace is fast. Even less factual information is presented than in adult ads, and there is even more of an overall association of the product with fun times. There is lots of alliteration (e.g., Frosted Flakes, Cap'n Crunch, Kit Kat) and word plays (e.g., "fruitiful," a character yodeling "Cheerio-ios"). Many use animated spokespersons, which increase the young child's level of attention, recognition, and positive attitude toward the product (Neeley & Schumann, 2004). The most common theme is fun, followed by taste and flavor. In contrast to adult ads, appeals based on price, quality, nutrition, or safety account for less than 1% of kids' ads each (Kunkel & Gantz, 1992). In terms of effects, such ads have been found to increase the intake of high-calorie foods, especially in overweight or obese children (Boyland & Halford, 2013).

Valkenburg and Cantor (2001) identified four stages that a child goes through in understanding advertising. During the first two years of life, the child primarily notices bright and colorful television images (many of the best of which happen to be in commercials) and starts asking for products seen on TV as early as 18 months to 2 years of age. In the preschool years (2–5), children understand TV literally and are very vulnerable to its appeals. By the third stage (ages 5–8), they have somewhat more cognitive sophistication and begin to develop strategies for negotiating with parents over purchases. In the last stage (ages 9–12) the child makes the transition to more adult styles of consuming. Although this model is still quite useful, some have questioned whether it applies as well to online and social media marketing as it does to TV (Lawlor, Dunne, & Rowley, 2016). Nevertheless, within this sequence of development, there are several particular issues of concern.

Differentiating Ads and Programs

One major concern about children and commercials is that very young children do not discriminate between commercial and program content and do not understand the persuasive intent of ads or the economics of television. Although children can identify commercials at a very early age, this identification seems to be based on superficial audio and video aspects rather than on an understanding of the difference between programs and commercials (Carter, Patterson, Donovan, Ewing, & Roberts, 2006; Raju & Lonial, 1990; S. L. Smith & Atkin, 2003). Children younger than 4 or 5 have little understanding that commercials are meant to actually sell products. Depending on how such understanding is tested, elementary school children show various stages of development in the understanding of the purpose of ads (Bever, Smith, Bengen, & Johnson, 1975; Carter et al., 2006; McAlister & Cornwell, 2009; Martin, 1997; Sheikh, Prasad, & Rao, 1974; Smith & Atkin, 2003; Stephens & Stutts, 1982; Ward, Wackman, & Wartella, 1977). The insertion of video and audio separators ("bumpers") to mark the transition between program and commercials has not made this discrimination easier (Hoy, Young, & Mowen, 1986; Stutts, Vance, & Hudelson, 1981). Perhaps the separators are just too brief to be noticed, or perhaps they look much like the adjacent programming. Discriminating between ads and programs is especially difficult if a primary character in the show or website is also the spokesperson in the ad, a situation called *host-selling* (Bucy, Kim, & Park, 2011; Hoy et al., 1986; Kunkel, 1988; Neeley & Schumann, 2004).

As they grow older, children show increased understanding of the selling purpose of ads (see Martin, 1997, for a meta-analysis). Only about a third of 5- to 7-year-olds understand this purpose, but almost all do by age 11 (Blatt, Spencer, & Ward, 1972; Ward et al., 1977; Wilson & Weiss, 1992). Typical explanations of middle elementary children center around the truth (or lack thereof) of the material; however, not until late elementary school is the distrust based on perceived intent and an understanding of the advertiser's motivation to sell the product.

Disclaimers

Another important issue in children's advertising is the question of *disclaimers*, those little qualifying statements like "some assembly required," "batteries not included," "some pieces sold separately," or "part of a nutritious breakfast." For obvious reasons these are seldom the central focus of the commercial. In fact, the disclaimers often occur in vocabulary far beyond the age of the targeted child and typically occur only in small script superimposed at the bottom of the screen or hurriedly read in a soft voice by an announcer. Of course, this is completely lost on a pre-reading child and probably on an older one as well, because the colorful activity in the background is so much more enticing and interesting. Unlike the rest of the ad, most disclaimers use adult terminology. Most preschoolers do not understand such language, although some disclaimers were less difficult to understand than others (Stutts & Hunnicutt, 1987). In a content analysis, Kunkel and Gantz (1992) found that over half of the commercials aimed at children had some sort of disclaimer, with 9% having two or more. These usually appeared as an adult voiceover, often in rapid hushed tones (Muehling & Kolbe, 1999). What's more, disclaimers often appear simultaneously with emotional appeals and other distractors (Fosu, Wicks, Warren, & Wicks, 2013).

Incidentally, disclaimers and other fine print information flashed at the bottom of the TV screen are not limited to children's ads. A content analysis of prime-time TV ads overall found two-thirds of them contained some sort of disclaiming "footnote" (Kolbe & Muehling, 1992). Such disclaimers are especially noticeable in the possible side effects mentioned during prescription drug ads on TV (for a more complete discussion of prescription drug ads, see the section dedicated to these products later in this chapter). Television disclaimers are just as problematic for adults as for children because of the inability of viewers to slow down the content enough to fully process it (Morgan & Stoltman, 2002). In fact, images like happy faces that appear during drug commercial disclaimers can be especially distracting (Russell, Swasy, Russell, & Engel, 2017).

Television, Toymakers, Gender, and Marketing

In 1983 Mattel's popular He-Man toy made the move to television (*He-Man and the Masters of the Universe*) and within a year became the second best-selling toy in the country. This successful marketing approach has been massively copied since then and raised a new issue in regard to children's TV ads, namely, the commercial-as-show phenomenon. In succeeding years, dozens of television shows were linked to toys in some way; for example, *The Transformers*, *Teenage Mutant Ninja Turtles*, *Power Rangers*, and *The Care Bears* (see Close-up 6.9 for historical background on how such shows became possible). Toy companies, TV networks, video game makers, processed food companies, and even restaurants routinely promote the toys and their tie-ins together (Pecora, 1997; Strasburger, Wilson, & Jordan, 2014). One of the most successful is the Pokémon craze that began in the late 1990s. Although beginning as 150 cartoon characters in a Japanese Nintendo game, Pokémon was simultaneously launched worldwide in 1998 as a TV cartoon, collector card series, video game, and toy merchandise. This was shortly followed by a Warner Brothers movie, Burger King kids' meal toys, children's clothes, and other merchandise (Strasburger & Wilson, 2002). Pokémon popularity saw a resurgence in the late 2010s as the *Pokémon Go* mobile game app became very popular, even among adults. Pokémon has also been extremely profitable for Nintendo, its parent company, which has leveraged the brand into a wide array of products, a number of movies, and an anime series. Thus, television and the toy industries have been wedded almost as significantly and profoundly as have been sports and TV (see Chapter 4).

A relatively new partner is the movie industry. Although toys tied to films have been around for some time (see the *Star Wars* franchise), movies based on toys began in the 2000s with big budget films like *Transformers*. In 2012, there was even a movie, *Battleship*, based on the old Milton Bradley board game. The movie in turn inspired the sale of additional toys and action figures. Although that movie was neither a critical nor a box office success, profitable movies were later made based on the Hasbro Ouija board game, Lego building blocks, and the Angry Birds mobile game (French, 2017).

This marriage of the film, TV, toy, video game, and food industries raises several concerns. Critics have argued that children's programming is driven too much by the marketability of associated toys rather than by the quality of the shows (Carlsson-Paige, 2008; Carlsson-Paige & Levin, 1990; Kline, 1992). Toy and broadcasting executives defend the policy by arguing that creative animated shows are preferable to tired syndicated sitcom reruns. Still, producers of non-toy-related children's programming report difficulty funding and selling their products.

Programming is now routinely initiated around an existing (or soon to be marketed) toy. Although merchandising toys from successful TV shows has long been practiced (*Mickey Mouse Club*, *Sesame Street*), until the 1980s, the show came first, not the toy. In large part, that is no longer the case. There is also some evidence that the combination of toys and TV shows that feature the toys have an inhibiting effect on imaginative play, especially for older children able to play more creatively than the toy's use in the show's context (Greenfield *et al.*, 1993). While the toy–show connection may help the youngest children see play possibilities, in the older children it restricts their play options to what is suggested by the show.

The toy–television alliance has also helped to produce increasing marketing segmentation by gender (Carlsson-Paige, 2008). The violent shows and accompanying toy weapons and action figures (never called "dolls" if marketed to boys) are sold to boys, whereas girls are offered the soft, cuddly shows and toys like My Little Pony and Barbie dolls. Successful "boy" toys have been repackaged and sold to girls, like pink Barbie Jeeps and computers or the "Adorable Transformables" that change from a dog into lipstick instead of from a car into a robot. Although food ads are likely to portray boys and girls together, ads for toys are usually gender-segmented, most often selling action figures or video games to boys and Barbie dolls and beauty products to girls. Also, the type of interactions was different; ads to girls showed cooperation 80% of the time, while only 30% of the ads to boys did so (Larson, 2001b). How do children themselves respond to such ads? One study (Zimmermann, 2017) that examined preschoolers' reactions to gendered toy ads found that boys especially adhered to gender stereotypes that appeared in ads, and this effect increased with age.

Many of the toy-related TV shows and games, especially those targeted at boys, are highly violent in nature. This in itself is not new; children's cartoons have always been the most violent shows on TV, in terms of numbers of violent incidents (see Chapter 9). A particular concern with the newer shows, however, is that the availability of toys makes it easier to act out the violence modeled by the cartoon characters. Whereas children have always played war games of sorts, in the past they have usually had to employ their imagination to make a stick into a sword or a cardboard cutout into a gun. In so doing, they also developed their creative capacities (Carlsson-Paige, 2008). A plastic Uzi or AK-47, however, can only be used to play killing people and thus requires no particular imagination. The more highly defined the violent purpose of the toy, the more it directs the child's play in a violent direction, even in a child who might not otherwise be inclined toward violent play. It also encourages the child to look on the real thing as just a toy. There are many serious consequences of the failure to distinguish toy weapons from the real thing: children using toy guns have been killed by police officers who thought they were about to be fired upon with real weapons. For this reason, some jurisdictions have banned such realistic-looking toy guns, though, curiously, the real guns are still legal.

Tobacco Advertising and Role Modeling
A final area of particular concern with marketing to children and teens is tobacco advertising, especially advertising that is allegedly aimed at nonsmoking youth. Historically, tobacco has been the most heavily advertised product in the United

States, all this in spite of a ban on broadcast advertising since 1971! Almost all smokers start in their teens, most often at ages 11 to 13 and almost never after age 20. Magazines are the major media outlet for tobacco advertising, and those publications that accept it tend to have less coverage of health-related issues than those which do not accept such ads (Haddock *et al.*, 2008). Over the past few decades, smoking rates have been falling in the United States. As a result, tobacco companies increasingly have been channeling their marketing energies to smokeless tobacco products, which are advertised heavily in magazines with large adolescent readerships (Morrison, Krugman, & Park, 2008). The tobacco industry is also investing heavily in electronic cigarettes (e-cigarettes), which are seen as a worldwide growth market. Although the long-term health risks of e-cigarettes are unknown at this time, big tobacco is charging ahead with marketing (Tavernise, 2016). Indeed, according to the Centers for Disease Control and Prevention, over 69% of youth have been exposed to e-cigarette advertising (CDC, 2016).

Movies are a particular concern. In spite of a huge drop in smoking among U.S. adults between 1960 and 2015 (down from over half to about 15%) and of smoking by TV series characters (down to 2% by the early 1980s), the rate of smoking in movies remained relatively high throughout the 1990s and was about three times the rate of smoking in the population. This may be in part due to product placements, which the tobacco industry claims to have discontinued; for example, Philip Morris reportedly paid over $350,000 to have Lark cigarettes smoked in the 1989 James Bond movie *License to Kill* (CDC, 2015; Strasburger & Wilson, 2002). Various studies showed tobacco use in 85–90% of the most popular movies in the 1990s, cutting across all genres of film (Roberts *et al.*, 1999). Even over half of the animated G-rated movies issued from 1937 to 1997 featured smoking, and many of these old films are still classics viewed by millions of modern children (Strasburger & Wilson, 2002). The good news is that as a result of public awareness and the work of some advocacy groups, smoking in U.S. movies finally appears to be on the decline. According to a report released by the Centers for Disease Control and Prevention, between 1991 and 2010, instances of smoking in movies seemed to peak around 2005, when 67% of top-grossing films contained smoking. By 2010, that percentage had dropped to 45% and to 41% by 2016 (Glantz *et al.*, 2011; Tynan, Polansky, Titus, Atayeva, & Glantz, 2017). However, young viewers may still be a target. Between 2005 and 2016, 58% of PG-13 movies depicted smoking or some other form of tobacco use (CDC, 2017).

There is also evidence that smoking by characters in movies, especially if they are admired characters and actors, can lead youth to start smoking (Dal Cin, Gibson, Zanna, Shumate, & Fong, 2007; Dalton *et al.*, 2002; Distefan, Gilpin, Sargent, & Pierce, 1999; Sargent *et al.*, 2001; Tickle, Sargent, Dalton, Beach, & Heatherton, 2001). Many teens perceive smoking in films as common and an accurate reflection of reality, seeing it as a model for dealing with stress and developing one's self-image, and as a marker of passage into adulthood (McCool, Cameron, & Petrie, 2001). This effect may be especially pronounced for youth who experience high levels of transportation, that is, those who can easily become immersed in the world of the story (Green & Clark, 2013). Indeed, as long as the "hot stars" like Angelina Jolie, Hugh Jackman, Brad Pitt, and Ben Affleck smoke onscreen, this behavior is likely to be modeled by their adoring fans. Ironically, most actors who smoke on screen are smoking relatively harmless prop herbal cigarettes (Hooton, 2016)

Advertising to children has always been regulated more than advertising to adults, but the extent of the oversight has varied considerably depending on the political whims of the time, and questions have been raised as to the ethics of advertising aimed at children (see Close-up 6.9). Whatever the government or industry regulation, there is still a tremendous need for media literacy in the home and elsewhere when it comes to kids and advertising.

> ## ❖ CLOSE-UP 6.9 THE POLITICS OF CHILDREN'S ADVERTISING AND FEDERAL GOVERNMENT REGULATION
>
> *In the United States, the consumer watchdog agency overseeing advertising is the Federal Trade Commission (FTC). The FTC was established in the early twentieth century during the trust-busting era of increasing concern over abusive monopolistic practices of large corporations. Its sister organization, the Federal Communications Commission (FCC), over-sees radio and television and was set up primarily to deal with such issues as assigning frequencies and channels and ensuring access and fair practices, although at times the FCC has gotten involved in perceived matters of decency.*
>
> *There have usually been stricter regulations and laws regarding children's advertising than for ads aimed at adults. For example, drug advertising aimed at children has usually been prohibited. In the late 1970s the FTC was probably at its most aggressive as a pro-consumerist organization, in such issues as deceptive advertising and children's ads. One interesting incident that apparently helped prompt this approach involved children's tele-vision host Soupy Sales in 1965. During an early morning show, Sales prompted his child viewers to go find their sleeping fathers' wallets and look for "some of those funny green pieces of paper with all those nice pictures of George Washington, Abraham Lincoln, and Alexander Hamilton, and send them along to your old pal, Soupy, care of WNEW, New York" (Sivulka, 1998, p. 323). Apparently, many did!*
>
> *In 1978, citing research that young children cannot understand the difference between television programming and advertising, the FTC made a bold proposal to ban all TV commercials aimed at young children. In addition, the FTC targeted commercials adver-tising sugary foods that caused dental problems in older children. This would include a ban on such commercials and a requirement that ads for kid foods include balancing nutrition and health disclosures (Niesen, 2015).*
>
> *The proposal went too far for many corporations, and soon the FTC's protective stance was strongly challenged. This was apparently a result of toy manufacturers, broadcasters, advertisers, and food companies like Kellogg's teaming up to raise money to oppose the FTC through political lobbying and lawsuits. Even the* Washington Post *labeled the FTC the "national nanny" in a 1978 editorial (Niesen, 2015). Such opposition worked. By the early 1980s, with increasing deregulation and the Reagan administration's pro-business philosophy, the FTC had lost much of its influence, especially with regard to children's advertising. For example, in 1983 the FCC abolished its children's TV guidelines, and in 1984 it lifted the limits on commercial time allowed each hour. In the 1980s the FTC also became far less aggressive in pursuing claims of misleading advertising based on the implication of a false claim. In the 1990s the pendulum started to swing the other way, as can be seen in the Children's Television*

Act (1990) that required broadcasters to air some educational programming ratings for television shows. The FCC later interpreted the 1990 Act to require at least three hours of "educational and informational" programming per week with limited commercials (Steyer, 2002). Such programming is denoted with a small "E/I" logo in the corner of the screen. In recent years, most broadcasters have shifted this E/I programming from animation aimed at young children to live action shows aimed at older children and preteens, a potentially more lucrative demographic. For example, CBS airs shows like Litton's Game Changers *(sponsored by the EA Sports video game company), and ABC has shows such as* Sea Rescue *(sponsored by SeaWorld theme parks). The corporate tie-ins can be heavy-handed on these programs, such as SeaWorld being referred to repeatedly on* Sea Rescue.

Some places have stricter regulation. For example, Norway, Sweden, and the Quebec province of Canada have all banned TV commercials targeting children. Italy permits no ads during children's cartoons, and Greece permits no ads for toys between 7 a.m. and 11 p.m. and no ads for war toys at all (Carlsson-Paige, 2008). If characters eat on kids' TV shows airing in the United Kingdom, the BBC requires them to consume healthy foods on camera (Fonda, 2004). Even in the United States, Sesame Street's *classic Cookie Monster has started eating vegetables. What do you think? Is advertising aimed at children ethical?*

Advertising in Newer and Unexpected Places

In recent years advertisers have had to scramble, trying harder and harder to attract and keep our attention. Although ads seem to be everywhere, we also have more technology to delete or subdue them (e.g., muting or fast-forwarding videos, pop-up blockers, delete keys, spam filters). In response, the advertisers have become increasingly clever in placing ads in places we can't ignore, sometimes even in places where we do not even realize they are ads. This section of the chapter looks at several of these.

High-Tech Billboards

Digital technology has allowed all sorts of more involving variations on the traditional outdoor advertising of the billboard (Tsiantar, 2006). Clear Channel LED billboards change image every 8 seconds along Interstate 90 in northeast Ohio and vary their products by the time of day. A digital Absolut vodka ad featuring Lenny Kravitz invites viewers to send a text message to enable their smartphones to download a free 4-minute digital track. Other billboards send digital coupons to passing cell phones, to be used in nearby stores. Digital LED screens on London's famous double-decker buses and escalators in its famed Underground change their ads frequently. Technology is even being developed that will allow electronic billboards to become "smart" by recognizing the make, model, and year of an oncoming car in order to tailor advertising messages to those who might drive such vehicles. What's more, such billboards may someday also be able to insert ads in mobile phones inside those passing cars (Johnson, 2017).

Product Placements

When your favorite actor in a TV show or movie drinks a Pepsi, smokes a Marlboro, or talks on an iPhone, is the choice of a brand coincidental? Hardly. The manufacturer has probably paid thousands of dollars through a placement agent or somehow contributed to the film or TV show as part of a deal to have those products used. Known as *product placement* (or sometimes "embedded advertising" or "product integration"), this technique is common in television shows, movies, and even video games. For example, on the family sitcom *black-ish*, Dre, the father character, works at an advertising agency. Some plotlines show him with his co-workers coming up with ad campaigns for real products and companies, like Buick. One episode also featured his daughter enjoying her new dream car—a Buick Enclave. Producers of *The Saint* actually shot more footage after the film wrapped, in order to include several scenes featuring Volvo's latest model, in response to Volvo's offer of an ad campaign to promote the car and the film together (Gornstein, 1997). Ramses Condoms paid over $10,000 to feature its product in *Lethal Weapon II*, while Safetex paid around $15,000 to have Julia Roberts pull a Gold Circle condom out of her boot while sitting on Richard Gere's desk in *Pretty Woman* (Wilson & Wilson, 1998). James Bond films are some of the most blatant and ubiquitous uses of product placements, including Visa, Avis, British Airways, Omega watches, L'Oreal makeup, and Mercedes, Land Rover, and Jaguar automobiles. Depending on the particular movie's sponsors, Bond has switched between his signature martinis (sometimes made with Smirnoff vodka, sometimes with Finlandia or Belvedere) to Heineken beer. Lately, he has also preferred a Sony mobile phone; Sony also happens to be the company that distributes the films (Barber, 2015; Rimmer, 2002). Reality-based TV shows like *Survivor* and *The Amazing Race* have brought product placement to new heights, including many scenes of the "cast" using the products (Nelson, 2002). Also don't think it's an accident when judges on *The Voice* sip Starbucks, and those on *America's Got Talent* enjoy their Dunkin' Donuts drinks.

Corporate mergers have had an effect on product placement, too. For example, Disney, which owns broadcast network ABC, often features Disney theme parks and movies on shows like *Good Morning America*. Cable company Comcast, which now owns NBC and Universal Studios (and also General Electric), frequently promotes across platforms, too. For example, Universal movies will frequently be heavily featured in interview segments on shows like NBC's *Today*. A newer strategy is to sell promotional time to outside corporations. For instance, NBC had an agreement with Microsoft to promote its Surface 3 tablet, in which the device appeared in the hands of NBC and E! cable network (also owned by Comcast) hosts. Comcast has named this marketing initiative Symphony (i.e., various pieces working together in harmony) and signed additional deals with companies like Disney and Chase (Ember, 2015a).

TV and movies are not the only modalities for product placement, however. Even video games routinely make these sorts of agreements with manufacturers. Called *in-game advertising* or IGA, corporate logos may appear in the background of some gaming environments. It's not always that subtle, though. For instance, in the game *EverQuest II*, Pizza Hut allowed players to order a real pizza and have it delivered to their real homes, all while staying within the game's virtual world. Political ads have even made appearances in games. In 2008, presidential candidate Barack Obama's campaign bought ads (appearing on virtual billboards) within the racing game *Burnout Paradise* (Freeman, 2014). Since most players now have their game systems connected to the Internet, some advertisers can even change their ads over time to suit specific geographic locations or changes in marketing campaigns.

Often the payment for such positioning is more subtle than a flat fee for appearance of the product. For example, Plantronics placed its headsets in *Minority Report* and *Die*

Another Day in 2002 by paying "marketing dollars" for costs toward promotion of the film (Rimmer, 2002). This way film advertising, trailers, and merchandising can promote both the product and the film at the same time.

Indeed, advances in technology are creating new opportunities for product placement. For example, in 2011 when a rerun of a 2006 episode of *How I Met Your Mother* aired, a movie poster for the 2011 movie *Bad Teacher* was digitally pasted into a scene (Stransky, 2011)! Sometimes, there are even product placements within other ads (Elliott, 2002b). For example, a Toyota ad displayed a Sony Vaio laptop computer inside the car to highlight its feature of a 110-volt outlet inside the car, at the same time burnishing the prestige of both products. Sometimes the juxtaposition can be more humorous for purposes of attracting attention. For example, Chevrolet featured a TV commercial with the two "lonely Maytag repairmen" cruising around in a Chevrolet. Guests on talk shows may even be product placements of a sort. For example, drug companies sometimes pay celebrities like Rob Lowe for pushing their products on talk shows (Eisenberg, 2002). These guest appearances are often not noted as paid appearances.

Although product placement may seem like a savvy new marketing phenomenon, it has been going on for years. For example, in *I Love Lucy*, Ricky and Lucy very conspicuously smoked Philip Morris cigarettes (a product line which actors Lucille Ball and Desi Arnaz also endorsed in commercials). Other radio and early TV shows even had product names in their titles, such as *General Electric Theater*, *The Dinah Shore Chevy Show*, and *The Colgate Comedy Hour*.

There are three different levels of product placement, according to a conceptualization known as the landscape model (Yang & Roskos-Ewoldson, 2007). The most shallow level is *background*, in which a product is shown onscreen but not used by a major character. The second level, *use*, is when the product is actually used by the character. Finally, at the *story connection* level, the product actually is an active "enabler" in the plot to help the character solve some problem; for example, when Elliott used Reese's Pieces candies to attract the alien in *E.T.*, or a Junior Mint candy is accidentally dropped into a patient during surgery on *Seinfeld*.

Do product placements work? As noted in the opening pages of this chapter, after Elliott used Reese's Pieces to lure the alien from his hiding place in the family's backyard in *E.T.* in 1982, sales of the candy increased by 65%. The Mars candy company later regretted declining an offer to use M&Ms in the movie (Rimmer, 2002). We also know that, generally, products are recalled better, especially in explicit memory measures, if they have deeper involvement in the plot (Yang & Roskos-Ewoldson, 2007). However, when viewers are aware that product placement is taking place, their attitudes about the brands being advertised and product placement itself are negative (Gillespie & Joireman, 2016). Although there has not yet been a lot of research on the behavioral effects of product placements, there is some emerging research with children, indicating that heavy product placement of high-calorie foods can increase consumption of those foods (C. L. Brown *et al.*, 2017; Matthes & Naderer, 2015).

Is there an artistic or ethical problem with product placements? If the script, the blocking, and the editing are driven by motivation to show a product rather than artistic and script-driven concerns, there may be a compromise of artistic quality. Particularly troubling is the case of modeling the use of unhealthy or dangerous products, such as tobacco or alcohol. For example, although instances of smoking on U.S. TV are very low, as discussed previously, smoking is far more common in movies.

Much of this difference has been attributed to product placement of tobacco in movies. Sometimes, product placement also seems in particularly poor taste. In 2016, Jeep had a product placement deal with the movie *Independence Day: Resurgence*. As is typical in such arrangements, the Jeep Grand Cherokee appeared prominently in the film. What was different this time, though, was that right before the movie's premiere, *Star Trek* movie star Anton Yelchin had been killed when his parked Jeep Grand Cherokee rolled down a hill and crushed him. Grand Cherokees had recently been recalled for a gear shift problem that sometimes resulted in the vehicles rolling away. However, the day after Yelchin's death, there was a shiny Jeep Grand Cherokee at the *Independence Day: Resurgence* red carpet premiere in Los Angeles, available for photos with the film's cast (Barnes, 2016).

Classrooms and Schools

As school districts and universities become increasingly financially strapped, they are turning to private industry for additional funds. One sort of arrangement is a sales contract whereby a school agrees to exclusively sell one brand of soft drink, for example, on its campus for some period of time in return for a substantial sum. One university concluded a contract with Pepsi to sell only its drinks on campus in return for $5 million for the university library. At a time when journal subscriptions and library hours were being cut, $5 million was a big help.

Public schools have long had corporate tie-ins, like the Pizza Hut Book-It campaign, in which an elementary school child receives a coupon for a free Personal Pan pizza from Pizza Hut if he or she completes an agreed-upon number of pages of reading per month. Sometimes if everyone in the class meets the requirements, the whole class gets an in-school pizza party at the end of the semester. Children are encouraged to read, and Pizza Hut socializes a new generation of customers for its restaurants.

Sometimes there are required sales quotas to actually receive the money. For example, a Colorado Springs, Colorado, school district was somewhat behind on its agreement with Coke to sell 1.68 million units of Coke products. Not wanting to risk losing the $8 million, 10-year contract, the district administrator moved vending machines to more accessible areas, encouraged principals to allow drinking Cokes in class, and generally exhorted staff and students to drink more Coke products as a way to support their school (Labi, 1999).

Advertising has become a major presence in schools. School buses and athletic scoreboards sell advertising space, and students watch the commercials on daily news summaries on CNN or Channel One, which is required viewing for an estimated 40% of American secondary students (Carlsson-Paige, 2008). It is now common for fast food chains like Taco Bell, Pizza Hut, and Chick-fil-A to sell their products in many food-court-like school cafeterias, and soft drink machines (usually selling only Coke or Pepsi products) are everywhere (Wartella & Jennings, 2001). Corporate-sponsored curriculum kits are also increasingly common, and one study suggested a strong bias in 80% of these, as when an Exxon curriculum emphasized the earth's resilience to recovering from oil spills (Carlsson-Paige, 2008).

Technology companies are also a marketing force in schools. Big companies like Apple, Google, Microsoft, and Amazon (as well as newer start-ups) have been frequent donors of tech software, equipment, and training to cash-strapped schools and teachers. These companies also sometimes host elaborate receptions and all-expense paid conferences for teachers as well as offering gift cards and other incentives if the teachers use their products in the classroom. Understandably, many teachers jump at the chance to give their students access to the latest learning technology. What's in it for the tech companies? The chance to hook children as lifelong users of their products (Singer, 2017).

Advertisers are forever finding new places to put ads; see Close-up 6.10 for some of the newest and most creative locations.

❖ CLOSE-UP 6.10 CAPTIVE MARKETING

The advertising and marketing industries are in a never-ending race to hawk their wares. Some of the newest agencies, with names like Flush Media, Cunning Stunts, and Captivate Network, take advantage of places where people find themselves necessarily looking at a flat surface for whatever reason. Public restrooms are one of the most potentially profitable of these newer "captive marketing" sites. Print ads or even video screens are appearing above sinks, urinals, and inside toilet stall doors in restrooms. The user is captive for a minute or so, a building owner can make some profit off the otherwise non-income-producing restroom, and very precise gender-targeted marketing can occur. Increasingly, we are also seeing video ads in theaters, airplanes, buses, taxis, and even golf carts. Movie theaters now routinely show a few commercials before their movie trailers, and British and Irish theaters sometimes present 3-minute live commercials before their nightly shows begin. In 2011, Budget Rent a Car started a marketing campaign in which it sold large advertising "wraps" that could be placed on its cars. These wraps, similar to those on some city buses, advertise products such as energy drinks. Car rental customers who agree to drive a wrapped car receive a discount on their rental rate (Haines, 2011).

Sometimes we meet marketing where we least expect it. Fans attending a Baltimore Ravens football game one Sunday in 2017 were given free DNA testing kits from the company Orig3n along with the message, "Purple and black are in your genes—now find out what else is" (Barker, 2017). Big Fat Promotions of New York has hired people to pose as bar customers and talk up certain drinks to the clientele, and mothers to talk up a laundry detergent at their children's ball games (Eisenberg, 2002). Harley-Davidson got Ryder, North Dakota (population 85), to change its name to "Riders," get all of its residents a motorcycle riding license, and paint its water tower with the company's logo (Sherman, 2017). A British agency even rented college students' foreheads to display corporate logos of semi-permeable color transfers made from vegetable dye. Cunning Stunts spokesperson Nikki Horton reports reaction from financially struggling students was "overwhelming" (Payne, 2003). A more permanent campaign offered employees of a real estate firm a 15% pay increase if they would have the company's logo tattooed on their bodies. At least 40 employees took the deal (Collen, 2013).

Advertising Online

Although it has been discussed throughout this chapter, Internet advertising is also unique in many ways. One is its growth rate. In 2010, web advertising revenue, totaling $26 billion in the United States, surpassed newspaper advertising for the first time (Worden, 2011). By 2016, it had grown to $72.5 billion, surpassing TV ad revenue for the first time (Richter, 2017). Even within the fast-growing realm of online advertising, advertising targeting mobile phones has seen the most explosive growth in recent years (Richter, 2017). However, Internet advertising has provided some distinct challenges to marketers as well. For one thing, most of the ad revenue goes to huge platforms such as Facebook and Google (Richter, 2017). Also, the pop-up, pop-under, and banner ads familiar to us on most webpages and mobile sites tend to be as annoying as they are ubiquitous; the more salient they are, the more aggravating they can be.

A newer (and perhaps even more annoying) technique is to embed video ads on webpages and mobile apps. This includes *pre-roll advertising*, which forces viewers to watch a video ad (or at least part of one) before continuing to the content they really want to see, such as a YouTube video. Some of the video ads are so invasive that clicking the "X" button to stop the video does not always work (Ember, 2015b). The ads that pop up and are hard to get rid of risk alienating the potential market, yet the advertiser has to get people's attention. Things get complicated from the viewpoint of the advertiser, too, because some websites employ "bots" to make it appear that many people have viewed an ad when that is not the case (Segal, 2014). This is an issue when websites set their advertising rates based on their number of online visitors. There are privacy concerns as well. You have no doubt noticed that sometimes when you search for a product or visit a merchant's website, an ad for that product will later appear in a completely different website. This is called *online behavioral advertising*, and is made possible with embedded cookies in web browsers (Ham, 2017).

One of the most attractive but also challenging new fields for ads has been social media, especially Facebook. The number of ads on Facebook has been increasing over the years, but so have the complaints about them. When Facebook went public with its initial IPO in 2012, its price fell far below what was expected. This was attributed in part to Facebook's inability to come up with a convincing business model of advertising income. The audience was huge but volatile, and Facebook feared losing numbers if it went too far with more obtrusive advertising. Although advertisers have gone on to spend billions of dollars on Facebook, the company has come under fire as fringe groups (like White Nationalists) and foreign powers (like Russia) have harnessed Facebook's ad-targeting tools to create fake ads in the hopes of swaying public opinion (Scheiber, 2017). See Chapters 7 and 8 for more on how social media are now being used to spread fake news in order to affect politics.

How effective are Internet ads, and how do people respond to them? Sagarin and his colleagues have conducted some research to begin to answer that question (Perloff, 2002; Sagarin, Britt, Heider, Wood, & Lynch, 2005). First of all, they found an extreme version of the third-person effect; practically everyone thought that they themselves paid no attention and were not affected at all by Internet ads. In fact, although they found the ads annoying, most people seemed willing to go along with the "exchange" of putting up with the ads in exchange for free Internet use and website access. However, there were some subtle ways that people were affected by Internet ads without viewers realizing it. For example, the ads did sometimes distract users doing a problem-solving task, even though they did not remember paying attention to them.

But do online ads really work in terms of getting people to buy products? Like other forms of advertising, it probably depends on how the consumer feels about the ad and the product. One group of researchers (Srinivasan, Rutz, and Pauwels, 2016) has proposed a three-step path from online ad to consumer purchase that is somewhat similar to the eight-stage model of ad processing discussed earlier in this chapter. First is *learning* (becoming aware of an ad and product), followed by *affect* (feeling toward the ad and product), and then *behavior* (buying the product or at least clicking to learn more). One study of pop-up ads discovered that although they may not require much cognitive processing, pop-up ads (particularly those images) do raise long-term awareness and intention to purchase products, thus affecting learning and affect (Courbet, Fourquet-Courbet, Kazan, & Intartaglia, 2014). However, marketers can walk a fine line between the learning and affect stages. They want to bring awareness to their products and services without the ads backfiring and annoying the consumer. For example, a study (Campbell, Thompson, Grimm, & Robson, 2017) examining pre-roll video ads discovered that when such ads are less visually complex, viewers are more likely to skip them. Interestingly, the authors propose that more complex ads engage the viewer more cognitively, allowing less cognition to be devoted to irritation and consequent skipping.

How has the more traditional advertising medium of television responded to increased Internet advertising? By finding other ways to hold our attention. Fox has begun airing 6-second commercials (similar to those seen on the Internet) during football games and some other programming (Maheshwari, 2017c). Some cable networks are adopting just the opposite strategy. Instead of running 30-second commercials, networks TNT and TBS are trying longer-format ads that tell more of a story. FX networks allow one sponsor to buy all the ad time when viewers watch their shows via streaming or on-demand platforms (Maheshwari, 2017b). TV viewership research for marketing purposes has also become more sophisticated. Using technology that monitors bodily movements, a company called TVision pays some families to let it use an Internet-connected device to collect data on their movements at home as they watch TV. For example, the device can tell if people are paying attention during ads, looking down at their mobile phones, or getting up to leave the room (Maheshwari, 2017a).

Prescription Drug Advertising

Although not a new place for advertising, one of the fastest growing areas of advertising, in terms of type of product, is the pharmaceutical industry. Prescription drug ads emerged from being almost nonexistent at the start of the 1990s to earning the TV industry an estimated $1.7 billion in 2000. By 2008, over $4 billion was spent on print and electronic ads. The market has only continued to expand, and the selling of prescription drugs directly to consumers (DTC) is considered a major growth industry (Belkin, 2001; Horowitz & Appleby, 2017; Howard, 2009). A 1997 loosening of requirements which formerly had required including all consumer warnings in every ad greatly facilitated this trend. One positive effect of this change is some increased empowering of the public to learn about these drugs and request them from their physicians. This probably has brought needed treatment to some who would otherwise remain undiagnosed, but it also has quite likely brought unneeded treatment to some looking for a quick fix to all of life's problems or those seeking treatment for ailments they do not actually have. Although a physician's prescription is usually still necessary, this is sometimes obtained without a consultation, particularly with drugs purchased over the Internet. Also, some (Horowitz & Appleby, 2017) have noted a correlation between rising prescription drug costs and the rising costs in advertising them.

DTC prescription drug advertising is unusual in several ways. Unlike most product advertising, it pitches to consumers who cannot directly purchase the product. However, they can and do request the drugs from their physicians. They also are subtly encouraged to think even more than previously in terms of chemical solutions to a wide variety of problems, many of which have not been traditionally thought of in this way, such as psychological disorders. Also, many of the ads are tailored to caregivers rather than those suffering from the medical problems themselves (Horowitz & Appleby, 2017). Consumers tend to hold DTC prescription drug advertising in higher esteem than most advertising, because they see it as providing useful information (Deshpande, Menon, Perri, & Zinkhan, 2004). However, this evaluation may be becoming more negative over time. There also seems to be a third-person effect in terms of the adverse effects of prescription drugs mentioned in the lengthy disclosures often included in TV ads (Ahn, Park, & Haley, 2014; Huh & Langteau, 2007). Consumers also see such ads as increasing their confidence in talking to their doctors and increasing their motivation to comply with treatment (Murray, Lo, Pollack, Donelan, & Lee, 2003). Physicians, however, are somewhat more skeptical, being concerned that consumers may be confused by the ads and may put undue demand on physicians for inappropriate drugs, although they do recognize that DTC ads have helped motivate some patients to seek care (Huh & Langteau, 2007; Murray *et al.*, 2003; A. R. Robinson *et al.*, 2004; Wilkes, Bell, & Kravitz, 2000).

Conclusion

This chapter is in no way a comprehensive review of all the psychological effects of advertising or even of all issues relevant to the perceived reality of advertising. Rather, the emphasis has been on looking at a few areas in which advertising attempts to create a reality within our minds that is conducive to purchasing a product. We are taught positive emotional associations about the product through classical conditioning or association of the product with positive experiences in our past. Natural information-processing tendencies like drawing inferences and invoking knowledge schemas to interpret ads are used by advertisers to encourage us to draw certain inferences and interpretations. Knowledge of the way that the mind processes information allows the advertiser to produce ads designed to encourage us to construct a meaning favorable to the advertiser's ends. On the other hand, knowledge of such processes also allows consumers to take steps to be less manipulated. Advertising is not going to go away and, in fact, new places will be found where it can be ensconced.

Media Applications, Chapter 6: Addressing Advertisers

As we saw in the Media Applications section of Chapter 5, individual media consumers can sometimes have great influence. This is especially true with advertisers. Also, people working together can often have more impact than single individuals. One community method to change advertising methods is the boycott, whereby people refrain from buying some product or using some publication, website, or broadcast station until desired changes are made. Even the threat of a boycott sends chills up the spines of advertisers and media companies. Newspapers have gone out of business when certain key economic interests have pulled their advertising. Nestlé changed its infant formula marketing campaign many years ago in response to a public outcry and boycott. Convenience stores have stopped selling sex magazines in response to public complaints and the threat of a boycott. Two single dads in Washington, DC, picketed local stores and the corporate headquarters of the manufacturer of *Grand Theft Auto*; this campaign eventually led to the DC government banning sales of M-rated video games to children (Carlsson-Paige, 2008).

In the hyper-polarized political climate we now live in, the mere thought of viewer boycotts over controversial political topics has begun to affect some news and interview shows. Now, advertisers themselves (often due to online public outcry and pressure) pull their ads from controversial programming. For example, when reporter Megyn Kelly planned to interview conspiracy theorist Alex Jones on NBC, several advertisers, including Chase, pulled their sponsorship (Battaglio, 2017a). Similarly, when highly-rated Fox News host Bill O'Reilly was accused of sexual harassment, big-name advertisers like Mercedes-Benz and Allstate fled. At one point, O'Reilly's show had lost over half of its advertisers, ultimately resulting in the show's cancellation and O'Reilly's firing (Maheshwari, 2017d).

Some organizations have established themselves as watchdogs on certain kinds of issues relating to advertising. For example, a grassroots group called Citizens' Campaign for Commercial-Free Schools identified all forms of commercialism in 30 Seattle schools and persuaded the Seattle school district to rescind a new policy selling wall space in schools to advertisers. Five years later, the group succeeded in goading the district to pass a comprehensive anti-commercialism policy prohibiting most kinds of advertising and commercial activities in Seattle schools (Carlsson-Paige, 2008). A similar group persuaded Boston mass transit to ban ads in subways for video games rated M (mature) or AO (Adults-Only). The national Parent Teacher Association (PTA) has at different times monitored children's advertising and violent and sexual content on television. Resulting public awareness, as well as the latent threat of a boycott, has probably had some subtle effects. For example, a PTA boycott of Pepsi once led to the company's cancellation of its sponsorship of a Madonna video and tour. As we know, the bottom line of most media in the United States is advertising revenue. When that revenue dries up because of media consumer unhappiness over advertising content, the medium becomes no longer viable.

Further Reading

Chapin, A. (2016, January 4). WD-40 and microwaved tampons: Secrets of food photography revealed. *The Guardian*. Retrieved from www.theguardian.com

Cialdini, R. B. (2006). *Influence: The psychology of persuasion*. Rev. ed. New York: Collins.

Common Sense Media (2014). Advertising to children and teens: Current practices. Retrieved from www.commonsensemedia.org

Eisend, M. (2011). How humor in advertising works: A meta-analytic test of alternative models. *Marketing Letters*, 22(2), 115–132. doi: 10.1007/s11002-010-9116-z

Strasburger, V. C., Wilson, B. J., & Jordan, A. B. (2014). *Children, adolescents, and the media*. 3rd ed. Thousand Oaks, CA: Sage.

Valkenburg, P. M., & Piotrowski, J. T. (2017). *Plugged in: How media attract and affect youth*. New Haven, CT and London: Yale University Press.

Useful Links

Ad Council:
www.adcouncil.org/

Federal Trade Commission:
www.ftc.gov/

Music backmasking:
http://jeffmilner.com/backmasking/

For more resources, please visit the companion website:
www.routledge.com/cw/harris

Chapter 7

News

Setting an Agenda about the World

Q: With so much online news available now, what percentage of adults say they still get their news primarily through television?

A: In a 2016 poll of U.S. adults, it was 57%, although among those 18–29, it was only 27% (Mitchell, Goddfried, Barthel, & Shearer, 2016). About 62% of adults also get news, at least occasionally, from social media sources (Gottfried & Shearer, 2016).

Q: How concerned are Americans about fake news?

A: In a survey following the 2016 U.S. presidential election, 64% said fake news causes a great deal of confusion about basic facts and current events (Barthel, Mitchell, & Holcomb, 2016). Other research has indicated that many voters blame Facebook for the spread of fake news (Roarty, 2017), although there seems to be widespread disagreement among the public about what exactly constitutes fake news. For some people, the term fake news has simply become a label for any reporting they dislike (Edwards-Levy, 2017).

Q: Why was a 14-year-old Muslim boy arrested at his school in Irving, Texas?

A: The boy, Ahmed Mohamed, had designed a homemade clock for his engineering class. Although the clock impressed Ahmed's engineering teacher, when his English instructor noticed the clock in her class later that day, she feared it was a bomb. Apparently, the combination of a young Muslim male and a pencil box with wires sticking out of it so alarmed school authorities that they called the police, who subsequently arrested Ahmed (Abramsky, 2017). The incident received an enormous amount of news coverage, which eventually led President Obama to invite the boy to the White House as an inspiration for other kids to like science.

Q: Why did a group of Mississippi parents pull their children out of a middle school in 2014?

A: They were concerned because of news reports of the Ebola virus spreading from Africa to the United States, and the school principal had recently traveled to Zambia. However, Zambia was not a country affected by Ebola. Apparently, like many Americans at the time, the parents had been influenced by sensationalized news reports about Ebola on cable television and social media (Abramsky, 2017; Steinhauer, 2014).

People watch, read, or listen to news in order to find out what happened in the world that day. However, their perceived reality may still diverge quite dramatically from the real world, where much more happened than can be reported in any day's news program, publication, or website. Even the most earnest attempt to accurately and fairly represent the day's events requires producers and editors to select which items to cover, how prominently to cover them, and in what manner to cover them. The typical daily newspaper, for example, only selects 25% of the daily Associated Press (AP) wire service material to print (McCombs, 1994). Similarly, local TV newscasts tend to be increasingly dominated by information that viewers want—weather, traffic, and sports reports—but not so much by actual news events (Waldman, 2013).

These choices necessarily involve some agenda setting (see Chapter 2), that is, telling us what to think about, what is important (Dearing & Rogers, 1996; McCombs & Reynolds, 2009; McCombs & Shaw, 1993). Agenda setting does not necessarily mean that media tell us what to think, although some sources quite unabashedly do that. The news is not a reflection of the day; it is a "set of stories constructed by journalists about the events of the day" (McCombs, 1994, p. 11). When the months-long U.S. presidential primary elections are given massive media coverage, for example, the public receives the implicit but unmistakable message that these campaigns are important. When a prominent celebrity has a substance-abuse-fueled meltdown, the extensive media coverage tells us we should care about that. Likewise, when stories receive little coverage, the implicit message communicated is that they are not important. Those in power know this well. For example, when the besieged Assad government in Syria closed its borders to reporters during the uprising of 2012, it was hoping that this limiting of news coverage would cause the world to forget about the atrocities being committed within its borders; see Boydstun (2013), Brosius and Kepplinger (1990), Edelstein (1993), McCombs and Reynolds (2009), and Sheafer and Weimann (2005) for different measures of agenda setting in regard to news.

The form of the narrative of the news can subtly set an agenda and tell us what is important. For example, Anker (2005) examined American news coverage of the September 11, 2001, terror attacks arguing that the attacks strongly fit a narrative of melodrama, meaning heavy use of emotionality, clear demarcation of good and evil, and salient unambiguous roles of victim, villain, and hero. Further, this type of coverage can have certain consequences, such as ensuring that the public sees the issue in very stark and moralistic good and evil terms and sees the power of the state as necessary and good to fight a terrible evil (Anker, 2005). Those who question its tactics are thus open to charges of lack of patriotism. The agenda can even be set by the use of a compelling metaphor. See Close-up 7.1 for an example of how a metaphor has driven popular thought and even foreign policy in dealing with terrorism and drugs.

❖ CLOSE-UP 7.1 THE POWER OF "WAR" METAPHORS IN SHAPING THE PUBLIC'S UNDERSTANDING OF NEWS

When U.S. President George W. Bush spoke on September 12, 2001, he framed the terrorism problem as war: "The deliberate and deadly attacks which were carried out yesterday against our country were more than acts of terror. They were acts of war." Linguist Lakoff

(2009) as well as Kruglanski and colleagues (Kruglanski, Crenshaw, Post, & Victoroff, 2007) argue that this metaphor has been accepted unquestioningly and should be examined.

What are the implications of using this war metaphor to think about terrorism? First of all, it conceptualizes terrorism as a national security problem, in which each side's interest, perhaps even its very existence, is threatened. Second, fighting terrorism becomes a zero-sum game, in which "victory" is only possible for one side, not both. It also requires national unity, such that the solution is seen only in military terms and dissent is seen as unpatriotic. The expansion of executive powers, including restrictions of civil liberties and brutal interrogation practices, is accepted.

How does the war metaphor not fit the problem of terrorism? Unlike in traditional wars, the opposition (Al-Qaeda) is not a state, though it sometimes takes refuge in weak nations. Second, victory is hard to define. It is not clear when the enemy is defeated, there is not likely to be a surrender by either side, and the "war" will likely drag on indefinitely, accompanied by increasing dissent among a weary population. Third, military force does not fundamentally weaken terrorism, though it may cause temporary setbacks. Military action also does not decrease motivation or morale to resist, and it may even increase them. Military force also obscures attention to the serious grievances of those drawn to terrorism, encourages stereotyping of Arabs and Muslims, diverts resources from other needs, and damages civil liberties.

Others (Perlman & Jordan, 2017) have argued that there are similar problems with the "war on drugs" metaphor, pointing out that news media as well as politicians frequently use that analogy as well as other military terminology like "capturing," "surveilling," and "targeting," when discussing drug users. Perlman and Jordan say that such language has the power to negatively affect perceptions of those who use drugs while at the same time obscuring the humanity and public health needs that underlie usage.

In conclusion, Kruglanski and colleagues, Lakoff, and Perlman and Jordan all recommend that no single metaphor be used to frame complex issues like terrorism and drug use. Furthermore, we need to recognize how metaphors guide thought and policy. Each metaphor highlights certain aspects and conceals others, and we need more political/policy debate on the metaphors themselves.

News programming is put in an especially tricky position by the economic realities of the media industry. Even though news divisions are separate from entertainment divisions at most television networks, and news has the explicit function to inform rather than entertain, the success of news is determined by ratings every bit as much as is the success of a sitcom or drama series, and that increases the pressure to entertain. Similarly, a newspaper, website, or magazine must try to maximize its advertising revenue, which is closely related to the number of viewers, readers, or subscribers. In deciding what news to include, pressures clearly exist to tell people what they want to hear and what will entertain them, in order to keep them coming back and to keep advertisers happy. If the public does not want to hear that its leaders are conducting an unjust war or if major advertisers do not care to see news coverage of studies showing their product to be harmful, those pressures are unlikely to be ignored (Demorest, 2009; Rinallo & Basuroy, 2009; Steyer, 2002).

Understanding the psychology of media news requires an examination of the nature of the medium itself as it transmits news. After some introductory comments on recent trends in coverage and consumption, this chapter examines what news is, in a psychological sense, and how the perceived reality about world events is constructed from reading or watching news reports. There is also a special section on what has become known as fake news. The rest of the chapter examines effects of consuming news, including effects on memory, decision making, evaluation of risk, and foreign policy. We conclude with a look at a how scientists try to communicate important research findings via news media.

Thinking about contemporary news coverage requires us to take a close look at television news, which has its roots in the movie newsreel of the early to mid-twentieth century (for examples, see Useful Links at the end of this chapter). With such news shorts, which were shown in theaters before feature films, the audience experienced an immediacy with distant world events, which, although initially delayed several weeks, had never been possible to experience before. This use of moving visuals to convey the news brought about the new technique of *montage*, the juxtaposition of images for dramatic effect. Reporters and editors reassemble the ingredients of the reality to best express what they perceive as the essence of that reality. Montage allows the telling of a news story using many of the dramatic narrative techniques from drama and fiction writing to make the event more compelling and entertaining. Do such techniques open the door for other elements of fiction to enter as well?

Television News History and Trends

Although news has been on television from its early days, the TV coverage of John F. Kennedy's assassination and funeral in November 1963 firmly established television as a serious, and for many years the predominant, player in news coverage. All other programming was preempted for three days as the country sat glued to their TV sets. There was a further unexpected surprise when the assassination of the alleged assassin Lee Harvey Oswald by Jack Ruby was captured on live TV from the basement of the Dallas police station. In the next five years, the U.S. TV news audience jumped 50%, the sharpest increase ever. By 1977, 62% of all adult Americans watched at least one TV newscast per weekday, making television the major source of news in the United States. More recently, the network share has fallen. In the 1990s, the audience for national news on the three major U.S. broadcast networks fell from 60% to 30% (Farhi, 2001), with much of the loss going to cable news channels like CNN, MSNBC, and Fox News, and, increasingly since 2000, Internet news sources. For years, cable news lost viewers to online news sources, but the 2016 presidential election and its aftermath saw cable news ratings soar, with the highest gains on partisan channels MSBNC and Fox News (Otterson, 2017). Since the mid-2000s, the audience for evening network newscasts has stabilized at about 23 million viewers per night. However, local TV newscasts, including weather and sports, remain popular and are critical for local stations in establishing their unique identity in the community, given that the large majority of programming is either network-produced or syndicated, both of which are identical regardless of the local station.

One interesting trend is for increasing numbers of people to get their news from late night comedy programs like *The Late Show with Stephen Colbert, Saturday Night Live Weekend Update,* and *The Daily Show.* Although late night talk show hosts of the past like Johnny Carson and David Letterman had frequently made fun of politicians, such shows turned more political and pointed after the 2016 U.S. presidential election. For example, modern hosts like Jimmy Kimmel and Seth Myers often tackle controversial issues such as Obamacare and mass shootings, sometimes addressing President Trump directly. Even when viewers can't stay up to catch the late night shows, segments often reappear online, especially in social media. Occasionally, newsmakers also appear on late night talk shows. Appearances on these entertainment shows, though often criticized by traditional news media as inauthentic, are frequently "repackaged" later by those same media as hard news (Edy & Snidow, 2011); for example, the president's comment on *The Tonight Show* may appear on news channels the next day. These shows are discussed in more detail later in the chapter.

Parasocial TV News Relationships

TV news reporters, especially network and local news anchors, can become familiar figures, even friends, in our lives. They may be a part of our mealtimes, almost like having the news anchor as a regular dinner or breakfast guest. We invite them into our homes through our choice to turn on the TV to a particular channel. It is not unusual for people to audibly respond to an anchor's greeting, such as responding "Hi, Al" back to NBC weatherman Al Roker as he signs on with "Good morning," during the *Today* show. News personalities can become substitute friends in the sort of parasocial interaction discussed in depth in Chapters 2 and 3 (Giles, 2002; Klimmt *et al.,* 2006; also see Hartmann, 2017, for how parasocial media relationships might relate to well-being).

Indeed, because of viewer interest, news reporters sometimes become news stories themselves. If the news anchor gets married, the meteorologist struggles with a chronic illness, or the sportscaster has a baby, that event is one of the featured stories of that day's broadcast. Such was the case when *Good Morning America's* Robin Roberts battled cancer and *Today's* Hoda Kotb adopted a baby. In perhaps the ultimate intersection of a news personality, news story, and real life, one pregnant TV reporter's water broke while she was live on the air. Of course, the subsequent birth became a popular story for her station (Sweeney, 2017).

As one person explained his relationship with long-time and much-trusted CBS anchor Walter Cronkite, "I grew up watching him. I guess I expect him to be there when I turn on the news. We've been through a lot together, Walter and me" (Levy, 1982, p. 180); also see Close-up 7.9 for a discussion of how Cronkite may have helped influence news events. That feeling of "being through a lot together" captures very well why news anchors are far more important people in our lives than merely folks who read us the day's events. In recent years some of these important personalities (e.g., Rachel Maddow, Anderson Cooper, and Sean Hannity) have become increasingly partisan, but our "relationships" with them are no less significant. Many liberals root for Maddow as she skewers Republicans. Likewise, conservative viewers may cheer as Hannity sticks it to the "liberal elite." We like to feel that our TV news personalities are on our side. We have no comparable relationships with newspaper or Internet editors or writers.

Internet News Trends

Many news consumers these days are finding websites and Internet blogs as useful sources of news, even though many of these are extreme in viewpoint and not always subject to institutional quality control present in mainstream media (Vraga, Edgerly, Wang, & Shah, 2011; Kim, 2016). Arguably, the best-known (and possibly one of the most extreme) of these is Breitbart News, whose co-founder briefly became a close advisor to President Donald Trump.

Indeed, the fastest-growing news source in recent years has been the Internet, including social media (see section below on the role social media have played in fake news). The Internet web pages for various newspapers, networks, wire services, television stations, and other sources are read by millions daily. There is some indication that this may be taking place primarily at the expense of newspaper subscriptions, although some of the most widely visited sites are newspaper homepages. Increasingly, Internet-only news sites such as the Huffington Post and Breitbart are taking larger shares as well. Websites are less constrained than either newspapers or television in terms of the amount of material that can be published, since they are not limited to a certain number of pages or minutes of air time. Most of the same biases of use hold true with Internet news sources as for traditional print or broadcast; for example, men tend to read more stories about achievement and performance, women read more about social or interpersonal topics (Knobloch-Westerwick & Alter, 2007), and people tend to seek out Internet news sources that align with their political beliefs. See Gunter (2003), and Tewksbury and Rittenberg (2012) for further discussions of Internet news.

What Is News?

We are all exposed to news content daily, but how is the concept of news best defined and characterized? Jamieson and Campbell (2006, p. 40) define *hard news* as: "any report of an event that happened or was disclosed within the previous 24 hours and treats an issue of ongoing concern." The event itself need not be recent, although it usually is, but it must at least involve some new revelation or previously unknown connection. Revelations that Abraham Lincoln may have suffered from depression or that DNA evidence confirmed that Thomas Jefferson fathered children with an enslaved woman, or the discovery of the asteroid crater that probably led to the extinction of the dinosaurs 65 million years ago, have all been news in recent years.

In contrast to hard news are *human interest stories*, which touch universal concerns and are less tied to place and time. Sometimes called *soft news*, these features have a narrative structure closer to fiction and are most prevalent on so-called slow news days (such as weekends). Soft news may include anything from a dog who shoplifted a chew toy from a supermarket in Utah, to a heartwarming story of a poor Mississippi sharecropper whose nine children have all graduated from college, to the mildly titillating story of a stripper who is working on her graduate degree.

Primary Characteristics of a Newsworthy Event

What characteristics do stories which receive a lot of news coverage have? Jamieson and Campbell (2006) identified five qualities of a newsworthy event. They need not all be present in every story, but no doubt several of them will be present for each hard news story. The more of these characteristics a story has, the more likely it is to be heavily covered in the news. An understanding of these qualities goes a long way toward explaining something most of us have wondered about at one time or another, namely, why certain events receive so much coverage and certain others so little. No one has decreed that news stories must have these characteristics; rather, they have evolved naturally.

Personalization

First, a newsworthy story is *personalized*—it is about individuals. This allows audiences to identify with the person and can help make a dauntingly complex event easier to comprehend. A personalized story also lends itself to photography and the interview format, which works well with TV, print, or Internet. However, this may be at the cost of oversimplifying (and possibly distorting) complex events and overemphasizing "stars" such as the political head of state, the Pope, a serial killer, or a terrorist looking for a media platform. Magazines like *People* and *Us Weekly* are known for focusing on stories with personalized angles, such as a feature on a birth in the British royal family or a profile of mass shooting survivor (see Close-Up 7.2 for an example of how such stories may be politicized). It is basically an entertainment model extended to news. Interestingly, such an individual frame for a news story may actually lead readers to hold more polarized opinions than those reading the same story with a group frame (Boyle *et al.*, 2006; Keum *et al.*, 2005).

❖ CLOSE-UP 7.2 AGENDA-SETTING POLITICS AT THE SUPERMARKET CHECKOUT

Do supermarket tabloids have a political agenda? According to Toobin (2017), they do. It may surprise you to learn that most of the familiar tabloids seen at U.S. checkout lines (like The National Enquirer, The Star, The Globe, *and* OK!*) are all owned by the same company, American Media, Inc. (A.M.I.). It may further surprise you that the chief executive of A.M.I., David Pecker, has been a friend of Donald Trump's for decades. Although best known for celebrity gossip (with headlines like "Mariah Carey's Weight Crisis!"), A.M.I.'s tabloids also get political at times. For instance, in 1987 the* Enquirer *made a splash by publishing a photo of Democratic presidential candidate Gary Hart on a boat with his mistress, effectively ending his political career. By the 2016 presidential election, the* Enquirer *had become blatantly partisan, with headlines identifying Hillary Clinton as a "criminal," a "racist," and a "sociopath." Toobin (2017) also reported that Pecker had killed numerous unflattering stories about Trump over the years. Perhaps Pecker and A.M.I.'s most prestigious publication is* Us Weekly. *Founded by the New York Times Company in 1977 and owned by various media conglomerates over the years,* Us Weekly *was bought by A.M.I. in March 2017. Long known for less salacious celebrity news,* Us Weekly *staffers now work in the same newsroom as the* Enquirer's *tabloid reporters. After A.M.I.'s acquisition of the magazine, it also began running sympathetic profiles of figures like first lady Melania Trump and first daughter Ivanka Trump. According to Toobin (2017), Pecker also has his sights set on acquiring additional companies like Time, Inc., and its familiar mainstream magazines* Time, People, *and* Fortune.

Another negative consequence of this highly individualistic frame of news stories is a failure to consider systemic issues. For example, pathological crimes such as presidential assassination attempts and mass shootings are usually covered through the frame of the demented criminal versus the threatened, vulnerable victim (Hoerl, Cloud, & Jarvis, 2009). While there certainly is a lot of truth to such a narrative in many, if not most, such cases, other important dimensions may be missed. For example, it took several years after the 1999 Columbine High School shootings and similar crimes of that era for public schools to seriously come to terms with the problems of bullying and its consequences and to take steps to combat destructive behavior long considered normal (Hoerl, 2002). A similar media coverage pattern arose when a mass shooting took place on the Las Vegas strip in 2017, and 59 concert goers were killed. In the aftermath, news outlets repeatedly pressed police for the shooter's motive, although one did not clearly emerge (Levenson, 2017). The media seemed to struggle with framing a mass shooter who apparently did not fit the mold of previous shooters as radically religious or outwardly mentally ill. At the same time, the fact that this shooting was the "deadliest" in U.S. history was stressed, and policy issues that might have prevented (or lessened) the mass carnage were often not discussed. As long as such crimes continue to be seen only through the frame of a demonic monster versus an innocent and vulnerable victim, such systemic and public policy problems are unlikely to receive much serious attention.

Drama and Conflict

The second primary characteristic of a newsworthy event is that it be dramatic and conflict-filled, even violent. This again follows the pattern of entertainment TV. Amateur videos of high-speed police chases make for more exciting news images than politicians debating economic policy. This emphasis on conflict helps to ensure coverage of opposing views, but on the negative side, may overemphasize the confrontational and violent nature of the story. Very infrequent violent events may be assumed by viewers to be the norm. Nonviolent events may be neglected, and very important issues which are not conducive to drama, conflict, or personalization may be underreported. Complex and protracted economic stories like the Eurozone currency and immigration crises are always a challenge to cover and often tend to be framed in terms of specific events like protests against a governmental policy or a story of an individual who lost his job.

There is reason to think that the emphasis on conflict has escalated more broadly in recent years. In a very provocative, and sadly prophetic, book, *The Argument Culture: Stopping America's War of Words*, Georgetown University sociolinguist Deborah Tannen (1998) argued that American society at all levels had become more confrontational and argumentative in recent decades, reflected in the contentiousness seen in the press, politics, the legal system, and even family and interpersonal relationships. At least for the press, Tannen traced much of this back to Watergate in the 1970s, when investigative journalism had indeed played a strongly, and constitutionally critical, adversarial role in rooting out the scandal in the Nixon administration. She worried that the mindset has never really changed, and news media, as well as office holders, continue to believe they must attack and challenge at every opportunity. Thus one sees, for example, candidates for office or nominees for appointed positions being subject to intense and unprecedented scrutiny of all aspects of their personal lives. Attacks from political opponents are also to be expected. Sometimes all of this is so unpleasant that highly qualified people withdraw from consideration rather than subject themselves and their families to such treatment. The rapid increase in acrimony on cable news, social media, and talk radio in the past few decades is further disturbing evidence of this. By 2016, all sides in Washington appeared to have lost interest in political compromise and seemed mainly concerned with their own partisan interests and (re-)election of their party's candidates.

Action

The third characteristic of a newsworthy event is that it contains action and some observable occurrence. This often becomes the "hook" on which to hang what is essentially a more abstract story. For example, trends in inflation or unemployment are covered by interviews with specific consumers expressing their views on rising prices and lack of job prospects. Important stories that do not have such a convenient hook or discrete encapsulating event receive less attention. For example, the dramatic shift in developing countries over the last 50 years from domestic-food producing to export agriculture is a profound change, but it is seldom mentioned in the news because it is not easily symbolized by discrete events. The action chosen as the frame can have serious consequences. For example, framing a news story on Moroccan immigration to Spain around the theme of the growth of crime led to more negative responses toward immigrants than the same story framed around the more positive frame of economic contributions of immigrants (Igartua & Cheng, 2009).

Novelty and Deviance

The fourth characteristic of hard news is that it is novel or deviant. Contrary to the "late breaking news" descriptor that is often used, most news is not particularly surprising. For example, much political and economic news is covered by the normal beat reporters who know in advance that certain speeches will be made, votes taken, or meetings held. Events outside this predictable range of news will stand a better chance of being covered if they are novel, with chances of coverage increasing as the events get more and more strange and bizarre. A drug addict being shot to death in Chicago may not be an exciting story, but it is big news when a Sunday school teacher is killed in a satanic ritual in rural Saskatchewan.

An event may be deviant in different senses (Arpan & Tüzünkan, 2011; Shoemaker, Chang, & Brendlinger, 1987; Shoemaker, Danielian, & Brendlinger, 1987). *Statistical deviance* refers purely to the frequency of an event, with highly unusual events being the most deviant. *Normative deviance* involves the violation of social and legal norms. Pritchard and Hughes's (1997) analysis of homicide reports found that normative deviance was a more important component of newsworthiness than statistical deviance. Lastly, *potential for social change deviance* refers to how much the existing status quo is threatened, a type of deviance very high in major events like the September 11, 2001, terrorist attacks, the election of Donald Trump as U.S. president in 2016, or the 2017 mass shooting at a concert in Las Vegas.

Link to Ongoing Themes

With the final characteristic of hard news, events are more likely to receive coverage if they are linked to themes of ongoing current interest. Some of these themes are deep-seated, even archetypal, at least within a given society. For example, *appearance versus reality* has always been a common theme in Western literature and drama. News stories about deception and hypocrisy make good copy; the Watergate scandal (1972–1974), which eventually led to the resignation of President Richard Nixon, was one of the hottest news stories in U.S. history. Second, *big versus little* is a powerful theme, nicely captured by some of the crusading stories on *60 Minutes, 20/20,* or consumer reporters on local TV stations. Closely related is *good versus evil,* a moral framework often imposed on news stories (e.g., the brave citizen versus the evil polluting corporation, righteous America versus the evil dictator). The fourth theme is *efficiency versus inefficiency,* commonly used in stories such as exposés of government or corporate waste or mismanagement. Finally, the *unique versus routine* highlights the unusual. New movements emerging make use of these classic themes; for example, the Tea Party movement in the United States cast government as evil, hypocritical, and inefficient. The Black Lives Matter movement framed police shootings of African Americans as rooted in racism and too-powerful law enforcement agencies.

Besides these underlying, archetypal themes we also have cyclical themes such as political cycles and seasonal, holiday, and weather themes. For example, we know we will see the Pope saying midnight mass on Christmas, the groundhog in Punxsutawney, Pennsylvania, looking for his shadow every February 2, stories about safe driving during a snow event, and Black Friday shoppers snapping up bargains the day after Thanksgiving. Such events appear in the news because they fit the cyclical themes, in spite of having few of the other characteristics of newsworthy events.

Secondary Characteristics of a Newsworthy Event

Besides the five primary characteristics of newsworthy events, there are four additional, more pragmatic, characteristics that are required for a story to receive extensive coverage.

Inoffensiveness

A story must be inoffensive or at least not blatantly offensive. Sometimes such concerns about taste keep a story from receiving coverage it might otherwise deserve. For example, the press was very slow to pick up on reporting on the AIDS epidemic in the early 1980s, in part because it was reluctant to mention the most common way to acquire the disease at the time, namely, anal intercourse by gay men (Meyer, 1990). After the terrorist attacks of 2001, the U.S. press only very cautiously addressed the issues of how U.S. foreign policy might have contributed to a climate spawning radical Islamic terrorism. Mainstream media concluded that most of the country did not want to hear that American foreign policy might be at least partially responsible for the climate that produced those horrible events. In 2018, some news outlets struggled with how to report that President Trump apparently referred to African nations and Haiti as "shithole countries" in a meeting. Issues like child pornography and human trafficking probably receive less coverage than they warrant because of media's concerns about the public being offended by specific depictions of how victims are treated.

Credibility

Second, a serious story must be perceived as credible. An occurrence so bizarre that readers or viewers would not believe it is less likely to be reported, at least by the mainstream press (Meyer, 1990). Although this requirement may sometimes have the salutary effect of weeding out tabloid-style oddities such as alien abductions or ghost sightings, it may also have a less benign effect, such as when news media self-censor a story that they do not believe their public would accept or want to hear, such as a report that a very popular and respected leader has been involved in corruption. This may have been the case when powerful Hollywood players like Bill Cosby and Harvey Weinstein allegedly began sexually harassing and assaulting women; it was only years later that allegations from scores of women began to receive press coverage. In recent years, many media consumers have questioned the credibility of news sources, even traditionally trusted outlets like the broadcast network news and newspapers like *The Washington Post* and *The New York Times*. See the section on fake news later in this chapter for a further discussion of this.

Sound Bites

Third, a story must be able to be packaged in small pieces, fit for a very brief TV news story or a short piece online or in print. A story that fits this packaging demand is much more likely to receive coverage than one that does not. The importance of this sound bite requirement is often underappreciated by those wishing their work would receive more coverage, such as scientists and others who are not very skilled in explaining their work to journalists in small, easy-to-digest pieces (see the Media Applications section at the end of this chapter for more discussion of how news media and researchers interact). Although the sound bite is often seen as a creation of television, some have argued that the pithy sound bite, whether or not it was actually uttered by its supposed author, has actually been with us for a long time (Wernick, 1996). For example, Louis XIV's "L'état, c'est moi" ("I am the state"), Julius Caesar's "Veni, vidi, vici" ("I came, I saw, I conquered"), or Harry Truman's "The buck stops here" have a lot in common with Nancy Reagan's "Just say no to drugs," Barack Obama's "We are the 99%," or Donald Trump labeling opponent Hillary Clinton as a "nasty woman" on TV. Sound bites have become increasingly important as the length of TV news stories has been decreasing; the average length of a TV news story about a U.S. presidential election campaign declined from 43 seconds in 1968 to 9 seconds by 1988, which is generally considered the norm these days (Hallin, 1992; Fehrman, 2011).

In the era of social media, Twitter (with its 280 character tweets) has become a new sort of sound bite vehicle for the 2010s. No one seems to have used Twitter more for this purpose than Donald Trump. During the 2016 presidential campaign and his presidency, Trump continually tweeted. Trump's topics included anything from taunting North Korean leader Kim Jong-un to falsely accusing Barack Obama of tapping his phone lines to deriding journalist Mika Brzezinski, whom he tweeted he had seen "bleeding badly from a facelift." In an especially odd late night tweet that caught the attention of the news media, in May 2017, Trump apparently mistakenly tweeted "Despite the negative press covfefe." Bewildered Twitter followers joked and tried to make sense of the non-word for the next few days; Trump never fully explained what had happened (Flegenheimer, 2017).

The Local Hook

A final secondary characteristic of newsworthiness is the local hook, the connection of the story to the community of the reader, viewer, or listener. At the local level, a newspaper or TV station will be much more likely to cover a national or international event if it has a local angle (e.g., a local resident caught in a foreign uprising, the closing of a local manufacturing plant because of Chinese economic policy). On a national level, the hook in the United States may be a current policy debate in Washington or the presence of U.S. troops abroad. Sadly, some very important stories are downplayed or missed altogether because of the lack of an obvious local hook. Simultaneously, American media may overlook the bigger picture in focusing on American lives above others. For example, when natural disasters or terrorist attacks strike abroad, U.S. media outlets also frequently highlight the number of Americans killed. U.S. media in particular are notorious for extensive foreign coverage during an immediate crisis, but very little before or after. Consequently, for the average person, foreign crises seem to emerge suddenly out of nowhere, because they have not been aware of some smoldering issues. Also, after the immediate crisis, the all-important follow-up period receives little coverage. For instance, the Afghanistan invasion during the fall of 2001 to oust the Taliban regime received extensive coverage, but the following important period of "nation-building" did not. The press had moved on to covering the invasion of Iraq to oust Saddam Hussein. Attention reverted from Iraq back to Afghanistan after U.S. troops were withdrawn from Iraq but more were committed to Afghanistan. Similarly, American media stories about the stability of Iraq's government have been in relatively short supply since most U.S. troops withdrew from that country in 2011. See Close-up 7.3 for an extended example of American news coverage from the same part of the world a generation earlier.

❖ CLOSE-UP 7.3 COVERAGE OF THE IRAN HOSTAGE CRISIS

The fact that Iran's 1979 Islamic revolution came as a surprise to many Americans was in part attributable to the almost total lack of coverage of Iran prior to that time (1% of international news stories on U.S. TV from 1972 to 1977) (Beeman, 1984; Mowlana, 1984). From November 1977 to January 1979, U.S. reporting on Iran increased, notably the autocratic pro-Western ruler's visit to Washington in 1977 and a demonstration against him. After his overthrow in January 1979, TV served as the major communication between the exiled Islamic leader Ayatollah Khomeini in Paris and a fragile caretaker government in Tehran. Although American media covered the return of Khomeini to Iran in February, coverage increased dramatically after the Iranian seizure of dozens of American hostages at the U.S. embassy in Tehran in late 1979, comprising nearly one-third of all international news stories in 1980. Television and, to a lesser extent, newspapers became major channels of communication between the two governments, as all diplomatic and commercial channels had been broken. A failed rescue attempt in 1980 and the safe return of the hostages on Ronald Reagan's Inauguration Day in January 1981 received heavy coverage, but the few subsequent stories on Iran originated elsewhere or occasionally from correspondents from other nations who were stationed in Iran (Larson, 1986).

This strong desire to play up a local connection and make the story relevant to readers can sometimes end up distorting the news (Goldberg, 2002). For example, when the media discovered the problem of the homeless, the homeless individuals actually interviewed tended to be very articulate, very needy, usually White, and often professional people down on their luck. In short, they were very much like the majority audience (Hodgetts, Cullen, & Radley, 2005). Never mind that the majority of the homeless had substance abuse or major mental illness problems and often were people of color. In another example, when AIDS started to receive wide coverage in the late 1980s, it was the relatively few heterosexual, non-drug-user AIDS victims who were interviewed. Just as with the homeless issue, the media believed that viewers would be most interested in the problem (thus higher ratings) if they felt it was a personal threat. As a result, the media chose "representative" individuals most like the majority audience in order to make the story connect with the most viewers. The consequence, however, was that many people were far more worried about contracting AIDS or becoming homeless than was warranted. At the same time, less attention was paid to the underlying systemic problems of what to do with the homeless mentally ill after state institutions closed and how to stop the spread of HIV among IV drug users, gay men, and others not practicing safe sex.

Subtle and not-so-subtle prejudice may also play a role in how local stories are reported. For example, when prescription opioid abuse and deaths started to become big news around 2016, news photos of drug victims began appearing, many of them White. In a thoughtful piece in the *Columbia Journalism Review*, Shaw (2017) argued that, in general, the news media was taking a "kind and gentle" approach to opioid abuse, especially as compared with coverage of heroin-related addictions and deaths, which were more likely to affect inner-city people of color. Opioid stories and accompanying photos also seemed more likely to focus on harrowing stories of families and options for recovery. In contrast, photos depicting heroin addiction appeared more likely to feature images of poverty, crime, and hopelessness. Ironically, heroin and prescription opioids are chemically similar drugs with similar effects.

The surest way to obtain coverage of one's activities is to imbue them with all of these primary and secondary newsworthy characteristics. The more of these an event has, the more likely the media will show interest in covering it. Perhaps the ultimate example of this is the double murder trial of former football legend and sometime actor O. J. Simpson in 1995. The Simpson story had all of the newsworthy characteristics. It focused on one person who was greatly admired but was accused of committing a shockingly violent act. It related to many of the central cultural themes (big vs. little, right vs. wrong, appearance vs. reality). The fact that the entire trial was televised also helped to ensure saturation coverage for several months. Even decades after Simpson was acquitted (on TV), interest in the case continued. In 2016, two separate miniseries about Simpson aired; one was a documentary, and the other was a dramatization. Both garnered large audiences and were acclaimed by critics (Poniewozik, 2016b). When Simpson was released from prison in 2017 (out on parole after serving nine years in a conviction not related to the 1994 murders), the focus was on how authorities managed to spirit Simpson out of the prison without media cameras capturing the action (Montero, 2017). See Close-up 7.4 for an interesting argument from Aristotle to explain the continued public fascination with the Simpson trial.

❖ CLOSE-UP 7.4 ARISTOTLE'S EXPLANATION OF INTEREST IN THE O. J. SIMPSON TRIAL

Although written around 400 BC, Aristotle's Rhetoric *offers some arguments about three elements needed to move an audience. Although Aristotle was talking about theater,*

Stonehill (1995) argued that these elements (pathos, logos, and ethos) also fit television and help to explain the intense public fascination with events like the O. J. Simpson trial of 1995. Pathos, the emotional appeal, was very high in this murder case, with overtones of sex, race, and deceit. Logos, the intellectual component, appeared in the mystery of whodunit but also in other questions such as why a low-speed car chase occurred and what all the DNA evidence meant. Finally, ethos is charisma, celebrity, or authority, which of course was very high in this case of a previously loved and respected athlete and movie star on trial for murder. Stonehill even argued that this case might be one of the highest ever on these three Aristotelian dimensions. However, not long after the Simpson trial faded, other high-profile events continued to capture the media's and the public's attention. The death of Britain's Princess Diana in August 1997, the Clinton–Lewinsky sex scandal of 1998, and the surprise election of reality TV star Donald Trump in 2016 likewise went off the charts in pathos, logos, and ethos—and press coverage. Aristotle was right!

Terrorists very often know all about how to stage a newsworthy event. This is why they are particularly fond of large public symbolic targets, like the Pentagon, World Trade Center, railroad stations or airports, and government buildings, especially in well-known places like New York, London, Paris, or Washington. They know there will be more reporters there and thus more news coverage, as well as more damage and deaths, due to the denser population.

Now that we have seen what makes a newsworthy event, we examine how the media create the story that is news.

News Media as Creating a Perceived Reality

As discussed in Chapter 1, mass communication mediates between the audience and some objective reality out there in the world. In Western culture, at least, we assume that such an external reality exists. However, what appears in the media are the news writers' and producers' interpretations of that reality, as seen through both their choice of topics and the amount of coverage they give (i.e., agenda setting). Although choices of media coverage are typically motivated from a sincere desire to present news stories to the public in the most complete and accurate way possible, there are instances when the construction of reality goes beyond the bounds of what most would consider acceptable (see Close-up 7.5).

❖ CLOSE-UP 7.5 WHEN NEWS REPORTERS BECOME NEWSMAKERS

In their desire to make "an invisible truth visible, dramatic, and entertaining" (Bogart, 1980, p. 235), even traditional media outlets have occasionally gone too far. In 1966, CBS helped to finance an armed invasion of Haiti in exchange for exclusive TV rights of the event; the invasion was aborted by U.S. Customs. The following year a U.S. soldier cut off the ear of a dead Vietcong soldier; it later came out in his court martial that he did so after being offered a knife on a dare by a TV news camera operator (Lewy, 1978). There were numerous accounts of TV news crews in the 1960s arranging for protest demonstrations or drug parties to be staged again for the cameras if the original event was not caught on camera. Reporter Janet Cooke lost her Pulitzer Prize in 1981 after admitting that her article, "Jimmy's World" was not based on a real Jimmy, but rather on different people who contributed to the fictional composite Jimmy that was published in The Washington Post.

NBC faked a crash test in 1993 to show that a car it believed to be dangerous would explode. In 1998, Stephen Glass, writer for the New Republic *and other magazines, was found to have fabricated all or parts of dozens of investigative journalism articles, even including a totally fictitious story about a cult that worshiped George H. W. Bush (Lacayo, 2003). Writer Jayson Blair and two editors lost their jobs at* The New York Times *in 2003 after numerous articles of Blair's turned out to be fabricated or plagiarized from other sources. It's important to note that the newspapers and magazines that originally ran these stories issued retractions and/or corrections detailing the reporters' deceit (also see the section below on fake news).*

In 2017, a number of powerful and high-profile male news media figures lost their jobs as a result of sexual impropriety. For example, network morning hosts Charlie Rose and Matt Lauer were both fired due to accusations of sexual harassment in the workplace; their stunned female co-hosts were then left to report on the story of their colleague having been terminated.

At other times, news journalists may become newsmakers in more positive ways. For example, Egyptian President Anwar Sadat's historic trip to Israel in 1977 was arranged not by the United Nations or U.S. State Department diplomats, but by CBS News anchor Walter Cronkite. It was Cronkite who persistently called Sadat and Israeli Prime Minister Menachem Begin to arrange their eventual meeting (Weymouth, 1981). For more on Cronkite, see Close-up 7.9.

Fake News

A recent news media development that has tremendous power to affect our perceptions of reality is the phenomenon that has become known as "fake news." Before the 2016 U.S. presidential election, fake news was not something many media consumers thought about. Fake news was also not a term that many people used; if they did, it was usually to refer to comedy shows like *The Daily Show with Jon Stewart,* which depicted parodies of news reporters. However, with those shows, viewers were in on the joke (Wisser, 2016). More recently, fake news has also taken on a more sinister meaning and has been attributed by some as one of the major reasons that Donald Trump won an upset victory over Hillary Clinton in the 2016 presidential election (Kwong, 2017). We may never know the full extent of fake news's influence on that election, but we do know that it has contributed to wildly irrational behavior, such as a man shooting up a Washington, DC, pizza parlor after having read a fake news account of Hillary Clinton running a child prostitution operation there (Kang & Goldman, 2016; also discussed briefly in Chapter 1). We also know that fake news is receiving increased attention, even from the likes of Pope Francis (Horowitz, 2018).

What exactly is fake news? Levinson (2016) defines *fake news* as "news in which falsities appear by deliberate intent rather than accident or error" (¶1). Although legitimate news sources sometimes make mistakes and report something that isn't accurate, that is not their intent. Legitimate news agencies also issue corrections or retractions when they discover something that they reported isn't right. Familiar and award-winning mainstream news outlets like *The New York Times*, *The Washington Post*, and *The Wall Street Journal* hate it when they have to run retractions because it calls their overall credibility into question. For that reason, they tap multiple independent sources before a story is published. Thus, in contrast to fake news, *real news* or *professional journalism* is "an honest attempt to find and report the truth, safeguarded by an honest attempt to identify and eliminate errors" (Levinson, 2016, ¶7). That's not to say that real news doesn't contain errors. Because news is produced by human beings, there will undoubtedly be errors or bias at times. But real, professional journalists also issue corrections when they are wrong and do everything they can to prevent reporting something that isn't correct.

In an odd irony, in two separate 2017 interviews, President Trump claimed to have coined the term fake news (Borchers, 2017; Schaub, 2017). However, an examination of Trump's Twitter history showed that the first time he used the term publicly was in a December 2016 tweet. By then (over a month after the presidential election), many media outlets had been reporting on how fake news might have affected the election (Borchers, 2017). Thus, Trump's claims about inventing the phrase fake news may itself have been fake news, if his intention was to deceive. In any case, Trump has gone on to use the expression fake news many times—up to eight times a day (Coll, 2017). Unfortunately, he seems to generally apply the label to any reporting he disagrees with or dislikes, even if it's credible. Claims of fake news coverage have also become popular among repressive regimes in countries such as Syria, Venezuela, and Russia (Erlanger, 2017).

In his provocative 2017 book *Weaponized Lies: How to Think Critically in the Post-Truth Era*, neuroscientist Levitin argues that part of the problem with separating fake and real news is the way we now use language about truthfulness, with terms like "post-truth," and "alternate facts," being thrown around. Cutting to the heart of the issue, Levitin says that the label fake news can be misleading in and of itself. "The phrase 'fake news' sounds too playful, too much like a schoolkid faking illness to get out of a test … There are not two sides to a story when one side is a lie … A post-truth era is an era of willful irrationality, reversing all the great advances humankind has made. Maybe journalists don't want to call 'fake news' what it is, a lie, because they don't want to offend the liars. But I say offend them! Call them on the carpet" (Levitin, 2017, pp. xiv–xv).

Why Did Fake News Emerge?

Most media consumers would probably agree that fake news is a troublesome development, but how did we get to a point in which it seems to be all around us? There's no clear answer to that question, but a starting point might be the public's general distrust of the news media. Two months before the 2016 presidential election, a Gallup poll indicated that only 32% of Americans trusted the news media to report the news "fully, accurately, and fairly." That was an all-time low in the 44-year history of that poll and was in stark contrast to earlier years, such as 1976, when 72% of respondents said they trusted the media (Swift, 2016). A 2017 Pew Research Center poll showed that distrust of the news media was even more pronounced among Republicans than Democrats (Barthel & Mitchell, 2017). President Trump has fanned the flames of the public's distrust as well, at one point even calling mainstream news outlets NBC News, *The New York Times*, and CNN the "enemy of the people" (Grynbaum, 2017a), although there was public backlash to that characterization (Ember, 2017a).

Why such distrust? Thompson (2016), among others, has suggested that media themselves may be at least partly to blame. In a world in which there are multiple cable news channels and thousands of online news sources (many with partisan bents), it has become easy to self-select the news that matches and supports our particular political worldview (Iyengar & Hahn, 2009; Reid, 2012). Indeed, an analysis by the *New York Times* and the web analytics company Chartbeat revealed that we may be curating our own media diets to reinforce what we believe while avoiding articles that might challenge our preconceptions (Quealy, 2017). More specifically, Chartbeat tracked web traffic to certain sites and identified readers who seemed to skew more liberal (with clicks on sites like The Huffington Post and Politico) or more conservative (with clicks on sites like Hannity and Breitbart). Interestingly, once on those sites, readers tended to avoid stories that could be considered as a challenge to their point of view. For example, in covering Trump's false claim that his inauguration crowd was the largest ever, conservative as well as liberal-leaning websites ran about the same number of stories. However, liberal readers spent far more time reading those stories than did conservative readers. It makes sense, then, that we might be vulnerable to fake news if we generally distrust news media while also selecting out news sources that match our own beliefs.

How is Fake News Created?

Although it's not clear exactly when and how fake news emerged, many fingers have pointed to the influence of social media. Certainly, we know that social media have become a huge part of news events. For example, in 2011, Facebook and Twitter were credited with helping revolutionaries organize and report on what became known as the Arab Spring (O'Donnell, 2011). Although some critics argued that social media's role in these revolutions may be been overstated (Rosen, 2011), there was a feeling that social media outlets were beginning to provide a platform for unfiltered news and information, particularly in places where news was underreported or not reported at all. By the time protests erupted in Ferguson, Missouri, in 2014 (in response to a police killing of an unarmed African American man), Twitter became especially active with everyday people tweeting live updates on the unfolding situation. By that point in social media's evolution, users also had the ability to live stream video. As a result, those who were interested in what was happening no longer had to wait for the filter of TV cameras or reporters (Deutsch & Lee, 2014). Nevertheless, the accuracy of some social media reports on Ferguson was questionable. For example, one Twitter user reported that police had arrested 12 protesters in a pickup truck for no reason. However, a *St. Louis Post-Dispatch* reporter who was there later reported that the pickup also contained guns and a Molotov cocktail. Unfortunately, with many re-tweets, the original misinformation spread quickly. When the newspaper reporter later weighed in with the truth, many Twitter users accused him of fabricating the story with a #mythicalmolotov hashtag (Bilton, 2014).

By the time of the 2016 U.S. presidential election, creators of fake news had become increasingly sophisticated. Conditions were also ripe for the spread of fake news. A deeply divided populace, skepticism about news media, and potential online advertising revenue all combined to help fuel a wave of fake news sites with stories relating to the election. Because online advertisers often pay websites based on the number of views they get, some sites were highly motivated to share or create false, sometimes outrageously false, stories to get clicks (e.g., "Michelle Obama holds feminist rally at her slave house," "Top officials set to testify against Hillary Clinton found dead"). Indeed, fake news propagators in both the United States and abroad have purposefully used this strategy to generate advertising revenue for themselves (Higgins, McIntire, & Dance, 2016; McCoy, 2016).

The motivation for spreading fake news may not always be about profit, though. The roots of one fake story revealed that the story's spread seemed to be more about partisan anger, quick Twitter fingers, and a reluctance to check facts. The night after the 2016 U.S. presidential election, Eric Tucker of Austin, Texas (who had about 40 Twitter followers), posted a photo of some buses he saw in Austin that day. He speculated in his tweet that anti-Trump protesters were being bused into town. Although it was later confirmed that the buses were there for a conference and had not been full of protesters, Tucker's tweet spread rapidly to conservative websites. It was also shared on Twitter over 16,000 times and on Facebook 350,000 times. Apparently having seen the false information about the bused-in protesters, then President-elect Trump also tweeted about "professional protesters" the next evening. The story was soon disproven by snopes.com as well as other fact-checking sources. Tucker even later admitted that he might have been completely wrong about the facts of his tweet and deleted it. However, by then the tweet and related stories had been seen (and no doubt accepted as fact) by thousands. When interviewed about the incident, Tucker said, "I'm also a very busy businessman, and I don't have time to fact-check everything that I put out there, especially when I don't think it's going out there for wide consumption" (Maheshwari, 2016, ¶9).

In another interesting analysis of the origins of a fake news story, it appeared that the story spread through a global version of the children's game "telephone," in which gossip is passed from one source to the next while facts are lost along the way. This particular story started with a grain of truth about a Russian warplane flying close to a U.S. Navy ship. From there, the story spread to a satirical Russian writer's website, in which he imagined that while flying by, the plane was able to perform a cyberattack on the ship's communication systems. Next, the story took off internationally on Facebook (with much of the satirical nuance lost). After that, the now fake story was picked up by Russian TV. Then, the story was featured in the British tabloid *The Sun*, which amped up the details to include a claim that the Russians might be able to disable the entire U.S. Navy's communication systems. Finally, the story was picked up by the Fox News website, where it was again shared widely on social media, although Fox News later took the story down (MacFarquhar & Rossback, 2017).

From most accounts, the Russian government has played a significant role in the spread of fake news, particularly in the United States. Although the extent of Russia's fake news campaign may never fully be known, in the weeks following the 2016 election, the sophistication of Russia's propaganda machine began to emerge. Apparently viewing Donald Trump as a more Russia-friendly candidate than Hillary Clinton (or perhaps simply seeking to sow distrust and chaos), Russia employed various strategies to help boost Trump's campaign. These included fake news sites, social media profiles for people who did not exist, and "trolls" who intentionally spread false information online (Timberg, 2016). Russian agents also reportedly bought fake news ads on Google and Facebook as well as publishing videos on YouTube (Carey, 2018). Also frequently used were "bots," or automated accounts for social media sites like Twitter. These bots could send or re-tweet identical fake news messages thousands of times (Shane, 2018). Not surprisingly, social media companies like Facebook and Twitter have been heavily criticized for not preventing, or at least not realizing the extent of, Russia's misuse of their platforms (Carey, 2018).

It's not just the United States where fake news has had an impact. In developing countries with little traditional news infrastructure, Facebook and Twitter can be major sources for news. In nations just becoming familiar with democracy and social media, fake news stories may also seem more likely to be true (Mozur & Scott, 2016). Even in established Western democracies like Britain, France, Italy, and Germany, fake news (spread by social media) is now seen as a considerable threat in elections (Horowitz, 2017; Isaac & Eddy, 2017; Scott, 2017; Scott & Eddy, 2017).

Who Consumes Fake News?

Because fake news as we now think about it is a relatively new phenomenon, the academic research to try to better understand it is still in its infancy. However, an interesting 2018 study was one of the first to shine light on how and why people are exposed to fake news (Guess, Nyhan, & Reifler, 2018). Using a representative sample of over 2,500 Americans, the researchers took a detailed look at Internet browsing histories around the time of the 2016 presidential election. They determined that about 25% of Americans had visited a fake news site in the month before the election, although even heavy fake news consumers also spent considerable time on mainstream news sites. It was also discovered that while supporters of both Trump and Clinton had read fake news stories, Trump supporters were much more likely to have visited fake news sites. Not coincidentally, about 80% of fake news stories had been supportive of Trump. Interestingly, Facebook also seemed to be a prime gateway to fake news because many visits to fake news sites were immediately preceded by time spent on Facebook. In addition, the researchers looked at whether study participants had spent much time on fact-checking websites (discussed further below). Sadly (but perhaps not surprisingly), those who consumed the most fake news had the least favorable opinions of fact-checking websites.

What Can Be Done About Fake News?

Although it is beyond the scope of this book to suggest ways that the news media itself might fight fake news, there are some lessons that individual media consumers can learn to combat it for themselves. One is to recognize fake news as such by taking the effort to fact check stories, particularly those that seem like they might be too strange to be true. This is often not an easy task. Before the days of the Internet, factual news sources looked authentic, and fringe literature looked like what it was—homemade. Now, of course, it's easy for anyone with some basic web design knowledge to throw up a fairly attractive fake news site (see Close-up 7.6 for a discussion of how fake sites may have deceived voters in a Florida congressional race).

Still, there are some tools that can help us tell the difference between real and fake news. For years, the website snopes.com has been a reliable source for uncovering and documenting truth relating to all sorts of rumors and urban legends; the website now also frequently takes on fake news claims. There are a number of other fact-checking websites listed at the end of this chapter as well. However, keep in mind that due to the sheer number of fake news stories (relative to the number of fact checkers), not all fake news stories are investigated. Also, it's certainly easier and faster to produce a false story than it is to check the facts behind it. In addition, even fact-checking websites themselves have at times been targeted by ads for fake news sites (Wakabayashi & Qiu, 2017).

❖ CLOSE-UP 7.6 DID FAKE WEBSITES AFFECT A CONGRESSIONAL ELECTION?

In 2014, a special election was held in Florida's 13th Congressional district because Congressman Bill Young had died while in office. The election pitted Republican David Jolly against Democrat Alex Sink, who both wanted to serve out the remainder of Young's term. Because they considered it a swing district, both the Democratic and Republican parties poured millions of dollars into their candidates' campaigns (Sullivan, 2014). That fact wasn't surprising, but what was remarkable about the race was that some voters may have unwittingly contributed money to the candidate they opposed. That's because local Republican offices created a website with the URL sinkforcongress2014.com. The website featured an attractive photo of Democrat Alex Sink along with her campaign's color scheme. However, in smaller print were the words "Make a contribution today to help defeat Alex Sink and candidates like her." Unless contributors read the small print, they may have easily mistaken the website for one supporting Sink while donating money toward her defeat. Not to be outdone, the Democrats soon used the same tactic, and created a website with the URL JollyforCongress.com (Levitin, 2017). In the end, Republican Jolly won a narrow victory over Sink and later also won re-election.

Some places are also putting education and information to use in battling fake news. For example, the European Union now employs a team of tech experts, diplomats, and former journalists whose job it is to scour the Internet and social media for fake news stories. When they find one, they do their best to debunk the false stories in real time on Facebook and Twitter (Scott & Eddy, 2017). In Italy, parliament has teamed up with Facebook and other digital companies to create a curriculum for school children that focuses on recognizing and not spreading fake news (Horowitz, 2017). A few U.S. universities are also beginning to offer courses that specifically address recognizing and dealing with fake news.

Whether or not you take such a course, there are some common-sense things to be on the lookout for when reading online news (Davis, 2016). For one, pay attention to the URL of the website. For example, abcnews.com is the legitimate address for the United States' ABC television network's news division. However, at one time, the web address abcnews.com.co also existed, which was a fake news site designed to look something like the real ABC News site, complete with a knockoff ABC News logo.

Another tip is to read the "about us" section of the website. Most legitimate news agencies have a mission statement that is fairly straightforward. Fake news sites often don't have such a section, or if they do, the language there is melodramatic. One site, for example, claims that its mission is "exposing the scientifically engineered lies of the globalists and their ultimate goal of enslaving humanity."

Yet another tactic in spotting fake news is to critically examine any quotations that appear. For example, almost all public comments made by national figures like Barack Obama, Donald Trump, and Hillary Clinton have been recorded or detailed in multiple sources. Google any quotes you see that seem suspect. If they are legitimate, you should be able to find them in more than one place, including familiar legitimate news sites.

You can also use Google to your advantage in other ways to spot fake news. If you type "link" before a URL, Google will come back with a list of websites that have linked to that URL. This can help you determine if legitimate or fringe sites tend to link to a particular URL (Levitin, 2017). You can also right-click images (in the Google Chrome browser) and do a Google search on the image itself (Davis, 2016). This can sometimes give you a good idea of where the photo originated, or at least where it has been widely used online. Keep in mind, though, that it can be very tough to tell when online photos have been digitally altered (Nightingale, Wade, & Watson, 2017). For additional tips on spotting fake news, see the Useful Links section at the end of this chapter for one communication professor's guide for her students.

The psychological research in how we understand and cognitively process fake news is still in its infancy, although there is emerging evidence that the kind of misinformation present in fake news can be hard for us to let go of, even in the face of conflicting evidence (Chan, Jones, Hall Jamieson, & Albarracín, 2017; De keersmaecker & Roets, 2017). We also know that it's easy to find and spread fake news. What's harder, and more important, is to critically evaluate what we see. Although it's sometimes helpful and informative to view social media live streams of breaking events, we must also remember that social media does not have built-in fact checkers the way that traditional news media outlets do. That puts the burden on us, media consumers, to be savvy about what we read and ultimately choose to believe.

Manipulation of News

Aside from fake news, legitimate news sources sometimes face other forces inside or outside of government that impinge on journalists and affect the news they report. Even in a thriving democracy with constitutional guarantees of a free press, there are always some limits on content. For example, release of classified information is not permitted, nor is libel or slander, obscenity, or language inciting people to violence.

Direct Censorship

In totalitarian nations with prior censorship, material must be submitted to government or military censors for advance approval before being aired or published, or sometimes the government owns and controls all news media. In such cases, a very selective piece of reality may be offered, so much so that history may be substantially rewritten. For example, Russian citizens' views of the West during the Cold War years (1945–1990) were very heavily colored by unflattering news stories about American crime, racism, homelessness, and imperialism that appeared in the Soviet press. Even if very little in these stories was actually untrue, one's overall perception was grossly distorted if, for example, crime was believed to be the rule rather than the exception. Today, most media in Russia are controlled by the government or at least are very pro-Kremlin. Present-day North Korea is an even more extreme example of media censorship. Most likely the most oppressive nation on earth, North Korea's government-controlled media present a very limited picture of the world to its citizens that typically involves the superiority of its leader and the probability of an imminent attack from abroad.

Direct censorship can come in other ways. For example, countries like Malaysia, Singapore, and China have laws forbidding discussion of topics that it deems potentially divisive (i.e., religion, interethnic violence, or anything that might make the government look bad). China also routinely blocks websites like Facebook, Wikipedia, Twitter, and YouTube. Sometimes, these sites are partially blacked out, sometimes completely, and sometimes just temporarily (like on the June 4 anniversary of the 1989 Tiananmen Square massacre) (Martz, 1998; Xu & Albert, 2017). Ironically, many of these nations' constitutions call for freedom of speech and the press.

Intimidation

Another way that news can be manipulated is when those in power try to coerce reporters. In an extreme example of a political figure trying to intimidate a journalist, Montana Republican candidate Greg Gianforte body slammed reporter Ben Jacobs of *The Guardian*, breaking his glasses. Audio recorders were running during the incident, in which Gianforte apparently became frustrated at Jacobs's questions. Despite widespread coverage of the incident, Gianforte won the election the next day. Later, he pleaded guilty to assault and was sentenced to community service hours and anger management classes (Mele, 2017). News media intimidation is not always so blatant, however, and sometimes journalists are bullied by forces which may or may not be connected to any government. For example, when the editor of Tijuana's newspaper *Zeta* wrote against the local drug cartel, he was visited by a team of assassins. Although he survived and continued to write, not everyone would have had the courage to do so. When Zairian freelance writer Jean Mbenga Muaganvita wrote a series of articles on then-strongman President Mobutu Sese Seko, he was arrested and held incommunicado, and soldiers raped his 14-year-old daughter when they searched his home (Martz, 1998). Noted Colombian investigative journalist Fabio Castillo was fired by Bogotá's *El Espectador* after implicating a government minister in a bank corruption scandal. Although the paper claimed he was dismissed purely for financial reasons, the fact that the minister under suspicion mysteriously received an advance copy of the article before publication suggests otherwise (Rosenberg, 2003). Sometimes the stakes for reporting are high; many journalists have been killed in recent years in Algeria, Mexico, Colombia, Cambodia, and other places.

Blocking Access

Certain news stories may be effectively censored purely through blocking the access of the media to the scene of the story. For example, during the apartheid era in South Africa (1948–1991), journalists were often forbidden to enter the Black townships. Similar policies by the Israeli government have sometimes kept the press out of the West Bank during times of Palestinian unrest. The Syrian government of Bashir Assad has largely closed off the country to international journalists in the hopes that the world would forget about his repressive policies and war (Malsin, 2014). In these cases, the governments involved clearly hoped that public attention to the problem would wane if compelling images could no longer be obtained for publication or broadcast.

One of the clearest and most controversial examples of blocking press access has come in the coverage of regional wars. Working on the conventional (although dubious) wisdom that unrestricted press coverage lost the Vietnam War for the United States (see Close-up 7.9), Britain in 1982 and the United States in 1983 forbade the press from accompanying troops in the island wars in the Falklands/Malvinas and Grenada, respectively (Strobel, 1997). The same policy was followed by the United States in the 1989 invasion of Panama to oust dictator Manuel Noriega. Only much later did the public learn that casualties were far higher than originally reported, including the nearly total destruction of a large, poor neighborhood in Panama City. Also see the section later in this chapter on media coverage of the Vietnam War.

One of the most widespread and pervasive cases of censorship through blocking access was exercised by the United States, Saudi Arabia, and their coalition allies in the six-week 1991 Persian Gulf War to oust Iraq from its occupation of Kuwait. Reporters were put in pools, ostensibly to protect them and prevent allied forces from being overwhelmed by reporters. Stories were subject to military censorship, supposedly to prevent the leaking of troop movement information. Sometimes stories were held up for days, and in some instances the Pentagon actually announced the story first at its briefings. There were total blackouts at the start of the air and ground campaigns, as well as a ban on photos of coffins of killed U.S. soldiers arriving home. Media were also used to help confuse the Iraqis. For example, reporters were frequently taken to the area near the southern Kuwaiti border with Saudi Arabia but not to the western border area where the real build-up for the ground invasion was occurring. Pools were taken to cover practice maneuvers for an apparent sea assault on Kuwait, an assault that never came but was rather used to divert attention from the planned ground thrust from the west.

Journalists were probably themselves highly supportive of the coalition effort, being determined not to allow themselves to be the scapegoats for a lost war (think Vietnam) and were not going to allow themselves to be called unpatriotic. This concern may not have been unrealistic; the little independent coverage that did occur sometimes elicited angry cries of traitor. Media coverage of the Gulf War continued to be debated and analyzed for many years (Greenberg & Gantz, 1993; Iyengar & Simon, 1993; Mowlana, Gerbner, & Schiller, 1993; Zelizer, 1992).

When the United States invaded Iraq in 2003, the American military took a different approach to media coverage, this time allowing "embedded" journalists to cover the war by traveling with select military units (Ignatius, 2010). However, some criticized cable news channels and the reports coming from their embedded journalists as largely pro-invasion propaganda (Ponce de Leon, 2015). Later, when the war did not go as quickly as anticipated (and no weapons of mass destruction were found), the media were again criticized for not asking tougher questions of those in power before the invasion began (Kurtz, 2013).

Indirect Censorship

In some nations, it is an official crime to broadcast or publish material that is in any way against the interests of the state. Such vague legislation is available for use according to the political whims of the current rulers. In other cases, the government and large business interests are so close that politically suspect TV stations and newspapers cannot find the advertising they need to survive. Even in most democratic countries, the government issues licenses for TV and radio stations. Sometimes these are withheld or delayed for political reasons; President Trump made such a threat toward NBC in 2017 (Baker & Kang, 2017). Some countries require journalists to be licensed, a practice consistently condemned by the International Press Institute as threatening freedom of the press. In other cases, the supply and distribution of newsprint is controlled by the government and may be allotted according to political considerations.

Manipulation by Timing

Sometimes "bad news" may be released at a time guaranteed to receive less coverage than average. For example, U.S. President Gerald Ford's 1974 pardon of ex-President Richard Nixon for any Watergate-related crimes was announced on a Sunday morning, after the Sunday morning TV news talk shows and newspaper distribution but before churchgoers would have arrived home from services. In 1992, President George H. W. Bush pardoned Iran-contra defendants on Christmas Day, when most people were busy with family activities. Several presidents have issued pardons to convicted felons during their last hours in office. President Trump even pardoned a controversial Arizona sheriff while a major hurricane was striking Texas and most news outlets were covering the storm heavily (Parker, 2017). These unpopular policies were deliberately announced at times likely to receive the least possible coverage and attention. Often, government sources strategically leak stories about upcoming policy to gauge public reaction (a practice known as a "trial balloon"). If the reaction is negative, the policy need never be officially announced, and the government will not be blamed for proposing it.

Media Self-Censorship

Sometimes censorship is self-imposed by the media, often due to pressure or fear of pressure from advertisers or the public. The largest commercial TV networks give limited attention to major corporate changes involving themselves or to any story reflecting unfavorably on their parent company, such as ABC and Disney or NBC and Comcast (Lee & Solomon, 1991; Stelter, 2016; Steyer, 2002). For example, in 1998 ABC News (owned by Disney) prepared a major investigative report on abuses of labor and safety practices at Walt Disney World (Steyer, 2002). The story was either killed by Disney executives or self-censored by ABC before it aired, as were other stories about large executive compensation (no one wanted to offend the very well-paid Disney chairman), lax screening procedures that allowed the hiring of pedophiles at the theme parks, and even a feature about the hit movie *Chicken Run*, produced by Disney rival DreamWorks (Mayer, 2000). Another example was when a young boy was killed by an alligator at a Walt Disney World resort hotel in Florida. CBS and NBC news reported that there were no alligator warning signs in the lagoon where the boy was swimming; ABC did not mention this fact (Stelter, 2016). See Chapter 1 for additional discussion of corporate self-censorship.

Advertising can play a role in media self-censorship, too. Magazines that accept tobacco ads publish fewer stories about the health risks of smoking than do magazines that do not accept tobacco ads (Strasburger & Wilson, 2002). Advertiser pressure may also have an effect. For example, the *San Jose Mercury News* published a lengthy consumer story on how to buy a car, including tips on negotiating with dealers and information on dealer incentives and money holdbacks and how customers could use the invoice to figure the actual cost of the car. In response, the Santa Clara County Motor Car Dealers' Association pulled $1 million of advertising from the newspaper. The editor published a letter apologizing for the article and extolling the paper's longstanding partnership with the local car dealers. There were no subsequent in-depth stories dealing with auto dealership issues (Lieberman, 2000).

Sometimes media are in possession of information that they choose not to reveal for some reason. This may include military information about troop movements, but it might also be information that some government official has lied. The press may conclude (rightly or wrongly) that the public just does not want to hear, or would not believe, certain highly negative news about their country or government. For example, when the Soviet Union shot down a South Korean commercial airliner in 1983, the Kremlin made the predictable Cold War charge that it was an American spy plane. Although this claim was widely reported in the United States, it was practically never taken seriously there. In a careful analysis of the coverage of this issue by magazines *Time*, *Newsweek*, and *U.S. News & World Report*, Corcoran (1986) concluded that all three publications, with an estimated combined readership of around 50 million, followed a virtually identical Reagan administration party line of anti-Soviet diatribe and paranoia (see also Entman, 1991). Outside of the United States (e.g., in reputable British publications like *The Guardian*) available evidence supporting the theory that the airliner was on a spy mission was fully examined and seen to be a credible explanation, though it was never definitively confirmed or discredited. Why was this perspective not heard in the United States? It was not due to government censorship but perhaps was due to the press sensing that the U.S. public did not want to seriously consider (or perhaps would not believe) such a claim.

In the Watergate scandal of the early 1970s, the press chose to call President Nixon and other high U.S. government officials liars only after a considerable period of time and the emergence of very compelling evidence. In the mid-1980s, the press was very hesitant to directly expose the very popular President Reagan's misinformation about Soviet involvement in Nicaragua. Only after the revelation in late 1986 that the Reagan administration had been sending arms to Iran with the profits being diverted to the Nicaraguan right-wing contra rebels did the press seem to give itself permission to seriously criticize the president. The Washington press corps long knew of the Reagan administration's disinformation campaign in attributing a Berlin disco bombing in 1985 to Libya's Muammar Gaddafi, but said nothing. More recently, U.S. news outlets reporting the mistreatment of prisoners by U.S. soldiers in the 2004 Abu Ghraib Iraq prison scandal tended to follow the Bush administration "party line," in spite of much public opposition to such frames by the political opposition (Rowling, Jones, & Sheets, 2011). Such behavior on the part of some U.S. soldiers (called "torture" by many) was a major threat to the positive national identity of the nation. Apparently the press was reluctant to stray too far from the official positive (or at least less negative) spin that the Bush administration put on the event.

A related way that news agencies sometimes do not report information they have is through *news embargoes* or media blackouts, in which news media agree to not report something or wait until a later time to do so. Often, this is due (at least ostensibly) to security concerns. Sometimes this may relate to a president or other high-level official's travel to a potentially dangerous area (Moniz, 2003). Another example is when British officials told many media outlets that Prince Harry was being deployed to Afghanistan, but asked that, for his safety, this fact not be reported until his deployment ended. However, Harry's cover was blown when an Australian magazine, unaware of the news embargo, broke the news (Squires, 2008).

Consolidation of News-Gathering Organizations

Although not exactly manipulation of news as such, another factor impacting the perceived reality of world events is the increasing consolidation of news-gathering organizations. As discussed in Chapters 1 and 6, recent years have seen many mega mergers among media companies. One large media conglomerate that has made no bones about being partisan is the Sinclair Broadcast Group. Having bought up U.S. TV stations for years, Sinclair owns more local stations than any other company. Although many of Sinclair's stations have their own local newscasts, the company also requires its stations to run company-produced opinion pieces that reflect the views of Sinclair's conservative owners (Ember, 2017b). Media consolidation can affect local markets in other surprising ways. For example, a late night train derailment in Minot, North Dakota, in 2002 spilled large amounts of toxic anhydrous ammonia. When emergency responders called the seven local radio stations to have them alert the public, there was nobody present at six of the seven stations, which were all owned by the Clear Channel corporation and were operating by broadcasting prerecorded material from corporate headquarters without any local on-air staff in the middle of the night (Collum, 2008). Still, not all large media companies are so lax or heavy-handed with their news coverage. Skyrocketing costs, plus the undeniable logic of efficiency, mandate a pooling of resources when it comes to news reporting. Clearly, not every newspaper, news magazine, website, or TV and radio station can afford to have its own reporter in every potential news spot in the world.

This consolidation, however, has reduced news gatherers to a very small club. In terms of newspapers, most news copy in most newspapers comes from a very few sources, most often the wire services of AP, Reuters, and Agence France Presse (AFP). Only a very few large dailies, such as *The New York Times* and *The Los Angeles Times*, have their own wire service. In terms of television, the U.S. commercial networks of ABC, NBC, CBS, Fox, and CNN (and their accompanying websites) have enormous influence worldwide. A few other major networks, such as the BBC and ITN in the United Kingdom and Brazil's TV Globo, take large pieces of the remaining pie. These few sources have enormous impact on our perceived reality of distant events. For example, even in nations ruled by stridently anti-American regimes, a large percentage of the news copy comes from the AP wire service. A small number of sources is not in and of itself cause for alarm. Large organizations like the AP take great pains to present diverse and balanced viewpoints, and it is strongly in their interest to be perceived by all as fair and unbiased. Still, the potentially enormous influence of any of these sources on people's knowledge worldwide is sobering, especially in light of the recent popularity of cable channels and websites with a very openly partisan agenda.

Another consequence of the financial realities of international news reporting has been a greatly decreased number of foreign bureaus and correspondents over the years. For example, by 1996 CBS was down from a high of 20 to 4 major foreign bureaus, with ABC having 8, NBC 7, and CNN 20. Many networks have also moved to having one-person foreign bureaus who report with their laptops, smartphones, and an Internet connection (Stelter, 2008). Most U.S. newspapers had also shuttered their foreign bureaus by 2010 (Enda, 2011). Although this reduction does not preclude a news anchor or Washington correspondent from reading a foreign story accompanied by visuals from file footage or freelance or government sources, the amount of international news reported by networks has decreased over the years, particularly since the 1970s (Moisy, 1997; Strobel, 1997).

As the number of reporters in the field has gone down, there is increasing sharing of reporters and content across TV channels, Internet sites, and other outlets. A lesser known trend is the increasing use of "video news releases" (VNRs). These are prepared by the newsmakers, often in prepackaged "news story" format and made available to news outlets. Although they are free to use these as they choose, including editing or ignoring them, tight budgets and reduced staff make it tempting to present these VNRs largely unedited and often without the public realizing their source, even if explicitly identified in the news story (Tewksbury, Jensen, & Coe, 2011).

"Disguising" the News as Entertainment

Increasingly, news appears in forums that are not even part of news departments. Soft news is becoming increasingly intertwined with hard news, especially on cable and Internet sources (Coe *et al.*, 2008). For example, television shows like *The View*, *Entertainment Tonight*, *Inside Edition*, and the late night network talk shows are produced by entertainment (not news) divisions, yet they frequently contain interviews and other material amplifying some current news story. Magazines like *People* or *Us Weekly* (see Close-up 7.2) are similar, and even established Internet news sites like MSNBC contain a large proportion of gossipy stories. What is the effect of such entities in conveying the news? These programs can effectively communicate news, particularly to people who are otherwise relatively uninvolved politically and low consumers of news media (Baum, 2002), although soft news may also contribute to increased political cynicism (Boukes & Boomgaarden, 2015).

News and Comedy Shows

One highly successful television format has been comedy news shows like *The Daily Show*, *The Colbert Report*, and *Last Week Tonight with John Oliver* (Baym, 2005; Trier, 2008a, 2008b). These shows have the format of a news show and are actually based on the day's events, complete with the host reading the news, followed by reports from (parodied) correspondents and interviews with (real) newsmakers. Current events are regularly lampooned, and venal or hypocritical newsmakers are sometimes ruthlessly taken to task, often by shameless editing to make them look as bad as possible. *The Daily Show* regularly has political candidates and office holders, other newsmakers, and famous entertainers as guests. Intriguingly, serious and probing interviews are also sometimes conducted which can be at least as enlightening as comparable efforts on real news programs. Occasionally, a comedy news show can actually take the lead in forcing legislative attention to a real problem. For example, on *The Daily Show*, an obviously outraged Jon Stewart once almost singlehandedly shamed the U.S. Congress into passing legislation restoring the health benefits of the 9/11 first responders. Similarly, late night comedian Jimmy Kimmel inserted himself into debate about repealing Obamacare in 2017. Telling a harrowing story of how his newborn son was saved with heart surgery (and lamenting the fact that poorer people might lose access to such procedures), Kimmel took Senator Bill Kassidy of Louisiana especially to task, as Kassidy had appeared on Kimmel's show months earlier saying a repeal bill would not affect health care for children (Russonello, 2017).

Kimmel, along with fellow late night co-hosts Seth Meyers and Stephen Colbert, has reshaped the late night network comedy talk show format into something much more political. Colbert, for example, initially struggled when he left his Comedy Central show *The Colbert Report* in 2015 to take over CBS's *Late Show* from David Letterman. Apparently finding it difficult to fill his predecessor's shoes and set a different tone than *The Colbert Report*, the *Late Show*'s ratings suffered. However, the 2016 presidential election seemed to re-energize Colbert, and he began pointedly taking on Donald Trump almost nightly.

This is in stark contrast to the old days when late night shows were hosted by the likes of Johnny Carson and Jay Leno. Those hosts often made fun of the president, but the comedy was usually gentler than the political jokes that Colbert and Kimmel dish out these days. Why the change? Comedians and comedy writers like Seth Meyers have said that it's hard to resist making fun of such a non-traditional president as Trump, who sometimes seems to write the jokes for them (Rutenberg, 2017b). Like other areas of television, ratings (and associated ad revenue) matter, too. Before the 2016 presidential election, NBC's *The Tonight Show*, hosted by Jimmy Fallon, was by far the most watched late night network show. During and after the election, Fallon chose to give his comedy less political bite than his competitors. As a result, Fallon's ratings were eclipsed by Colbert's and are also frequently challenged by Jimmy Kimmel's on ABC (Koblin, 2017). Although perhaps reflecting the deep political divides in the United States, some have argued that this pointed political comedy also deepens the rift by further alienating those who disagree and see the kind of jokes that Kimmel and Colbert offer up as attacks by liberal show business elites (Flanagan, 2017).

Of course, being comedians, Colbert, Kimmel, and others do not have to adhere to any of the ethical norms of journalism (Borden & Tew, 2007). They regularly take quotes from newsmakers out of context and make fun of them, "report" outrageous events that never happened, and need show no constraints to present a fair representation or even to check the accuracy of what is reported. When Jon Stewart regularly framed his reports about the Iraq War with a "Mess-O-Potamia" background slide, he was not being biased, simply entertaining. Nonetheless, such shows may have something to say about journalistic ethics. Colbert and others "do not inhabit the role of journalists but, rather, adopt the performance of journalists to draw attention to lapses in journalistic integrity" (Borden & Tew, 2007, p. 311).

Stewart especially has used his fame to encourage a higher ethical standard of news journalism. Most notably, he used a 2004 guest appearance on CNN's *Crossfire* to criticize that program for "hurting America" with its strident adversarial format. He called the show's protagonists "partisan hacks" and said "You have a responsibility to public discourse, and you failed miserably" (Baym, 2005). Does comedy news have higher standards than real news? Some credit Stewart's critique for leading to the subsequent demise of *Crossfire*.

The Docudrama: Fact or Fiction?
Sometimes the line between media news and fictional entertainment becomes blurred. A particularly controversial format is the *docudrama*, a fictional story based on real events. Although it is certainly not new to take some historic events and build a story around them, embellishing where facts are unavailable or undramatic (Shakespeare did it all the time), there is greater concern with TV dramas or movies based on spectacular crimes, political and international figures, and other news stories. Such programming was especially popular in the 1990s. For example, one weekend in January 1993, CBS, NBC, and ABC all aired premiere TV docudrama movies based on the same story of the teenager who only months earlier was accused of trying to kill her alleged lover's wife. All three movies did at least reasonably well in the ratings. Although docudramas became less common in the 2000s, they saw a resurgence in 2017 and 2018, with depictions of the O. J. Simpson, Menendez, and Versace murder cases. Ironically, all of those crimes occurred in the 1990s.

At times, docudramas have so quickly followed the news events they dramatize that it becomes difficult to distinguish them from news. In one sweeps week in late May 1993, networks aired TV movies about the first World Trade Center bombing

(February, 1993), Hurricane Andrew (August, 1992), and the siege of the Branch Davidian cult in Waco, Texas (April, 1993). The latter script was written and came to the screen in record time. From the initial shootings of federal agents in late February to the final FBI assault on the compound on April 19, the country waited for news of how the siege would be played out. All the while, the TV movie was in production, with the script being written and rewritten in response to each day's news. The movie aired on May 23, only 34 days after the real death of its lead character David Koresh and dozens of his followers. For millions of people, that script's interpretation of the Waco events became reality.

There may be limits on what the media believe the public will find acceptable. For example, in contrast to those events of the 1990s, it was five or more years after the terrorist attacks of September 2001 before any movies or TV shows based on those events appeared. Entertainment based on events that horrible carry a public relations risk of being perceived as attempting to profit from a catastrophic tragedy. There is also the issue of when the public is ready to watch entertainment based on very recent tragedies. For example, there were several theatrical movies set in the Iraq War released in the 2005–2010 time period, including one Oscar winner (*The Hurt Locker*), but the audiences for such films were modest at best.

Producers are hungry for docudrama deals and have little compunction about changing the facts to suit entertainment needs. For example, when North American peace worker Jennifer Casolo was approached about a movie contract about her experiences working in El Salvador in the 1980s and being falsely arrested for being a revolutionary, the producers wanted her permission to make two changes in the story. They wanted her to (1) be actually guilty instead of innocent, and (2) fall in love with one of her captors. Unimpressed, Ms. Casolo turned down a lucrative offer.

Sometimes details of the story and its marketing are subtly changed for different audiences. For example, the 2001 film *Pearl Harbor* played up the love story and played down the battle scenes for its Japanese debut. A scene in which an American major tells his men that, should an upcoming raid on Tokyo not succeed, he would "kill himself and as many Japanese as possible" was deleted. There were also certain changes in language. For example, the phrase "a few less dirty Japs" was softened to "a few less Japs" (Kleiner, 2001).

In fact, the whole genre of the docudrama is merely a continuation of filmed interpretations of the past. In a fascinating study of cinematic stories of American historical events, historian Robert Toplin (1995) argued that famous period films such as *Mississippi Burning, Sergeant York, JFK, Bonnie and Clyde, Patton*, and *All the President's Men* all significantly distort the historical record but yet at the same time convey a fairly accurate sense of the time and place to many people who would never be reached by purely historical writing.

Sometimes telling the story accurately risks distorting it in a broader sense. For example, Clint Eastwood's two critically acclaimed 2007 films, *Flags of our Fathers* and *Letters from Iwo Jima*, about the six men who planted the flag on Mount Suribachi on Iwo Jima in World War II were quite accurate historically. True to that racially segregated period, however, Whites and African Americans were trained separately and the latter were limited to supportive, though still dangerous, supply roles. The film portrayed the six heroes all as White, which they actually were, but some, including director Spike Lee, argued that Eastwood should have used a metaphorical "wider-angle lens" to include African American roles in this iconic battle (Altman, 2008).

Although there is often an under-emphasis on examining the deeper motivations for the behavior of historical figures (Hoekstra, 1998), docudramas are compelling and make events of the past accessible to many people. How does one balance the distortion of the historical record with the advantage of telling more people an important story? See Close-up 7.7 for a detailed comparison of fiction and reality in one docudrama.

❖ CLOSE-UP 7.7 CASE STUDY OF THE DOCUDRAMA AMISTAD (1997)

Steven Spielberg's film Amistad *told the previously little-known story of a rebellion by 53 kidnapped Africans aboard a Portuguese slave ship bound for the United States in 1839. They killed all but two of their captors. Double-crossed by these two survivors, who kept sailing to America at night instead of back to Africa, the Africans ended up in a Connecticut jail. However, their cause was taken up by Christian abolitionists, who hired ex-President John Quincy Adams to argue their case up to the U.S. Supreme Court, which eventually released them. The movie left out or downplayed certain major protagonists and enhanced the roles of others or combined them into fictional composites. For example, Adams's stirring speech to the U.S. Supreme Court never happened, according to Amistad historian and film consultant Clifford Johnson. The Africans' earlier attorney Roger Baldwin is portrayed as a more minor and inept character than he was in reality. Abolitionism as a social movement almost disappeared in the film, except for the abolitionist Lewis Tappan, who is played as a hypocrite with a more minor and far less noble role than the historical Tappan had. The central driving role of Christianity in the lives of the abolitionists is largely absent, in keeping with the general invisibility of religion in American popular culture (see* Chapter 4). *Still, for all its rewriting of history, the film* Amistad *brought this important but previously largely unknown incident to the consciousness of millions in a way that historians could never hope to do (Goldstein, W., 1998; A. Schneider, 1998).*

In a curious footnote to this film, an egregious historical error came to light. The revolt's leader Cinqué, portrayed as a hero in Spielberg's film, has been identified in several sources as having later returned to Africa and himself become a slave trader, although this was not part of the movie. In a bit of bibliographic sleuthing, Amistad historian Howard Jones traced the historical source of this claim to several history textbooks by Samuel Eliot Morison in the 1950s and 1960s. The sole source cited in these texts is a 1953 novel Slave Mutiny *by William Owens. Apparently, several historians adopted Morison's interpretation without checking primary sources. Although novelist Owens apparently reported seeing some document somewhere confirming Cinqué's role as a slave trader, researchers at the Amistad Research Institute could find no record of such activity (Hot Type, 1998).*

Now that we have looked at how the media mediate between the reality of the news and the reports we receive, let us examine some effects of news coverage.

Effects of News Coverage

Long after the events reported in the news, what is primarily remembered is the media coverage. As Lang and Lang put it, "the reality that lives on is the reality etched in the memories of the millions who watched rather than the few who were actually there" (1984, p. 213). Now let us turn to examining the impact and effects of consuming news coverage, including the importance of different points of view, memory for the news, effects on decision making and other behaviors, effects of crime coverage, and the effect of news reporting on foreign policy.

The Impact of Different Points of View

Part of the reason that people in different nations or with different political leanings tend to perceive the same situations so differently is that the reality they construct in response to news is so different (Quealy, 2017; Schmitt, Gunther, & Liebhart, 2004). Not only does the reporting of such events in the media vary in different places, but even more basically, the interpretation of the same events differs, depending on the knowledge, motivations, and experiences of those who hear or see the news (David, 2009; Iyengar & Hahn, 2009). To illustrate, let's look at a few examples.

White and African American audiences responded quite differently to news reports of Hurricane Katrina damage in 2005. Blacks overwhelmingly blamed the federal government and were not affected by whether or not a news story contained pictures of victims and, if so, the victims' race. White media consumers, however, attributed less government blame overall (Ben-Porath & Shaker, 2010). Similarly, Israeli Arabs perceive news very differently than their Jewish neighbors (Baden & Tenenboim-Weinblatt, 2017; Tsfati, 2007). Different groups of people also choose to read about different kinds of people; in a study of online news stories selected to read, African American readers disproportionately read more stories about Blacks, while White readers showed no comparable differences (Knobloch-Westerwick, Appiah, & Alter, 2008).

Technology may be making it easier for us to interpret news events differently, too. For example, it is increasingly common for different news consumers to watch a mainstream broadcast of an event (like CBS coverage of the president's State of the Union address) while simultaneously watching more partisan coverage on another device (like monitoring liberal websites on a tablet or watching conservative tweets about the State of the Union on a smartphone). This phenomenon has been called *second screening* (Gil de Zúñiga, Garcia-Perdomo, & McGregor, 2015), and it may have an effect on political attitudes as well as political participation (McGregor & Mourão, 2017).

The actual framing of the news can have a great impact. For example, the 2011 popular uprising in Egypt which ultimately led to the overthrow of Hosni Mubarak was framed by government newspapers as "A conspiracy on the Egyptian state," while independent news sources and social media posting framed it as "a revolution for freedom and social justice" (Hamdy & Gomaa, 2012). That same dichotomy has appeared in the conflict against the Assad regime in Syria. Social media now allow the publication of material in ways that would have been very difficult if not impossible in authoritarian regimes previously. The impact of the wider variety of framing of public events now possible through social media is hard to overestimate (Lim, 2012; Nisbet, Stoycheff, & Pearce, 2012; Wasike, 2017). Indeed, someone reading everything framed in a particular way would get a very different idea of events than someone who only read everything framed in the opposite way.

Many of the most intractable and chronic world conflicts have at their heart a gigantic divergence in point of view, a chasm that causes the two sides to interpret reports of the same events totally differently. They also consistently fail to appreciate how differently other people view the same events. For example, during the Cold War (1945–1990), the Soviet Union and Western nations viewed each other through their own mirror-image biases (Hirschberg, 1993); the same is probably true today for those same Western nations and North Korea. Israelis and Palestinians on the West Bank, Christians and Muslims in Lebanon, and liberals and conservatives in the United States see themselves besieged and oppressed by the other. In the 1990s, when the West moved to expand NATO, that development looked very threatening to Moscow, which saw it as an aggressive move. From the Russian perspective, it looked like preparation for war to the east. When the United States moved hundreds of thousands of troops to the Persian Gulf and invaded two countries (Afghanistan in 2001 and Iraq in 2003) to remove unfriendly regimes, neighboring countries quite reasonably wondered if they would be next, even if that concern seemed ridiculous to many Americans. See Close-up 7.8 for a more extended example of the sharply divergent points of view of Islam and the West on political, social, and religious issues.

❖ CLOSE-UP 7.8 THE COGNITIVE GULF BETWEEN ISLAM AND THE WEST

Islam as a religion is very poorly understood in the West, a fact especially troubling to Muslims, given its position, with Christianity and Judaism, as one of the three related mono-theistic Abrahamic faiths (Easterbrook, 1989; Shaheen, 2014); also see Chapter 5. *Events of the last 30 years, particularly the unprecedented Muslim migration to the West and the heightened Islamist terrorist threat of the new millennium, bring a new urgency to bridging this gap. There are some fundamental differences in the faiths and associated cultures that both sides would do well to better understand. It is very much against the dictates of Islam to criticize the theology of Judaism or Christianity, which are seen as part of the foundations of Islam, although considerable criticism of Western politics is permitted. In a similar vein, it is acceptable for Christians to make gentle jokes about Jesus, but in Islam there exist strong proscriptions against discussing the personal life of the prophet Mohammed or even of having any pictorial representations of him. This explains the worldwide Muslim outrage at the Danish publication of a cartoon picturing Mohammed as a terrorist. Intellectual debate and disagreement about the prophet's actions is quite acceptable, but anything personal or disrespectful is not. Finally, Islam is no more monolithic than is Christianity, and Muslims are understandably offended when Western media portray some radical Islamic terrorist as a typical Muslim.*

There is also a fundamental difference between Islam and the West in the relationship between church and state. Most Muslim countries accept some degree of theocracy, although the degree varies. Thus, insulting Mohammed is an insult to all Muslim nations and all Muslims, even those not actively practicing their faith. This is somewhat like nonreligious Jews' abhorrence of anti-Semitism, although there is no real parallel in Christianity, which has much less nonreligious cultural identity than does either Judaism or Islam.

One of the most basic beliefs in Western Europe and especially in North America is the separation of church and state, a belief whose deep ideological character and ramifications are
not well understood by Muslims. In the West, it is unacceptable for one person's religious
beliefs to infringe on another person's political freedom. Although it is a political belief, this
tenet is highly ideological, almost religious in character, especially in the United States.
Furthermore, the Western democratic tradition of free speech is also practically like a religious belief to most people in the United States and the European Union. The treatment
of women is seen in the West as a political right, not a religious decision, although most
Western religions support equality of the sexes as well. If some stories from Muslim news
sources of violence against women tend to blame the victim and downplay responsibility of
the perpetrator (Halim & Meyers, 2010), this does not sit well with Western eyes and ears.

Memory for the News

News offers an interesting case to test people's memories in a real-world setting, with
obvious applied, as well as important theoretical, relevance (McCombs & Reynolds,
2009; Meeter, Murre, & Janssen, 2005; Saux *et al.*, 2017). News stories in all media are
most typically fairly short, self-contained pieces, which happen to be very useful units
for experimental research on memory.

Schneider and Laurion (1993) studied meta-memory for radio news, finding that
people's assessment of what they had remembered from news was fairly accurate. In the
case of television, however, the information involves more than the verbal content. The
simultaneous presence of both visual and auditory information provides the potential
of their either (a) complementing or (b) interfering with each other in the processing
of and memory for news content. With television news, memory for visual content is
generally better than memory for verbal content (Graber, 1990), and memory is better
if there is a close fit between the video and the audio component, such as when the
video illustrates exactly what was being described by the reporter (Fox, 2004). When
the relationship is less clear or when the video and audio portions evoke different previous information from the viewer's memory, comprehension and memory for the new
information suffers (Fox *et al.*, 2004; Grimes, 1990, 1991; Mundorf, Drew, Zillmann, &
Weaver, 1990).

More recent research has focused on how our memories for news reports can
become distorted. Children may be especially vulnerable to such false memories of the
news. While one study found that half of adults could recall a frightening news story
from childhood (Riddle, 2012), other researchers found that 7- to 8-year-old Dutch
children's exposure to a false newspaper report about UFO abductions led to 70% of
those children later falsely "remembering" themselves as having been abducted (Otgaar,
Candel, Merckelbach, & Wade, 2009). Similarly, Loftus and colleagues (e.g., Patihis &
Loftus, 2016) have consistently found that adults can report false childhood memories
of seeing news video footage. For instance, some people recalled seeing images of a
plane crashing in Pennsylvania during the September 11, 2001, terrorist attack when
they were children, even though such footage does not exist. Other research has found
that memory for news also can become distorted, particularly when the news reports
focus on sensational details like injuries (Lawson & Strange, 2015).

Indeed, some of the most distressing events ever to be broadcast on television
were the terrorist attacks of September 11, 2001. Thanks to a fortuitous longitudinal

study of dreams in progress from August to December 2001, researchers were able to document an increase in troubled dream content after 9/11. These included threats or specific reference to events of that day. The authors argued for a causal connection between the disturbing news footage shown repeatedly on television in those days and the disturbed dreaming (Hartmann & Basile, 2003; Propper, Stickgold, Keeley, & Christman, 2007).

Whether people are in a good or bad mood can affect what they remember from the news as well. German high school students read either a news story about the World Championship Soccer German victory or a depressing article about child soldiers in Congo. Their memory for six subsequent news articles was affected by the tone of the first article. Students reading about the soccer championship recalled more positive than negative information from the subsequent articles, while those reading about the child soldiers in Congo recalled more negative than positive information from subsequent articles (Baumgartner & Wirth, 2012).

Memory for persons in the news can also be affected by viewers' social attitudes. For example, Whites are more likely to identify an African American, rather than a White person, as a criminal suspect (Gibbons, Taylor, & Phillips, 2005; Oliver & Fonash, 2002; Oliver, Jackson, Moses, & Dangerfield, 2004), although such an effect was not demonstrated with photos of men who appeared to be of Middle Eastern descent (Hoewe, 2014). However, as predicted by cultivation theory, Whites who watch more local TV news with a disproportionate number of African Americans presented as criminals were more likely to perceive Blacks as violent (Dixon, 2008a) or poor (Dixon, 2008b) or to identify race-unidentified perpetrators as Black (Dixon, 2007).

Effects of News on Attributions and Decision Making

Comprehension of news media has implications beyond memory. How the news is reported can affect our knowledge about the topic. One example of this is our perception of crime. Studies have found that those who are frequent consumers of print and television news may perceive violent crimes such as carjacking as more frequent than they actually are, in a cultivation effect (Gibson & Zillmann, 1994; Pinker, 2018). Such an effect has not been found for online news consumers (Roche, Pickett, & Gertz, 2016), although one study revealed that frequent use of social media (that no doubt contained news stories of crime) was related to an overall fear of crime (Intravia, Wolff, Paez, & Gibbs, 2017). Also see the section later in this chapter on news media coverage of crime.

Cultivation effects also seem to be present with our perceptions of the larger world. Brown and Siegler (1992) found that the amount of media coverage of a country predicted people's rated knowledge of that country and also its estimated population. Countries receiving more media coverage were believed to be more populous than those receiving less coverage. Gibbons, Lukowski, and Walker (2005) found that merely being exposed repeatedly to initially unbelievable headlines over time led readers to find them more believable. News consumers continually update their mental models of the content being described, for example, drawing causal inferences from material mentioned (Blanc, Kendeou, van den Broek, & Brouillet, 2008; Blanc, Stiegler-Balfour, & O'Brien, 2011). News readers also sometimes interpret news headlines as indicative of cause-and-effect relationships that may not really exist (Adams *et al.*, 2017).

Viewers' goals in watching TV news and their expertise on the topic also affect how carefully and systematically they extract information from a news story (Tewksbury, 1999). For example, people relatively high in need for cognition (i.e., enjoying thinking) like the cognitive processing of news stories, regardless of their level of skepticism or trust of the source (Tsfati & Cappella, 2005). In addition, online news stories that contain hyperlinks increase readers' further seeking information about the news topic while also increasing the perceived credibility of the story (Borah, 2014).

Another issue is the effect of media publicity on juror decision making, specifically pretrial publicity about a case. Jurors' exposure to information about a particular case affects verdicts. For example, lurid pretrial information about a rape or murder case increases the likelihood of a conviction vote (Ruva, McEvoy, & Bryant, 2007). This knowledge is not necessarily erased by a judge's direction to disregard the information (Ruva & Guenther, 2015).

Responses to Crime Coverage in Media

Several provocative books, most notably Abramsky's (2017) *Jumping at Shadows: The Triumph of Fear and the End of the American Dream*, Glassner's (1999) *The Culture of Fear: Why Americans Are Afraid of the Wrong Things*, Gardner's (2008) *The Science of Fear: Why We Fear the Things We Shouldn't—and Put Ourselves in Greater Danger*, and Best's (1999) *Random Violence: How We Talk About New Crimes and New Victims*, address the question of the effect of media coverage of crimes on the public perception of different dangers. In particular, news may help warp the accuracy of our ability to assess risk.

How News Distorts the Reporting of Dangers

There's little that people fear more than being the target of violence. Best (1999) identified three unwarranted, yet widely believed, assumptions about so-called "random" violent crimes. First of all, violence is believed to be pattern-less, with everyone equally likely to be a victim. However, the facts are otherwise. Young adult men, especially if they are young men of color, are much more likely to be victims of violent crime than anyone else (except for women as sexual assault victims). Second, violence is seen to be pointless; that is, perpetrated for no apparent reason. On the contrary, there is almost always some motive for violent crimes, although the rare, exceptional cases when there is not a motive receive heavy coverage and seem particularly threatening. Finally, violent crime is perceived to be getting worse, while in fact most violent crime rates in the United States have been falling sharply since the early 1990s (Gramlich, 2017). If violent crime rates are falling and violent crime is not pattern-less or pointless, why do most people believe otherwise?

One reason is that very often in crime reporting, scenarios substitute for facts. Vivid cases are reported without reference to a base rate of incidence for that type of crime. The vivid case is thus made to appear typical, even representing an "epidemic." For example, Glassner (1999, 2010) looked at the trendy 1990s crime of "road rage" when we started hearing about people being shot at on the freeway for no apparent reason, and people thus became afraid of what might happen when they were driving their daily commute. However, when looking at base rates instead of vivid cases, Glassner found that five drivers died from road rage crimes in the years 1993 to 1998, amounting to less than one-thousandth of the 250,000 road deaths from 1990 to 1997; 85 times as many motorists died as a result of accidents caused by drunk drivers. Besides that, statistically speaking, driving puts us at a greater risk of injury or death than almost any other daily activity (Abramsky, 2017). Yet all the distraction about "road rage" kept us from looking at deeper systemic problems like increasingly long commutes, distracted driving, and inadequate investment in transportation infrastructure.

It's natural for adults, particularly parents, to be concerned about the well-being of children. However, one of the most sensationalized crimes in the media is child abduction. For example, a *USA Today* headline screamed "MISSING CHILDREN: A FEARFUL EPIDEMIC." The CBS program *48 Hours* set up a mock abduction to show how easily children could be lured out of a mall store by a stranger claiming to need help finding his dog, even though there was no evidence such a crime had ever happened! Fox News host Bill O'Reilly once spoke of "100,000 abductions of children by strangers every year in the U.S.," although the U.S. Office of Juvenile Justice reported only 115 such abductions that year (Glassner, 2010). That is 115 too many, but hardly an epidemic.

Such media sensationalism can affect our perceptions of the world. The reality is that although a few notorious cases receive publicity on the local or national news, most missing children are runaways, not kidnap victims, and most of the small minority that are true abductions are by noncustodial parents in child custody disputes. In fact, only 0.1% of child abductions are by nonfamily members, and reports of missing children have declined by 40% since 1997 (Ingraham, 2015). Nevertheless, parents drag their children to the mall to be fingerprinted or have dental identification implants with apparently no thought to the fear and insecurity they might be inducing by telling their child they are doing this in case the child is abducted and murdered so that their remains could be identified!

Is there a cost to inducing disproportionate fear in children by overreacting to extremely rare crimes like child abduction? Many fewer children walk to school or play outside than did so a generation or two ago, often out of parents' disproportionate fears of abduction and other crimes. This contributes to poorer fitness and greater obesity. One of your authors (RJH) once noted another dad at a parent soccer meeting for a second-grade team speak out strongly against putting children's names on the back of their soccer jerseys because "then someone could call him by name and kidnap him." In two separate instances (one in a small town in South Carolina, the other in a Maryland suburb, neither particularly dangerous areas for children) authorities were so concerned with unaccompanied children playing in parks or walking home that they arrested the children's parents. This was despite the fact that the parents were well aware of the location of their children. Of course, these cases got widespread coverage by local TV news (Abramsky, 2017).

The thought of children being gunned down in a mass school shooting is terrifying, too. However, the chance of a child being killed at school was actually less in 2000 after highly covered tragedies like the Columbine High massacre in 1999 than it was in 1990 (Gardner, 2008). The tragic 2012 school shooting in Sandy Hook, Connecticut, claimed the lives of 20 children and 6 adults. Yet, that same day, "somewhere in the region of 4,000 people globally died of tuberculosis. More than 300 of those who died were children. That same day, globally another 3,500-plus people died of HIV/AIDS ... The same day that 130 people died at the hands of ISIS fanatics in Paris, roughly the same number of people died in the United States of drug overdoses. The same number had died the day before and would die the day afterwards" (Abramsky, 2017, p. 224). Still, the Sandy Hook shooting received tremendous national news coverage.

Effects of Sensationalized Reporting

There are impacts of such reporting, beyond the fear induced in the public. Typically, some vicious stranger is blamed for the crime, with no mention of bad policies creating conditions that increase its likelihood. "In large part, this has happened because of how we mentally categorize events such as school shootings or outburst of terrorist violence. We think of them as crimes—which of course they are. But we don't think of them as public health disasters" (Abramsky, 2017, pp. 222–223). Thus, we worry about encountering the crazed gunman on the freeway or in a school but don't think much about policies that allow anyone to buy a deadly weapon at a gun show without a background check or the lack of a social support network that leaves inner-city youth nowhere to turn but to drugs and crime. Sometimes there are major financial interests that have reason to profit by fomenting irrational fears of crime. For example, large political donations from pharmaceutical companies may discourage elected officials' criticism of prescription drug abuse, especially when it is easier to focus on illicit drug abuse, whose purveyors have no powerful legislative lobby.

Just as there are threats that we worry about too much, there may be others that we do not worry about enough. With regard to violence, for example, Glassner (1999, 2010) argues that we are worrying about the wrong things. Although middle-class communities generally remain very safe places, some poor communities are extremely dangerous. The high chronic violent crime rate in minority communities receives far less media attention than a single sensational crime in a middle-class suburb. The easy availability of guns in the United States has led to far higher rates of death from handguns in that country than elsewhere. More teen suicide attempts succeed today than formerly because more (about 60%) use guns.

Another area in which we may be worrying about the wrong things concerns medical risks. For example, in almost all cases, the danger from not receiving a vaccine is far larger than the extremely unlikely danger of a dangerous side effect from the vaccine. Before 1949, 7,500 children died from whooping cough and 265,000 were sick annually, whereas the actual deaths from DPT vaccine were zero or almost zero (Glassner, 1999). During a vaccine scare in the United Kingdom that led to a 40% drop in immunizations, 100,000 whooping cough cases appeared over 8 years. Japan had a tenfold increase in cases and a threefold increase in deaths after a temporary ban on the vaccine.

Fueled by websites purporting a link between autism and childhood immunizations, some parents recently have chosen to delay or avoid having their children vaccinated. This panic can be traced primarily to a 1998 study published in the British medical journal *The Lancet*. However, after most subsequent research failed to replicate the original study's results linking vaccinations and autism, it later came to light that the study contained serious ethical violations that may have affected the data. The article's primary author was subsequently barred from practicing medicine, and the study was retracted (Abramsky, 2017). Meanwhile, this kind of focus draws attention away from the very real challenges of individuals and families living with autism in a broken mental health system (see Donvan & Zucker, 2017). Also see Offit (2011) for an excellent and detailed look at the history and costs of the anti-vaccine movement and Lo and Hotez (2017) for a study examining the incredible costs of avoiding the measles vaccine.

TV News and Crime Fears

Why did the American public in the late twentieth century show a jump from 5% to 52% in those who believed crime to be the "most important problem" facing the country? From looking at TV news broadcasts and crime statistics from 1978 to 1998, Lowry, Nio, and Leitner (2003) concluded that changes in network TV news accounted for four times as much of the variance in public perceptions as did actual crime rates!

Abramsky (2017) suggests that TV news has gone from a "if it bleeds, it leads" approach in the 1990s to a "if it scares, it blares" mentality in the twenty-first century. This kind of coverage is related to our fears of the world. Indeed, one of the best individual predictors of fear of crime is the sheer amount of time individuals devote to watching news accounts of crime. Coming from the cultivation theory perspective, Romer, Jamieson, and Aday (2003) and Slater and Rasinski (2005) found that the amount of exposure to crime-ridden local TV news was a good predictor of the amount of fear and concern about crime. People also can recall media examples of crime very readily, especially for events in which personal life experience is limited, such as murders, drug busts, and courtroom trials (Busselle & Shrum, 2003). Vivid and compelling images of crime are likely to influence people low in quantitative literacy, as are on-camera comments by the public (Gibson, Callison, & Zillmann, 2011; Lefevere, de Swert, & Walgrave, 2012; Zillmann, Callison, & Gibson, 2009). More recent studies have also demonstrated a link between viewing crime stories on social media and fears of crime (Intravia *et al.*, 2017). However, in a study of TV viewers in Trinidad, perceived personal risk of crime victimization was a much more powerful predictor of crime fear than was consumption of crime shows or television news (Chadee, Smith, & Ferguson, 2017).

Counteracting Fear
Can these kinds of media effects be neutralized? Exposure to base-rate information (e.g., information about population increasing faster than associated crime rates) has been shown to lead to lower levels of apprehension and perceived victimization risk in men (though not in women) compared to those receiving only frequency information, such as reports of increasing numbers of crimes over time (Berger, 1998, 2000). In a study of estimated risks of terrorist events, one research team found that a fear-inducing manipulation led participants to raise their perceived likelihood of risks, though an anger manipulation intervention actually caused them to reduce the risk estimates (Fischhoff, Gonzalez, Lerner, & Small, 2005). Inducing fear and raising estimated likelihoods of negative events may not always be bad. For example, Slater, Hayes, and Ford (2007) found that adolescents' increased attention to news coverage of alcohol-related vehicle accidents led to increased judgments of likelihoods of such accidents. This is of course the logic behind showing gory films of traffic accidents in driver education classes. Another research approach (Comer, Furr, Beidas, Weiner, & Kendall, 2008) trained mothers to discuss frightening news stories with their children by modeling calm behavior and discussing the likelihood of such events. Compared to a control group, children of these mothers displayed less perceived threat after watching a news clip about terrorism.

In the realm of health communication, much research has been done on how we process potentially frightening information about our health, such as news stories or PSAs about health risks like heart attack, diabetes, and cancer. One of the leading research paradigms in this area is the *extended parallel process model (EPPM)* (Witte, 1992b). The EPPM framework proposes that when we encounter possibly threatening information that might relate to our own health, we tend to have one of two responses. The first, *danger control*, leads us to adaptive responses like accepting the message and possibly changing behaviors relating to our health. The other response, *fear control*, happens when we are truly frightened, and this can lead us to outright reject the health message because we find it too scary and too much of a threat. Interestingly, then, if we are too frightened about news reports or PSAs relating to health, we may just choose to ignore them (Abril, Szczypka, & Emery, 2017; Goodall & Reed, 2013).

Do We Actually Like Sensational Reports?

Although everyone loves to complain about it, does sensationalized news reporting still actually appeal to people? In an interesting study of channel-switching, Lang and colleagues (2005) found that a major reason that news viewers change the channel is a decrease in physiological arousal. However, this may not be the whole story either. Another study on "viral" news stories found that online news content was most likely to be shared (e.g., re-tweeted) when it provoked relatively high levels of positive emotional arousal (like awe) or negative emotional arousal (like fear) (Berger & Milkman, 2012). Vettehen, Nuijten, and Peeters (2008) found that the more sensational aspects a news story had (defined by both negative content and various production techniques like background music and close camera zooms), the higher the emotional arousal. This arousal then increased people's liking for the story but only up to a point. Apparently we prefer a moderate level of arousal more than either very low or very high arousal. Thus it would appear that increasing sensationalism raises arousal, which in turn increases liking for a while, after which it starts to decrease. For example, a news story that is extremely graphic or disturbing may not be liked as much as one that is only moderately so. Clearly, the way crimes are reported has a huge, although complex, influence in the way we think about specific crimes and the likelihood of ourselves being victimized.

Occasionally there is one particular news event whose graphic coverage triggers unusually strong responses in the public. One of the most striking of these were the September 11, 2001, terrorist attacks (Marshall *et al.*, 2007; Schlenger *et al.*, 2002; Silver, Holman, McIntosh, Poulin, & Gil-Rivas, 2002; Torabi & Seo, 2004). Research in the aftermath of the attacks indicated that there were strong correlations between exposure to TV coverage and the diagnosis of anxiety and other symptoms of post-traumatic stress disorder (PTSD) in viewers throughout the United States (Marshall *et al.*, 2007; Neria & Sullivan, 2011). This was not limited to those geographically near the attacks and also was not explainable by the media coverage as only exacerbating symptoms already present.

Marshall and colleagues argue that the cognitive notion of *relative risk appraisal* (Slovic, Finucane, Peters, & MacGregor, 2004) is important to understanding media effects in such cases. Persons are continually making relative judgments of risk of various outcomes, and these judgments are very intuitive and involve emotional responses to the situation. Assessments about the relative risks of terrorism may be particularly elevated because such events are high on both dimensions of risk: *dread risk*, which comes in response to catastrophic and uncontrollable events (nuclear war, major toxin accidents) and *unknown risks*, in which one does not know when he or she is exposed or how he or she might be injured. Because the media reports necessarily stress these two factors (an unprecedented catastrophic event that could happen anywhere), the assessment of risk in the public would be especially high. This then would explain the unusually high level of PTSD and anxiety disorder diagnoses after 9/11. One could imagine that similar reactions may continue to result from the more recent (and seeming endless) news coverage of terrorism, mass shootings, and natural disasters. Interestingly, but not surprisingly, news reports about PTSD itself tend to spike during terrorist attacks and military conflicts (Houston, Spialek, & Perreault, 2016).

How Media Affect Governmental Policy

Just as the news media affect us personally, they also can have an influence on broader government policies. The news, especially television news, can even affect foreign policy and foreign relations (Gilboa, 2002; Larson, 1986; Naveh, 2002; Price, 2009). The transnational character of media news-gathering necessarily involves it in policymaking issues. The sharing of wire service stories and TV footage is common. Reporters in a foreign locale depend on local facilities to transmit news stories home, and often they must cope with local censorship or interference with such coverage. Governments sometimes try to manipulate the perceived reality by limiting the coverage. For example, Saudi Arabia has prevented Western reporters from covering repression of women in its country.

Compelling Images

The availability of relevant and appropriate video material affects the choice of stories. This clearly leads to over-coverage of some photogenic issues and under-coverage of others that are less so, thus covertly setting the agenda. It also favors coverage from places where networks or wire services have correspondents on site, which historically for U.S. media has meant primarily Western Europe, with many other places covered firsthand only if there is a current crisis or American military involvement.

A particularly compelling visual can galvanize world opinion and may affect government policy decisions as well as public discourse. Images of NFL players kneeling during the national anthem in 2017 spurred discussions of the Black Lives Matter movement and police treatment of African Americans, including public condemnations by President Trump. The picture of a lone person standing in front of a line of tanks in Tiananmen Square in Beijing in 1989 helped to increase the world's condemnation of the Chinese government's squelching of the prodemocracy movement. In the late 1960s, Pulitzer Prize-winning photos of a Vietcong prisoner as he was being shot in the head and a naked little girl running from an explosion in Vietnam were thought to help turn U.S. public opinion against that war.

Policy problems may also be created or exacerbated by the lack of media attention to basic processes of social and cultural change in developing nations. The bias in international news coverage by U.S. sources toward greater coverage of developed nations and those of obvious geopolitical importance at the moment has long been known. Western Europe, Japan, and Russia receive heavy coverage in the United States, whereas Africa, Latin America, and much of Asia have traditionally been largely invisible (Larson, McAnany, & Storey, 1986; McAnany, 1983). Only in a crisis or when events thrust the United States into immediate involvement does the focus shift to such places, as was seen in Iran in 1979 (see Close-up 7.3), Iraq in 1990 and 1991, Somalia in 1992, Bosnia in 1993, Rwanda in 1995, Afghanistan in 2001, Iraq (again) in 2003, or North Korea in 2017. Thus the perceived reality of a particular crisis often comes across as heavily ahistorical, with no background provided for understanding the puzzling present events. Crises seem to pop up out of nowhere, and the public often has little understanding of why they occurred.

The Vietnam War

Media can change public perceptions about foreign affairs, particularly when they convey new visual information and when such information is repeatedly presented over a long period of time. The dramatic change in U.S. public opinion about the Vietnam War from 1965 to 1969 is perhaps the most compelling example. In addition to being the first war ever lost by the United States, Vietnam was the first televised war. That aspect is sometimes cited as a major reason why the war lost support among the American people to an extent not seen in modern history in the United States. Although there were many other reasons for the lack of public support for the Vietnam War, the fact that the public could see the horrors of war every night while they ate dinner brought home the reality of how violent and deadly it truly was. The romantic ideals that some soldiers traditionally have taken to war, and that some family members back home had clung to, simply could not continue to be embraced. This war (like all others) was hell, but this time everybody could see that firsthand.

The effect of bringing war into our homes through television has been a hotly debated topic, however (Cumings, 1992; Strobel, 1997). Some (e.g., Strobel, as discussed earlier in this chapter) argue that the role of the media in changing public opinion about Vietnam was far less influential than generally believed. Critical media coverage, starting around 1967, followed public opinion, rather than preceded it (see Close-up 7.9). The change in public opinion away from supporting the war occurred similarly for both the Korean (1950–1953) and Vietnam (1963–1975) wars and was more due to increases in U.S. casualties and a prolonged stalemated situation than to the nature of news coverage (Strobel, 1997). Although the worry that news coverage influences neutral people is widespread, such influence may be less than we believe. Even if the media influence policy less than is often believed, the fact that many policy makers firmly believe in that power can itself affect policy, most notably in the restriction and censorship of military operations post-1980, in order to avoid "another Vietnam." Indeed, over 40 years later, Vietnam War images are no less compelling, disturbing, and interesting to the public. A 2017 10-part Ken Burns documentary on Vietnam garnered enormous ratings for PBS (de Moraes, 2017).

❖ CLOSE-UP 7.9 DID A NEWS ANCHOR CHANGE THE COURSE OF A WAR?

In 1962, journalist Walter Cronkite took the helm of The CBS Evening News, *serving as its anchor for almost 20 years. In those tumultuous decades, Cronkite calmly reported to Americans the many disturbing news events of the day, from the assassination of President Kennedy to Watergate. Although he looked like someone's family dentist, there was something about Cronkite's earnest Midwestern delivery that put many viewers at ease as they digested troubling news stories. It's hard to overestimate the respect that Cronkite held among the general public. Although not universally admired, he was voted "the most trusted man in America" in a 1972 opinion poll (Plissner, 2003), and that label became associated with him throughout the rest of his career. One TV critic said, "Americans got their news from Cronkite but, more than that, joined him in shared experiences that could be inspiring, frightening or almost indescribably painful" (Shales, 2009, ¶7).*

Cronkite had perhaps his greatest influence as a newsman during the Vietnam War. In 1965, he reported from Vietnam, telling America that the war was going well and that bombing had been effective. He even flew along on one mission and was seen crawling out of the cockpit saying, "Well, colonel, it's a great way to go to war" (Solomon, 2009). However, Cronkite returned to Vietnam in 1968 and came back to air a very different CBS News Special Report. Having become convinced that the war was hopelessly intractable by that point, Cronkite went so far as to say on air, "It is increasingly clear to this reporter that the only rational way out then will be to negotiate, not as victors, but as an honorable people who lived up to their pledge to defend democracy, and did the best they could." There were some reports that when President Johnson heard this proclamation, he turned to his press secretary and said, "If I've lost Cronkite, I've lost the country" (Folkenflik, 2009). Did Cronkite turn public opinion against the war? According to Gallup polling, support for the war had been deteriorating since about 1966, but it was not until August of 1968 that over 50% of Americans said they thought sending troops to Vietnam was a mistake (Cronkite's report aired in February of 1968) (Newport & Carroll, 2005). It's probably giving one news reporter too much credit to say that he so dramatically altered public opinion, and thus, history (and Cronkite frequently denied having such power), but it's also difficult to imagine any journalist today commanding the kind of public respect and trust afforded Cronkite during his career.

Iraq and Afghanistan

Even though post-Vietnam war coverage was greatly censored both by governments and military and by self-censorship of the press, the criticism that the press was not being adequately supportive of a national war effort has continued. For example, the George W. Bush administration complained that news coverage of the wars in Iraq and Afghanistan was unfairly negative and led to eroding national support for those efforts. Was there any truth to these claims? Aday (2010) analyzed all war reports on *NBC Nightly News* and *Fox News' Special Report with Brit Hume* during 2005. Results found that, while both channels focused a lot on negative stories, overall they both actually underreported the violence in Iraq and Afghanistan. Moreover, although Fox News was much more sympathetic to the Bush administrations than was NBC, both were more positive than events may have warranted. In an analysis of British media coverage of the 2003 Iraq War, considerable support was also found for the elite-driven (i.e., government-supporting) position, but there was also some evidence of some independent and oppositional coverage (Robinson, Goddard, Parry, & Murray, 2009). In addition, an analysis of Swedish blogs found that most of them supported, rather than challenged, that country's governmental contribution to the war in Afghanistan (Hellman & Wagnsson, 2015). Interestingly, another investigation found that merely watching *The Daily Show* also increased politically inattentive viewers' focus on the war (Cao, 2010).

Terrorism

Although a terrorist incident is often a highly newsworthy story in terms of the characteristics discussed earlier in this chapter (Weimann & Brosius, 1991), terrorism stories place a difficult set of pressures on the media. Wittebols (1991; see also Herman & Chomsky, 1988; Herman & O'Sullivan, 1989) has distinguished between institutional and grievance terrorism. *Grievance terrorism* challenges the powers that be and actively seeks media to help advance its cause and publicize its side of the story. For example, radical Islamic suicide bombers or those who shoot abortion providers are grievance terrorists. On the other hand, *institutional terrorism* has the purpose of maintaining the status quo and generally shuns media coverage, even actively threatening those who try to cover it; for example, paramilitary death squads in Colombia or Zimbabwe. Institutional terrorists most often have the complicit or at least grudging implicit support of some government.

The most likely trap that media fall into with grievance terrorism is excessive coverage that risks legitimizing or glamorizing the terrorists, a very frequent criticism of coverage of terrorism in the 1970s and 1980s. Since that time, the press has learned a bit better how to handle terrorism and avoid giving the extremists their desired media platform. On the other hand, the media risk with institutional terrorism is failing to cover it at all, or failing to identify those really responsible for it, in cases where such responsibility can even be determined; see Alali and Eke (1991), Kushner (2001), McLeod and Shah (2014), Paletz and Schmid (1992), and Picard (1993) for further examinations of media coverage of terrorism.

Conclusion: News and Perceived Reality

As we have seen, there are distinct characteristics that define the news. We tend to find stories that are dramatic, full of conflict, and about individual people the most interesting. News about crimes, particularly violent crimes, fit all of those parameters. However, being exposed to too much crime coverage can cause our sense of reality to be distorted such that we perceive the world as a more dangerous place than it actually is.

Indeed, the news media sometimes walk a fine line between reflecting reality for their audience and creating an alternate reality for them to consider. For years, newsmakers have found ways to manipulate the news, from censoring what is reported, to manipulating how and when the news media receive information. The relatively new trend of fake news is an especially troubling one, though, because it has caused many media consumers to be wary of any news they see.

The lines between news and reality also become blurry when stories about the media often become news in themselves. The weekly top-10 Nielsen ratings and movie ticket sales figures are reported in the news. Certain blockbuster TV entertainment shows become news events in themselves, receiving coverage throughout print and broadcast media. For example, the final episodes of *Friends* in May 2004 and *The Oprah Winfrey Show* in 2011 were major news stories as were the debuts of rebooted series like *Will and Grace* (2017) and *Roseanne* (2018). The cost of running commercials during the Super Bowl is announced in all media. The release of blockbuster movies like every new *Star Wars* film is a major news story. Such news coverage effectively serves as highly effective and free advertising, greatly boosting the audiences for the films.

In spite of the enormous influence of news media, we must be careful not to attribute an even larger role to media in the perceived reality of our world than is appropriate. Even if news is not quite the preeminent influence it is sometimes believed to be, it clearly occupies a major place in the popular imagination. The coverage of news has itself become news, sometimes bigger news than the event being covered. On the eve of the Iowa presidential caucuses one year, a voter in the studio was asked if she planned to attend the caucus and thus participate in the historical selection of a nominee for president. Her reply was to look around the studio and say, "Oh, I guess so, but I hate to miss all the excitement here." In other words, for her the act of reporting had become the newsworthy event, eclipsing the event being reported. This example suggests the continuation of this discussion in the context of the specific area of politics, which is the subject of Chapter 8.

Media Applications, Chapter 7: Understanding Research Findings Reported in the Media

In the reporting of science to the general public, the scientist's "truth" and the reporter's "news" are often quite different. For example, an editor may not consider a particular background feature story about pornography research as newsworthy because the paper has already carried two stories that week on that particular topic. The scientist looking at the same situation may not be convinced of the overlap, given that one article was a story about citizens seeking better curbs on pornographic websites and the other was a feature about a woman who acted in pornographic videos, neither of which at all overlaps with a report of behavioral research on effects of pornography.

In their desire to fairly present all sides of an issue, journalists may disproportionately emphasize controversy and thus inadvertently play up and legitimize a fringe position given little credibility in the scientific community. As discussed throughout this chapter, conflict and controversy are highly newsworthy. For example, subliminal advertising greatly intrigues and even alarms the general public, whereas the research community has long realized that its feared effects are at most vastly overrated and are probably nonexistent (see Chapter 6). Such a topic may make for compelling journalism, but it is bad science. As discussed in Chapter 9, attempts to be fair and balanced in the treatment of media violence research have led to the mistaken view in the popular press that the research community is evenly split or undecided on whether violent media have negative effects. The perceived reality of readers in response to such stories may be significantly at variance with the scientific reality. Also, journalists and scientists use language in very different ways. As Tavris (1986, p. 25) said:

> To the academician, the language of the reporter is excessively casual, trivializing, and simple-minded, if not downright wrong or silly. To the journalist, the language of the academicians is excessively passive, technical, and complicated, if not downright wordy or pompous. Academic language strives to be informative and accurate. To the reporter, though, the result sounds like nit-picking; it encumbers the research with so many qualifications and exceptions that the results seem meaningless.

It is not unusual to encounter the impression that social science is inferior, immature science. Not surprisingly, this feeling is common among the relatively few journalists trained in science. More surprising, however, is that this view is also not unusual among social scientists themselves, some of whom see themselves as doing work that is inferior to that of their colleagues in physics or biology. If many social scientists do not see themselves as true scientists, is it surprising that others do not perceive them that way?

This collective feeling of inferiority may stem from the fact that social science is by its very nature probabilistic, not deterministic. One can never predict for sure the effect on a particular person of seeing a violent movie, in the sense that one can predict with absolute certainty that $2 + 2 = 4$. One particular burden of social science is the challenge to communicate about uncertainty to a world that seeks and values deterministic answers (Friedman, Dunwoody, & Rogers, 1999). Too often discussion of statistical uncertainty comes across to the public as a wishy-washy lack of commitment which falsely conveys a state of inconclusiveness of the scientific research.

As advances in neuroscience, genetics, and other interfaces of biology and psychology become more prominent and of more interest to the public, new challenges and possibilities for misinterpretations will emerge. Conrad (2001) examined news coverage of genetics and mental illness research over a 25-year period and found a dominant frame he called *genetic optimism*. This frame had three elements: a gene for every disorder exists, that gene will be found, and this is good. This frame has the effect of encouraging people to believe in overly simplistic and optimistic solutions for mental illness treatment, such as there being a discrete gene that in and of itself causes the disorder, and that dealing with this gene will effectively treat the illness. As another example of a very complex research field, Thompson and Nelson (2001) discuss research on early brain development and the challenges of communicating those findings to the public. Researchers, including social science researchers, have not always been very successful at, or even interested in, communicating the results of their research to the public. Sometimes the few highly respected scientists who do so very well are actually scorned by their professional colleagues (Diamond, 1997; Ferris, 1997). They certainly are not rewarded by the academic profession, which primarily rewards the obtaining of research grants and publication of scholarly research papers in scientific journals. Even writing textbooks is held in relatively low esteem in terms of professional advancement (few professors ever write textbooks before they have tenure!), and talking to the press and the public is often not valued at all and possibly even scorned. Professors and researchers typically receive no training at all in their doctoral programs or elsewhere in how to speak with the press and often have no clue how to talk to reporters about their work in a way that gives the journalist something he or she can use in writing a story. Sometimes the opportunities we do get and the end products from such interviews are not particularly enlightening or encouraging to anyone, nor are they likely to make us eager to seek out more such opportunities. See Close-up 7.10 for a personal example.

❖ **CLOSE-UP 7.10 ONE OF YOUR AUTHORS' APPEARANCE ON THE TODAY SHOW: DID THIS ADVANCE THE CAUSE OF UNDERSTANDING RESEARCH ON ROMANCE AND MEDIA?**

As media researchers, we are occasionally contacted by the media for our views of various aspects of topics discussed in this book. Perhaps the one with the most exposure was my (RJH) 2008 appearance on NBC's Today *show on a Valentine's Day themed story. A producer called me about my research on young adults' movie-going experiences, in this case watching romantic movies (Harris et al., 2004). This was a complex pair of studies asking people to retrospectively recall and evaluate an experience watching a romantic movie on a date. We looked at how that experience had affected the relationship, how men and women viewed it differently, and how they would fantasize about their own lives interacting with the movie. A producer and photographer came from New York and spent over an hour setting up a television-ready "office" in a seminar room (my real office was too small for all their equipment). Once this was completed, they taped about a 15-minute interview in which they asked me good questions, and I tried to communicate as best I could in terms everyone could understand what we had found in our research.*

The story that appeared on the air a few days later was something else again. Although the whole piece lasted 6 to 8 minutes, very long for a TV news story, I was on air for about 30 seconds and basically said that men like romantic movies, though not as much as women do. Obviously our published paper contained a bit more sophisticated and complex results than that, though I guess I should be grateful that the brief appearance did not distort what I said or make me look totally stupid or incoherent. After my short statement, Matt Lauer and Meredith Vieira bantered a bit about their opinions, while the several minutes remaining were entirely devoted to an argument between two people, a woman identified as a therapist and a man identified only as a "relationship expert." While the woman made some thoughtful comments, the man consistently countered with multiple ways of stating basically that real men wouldn't be caught dead watching romantic films. What the producers wanted was controversy, shouting back and forth, and my academic piece was only a small chunk of evidence for one side. I ended up not thinking that I had contributed anything substantial to the viewers' understanding of the topic. Should I have declined this interview? Should I accept such offers in the future? This experience left me pessimistic about the worth of doing so, although I have no doubt that any producer could easily find someone with fewer scruples than I willing to talk to them if I did not.

One study showed that neither journalists nor scientists believed that media do a good job communicating scientific information to the public (Chappell & Hartz, 1998). Indeed, sometimes the impression conveyed in the popular press is entirely opposite to the state of the research, as seen in Chapter 9 in the study of popular press coverage of conclusions from media violence research (Bushman & Anderson, 2001).

Does any of this matter? There are increasing cries of the dangers of scientific illiteracy. See Mooney and Kirshenbaum (2009) for a particularly cogent and compelling argument about this issue. Science is presented so poorly in the media, and it is so shamelessly manipulated by some political interests, that the general nonscientific public has little understanding either of the general principles by which science proceeds or of specific findings in fields of a particular scientific endeavor. About 46% of the American public holds young-earth-creationist views of the formation of the earth, in spite of a total lack of scientific support (Mooney & Kirshenbaum, 2009). The debate over global warming being caused, at least in part, by human activity, is largely settled in the scientific community but appears to much of the public to still be a matter of scientific debate, thanks to scientifically irresponsible political demagoguery. Valuable time in dealing with this issue is being lost while a bewildered public confuses a scientific issue with a political one. Also see Media Applications, Chapter 8.

Further Reading

Abramsky, S. (2017). *Jumping at shadows: The triumph of fear and the end of the American dream*. New York: Nation Books.

Bennett, W. L. (2016). *News: The politics of illusion*. 10th ed. Chicago: University of Chicago Press.

Hartmann, T. (2017). Parasocial interaction, parasocial relationships, and well-being. In L. Reineke & M.B. Oliver (Eds.), *The Routledge handbook of media use and well-being* (pp. 131–144). New York: Routledge.

Levitin, D. J. (2017). *Weaponized lies: How to think critically in a post-truth era*. New York: Dutton.

McLeod, D. M., & Shah, D. V. (2014). *News frames and national security: Covering Big Brother*. New York: Cambridge University Press.

Tewksbury, D., & Rittenberg, J. (2012). *News on the internet: information and citizenship in the 21st century*. New York: Oxford University Press.

Useful Links

A communication professor's guide for spotting fake news:
https://docs.google.com/document/d/10eA5-mCZLSS4MQY5QGb5ewC3VAL6pLkT53V_81ZyitM/edit

Fact-checking websites:
www.factcheck.org/
www.snopes.com/
www.politifact.com
www.washingtonpost.com/news/fact-checker

Newsreel archives:
www.newsreelarchive.com/

For more resources, please visit the companion website:
www.routledge.com/cw/harris

Chapter 8

Politics

Using News and Advertising to Win Elections

Q: How did TV comedian John Oliver plot to get the attention of President Trump?

A: After learning that Trump apparently gets much of the information that he tweets about from morning cable news shows, Oliver convinced HBO to buy ad time on those shows in the Washington, DC, area. Oliver even employed a folksy actor dressed as a cowboy to star in commercials that briefly explained topics like "clean coal" and nuclear arsenals. Oliver said his goal was to educate Trump about things he didn't understand. It didn't hurt that the commercials also made for funny segments on Oliver's HBO show, although there's no evidence the messages actually got through to Trump (Genzlinger, 2017).

Q: In the lead up to the 2016 U.S. presidential election, what media sources did news consumers say they found most useful for learning about the candidates?

A: In a Pew Research Center poll, cable TV news and social media were rated as most helpful (Gottfried, Barthel, Shearer, & Mitchell, 2016).

Q: How did President Trump help MSNBC, whose news coverage and hosts he repeatedly berated on Twitter?

A: MSNBC had been struggling with low ratings for years, especially in comparison to rivals Fox News and CNN. After the 2016 election, MSNBC's ratings soared. Apparently, the left-leaning network had become a place of television solace for liberals disturbed by Trump and his administration (Grynbaum & Koblin, 2017).

Politics and media have long been intimately involved with each other, with media strongly setting the agenda that politics is very important. As we know, both the nature of media and politics can change in a very short time period. At times, the changes we see in media technology and how political candidates use it can seem staggering. Sometimes, scholarly research struggles to keep up with such rapid changes, too (Perry, 2008). However, although television and more recently the Internet have made some drastic changes in the relationship between media and politics, the connection between the two is certainly not new. Print media have long covered political campaigns, and the level of political rhetoric has sometimes been even more vicious than it is today.

For example, the U.S. presidential campaign of 1884 saw Democrat Grover Cleveland's alleged fathering of an illegitimate child as a major campaign issue ("Hey, man, where's my pa?/Gone to the White House, ha, ha, ha!").

Still, from the first tentative and fragmented radio reporting of Warren Harding's U.S. presidential victory in 1920 to today's framing of whole campaigns around the use of television and Internet news and advertising, broadcast media have transformed political campaigns beyond recognition from Grover Cleveland's days. Franklin D. Roosevelt (1933–1945) was perhaps the quintessential radio president; his lofty mellow tones electrified listeners in ways that watching his body in a wheelchair could never do. In recent decades, candidates have been forced to deal with the visual and social media aspects of modern media, and some of them have done so only grudgingly. For another historical example, see Close-up 8.1 for more on the political use of the media by abolitionists in pre-Civil War United States.

❖ CLOSE-UP 8.1: ABOLITIONIST MEDIA CAMPAIGNS IN THE NINETEENTH CENTURY

One of the major political and philosophical issues in nineteenth-century America was slavery, a controversy so divisive that it eventually led to the calamitous American Civil War (1861–1865). The abolitionists successfully used pre-electronic media to gradually turn the nation's thinking against slavery (Jakes, 1985; Risley, 2008).

Abolitionism was considered a rather extreme position in its early days in the 1820s, in that it advocated the end of all slavery on moral grounds, not merely prohibiting its extension to the new Western territories. The Quakers were the first to publicly denounce slavery, and one of the earliest abolitionist newspapers was published by Quaker Benjamin Lundy. Soon, more abolitionists ran their own newspapers and had supporters in the editors' chairs at many publications, such as William Lloyd Garrison's Liberator, *Frederick Douglass's* North Star, *Horace Greeley's* New York Tribune, *and even a children's newspaper called* The Slave's Friend. *Eventually, more mainstream newspapers like* The Chicago Tribune *and* The New York Evening Post *also took strong stands against slavery. Several books were also tremendously influential. Narratives of escaped slaves became popular in the 1840s, with the preeminent example being Frederick Douglass's autobiography. Far eclipsing all other books in influence, however, was Harriet Beecher Stowe's* Uncle Tom's Cabin *(1852), written more out of religiously motivated concern for the treatment of slaves than from any political conviction or true egalitarian sentiment (Stowe favored sending freed slaves back to Africa). In fact, the novel was based only on Stowe's one short visit to a Kentucky plantation and contained very condescending portraits of African Americans. Still, it had substantial political impact. In fact, upon meeting Stowe, Abraham Lincoln is said to have remarked (some say apocryphally): "So you're the little woman who wrote the book that made this great war!" (Vollaro, 2009).*

Highly newsworthy events that received wide coverage polarized already strong opinions to help lead the nation to war. Public meetings led by White clergymen or escaped slaves drew increasing crowds. Protests over the Fugitive Slave Law allowing Southern slaveholders to hunt and retrieve runaway slaves in the North occasionally led to dramatic countermeasures,

> such as the founding of the Underground Railroad to help runaway slaves escape to Canada. Garrison once burned a copy of the U.S. Constitution, calling it "a covenant with death and an agreement with hell." In 1859 abolitionist John Brown and 21 followers tried unsuccessfully to seize arms from the federal arsenal in northern Virginia. He was caught, tried, and hanged, but coverage of the trial split the country more sharply than ever.

Closing the Distance between the Candidate and the Public

Meyrowitz (1985) argued that television coverage forever changed politics by decreasing the psychological distance between the politician and the voter. Although it was no longer necessary to cross the gulf between oneself and the voters by being an imposing physical presence in a crowd or an accomplished orator, it was imperative to know how to use the more intimate medium of video to one's advantage. Analysts of various political persuasions have acknowledged that U.S. presidents Ronald Reagan (1981–1989) and Bill Clinton (1993–2001) were highly effective television politicians, as was John F. Kennedy (1961–1963) in an earlier period. President Donald Trump (2017–) has made use of television, too, although in a different way. Rarely seen as having the kind of television charisma of Reagan, Kennedy, or Clinton, Trump can nonetheless be mesmerizing when speaking to a rally full of his supporters. As discussed throughout this chapter, Trump has also been adept at closing the psychological gap between himself and the public with his use of social media, particularly Twitter.

With social media, cell phone cameras, and television crews present nearly everywhere politicians go, political audiences are also not as segmented as they used to be. A candidate cannot deliver one speech to an audience of factory workers and a contradictory address to a group of business leaders, because both will be reported on the evening news and posted on the Internet, especially if reporters perceive any inconsistency. A single unfortunate statement or behavior may have a lasting negative effect through the magic of television transferring that one place to all places, to say nothing of the gaffe being available for all to watch repeatedly on YouTube. Democratic presidential candidate Edmund Muskie was the front-runner for his party's nomination in 1972 until he was seen on television shedding a tear in New Hampshire in response to a newspaper editor's unfounded character attack on his wife. This reaction, however noble and loyal, was then interpreted as weakness and may have cost him the nomination. One would hope the public has become more forgiving over time, yet when House Speaker John Boehner shed some tears in 2010 it became frequent fodder for late night comedians' political satire.

A candidate's insensitive comment about some group sometimes has costly career effects because of the instant widespread dissemination of the comment on television, YouTube, social media, and the Internet as a whole. In 1990, Texas Republican gubernatorial candidate and political novice Clayton Williams seemed to bring insensitivity to new depths when he commented that bad weather was like rape, "If it's inevitable, just relax and enjoy it," a remark that drew shocked and widespread condemnation. Slow to learn, Williams went on to say that during his youth, crossing into Mexico and "being serviced by prostitutes" was part of a healthy Texas boy's coming of age. Although Williams began over ten points ahead, he became an acute embarrassment to Texas Republicans and lost the election. Internet and new media have only enhanced the possibilities for sharing one's weaknesses and gaffes. In 2011, New York Congressman Anthony Weiner (yes, it's pronounced "ween-er") was forced to resign after first denying and then admitting sending lewd cell phone photos of himself to young women. Not only did this story dominate the news for a week or so but the pictures of his bulging underwear circulated widely on the Internet. By late 2017, the "Me Too" movement had brought to light numerous accusations of sexual misconduct by powerful men in the media spotlight. This included Senator Al Franken when an old photo surfaced of Franken joking about groping a sleeping woman's breasts. After initially apologizing and saying he would stay in office, Franken gave in to pressure (including demands from fellow female senators) and resigned.

In discussing the infamous Watergate tapes of the 1970s Nixon White House, Meyrowitz (1985) suggested that Nixon always saw those tapes as private conversations rather than as public statements. In private most people say some things on occasion that they would not deem appropriate for a public forum, due to language (e.g., profanity), content (e.g., prejudicial or judgmental comments), or style (e.g., imitation of someone). Another infamous example is when then-reality-TV star Donald Trump was overheard on an *Access Hollywood* microphone crudely bragging to a host about his sexual conquests. When an audio recording of the conversation surfaced years later during the 2016 presidential campaign, it did not prevent Trump from being elected. Limited to the private world, such conversations, though regrettable, may not be unusual. As public discourse, however, they appeared highly inappropriate, insensitive, and even shocking. Electronic media technology has broken down that public–private barrier by bringing formerly private discourse into the public world. No longer can a public figure assume that private comments will remain private. Indeed, it seems rather naïve when a public figure seems surprised when that happens.

Cognitive Processing of Political Media

People process media information, including political information, in multiple ways. As discussed in Chapter 6, media processing may be central, with elaboration and careful consideration of arguments of each candidate, or it may be peripheral, with little elaboration and noting primarily superficial aspects like a candidate's appearance or some lighthearted comment. Central or peripheral processing can be either *online*, meaning it is processed while it is perceived, or *memory-based*, meaning it is thought about later (note that in this context "online" doesn't refer directly to the Internet). Thus, a person consuming political news is likely processing it in all of these ways at different, or possibly the same, times, and different audience members are processing the same message very differently (Choi, 2011). This is the challenge of measuring effects of political news and advertising.

In this chapter we begin by looking briefly at a few ways that the Internet, and particularly social media, has changed politics. Next, we more closely examine news media coverage of political campaigns, including televised candidate debates. Then we examine how politicians can manage the news coverage that their campaign receives. This is followed by a case study of the media coverage of the closest presidential election in U.S. history. Next we take a careful look at political advertising, when candidates pay to say exactly what they want. Finally, we briefly look at the cultivation theory thesis that television cultivates politically moderate attitudes.

Politicians consistently hope to use media to create a favorable reality about themselves in the public mind. The examples discussed are primarily from the United States, because that is the area known best to your authors and the one most studied by scholars examining politics and the media. Most of the principles discussed, however, are also applicable elsewhere.

Political Behavior on the Internet

As discussed in Chapter 7, the Internet has greatly changed the interaction of news and politics, particularly with regard to the 2016 U.S. presidential election. Before we look more closely at news coverage of politics in the next section, let us discuss some of the research that has been conducted regarding online political behavior.

As we know from Chapter 3, many of us enjoy multitasking our media (that is, watching two screens at the same time). Called *second screening* (sometimes also labeled *dual-screen viewing*), this behavior can be especially common when consuming live media events, including those that are political. For instance, while viewing a live presidential candidate debate on TV, you might also be sharing your personal opinions about what is happening by tweeting to your followers. Likewise, you might be closely monitoring your Facebook feed to see what your friends are saying about the president's State of the Union address as he speaks live on your television. Despite the kind of research cited in Chapter 3 (e.g., Brasel & Gips, 2011) indicating that our attention suffers when we second screen, other studies (e.g., Wang & Tchernev, 2012) from a uses and gratifications perspective point out that multitasking media may meet important individual media consumer needs; these needs include discussion and information that traditional forms of media cannot or do not immediately provide. This may be especially true for political media. For example, one study found that second-screeners were especially likely to say they would take part in political engagement activities, such as discussing politics with people in person or online (Vaccari, Chadwick, & O'Loughlin, 2015). A related analysis found that second screening behavior was a predictor of online political participation (such as creating online petitions) (Gil de Zúñiga *et al.*, 2015).

Social Media

As discussed throughout this book, the advent of social media has changed almost all aspects of communication. Of course, this is also true when it comes to politics. Because of the availability and ease of use of social media platforms like Facebook and Twitter, users, including political candidates, have ready-made platforms for expressing their political beliefs (Gil de Zúñiga, Molyneux, & Zheng, 2014). Although some have argued such activity strengthens democracy by giving more people voice (Gil de Zúñiga *et al.*, 2015), it's also true (as seen in Chapter 7) that social media are especially vulnerable to fake news, particularly regarding politics.

As this chapter is being written, Donald Trump, having been elected U.S. president in 2016, is serving his first term in office. As discussed in Chapter 7, Trump was not predicted to win the presidency, and media scholars are still trying to understand the role that media, particularly social media, may have played in his electoral victory. Without a doubt, Trump has used Twitter to his advantage more than any other politician. Touting his tweets as a way to cut through the "fake news," many of Trump's

Twitter followers appreciate being able to receive unfiltered information directly from the president. One study indicates that Trump may be on to something. Lee and Oh (2012) found that personalized, first-person tweets from politicians enhanced the perceived intimacy with their followers who have strong affiliation needs (i.e., those who especially like being part of a group). Trump excels at such personalized social media messages. In fact, one of his most popular re-tweets ever was of a doctored video of him wrestling "CNN" (the CNN logo having been superimposed over the face of World Wrestling Entertainment's Vince McMahon. The video existed because Trump had "wrestled" McMahon on TV in 2007, long before he was a political candidate) (Silva, 2017).

Although perhaps not as omnipresent as Trump, other politicians also have certainly used social media to their advantage. In 2008, Barack Obama's victory was credited largely to his campaign's savvy use of online support to raise awareness of his candidacy—and to raise campaign funds. This was in stark contrast to his opponent, John McCain, who was 72 at the time, and whose campaign was not adept at using social media (Fraser & Dutta, 2008). However, being older does not necessarily mean that a candidate cannot be skillful at employing social media. After all, Trump is in his seventies. Also, in examining the 2016 Bernie Sanders campaign for president (Sanders was 74 at the time), Penney (2017) found that there were two channels of Twitter communications. One included the official, tightly controlled tweets that came out from Sanders himself and his campaign. The other route included unofficial grassroots Twitter activity from individuals who strongly identified with Sanders and his message.

These days, traditional news outlets (like CNN and *The New York Times*) regularly report on politicians' social media activity. When Trump, for example, tweets on immigration or a terrorist attack, it can be a story on NBC. Most mainstream media outlets also maintain their own social media accounts, where they post information about breaking news and upcoming stories. But how might coverage of political events differ on social media and in traditional media? In a thoughtful analysis of a German election, Jungherr (2014) discovered some interesting similarities and differences. By analyzing Twitter hashtags as well as TV and newspaper coverage, Jungherr found that all stressed familiar aspects like horserace aspects (i.e., "Who's ahead?"). However, tweets were more likely than traditional media to challenge public statements by politicians.

News Coverage of Politics and Political Campaigns

Because news and politics are so closely entwined, in most nations of the world, the media strongly set the agenda that politics is a very important concern. Political news can set more subtle agendas as well. For example, people who attended highly to political news or news from social media sources were less likely to hold scientifically accurate beliefs about climate change and were less likely to see it as a high risk than were those who attended highly to science and environmental news (Happer & Philo, 2016; Hwang & Southwell, 2009; Southwell & Torres, 2006; Zhao, Leiserowitz, Maibach, & Roser-Renouf, 2011). This was no doubt a reflection of the high degree of scientific consensus about the human causes of climate change and the high level of political rhetoric from some quarters questioning those scientific conclusions. This is discussed further in the Media Applications section of this chapter.

Although political campaigns, candidates, and issues, especially at the national level, receive heavy media news coverage, a closer look at this coverage reveals that some political news receives more media attention than others.

What Is Heavily Covered?

Certain aspects of political campaigns are inordinately heavily covered and others more lightly covered, in large measure depending on how newsworthy they are, in the sense discussed in Chapter 7. First, major pronouncements receive press attention, especially formal announcements of intent to run for office or to withdraw from a race. Other types of strong statements, like a strident attack on an opponent, also have high visibility.

Second, any type of major gaffe or blunder, even if substantially inconsequential in the long run, receives wide attention (Baker, 2004). One of the most notorious gaffes historically was President Gerald Ford's statement in the 1976 presidential debates that Poland was a "free country," not dominated by the Soviet Union. Although this was clearly incorrect at the time (he later claimed he meant the Polish "spirit" could never be dominated), the press did not let the public forget. Vice-presidential candidate Sarah Palin's comment in a 2008 campaign interview suggesting that she had foreign policy experience because she could "see Russia from land here in Alaska" produced widespread derision and many *Saturday Night Live* parodies ("I can Russia from my house!"), and helped to frame her as an uninformed lightweight (Harp, Loke, & Bachmann, 2010). Even press coverage of candidate spouses tends to disproportionately cover controversies involving that spouse (Shoop, 2010). Sometimes, however, the public may weigh the blunders less heavily than the media. Candidate and later President Trump has been forgiven (at least by his strongest supporters) for saying everything from former POW John McCain was not a hero to calling a book of the Bible "Two Corinthians" instead of the correct "Second Corinthians" (Kruse & Gee, 2016).

A third aspect of campaigns which receives heavy coverage are the colorful public responses to a political speech or event. Cheering masses and especially angry demonstrations draw cameras. When candidate Barack Obama spoke to an estimated 200,000 in Berlin in 2008, that cheering crowd provided quite a boost to his campaign. In many countries, rulers of questionable legitimacy regularly pay people to attend a speech and "spontaneously" cheer. Likewise, protests against a leader are carefully orchestrated primarily for the TV cameras, not for the speaker. Protests for democracy in nations like the Philippines, South Korea, Egypt, and the Baltic nations have been televised around the world and eventually forced repressive regimes to yield power. Protesters worldwide routinely have sets of posters and banners in several languages to display as appropriate, depending on which nation's camera crew is present. The world media audience, not the local one, is the most important.

Fourth, meetings of a candidate with important people receive press coverage. This is particularly important for candidates without wide experience in some areas. For example, candidate Barack Obama's July 2008 trip to the Middle East and Europe produced lots of good photo opportunities with American generals in Iraq and Afghanistan, as well as meetings with heads of state in Israel, Germany, Britain, and elsewhere, important tactics in burnishing the image of a candidate without much foreign policy experience. Similarly, candidate Donald Trump met with the president of Mexico in 2016 to reinforce his campaign message that he would be tough on immigration.

Finally, and probably most importantly, any aspect of a campaign that emphasizes the so-called horserace (who's currently ahead and who's behind in the polls) receives coverage. Poll results are reported widely and promptly, as are predictions by experts and any event that "upsets" the relative standings of the "players." In the 2000 U.S. presidential campaign coverage, 71% of the TV news stories were concerned with the horserace, rather than the issues (Lichter, 2001), and less than a third mentioned any issue at all (Jamieson & Waldman, 2003). A large majority of TV news election stories are on horserace and superficial campaign events, rather than on substantive issues or a candidate's qualifications (Fox, Angelini, & Goble, 2005). The number of poll-related stories and the relative prominence of such stories have risen greatly in the last 50 years, with the agenda increasingly being set that what is important in the campaign is primarily the change in poll results since the last report, especially if the race is tight (Craig, 2000; Jones, 2016). By 2008, using statistical software, some media sources began projecting the probability of certain candidates winning an election. According to one study, such predictions were mentioned an average of 16 times per day on cable news channels during the 2016 election cycle (Messing, 2018). Such probabilities can be difficult for the general public to understand, particularly when the outcome is surprising (Leonhardt, 2017). Notably, on the morning of the 2016 presidential election, Hillary Clinton was given an 85% probability of winning (Katz, 2016b).

What are the effects of such preoccupation with who's ahead and who's behind? Relatively unknown candidates who are suddenly perceived as serious contenders or even frontrunners receive a rapid and substantial increase in coverage. At least in primary elections, they do not necessarily have to win; a simple "better-than-expected" showing is often enough for a media-framed "victory." Dark horse anti-Vietnam War candidate Gene McCarthy's surprisingly good showing in the New Hampshire Democratic primary in 1968 may have been instrumental in President Lyndon Johnson's surprise decision not to seek re-nomination himself. Early Republican primary victories, or "better-than-expected" showings, in 2012 by relatively unknown candidates Ron Paul, Herman Cain, Rick Santorum, and Michele Bachmann temporarily catapulted them from the relatively obscure group of minor candidates to being serious contenders. In 2016, the big story in primary elections was Donald Trump's continuing edge over more traditional and favored candidates like Senators Marco Rubio and Ted Cruz.

This heavy coverage of horseraces has probably encouraged the proliferation of more and earlier contests. With the New Hampshire presidential primary established by law as two weeks before the earliest primary of any other state, that state ensures the continued attention and economic development benefits of all the media coverage; in 2016 it occurred in early February, 9 months before the general election. Other states such as Iowa have attempted an end run by having non-primary caucuses or statewide straw polls even earlier. These contests end up drawing considerable coverage far out of proportion to the few delegates (if any) at stake. Most primary states have moved their primaries earlier in recent years in the hope of having some influence before the contest is decided. The primary system has now become so front-loaded that the two major candidates are often effectively chosen by March or April, 7 to 8 months before the general election in November! This extensively protracted campaign period is a major reason for both the rapidly escalating cost of campaigns and the public's increasing weariness of them. They simply last too long, a fact almost everyone acknowledges but no one knows quite how to fix. Most other nations typically have national election campaigns that last no longer than several weeks.

The race aspect that is covered the most heavily of all is, of course, the result of the actual election. There is a lot of concern that knowledge of the results, or predicted results, in the case of network projections of winners, may actually affect the outcome of the election by influencing voters who have not yet gone to the polls. See Close-up 8.2 for further discussion of this issue.

❖ CLOSE-UP 8.2 PUBLIC OPINION POLLING AND ELECTION RESULTS: CREATING OR REFLECTING REALITY?

Started by newspapers in the 1800s but greatly improved scientifically since 1950, public opinion polls are an integral part of modern political life most everywhere. The famed Gallup Poll began in the 1930s and held a margin of error of 4% in the period from 1936 to 1950, although this had fallen to 0.3% by 1984. It is larger if there are three, instead of two, candidates, as in 1980 when the Carter–Reagan–Anderson contest produced a margin of error of 4.7%. However, by the time of the 2016 election, Gallup decided to no longer do presidential horserace polls. With increased polling competition from media outlets like CNN and websites like FiveThirtyEight and RealClearPolitics, Gallup decided to focus its polls more on issues that might matter to voters (White, 2015).

One of the most notorious blunders in polling history occurred in the Literary Digest presidential poll in 1936. Mailed to auto and phone owners in the heart of the Great Depression, the poll came back favoring Republican Alf Landon, who in fact lost to incumbent Franklin Roosevelt by a landslide. The poll, so inaccurate due to a skewed sample of more affluent than average voters, was such a point of disgrace that it helped lead to the demise of the magazine.

More recently, there were also problems with polls surrounding the 2016 presidential election. In the days before the election, national polls predicted that Democrat Hillary Clinton would win the popular vote by about four percentage points; she won by about two points (Marcin, 2017). Of course, what matters more for presidential elections is the winner of the Electoral College. For that reason, many polling agencies focused their attention in 2016 on battleground states with many electoral votes like Pennsylvania, Michigan, and Ohio. Before the election, most polls indicated Clinton would win these states and thus the election. So what happened? Although that question will be debated for some time, a few explanations have been suggested. For example, many voters who were undecided at the time the polling took place may have ended up choosing Trump on election day (Cohn, 2017). Because candidate Trump had said some outrageous things before the election, such voters may also have been hesitant to say they supported him in a poll, although they ended up choosing him once they were in the voting booth. It's also possible that many of the polls simply missed Trump voters and therefore underestimated his support in key states. This may have occurred because Trump voters did not care to respond such polls. It has also been suggested that the polls relied too heavily on educated respondents, who are generally more likely to respond to polls and who were more likely to vote for Clinton (Cohn, 2017; Mercer, Deane, & McGeeney, 2016).

One particularly controversial issue concerns the broadcasting of election results and projection of winners before the polls have closed in all states. In the days of paper ballots counted by hand, no substantive results could be obtained for several hours, but that is no longer the case. Four studies done many years ago assessed U.S. West Coast voters' exposure to election results and projections before they voted (Fuchs, 1966; Lang & Lang, 1968; Mendelsohn, 1966; Tuchman & Coffin, 1971). These studies show only modest exposure to the projections and very small proportions that indicate a change in their vote or a decision not to vote (1–3%). Still, these studies were done before the widespread use of exit polls and, in any case, many elections are decided by very close margins.

Since these studies were done, sampling techniques have improved, and TV networks today take exit polls by asking voters as they leave the polling places which candidate they voted for. Assuming appropriate sampling and truthful responses, exit poll results can project winners with great accuracy before the polls close. Networks and news sites, in a race to scoop the competition, routinely declare projected winners in races with only a tiny percentage of the votes counted (often less than 10%). Although this may be statistically sound, based on the science of representative sampling, it may nonetheless convey a troubling message to viewers. If results can be obtained with only 5% of the votes in, it may not seem to an individual voter that a single ballot can make much difference. The United States has consistently had one of the lowest voter turnout rates in the world, frequently less than half of the qualified voters. There is not much incentive to go and vote after you have already heard the results announced on television.

What Is Lightly Covered?

Just as some aspects of political campaigns are heavily covered, others are relatively lightly covered. Candidates' qualifications in intangible, but highly important, ways are relatively difficult for the press to cover. What have candidates gained from being governor of Texas, senator from Arizona, CEO of a financial firm, or first lady for a previous president, that would help qualify them to be president? Very abstract issues such as character are in one sense extremely important but in another sense very difficult to assess. Coverage that does occur tends to focus on superficial, though not necessarily completely irrelevant, indicators of integrity (or more often lack thereof), like marital infidelity or questionable business dealings. For example, although there was much talk early in the 1992 presidential campaign of Democrat Bill Clinton's apparent extramarital affairs some years before, the exact relevance or irrelevance of this to his possible performance as president was never clarified.

Also relatively lightly covered are positions on issues, especially complex ones. Television news especially is ill-suited to detailed presentations of positions on complex issues like the economy. Print media or the Internet can do much better, as in publication of a candidate's lengthy position paper on some issue. However, few people read such reports; they listen instead to a television commentator's 30-second interpretation of it, which may focus on peripheral aspects that are more "newsworthy" than the main argument. Many candidates and incumbents have written scholarly books or papers carefully outlining comprehensive positions on complex issues; such positions may be vitally important to predicting their performance in office, yet such positions are difficult to cover adequately in the media, especially on television. A 200-page treatise on economic issues simply does not translate well to a 15-second news story. Most TV campaign coverage is even shorter than that; the length of an average TV political news story fell from 43 to 8 seconds from 1968 to 2000 (Bucy & Grabe, 2007; Hallin, 1992; Lichter, 2001). There is also some evidence that so-called "image bites" (e.g., seeing video footage of a candidate speaking to someone without hearing his or her words) are increasing over time (Bucy & Grabe, 2007; Fehrman, 2011). Interestingly, though, one analysis indicated that people are willing to watch much longer news videos on YouTube (over 2 minutes), and politics is one of the most popular news categories on that medium (Pew Research Center, 2012).

Interpretation by the Press

When more abstract issues such as economic or health care policies are covered, they tend to be seriously distorted. For example, in the protracted 2008 Democratic primary fight between Hillary Clinton and Barack Obama, the press highlighted their few differences rather than their many similarities. Because of the media's highlighting of differences (remember, conflict is more newsworthy), the truth can suffer. Similarly, when Hillary Clinton published an extensive health care policy proposal on her candidate website in 2016, one of the main aspects that was highlighted by the media was how it contrasted with ideas from her primary opponent, Bernie Sanders (Rappeport & Sanger-Katz, 2016). By the time of the general election and the emergence of Donald Trump as the Republican nominee, there was little press coverage of Clinton's plan or of the fact that Trump never offered a competing health care proposal.

Sometimes the political and general culture of a society will affect how certain aspects of a campaign and other political news are covered. Perhaps the most striking example of this is the response to sex scandals of high officials (see Close-up 8.3 for a historical view). When reports of President Bill Clinton's relationships with several women began to surface in early 1998, the domestic and international press did not quite know what to make of it. On the one hand, allegations and rumors were reported in great detail, along with rampant speculation of how the president may have lied about these affairs, possibly to the point of a legally impeachable offense. Even as the media wallowed in this saturation coverage and tabloid-like reporting, a curious thing happened. The president's popularity in the polls actually increased to some of his highest levels. Many constituencies were in a quandary. Opposition Republicans were presented with an opportunity for potential political gain but one with definite risks. If they succeeded in impeaching and removing the Democratic President Clinton, they would have an incumbent President Al Gore (as vice-president, he would be Clinton's replacement) to face in the next election, instead of a less experienced challenger. Likewise, more liberal constituencies were heavily embarrassed by the apparently sexist, insensitive behavior of their president, who had otherwise done more to advance the cause of women than had any of his predecessors. It is probably no coincidence that presidential candidates of the next few elections (George W. Bush, Al Gore, Barack Obama, John McCain, and Mitt Romney) were all completely above reproach in terms of marital infidelity. No one wanted to deal with the gossip. Once candidate Trump entered into the political news cycle, gossip and controversy became a new way of life, although media outlets sometimes struggled with how to cover a highly unconventional politician. See Close-up 8.4 for more details on how Trump has changed the news coverage of politics.

❖ CLOSE-UP 8.3 PROMISCUOUS PRESIDENTS: HOW MUCH DO WE WANT TO KNOW?

Having been a celebrity in the public eye for decades, Donald Trump's (2017–) extramarital affairs had been frequent tabloid fodder, especially the one involving his breakup with first wife Ivana in the early 1990s. However, it was only after he became president that it came to light that he allegedly had an affair with a porn actress and had her paid to keep quiet about it. However, among presidents, the most media attention may have gone to President Bill Clinton's (1993–2001) alleged extramarital adventures. Indeed, those exploits received far greater coverage in the late 1990s than had indiscretions of his predecessors in earlier times, although such behavior is hardly unprecedented among U.S. presidents. With a few exceptions, such as Grover Cleveland's alleged out-of-wedlock child who surfaced in the 1884 campaign, relatively few people knew of such liaisons, and those who did either did not care or chose not to make them issues. For example, John F. Kennedy (1961–1963) and Lyndon B. Johnson (1963–1969) were both long rumored to have had extramarital affairs, but the press refrained from pursuing the specifics too aggressively. Earlier, Warren Harding (1921–1923) and Franklin D. Roosevelt (1933–1945) were known to have mistresses, but both also had strong wives highly respected in their own right. Woodrow Wilson (1913–1921) was widowed while in office and later married Edith Bolling Galt, with whom he had been rumored to have had a long-term relationship. The second Mrs. Wilson later acted as de facto president after her husband became physically incapacitated, a condition hidden from the public by Mrs. Wilson. Founding Father Thomas Jefferson (1801–1809) was widowed early in life and never remarried but later apparently had a long-term relationship, including children, with one of his slaves, Sally Hemings. It may have been as hard for the public of Jefferson's time to accept that he might have had a long-term relationship with an enslaved Black woman as to accept that he had children with her.

More potentially controversial, and less well-known, are claims that the United States' only bachelor president, James Buchanan (1857–1861), was gay and lived for several years with a senator from Alabama, a disturbing piece of news that, when discovered by his fiancée Anne Cole, allegedly led to her suicide. It is also possible that the married James Garfield, killed after being in office only months, had frequent flings with men (Hurst, 1998). If the press had not shown some restraint, how might these stories have played out? Is the public better off knowing or not knowing?

The international press responded to Clinton through their various cultural lenses. Some Middle Eastern countries presented Bill Clinton as a sort of immoral clown totally unfit for his office. They wondered how such a powerful country could permit such an irresponsible person to hold office. On the other hand, many Western European nations wrung their journalistic hands at how a puritanical nation was threatening to destroy a highly successful presidency over details of his private life, which should remain private and have no bearing in evaluating his public performance in office. Only a few years earlier, the state funeral of former French President François Mitterrand prominently featured both his wife and his longtime mistress, and his children with each woman, among the mourners. In 2012 François Hollande was elected President of France, in spite of not being married to his long-time partner, with whom he had children. Hollande was succeeded by Emmanuel Macron, who married his one-time high school teacher.

❖ **CLOSE-UP 8.4 HOW TO REPORT ON AN OUTRAGEOUSLY NON-TRADITIONAL PRESIDENT?**

From the time Donald Trump announced his campaign for president in 2015, the news media have seemed to simultaneously delight in and be perplexed by the task of reporting his words and behavior. Previously known as a celebrity real estate developer and star of the reality TV show The Apprentice, *Trump chose to stage his presidential candidacy announcement at Trump Tower (where much of* The Apprentice *had also been shot). At first, many media outlets seemed to focus on the spectacle of it all (Trump was famously filmed riding down a gold and marble-trimmed escalator on his way to his press conference), while others seemed more concerned with Trump's claims that many Mexican immigrants were rapists and criminals (M. Y. H. Lee, 2015).*

Early in the campaign and during the beginning of the Republican primary season, news outlets seemed to treat Trump as a novelty. After all, he did not look like other politicians (with his uniquely styled hair and orange tan) or behave like them (frequently tweeting provocative comments, holding raucous rallies, and flying around the country in his own jet emblazoned with the Trump name). However, as Trump continued to win primary after primary, the press began to take his candidacy more seriously, and increased coverage followed. When Trump was able to pull out an election-night electoral victory in November of 2016, no one was more surprised than many of the journalists who had been closely following his every move. For example, when the election returns were in and Trump was declared the winner, Rachel Maddow told her MSNBC audience that they were awake and not having "a terrible, terrible dream." A couple of weeks after the election, Trump summoned journalists to a private meeting in Trump Tower, including star anchors from ABC, NBC, and CNN. Although the journalists agreed to keep the meeting off the record, some news agencies reported that Trump berated them for their coverage of him (Grynbaum & Ember, 2016a).

Why would journalists agree to a dressing down from Trump? One reason could be that he has been very good for the news media business. As discussed earlier in this chapter, coverage of candidate and President Trump has significantly boosted ratings at cable news networks, particularly left-leaning MSNBC (Battaglio, 2017b). Similarly, since Trump was elected, The New York Times *(which Trump has frequently labeled as "failing" in his tweets) has seen large increases in subscriptions as well as its stock price (Wojcik, 2017).*

Still, journalists struggle to keep up with such an unpredictable president. When Trump seemed to defend White nationalists who had gained infamy at a deadly Charlottesville, VA, rally, cable TV hosts were at a loss. Covering Trump's remarks live, CNN's Jake Tapper said, "Wow. That was something else." MSNBC's Chuck Todd said that he was shaken and had "the wrong kind of chills." Even Fox News personality Kat Timpf said she was "wondering if it was actually real life" (Grynbaum, 2017b). While TV reporters keep track of Trump, he also apparently keeps close tabs on TV news. At times, Trump has appeared to take his day's comments (and tweets) directly from the talking points on cable morning news shows, especially those on Fox News (Baker & Chan, 2017). See the first page of this chapter for a brief discussion of how TV comedian John Oliver decided to use this for comedy fodder.

What are the news themes covered relating to President Trump? One analysis found that in the first three months of Trump's presidency, the most commonly reported topics relating to him and his administration were political skill (or lack thereof), immigration, appointment of staff nominees, and U.S.–Russian relations. Compared to previous presidents' first few months in office, the news coverage also included more negative assessments (62% negative for Trump in 2017, 20% negative for Obama in 2009, and 22% negative for Bush in 2001) (Mitchell, Gottfried, Stocking, Matsa, & Grieco, 2017).

A special challenge in reporting on Trump relates to some of his off-color, off-camera remarks. Although many presidents (e.g., Truman, Johnson, Nixon, Obama) were known to use coarse language at times, Trump's comments were seen by some journalists as more relevant and more outrageous. In one such remark, the infamous Access Hollywood *audio tape from 2005 (released in 2016), Trump, talking about meeting beautiful women said, "And when you're a star, they let you do it. You can do anything. Grab them by the pussy." The story was reported widely across the news media. Most television outlets chose to censor Trump's words, while many online and print sources published the remarks verbatim. By 2018, when Trump reportedly referred to some developing nations as "shithole countries,"* The Washington Post *(which broke the story) even included the offensive language in a front-page headline. TV reporters were less shy this time around, too. Although some who quoted Trump said things like "blank-hole countries," others, like CNN's Anderson Cooper and NBC's Lester Holt, repeated the profanity.*

News agencies also struggle with how and whether to cover Trump's frequent tweets. On the one hand, almost any comment a sitting president makes is news in and of itself. On the other hand, Trump tweets so frequently, and on so many topics, it's almost impossible to report everything. Some have also wondered if at times Trump intentionally tweets something provocative in order to distract from other negative coverage he's receiving (Grynbaum & Ember, 2016b). Indeed, in his first press conference after being elected, Trump commented heavily on the "disgraceful" news media coverage he had received and called CNN "terrible" and "fake news." Of course, those comments were a leading story on news outlets in the next few days (Rutenberg, 2017a).

The increasingly nasty political landscape in the second decade of the new millennium has been a cause for concern. What is the effect on voters by reporters and opposition candidates continuing to harp on long-discredited or irrelevant issues like whether Barack Obama was actually born in the United States (he was), whether Mitt Romney bullied a fellow student in high school (he didn't remember), or whether Hillary Clinton was in failing health during the 2016 campaign (she had pneumonia but recovered)? A long line of research has indicated that when we are strongly on one side of the political fence (conservative or liberal), we tend to see even neutral news reports as biased in a *hostile media effect* (Perloff, 2015b). Relatedly, an interesting study was done to test the effects on the audience of different types of hosts on political talk shows (Vraga *et al.*, 2012). College students viewed one of three prepared political talk shows with a host and two guests discussing environmental policies. The three versions contained identical factual information but varied the style of the host. One host (the "correspondent") asked the guest questions but did not critique the responses, using the style of *Meet the Press* or *Face the Nation*. A second (the "comic") used humor as he pointedly questioned his guests, using the style of *The Daily Show*, *Full Frontal with Samantha Bee*, or *Real Time with Bill Maher*. The third host (the "combatant") used a very aggressive style to elicit information and challenge claims of the guests, in the style of Chris Matthews or Sean Hannity. Results showed that the correspondent and his program were seen as the most credible, while the combatant and his program were seen as the least credible. Participants also rated the correspondent's program the highest in information value, and the combatant's program led to the lowest level of perceived general media trustworthiness. Interestingly, the three programs did not differ in rated entertainment value.

Political Candidate Debates

An exception to television not dealing well with complex candidate positions might be televised debates between candidates, when there is more time to articulate positions and challenge the opponent. U.S. televised debates began in 1960 with the presidential candidate debates between John F. Kennedy and Richard Nixon. These quadrennial debates were not repeated in the next three elections but have occurred regularly since 1976; see Hinck (1992), Kraus (1988, 1996), and Minow, LaMay, and Gregorian (2008) for analyses of these debates. Here the candidates have a chance to put forward their positions in more detail than is usual for television and, most importantly, in perhaps the only forum where partisans of the other candidate will actually listen to them.

Still, however, the debates are typically analyzed by both media commentators and the public primarily in terms of superficial appearances and performances. Polls and scholars indicated that Kennedy "won" in 1960 with those who watched on TV, while Nixon "won" with those who listened on radio (Kraus, 1996). Apparently, Nixon's sweating and lack of TV makeup contrasted poorly to the relaxed-looking Kennedy. Reagan "won" the 1980 and 1984 debates because he seemed friendly and trustworthy and stuck to generalities; the only exception was the one debate that he "lost" because he became too bogged down in facts and was perceived as not comfortable, eloquent, or accurate. Bill Clinton "won" the third 1992 debate, which involved talking directly to audience members, a format at which he excelled. Although media analysts usually attributed "wins" to his debate opponents, Donald Trump often had the most memorable lines, giving derisive nicknames to the likes of Marco Rubio ("Little Marco"), Ted Cruz ("liar"), and Hillary Clinton ("nasty woman").

Televised Debate Coverage

The media mediate between the debate itself and the viewers' interpretation of it. There has long been criticism of presidential debate coverage as being too superficial. However, Kraus (1988, 1996) argued that such critics often fail to accept the reality of debates and campaigns. In spite of their stated intent to inform, people expect the debates to produce winners and losers. They are an integral part of a candidate's campaign strategy designed to produce a winner. The debates are part of a society that loves a contest and expects to be constantly entertained by television. The horserace type of debate coverage has always predominated. In a study of the 1980 debates, Robinson and Sheehan (1983) found that CBS and a newspaper wire service both devoted more space to horserace aspects of a debate than to any other, and 55–60% of the stories failed to contain even one sentence about an issue.

The specific format of a particular debate is whatever the candidates themselves decide, because they will only agree to what they think will help them. Most of this is not really new. The Lincoln–Douglas debates of 1858 in Illinois are often seen as a prototype of pure political debate, but in fact they actually were much more like today's televised candidate debates than we often realize. Candidate Abraham Lincoln manipulated the press and used the occasion to launch his national platform and campaign for the presidency in 1860. At least today technology allows the accurate recording of a debate; Lincoln and Douglas had to rely on the biased memories of each side.

In a careful review of the 1996 debates and their predecessors, Hart and Jarvis (1997) concluded that, despite their problems, the presidential debates have had a positive influence on the political process. "Debates cut through some of the campaign baloney, ground political discourse a bit, sharpen points of difference, make the candidates at least faintly introspective, and restrain overstatements" (p. 1120). Even if they do not do any of these to the extent we might hope for, they do so to a substantial degree. As for how presidential debates changed between 1960 and 1996, Hart and Jarvis conclude that the major change was a decreasing certainty and more tentativeness of statements and increasing conviviality and sociability. This may be due to what Hart (1994) called the "phenomenology of affect" engendered by the highly intimate medium of television, whereby everything and everyone on television strives to connect more with the viewer at the emotional level. Candidates have increasingly learned this lesson, though some have learned it better than others.

Effects on Viewers

What are the effects of the debates on the public? To begin with, at least the presidential debates draw large audiences (Jamieson & Waldman, 2003). In fact the Clinton–Trump debates in 2016 were the most watched ever (Katz, 2016a). Debates are regularly followed by polls about the candidates' debate performance. Campaign handlers know this and carefully plan to try to make a strong impact first.

One very important function is to activate the electorate through engaging citizens, expanding audiences, and creating interest and discussion among voters. One interesting study found that watching Barack Obama (a highly composed Black speaker) perform in presidential debates provided enough of a positive and salient impression to counter some negative stereotypes of African Americans (Meirick & Dunn, 2015). However, the research is inconsistent in regard to the effects of debates on actual voting. They certainly reinforce and crystallize existing attitudes and may actually influence some votes, especially those who are undecided (Benoit & Hansen, 2004; Schill & Kirk, 2014, 2017). Although viewers may acquire information about candidate positions from watching debates, that information may not always be accurate. For example, careful studies of a 2002 German general election debate between Chancellor candidates Gerhard Schroeder and Edmund Stoiber found that viewers did in fact learn economic information from the debates, but much of this was misinformation stemming from candidates' selective presentation of facts (Maurer & Reinemann, 2006). Furthermore, attack statements and disrespectful dialogue in debates tend to polarize supporters on both sides (Mölders, Van Quaquebeke, & Paladino, 2017; Reinemann & Maurer, 2005). Prior exposure to counterarguments against one's preferred candidate also has had some success in "inoculating" people against persuasive attempts by the other candidate (An & Pfau, 2004).

The framing of debate coverage is important as well. In a study of post-debate coverage of U.S. presidential debates, Pingree, Scholl, and Quenette (2012) found that a "game-framed" story (who won, who lost) decreased viewers' thinking about issues, while a "policy-framed" story increased such thought, relative to a control group seeing no post-debate story. Overall, debate viewing tends to move partisans of the two candidates further apart, compared to partisans who did not view the debates (Holbert, LaMarre, & Landreville, 2009).

Candidates' Use of News Media

Next, let us turn to looking at how candidates can use media news coverage to their advantage. Campaign strategists devote considerable energy to examining how to use news coverage most effectively to create a positive and electable image of their candidate. This is both much cheaper and more believable than using advertising.

Setting the Agenda

Using the news for political gain can be done in many different ways, some of which are an integral part of the daily life of newsmakers. For example, an elected official may have more or fewer news conferences, depending on the desire for press coverage at the time. An incumbent has considerable advantage over the challenger in such matters (Hopmann, de Vreese, & Albaek, 2011). One of the most famous historical examples of skillfully using the incumbency occurred in early summer 1972. While hopeful Democratic presidential candidates were squabbling among themselves, Republican candidate (and incumbent president) Richard Nixon captured media attention with a historic trip to China. His landmark voyage opened up the world's largest country to the West and contrasted sharply to the petty bickering of his Democratic opponents attacking each other in their primary campaigns. More recently, during the 2012 presidential campaign, President Barack Obama issued an executive order halting deportation of undocumented young adults who had been brought to the country as children. Predictably, his opponent Mitt Romney criticized this as a political move to woo Latino voters, though Obama responded that the Republican House had blocked an earlier attempt to pass a similar law. See Gruszczynski and Wagner (2017), Kiousis, McDevitt, and Wu (2005), and Walgrave, Sevenans, Camp, and Loewen (2017), for models of political agenda setting.

Candidates help to set an agenda by telling us what issues are important in the campaign. Ronald Reagan in 1980 and 1984 told us that it was important to "feel good" about America, and that struck a responsive chord in a nation weary of inflation, Watergate, and international terrorism. The same appeal by incumbent George H. W. Bush in recession-weary 1992 failed to resonate with voters who did not "feel good" about their economic distress. In 2008, Barack Obama campaigned on the idea of "hope and change," which electrified many young voters. Hillary Clinton tried to set an agenda in the 2016 election with slogans about the power of unity. However, that year, Donald Trump's messages about a Mexican border wall and Hillary Clinton ("lock her up") got more media play. Sometimes candidates' agenda can affect their opponents, by eliciting certain attitudes (see Close-up 8.5) or even forcing them to deal with issues they may prefer to avoid (Dunn, 2009). Agenda setting then helps to crystallize political attitudes, which can subsequently affect voting behavior (Kiousis & McDevitt, 2008).

❖ **CLOSE-UP 8.5 YOUR EMOTIONS CAN AFFECT YOUR POLITICAL ATTITUDES**

People often have very strong feelings about political candidates and issues, but do these emotions affect our attitudes, and, if so, how? One study found that Americans' emotional responses of anger and anxiety affected attitudes to the Iraq War but in the opposite direction (Huddy, Feldman, & Cassese, 2007). Those who were angered by news reports of the war showed increased approval of the 2003 invasion, perhaps because their anger and associated heightened physiological arousal caused them to reduce their evaluation of the risk. On the other hand, those who responded with anxiety showed reduced support. With regard to social media, another study indicated that when we expose ourselves to a lot of partisan online news that coincides with our own political beliefs, this tends to stir anger. In turn, this anger seems related to increased sharing of such news on social media (Hasell & Weeks, 2016). Positive emotions can also have their effects. Following the 9/11 attacks, people experiencing the emotions of pride and hope showed greater confidence in institutions (Gross, Brewer, & Aday, 2009). Feelings of happiness that some feel when watching shows interest in politics (Weinmann, 2017). Thus, the powerful role of emotion in helping to set a political agenda gives considerable food for thought in this era of increasingly strident political rhetoric and advertising (González-Bailón, Banchs, & Kaltenbrunner, 2012).

In trying to set a media agenda, should candidates talk more about what they have done in the past (retrospective) or what they would do in the future if elected (prospective)? Benoit (2006) performed a content analysis of U.S. presidential campaign messages from the 1940s to the 2000s. He found no differences between winners and losers in the primary campaigns in terms of the proportions of retrospective and prospective messages. However, in the general election campaigns, winners, especially if they were incumbents, used a larger proportion of retrospective and smaller proportion of prospective messages. This would suggest that candidates would be advised to talk more about what they have done in the past than what they would do in the future. Perhaps voters find this information more useful because it is a "known quantity," rather than speculative promises.

Framing the Candidates

Candidates sometimes come to have a prevailing image that becomes the frame through which all their actions are viewed. Once they are cast in such images, the media and the public begin to view candidates through particular lenses.

The Unstable Rebel and the Frail Criminal

In the 2016 presidential election, candidates Hillary Clinton and Donald Trump were roughly the same age (Trump is about a year and a half older) and seemingly both in good health. However, Clinton was frequently cast (often by Trump himself) as concealing potential illnesses and having low stamina. It didn't help when Clinton was seen on cell phone video stumbling and apparently weak while getting into an SUV. Clinton later revealed that she had been fighting pneumonia and dehydration (Martin

& Chozik, 2016). Another frame that came to characterize candidate Clinton, at least among some, was that of criminal. Having weathered numerous scandals while her husband was president, questions about Clinton's handling of classified e-mails added to a narrative that Clinton could not be trusted and had perhaps been doing things illegally for years. Trump and his supporters fanned these flames, chanting "lock her up" at rallies and even during the Republican National Convention (Finnegan, 2016).

Meanwhile, on his side of the campaign, Trump had frequently been saying outrageous things that challenged the status quo. From insulting Clinton (with the nickname "Crooked Hillary") to claiming he knew more about ISIS than military generals, Trump became framed as unstable, unpredictable, and a rebel against the Washington establishment. Psychohistorian Mark Anderson (2017) says that Trump also tried to cast himself in a familiar U.S. political narrative as a great savior of White America. Thus, in the vein of manifest destiny and White men conquering a savage continent in the early years of the United States, Trump wanted to be seen as a leader who could expel undocumented immigrants and "make America great again."

The Weeping Woman and the Militant Black Couple

In an interesting analysis of non-verbal candidate behavior in the 2008 Democratic primaries, Manusov and Harvey (2011) focused on some non-verbal gestures by Hillary Clinton and Barack and Michelle Obama. First, after not having done well in the Iowa caucuses, Clinton responded to a New Hampshire voter's question in a surprising way. Clinton commented that the campaign was "very personal for me. It's not just political. It's not just public." As she said those words, her voice cracked, and tears seemed to well up in her eyes. In the following days, much media attention was focused on Clinton's response, especially her tears. Some media outlets framed the response as a positive in that Clinton was displaying authentic emotions, having been characterized in the past as cold or "plastic." Others saw Clinton's tears as calculated and staged, a way for her to consciously present herself as someone who was "real."

Later in 2008, when Barack Obama had clinched the Democratic nomination for president, his wife introduced him before his acceptance speech at the Democratic National Convention. As she exited the stage, Michelle Obama gave her husband a fist bump. Perhaps not a mainstream gesture at the time, the Obamas' fist bump received a good deal of media attention. Conservative media outlets especially wondered whether the gesture was some sort of secret terrorist handshake of "Hezbollah-style fist jabbing," which played on the rumors that Obama was, or had been, Muslim (he was not). Later, *The New Yorker* had fun with this characterization, going so far as to publish a cover art cartoon depicting the Obamas in the Oval Office fist bumping, Barack dressed in traditional Muslim garb and Michelle with a machine gun on her back (see Close-up 8.6 for a more detailed discussion). Other media chose to frame the fist bump in a positive light, writing about how the gesture seemed to indicate that the Obamas were hip or just regular people (Manusov & Harvey, 2011).

Pinocchio and Dumbo

In the 2000 U.S. presidential election, Democrat Al Gore came to have the "lying panderer" ("Pinocchio") frame, while Republican George W. Bush had the "inexperienced dolt" ("Dumbo") frame (Jamieson & Waldman, 2003). Bush was seen as more trustworthy and Gore as more knowledgeable. Such frames sometimes evolve from the media's attempt to play amateur psychologist and identify and explore the candidates' characters. All too often, however, the deep probing of character and its potential effects on qualifications for office do not occur, leaving the frame with a life of its own with everyone interpreting a candidate's actions simplistically around it.

Because of the Pinocchio frame, Gore's statements were scrutinized much more carefully than Bush's for possibly misleading information. For example, Gore was often chastised for claiming to having invented the Internet. His actual statement, made in an interview with CNN's Wolf Blitzer, was, "During my service in the U.S. Congress, I took the initiative in creating the Internet" (Jamieson & Waldman, 2003, p. 48), reflecting that he had in fact played a large role in securing funding for expanding that new system. Once the word "invented" became attached to that statement, however, there was no correcting it. On the other hand, George Bush's malapropisms like "misunderestimate" were given much more attention than Gore's. Bush's, but not Gore's, speech errors were front-page news, as was his poor performance on an impromptu quiz of naming world leaders.

Because of the well-known and validated principle of the confirmation bias, we tend to seek, notice, and remember information consistent with our prior beliefs about the candidate and forget or ignore information incongruent with those same beliefs. This bias works with both journalists and the public. This much greater intentional exposure to political messages we agree with than those we disagree with also reinforces what some have called the political self (Knobloch-Westerwick & Meng, 2011).

These frames were reinforced not only by many journalists but also by comedians. Late night comedians continually poked fun at Bush's intelligence and speech errors and at Gore's exaggerations and stiffness. Since the early 1990s, TV comedy and talk shows have become increasingly important formats not only for what they say about the candidates but also as expected venues for the candidates to visit. In recent elections, visiting programs like *The Tonight Show* or *The Late Show* have been as necessary as visiting the Iowa caucuses and the New Hampshire primary. Some have argued that this development only goes to show that political news, and perhaps news more generally as well, has become subordinate to entertainment and just another part of television's overriding aim of entertaining its audience.

Changing Frames

Sometimes for various reasons a candidate's frame may no longer be desirable and cease to be useful (Graber & Dunaway, 2018). One of the most dramatic illustrations of this occurred in the United States in 2001. Although the dim, inexperienced "Dumbo" image of George W. Bush persisted several months into his presidency, the terrorist attacks of September 11 changed all that. Suddenly, we did not want Dumbo leading us in those tragic times when difficult decisions had to be made. Overnight, press descriptions of Bush radically changed. His speech errors were no longer noted. He was now described with language like "eloquent," "thoughtful," and a "strong leader." Many wrote about how the president had been transformed by September 11, but there are some good arguments that it was actually journalists who had been transformed (Jamieson & Waldman, 2003). Comedians also changed; Bush was the butt of 32% of all late night jokes in 2001 up until September 11, but only 4% thereafter. Although the predominant frame for George Bush before the attacks was Dumbo, afterwards we did not want to think of our leader in that way, so the idealized frame of the wise and strong leader took hold. Using the confirmation bias, reporters and the public noted Bush's statements and behaviors that fit this new image and neglected those congruent with the old Dumbo frame.

Creating Pseudo-Events

One way to increase news coverage beyond what is routinely expected is to create "pseudo-events" to capture media coverage and, in effect, produce many hours of free advertising. One of the most creative and successful was when Bob Graham ran for governor of Florida in 1978. Although he began as an unknown state legislator with 3% name recognition and 0% of the projected vote, he overcame this largely because of his "work days" project. During the campaign he worked for 100 days doing different jobs around the state, one job per day, apparently to learn the demands and needs of different sectors of the electorate. These were heavily covered by the media and worked greatly to Graham's advantage, in spite of the obvious self-serving motivation behind them. He defused some of the predictable criticism of opportunistic gimmickry by dressing appropriately and actually working a full 8 hours on each job. The first 9 days were done before the media were invited in, so Graham had time to fine-tune his program. Photos from the work days were of course used in his campaign advertising, but, more importantly, they were also widely covered as news (see the Useful Links section at the end of this chapter for some of these photos). In his campaign speeches he made references to insights he had gained from these days, and he continued them intermittently after becoming governor, all in all confirming the impression that he had actually learned from them and was not merely dealing in transparent political grandstanding. It was a brilliant example of the use of news media for one's own political gain; no amount of paid advertising could have bought what he gained for free in the news coverage.

Creating pseudo-events can backfire, however. In 1988, modest-sized Democratic candidate Michael Dukakis sat in a tank to try to project a "strong-on-defense" image but instead looked more like a small turtle sticking his head out of a large shell. Likewise, Ivy Leaguer George H. W. Bush's occasional attempts to don cowboy boots and eat pork rinds to appear like a "true Texan" did not always ring true. His son George W. Bush, who actually grew up in Texas, came across more believably in this role.

Perhaps reflecting the divided political times, Donald Trump seems to have had mixed success with attempts at pseudo-events. After being accused by some opponents of not being a great businessman during the 2016 Republican primary season, Trump staged a press conference that featured many products branded with his name, including Trump steaks and Trump wine. However, it was later revealed that some of the products were no longer available for sale or were not owned outright by Trump (Neely, 2016). When President Trump later had a showdown with Democratic Congressional leaders, he staged a photo opportunity with empty chairs, supposedly for Democrats Nancy Pelosi and Chuck Schumer, who had declined a meeting. Trump chose to pose for photos with the empty chairs to demonstrate that he was willing to talk, even if the Democrats were not (Kaplan, 2017). However, the photo became something of a comedy meme, with online users pasting digital pictures of various public figures in the chairs, including Vladimir Putin.

Dealing with Attacks from the Opponent

In the 1992 Democratic primary campaign, candidate Bill Clinton had been accused of an extramarital affair that allegedly occurred years before. The forum he chose to respond to this was a *60 Minutes* TV newsmagazine interview in which he and his wife Hillary admitted that there had been "problems" in their marriage but said that those had been worked through and they were thoroughly reconciled. It was a masterful combination of confession and avoidance of admitting critical information. Clinton's story of how his daughter Chelsea hugged him after hearing of the accusations melted people's hearts as did his embrace of wife Hillary after a lighting camera nearly hit her as it fell during the interview. Viewers were ready to forgive, interpreting what they saw on TV as sincere repentance and love for family. Shortly after the interview, the alleged affair ceased to be a campaign issue. It is hard to imagine how it could have been so effectively refuted and defused in a traditional press conference or interview. Later, when confronted with other allegations of personal and real estate scandal, Clinton apparently forgot his own lesson and did not meet criticism so directly. When Barack Obama was embarrassed by the publication of his former pastor Jeremiah Wright's apparently racist and unpatriotic comments in 2008, he confronted it directly by publishing a lengthy and thoughtful paper about issues of race in America, defusing the criticism while at the same time contributing something positive to discussion of a major unspoken campaign issue.

By the 2016 election, the rules seemed to have changed. When criticized during the Democratic primaries about issues like initially supporting the Iraq War or benefiting from giving speeches to Wall Street executives, Hillary Clinton acknowledged the issues as "fair questions" or "fair criticisms" (Reilly, 2016). When controversy grew over Clinton's use of a private e-mail server while she was Secretary of State, Clinton said, "I take responsibility" (Gearan, 2015). However, the e-mail issue came back to haunt Clinton again and again, and may have played a part in her eventual defeat by Trump; at least Clinton herself later blamed her loss partially to the FBI's announcement that they were re-opening the e-mail investigation shortly before the election (Chozik, 2016).

There always exists the danger of a backlash of sympathy for the opponent if an attack is perceived as too unfair or mean-spirited. This tends to keep potential mudslinging in check. However, sometimes this fear may also suppress useful dialogue. For example, in the historic 2008 Democratic primary, which pitted the first serious female candidate against the first serious African American candidate (Hillary Clinton versus Barack Obama), these candidates and other challengers meticulously avoided any criticism that might suggest women or African Americans were not qualified for the office. Similarly, Obama made little mention of Republican John McCain's advanced age (72) in the general election campaign. At the same time, all candidates were squarely attacked for their policies, a sure sign they were being taken seriously. If a candidate is not attacked by opponents, the perception is of a less-than-serious candidate. If a candidate is far ahead in the polls, he or she usually refrains from attacking the opponent at all, because an attack only tends to legitimize that opponent.

The Need to Be Taken Seriously

For lesser-known candidates, the most difficult aspect of their campaign is convincing the media to take them seriously. If the public and the media do not perceive someone as having a realistic chance of winning, the public acceptance or rejection of that candidate's stand on issues or themselves as persons is largely irrelevant. Although polls showed that large numbers of Americans favored the positions of moderate Independent candidate John Anderson in the 1980 presidential race, less than 10% eventually voted for him, largely because they felt that he had no chance of winning. In 1992, early summer polls showed Ross Perot's support substantial enough to conceive of his winning the presidency. However, his support gradually eroded by November, although he still acquired a larger share of the vote (around 20%) than any other third-party candidate in modern times. When he ran again in 1996, he failed to do as well. Because no one other than a Republican or Democrat has been elected President of the United States since 1848, people perceive such an outcome as highly unlikely, a social perception that can quickly become a self-fulfilling prophecy.

Case Study: Press Coverage of the 2000 U.S. Presidential Election

The historic 2000 presidential election on November 7 was the closest race in U.S. history. Republican George W. Bush and Democrat Al Gore were virtually tied in electoral votes the morning after the election. For the next 36 days, the outcome was uncertain as the controversy swirled around the count in the state of Florida. The election was only finally decided on December 12, when a close decision by the U.S. Supreme Court favored the claims of George Bush. After this decision, Al Gore conceded; but it probably will never be definitively established which candidate actually won Florida, where the popular vote was within a hundredth of a percent, with the winner receiving the entire electoral vote. The role of the press in covering this election and the postelection process was carefully examined in an illuminating book by Jamieson and Waldman (2003).

Election Night Coverage

When networks make projections that turn out to be accurate (as most do), they tend to take credit for their skill. However, when they have to retract their projections, as they did repeatedly with the 2000 Florida presidential returns, they tended to blame "bad data," even though all networks were drawing on basically the same data, from the Voter News Service (VNS).

Premature Overconfident Projections

On election evening, the networks projected Florida first for Gore and later reversed themselves and called it for Bush. Around 10:15 p.m. Eastern Time they retracted both and placed the state (and thus the whole election) back into the "too-close-to-call" category. Several smaller states were also very close and undecided until well into the next day or days. At 2:20 a.m. the networks called the election for Bush but retracted this call at 3:50 a.m.

As the election results became increasingly uncertain as more returns came in, the opposite of the usual trend, reporters and pundits struggled in their interpretation. There was much discussion about "egg on their faces" and "eating crow," as well as extended discussions of possible scenarios ("if Gore wins these three states, he could still lose Florida and win …"). Some of this discussion was accompanied by the startlingly low-tech graphics of network analysts and anchors drawing scribbles on paper with a crayon and holding them up to the camera!

Framing the Electoral Uncertainty

Jamieson and Waldman (2003) argued that, during the next five weeks, the prevailing frame for discussing the outcome of the election gradually came to increasingly favor Bush over Gore, although the objective data coming in over that time did not necessarily do so. The three possible frames, each drawing on true information, would be that (1) Gore had won the popular vote and was ahead in the electoral vote, and the final outcome in the Electoral College was uncertain; (2) Bush was ahead in the key state that would decide the final electoral vote and thus was the presumed victor unless Gore's campaign proved otherwise; or (3) neither candidate was ahead nor held an advantage over the other. In the news coverage over the next five weeks (especially the influential Sunday morning network news shows), the bias favoring the second frame with Bush as presumed victor gradually emerged, as Bush's campaign people managed the media more effectively than Gore's people. See Wicks (2001) for discussion of the idea of framing of news events.

How did they do this? First of all, Republicans began to frame the postelection hand recount as flawed and unfair. The Bush camp framed the initial machine count, which showed him ahead by a few hundred votes out of several million cast, as legitimate and the subsequent statewide hand recount as suspect and unreliable. The latter was always referred to by Republicans as a "recount" rather than a "full count," "complete count," or "hand count." Attempts to force a recount were described as attempts to "overturn the results." Also, the Bush campaign talked openly of challenging Gore's winning results in other close states like New Mexico, Oregon, Wisconsin, and Iowa, but Gore's camp did not aggressively do likewise.

Perhaps the most telling reframing came in the decisions about the legitimacy of the overseas absentee ballots, which came in late and had to be counted by hand. Gore attempted to have those strictly evaluated, with those not meeting specified criteria (such as containing a postmark no later than election day) thrown out, while the Bush campaign framed those ballots as "military ballots" (which only some of them were) and questioned the patriotism of those trying to "disenfranchise" the voting of our "brave men and women defending our country." Both sides insisted on strict adherence to the law only when it favored their candidate. In the case of the absentee ballots, whose legitimacy was decided very idiosyncratically by each county, the Bush frame of casting Gore's adherence to the law as an attack on the patriotism of the military came to be adopted by the news media, who came to see Gore's moves as illegitimate and as a desperate attempt to overturn the election results favoring Bush. Thus, 680 questionable votes were accepted and counted, even though some had no postmark or a postmark after election day, and in some cases were from people who had already voted. These may well have determined the election, where Bush's final certification of victory was only a 537-vote margin.

The frame of Bush as the apparent winner and Gore as the stubborn loser had become the prevailing network news frame by late November. Frequent photo shots of Bush supporters holding "Sore Loserman" signs parodying the Democratic "Gore Lieberman" placards supported this frame. When Bush starting naming people to his cabinet but Gore did not, this perception of the inevitability of a Bush victory was further reinforced. Implications of "stealing the election" were raised for Bush only three times in the five weeks of Sunday news shows but 12 times in connection with Gore. Also, 20 out of 23 times the word "concession" appeared in a question over these weeks, it was applied to Gore.

The contest finally ended 36 days after the election when the U.S. Supreme Court ruled to halt the further counting of votes, arguing that the petitioner Bush would be "irreparably harmed" by continuing the count and "casting a cloud upon what he claims to be the legitimacy of his election" (Jamieson & Waldman, 2003, p. 127). The vote was 7–2 that there were constitutional problems with the state-court-mandated recount and 5–4 to halt the count and declare Bush the victor. After the ruling in Bush vs. Gore, Al Gore promptly conceded the election, his legal recourses exhausted.

Once Bush had been declared the victor and especially after he assumed office on January 20, 2001, the press seemed eager to assert his legitimacy and downplayed any consideration of the possibility that the wrong man may have assumed the presidency. In fact, in 2001 there were two largely unknown recounts of the Florida votes, designed to answer the question for the historical record. The first, by the *Miami Herald*, *USA Today*, and Knight Ridder, produced eight alternative sets of results, depending on the standard used to judge the acceptability of ballots; five of these favored Bush and three favored Gore. The second, more comprehensive, recount was conducted by the Associated Press, *The New York Times*, *Washington Post*, and the *Wall Street Journal*. This count produced 44 separate results, 22 favoring Bush and 22 favoring Gore! Because these were not available until shortly after the terrorist attacks of September 11, 2001, their release did not receive much attention by a press and country too traumatized from terrorism to consider it might have made a mistake at the last presidential inauguration. The fact remains, though, that we will never definitively know which candidate actually received more votes in Florida and thus actually "won" the election. It truly was "too close to call," but that is not an option in an election when a country needs a winner to assume office.

Now that we have considered the candidate's use of news for one's political advantage, let us consider the most directly partisan form of political media, namely political advertising. Although political advertising has much in common with advertising in general (see Chapter 6), there are also some important differences (Thorson, Christ, & Caywood, 1991).

Political Advertising

One of the major political issues of our time is the rapidly escalating costs of running for office, in large part due to the increased purchase of television time and hiring of media consultants. This trend was greatly accelerated in the United States by the 2010 Supreme Court decision *Citizens United vs. Federal Election Commission*. The ruling essentially removed all limits on campaign spending by political action committees, which are not formally linked to candidates but nonetheless support them and which can still be formally disavowed if their strong claims are determined to go too far. Although the political process has always been unduly influenced by the wealthy, that trend has since 2010 accelerated to an alarming degree (Frank, 2012). By the time of the 2016 elections, political advertising costs were actually less overall than had been estimated the year before. However, compared to previous elections, candidates were spending less on TV advertising and more on digital media ads, especially ones that could target particular kinds of voters through social media (Kaye, 2017). We are still learning the extent of such analytics as used by candidates, private firms, social media platforms, and foreign powers in the 2016 election (Granville, 2018). Although the arguments of the campaign finance reform debate and the use of voter data analytics are outside the scope of this book, we want to examine the purposes and effects of political advertising, whose aim is to affect the perceived reality of that candidate in our minds.

Purposes

Name Recognition

A primary purpose for lesser-known candidates and those campaigning outside of their previous constituency (e.g., a senator or governor running for president) is simply awareness and recognition of their name. Voters must have heard of a candidate before they can be expected to have any image of or attitude about that candidate (although this was not the case in the 2016 presidential election as Hillary Clinton and Donald Trump had both been in the public eye for decades). Name recognition is the perennial problem of "dark horse" challenger candidates for any office. In this sense, the goal of political advertising is not unlike the goal for advertising a new product on the market.

Agenda Setting

Political advertising can also set the agenda on issues by conveying to us what issues we should feel are particularly important (Dermody & Scullion, 2001; Schleuder, McCombs, & Wanta, 1991). Obviously candidates emphasize those issues on which they believe they are strongest. For example, an incumbent president with several foreign policy successes but economic problems at home will try to position foreign policy as a major issue in the campaign, whereas the opposing candidate may try to set the agenda toward domestic economic issues. Sometimes such decisions are not so clear-cut. For example, Democrats in 2008 had to decide whether to make age an issue in regard to Republican John McCain, who, if he had won, would have been the oldest president ever elected. On the one hand, they stood to gain if voters became concerned that 72 was too old to begin the job. On the other hand, they stood to lose if voters perceived them to be too mean-spirited and unfairly attacking a nice older gentleman (and decorated veteran) fully capable of competently functioning in office. For better or worse, Democrats chose not to make age an issue, the same choice they had made running against Ronald Reagan (age 69) in 1980 and 1984 or against Bob Dole (age 72) in 1996. In an interesting twist, during the 2016 election, both candidates were older (Hillary Clinton was 69, Donald Trump was 70), and Trump became the oldest person ever inaugurated president.

If a viewer is primed by exposure to a prior story about the economy, for example, associations from that initial concept activate related information on the economy to a more conscious level in one's memory than are other topics (Collins & Loftus, 1975; Schleuder et al., 1991). In this way, the agenda is set that this issue is important when it comes to processing later information such as a political ad. Either a prior ad or a news story could serve a priming function and thus set the agenda for interpreting a subsequent ad. Thus, a candidate must be concerned about an ad appearing immediately following a news story that inadvertently sets a different agenda. For example, a candidate vulnerable on economic issues would not want his or her ad to follow a news story about gloomy economic indicators.

Sometimes an agenda of a different sort is set by political advertising, often in ways perhaps not intended by the creators of the ads. Certain social, ethnic, or racial groups may be marginalized simply by their non-appearance in advertising. For example, a careful analysis of television advertising in the Guatemalan presidential election of 2007, in which for the first time a Mayan candidate (Rigoberta Menchu) competed, revealed that ads for all candidates, including Menchu, showed few indigenous peoples and only in minor roles like background crowd members (Connolly-Ahern & Castells i Talens, 2010). One would never know from seeing these commercials that a majority of the population of Guatemala was indigenous Maya, although they had long been politically marginalized.

Unfortunately, ethnicity has come to play an increasing role in some political advertising in the United States. A good example is some of the ads run by candidates for Virginia governor in 2017. The Republican, Ed Gillespie, apparently thought he could gain political traction by echoing some of the sentiments espoused by President Trump. Gillespie ran ads saying he would crack down on illegal immigration and "sanctuary cities" (even though there were none in Virginia at that time) (Tackett, 2017). In contrast, an ad was run on behalf of Democrat Ralph Northam that depicted an angry White man in a pickup (Confederate flag flying off the back) who seemed to be terrorizing minority children in his neighborhood (see the Useful Links section at the end of this chapter for a link to see some of these ads). Northam won the election with about 9% more overall votes than Gillespie.

Image Building

Political advertising also seeks to express an image of a candidate, or perhaps reinforce, soften, or redefine an existing image. This construction of an image is done especially effectively by television, which communicates nonverbal as well as verbal behaviors. One effective way to communicate an image is through eliciting emotional responses in the viewer (Englis, 1994). Another is to cultivate a candidate's particular image of morality (Page & Duffy, 2009). The widespread use of media consultants testifies to the importance of image building. As mentioned elsewhere in this chapter, it is also increasingly common for politicians to seek out particular kinds of voters, using analytical tools from social media. It is even possible for politicians (and celebrities) to appear more popular online than they actually are by buying fake media followers through online companies devoted to just that task (Confessore, Dance, Harris, & Hansen, 2018). In addition, polls are continually taken by a candidate's campaign staff to determine what issues voters are concerned about and what aspects of their own and their opponent's campaigns attract or trouble them. Then the candidate's image is tailored accordingly.

Some studies of candidate image have focused on general affective traits or personality or social attributes and compared the image a voter has with actual voting behavior (Andersen & Kibler, 1978; Dimitrova & Bystrom, 2013; Nimmo & Savage, 1976). More situational approaches have demonstrated a relationship between voters' ratings of candidate behaviors and voting preference (Balmas & Sheafer, 2010; Husson, Stephen, Harrison, & Fehr, 1988). Another approach has been to study how voters use their cognitive schemas to form an image of a candidate, which subsequently affects their evaluation (Garramone, Steele, & Pinkleton, 1991; Spezio, Loesch, Gosselin, Mattes, & Alvarez, 2012). Lau (1986) argued that there are four general schemas that people use to process political information: candidate personality factors, issues, group relations, and party identification. Many voters fairly consistently use one of these schemas more than the others. There are limits, of course, to what a media campaign can do; an urban candidate may never look comfortable and convincing astride a horse making a political ad for the rural West. Also, one cannot assume that all voters will understand an ad in the same way. The image that different members of the public construct in response to the same ads may be strikingly different because of their unique experiences and political predilections. What one viewer sees as a sincere interest in the common people looks to another as offensively hokey and opportunistic.

Issue Exposition

Occasionally, ads develop a candidate's position on issues. Such appeals are most conducive to lengthy print or Internet ads but few voters will read such material. Of course, due to the mass nature of media communication, even a minuscule percentage of the population reading a newspaper ad might be considered a success for the candidate. If the issue appeal is simple, even a TV spot can effectively communicate a candidate's position as well (Just, Crigler, & Wallach, 1990).

Fund-Raising

Finally, ads may be used to raise money. Barack Obama was incredibly successful raising money from many small donors over the Internet in 2008 as was Bernie Sanders in 2016 (see Close-up 7.6 for a discussion of how fake websites may have helped raise online funds for the wrong candidates). Although ads are a major expense, they may also bring in money. Of course, they also do so indirectly by keeping the candidate's name in the public consciousness, a prerequisite for any successful fund-raising.

Appeals in Political Advertising

Political ads use most of the same types of appeals as discussed in Chapter 6 on advertising. Various psychological appeals are quite common. Basic appeals to security come out in the "strong national defense" and "law-and-order" appeals. Fear appeals can be especially powerful in political advertising. For example, in George H. W. Bush's infamous Willie Horton ad of the 1988 presidential campaign, viewers were encouraged to fear that Democratic opponent Michael Dukakis would let dangerous criminals go free, citing the example of Massachusetts felon Willie Horton, who had been released on parole and then committed murder. The fact that Horton was an African American subtly played to White fears about Black criminality and may have reinforced racist stereotypes of African American men. Fear appeals, in general, are most often used by incumbents, playing on voters' fear of the unknown quality of what the challenger's work in office would be like.

Patriotic appeals are particularly common in political advertising, with certain national symbols like the flag very commonly present, even for regional and local races. Other patriotic symbols like familiar public buildings, monuments like the Statue of Liberty, and national historical symbols are also widely used.

Family and affiliation appeals are seen in the typical family campaign ad photo of a candidate with smiling supportive spouse and children, as if being married or a parent somehow qualified one to hold public office. It is interesting and ironic that an occupation virtually guaranteed to take enormous amounts of time away from family is so heavily "sold" with such family appeals. Using only pure logic, one might argue that an appeal from an unmarried, childless candidate who could say, "I have no family responsibilities; I'll spend all my time in office working for you" would be the most successful. However, such an appeal would probably be a dismal failure.

Testimonials are often used, sometimes by famous endorsers such as a senator or president plugging for the local candidate, sometimes by the man or woman in the street saying how much they trust a candidate to look after their interests if elected. A popular president or other office holder of one's party is eagerly sought for testimonial purposes; an unpopular one may be an embarrassing liability for their party's candidates for other offices, as Republican candidates tried to keep their distance from the relatively unpopular incumbent George W. Bush in 2008. The same thing happened with Barack Obama in 2014, especially in some swing states where Obamacare was unpopular (Martin, 2014).

Sometimes certain types of appeals are effective with particular demographic groups. For example, a study of American TV ads targeting Latinos found that these ads were very positive in nature and tended to focus on this group and encourage their identification with the candidates and invite them to see their political role as valued and important (Connaughton & Jarvis, 2004). Although most people learn something from political advertising, those who are more politically aware learn even more, especially when it comes to making inferences beyond what was explicitly stated in the ad. However, the least politically aware may actually be the most susceptible to persuasion by the ads (Valentino, Hutchings, & Williams, 2004).

Negative Advertising

The issue of how stridently and directly to attack the opponent in advertising is a major question that all political campaigns must deal with. Attack ads have a long history in American politics (Geer, 2006), and attacks on the opposition may be highly effective if they are perceived as fair. Regardless of their factual merit, or lack thereof, if the ads are perceived as mean-spirited "cheap shots," they can disastrously boomerang against the candidate making them (Garramone, 1984, 1985). Fear of such a scenario sends shivers up the spines of all politicians and often causes them to not take chances in this area, as seen in the Democrats' decision not to make John McCain's or Ronald Reagan's age an issue. Nonetheless, negative political advertising continues to be widely used (Geer, 2006; Wallace, 2016; West, 2005).

It is not clear if or how much negative advertising has increased in recent years. By some counts (Kaid & Johnston, 1991), negative advertising increased in the 1980s over the 1970s to about one-third of the TV ads in the presidential campaigns. On the other hand, the Campaign Discourse Mapping Project concluded that attack ads had been roughly constant in percentage since from 1960 through the late 1990s (Jamieson & Waldman, 1997). Some argue that the outrage at negative advertising that was common in an earlier era has become much more muted since the late 1980s, as voters apparently have accepted some degree of mudslinging and even falsifying the opponent's record as normal (Jamieson, 1992). Still others argue that it is not even conceptually clear what constitutes a negative political ad (Richardson, 2001). As is the trend with all forms of media, negative political advertising has also moved online. One study (Auter & Fine, 2016) that examined the use of attack ads on Facebook found that they were very common in tight political races. However, in contests that were not close, negative ads were much more likely to be used by political underdogs, perhaps out of desperation.

Attacks may be strong without being direct or even mentioning the opponent by name. For example, one of the most notorious historical instances was incumbent President Lyndon Johnson's 1964 TV ad (withdrawn after one airing due to complaints) showing a little girl in a field of daisies. Suddenly an atomic bomb explodes and we hear Johnson's voiceover: "These are the stakes: to make a world in which all God's children can live, or go into the dark" (cited in Devlin, 1987). Republican candidate Barry Goldwater was never mentioned, but the ad clearly played on viewers' fears of his hawkishness. Similarly, an ad was run for Hillary Clinton in 2016 that featured news video of many prominent Republicans' (Jeb Bush, Mitt Romney, Ted Cruz, Marco Rubio) negative assessments of Trump. However, the ad never showed Clinton herself or mentioned her name.

Does negative advertising work? The answer seems to be yes and no. Research suggests that negative ads are remembered well, even though they are generally disliked (Garramone, 1984; Garramone, Atkin, Pinkleton, & Cole, 1990; Klein & Ahluwalia, 2005; Lau, Sigelman, Heldman, & Babbitt, 1999; Meffert, Chung, Joiner, Waks, & Garst, 2006; Newhagen & Reeves, 1991; Phillips, Urbany, & Reynolds, 2008). This finding is quite consistent with the widespread negative attitudes about political attack advertising and the popular perception that such ads apparently work (Kaid & Boydston, 1987). Negative emotional ads are remembered better than positive emotional ads, perhaps due to their greater use of automatic, as opposed to controlled, cognitive processing (Lang, 1991, 2000) and peripheral rather than central processing (Kahneman, 2011; Petty et al., 2002; Schemer, 2012). There is also evidence that negative ads engender cynical attitudes (Dardis, Shen, & Edwards, 2008; Schenk-Hamlin, Procter, & Rumsey, 2000). It may also be important whether the negative message is embedded in a positive or negative context. Messages that contrast with their context are recalled better (Basil, Schooler, & Reeves, 1991). This negative attitude toward attack ads may have two undesired effects for the candidate: it may erode support among current partisans, and it may lead opposing partisans to draw up defenses to strengthen their position (J. M. Phillips et al., 2008). See Close-up 8.6 for a few examples of times when political satire has been interpreted by some as a low-blow attack.

❖ CLOSE-UP 8.6 WHEN IS IT SATIRE AND WHEN IS IT JUST PLAIN MEAN?

During the U.S. presidential campaign of 2008, The New Yorker *magazine published what turned out to be an extremely controversial cover illustration. The cartoonish drawing showed Michelle and Barack Obama dressed as Muslim terrorists fist-bumping each other in the Oval Office. She carried a machine gun and sported a large Afro. He was dressed in a caftan and turban with a portrait of Osama bin Laden on the wall and an American flag burning in the fireplace. Although editor David Remnick and artist Barry Blitt professed surprise and disbelief at the critical offense taken, Harvard social psychologist Mahzarin Banaji (2008) argued that they should not have been. The magazine claimed that the drawing was a satirical piece attempting to skewer the political far right's distortion of Obama's record and exploitation of racial and religious prejudice by depicting the future president as a Muslim apologist for Islamic terrorism.*

However, Banaji argued the simple associative power of the image (Obama = terrorist) far overshadowed the intended, more intellectual appeal of satirizing the far right. For example, she says, would anyone seriously find a cartoon of an older man and young teen boy fist-bumping after having enjoyed sex to be a satirical condemnation of pedophilia? She concludes (p. B13) that "it is the moral responsibility of the artist to know about how art is received by its intended audience."

As mentioned elsewhere in this chapter and the previous one, comedy TV shows have long enjoyed satirizing politicians. None has been more adept at this than NBC's long-running Saturday Night Live. Starting out by mocking 1970s pols like Gerald Ford (with Chevy Chase frequently portraying the accident-prone president), SNL's parodies continue to this day. As was the case with other forms of media, the 2016 presidential race was a ratings boon to SNL. In particular, Alec Baldwin's memorable portrayal of Trump before and after the election boosted SNL's ratings (O'Connell, 2017); in fact, some of the show's spoofs of events like the Trump/Clinton debates actually got higher ratings than the real debates (Graber & Dunaway, 2018). Ironically having served as a guest host of the program in 2015, once elected president, Trump was no longer a fan. Tweeting that the show was not funny and unwatchable, Trump got into public spats with Baldwin, who frequently stated how poorly qualified Trump was (Itzkoff, 2018). Trump press secretaries Sean Spicer and Sarah Huckabee Sanders were also parodied on SNL. Although the primary focus of Aidy Bryant's impersonation of Sanders seemed to be her alleged lies, some criticized the portrayal as especially harsh in depicting Sanders's appearance, weight, and Southern accent (Strause, 2017).

Whether negative ads directly affect voting behavior is less clear. It may depend what the source of the negative message is, whether the focus is issue- or person-oriented, at what point in the campaign they are used, and what sort of response is made to the negative attack. In a study of a U.S. Senate race, Lemert, Wanta, and Lee (1999) found that attack ads by a Republican candidate, coupled with a pledge from the Democrat not to use negative advertising, led to a lower voting rate by Republicans but not Democrats. Negative ads, in the framework of comparing the two candidates directly, may be the most effective way to produce attack advertising. Some studies have shown that negative comparative ads can reduce preference for the targeted candidate without much backlash against the sponsoring candidate (Pinkleton, 1998). The repetition of negative ads seems to matter, but only up to a point. For example, one study found that attack ads can influence voter behavior, but if the ads were seen more than three times, this effect backfired, perhaps as viewers began to see the sponsor of the ads as mean-spirited (Fernandes, 2013). Negative ads can also stimulate voter turnout (Goldstein & Freedman, 2002; Meirick & Nisbett, 2011), and negative ads are more effective than positive ads in reinforcing commitment of prior supporters (J. M. Phillips *et al.*, 2008). Finally, in yet another example of the third-person effect (defined in Chapter 2), people believe strongly that negative ads affect other people and other political parties more than themselves and their party (Gardikiotis, 2008; Hoffner & Rehkoff, 2011; Wei & Lo, 2007).

Sometimes there are other negative influences besides advertising and news. See Close-up 8.7 for a discussion of a popular political documentary film that influenced the political landscape in the U.S. 2004 election.

❖ **CLOSE-UP 8.7 THE EFFECT OF A DOCUMENTARY FILM ON POLITICAL PERCEPTIONS: THE CASE OF FAHRENHEIT 9/11**

All sorts of influences may affect political attitudes and perceptions, including some surprising ones. One unusual piece in the 2004 U.S. presidential campaign between incumbent George W. Bush and challenger Massachusetts Senator John Kerry was the release of Michael Moore's polemical documentary Fahrenheit 9/11. *Although Moore had long been known for hard-hitting documentaries in the classic muckraking tradition, including the previous* Bowling for Columbine *and* Roger and Me, Fahrenheit 9/11 *drew his largest audience and became one of the most seen documentaries in U.S. film history, favorably competing with blockbuster summer films.* Fahrenheit 9/11 *was a scathing portrayal of the Bush administration and seemed designed to evoke strong anger against George W. Bush. It used accepted historical and news footage but put them together in creative ways. One of his most famous scenes was the shot of the president reading a story to a group of children just after he had heard the World Trade Center was attacked. The film was praised as a brilliant political documentary and decried as a grossly unfair and biased piece of propaganda. It may have been both.*

What effect did viewing this film have? Communications researchers Lance Holbert and Glenn Hansen (2006, 2008; see also Holbert, Hansen, Caplan, & Mortensen, 2007) attempted to answer this question. Examining Bush and Kerry supporters who either had or had not seen Fahrenheit 9/11, *Holbert and Hansen found that anger toward Bush after seeing the film mediated impressions of his performance in the televised debates. Those who saw the film (both Bush and Kerry supporters) increased their anger toward Bush and this led them to rate his debate performance as poorer. Holbert and Hansen argue that a potent emotional stimulus like this film can have a crucial role in forming political opinion.*

Effects of Political Advertising

The effects of political ads, as well as other forms of political communication in media, can be many. The study of such effects has come from the perspectives of political science, advertising, social psychology, and communication. In spite of the prevalent perception that the overriding intent of political ads is to cause attitude change in people, relatively few political ads actually change anyone's mind, in the sense of causing them to switch loyalties from one candidate to another (Blumler & McQuail, 1969; Cwalina, Falkowski, & Kaid, 2000; Liasson, 2012). This is not to say that they are ineffective, however. Political ads frequently help crystallize existing attitudes by sharpening and elaborating them. For example, perhaps someone was slightly leaning toward Hillary Clinton for president in 2016 because of her experience as a New York senator and Secretary of State. Political advertising for Clinton may help flesh out that attitude by providing more information about her positions, past performance as Secretary of State, and general intangible impressions about the candidate. In a related vein, political advertising may reinforce existing attitudes in voters to keep in the fold a voter who is leaning toward a candidate but not strongly committed. Such an attitude that is so reinforced is more likely to translate into voting on election day and greater resistance to an opposing candidate's attempts to change that attitude. There is also evidence that political advertising, at least on a local level, leads to more political information-seeking through television, the Internet, and social contacts (Cho, 2008, 2011).

Political strategists are always concerned about reinforcing "soft" support from voters who are leaning toward their candidate but not strongly committed. Many ads are targeted at such people to help ensure that they turn out on election day. As discussed elsewhere in this chapter, ads targeting social media users with particular demographics may help with this, too. Such data-driven, tailored online advertising will no doubt continue in upcoming elections (Fulgoni, Lipsman, & Davidsen, 2016).

Occasionally political advertising may actually convert a voter from one candidate to another, but this is fairly rare and did not increase substantially with the advent of television (see Berelson, Lazarsfeld, & McPhee, 1954; Lazarsfeld, Berelson, & Gaudet, 1948, for pre-TV studies). Of course, because some elections are decided by a tiny fraction of the vote, such swing votes are not unimportant.

Reactions to political advertising may also depend on the connection that the voter feels with the candidate (Alwitt, Deighton, & Grimm, 1991; Winfrey, Warner, & Banwart, 2014). Such an attitudinal bond may be based on an objective belief ("I support her program for the economy") or a subjective emotion ("I feel good about him") criterion. Sometimes the two may be opposed, as in the case when there is intellectual agreement with the candidate's positions on issues but passionate opposition on more emotional levels, or vice versa.

Conclusion

Now more than ever, our perceived reality of the political world is largely a product of the media. The role of media in politics will continue to be hotly debated. The loudest critics some years ago decried how TV was corrupting the democratic process and reducing political discourse to banal superficialities. The same concern is directed toward the Internet and social media today. There is also a historical trend of people being the most critical of the newest medium or newest uses of old media. "If one goes back through the history of press criticism, a distinct pattern emerges: the most modern medium is always regarded as the most issueless, the most frivolous—first in print, then daily press, then radio, then television … newest medium attracts the loudest complaints" (Robinson & Sheehan, cited in Kraus, 1988, p. 88). Predictably, in recent years there have been loud criticisms of candidates' using talk show TV formats in campaigning. An even louder outcry about the political use of the Internet, particularly social media, has also arisen recently (Gil de Zúñiga, Weeks, & Ardèvol-Abreu, 2017; Jacques & Ratzan, 1997; Selnow, 1997; Whillock, 1997; Wojcieszak & Mutz, 2009), in spite of its considerable promise in increasing civic engagement of voters, especially young ones (Verser & Wicks, 2006; Xenos & Moy, 2007).

What is certain, however, is that media do create a political world that is the basis of most of our perceived political knowledge and subsequent political behavior, most notably voting. That role is not likely to change, so it behooves us to understand it better. Specific media use will evolve, such as increased use of the Internet by candidates. However, it is still media which offer the interpretation of political events and candidates, allowing us to construct our reality of these candidates. The almost-tied 2000 U.S. presidential election and the extremely close 2016 election remind us of the potentially very high stakes of constructing that political reality in a responsible fashion.

Media Applications, Chapter 8: Can We Moderate Our Political Attitudes Through Our Media Choices?

Before leaving the topic of politics and media, let us examine the argument of one group of researchers who believe that television, in a very general sense, may shape our political attitudes and perceived reality about politics in some subtle ways. Using cultivation theory, Gerbner, Gross, Morgan, and Signorielli (1982, 1984; see also Morgan *et al.*, 2009) examined the relationship between television viewing in general and political attitudes.

Using data gathered for several years by the National Opinion Research Center in their General Social Surveys, Gerbner and colleagues (1984) looked at the correlation of the amount of TV viewing (and other media use) and political self-designation on a liberal–moderate–conservative dimension. Frequent TV viewers were most likely to label themselves as politically moderate, whereas frequent newspaper readers labeled themselves conservative, and heavy radio listeners labeled themselves liberal. This relationship was quite consistent within various demographic subgroups, especially so for the conservatives and the moderates. Among light viewers, there was consistently greater difference of opinion between liberals and conservatives on several different specific issues than there was between the liberal and conservative heavy viewers. One conclusion of these studies was that television, with its mass market appeal, avoids extreme positions that might offend people and thus, by default, it cultivates middle-of-the-road perspectives.

This sort of political cultivation effect is not limited to North American culture, although the specific effects may differ in different places. For example, in Argentina, Morgan and Shanahan (1991, 1995) found that adolescents who were heavy TV viewers were more likely to agree that people should submit to authority, approve of limits on freedom of speech, and believe that poor people are to blame for their own poverty. In a country having recently come out from under a repressive military dictatorship, it appeared that television "cultivates views that provide legitimacy to authoritarian political practices" (Morgan & Shanahan, 1991, p. 101). Similarly, Toepfl (2011) found that government-controlled TV in Russia was effective at directing public outrage at political scandals from top-level government officials to lower-level ones.

Has Our Polarized Media Affected TV's Moderation Effect?

How might changing media consumption trends have changed this moderation effect? For one thing, heavy and light television viewers may use information differently. Cho (2005) found that high TV news viewers were more likely than low TV news viewers to decide on a candidate based on image perception and were less likely to vote based on policy issues. More recent research has indicated that as fewer people watch mainstream TV news (and turn online for more partisan news sources that may reinforce political biases), this sense of moderation may be declining (Liu, 2017). This effect may be magnified with increasingly high ratings for our polarized cable news channels, such as Fox News and MSNBC (Levendusky, 2013).

Such political division may even stretch into advertising and consumer product preference. In a fascinating study, Hoewe and Hatemi (2017) manipulated some Coca-Cola ads to include (or not include) images of Middle Eastern looking men and women in hijabs as "America the Beautiful" was sung in Arabic. Before seeing the ads, participants indicated their political orientation (extremely conservative to extremely liberal) and their preference for either Coke or Pepsi. After seeing the ads, participants were rewarded with pizza and a beverage—their choice of a Coke or Pepsi. Conservatives who initially preferred Coke and saw the Arabic/Coke ad were significantly more likely than liberals to have a post-viewing Pepsi.

Even our political TV dramas have become polarized and dystopian. In the 1990s and early 2000s, one of the most highly rated political shows was *The West Wing*, which depicted many politicians, especially the fictional President Bartlet, as honorable. One study (Holbert *et al.*, 2003) even found that watching *The West Wing* increased participants' favorable impressions of real-life presidents Clinton and Bush. These days, however, popular political dramas tend to revolve around more sinister topics like political scandal (*Scandal*), double dealing (*House of Cards*), and compromised ethics (*The Good Wife*) (Tryon, 2016).

What Can Individual Media Consumers Do?

In this polarized media landscape, is it possible for media consumers to moderate their political views? A theme of this entire book has been that media help us create a reality. However, when we isolate ourselves in our own political media bubbles, we are creating a very stark reality. Some researchers suggest that broadening our political media diet may make a difference.

Crosscutting Media

When political media consumers engage in *crosscutting*, they take in media not only from sources that match their own ideology but also from sources that may contradict it. How possible is it for us to crosscut our media consumption? Yun and colleagues (Yun, Park, Holody, Yoon, & Xie, 2013) examined that question by investigating one area of online media that might be considered an extreme echo-chamber of likeminded people reinforcing one another's views. Specifically, they looked at popular blogs about abortion—those with prolife, prochoice, or neutral positions. The researchers also monitored how the blog administrators handled comment posts by new readers of the blogs. Interestingly, they discovered that most blogs did include user comments sections, and the comments were very infrequently moderated by administrators (even when the comments were in opposition to the overall position of the blog). Another study that examined online remarks in newspaper comments sections found that such forums can actually serve as a place for moderate views to be expressed (Harris, Morgan, & Gibbs, 2014).

There is also some evidence that once we begin to crosscut, our views may become more moderate. In a series of experiments, Levendusky (2013) discovered that the effect is somewhat complicated, though. One experiment showed only a small moderating effect from crosscutting, and in fact those who had especially strong views to begin with became even more extreme in their views after crosscutting. However, that effect differed based on the perceived credibility of the crosscutting source. When people crosscut with a highly regarded source, those people "became much more moderate" (p. 77). Other experiments revealed that for the moderation effect to take place, people have to be open to crosscutting sources and actually like consuming media with different viewpoints. Crosscutting media seems to work in non-Western cultures as well. For example, a study in Ghana (Conroy-Krutz & Moehler,

2015) found that commuters who listened to political radio programming that opposed their own views tended to moderate their opinions to a more middle-of-the-road stance.

It also seems that *not* crosscutting can have significant implications for our beliefs. One case in particular might be our beliefs about climate change. Bennett (2016) argues that much of the importance of the issue has been lost by the media's coverage of climate change skeptics. Although the science of human-made climate change is virtually undisputed among most scientists (Cook *et al.*, 2016; Shermer, 2015), the news media's desire to present "balanced" viewpoints may be creating a false equivalency between climate change experts and skeptics. To make matters worse, "many people do not fully understand or trust science, particularly because scientists themselves typically portray their findings in terms of complex ideas, probabilities, and degrees of uncertainty" (Bennett, 2016, p. 96); see Media Applications, Chapter 7 for further discussion of this.

One of the biggest platforms for climate change skeptics has been the conservative Fox News. In studies comparing the effects of consuming Fox News and "not-Fox news" (ABC, CBS, NBC, CNN, and MSNBC news), Krosnick and MacInnis (2015) unsurprisingly found that more self-identified Republicans watched Fox News than Democrats or Independents. Also unsurprising was the fact that climate change skepticism views were much more likely to be expressed on Fox News than non-Fox sources. However, the researchers also discovered that heavy Fox News viewers were also much more likely than non-Fox viewers to express skepticism that climate change was real and caused by humans. Taken together, Krosnick and MacInnis's analyses led them to conclude that, "it appears that Republicans and Democrats diverge in their opinions about global warming due to selective exposure to different news sources" (p. 85).

Thus, as is the case with so many other examples throughout this book, it appears the burden sits on the shoulders of us, the media consumers. If we want to have the most accurate view of politicians and political issues, we must think carefully about how we choose our information sources.

Further Reading

Bennett, W. L. (2016). *News: The politics of illusion*. 10th ed. Chicago: University of Chicago Press.

Geer, J. G. (2006). *In defense of negativity: Attack ads in presidential campaigns*. Chicago: University of Chicago Press.

Graber, D. A., & Dunaway, J. (2018). *Mass media and American politics*. 10th ed. Thousand Oaks, CA: CQ Press/Sage.

Gruszczynski, M., & Wagner, M. W. (2017). Information flow in the 21st century: The dynamics of agenda-uptake. *Mass Communication and Society*, 20(3), 378–402. doi: 10.1080/15205436.2016.1255757

Levendusky, M. (2013). *How partisan media polarize America*. Chicago: University of Chicago Press.

Perloff, R. M. (2015). A three-decade retrospective on the Hostile Media Effect. *Mass Communication and Society*, 18(6), 701–729. doi:10.1080/15205436.2015.1051234

Tryon, C. (2016). *Political TV*. New York: Routledge.

Van Steenburg, E. (2015). Areas of research in political advertising: A review and research agenda. *International Journal of Advertising*, 34(2), 195–231. https://doi.org/10.1080/02650487.2014.996194

Useful Links

Bob Graham's 100 work days:
www.floridamemory.com/photographiccollection/photo_exhibits/bobgraham/

John Oliver's ads targeting President Trump:
www.youtube.com/watch?v=i296CJMOZpk

Some political ads from the 2017 Virginia governor's race:
www.theroot.com/va-governor-s-race-conservatives-shed-white-tears-aft-1820006787

For more resources, please visit the companion website:
www.routledge.com/cw/harris

Chapter 9

Violence

Media Mayhem Matters

Q: How did depictions of gun violence change in PG-13 movies between 1985 and 2015?

A: For one thing, the number of scenes with gun violence more than doubled in those years. Also, a greater proportion of movies were rated PG-13 in 2015 than in 1985, and fewer were rated R. Alarmingly, compared to R-rated movies, instances of gun violence were more common and consequences of violence were less common in PG-13 movies (Romer *et al.*, 2017).

Q: How concerning is video game violence to media researchers, parents, and pediatricians?

A: In one study that surveyed these groups, 66% of researchers, 67% of parents, and 90% of pediatricians said they believed that violent video game play results in increased aggressive behavior in children (Bushman, Gollwitzer, & Cruz, 2015).

Q: Why have Hollywood movie studios increasingly produced action-adventure movies, many of which are chock full of violent content?

A: One reason may be the movie markets overseas. China in particular is a large consumer of American movies. Some of the most popular American movies there include the *Transformers* and *Star Wars* series. Such movies are easy to translate into different languages since a large proportion of the movies are action. Hollywood studios also sometimes count on overseas viewers to make up for poor ticket sales at home. For example, in 2016 *World of Warcraft* was a flop in U.S. theaters on its opening weekend, but it generated five times as much revenue in the same period in China (Beech, 2017).

How common is media violence? Although specific frequency figures depend on our precise operational definition of violence, the reality of media, especially television and film in the United States, Asia, Europe, and elsewhere, is a highly violent world. For at least the past several decades, about two-thirds of American TV programs and about 90% of movies have contained some sort of violence (Bleakley, Romer, & Jamieson, 2014; Gabrielli, Traore, Stoolmiller, Bergamini, & Sargent, 2016; National Television Violence Study, 1997; Smith, Nathanson, & Wilson, 2002). By one estimate, on U.S. television, there are 7.9 violent acts per hour in programming aimed at children, compared to 4.7 violent acts per hour in adult prime-time programs. Even without counting the cartoon violence, there are still 6.3 violent incidents per hour on children's TV (Carlsson-Paige, 2008), much of which is trivialized, glamorized, and sanitized (Wilson, Smith *et al.*, 2002). Considerable violence even occurs in programming we do not immediately associate with aggression, such as news, music videos, and even commercials aimed at children.

Kids are watching all this violence, too. One study found that almost 50% of 10- to 14-year-olds had seen very violent (R-rated) movies that had been recently released; among African American boys, it was 80% (Worth, Chambers, Nassau, Rakhra, & Sargent, 2008)! Clearly, violent movies are popular. Another analysis discovered that among PG-13 movies, increased levels of violence were associated with increased ticket sales (Barranco, Rader, & Smith, 2017).

How about the response that media violence only reflects an imperfect world that is very violent? Yes, there is violence in the real world but much less than what is portrayed in the media. For example, on TV crime dramas, violence is wildly overrepresented (Bushman & Anderson, 2001; Oliver, 1994; Surette, 2015). On those shows, murder, robbery, kidnapping, and assault are present 90% of the time, with murder present about 25% of the time. However, according to FBI statistics, murders actually account for less than 1% of crime. In contrast, about two-thirds of actual crimes involve theft, although on TV dramas, it only happens about 6% of the time (Surette, 2015); watching someone steal something apparently is less entertaining than seeing someone murdered. Interestingly, over the past few decades, the level of violent crime in the United States has generally been dropping; one would never know that by watching movies, however, in which the levels of violence have steadily increased over the years (Barranco *et al.*, 2017). We have already seen in Chapter 7 how the sensationalist news reporting of unusual but grisly crimes leads people to hugely overestimate the frequency of their occurrence in reality.

Consistent with the definition of most, though not all, researchers, *violence* is defined here as behavior intended to cause physical harm or pain to another individual. Excluded from this definition are accidental injury, vandalism of property, and various behaviors sometimes called "psychological," "relational," or "verbal" aggression, including emotional abuse and the "alternative aggressions" often used by girls to intimidate other girls by threatening to withdraw relationships (Simmons, 2002). These issues are all very important and deserve serious study in regard to media images. However, they have not received much research attention as yet (but see Coyne & Archer, 2004, 2005; Coyne & Whitehead, 2008; Glascock, 2014; Martins & Wilson, 2012; Mehari & Farrell, 2018), whereas the effects of physical violence have been the subject of intense research scrutiny for the last half century. Although the term is not always used precisely or uniformly, *aggression* is the internal motivation behind violent behavior; the behavior may be observed directly; the motive of aggression must be inferred from those acts.

Media violence on television has long been a contentious political issue, and there has probably been more psychological research on the topic of violence than on all other topics in this book put together—by some estimates at least 3,000 to 4,000 studies by the 1990s alone (Grossman & DeGaetano, 1999). This chapter makes no claim to comprehensively review all of that literature; thorough reviews and discussions in varying detail are available elsewhere (see Anderson, Berkowitz, *et al.*, 2003; Arriaga, Zillmann, & Esteves, 2016; Christensen & Wood, 2007; Kirsh, 2006; Murray, 1999; National Television Violence Study, 1997; Potter, 1999; Sparks, Sparks, & Sparks, 2009).

This research has most often been conducted within the theoretical frameworks of social cognition and cultivation theories (see Chapter 2), although other perspectives have also been useful. Often the discussion of the scientific issues has been clouded and colored by the economic interest or ideological perspectives of those involved, and much of the popular writing on the topic has taken the form of either (1) polemical and unfounded media bashing (e.g., "It's all the media's fault") or (2) a defensive apologia to support one's economic self-interest (e.g., "It's all just make-believe"). Either of these positions blatantly ignores the large body of research that is readily available. In addition, in these types of arguments, crucial distinctions among diverse types and contexts of violence and among different populations are often lacking.

In considering the effects of media violence on society, we must not make the mistake of imagining media to be the only factor, or even the major factor, which contributes to violence in society. Negative social conditions like poverty, racism, crowding, drugs, parental neglect, weakened family values, availability of weapons, and the underclass subculture doubtlessly contribute far more than television, movies, or video games. Negative family or peer role models also have substantial effects. However, even if media violence is responsible for only 5–15% of societal violence, as estimated by some researchers (Huesmann, 2007; Sparks & Sparks, 2002; Strasburger, 1995), that is still very important. Because of the nature of mass communication, even a very small effect of media can be substantial. For example, suppose a violent movie incites 0.001% of viewers to act more violently. Although the percentage may be minuscule, 0.001% of an audience of 20 million is still 200 people! Also, when examining the public health threat of media violence, effect sizes are similar to dangers such as smoking and sexually transmitted infections (Bushman & Huesmann, 2001).

We approach the study of media violence in this chapter by looking at the various effects of the violent view of the world presented in media. This study of the perceived reality of media violence focuses on the psychological processes involved and the weight of the evidence supporting the existence of those effects. Later in the chapter we look at individual differences among those who are attracted to or repelled by media violence and longitudinal studies probing for long-term effects. Next we look at one of the newer areas of concern, violent video games. Finally, we address the question of what may be done to provide balance to this perceived reality of violence. As we will see, most of the public concern and scientific study of the perceived violent reality of media centers on the effects of viewing televised violence, especially on children.

Effects of Media Violence

The effect of media violence that many think of first is behavioral, when people imitate or model violent behavior that they see on the screen. However, this is only one of several effects. The research on the different effects has been driven by diverse theoretical frameworks (see Chapter 2); for example, studies of behavioral effects have most often been heavily influenced by social learning/cognitive theory, and studies of attitudinal effects often draw on cultivation theory. The following section examines various effects of media violence in turn and the evidence supporting each of them. We begin with what is perhaps the most immediate effect of viewing violence, the idea that watching violence induces fear.

Fear

Much of the research on fear responses to violent media comes from the laboratory of Cantor (1996, 1998a, 2002, 2006, 2009, 2011; Cantor & Riddle, 2014), who concludes that "transitory fright responses are quite typical, that enduring and intense emotional disturbances occur in a substantial proportion of children and adolescents, and that severe and debilitating reactions affect a small minority of particularly susceptible individuals of all ages" (Cantor, 1996, p. 91). Overall, we also know that there is a correlation between the amount of television viewed and the prevalence of symptoms of psychological trauma like anxiety, depression, and post-traumatic stress (Dempsey, Howard, Lynch, Owen, & Dunstan, 2014; Singer, Slovak, Frierson, & York, 1998).

Fear-Inducing Images

Different categories of stimuli and events differentially produce fear responses in viewers of different ages. Distortions of natural forms (e.g., monsters and mutants) are very scary to preschoolers but typically less so to older children. Depictions of dangers and injuries (e.g., assaults, natural disasters) are more scary to older elementary school children than they are to preschoolers. This is in part because the older children are cognitively able to anticipate danger and its possible consequences and thus become fearful before the actual event occurs. As we know from developmental psychologists like Piaget (1972), the older the child, the more able he or she is to think abstractly and be frightened by watching situations of endangerment to others. Sometimes two siblings viewing together may be afraid of very different aspects of a movie, or one (not necessarily the younger) may be afraid while the sibling is not. For example, consider two brothers watching E.T., a movie about a benevolent alien visiting from outer space. The preschooler may be afraid of the fantastic form of the alien, while the older child may be afraid during the scenes in which he recognizes that the friendly alien or sympathetic humans may be in potential danger from others. Alternatively, the younger child may not be afraid at all—in fact, he may love the cute little alien—and may not be able to think abstractly enough to understand why his brother is afraid of the potential endangerment.

Responses to Fear

Cantor and Oliver (1996; see also Cantor, 1998a, 2002, 2006, 2009) identify some principles to predict fear responses in children. First, the older the child, the more that a character's behavior, relative to appearance, is important in predicting fear responses, although all children will be more fearful of an ugly than an attractive character. Second, as children grow older, they become more responsive to realistic dangers and less responsive to fantasy dangers in the media. Third, and closely related, the older the child, the more able he or she is to be afraid of increasingly abstract dangers. In fact, very young children tend not to be very afraid of abstract threats. For example, fear responses to a 1980s TV movie about nuclear war in the heartland of the United States found young children to be the least afraid and adults the most afraid (Scholfield & Pavelchak, 1985), with the number of parental reports of their children discussing the movie with them increasing with the age of the child (Cantor, Wilson, & Hoffner, 1986). Similarly, compared with younger children, kids over the age of 10 showed heightened stress over media exposure to terrorism (Becker-Blease, Finkelhor, & Turner, 2008).

When they are afraid of watching something scary, preschoolers tend to cope by using non-cognitive strategies like eating, drinking, covering their eyes, or clutching a beloved object. School-age children tend to use and respond well to cognitive strategies like verbal explanations, reminders of the unreality of the situation, or instructions to think about the danger in a new, less threatening way, provided that the explanation is at an appropriate level. However, as many parents know, it can be quite difficult to totally reason away a strong media-induced fear in a young child. Interestingly, one study (Paavonen, Roine, Pennonen, & Lahikainen, 2009) indicated that parents may not always be comforting to children who encounter scary media. In fact, Paavonen and colleagues discovered that parental co-viewing of scary TV actually increased TV-related fears among children, indicating that mere parental presence is not always effective at reducing fears. The authors suggest that what may be most important in reducing children's fears of media violence is the nature and quality of the discussion that accompanies co-viewing. Others (Carroll, 2009) have speculated that in an attempt to comfort children frightened by media (by, say, cuddling them), parents may some-times actually be reinforcing the frightened reaction.

Fearful Media Memories

Several studies (e.g., Cantor & Oliver, 1996; Harrison & Cantor, 1999; Hoekstra, Harris, & Helmick, 1999; Riddle, 2018) found that practically all young adults were readily able to remember an incident of being extremely scared by a movie as a child or teen. Such memories, and perhaps some of the effects as well, are long lasting. Some effects reported are general fear/anxiety, specific fears (e.g., fear of swimming after seeing *Jaws*), sleep disturbances, and nightmares (see Close-up 9.1 for some actual memories reported by Cantor's participants). These kinds of effects may also translate into perceptions of the world. For example, one investigation (Riddle, Potter, Metzger, Nabi, & Linz, 2011) found that most college students sampled could remember a specific, graphic instance of media violence they had viewed between the ages of 5 and 23. Further, those who had vivid memories of the gory media (usu-ally movies) tended to overestimate the prevalence of real-world violent crimes. One possible reason that so many of us are able to remember frightening movies is that the intense emotions we experience during the scary scenes may make the memories more vivid (Riddle, 2014).

❖ **CLOSE-UP 9.1 MEMORIES OF BEING SCARED BY MOVIES SEEN AS A CHILD**

Cantor, in her research on the inducement of fear by violent media, has interviewed and tested hundreds of young adults about their memories of being scared by a movie seen in childhood. Here are two actual accounts of these experiences (Cantor, 1998b, pp. 9–10).

After the movie [Jaws], I had nightmares for a week straight. Always the same one. I'm in a room filled with water with ducts in the walls. They would suddenly open and dozens of sharks would swim out. I felt trapped with no place to go. I would usually wake up in a sweat. Occasionally I'll still have the exact same dream. The movie didn't just affect me at night. To this day I'm afraid to go to the ocean, sometimes even a lake. I'm afraid that there will be a shark even if I know deep down that's impossible.

> *I watched [Friday the Thirteenth, Part 2] when I was 14 years old and it scared me so much that I couldn't sleep for a whole month. I was scared of the name Jason, and I hated standing under a thatched roof. At night I needed a night light so I could see everything around me. I was very conscious of the smallest little noise, I had nightmares about knives, chain-saws, blood, screams, and hockey masks. I was very jumpy. This kind of slaughter film still has these effects on me.*

Sometimes self-reports may not be a completely adequate measure of induced fear. For example, Sparks, Pellechia, and Irvine (1999) found that certain "repressor" personality types reported low levels of negative emotional responses while watching a 25-minute segment from the horror film *When a Stranger Calls* but high levels of physiological arousal responses, as measured by skin conductance. In a similar vein, Peck (1999, as cited in Cantor, 2002) discovered that, in general, women's verbal reports of fear in response to watching scary scenes from *A Nightmare on Elm Street* were more intense than men's, but in some cases men's physiological responses were more intense than women's, especially if the victim in the scene was male. Thus, it is possible that in some circumstances some people either cannot or do not accurately report the fear they experienced, and we cannot assume that self-reports of fear completely reflect their internal emotion.

Clearly, violent media do induce fear in viewers. Further, the type of image that induces the most fear varies greatly with the age and cognitive developmental level of the viewer. However, any expression of fear by a child should be taken seriously by the parent or caretaker, not ignored, and never belittled. Even if the danger is very unreal or even silly from an adult perspective, the child's fear is very real, and that is what both parents and children must address.

Brain Correlates

Some exciting work with brain imaging suggests that our brains respond differently to violent and nonviolent stimuli (Murray *et al.*, 2006). Children aged 8 to 13 watched an 18-minute violent (boxing segment from *Rocky IV*) or nonviolent (National Geographic documentary or *Ghostwriter* children's literacy TV program) video segments while fMRI mapped their brain activity. Although both videos activated certain brain regions routinely involved in visual and auditory processing, only the violent film activated parts of the amygdala and right cerebral cortex involved with arousal, threat detection, and unconscious emotional memory. This suggests a neural basis of the fear response from violent video. It also suggests that areas such as the right hemisphere and amygdala, known to be involved with other kinds of emotional responding, are also active while watching violent media. Such emotional memories often endure long after the associated cognitive memories have faded, explaining, for example, why someone might be afraid of swimming in the ocean years after watching *Jaws* (Cantor, 2006). More recently, there have also been a number of fMRI studies done relating to how violent video game play affects brain activity. See the section on video games later in this chapter for details.

Modeling

Research on modeling media violence comes primarily out of social cognitive theory (see Chapter 2), which applies principles of learning to social situations.

How Modeling Works

From the modeling/social learning/social cognitive perspective, people see a violent act in the media and later, as a result, behave more violently themselves than they otherwise would. For this to happen, first the relevant behavior of the model must be attended to. For example, a child must notice and pay attention to a violent horror movie like *Saw*. Second, the model behavior must be retained and encoded into memory in some form; this usually occurs as the behavior is being analyzed and interpreted through cognitive processing. Using the earlier example, the child would need to think about the events in the *Saw* movie, perhaps even days after it was viewed. Whether the learned behavior is later actually produced by the viewer will depend on many factors, such as motivation and the strength of prevailing inhibiting factors. Thus, the hypothetical child viewer mentioned earlier might re-enact some of the punching seen in the movie while playing with friends.

The process of modeling may actually teach new behaviors, much as one might learn a new athletic skill by watching a coach demonstrate it. When a group of teenagers play Russian roulette after seeing a film with a similar scene in it, they may not have thought much about behaving that way before seeing the movie. This would appear to be a particularly troublesome example of the common phenomenon called observational learning. A well-documented example is the notorious New Bedford gang rape case of the mid-1980s, when several men raped a woman on a pool table in a bar (later the basis of the movie *The Accused* in which a character played by Jodie Foster was gang raped on a pinball machine). The rapists had recently seen a movie with a barroom gang rape scene in a nearby theater. Many (e.g., Follman, 2015) have suggested that the now too-common mass shootings in the United States, particularly those in schools, may be sparked in part by shooters modeling their behavior off of past shootings. It doesn't help that the shooters often receive extensive news coverage after the shootings have occurred. See Close-up 9.2 for the story of some especially tragic cases in which legal charges were filed against media for teaching violent behaviors.

❖ CLOSE-UP 9.2 ARE MEDIA CRIMINALLY LIABLE FOR EFFECTS OF VIOLENT CONTENT?

From time to time, defense attorneys representing violent crime perpetrators who appear to have been affected by television have used rather creative defenses, which inevitably come up against First Amendment freedom of speech issues. For example, in 1977, Ronald Zamora, 15, killed his 83-year-old neighbor in a robbery attempt after she discovered Zamora in her home and threatened to call the police. What was particularly unusual was that the defense attorney argued for temporary insanity at the time of the crime, arguing that Zamora was "suffering from and acted under the influence of prolonged, intense, involuntary, subliminal television intoxication" (Liebert & Sprafkin, 1988, p. 127). He further argued that the shooting was a TV-learned conditioned response to the stimulus of the victim's threatening to call the police. Television was thus an accessory to the crime. In the end, however, the jury failed to accept this reasoning, and Zamora was convicted on all counts and sentenced to life. He was released after serving 27 years and deported to Costa Rica.

A second case involved 9-year-old Olivia Niemi, who in 1974 was assaulted and raped with a bottle by three older girls and a boy. Four days before, a TV movie, Born Innocent, had been aired, showing a scene of a girl being raped with a toilet plunger. Olivia's mother then sued NBC for $11 million for alleged negligence in showing the movie in prime time. Her lawyer argued for vicarious liability and claimed that the movie had incited the children to criminal activity. After a series of appeals and countersuits, the case was finally thrown out when a judge ruled that the plaintiff had to prove that the network had intended its viewers to imitate the violent sexual acts depicted. However, when NBC aired Born Innocent as a rerun, it aired at 11:30 p.m. with most of the critical rape scene edited out (Liebert & Sprafkin, 1988).

There have also been lawsuits involving mass shootings. In 1999, the families of some high school shooting victims in Kentucky sued video game companies, pornography websites, and movie companies who distributed The Basketball Diaries and Natural Born Killers, which the plaintiffs argued had influenced the shooters. Part of the evidence was that The Basketball Diaries contains a scene in which Leonardo DiCaprio's character shoots students in a classroom. In 2001, the families of several victims in the Columbine High School shooting filed a similar lawsuit against media companies, including the makers of the first-person shooter video game Doom, which the killers apparently played frequently. Both lawsuits were later dismissed.

More often, however, it is not the specific behavior itself that is learned from the media. A second process by which modeling can work is when watching media violence produces *disinhibition*; that is, it reduces the normal inhibitions most people have against acting violently or perceiving violence as acceptable. For example, watching a movie with scenes of street fighting might produce disinhibition by weakening a viewer's usual proscriptions against fighting. In this scenario, the viewer already knows how to fight, and the medium cannot be blamed for teaching that behavior. However, TV may be breaking down the normal inhibitions that we would otherwise have against engaging in such violence. Thus, actual violent behavior may occur in the future with less provocation than would have been necessary to evoke it prior to the disinhibition.

Disinhibition may also occur through the teaching of more accepting attitudes toward violent behavior. Although most people are raised with the general belief that violent behavior is bad (specific circumstances when it might be acceptable may vary), exposure to repeated media violence may break down these attitudinal inhibitions against thinking violence is acceptable. This change toward a more accepting attitude about the appropriateness of using violence to settle disputes may subsequently and indirectly lead to violent behavior, although such an unequivocal causal connection is very difficult to empirically demonstrate.

Most of the concern with modeling effects of media violence assumes that persons may become violent in their own behavior in a somewhat different way than the media model; that is, the effect generalizes beyond the specific behavior demonstrated in the media. A person who watches a war movie may be disinhibited from violent behavior generally, and a viewer may subsequently punch or kick another person but not necessarily start shooting with an AR-15 exactly as a character in the movie did. This generalized type of modeling is far more common than the modeling of a very specific behavior.

Sometimes the nature or timing of the response can be taught through media. For example, some researchers (e.g., Grossman, 1996; Grossman & DeGaetano, 1999; Hartmann & Vorderer, 2010) have argued that violent TV and movies, and especially violent video games, train children to shoot rapidly at the appearance of certain stimuli without thinking or caring about the consequences. The normative behavior in many video games is to shoot as soon as some target appears, with the fastest reaction being the best one. Thus, Grossman argues that the child playing video games is learning to shoot first and ask questions later. Does this learned shooting behavior transfer to other situations? Grossman cited one of the boys charged in a 1998 Jonesboro, Arkansas, schoolyard shooting who had little if any experience shooting real guns but a lot of experience playing video games. He and his buddy were good enough shots to hit 15 people with 27 shots from a distance of 100 yards! Research on violent video games is discussed later in the chapter.

There are other, even more indirect ways in which modeling may occur. Violence may alter the general emotional responsiveness of the viewer, which could in turn lead to violent behavior. It may also raise the overall arousal level, which could prime the person for (among other behaviors) violence. Now let us turn to some of the research done to test the modeling hypothesis and to identify the conditions under which modeling occurs.

Basic Social Learning and Field Research

The best-known early research studying modeling of media violence was social psychologist Albert Bandura's Bobo doll studies (Bandura, 1965; Bandura *et al.*, 1963; see also Hicks, 1965). In a typical Bobo doll study testing modeling, Bandura had young children watch someone else behave aggressively toward a large plastic inflatable doll known as Bobo the clown. The child's own behavior with the Bobo doll was subsequently observed. Studies of this type consistently demonstrated that children imitated violent behavior previously observed in a live model. Most importantly for our purposes, the same effect was found when the violent model was on film rather than live (Bandura *et al.*, 1961; J. P. Nelson, Gelfand, & Hartmann, 1969; Rosencrans & Hartup, 1967; Walters & Willows, 1968). Many laboratory studies have replicated these effects over the years and have demonstrated generalization to other behaviors. For example, participants who had seen a series of violent films were more likely to respond negatively in an "unrelated" study to a research assistant who had written insulting comments on a questionnaire they had completed (Zillmann & Weaver, 1999). See Oates (2012) for additional discussion of the social learning process as applied to media.

Although these experimental studies were groundbreaking, they were not without criticism. Primarily, they were attacked for being too artificial and of questionable application to the real world. However, later research moving away from the laboratory also found corroborative evidence for modeling (Huesmann, Lagerspetz, & Eron, 1984; Joy, Kimball, & Zabrack, 1986; Lefkowitz, Eron, Walder, & Huesmann, 1977; Leyens, Camino, Parke, & Berkowitz, 1975). It also should be noted that the rates of violent crimes rose in societies following the introduction of television with its steady diet of violence. For example, although the homicide rate for White Americans and Canadians rose 93% and 92% respectively between 1945 and 1974, it declined by 7% in the same period for White South Africans, living in comparable economic conditions, except for the lack of television, which was not introduced in South Africa until 1975 (Centerwall, 1989, 1992; Joy *et al.*, 1986). After the introduction of TV, the homicide rate rose there as well. Centerwall rules out other explanations like economics, age, firearms availability, and civil unrest as accounting for these changes. Thus, there is evidence that modeling media violence is not purely an artificial laboratory phenomenon.

Sensitization

Sensitization is a sort of reverse modeling effect, whereby viewers react so strongly to seeing some violence and have such a traumatized perceived reality that they are actually less likely to imitate it as a result. This may happen with actual events or fictionalized entertainment. With regard to entertainment media, sensitization is most likely to occur with very extreme violence and might be the reaction, for example, of someone who has never seen anything stronger than a G-rated Disney movie when he or she sees a graphically violent R-rated film. The behavioral tendency away from violence might arise from the arousal of anxiety about the violence and/or the arousal of empathy for the victim of the violence.

The Role of Empathy on Sensitization

Broadly speaking, *empathy* is the ability to understand another person's emotional point of view, and psychologists have various ways of measuring that ability. Some measures of empathy have been researched with regard to media violence. For example, Hoffner and Levine (2007) concluded from a meta-analysis that relative to others, people high in the "personal distress" and "empathic concern" measures of empathy showed less enjoyment of fright and violence. Using a different conceptualization of empathy, several studies in Germany (Krahé & Möller, 2010; Mößle, Kliem, & Rehbein, 2014) found that in children and adolescents, trait empathy was a longitudinal mediator between violent media consumption and later aggressive behavior. In other words, those who were high in empathy were less likely to be negatively affected by consuming violent media. This effect may exist because there seems to be a relationship between disliking watching graphic violence (i.e., being especially sensitized) and higher levels of empathy (Tamborini, Stiff, & Heidel, 1990). Thus, empathic people can easily imagine themselves in the position of the victim of the violence and vicariously experience the negative emotions that person would feel. Someone who cannot easily do this would also be aroused but would be more likely to enjoy the violence, because the negative emotions would not be so strongly felt. Other research has also shown a link between decreased levels of sympathy (i.e., feeling sorry for someone) and increased levels of violent media use (Vossen *et al.*, 2017). Empathy relating to media violence is discussed elsewhere throughout this chapter.

Sensitization and Graphic Violence

It is likely that the strongest sensitization effects could come from very graphic violence that is clearly understood as real (i.e., the news). As we saw in Chapter 7, extensive news media coverage of large-scale violence can induce fearful cognitive misperceptions in the viewing audience. One meta-analysis (Hopwood & Schutte, 2017) found that across 18 different studies, there was also a pattern of violence sensitization from exposure to media reports of natural disasters (e.g., hurricanes), major accidents (e.g., plane crashes), and acts of war or terrorism, with negative psychological effects such as anxiety and fear. Sometimes producers face a difficult decision about whether or not to air an extremely violent scene from a news story (see Close-up 9.3 for some especially compelling examples). Once in a while they may be unable to legally block the image, for example, if it comes in a political ad, which may not legally be censored.

❖ CLOSE-UP 9.3 EXTREMELY VIOLENT NEWS IMAGES

Sometimes television networks and stations or print media are faced with a difficult decision about whether to air a graphically violent news image. One of the most agonizing decisions came in July 2003 after the deaths of deposed Iraqi dictator Saddam Hussein's sons Oday and Qusay in an assault by the U.S. military on a fortified house in Mosul, Iraq. At this point, Iraq was occupied by U.S. and U.K. forces, but Saddam was still alive and in hiding. The two sons were notoriously hated and feared for perpetrating crimes of incredible cruelty. Although the United States generally had a policy of not releasing photographs of people killed in military action, it decided that at least the Iraqi public needed concrete evidence that the hated brothers were really dead. Thus the gruesome photos of the dead brothers were published.

Another Iraq War image came when an Islamist website offered video footage of terrorists slowly sawing off the head of a captured 26-year-old American contractor. Although nearly all networks declined to run the video in its entirety, most did describe the scene quite graphically, arguing that was necessary to fully communicate the horror of the act. Unfortunately, such spectacle beheadings have become common overseas, and are widely available online, although most American TV outlets do not air the images. In 2011, the White House struggled with the notion of releasing a photo of the recently killed Osama bin Laden to prove that he had really been captured. Ultimately, President Barack Obama decided that the image was too gruesome, and the news media were denied access to it.

Decades earlier, an AP photographer working in Saigon during the Vietnam War in 1968 captured a disturbing photo of a Vietcong operative being executed at point blank range. The photo (and accompanying TV news footage) appeared in media outlets around the world. The photographer later won a Pulitzer Prize for the image.

Sometimes cameras fortuitously happen to capture a gruesome image. Local media photographers covering a routine 1987 news conference by Pennsylvania State Treasurer Budd Dwyer caught the unexpected image of Dwyer putting a pistol in his mouth and pulling the trigger, killing himself instantly. Network news, TV stations, and newspapers then faced the decision of whether to run the grisly sequence. Most TV stations chose not to air the tape or did so only to the point of Dwyer placing the gun in his mouth. A few TV stations and newspapers carried pictures of what happened after that, saying it was "an important historical event" and should be covered. In a 1993 case, a Florida woman being interviewed by a television crew in a park in broad daylight was suddenly accosted and shot several times by her estranged husband. Although the unexpected murder photos later provided important legal evidence, networks were faced with the decision of whether or not to air the footage on the news. Many (including CNN) did air the pictures. In a somewhat similar 2015 incident, a reporter for a CBS station in Virginia and a photojournalist were shot and killed live on the air as she was conducting an interview. This time, there was an odd twist; in addition to the footage the photojournalist had been capturing, the shooter was himself a former reporter and was video recording the shooting as it happened. Some news outlets chose to show parts of the shooter's video, others used still frames (Bowerman, 2015). Another twist was the fact that the story showed up in many people's social media feeds, some with autoplay video (i.e., the video rolls as soon as the user gets to that story) of the murders (Gibbs, 2015).

The public has a right to know, but how much does the public have a need or right to know and see explicitly? The answer is obviously an ethical and policy question, although one study suggested a positive effect of learning at least some gory details. College students who read a newspaper report of a wife-battering incident rated it as more serious and rated the batterer more negatively if the victim's injuries were described in detail, compared to a situation in which they were not explicitly described (Pierce & Harris, 1993). These descriptions, however, were much less graphic than the pictorial images described above.

Although product and political advertisers generally are reluctant to risk offending the public, once in a great while a political candidate may wish to do so. For example, in the fall 1992 U.S. election campaigns, several antiabortion candidates for Congress and other offices chose to air photos of what they said was an aborted fetus. Their explicit goal was to offend viewers, in order to convince them that abortion really is offensive. Such tactics are risky, however, because viewers might be even more offended by a decision to use such an image.

Although sensitization effects are hard to study scientifically for ethical reasons (e.g., we cannot show young children highly graphic violence), general sensitization effects are probably not too widespread and do not occur nearly as often as their opposite, desensitization (discussed in the next section of this chapter).

In general, situations in which sensitization effects might seem present can often be interpreted equally plausibly in terms of desensitization. For example, people have argued that daily news broadcasts of the Vietnam War sensitized us to the horrors of war and eroded public support for that conflict, in contrast to previous wars. On the other hand, others have argued that the same news broadcasts desensitized us to war, and thus we now are not as bothered by seeing images of other conflicts (see Chapter 7 for more detail on how news media cover war). Also see Close-up 9.4 for a history of the treatment of war in films.

❖ CLOSE-UP 9.4 HOLLYWOOD GOES TO WAR

The 1966 pro-Vietnam War film The Green Berets *starred John Wayne in a stylized epic with good guys and bad guys. Two years later, such a simplistic approach to Vietnam rang very shallow and false for many. Shortly after* The Green Berets, *sentiment in the United States had turned completely around, and whatever glory there had been to the Vietnam War had all but disappeared. The 1974 Oscar-winning documentary* Hearts and Minds, *by Peter Davis, was very graphic and carried such a strong antiwar message that some newspapers refused to publish reviews of the film. Although the last U.S. troops left Vietnam in 1973 and Saigon fell in 1975, there were no commercially successful film images of Vietnam before 1978, when* The Deer Hunter *and* Coming Home *picked up seven Oscars between them. Both of these (along with* Apocalypse Now *in 1979) carried a strong antiwar message and reflected the country's disgust with the war in Vietnam, a wound that had just started to heal.*

That healing proceeded slowly until 1986, when Oliver Stone's graphic and realistic Platoon *and Sylvester Stallone's live-action comic book* Rambo: First Blood Part II *appeared. Both were huge successes, but* Platoon *was the greater commercial gamble, having taken years to acquire the necessary funding. The Pentagon refused to help the producers, although it enthusiastically aided the makers of the heroic* Top Gun, *on the grounds that it wanted to ensure a realistic portrayal of the military! Widely hailed as a critical success (including winning the Best Picture Oscar),* Platoon *astounded everyone with its huge commercial success as well. It was then followed by a spate of realistic Vietnam films like* Gardens of Stone, Casualties of War, The Hanoi Hilton, *and* Full Metal Jacket, *none of which received close to* Platoon*'s critical or commercial success.*

*By 1988, the wounds of Vietnam had healed enough to allow the production and modest commercial success of the first two Vietnam War TV series (*China Beach, Tour of Duty*) and big-screen comedy* Good Morning, Vietnam. *A comedy about Vietnam would have been unthinkable much before that time. Not too long after followed another antiwar film,* Born on the Fourth of July, *the biographical story of gung-ho soldier turned antiwar protester Ron Kovic.*

As the themes of Vietnam War movies changed over time, there was a somewhat similar evolution with World War II films. In particular, an interesting contrast can be made between the movies The Longest Day *and* Saving Private Ryan. The Longest Day, *produced in 1962, depicts the D-Day invasion of Normandy as difficult, but manageable by brave and smooth-talking leaders.* Saving Private Ryan, *released 36 years later, sought to portray the same event in a much more realistic way. In the latter film, the horrors of war are graphically depicted, with mass fear among troops, close up shots of terrified soldiers, widespread death, and severed body parts. Although difficult to watch, many (including some Normandy veterans) praised the film's battle scenes for their realism (Wallace, 1998).*

*By the late 2000s and early 2010s, the U.S.-led wars in Afghanistan and Iraq had been going on for years. War movies of this era began to reflect the personal toll that many soldiers were paying, including post-traumatic stress disorder (*The Hurt Locker*), strained family relationships with extended tours of duty (*American Sniper*), and torture techniques (*Zero Dark Thirty*). Although U.S. involvement in the Iraq War ostensibly ended in 2011 with the withdrawal of troops, the wars with ISIS and in Afghanistan continue. There will no doubt be additional war movies to follow.*

Desensitization

Although the primary concern of public debate about the effects of media violence typically involves the inciting of violent behavior, there may be far more pervasive attitudinal effects, especially in the area of *desensitization*. The basic principle here is that viewing a steady diet of violence in the media makes us less sensitive to it, more jaded, and less aroused and bothered by it. We become so used to seeing people wasted, blown apart, or impaled that it no longer particularly troubles us. For example in an early study on desensitization, sixth graders who had seen a violent TV show were less sensitive to violent images in a subsequent film than were children who had seen a nonviolent film first (Rabinovitch, McLean, Markham, & Talbott, 1972). Desensitization is typically measured experimentally through physiological or attitudinal measures.

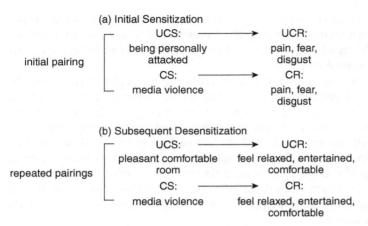

Figure 9.1 Desensitization as classical conditioning

How Desensitization Works

The process of desensitization may be seen as a straightforward example of classical conditioning (see Figure 9.1). The normal, unlearned responses to being physically hurt include pain, fear, and disgust. The first time one sees media violence, it probably evokes such negative emotional responses, due to its similarity to real violence (Figure 9.1a). Such a single occurrence may actually produce sensitization as discussed previously.

What happens with repeated viewing of violence in comfortable surroundings is quite different, however (Figure 9.1b). Suppose, for example, that the normal, unlearned response to sitting at home in one's easy chair is feeling relaxed and happy. When this is repeatedly paired with violence on TV and movies, vicarious violence in a pleasant home context gradually becomes associated with that situation and itself comes to be seen as entertaining, pleasant, and even relaxing. The natural association of filmed violence and real-life violence has been weakened as the new association of video violence with recreation is strengthened. We repeatedly see violence without experiencing pain or hurt ourselves and thus the normal negative responses to it weaken. Given what we know about classical conditioning in psychology, it is unlikely that such frequent and repeated exposure to stimuli could *not* have a substantial effect. In the adolescent subculture, part of the male gender-role socialization has also been for a boy to desensitize himself so that he can watch graphic violence and not appear to be bothered by it (Harris *et al.*, 2000; Kivel & Johnson, 2009; Mundorf, Weaver, & Zillmann, 1989; Zillmann & Weaver, 1996; Zillmann *et al.*, 1986). Demonstrating desensitization to violence thus becomes a way to impress peers or a date.

Consequences of Desensitization

What are the implications of people becoming desensitized to violence from the media? Becoming jaded to news of war and mass shootings will cause such stories not to bother us so much anymore. Even if we never come to actually like violence or behave violently ourselves, we may come to not really be bothered by it deeply; it does not seem all that serious. This has important implications for behavior. For example, Drabman and Thomas (1974, 1976) had 8- to 10-year-old children watch a violent or nonviolent film and later watch younger children at play. When the younger children started to get rough, the older children who had watched the nonviolent film called an adult sooner than did the older children who had watched the violent film, thus showing some generalization of the desensitization effect.

More recent research has confirmed that desensitization has physiological effects, such as decreased blood pressure with increased media violence exposure (Mrug, Madan, Cook, & Wright, 2015). Similarly, Krahé and colleagues (2011) found that habitual exposure to media violence in college students correlated positively with factors such as pleasant arousal and negatively with factors such as sweating while watching a violent movie clip. Interestingly, these correlations were not present while students watched sad or funny film clips, suggesting a desensitization effect specific to violence. Amazingly, media violence desensitization effects have also been demonstrated over exposure in a relatively short time period, like a couple of hours (Fanti, Vanman, Henrich, & Avraamides, 2009).

One of the major areas of concern with desensitization has to do with tolerance of violence toward women. For example, in one older study, male college students who viewed a series of slasher horror movies later showed less empathy and concern for victims of rape (Linz, Donnerstein, & Penrod, 1984). This kind of attitude may reflect what is sometimes called a *rape myth,* "prejudicial, stereotyped or false beliefs about rape, rape victims, and rapists" (Burt, 1980, p. 217). Such thinking and attitudes toward sexual violence can be hard to change, particularly in males (Emmers-Sommer, Triplett, Pauley, Hanzal, & Rhea, 2005). Sexual violence is one of the major current concerns among media researchers studying violence; we examine this aspect of violence in some detail in Chapter 10.

Cultivation

Another type of attitudinal effect in regard to violence is cultivation. As discussed in Chapter 2, cultivation theory argues that the more exposure a person has to television, the more that person's perception of social realities will match what is presented on TV (Bryant et al., 2013; Gerbner et al., 2002; Morgan et al., 2009, 2015). As a matter of fact, cultivation theory was originally developed in regard to studying media violence. In contrast to modeling, cultivation attributes a more active role to the viewer, who is interacting with the medium, not being passively manipulated by it. Nevertheless, there is a coming together of the outlook of the viewer and that of the medium, whereby the person's perceived reality gradually approaches that of the media world.

Cultivation theory is best known for its research on the cultivation of attitudes related to violence (Gerbner, Gross, Signorielli, & Morgan, 1986; Morgan et al., 2009; Riddle et al., 2011). Such studies show that frequent viewers believe the world to be a more dangerous and crime-ridden place than infrequent viewers believe it to be. As discussed earlier in this chapter, television also portrays violent crimes as much more common than they actually are. Indeed, the world of TV portrays about 50% of characters involved in violence and murder each week, compared to less than 1% of the population per year in real life (Bushman & Anderson, 2001; Surette, 2015). This cultivation effect could be due either to media teaching that this is what the world is like or to the fact that more fearful people are drawn to watching more TV. If it is the former, and cultivation theorists believe it is, media can induce a general mindset about the position of violence in the world, completely aside from any effects it might have in teaching violent behavior.

Finally, cultivation theory speaks of media teaching the role of the victim. From watching a heavy diet of crime and action-adventure, viewers learn what it is like to be a victim of violence, and this role becomes very real to them, even if it is completely outside of their own life experience.

The effects of media violence just discussed are not presented as an exhaustive list but rather as general classes into which most proposed effects fall. Occasionally an effect falls outside of those classes, however; see Close-up 9.5 for some interesting evidence of violent media causing amnesia in viewers.

❖ CLOSE-UP 9.5 DO VIOLENT IMAGES CAUSE AMNESIA?

Amnesia is not on the typical list of media violence effects, but evidence for just such an effect has been offered (Christianson & Loftus, 1987; Newhagen & Reeves, 1991). It has been known for some time that a physical injury to the brain can result in a loss of memory for events immediately preceding the impact (retrograde amnesia). For example, the shock of one's head flying against the headrest in an auto collision may lead to amnesia for events immediately preceding the impact. It is as if the brain had not yet had time to transfer the event from working memory to long-term memory. Loftus and Burns (1982) demonstrated that such an effect may also occur solely from the mental shock of seeing graphic violence on the screen. Research participants saw a 2-minute film of a bank robbery, in either a violent or nonviolent version. In the violent version, the fleeing robbers shot their pursuers and hit a young boy in the face, after which he fell, clutching his bloody face. The nonviolent version was identical up to the point of the shooting, at which point the camera cut to the interior of the bank. Measured using both recall and recognition measures, people seeing the nonviolent version of the film remembered the number on the boy's T-shirt better than those seeing the violent film, although the shirt was shown for the same amount of time in both. A second study ruled out the possibility that the effect could have been due to the unexpectedness or surprising nature of the shooting.

Media violence may affect our memories relating to advertising, too. A meta-analysis that examined various studies on memory and ads found that brand names were remembered less frequently in advertisements that contained violence than those without violent or sexual content (Lull & Bushman, 2015). Similarly, video game players who played a violent version of a game remembered fewer in-game advertisements than those who played the game in a nonviolent version (Lull, Gibson, Cruz, & Bushman, 2018).

Important Interactive Factors

Now that we have looked at the major effects of watching media violence, it is time to examine important moderating variables that affect how much the violent behavior will be modeled or how strongly induced the attitudinal effects of desensitization, cultivation, or fear will be. Consistent with the conditional effects model discussed in Chapter 2, it should be understood that individual differences are important to models of media violence effects. Thus, these effects models do not apply to everyone the same way under all circumstances. Numerous important variables such as modeling or desensitization heighten or lessen effects. To be sure, violent media do not affect everyone in all circumstances in the same way.

Model Attributes

First, several characteristics of the violent model are important. People are more likely to imitate or be disinhibited by viewing the violent behavior of an attractive, respected, prestigious model (such as a movie superhero) than by one who does not have such qualities. Also, the more deeply we identify and empathize with a model, the more likely we are to imitate that person (Huesmann *et al.*, 1984; Huesmann, Moise-Titus, Podolski, & Eron, 2003). These points suggest that violence by the characters we admire and identify with is a stronger influence than violence by the bad guys. For example, when a heroic character shoots a bad guy point blank in the chest, there may be more of a lasting impact on the viewer than when a villain performs a similar act. This kind of effect has important ramifications for assessing the implications of viewing action-adventure and police shows. An important qualification to this pattern is some alienated youth who may actually identify with perpetrators of mass school shootings and see them as a model. For this reason, some news agencies have started focusing less on the shooter when covering such mass killing.

Reinforcement and Justification of Violence

Whether or not the violence is reinforced in the plot is also a very important moderating variable. One of the central principles of operant conditioning, and indeed of all psychology, *reinforcement* occurs when some event follows a response and increases the likelihood of that response occurring again. The connection (*contingency*) between the response and the reinforcement is learned; thus the response is made in anticipation of receiving the reinforcement. A dog learns to fetch a stick because he is reinforced with a treat when he performs the act. A girl does her homework each night because she is reinforced by being allowed to watch TV after she is finished. A police officer is reinforced for using excessive force by catching the bad guy and sending him to prison and earning a promotion for himself. After the learning has occurred, responses continue to be made for some period of time without the reinforcement, until they gradually diminish and are finally extinguished altogether.

If acting violently appears to pay off for the violent character (in money, power, social recognition, relationship status, etc.), it is thus reinforced in the context of the story. Classic research suggests that reinforced violence is more likely to desensitize or be modeled than non-reinforced or punished violence (e.g., Bandura, 1965). Krcmar and Cooke (2001) found that 4- to 7-year-olds thought unpunished violence in a video clip was more acceptable than punished violence. In a typical TV storyline, violence by the hero is more likely to be rewarded (reinforced) than is the violence of the villain, although the latter may have been reinforced for much of the show. Model characteristics and reinforcement suggest that a particularly troubling type of violent perpetrator is the violent child or teen character. Content analyses show that, compared to adult models, violent child models in media are more attractive to children and less likely than adults to be punished or to experience other negative consequences of the violence (Wilson, Colvin, & Smith, 2002); both of these characteristics make modeling by young viewers more likely.

Sometimes media do not necessarily reinforce specific behaviors but rather reinforce certain values about the use of violence. For example, characters in action-adventure TV shows and movies frequently use violence to settle interpersonal disputes. As such, they subtly reinforce the value that violent behavior is a realistic and morally acceptable manner of dealing with conflict, a value that may become part of the viewer's perceived reality. Children seeing a fantasy movie clip ending in violence later rated a different story with violence as more morally correct than children seeing the same clip but without the violence (Krcmar & Curtis, 2003). In sports, when sportscasters legitimize on-field violence as necessary or regrettably acceptable in the context in which it occurred, or when an athlete receives only a slap on the wrist for assaulting another player, such treatment reinforces violence as a way of dealing with the stresses of the game (Bryant *et al.*, 1998).

Related to the concept of rewarded media violence is the depiction of violence as justified. If the narrative of the TV show, movie, or video game makes it seem that the one behaving violently has a good reason for doing so, the violence seems more acceptable. We know that unjustified media violence (e.g., the Joker blowing up a hospital in a Batman movie) causes more physiological arousal than violence that is presented as justified (e.g., when Batman retaliates against a violent criminal) (Samson & Potter, 2016). People can also see the same instance of media violence as less extreme and more attractive when it is presented with a narrative of justification (Moore & Cockerton, 1996; Vidal, Clemente, & Espinosa, 2003).

Interestingly, King and Hourani (2007) found that viewers of horror films with alternative endings strongly preferred the "traditional" ending in which the evil antagonist is punished and destroyed over a "teaser" ending in which the evildoer revives, perhaps setting the stage for a sequel. People not only liked the traditional ending better but, surprisingly, found it less predictable, perhaps reflecting the large number of teaser endings and sequels for horror movies at that time. This result held for viewers strongly motivated by gore and thrill factors, as well as the general population.

A relatively recent trend in Hollywood narratives has been storylines that emphasize *antiheros*, "protagonists whose conduct is at best morally ambiguous, questionable, and at times unjustifiable" (Janicke & Raney, 2017, p. 1). Antiheros also frequently possess heroic characteristics while simultaneously displaying negative qualities like selfishness or vanity. Examples of violent antiheroes include Batman from *The Dark Knight*, Captain Jack Sparrow from *Pirates of the Caribbean*, and Walter White from *Breaking Bad*. Research indicates that audiences enjoy antihero narratives (Krakowiak & Oliver, 2012). In fact, the more that people are able to accept violence and suspend morality, the more they like and identify with antiheroes (Janicke & Raney, 2017). In the realm of video games, players who played a violent game as an antihero character displayed more postgame aggression than those who played the game as a violent hero (Sauer, Drummond, & Nova, 2015).

Perceived Reality

Another important moderating factor is whether the violence is seen as real or make-believe, that is, the degree of *perceived reality* (van der Voort, 1986). There is some evidence of stronger effects of violence that is perceived as real than of violence that is perceived as unrealistic. Although children's cartoons are by far the most violent genre of TV show, cartoon violence is also the most stylized and unrealistic. Other than very young children, few people believe that someone could survive falls from high cliffs or being flattened under an anvil. However, although cartoon violence is generally perceived as less realistic than live-action violence and in many instances is less likely to induce fear or desensitization or be imitated, numerous moderating factors are important, including how graphic the violence is and whether it is perceived as humorous or factual (Bartsch *et al.*, 2016; Kirsh, 2006).

In understanding the perceived reality of violent media, it is always important to consider the viewer's cognitive understanding of television at any given time (e.g., Bartsch *et al.*, 2016; Cantor, 1998b, 2002; Kirsh, 2006). For example, a very young child might think that a violent death on a police drama actually shows someone dying, rather than merely an actor pretending to die. Children who believe such staged violence to be real are often more disturbed by it than those who understand the convention of acting. The greater the perceived realism of media violence, the more likely that aggressive behavior or intentions will increase (Huesmann *et al.*, 2003; McGloin, Farrar, Krcmar, Park, & Fishlock, 2016). Continuing this line of reasoning, the most difficult forms of TV violence for children to deal with are probably news and documentaries, because violence on these programs is real and not staged. Beyond the issue of perceived realism, the whole area of how the viewer interprets the violence is very important; such variables often account for more of the statistical variance in studies than stimulus factors (e.g., amount of violence in a media example) manipulated by the experimenter (Jeong, Biocca, & Bohil, 2012; Potter & Tomasello, 2003).

The sophisticated technology of video games provides some of the most realistic presentations of media violence. See the section later in this chapter on violent video games for a discussion.

Personality Characteristics of the Viewer

Research has also generally found larger modeling and attitudinal effects in people more naturally inclined toward violence in terms of personality (Alia-Klein *et al.*, 2014; Kirsh, Olczak, & Mounts, 2005; Scharrer, 2005; Swing & Anderson, 2014). However, this result has not been found consistently (e.g., Huesmann, Eron, Lefkowitz, & Walder, 1984), perhaps due to trait aggression being a complex, multifactor construct (Scharrer, 2005). Violence in the media may reinforce dispositional violent tendencies already present in the viewer, even if it is not the cause of those tendencies. The more that such tendencies are reinforced, the more likely they are to manifest themselves in behavior. Regrettably, the lack of a uniform effect on viewers has often been used to argue that there is no substantial impact of media violence. As suggested previously, however, a modeling effect on even a tiny percentage of the population may be cause for serious concern. The fact that people less naturally inclined toward violence do not respond as strongly as those more inclined toward violence is not an argument that media violence has no effect! The role that individual differences and personality factors play in who is attracted to violent media is discussed later in this chapter.

Viewer Cognitions

Another important factor in moderating the effects of media violence perceived by the viewer may be the thoughts that one has in response to viewing media violence

(Berkowitz, 1984; Yukawa, Endo & Yoshida, 2001). Those thoughts may focus on the suffering of the victim, the triumph of the violent person, the relation of the violence to one's own experience, and so on. Depending on the nature of these thoughts, their mediating role in facilitating violent behavior may vary substantially. For example, someone who is overwhelmed by the suffering of the victim is probably less likely to behave violently than one who identifies strongly with a heroic and attractive character like James Bond (McCauley, 1998). Even preschoolers exposed to one violent cartoon give more aggressive story endings than children seeing a nonviolent cartoon or still picture. See Alia-Klein and colleagues (2014), Krcmar and Kean (2005), and J.H. Goldstein (1998) for discussions of individual differences in reactions to media violence.

Arousal

The variable of arousal level of the viewer is important in understanding media violence and viewer behavior. Studies from decades past revealed that a person who is already physiologically aroused for whatever reason is more likely to engage in violence after seeing a violent media model than is a non-aroused person (Tannenbaum, 1971, 1980). The arousal may come from the film itself, given that violent films tend to be emotionally arousing and exciting, or it may come from some prior and unrelated source, such as the manipulation in some experiments that makes one group of participants angry before exposing them to a violent media model (e.g., Berkowitz, 1965; Hartmann, 1969; Zillmann, 1978). However, there is not a consistent level of media arousal across studies (Hoffner & Levine, 2005), and there is a difference between "anxious arousal" (i.e., feeling uncomfortable) and "pleasant arousal" (e.g., feeling anticipation or enjoyment). Interestingly, long-term viewing of media violence has been associated with lowered anxious arousal and heightened pleasant arousal while watching a violent movie clip (Krahé et al., 2011). This issue of the interaction of arousal and a violent model becomes important when considering sexual violence, which is examined in Chapter 10, as well as video game violence, which is discussed later in this chapter.

Age and Gender

In terms of age and gender, modeling effects typically increase up to about ages 8 to 12 and slowly decrease thereafter. After this age, children have developed their own viewing schemas and are better able to separate video experience from reality. Although boys consistently both watch more violent media and are themselves more violent than girls, there is no clear evidence of a stronger modeling effect as such on either boys or girls, at least not before about age 10 (Hearold, 1986; Kirsh, 2006; Krahé & Möller, 2011).

Context of Violence

One moderating variable that has not yet been studied very extensively is the embedding of graphic violence in a humorous context. For example, violent characters can utter humorous wisecracks, a laugh track can accompany violent scenes, and acts of violence can be presented with humorous consequences. Sometimes technical or editing devices can serve to reinforce violence in such a context. For example, when the hero in the 1994 film *Natural Born Killers* drowned his girlfriend's father in a fish tank and killed her mother by tying her to a bed, dousing her in gasoline and burning her alive, a background laugh track encouraged us to see this brutality as humorously entertaining, possibly reinforcing positive responses within the viewer. A similarly gruesome scene played out in the 2008 Batman movie *The Dark Knight* when the Joker made a pencil "disappear" by ramming the eye socket of a Mafioso onto it. Director Quentin Tarantino is known for mixing extreme violence with humor in his movies, like when assassins Samuel L. Jackson and John Travolta casually discuss the merits of various hamburgers with a few young men just before killing them in *Pulp Fiction*. Advertising also frequently mixes humor and violence. In fact, one analysis found that about 60% of Super Bowl ads use this technique (Blackford, Gentry, Harrison, & Carlson, 2011). Another empirical study of the effects of viewing wisecracking heroes and villains in a violent action film (*The Hit-man*) found a different pattern of results in men and women (King, 2000). The presence of humor in the hero increased distress in women but not in men, while their reactions to a subsequent nonfiction film showed the reverse effect.

This embedding of violence in comedy is a specific instance of the broader situation of violent behavior being reinforced by virtue of its occurrence in a context that is overall very reinforcing. For example, because viewers may choose to identify more with the glamorous opulence of shows like *Empire* or *Dynasty* than with the gritty seediness of the *CSI* shows, the violence on the former shows may have a greater effect, even if the actual violence is less frequent or less graphic. However, this effect may be mitigated by the fact that the more realistic shows may have a greater impact than the less realistic ones due to their closer connection to the viewers' own experiences. Thus, we see that many factors are at work to produce modeling effects. We turn now to a final alleged psychological effect of violence: catharsis.

Catharsis

The notion of catharsis extends all the way back to Aristotle's *Poetics*, in which he spoke of drama purging the emotions of the audience and leading to a ritual purification (Scheele & DuBois, 2006). In modern times, however, the notion was developed largely in psychoanalytic theory, with emphasis on the purging, more than the purifying, function. According to Freud, the id, ego, and superego are locked in battle, with anxiety resulting from id impulses trying to express themselves and, in so doing, coming into conflict with the moralistic superego. The threatening unconscious impulses like sex and aggression are repressed from consciousness but may cause anxiety when they creep back. These repressed impulses and the anxiety that they produce may be dealt with directly by overt sexual or violent behavior or indirectly through some sublimated substitute activity, such as watching others act sexually or violently onscreen.

The emotional release called *catharsis* comes from venting the impulse (i.e., expressing it directly or indirectly). This purging of emotion has been a notoriously difficult concept to operationally define and test, but it has continued to have a lot of intuitive appeal and anecdotal support (e.g., people report feeling better after watching a scary movie).

Catharsis theory, however, does make one very clear prediction about the effect of screen violence on behavior, a prediction that is eminently testable and exactly opposite to the prediction of modeling theory. Whereas modeling predicts an increase in violent behavior after watching media violence, catharsis theory predicts a decrease in such behavior (Feshbach, 1955). If the substitute behavior of watching the violence provides the emotional release that would normally result from actually acting violently, then violent behavior should decrease after watching media violence. For example, catharsis theory would predict that a girl who is angry at her sister and then watches a violent cartoon would be less likely to actually hurt her sister than if she hadn't watched the cartoon.

Thus, the catharsis and modeling theories are clearly and competitively testable. When such tests have been done, modeling theory has been consistently supported (e.g., Siegel, 1956), whereas catharsis theory has received little support. In spite of consistent failures to be supported by scientific evidence over many years (Bushman, Baumeister, & Stack, 1999; Bushman, Chandler, & Huesmann, 2010; Geen & Quanty, 1977; Zillmann, 1978), catharsis continues to occupy a prominent though undeserved place in the conventional wisdom about the effects of media violence. Indeed, many intuitively believe that consuming violent media prevents them from behaving aggressively. Unfortunately, research evidence does not support this belief, and in fact supports just the opposite.

Later refinements of catharsis theory have been proposed (e.g., Feshbach & Singer, 1971). It may be that the media violence elicits fantasizing by the viewer, and that fantasizing, rather than the media violence per se, is what leads to catharsis. Another version of catharsis theory argues that watching media violence reduces one's arousal level, and thus one is less prone to violence. There is evidence that a reduction of arousal level is associated with decreased violent behavior. Third, media violence may elicit an inhibition response, which puts a brake on tendencies toward violent behavior. This is very similar to a sensitization hypothesis. None of these explanations, however, has offered a serious challenge to the overall conclusion that viewing media violence leads to increases in violent behavior.

Who Watches Media Violence and Why?

As noted earlier in this chapter, violent movie content results in increased movie ticket sales (Barranco et al., 2017). But who is watching violent movies? Another approach to studying media violence has been to examine what attracts viewers to violence and why some are attracted to it much more than others (Goldstein, J.H., 1998; Krcmar, Farrar, Jalette, & McGloin, 2015; Sparks & Sparks, 2000). What is it that is appealing about violence as entertainment? Some answers that have been suggested are its novelty, sensory delight, and the violation of social norms. It also may have some social utility; for example, in allowing the display of mastery of threats or dependence on a loved one (Zillmann & Weaver, 1996).

Social Factors

Although there has not been a tremendous amount of research regarding the social and cultural contexts in which people consume violent media (Glackin & Gray, 2016), there have been some interesting findings. In a historical sense, very violent films, especially horror films, have generally been the least popular during wartime and have shown very strong popularity during times of overall peace accompanied by high degrees of social unrest. In his book *The Monster Show*, cultural historian David Skal (1993) traces the history of horror movies in the United States throughout the twentieth century, pointing out that these films often reflect cultural angst that precedes and follows wars. For example, in the 1930s, films such as *The Black Cat* (1935) and *King Kong* (1933) may have foreshadowed Nazi atrocities and the leveling of large cities by a tyrannical force. The 1937 French film *J'Accuse* even used maimed World War I veterans as actors portraying monsters who were reincarnated war dead (also see Fahy, 2010, for a further discussion of motivations behind consuming horror media).

In terms of gender socialization in adolescents, Zillmann and Weaver (1996) developed and tested a model of the role of social motives in consuming horror films. Specifically, they argued that preadolescent and adolescent boys use horror films to develop mastery over fear and to perfect their displays of fearlessness and protective competence. Girls, on the other hand, use the same films to develop their displays of fearfulness and protective need. Although girls actually enjoy the films less than boys do, both find them socially useful as they practice the very traditional gender roles in dating, whereby the boy is the fearless protector and the girl the dependent and fearful companion. The boy's expression of boredom or amusement in response to graphic violence is thus a statement of his apparent mastery over fear. This mastery then may actually mediate a feeling of pleasure. This pleasure, however, was much greater in the presence of a fearful young female companion than in the presence of a fearless female companion who expressed less dependence. Young men, compared to women, are much more desirous that their date not know how scared they felt while watching a scary movie (Harris *et al.*, 2000). See Mundorf and Mundorf (2003) for a further discussion of gender socialization through horror films.

Individual Differences

Several researchers have examined the relationship between personality factors and preference for violent media (e.g., Haridakis, 2002; Krahé, 2014; Slater, Henry, Swaim, & Cardador, 2004). Such personality characteristics may interact with social and situational factors to produce interpretations of the violent media, and sometimes behavior. Anderson and Bushman (2002) call this interaction the *General Aggression Model*.

For example, empathy, discussed earlier in this chapter, is one of the most-studied traits in this regard. Empathy is itself a multidimensional construct (Davis *et al.*, 1987; Zillmann, 2006a) which tends to be negatively associated with a preference for violent media. Tamborini (1996) developed a complex cognitive-motivational model of empathy as a predictor of reactions to viewing violence. Empathy may be evoked to different degrees by certain editing techniques and formal features. For example, extended close-ups of faces encourage empathic responses more than rapid-fire wide-angle camera shots. Raney (2002; see also Raney & Bryant, 2002) argues that the elicitation of empathy may evoke sympathy for the victim of violence, which in turn predicts lesser enjoyment of the violence. Unjustified media violence (discussed earlier in this chapter) also is especially bothersome to people high in empathy (Hartmann, Toz, & Brandon, 2010; Samson & Potter, 2016). Also, prolonged exposure to media violence has been shown to reduce levels of empathy in adolescents (Krahé & Möller, 2010). This effect has also been demonstrated with violent video game play (Anderson *et al.*, 2010), although feelings of empathy can also depend on whether the gamer is playing as a "good" (e.g., Batman) or a "bad" (e.g., the Joker) character (Happ & Melzer, 2014). There is more on video game violence later in this chapter.

Another personality variable studied in relation to violent media consumption is *sensation seeking* (Xie & Lee, 2008; Zuckerman, 1994, 1996, 2006), the "seeking of varied, novel, complex, and intense sensations and experiences, and the willingness to take physical, social, legal, and financial risks for the sake of such experience" (Zuckerman, 1996, p. 148). Sensation seeking is positively correlated with an enjoyment of media violence (Xie & Lee, 2008) and preference for viewing violence (Krcmar & Greene, 1999). However, this relationship is tempered by the degree of alienation experienced and by the fact that high sensation seekers tend to prefer real-life over vicarious media experiences and thus tend to be lighter-than-average media viewers overall (Slater, 2003; Slater *et al.*, 2004). High sensation seekers also tend to prefer to view more intense images (e.g., graphic violence or sex) and to experience higher levels of arousal than do low sensation seekers (Zuckerman, 2006). In addition, there is a relationship between preferences for violent video games and sensation seeking in children (Jensen, Weaver, Ivic, & Imboden, 2011).

Hostility (perceiving others' actions, especially those that are ambiguous, as intending harm) is another individual difference that can interact with media violence. In particular a meta-analysis of 37 previous studies discovered a strong relationship between media violence exposure and hostility. The effects also seemed to be correlated with age, which might indicate cumulative effects (Bushman, 2016). Another study on video game play also found a link between hostility, media violence consumption, and aggression (Bartholow, Sestir, & Davis, 2005).

Perhaps the most dramatic individual difference variable comes in the area of psychopathology. Although there have been few studies of effects of media violence on people with particular diagnosed psychiatric disorders, one interesting recent study showed significantly different psychophysiological and behavioral responses in boys ages 8 to 12 who had been diagnosed with one of the disruptive behavioral disorders (DBD), which include attention deficit hyperactivity disorder (ADHD), oppositional defiant disorder (ODD), and conduct disorders (Grimes *et al.*, 2008). Compared with a control group not diagnosed with DBD, the boys with DBD showed several differences while watching three violent movie clips—less physiological arousal but more frequent anger in their facial expressions, though the two groups did not differ in their verbal reports of anger. Grimes and colleagues claim this may be because they were not cognitively processing the film thoroughly enough to respond with appropriate autonomic reactions; they were not interpreting social cues accurately enough to direct their anger in a mature fashion. The authors argue that the responses of such people are what we should worry more about than effects of violent media on the population as a whole. Still, the individual difference research discussed in this section of the chapter overall seems to support the idea that some personalities can interact with certain kinds of violence, but maybe not others, to produce aggression, as predicted by the General Aggression Model.

Longitudinal Studies

Although literally thousands of studies have shown some negative psychological effects of media violence, most of those have been short term and conducted in a laboratory setting, often using the methodology of showing participants a film or film clip and subsequently measuring their behavior or attitudes in some way. Although these findings are important, they do not directly address the long-term cumulative effects of watching hundreds of hours of violent television and movies as recreation throughout one's childhood. There have been a few studies that have addressed this issue, most notably those by Huesmann and Eron and their colleagues. Because of their long-range view, such longitudinal studies are especially powerful in understanding the real-world effects of media violence.

Longitudinal studies over as long as 30 years in the United States, Finland, Germany, and Spain provided the first evidence of a causal relationship between real-world viewing of TV violence through childhood and violent or aggressive behavior as a child or a young adult (Eron & Huesmann, 1984; Eron, Huesmann, Lefkowitz, & Walder, 1972; Hopf, Huber, & Weiß, 2008; Huesmann & Eron, 1986; Krahé, Busching, & Möller, 2012; Krahé & Möller, 2010; Lefkowitz et al., 1977; Orue et al., 2011; Pitkanen-Pulkkinen, 1981). The kind of aggression can vary, too. At least one longitudinal study found that the aggression linked to viewing TV violence can be physical, verbal, and/or relational (Gentile, Coyne, & Walsh, 2011).

Through careful design and control of other variables, Eron and colleagues (Eron et al., 1972) as well as Lefkowitz and colleagues (1977) concluded that they could rule out other plausible third variables, such as dispositional violence, as being the cause of both violent TV viewing and violent behavior. Strikingly, Huesmann and Eron's research has shown that the amount of television watched at age 8 was one of the best predictors of criminal behavior at age 30, even after controlling for individual aggressiveness, IQ, and socioeconomic status. Those who were heavy TV viewers in preadolescence were also more likely to more severely punish their own children many years later than were those who watched less TV during the critical years of ages 8 to 12; watching more TV in adolescence did not seem to matter.

In a three-year longitudinal study, Huesmann and colleagues (1984) further explored the role of several intervening variables on the relationship between viewing media violence and violent behavior in U.S. and Finnish children in elementary schools. The study collected data over three years from the children, their parents, the children's peers, and the schools. Data gathered included measures of TV viewing, attitudes, behaviors, ratings of self and others, and family demographics. A few of the highlights are presented below.

As had been found in many other studies, there was a positive correlation between violent TV viewing and peer-rated aggression, which was stronger for boys than for girls and for Americans than for Finns. The overall level of violent behavior was also higher in the U.S. children. One of the most striking results for both samples was the strong correlation of violent behavior and self-rated identification with violent TV models, especially in boys. The best predictor of later violent behavior was the interactive product of violent viewing and identification with violent characters. There was no evidence that violent TV affects only those children naturally more predisposed to violent behavior or that children who fantasize more were affected any differently. In addition, neither parents' level of violent behavior nor parents' TV viewing had any significant effect on children's level of violence.

More recent longitudinal research presents the strongest evidence yet that exposure to media violence from ages 6 to 10 predicts violent behavior in young men and women in early adulthood (Huesmann et al., 2003). Following up on children first tested between 1977 and 1978 (Huesmann & Eron, 1986), all of the same persons who could be found (about 60% of the original sample) were tested as young adults over three years. Data were obtained on their adult TV violence viewing and their adult aggressive behavior, the latter obtained from self-reports, spouse/significant other reports, and archival crime and traffic-violation data. Results showed that childhood TV violence viewing was a significant predictor of adult aggressive behavior. These effects were most pronounced if there was strong viewer identification with the aggressive model and if the perceived realism of the violence was high. Unlike the earlier longitudinal studies, the 2003 study found these predictive effects for both men and women. The effects persisted even when the factors of socioeconomic status and intellectual ability were controlled. These results were replicated by another 17-year longitudinal study of 700 children (Johnson, Cohen, Smailes, Kasen, & Brook, 2002). The results of these many longitudinal studies are strikingly important because they appear to show the direct, long-term effects of violent media on individuals.

Violent Video Games

Although violent video games have been discussed throughout this chapter, they also warrant their own section because they are different from other forms of violent media in some important ways. Unlike TV or movie violence, video games are interactive and allow players to participate in the violence as aggressors themselves. If the games are online, gamers can also use computer-generated violence on other players they may never see in person. Some games also employ virtual reality technology, so that the player's senses become immersed in the gaming world.

Video game play is popular. According to one survey, 84% of boys and 59% of girls age 13–17 reported regularly playing video games (Lenhart, 2015). Video games are relatively popular with adults, too, with 47% of men and 39% of women over 18 reporting that they play video games as least sometimes; not surprisingly, the percentages are higher among younger than older adults (Brown, 2017). To be sure, not all video games are violent. Some games involve strategy (like chess or *Bejeweled*) or word play (like *Scrabble* or *Words with Friends*). Many video games are also designed or adapted for mobile devices like tablets and phones. Make no mistake, however—the highest selling video games contain high levels of violence and are meant to be played on graphically rich console systems like PlayStation and Xbox. For example, a report by the video game industry itself reported that the top three selling games in 2016 were the extremely violent *Call of Duty: Infinite Warfare*, *Battlefield 1*, and *Grand Theft Auto V* (Entertainment Software Association, 2017).

Indeed, the major concern with video games is the high level of violence. For example, *Grand Theft Auto* allows gamers to commit carjacking and murder police officers as they drive through a virtual criminal playground. You can pick up a prostitute and take her to a dark alley. She takes your money (as the car rocks excitedly) but you can get it back by killing her. You're also free to drive drunk (in one setting) and torture people with pliers or electricity. When playing *Postal*, you become a paranoid psychopath and kill hostile people, with no penalty for shooting innocent bystanders. Once you have wounded people, you can stand above them while they beg for mercy, and then shoot them. In *Carmageddon*, players knock down and kill innocent pedestrians. In *Duke Nukem*, the shooter murders female prostitutes, who are often naked and tied to columns pleading, "Kill me, kill me." There's even a video game version of the *Friday the 13th* movies, in which players can take on the role of hockey-masked murderer

Jason, killing other players with weapons or bare hands. The female victims are scantily dressed or naked as they skinny dip.

One type of video game provoking particularly great concern is the first-person shooter games, in which the player controls interactive guns that he or she has to learn to hold, aim, and fire at a moving target. One of the most popular of these is the *Call of Duty* series, in which players become shooters in various wartime scenarios. There have been at least 15 iterations of *Call of Duty*, but they are all first-person shooter games. In one version of the game, a player can choose to be a terrorist and massacre a group of unarmed civilians in an airport. Although a rating system exists to flag video games with violent content (the Entertainment Ratings Board), one study found that it was inadequate at identifying gratuitous violence like torture and the killing of civilians (Krantz, Shukla, Knox, & Schrouder, 2017).

Technology advances have helped bring increasing realism to first-person shooter games. For example, some games have a built-in vibrating system called a rumble pack, which vibrates the controller whenever a bullet is fired. *Time Crisis* has a kickback function to simulate the feel of a real weapon. The player also has a foot pedal that can control when the character takes cover to reload or steps out and shoots. Some games are also customizable, in which a player can scan in photos of one's school, neighborhood, or "enemies." Even back in 1999, the computer of one of the Columbine High assassins contained a customized version of *Doom*, in which the killer had used photos of his school and classmates he despised so he could practice killing them. This level of realism matters. Several studies have shown increases in aggression associated with more realistic game controllers (i.e., those more like a real gun) (McGloin, Farrar, & Fishlock, 2015; McGloin, Farrar, & Krcmar, 2013).

Do first-person shooter games teach anything more than the military and police training do? See Close-up 9.6 for some surprising research from military psychology about how eager and effective soldiers have, or haven't, been in battle.

❖ CLOSE-UP 9.6 WHO SHOOTS BETTER, SOLDIERS OR VIDEO GAMERS?

In studying historic battles, military psychologist Grossman (1996) discovered that there was often more posturing than killing. For example, 90% of the muskets picked up from dead and dying soldiers at the Battle of Gettysburg in 1863 were loaded, over half of them with multiple loads. This was surprising, considering that it took 19 times as long to load a musket as to fire one. Such findings suggest that there was a lot of loading and posturing by basically decent young soldiers who could not bring themselves to actually fire their weapons. Another study found that only 15–20% of World War II soldiers could bring themselves to actually fire at an exposed enemy soldier. Once the army discovered this, they set out to improve this record through training involving classical and operant conditioning, desensitization, and a heavy dose of brutalization. Such efforts worked. In the Korean War, 55% of the soldiers were willing to fire, and over 90% did so in the Vietnam War.

Grossman (1996; Grossman & DeGaetano, 1999, 2014) argues that we are doing the same thing with video games and violent movies, except that we start training shooters much younger. Teaching people to shoot immediately in response to the sight of the enemy is not always good soldiering or effective police behavior, but it is successful video game playing. Associating brutal killing with entertainment greatly lessens the distress and inhibitions we normally have about such behavior, and that is what is going on all the time with teens playing a steady diet of violent video games as regular amusement. "We have raised a gen-eration of barbarians who have learned to associate violence with pleasure, like the Romans cheering and snacking as the Christians were slaughtered in the Colosseum" (Grossman, 1996, p. 5).

Violent Video Game Effects

Much of the media violence research and its theories discussed earlier in this book have guided the research on the effects of playing violent video games. Following predictions from social learning theory (Bandura, 2002), game players learn shooting behaviors from playing the video game and imitating violent characters in the game. We also know that children behave more aggressively after playing a violent video game than a nonviolent one (Anderson & Morrow, 1995; Bartholow & Anderson, 2002; Bushman & Anderson, 2002; Kirsh, 1998; Lightdale & Prentice, 1994; Willoughby, Adachi, & Good, 2012).

Results from a meta-analysis of over 80,000 participants indicated that engaging in "active" violent media such as video games was associated with risk-taking behaviors in real life (Fischer, Greitemeyer, Kastenmuller, Vogrincic, & Sauer, 2011). Playing violent video games also elevates the overall arousal level, thus raising physiological indicators like heart rate and cortisol levels and priming the person to behave violently with relatively less provocation than would otherwise be the case (Anderson & Dill, 2000; Anderson *et al.*, 2004; Fleming & Rickwood, 2001; Gentile, Bender, & Anderson, 2017; Panee & Ballard, 2002).

In addition, playing violent video games can elicit hostile expectations, leading one to expect that others will respond aggressively (Bushman & Anderson, 2002; Eastin & Griffiths, 2006). It also heightens negative emotions in a way that is similar to possessing high trait hostility (Barlett, Harris, & Baldassaro, 2007; Hasan, Bègue, & Bushman, 2012, 2018; Kirsh *et al.*, 2005). For instance, participants playing a violent video game with the "blood on" (versus no blood) condition show more hostility and arousal (Barlett, Harris, & Bruey, 2008) and more physically aggressive intentions (Farrar, Krcmar, & Nowak, 2006) than those playing the same game with the blood option off.

Reinforcement matters, too. When violent game actions are rewarded within the world of the game, hostile emotions, aggressive thoughts, and aggressive behavior all increase; when the violent actions are punished, only hostile emotion increases (Carnagey & Anderson, 2005). Perhaps not surprisingly, technologically more advanced games have stronger effects on arousal than do older games (Ivory & Kalyanaraman, 2007).

Violent Video Games and the Brain: fMRI Research

Several fMRI studies done on people's brains while they play violent video games have been eye opening. One such study (Hummer, Kronenberger, Wang, & Mathews, 2017) asked males age 18–29 who had little experience playing video games to play the very violent *Call of Duty 4: Modern Warfare* extensively for a week. In contrast to a con-trol group, the men who played the violent video game showed decreased activity in areas of their prefrontal cortex as well as their right cerebellum during a cognitive task.

Other studies (e.g., Hummer *et al.*, 2010; Wang *et al.*, 2009) have similarly found that violent video game play may have an impact on the prefrontal cortex, in areas such as cognitive inhibition (Hummer *et al.*, 2010) and emotional suppression (Gentile, Swing, Anderson, Rinker, & Thomas, 2016; Wang *et al.*, 2009). Because the prefrontal areas of the brain are involved in decision making and are also the latest to mature during development, if such areas of the brain are significantly affected by violent video game play, there could be serious implications for children who play such games. In addition, Weber and colleagues (2006) found that brain activation during violent video game play was remarkably similar to real-life experiences when behaving violently and dealing with violence.

Meta-Analyses on Violent Video Game Effects

Sherry (2001) and Anderson and Bushman (2001) independently conducted meta-analyses of 25 to 35 studies conducted between 1975 and 2000 on the effects of violent video game play on violent behavior. Results showed a consistent effect that playing violent video games led to more violent behavior. The results were stronger for fantasy and realistic-violence games than for sports games, with larger effect sizes for studies with better methodologies (Anderson, Berkowitz, *et al.*, 2003). Violent video games were also shown to increase physiological arousal and aggressive affect and cognitions. Interestingly, Sherry (2001) found that the effects became weaker the longer the games were played, unlike findings from TV violence research exposure.

An extensive meta-analysis published in 2010 that examined 136 studies on violent video game play (comprising over 130,000 participants in multiple countries) concluded, "The evidence strongly suggests that exposure to violent video games is a causal risk factor for increased aggressive behavior, aggressive cognition, and aggressive affect and for decreased empathy and prosocial behavior" (Anderson *et al.*, 2010, p. 151). Commenting on the results of this meta-analysis, Huesmann (2010) said, "violent video games stimulate aggression in the players in the short run and increase the risk for aggressive behaviors by players later in life. The effects occur for males and females and for children growing up in Eastern or Western cultures" (p. 179). A study commissioned by the American Psychological Association examining research conducted after 2009 reached much the same conclusion: "the use of violent video games results in increases in overall aggression as well as increases in the individual variables of aggressive behaviors, aggressive cognitions, aggressive affect, desensitization, physiological arousal, and decreases in empathy" (Calvert *et al.*, 2017, p. 142).

Although the overwhelming majority of research links violent video game play with aggression, not all researchers agree about the effects. See Ferguson and Konijn (2015) for a discussion of some research differences. Also see Anderson, Birkowitz, *et al.* (2003), Brockmyer (2015), Bushman and Huesmann (2014), Huesmann (2010), Lee and Peng (2006), Sherry (2007), and Weber, Ritterfeld, and Kostygina (2006) for reviews of the literature on the effect of playing violent video games on violent behavior.

Putting This All Together: Making Sense of the Body of Research on Violent Media

Although the evidence from meta-analyses, longitudinal, and other studies has consistently supported the existence of significant negative effects of viewing media violence, studies that look at multiple contributors to societal violence typically estimate that media account for 10–15% of the variance in the dependent measure of the variance attributable to other factors (Perse, 2001; Perse & Lambe, 2017). In fact, however, this 10–15% range is neither surprising nor insignificant. In any complex social behavior, there are naturally going to be multiple causes. In the case of interpersonal violence, there are numerous known strong causes such as parental behavior, poverty, drugs, gangs, absent parents, and easy access to weapons, all of which clearly contribute greatly to this problem. Thus, it would be surprising, indeed completely incredible, to expect media to account for half of societal violence! Media violence's importance is further demonstrated when we realize that media may be one of the easier causes of societal violence to control. There are also some good reasons to think that the contribution of media to societal violence may be, if anything, underestimated by these studies (Perse, 2001).

Nevertheless, there are some critics who argue that the negative effects of media violence are less widespread and serious than most researchers believe. Although some of these critics have obvious self-interest (e.g., television network executives or movie producers), there are a few who offer more reasoned arguments. See Grimes and colleagues (2008) for one of the most careful and articulate of these arguments. Grimes *et al.* argue that media "causationist" researchers, as they call them, are in fact driven by ideology rather than science. Another argument they make is that one cannot generalize the negative effects beyond very specialized populations, whom, they acknowledge, may be strongly adversely affected.

However, the clearest conclusion about the mass of research on the effects of media violence requires taking a convergent evidence approach. Any study taken by itself is subject to some criticism in terms of methodology, interpretation, or validity. When looking at the big picture, however, the weight of the evidence clearly falls on the side of violent media having several negative behavioral and attitudinal effects, especially modeling and desensitization. These effects typically are not uniform and frequently are moderated by other variables, but they do seem to be causal in nature.

By the 1990s, the pattern of research findings was clear. According to one estimate (Grossman & DeGaetano, 1999), of the 3,500 research studies conducted between 1950 and 1999 studying the effects of watching media violence, all but 18 (i.e., 99.5%) showed negative effects of consuming violent entertainment. Murray (2008), in a thorough review of over 50 years' worth of research (1,945 studies) on TV violence effects, found a very similar pattern: "the inescapable conclusion that viewing media violence is related to increases in aggressive attitudes, values, and behaviors" (p. 1212). Another review of the decades of research said, "What is supported by the vast body of research is the following: Media violence is an important causal risk factor for increased aggression and violence in both the short and long term" (Anderson, Bushman, Donnerstein, Hummer, & Warburton, 2015, p. 15). The effects cross cultural lines, too. Other studies have found clear links between media violence and aggression in countries across North America, Europe, Asia, and Australia (Anderson *et al.*, 2017; Huesmann, 2013).

When the large majority of thousands of studies, using a wide variety of methodologies, point in the same direction in terms of results, this cannot be discredited by pointing to particular flaws or limitations of experimental design in individual studies. Further, a 1993 American Psychological Association report summed up the research in this area by saying this: "Nearly four decades of research on television viewing and other media have documented the almost universal exposure of American children to high levels of media violence ... there is absolutely no doubt that higher levels of viewing violence on television are correlated with increased acceptance of aggressive attitudes and increased aggressive behavior" (American Psychological Association, 1993, pp. 32–33). The strength of these conclusions has only grown stronger in succeeding years (Anderson *et al.*, 2015; Bushman & Anderson, 2001; Krahé, 2014).

A useful way to look at effects of media violence is in terms of risk and protective factors (Kirsh, 2006). Strong negative effects will only be observed in someone who exhibits or is exposed to multiple risk factors. Some of these risk factors are demographic (being male, young, living in high violence environments, heavy exposure to media violence, using drugs, being in gangs). Others are personality and mental health factors (high alienation, proneness to violence, hopelessness, high sensation seeking, lacking social support, being angry, having been diagnosed with a behavioral disorder, being low in empathy). Finally, there are risk factors in the media itself (violence that is reinforced, realistic, perpetrated by admired characters with whom one identifies). The alienated youth who starts shooting classmates has not merely watched bloody movies and played first-person shooter video games; he almost surely has multiple risk factors to a high degree. It is thus quite understandable that most people watching violent media do not show clear ill effects. However, given the mass audience, serious negative effects on a few individuals is still cause for great concern.

Just as there are risk factors which push a child toward experiencing more negative reactions to watching media violence, so are there protective factors which may reduce the likelihood of exhibiting negative effects. Like the risk factors, some of these are dispositional attributes of the person, such as low sensation seeking, high empathy, low violence proneness, slowness to anger, and generally easy temperament. There are also protective factors in the environment, such as positive and engaged parenting, mediation from parents about media, safe and nonviolent surroundings, absence of drugs and gangs, and lower rate of exposure to screen violence. Parents seeking to protect their children from negative effects of media violence should seek to minimize as many of the risk factors and maximize as many of the protective factors as possible, keeping in mind that the risk will never be zero.

No one but the most strident media bashers seriously argues that violence in media is to blame for all societal violence. However, the conclusion of "no effects" or "no clear picture yet" from the research is simply not tenable scientifically, although it is surprisingly the view that is increasingly presented in popular news reporting.

Research versus the Public Perception

Bushman and Anderson (2001) conducted a meta-analysis of over 200 studies on the effects of media violence, collectively involving over 43,000 participants. They concluded that the evidence for negative effects of media violence is strong and its strength is increasing, especially in the post-1990 research. Overall, effects are larger for experimental than correlational studies, as one would naturally expect, though the trend is the same. Interestingly enough, however, during this same period when the research evidence on the negative effects of media violence was becoming stronger, the popular news reporting of the same research erroneously suggested that these effects were becoming weaker over time.

Media Factors

What are some possible reasons for this serious deviation from reality? Bushman and Anderson (2001) suggest three possible explanations relating to the media itself. One, certain segments of the media and entertainment industries have a strong, vested interest in denying a strong link between media violence and violent behavior, given that they make enormous profits from selling violent entertainment (Hamilton, 1998). Television networks, movie studios, cable channels, and sometimes print media outlets as well, are part of the same huge conglomerates with considerable pressure to maintain or increase their audience size for their advertisers.

A second reason suggested by Bushman and Anderson is what they call a "misapplied fairness doctrine." One of media's strongest abiding principles is balance and fairness—presenting all sides of an issue. This causes media to look very hard for an opposing view (e.g., pro vs. con opinions on the negative effects of media violence), even when evidence on one side of an issue is weak. The resulting presentation of both sides of this issue leaves the reader/viewer with the mistaken impression that research opinion is more or less evenly divided on the issue. This laudable attempt to be fair ends up obscuring the fact that, although there are two sides of opinion on the issue (violent media do or do not cause violent behavior), the overwhelming majority of scientific opinion comes down on the negative effects side. Unfortunately, one content analysis on news coverage about media violence (Martins et al., 2013) found an increasing trend toward neutral conclusions.

Finally, Bushman and Anderson argue that the research community has often failed to advocate its position with strength and clarity. Researchers by training are very cautious and conservative about overgeneralizing the effects of their research, and most have no training and little or no experience in talking to the press. Thus, when appearing on TV to argue the case against media violence, researchers may not seem all that compelling to the viewing audience. See Chapter 7 Media Applications for a further discussion of researchers relating to mass media.

Psychological Factors

Although market factors no doubt drive some of the misperceptions about media violence, the most influential elements of disbelief are probably our own cognitive processes. Huesmann, Dubow, and Yang (2013) argue that there are four especially important psychological processes involved here. First, as we have discussed earlier in this chapter, is desensitization. We know that a steady diet of media violence results in us being less bothered by violence we see on a screen. It follows, then, that after having been exposed to it our entire lives, at least in some sense we no longer "see" TV, movie, or video game violence as a big deal and thus see it as having little power to influence behavior.

A second psychological factor is *reactance*, an attempt to exert control, especially in the face of opposition (Huesmann et al., 2013). Huesmann (2010) argues some may be unwilling to embrace the fact that violent media are related to real-life aggression due to a misguided concern that this acceptance may lead to limits on freedom of expression. Those who make violent media may also find it hard to reconcile their art with negative outcomes and in turn may experience reactance. As media consumers, we might also defiantly consume violence, thinking it cannot affect *us*.

Denying research findings on violent media may also reflect a need for *cognitive consistency* (Huesmann et al., 2013). As discussed earlier in this book, classic studies on cognitive dissonance (Festinger, 1957) have shown that we become very uncomfortable when we have thoughts, behaviors, or attitudes that don't align with one another. This effect may carry over into our understanding of media violence in that if we have grown up enjoying media that contains violence, we may find it hard to accept that there could be negative effects. Producers of violent media may also have difficulty reconciling the notions that they are creating valuable art while at the same time creating content that may damage society and individual lives.

Finally, the *third-person effect* (discussed in detail in Chapter 2 as well as elsewhere in this book) may well play a role in denying the power of violent media images (Huesmann *et al.*, 2013). It seems very easy to reason that violent media may affect others but "not *me*." The third-person effect works hand in hand with the need for cognitive consistency and reactance. Thus, one could hear or read about research findings on violent media (like many of the studies described in this chapter), resolve any cognitive inconsistencies by reasoning, "that doesn't happen to me," and then reactively, perhaps defiantly, continue watching violent movies and playing violent video games. Interestingly, one cross-cultural study on violent video games found a larger third-person effect on U.S. participants than those in Korea. Unsurprisingly, Koreans also were more open to the idea of censoring and regulating violent video games than were Americans (Hong, 2015).

Conclusion

What, then, may we conclude from this mass of research on media violence inside and outside of the laboratory? Although no single study by itself is definitive in establishing the deleterious effect of TV violence on children, the evidence overall strongly converges on the conclusion that media violence does have harmful effects, especially on children, primarily in three areas. After exposure to media violence, there is an increase in fear, violent behavior, and desensitization (Anderson, Berkowitz, *et al.*, 2003; Bushman & Anderson, 2001; Dubow & Miller, 1996; Kirsh, 2006). The laboratory research generally has yielded stronger conclusions than the field studies, which is exactly what would be expected. The majority of the opinion clearly concludes that there is strong evidence of those three negative effects.

Although most of the longitudinal field studies have shown a significant positive correlation between viewing televised violence and subsequent aggressive behavior, such correlations have typically been small in magnitude (e.g., Pearson r correlations between 0.15 and 0.30, statistically accounting for 2–9% of the variance). The fact that this amount is small, however, should not be surprising. Social cognitive theory, for example, would predict such a modest effect, because television is, after all, only a small part of the matrix of influences in people's lives (Perse & Lambe, 2017). It is, however, clearly one of those influences, and no doubt an important one.

The effects of media violence, however, do not fall equally on all viewers. Some people are affected more than others, and some portrayals of violence and some shows have more effect than others. The more risk factors that are present and the fewer protective factors, the greater the negative effects on viewers. In proposing policy, either legislative regulation or industry guidelines, such issues must be considered. All violence is not equally harmful to all people. This is also the challenge to those implementing the V-chip and industry ratings, discussed in the Media Applications section of this chapter.

A final issue that complicates policy-setting questions is the fact that violent themes are very widespread in media. Certainly most prevalent in entertainment TV programming, films, and video games, violence is also widespread in cartoons, news, song lyrics, sports, and other places we do not always think about when discussing media violence. The debate over the effects of media violence has been strident and heated and probably will continue at that level. Predictably, the television, film, and video game industries in general have questioned the conclusions of much of the behavioral research. Although the negative effects of TV may not be quite as widespread or serious as suggested by the strongest critics, they are not nearly as benign as suggested by the apologists. We have not yet seriously addressed one of the types of media violence causing the greatest concern today (i.e., sexual violence). We examine this issue and research on the problem in detail in the next chapter after a look at sex in the media.

Media Applications, Chapter 9: Helping Children Deal with Violent Media

With the many concerns identified by the research combined with the impossibility of totally shielding our children from violent media, what can we do to help mitigate these negative effects, especially on kids? Possible solutions come in several different areas, which we will examine in turn.

Institutional Solutions

Given the probable negative effects and influences of violent television, what can a parent do, short of prohibiting viewing or game-playing altogether? There are some technological options that may be of help.

The V-Chip

Technology built into all televisions sold in the United States includes what's become known as the "V-chip." This technology was mandated by the Telecommunications Act of 1996 (Price, 1998), but it must be programmed in each TV set to block out the violent shows, as determined by the rating. To the surprise of its proponents, the V-chip has been used very little over the decades it has been available, even though most parents are aware that the technology exists (Vaala, Bleakley, Castonguay, & Jordan, 2017). The reasons for this are not completely clear, but it is probably due to a combination of ignorance of its presence, lack of knowledge about how to program and implement it, a reluctance to block out a large number of programs of possible interest to the parents, tech-savvy kids' ability to get around the technology, and questionable criteria for blocking programs (Kunkel *et al.*, 2002). In addition, cable and satellite TV providers may have their own content-blocking systems, which may or may not work well with V-chips. The V-chip is also increasingly irrelevant with online streaming media, particularly if it is streamed on a mobile device rather than a television (Grossman, 2018). Although many streaming services offer parental controls, they also seem underused. For example, one survey found that about 60% of parents had never used YouTube's parental controls and/or didn't know they existed (Common Sense Media, 2018).

Television Content Ratings

First implemented in the late 1990s in the United States as a parallel to the more familiar MPAA movie rating systems, TV ratings attempt to specify appropriate ages for viewers (e.g., TV-14—not suitable for children under 14). These ratings continue to be the subject of criticism and refinement in an attempt to make them more useful. One criticism is that the ratings may lack uniformity because networks voluntarily set the ratings for each show themselves. It can also become more difficult to block content if shows are watched over streaming devices such as Roku. As with movie ratings, indications are that sex, more than violence, drives the ratings (Leone, 2002). Over the years, the television industry has modified its rating system somewhat to include codes (e.g., "V" for violence, "L" for language) signifying specific content that parents may want to avoid (Timmer, 2013).

Mediation and Media Literacy Training

Although mitigating the effects of TV violence has not been the major thrust of the research, there have been some interesting findings that speak to this issue.

Classroom Training

Back in the 1980s, a group of researchers (Huesmann, Eron, Klein, Brice, & Fischer, 1983) developed a treatment designed to change children's attitudes about violent TV. One hundred sixty-nine first and third graders who watched a lot of violent TV were exposed to an intervention in which the children were asked to develop arguments about the negative effects of TV violence, write a paragraph on the topic, and make a group video with everyone reading his or her essay. This treatment (but not the control) led to reduced violent behavior and a weaker relationship between aggression and violent TV viewing. In terms of attitudes, the treatment had a substantial effect on children's responses to two questions ("Are television shows with a lot of hitting and shooting harmless for kids?" and "How likely is it that watching a lot of television violence would make a kid meaner?"). The mitigation effect was strongest in children who identified least with the violent characters, suggesting the important role of identification with the aggressive model.

Another interesting study (Robinson, Wilde, Navracruz, Haydel, & Varady, 2001) tested a 6-month training session for third and fourth graders and their parents designed to reduce television, video, and video game use. Children were encouraged to watch no TV or video for 10 days and stay on a one-hour-per-day regimen thereafter. Children also received lessons on various aspects of media literacy, and parents were encouraged to help their children follow the schedule and to encourage the family to do likewise. Compared to a control group, the experimental group showed less peer-rated aggression and observed verbal aggression.

More recently, research conducted in Croatia (Velki & Jagodić, 2017) examined the relationship between the amount of time elementary school students reported consuming media (TV, video games, Internet) and the frequency with which they behaved aggressively toward their peers (physically, verbally, and/or electronically). Interestingly, the social context in which they consumed violent media seemed to matter. Specifically, when children played violent video games in the presence of peers, they were less likely to display physical aggression toward peers. Further, consuming Internet media in the presence of parents or peers was associated with decreased physical and electronic peer aggression. The authors speculate that the results may be reflective of discussions taking place as violent media is consumed. In any event, such discussions certainly cannot take place if children are consuming violent media while they're alone.

Personality Development
Another approach to mitigating negative effects of media violence is suggested by the individual differences research of Tamborini and colleagues (Hahn *et al.*, 2017; Tamborini, 1996; Tamborini & Stiff, 1987; Tamborini, Stiff, & Zillmann, 1987; Tamborini *et al.*, 1990). If certain types of personalities (e.g., highly empathic) find graphic violence distasteful and disturbing, and others (e.g., sensation seeking) find it pleasantly arousing, cultivating empathic qualities in one's children and discouraging sensation seeking presumably should help in ensuring that they will not find viewing violence to be pleasurable. Similarly, encouraging psychological identification with the victims rather than the perpetrators of violence should decrease the enjoyment level of violent TV or movies (Waddell, Bailey, & Davis, 2017). Anything to lower the risk factors or raise the protective factors will help lessen the negative effects of media violence on children (see Cantor & Wilson, 2003, for a thorough review of strategies to reduce negative effects of media violence in children).

Parental Mediation
As we have seen throughout this book, whatever the negative effects of media on children, they can be mitigated, and perhaps even redirected to positive changes, through positive interaction and dialogue in the home. Such parental mediation, as it is called, can take any of three general forms (Nathanson, 1999). *Active mediation* involves talking with children about the media they encounter. This mediation may be either positive (e.g., endorsement of content) or negative (e.g., criticism of content). It may be fully intended as mediation (strategic mediation) or only thought of by those doing it as incidental conversation (nonstrategic mediation) (Buerkel-Rothfuss & Buerkel, 2001). It also starts very early in life, as young as the first year (Barr, Zack, Garcia, & Muentener, 2008; Fidler, Zack, & Barr, 2010), although parents may overestimate the extent to which they actually engage in mediation (Gentile, Nathanson, Rasmussen, Reimer, & Walsh, 2012). Resources are available to help; for example, Niemiec and Wedding (2008, 2014) have authored books on using films to build virtues and character strengths.

Restrictive mediation involves setting rules and limits on media use or screen time, a strategy used by most parents at least occasionally. This could come in the form of preventing viewing certain programs, websites, or media use outside certain allowed hours. In other families it takes the form of limits on overall TV viewing or screen time.

The final form of parental mediation is *co-viewing*, that is, watching television with children. Most scholars (e.g., Rasmussen, Keene, Berke, Densley, & Loof, 2017) agree that co-viewing TV with children is very helpful, though admittedly not always realistic, especially as the child grows older.

These three mediation categories are not mutually exclusive and in fact often coexist. For example, parents may limit children from watching certain shows and may co-view others with their children, while making both positive and negative active mediation comments. All of these types of mediation probably occur in all families at some point, but parents would be well-advised to recognize the mediation they do and be more intentional about it. Restrictive mediation is the most common type of parental mediation overall in all social classes but especially so among lower-income parents (Warren, 2005).

Although it is seldom possible to do all the mediation one might like, even occasional mediation by parents can be helpful. As the family watches television together or discusses shows previously watched, conversation may occur about deceptive advertising, stereotyped group portrayals, antisocial values, or excessive sex or violence. Parents may offer factual ("Those people are really actors and that isn't real blood") or evaluative comments ("That man is mean. People don't like people who act like that") appropriate to the age of the child (Buijzen, 2007; Nathanson, 2004). Parents can also question children about their reactions to what is on TV, thus better understanding the perceived reality constructed by the child (e.g., "Do you think most grown women look that that model?"). They may comment about their own reactions, thus providing a balance to what may be a skewed media portrayal. For example, parents could voice their concern about a violent scene and share that they remember being scared by such scenes as a child (Nathanson & Yang, 2003). They do need to talk, however. It is unfortunate that parents often do not talk to their children as much while they are watching television together as while they are reading or playing with toys (Nathanson & Rasmussen, 2011); these can be important missed opportunities.

Parental mediation has measurable effects. For example, there is some meta-analytical evidence that restrictive and co-viewing mediation (but not active mediation) may be associated with positive child outcomes such as reduced substance use and sexual activity (Collier *et al.*, 2016). Negative active mediation can induce a mistrust of television, lower levels of aggression, and skepticism toward television news, while positive active mediation is related to positive attitudes toward television and improved understanding of cognitively complex material (Austin, 1993, 2001; Austin, Bolls, Fujioka, & Engelbertson, 1999; Austin, Pinkleton, & Fujioka, 2000; Nathanson, 1999, 2004). A study of parental mediation with children following extensive news coverage in the Netherlands of the assassination of filmmaker Theo van Gogh in 2004 found that active mediation had some effect of reducing fear, worry, and anger in young children, but not older ones, and restrictive mediation was not helpful and was sometimes even counterproductive (Buijzen, Walma van der Molen, & Sondij, 2007). However, the approach parents take with restrictive mediation matters, too. Another study in the Netherlands (Fikkers, Piotrowski, & Valkenburg, 2017) found that restrictive mediation with an autonomy supportive style (e.g., explaining the rationale for rules and listening to the child's perspective) was more effective than active mediation and other forms of restrictive mediation at decreasing young adolescents' aggression, at least in the short term.

Further Reading

Bartsch, A., Mares, M.-L., Scherr, S., Kloß, A., Keppeler, J., & Posthumus, L. (2016). More than shoot-em-up and torture porn: Reflective appropriation and meaning-making of violent media content. *Journal of Communication*, 66(5), 741–765.

Bushman, B. J., Gollwitzer, M., & Cruz, C. (2015). There is broad consensus: Media researchers agree that violent media increase aggression in children, and pediatricians and parents concur. *Psychology of Popular Media Culture*, 4(3), 200–214.

Calvert, S. L., Appelbaum, M., Dodge, K. A., Graham, S., Nagayama Hall, G. C., Hamby, S., & ... Hedges, L. V. (2017). The American Psychological Association Task Force assessment of violent video games: Science in the service of public interest. *American Psychologist*, 72(2), 126–143. doi:10.1037/a0040413

Ferguson, C. J., & Konijn, E. A. (2015). She said/he said: A peaceful debate on video game violence. *Psychology of Popular Media Culture*, 4(4), 397–411. doi: 10.1037/ppm0000064

Gentile, D. A. (Ed.). (2014). *Media violence and children: A complete guide for parents and professionals*. 2nd ed. Santa Barbara, CA: Praeger/ABC-CLIO.

Niemiec, R. M., & Wedding, D. (2014). *Positive psychology at the movies: Using films to build character strengths and well-being*. 2nd ed. Boston, MA: Hogrefe.

Oates, J. (2012). Learning from watching. In N. Brace, & J. Byford (Eds.), *Investigating psychology: Key concepts, key studies, key approaches* (pp. 100–138). New York: Oxford University Press.

Surette, R. (2015). *Media, crime, and criminal justice: Images, realities, and policies*. 5th ed. Stamford, CT: Cengage Learning.

Useful Links

Entertainment Software Ratings Board description of video game ratings:
www.esrb.org/

How to Set Parental Controls on Streaming Devices:
www.lifewire.com/set-parental-controls-on-streaming-devices-4154531

Parental Controls on Netflix and YouTube:
www.ebuyer.com/blog/2017/01/how-to-set-up-parental-controls-on-youtube-and-netflix/

Television Content Ratings System:
www.tvguidelines.org/ratings.htm

For more resources, please visit the companion website:
www.routledge.com/cw/harris

Chapter 10

Sex

Is Tuning In Turning Us On? Sexuality through a Media Lens

Q: What percentage of adolescents have seen pornography online?

A: In a survey of British children between the ages of 11 and 16, 28% of 11-year-olds said they had seen online porn, but the percentage rose to 65% among 15- to 16-year-olds. Fifty-three percent of the 15- to 16-year-old males also reported that they thought the sexually explicit material they had seen was realistic (Martellozzo *et al.*, 2017).

Q: What percentage of TV shows contain sexual content?

A: In one sample, it was 53%, with an average of 0.26 seconds of every minute containing sex. Among shows rated TV-MA, the percentage was 90.5%, with 0.8 seconds of every minute devoted to sexual behavior (Gabrielli *et al.*, 2016).

Q: Is "sexting" related to teenage self-esteem?

A: One cross-cultural study found that the higher an adolescent's self-esteem and self-control, the less likely he or she was to engage in sexting behaviors (Wachs, Wright, & Wolf, 2017).

Some of our major sources of information about sex come from media (Chia, 2006; Sutton, Brown, Wilson, & Klein, 2002; Wright, 2015). Everything from the mildest innuendo on a network sitcom to the most explicit pornographic Internet video can contribute to our perceived reality of what sex is all about and what people expect from it.

Of course, adolescence is a prime time in life when people want to learn more about sexuality. According to one study (Bleakley, Hennessy, Fishbein, & Jordan, 2009), 57% of 14- to 16-year-olds said media was a primary source of information about sex. Television and movies were identified by these adolescents as the most informative kind of media for learning about sex. The Internet is another big source of sex information for teens (Simon & Daneback, 2013; Smith, 2013), with well over half of 16- to 19-year-olds (61% of females, 93% of males) reporting having viewed online porn (Weber, Quiring, & Daschmann, 2012). Interestingly, sexually explicit media sometimes may be the only source of information for sexual minority youth because while pornography targeting LGBT people is widespread, sexual health information for that population may be harder to find (Arrington-Sanders *et al.*, 2015). What do parents think about their kids accessing media sex? A survey indicated that although most parents believed that adolescents should use parents as a source for sex information, the parents thought that their kids probably obtained more information from friends and media (Lagus, Bernat, Bearinger, Resnick, & Eisenberg, 2011).

We are continually learning more about sex and modifying our constructed reality of its nature. How we act on that information may have serious consequences for our lives and the lives of others. In this chapter we first examine how sex is presented in the media and then turn to the research on the effects of exposure to that material. Toward the end of the chapter, we focus on one of the most controversial varieties of media sex, namely, sexual violence and discuss some ways to mitigate the effects of consuming such media.

The Nature of Sex in Media

Whenever we speak of sex in the media, we must clarify what we are including in that term. There is a class of media often explicitly labeled erotic, pornographic, or sexually explicit, which comprises magazines, videos, films, and Internet websites. These materials have typically been marketed separately from nonsexual media and have been at least somewhat restricted from children, although this is becoming increasingly difficult to do effectively, especially with the few restrictions imposed by the Internet.

Definitional Issues

When people first think about sexual media, pornography probably comes to mind. It's estimated that the pornography industry reaps billions of dollars every year, although, as you might imagine, not all porn producers keep exacting accounting records (Pinsker, 2016). Interestingly, however, changes in Internet usage patterns are increasingly providing financial challenges to the business of pornography. Specifically, YouTube-type porn sites seem to be leading to pornography piracy and user-submitted videos that can be accessed without fees, which in turn leads to less traffic on pay porn websites (Chiang, 2009). Of course, that doesn't mean that there is less interest in online pornography—it just seems that it is becoming easier, and cheaper, to locate as the Internet matures. Indeed, one of these sites, Pornhub, receives more daily Internet traffic than Pinterest, Tumblr, or Paypal (Jones, 2018).

Pornography can be difficult to define; an Associate Supreme Court Justice once famously said, "I know it when I see it" (see Close-up 10.9 for further discussion of pornography and politics). However, traditionally, *pornographic media* have been recognized as being for sexual purposes only and without recognized literary or artistic merit, although there are a few signs that pornography is becoming more mainstream (Sigesmund, 2003). For example, porn film stars are becoming more widely known, and several mainstream movies and TV series have dealt with the pornography industry (*The People vs. Larry Flynt, Boogie Nights, The Girl Next Door, Wonderland*; TV series like *Skin* and *The Deuce* and documentary series like *Pornucopia, Family Business*, and *Hot Girls Wanted* feature porn producers as the major characters). Because pornography is so readily available online, the widespread, private availability of porn on the Internet has had a huge role in spreading its influence. Interestingly enough, as the new technology has spread sexually explicit media in unprecedented ways, some traditional sex media, especially magazines, have fallen on hard times. Most sexually explicit magazines have lost at least 10% of their circulation per year since the mid-1990s. For example, *Penthouse* has fallen from publishing 5 million copies a month to about 100,000 (Audit Bureau of Circulations, 2011; Sigesmund, 2003; Somaiya, 2015). Trying to raise circulation, *Playboy* eliminated nudity in its issues … and then brought it back again (Snider, 2017).

Defining Sexual Violence

Scholars have found it helpful to distinguish between *sexually violent* material, which portrays rape and other instances of physical coercion and harm to persons in a sexual context, and *nonviolent sexual material*, which may or may not depict degradation, domination, subordination, or humiliation. Nonviolent and non-degrading material typically depicts a couple having intercourse with no indication of violence or coercion. Research has consistently shown more negative effects from viewing sexual violence than from the nonviolent, non-degrading material, with intermediate results from the nonviolent degrading material.

Because minors cannot legally give consent for sex, child pornography is often considered a form of sexual violence as it is coercive. Child pornography portrays minors and, although illegal to produce, distribute, and possess in most countries, it still circulates widely through personal distribution channels, especially the Internet (Jenkins, 2001; Pullido, 2014). For obvious ethical reasons, there has been little scientific research on the effects of child pornography, though see Paul and Linz (2008) for a creative attempt to measure effects of showing participants "barely legal" photos of women who appear to be minors.

Of course, sex occurs in many other media outlets besides these explicitly sexual materials. As we know, it is rampant in advertising, certainly for products like mouthwash, perfume, cologne, and after-shave, but also for tires, automobiles, and faucets (see Chapter 6). Sex in media is not limited to explicit portrayals of intercourse or nudity, but rather may include any representation that portrays or implies sexual behavior, interest, or motivation. Indeed, the most common category of sex in media is talking about sex, the sort of dialogue rampant on sitcoms and dramas like *Game of Thrones*, *Grey's Anatomy*, *The Big Bang Theory*, or *How to Get Away with Murder*. Although much of this chapter deals with explicit sexual materials, we consider sexual talk as well, which can also convey strong messages about sex. Because the term "pornographic" is highly value-laden but scientifically imprecise, from here on we will generally refer to such materials as sexually explicit.

History of Sex in Media

Sexual themes in fiction have been around as long as fiction itself. Ancient Greek comedies were often highly sexual in content, such as Aristophanes' *Lysistrata*, an antiwar comedy about women who withhold sex from their husbands to coerce them to stop fighting wars. Literary classics like Chaucer's *Canterbury Tales* and Shakespeare's *The Taming of the Shrew* are filled with sexual double entendres and overtly sexual themes, some of which are missed today due to the archaic language and the classic aura around such works. Throughout history, the pendulum has swung back and forth in terms of how much sexual expression is permitted in literature, art, and entertainment at any given time and how explicit it may be.

Since the advent of electronic media, standards have usually been more conservative for movies, radio, and television than for print, because it is easier to keep sexually oriented print media from children than it is radio or TV. The issue is more complex with movies, because although there is a movie ratings system in place (see Close-ups 1.2 and 10.1), it is not always enforced. With the advent of widespread cable and digital technology, a sort of double standard has arisen, with greater permissiveness for streaming and premium cable channels than for network television, using the logic that premium cable and streaming video are invited into the home, whereas broadcast network programming is there uninvited whenever a TV set is present. Of course, the biggest access issue is the ready availability of sex on the Internet and how to restrict its access to minors. Online pornography filters have some success, although they raise free speech issues and sometimes unintentionally restrict nonsexual sites (e.g., breast cancer information); also, entrepreneurs of sexually explicit websites are usually one step ahead of the screeners in designing ways to avoid the filters (also see Close-up 10.4).

❖ CLOSE-UP 10.1 SEX, MOVIE CENSORSHIP, AND THE HAYS CODE

Most moviegoers in the United States today are familiar with the film rating system employed by the Motion Picture Association of America (MPAA) in which films are given the ratings G, PG, PG-13, R, and NC-17 (also see Close-up 1.2). What is probably less known to modern movie audiences is the surprising history that predates the use of these ratings.

Almost as soon as movies began to be produced, there was concern about their content, particularly as it related to sex. There may have been good reason to be worried. You may think of old movies as generally tame and "family friendly," but many films from the 1920s to mid-1930s were anything but. In this era before much regulation was in place, movie producers often pushed the envelope with racy content such as graphic violence, adultery, promiscuity, out-of-wedlock births, rape, and prostitution. No one pushed the envelope more than writer and performer Mae West. In movies such as She Done Him Wrong *(1933) and* I'm No Angel *(1933), West sang seductive numbers like "A Man What Takes His Time," alluding to the benefits of sexual foreplay. She also purred snappy one-liners including, "It's not the men in your life that matters, it's the life in your men," and "When I'm good, I'm very good, but when I'm bad, I'm better." This sort of innuendo, combined with themes of organized crime, prostitution, and even brief glimpses of nudity and lesbian relationships delighted some and outraged others (Black, 1994; Doherty, 1999).*

Interestingly, even while some of the most scandalous early movies were made, there was a detailed film censorship policy in place. Formally called the "Motion Picture Production Code of 1930," it became better known as the "Hays Code" after Will Hays, who at the time was president of the Motion Picture Producers and Distributors of America (MPPDA). The Hays Code contained very specific dos and don'ts relating to topics like vulgarity (e.g., "the name Jesus Christ should never be used except in reverence"), costume (e.g., "nudity is never permitted"), and location (e.g., "brothels and houses of ill fame, no matter of what country, are not proper locations for drama"). Later additions to the Code forbade depictions of seduction, rape, venereal disease, scenes of actual childbirth, and miscegenation (sex relationships between the Black and White races).

Despite this specificity, the MPPDA (which would later become the MPAA mentioned above) at first was a largely symbolic organization constructed by the big movie studios as a way to quell talk of government censorship. Thus, the Hays Code was rarely followed or enforced. However, as movies became particularly edgy in the early 1930s, there was increased opposition from various fronts including religious leaders, the Roosevelt administration, and academics, who began to report on the negative effects of viewing provocative movies. Seeing the writing on the wall (and wanting to avoid outright governmental censorship, or worse—box office boycotts), Hays and the MPPDA began to enforce the Code by 1934 (Doherty, 1999; Skal, 1993). The turnaround was profound. "Now truly under the Code, the landscape of American cinema underwent a tectonic shift. In a matter of months, the genres, tones, and textures of pre-Code Hollywood were erased from the screen" (Doherty, 1999, p. 331).

The Hays Code was strictly enforced throughout most of the rest of the 1930s, 1940s, and 1950s, giving rise to squeaky clean movies starring performers such as Shirley Temple and Judy Garland. It wasn't until the 1960s that the Code was replaced with the current MPAA rating system, although by that time, the Code was again largely being ignored by producers as audiences seemed to demand more sophisticated movie fare.

Media Sex Today

Content analyses of media show that sexual innuendoes and, less often, behaviors are common, very frequently occurring in a humorous context. For example, estimates are that sex in some form is an element in over 80% of movies and TV shows (Fisher, Hill, Grube, & Gruber, 2004; Jamieson, More, Lee, Busse, & Romer, 2008). More TV programs contain talk about sex (68%) than actual sexual behavior (35%), though intercourse is depicted or strongly implied in about 11% of the shows (Kaiser Family Foundation, 2005; Kunkel *et al.*, 2007). Only about 15% of TV shows mention any concerns with abstinence, birth control, or consequences of sex like pregnancy or sexually transmitted infections (STIs) (Kaiser Family Foundation, 2005; Pariera, Hether, Murphy, de Castro Buffington, & Baezconde-Garbanati, 2014). TV show mention of such concerns has slowly increased over the years, but the depiction of sex as behavior without serious consequences remains a major distortion of reality in the media presentation of sex.

The portrayals of sex in media have changed over time. A meta-analysis on sexual content appearing on U.S. prime-time broadcast network programming (NBC, ABC, CBS, and Fox) found a decrease in the frequency per hour for passionate kissing, touching, and intercourse from the early 1990s to the mid-2000s (Hetsroni, 2007). Interestingly, however, the amount of sex talk steadily increased from 1999 to 2004. Another change over time has been the portrayal of casual premarital and extramarital sexual encounters; these days, media references to such behaviors outnumber references to sex between spouses in TV and movies, sometimes by as much as 32:1 (Greenberg & Hofschire, 2000; Timmermans & van den Bulck, 2018).

Portrayals of LGBT sexual relationships have become relatively common in everyday media, too. Virtually absent from TV and movies until the 1990s (see Chapter 5), sexual minority characters are now quite commonly seen engaging in dating and marital relationships. However, one content analysis found that compared to heterosexual sexual relationships, same-sex relationships are underrepresented in mainstream media (Bond, 2014). Interestingly, though, LGBT sexual relationships are portrayed more positively in media targeted specifically to the LGBT community than in mainstream media (Bond, 2015).

We clearly have come a long way from the early 1950s when network censors required Lucy and Ricky Ricardo on *I Love Lucy* to have twin beds and refer to her expectant state as "having a baby," never as "pregnant," but there are still firm standards that no network or basic cable TV shows dare cross, such as frontal nudity, explicit sexual intercourse, or use of the notorious "F-word." Even now, though, standards for television are more conservative than for radio, which is in turn more conservative than the recording industry. These differences are especially clear in terms of music lyrics. When Mick Jagger and the Rolling Stones appeared on *The Ed Sullivan Show* in the 1960s, they had to change the line "Let's spend the night together" to "Let's spend some time together." When Jagger performed this line, he did so with exaggerated gestures, rolled eyes, and body language to communicate his attitude about the censorship. These days, it's common for artists to record two versions of songs, one a "radio edit" with less explicit lyrics that can get airtime on the radio and TV.

Sex in media is one area in which we clearly tolerate some limits on freedom of speech, and that fact is generally accepted. The sharp differences of opinion come in deciding just where those limits should be. Few are arguing that a network sitcom should show frontal nudity or child prostitutes, although it is highly unlikely that the producers would ever care to do so. One important issue in discussion of where the limits should be is the age of the consumer. There is far more concern about the effects of sexual media on children than on adults. Even a highly libertarian person probably does not want a 6-year-old surfing porn sites on the Internet, whereas even a morally conservative person would be less alarmed about adults viewing X-rated videos than young children seeing them. The whole area of the effects of sexual media on children is a difficult area to study for ethical reasons; however, there are some ingenious ways to probe their effects without actually presenting children with stimuli that many of their parents would object to (see Close-up 10.2).

❖ CLOSE-UP 10.2 STUDYING EFFECTS OF SEXUAL MEDIA ON CHILDREN AND ADOLESCENTS

One empirical question we would like to know the answer to is almost impossible to study for ethical reasons: what is the effect of sexual media on children and adolescents? What parent would approve of his or her young child watching sexually explicit media, or even an R-rated movie, for research purposes? Nevertheless, we all know that children do sometimes see sexual media. One clever methodology to examine this problem involves the use of the retrospective method which entails questioning adults about their memories of watching sexual content as children. The researchers are not exposing any children to questionable stimuli, but merely asking people about material they have already seen a long time ago on their own. Cantor, Mares, and Hyde (2003) asked 196 college students to remember an exposure to sexual media between the ages of 5 and 12 or during the teen years. Almost 92% could do so, 39% remembering something seen between the ages of 5 and 12 and 61% age 13 and over. Most often (79%) the content was R or NC-17 rated movies, and 80% were viewed with someone else (only 17% with parents, however). Disgust, shock/surprise, interest, and embarrassment were the most common emotional responses remembered (21% to 25% each), with sexual arousal (17%) and avoidance (14%) the most common physical reactions.

Memories from younger ages (5–12) tended to focus on salient sensory aspects like nudity, kissing, and "sexual noises," while the older children's memories focused on dialogue or themes like rape or same-sex sexual behavior. Overall, men's memories were more positive and more likely to focus on physical aspects than women's. Although there is no way to verify the accuracy of these students' memories, the vividness of memories years after the exposure testifies to the powerful effect of seeing this sexual content relatively early in life.

Other insights come from a review (Peter & Valkenburg, 2016) of 20 years of research on adolescents' experiences with sexually explicit media. The patterns across various studies indicated, perhaps not surprisingly, that males were more likely than females to access sexually explicit media as an adolescent. Interestingly, though, use of such media was also associated with sensation seeking, more permissive sexual attitudes, weak/troubled family relationships, and gender-stereotypical beliefs about sexual behaviors.

Explicit sexual materials have traditionally been designed by and for heterosexual men. As such, they have a distinctly macho and hyper-masculinized orientation. Although all varieties of heterosexual intercourse are shown, there is typically little emphasis on associated foreplay, afterplay, cuddling, relationships, or tenderness in general. Women are typically seen as eagerly desiring and participating in intercourse, often with hysterical euphoria (see Chapter 5 for a discussion of the sexualization of females in the media). There is little presentation of any consequences of sex or the relational matrix within which most people experience it.

Over the past few decades, there has been some increase in sexual materials with more emphasis on relationship, pre- and post-coital behaviors, and the woman's point of view generally, developed primarily to be marketed to women (Barber, 2013; Mosher & Maclan, 1994; Senn & Desmarais, 2004; Smith, 2007; Reese-Weber & McBride, 2015). However, these comprise only a minuscule part of the worldwide porn market. Although men are much more active seekers and users of sexual material than are women, this cannot necessarily be attributed to greater intrinsic male interest in explicit sexual media; it may merely reflect the pornography industry's extreme slant to the traditional male perspective.

Media are clearly major sources of information about sexual issues that we use to construct our reality of what sexuality and sexual behavior and values are all about (Fabes & Strouse, 1984, 1987; Kunkel *et al.*, 2007; Strouse & Fabes, 1985; Sutton *et al.*, 2002; Ward, Seabrook, Grower, Giaccardi, & Lippman, 2018). To better understand this perceived reality, let us examine some effects of consuming sex in the media. How do we change after exposure to such material?

Effects of Viewing Media Sex

Although many people might wish it otherwise, sex—even very explicit sex—does sell, though see Close-up 10.3 for an interesting exception. Sexually oriented media are highly profitable, and this fact has ramifications for all media. However, this economic issue is not the focus of this book, and we turn now to the various psychological effects (see Gunter, 2001; Harris & Barlett, 2008; Mundorf, Allen, D'Alessio, & Emmers-Sommer, 2007; Peter & Valkenburg, 2016, for reviews of the literature on the effects of viewing sexual media).

❖ CLOSE-UP 10.3 DOES SEX ON TV HELP SELL PRODUCTS?

Bushman (2005) showed 336 adults aged 18 to 54 a TV show containing one of four possible content conditions: violence, sex, violence and sex, or neither violence nor sex. All groups saw the same 12 commercials embedded in the program. Those who had seen programs with violence or sex were less likely to remember the advertised brands and showed less interest in buying or selecting a coupon for that brand. This held for both men and women of all ages, regardless of their preference for content with sex or violence.

What if the sex is in the ad itself? Parker and Furnham (2007) showed viewers either sexual or nonsexual ads in the context of a sexual (Sex and the City) or nonsexual (Malcolm in the Middle) TV show. People remembered more content from the commercials in the nonsexual show, although there was no difference in the recall of sexual and nonsexual ads. Overall, men recalled sexual ads better and women the nonsexual ads. Similarly, Leka, McClelland, and Furnham (2013) had four groups of participants: two of the groups watched a TV show with high sexual content (Californication), and the two other groups watched a show without sexual content (Bored to Death). The groups were further subdivided such that one of the Californication and one of the Bored to Death groups saw either a group of sexual or nonsexual commercials during the programs. The participants were then asked about their memories of the products being advertised. The type of show didn't seem to affect how well people remembered the ads, but males remembered the sexual ads better than the nonsexual ones.

Arousal

The most straightforward effect of sex in media is sexual arousal, the drive that energizes or intensifies sexual behavior. Sexually oriented media do arouse people, especially men, in terms of both self-ratings of arousal level and physiological measures such as penile engorgement (Golde, Strassberg, & Turner, 2000; Lohr *et al.*, 1997) and body temperature (Kukkonen, Binik, Amsel, & Carrier, 2007; Landry, Goncalves, & Kukkonen, 2016). See Chivers, Seto, Lalumière, Laan, and Grimbos (2010), for a meta-analysis of sexual media consumption and the degree of agreement between self-report and physiological measures of arousal.

Overall, men tend to be more aroused by sexual media than women are (Allen, Emmers-Sommer, *et al.*, 2007; Malamuth, 1996; Murnen & Stockton, 1997), although there is some evidence that women may be more aroused by sexual media developed by and for women that does not portray sex from an extreme hyper-masculine fantasy point of view (Mosher & Maclan, 1994; Quackenbush, Strassberg, & Turner, 1995). Sexual violence is particularly arousing to sex offenders and much less so to other men, unless the victim is portrayed as being aroused by the assault; this issue is discussed in more detail later in the chapter.

Sexual arousal to stimuli not naturally evoking such a response may be learned through classical conditioning, discussed earlier in Chapters 6 and 9. This process could account for the vast individual differences in what specific stimuli arouse people sexually. Through our different experiences, we have all been conditioned to different stimuli through their associations with those we are attracted to and/or love. Because of its association with a particular person, someone may be aroused by a certain perfume or cologne, type of clothing or food, or specific behaviors.

Contrary to what one might expect, the degree of arousal is not necessarily highly correlated with the degree of explicitness of the media. Sometimes people are actually more aroused by a less sexually explicit story than a more explicit one. Censoring out a sex scene may sometimes actually make a film more arousing, because sexual arousal is highly individual, and some viewers prefer to fill in their own fantasies. When people are allowed to use their own imaginations to construct the ending of a romantic scene, they are more likely to construct a scenario that is more arousing to them personally than if they view someone else's idea of what is arousing. There is some validity to the old truism that the most important sex organ is the brain. See Close-up 10.4 for some examples of how technology has been used to censor sexual content in movies.

❖ CLOSE-UP 10.4 MOVIE SANITIZERS: WELCOME INFLUENCE OR ARTISTIC INTRUSION?

There are several options available for viewers who want to watch some movies without the full measure of violence, sex, or rough language. Companies like MovieMask, ClearPlay, and VidAngel have offered software loaded onto home computers, a box connected to the television, or through online streaming services. This software offers several levels of editing to remove as much or as little offending material as the viewer desires. Although most changes involve removing questionable material, sometimes other avenues are taken, such as when MovieMask gave Kate Winslet a digital corset for the nude sketching scene in Titanic *or replaced the swords in* The Princess Bride *with what looked like light sabers from* Star Wars *(Lyman, 2002). Many Hollywood directors have decried such editing on artistic grounds, and movie studios have filed copyright infringement lawsuits (Johnson, 2016). Is this unfair tampering with an artistic work or a long-overdue option welcomed by parents?*

Attitudes and Values

Some of the major effects of media sex are in the areas of effects on attitudes and values. In exploring sexual attitudes and values, we now turn to several specific value issues.

Sexual Details in the News

Although the discussion of sexual violence so far has dealt with the effects of fictional portrayals, there is another type of material with this content, namely, news coverage of sexually violent crimes. This too is part of our exposure to sexually violent content.

How explicit should the media be in reporting news of sex-crime trials? When is the public's right to know overshadowed by its right to standards of good taste? When does reporting turn into voyeurism? Consider some actual examples.

1. A small city is the scene of a child sexual molestation trial of a prominent businessman accused of abusing two 13-year-old boys. Each day's court proceedings are reported in great detail in front-page stories in the local newspaper, always identifying the accused, though never the boys. Sexually explicit materials and alcohol in the man's home were described in detail, along with extensive direct quotes from the victims' testimony: "He rubbed our butts in the shower," "He called me to where he was sitting and told me to play with his penis," "He also made me and [the other boy] lay on the floor and have oral sex with each other while he watched." Other episodes such as the man asking the boys to reach inside his underwear and squeeze his penis were also explicitly described.

Predictably, this coverage provoked some community comment, although even the most outraged people nevertheless always seemed to thoroughly read the articles. Although no one defended the abuse that had occurred, some argued that young readers should not be exposed to such explicit descriptions in the newspaper. Others countered, however, by saying that such events are serious and need to be reported in detail to show everyone how horrible they are and thus increase commitment to ensure that they would not happen again.

2. In a somewhat similar 2012 case, Pennsylvania State University football coach Jerry Sandusky was on trial for multiple counts of child sexual abuse. One victim testified that he had been anally raped in the basement of Sandusky's home, screaming for help while Sandusky's wife was upstairs. When another witness testified, it was widely reported that Sandusky had been seen naked in locker room showers holding young boys while a "skin-on-skin slapping sound" was heard (Belson, 2012).

3. In 2011, New York Congressman Anthony Weiner was caught in a "sexting" scandal in which it was revealed that he had been using his Twitter account to send sexually explicit photos of himself to a college student. Initial waffling and denials by Weiner only led to additional media coverage including (eventually) the photos being published online and in some newspapers. Weiner resigned soon after. He briefly tried to revive his political career in 2013 by running for mayor of New York City. His campaign was derailed when it was revealed Weiner, using the alias Carlos Danger, had sexted again with another woman. By 2016, Weiner was at it again, this time with his young son nearby. *The New York Post* reported "Weiner then hit 'Send' on the cringe-inducing image, which shows a bulge in his white, Jockey-brand boxer briefs and his son cuddled up to his left, wrapped in a light-green blanket" (Rosenberg & Golding, 2016, ¶7). Weiner eventually pled guilty to transferring obscene material to a minor and served a prison sentence.

4. Some of the most celebrated cases of sexually explicit language in the news have involved two U.S. presidents. The first came with the release in September 1998 of U.S. President Bill Clinton's grand jury testimony about his alleged affair with White House intern Monica Lewinsky. The critical legal, and potentially impeachable,

question here was whether the president had perjured himself in grand jury testimony about the specific sexual behaviors. The video footage and news commentary on them had the look of both high political drama and sleazy tabloid reporting. Although not as protracted, the news media also reported extensively on a "dossier" apparently put together on Donald Trump that included titillating details of purported exploits with Russian prostitutes. There was also the extensive coverage of Trump's alleged affair with a porn actress, including details of hotel rendezvous. Although some questioned the authenticity of these accounts, the news media still reported. With both the Trump and Clinton scandals, parents were in a quandary as to how to explain these matters to their children. Many lamented the depth to which news reporting had fallen, but no one quite knew what to do about it. Such a story involved the leader of the free world in a possibly illegal offense and thus could not be ignored.

Although such sexually explicit language as occurred in these news stories would not generally be acceptable on prime-time entertainment programming, because these stories were news, their use was not covered by entertainment standards. Still, however, it caused some concern, especially insofar as many people watch TV news and read the newspaper for entertainment purposes.

Casual Sex

Sex before marriage, often shortly after one's first meeting, seems to be the norm in TV and film entertainment today. However, there is somewhat of a double standard depending on whether adolescents or adults are involved. Often for teens, but seldom for adults, the choice of whether to have sex is a difficult or complex decision and consequences are not typically portrayed (Eyal & Finnerty, 2009). Traditional values are far more likely to be affirmed in the end if the storylines involve youth. A teenager may consider having sex with a boyfriend or girlfriend and discuss it openly with family and friends. In the end, however, the teenager may decide that he or she is not ready, choosing to abstain. Even when the decision is affirmative, however, there is considerable moralizing and prior discussion of the behavior, often with parents. Moreover, sometimes there is clear regret afterwards. In such cases, traditional values are more or less affirmed.

In contrast to this moral angst of teen decisions about premarital sex, between adults it appears to be a nonissue in entertainment media. Dramatic TV shows and movies seem to presuppose a norm of early sexual activity on the part of adult dating couples, usually with little if any concern about either moral propriety or protection against pregnancy or sexually transmitted diseases. Casual sex between adults is portrayed as routine and noncontroversial with little indication of either party struggling with the decision. In fact, there is seldom any discussion by either party about whether that is right or whether it is too soon in the relationship. Only in storylines with adolescents does it seem to be considered a moral or developmental issue. Casual and premarital sex are thus treated fairly conservatively in regard to teens and very permissively in regard to adults. For example, on *Glee*, an entire episode was devoted to whether couples Kurt and Blaine and Rachel and Finn were going to have sex. Similar plotlines have played out on shows such as *Gossip Girl*, *Gilmore Girls*, and *Riverdale*. In contrast, even the nerdy single adult characters on *The Big Bang Theory* seem to have sex fairly often.

One concern is a desensitization to certain expressions of sexuality deemed by others to be inappropriate. For example, sitcoms showing teenagers considering being sexually active may disinhibit and thus weaken family-taught values against premarital sex. Fashion ads that sell clothing by showing a scantily clad woman being physically dominated by a man may desensitize readers to violence toward women.

Sometimes the media may actually change one's values or attitudes, rather than merely desensitizing or reinforcing an existing one. For example, if a teen boy watches his favorite sitcom character consider having sex, the teen viewer may approach his own girlfriend about making their relationship sexual. This kind of modeling is especially likely to happen if the TV characters demonstrating certain values are respected characters with whom viewers identify. Sexual promiscuity by a prostitute character is less likely to influence the values of a viewer than promiscuity by a character who is a respected suburban wife and mother.

Extramarital Sex

Although less frequently portrayed than casual and premarital sex, extramarital sex is also not unusual in TV and film and is especially common in soap operas and nighttime dramas like *Scandal*. Depending on the situation, it may be treated comically or seriously. If treated humorously, it may discourage taking seriously the consequences of marital infidelity. If treated seriously, either it may carry the implicit message that adultery is okay, or at least that it does not have terribly serious consequences, or it may convey the message that adultery has serious repercussions for all concerned. The effect on viewers may be very different in these two cases.

In thinking about portrayals of extramarital sex, the first shows that come to mind are soap operas, in which adultery is a frequent theme, even an accepted way of life for many of the characters. In terms of values, both approval and condemnation come through at different times. A sympathetic character who is trapped in an unhappy marriage uses an affair as a relatively healthy outlet for her needs. The inevitable pain and hurt resulting from the adultery may or may not be dealt with in the plotline. Demonstrating a cultivation effect, Buerkel-Rothfuss and Mayes (1981) found that college students' heavy viewing of soap operas was positively correlated with higher estimates of the percentages of people having affairs, divorces, abortions, and illegitimate children, although it was unrelated to their perception of how many people were happily married. The perceived reality constructed from such shows apparently depends not only on the program content, but also on the viewer's motives and uses of the medium, as well as parental values and parent–child discussion and co-viewing (Carveth & Alexander, 1985; Greenberg *et al.*, 1982; Greenberg & Woods, 1999; Perse, 1986). One study, for example (Busselle, 2001), found that the more people had been exposed to TV overall and the more they thought dramatic portrayals were realistic, the more likely they were to believe that adultery was commonplace. Another study found a relationship between the viewing of sexually explicit media and attitudes supporting extramarital sex (Wright, Tokunaga, & Bae, 2014).

Just as extramarital affairs are presented as common, sometimes marital sex is actually denigrated. For example, one episode of the old family sitcom *Married with Children* had the father eye his wife dressed very seductively and say, "Geez, if I weren't married to you, I'd really be turned on about now!" The message is clear: sex within marriage is boring, uninteresting, or otherwise devalued. The good stuff lies elsewhere.

STI Education and Birth Control

Although we accept great amounts of implied or semi-explicit sex on TV, even after the onset of AIDS in the mid-1980s, contraceptive and prophylactic ads were for a long time felt to be too controversial for most U.S. television audiences, although such ads had appeared regularly in magazines for years. It is as if the action of having sexual intercourse is acceptable if done in the heat of a passionate moment, but that planning for it is somehow unseemly or dirty. This communicates a potentially dangerous reality! The teen pregnancy rate is higher in the United States than in any other industrialized country, and such rates elsewhere fell dramatically after media campaigns that included televised birth control ads. It is an interesting paradox that all sorts of non-marital sex, at least some of which would clearly be against the personal values of most Americans, were considered acceptable for story content, but that the use of birth control, a practice consistent with the values and practice of most citizens, was seen as too controversial to advertise or to even mention in storylines. Thus, we see another paradox of fairly extreme permissiveness in regard to non-marital media sex coexisting with extreme conservatism in regard to birth control and protection. Why are premarital and extra-marital sex so acceptable but birth control and a reasonable concern about acquiring sexually transmitted infections perceived as unseemly?

The advertising of condoms had cautiously crept into some cable channels like MTV by the 1990s, but it is still rare. In terms of entertainment programming, storylines continued to portray very casual attitudes toward non-marital sex and its consequences, especially among adults. Although there have recently been increasing numbers of storylines indicating some concern about HIV and other STIs or the use of protection (so-called safe sex), that is still much more the exception than the rule (Kaiser Family Foundation, 2005; Pariera *et al.*, 2014).

Comedic vs. Serious Sex

Another concern about the effects on values and attitudes is that sexually oriented media may encourage people not to take sexual issues seriously. When *Family Guy* has the perpetually aroused and kinky Quagmire as well as a recurring pedophile character, many argue that this is an inappropriately light treatment of an extremely serious subject. It's now commonplace for porn films to parody popular movies and TV shows, with titles like *Game of Bones* and *Edward Penishands*. Although few would be likely to argue that sex should never be comedic, there are for most people some sexual subjects, for example child sexual abuse, that do not seem appropriate for light treatment.

Sometimes a comedic treatment of sex can send a serious message. When the father on *Married with Children* chastised his daughter for receiving a bad grade, upon closer scrutiny he was relieved because "at least it was in sex education." Ironically, this sexually permissive sitcom confirmed a very conservative, and in this case scientifically unsupported, belief that having more knowledge about sex and contraception leads to promiscuity. Even mainstream ads communicate sexual values. When a car ad features two women discussing whether men drive big cars to compensate for the size of their penises ("I wonder what he's got under the hood"), they send a message about what is important about men in the eyes of women. A pizza commercial shows a couple with the wife saying, "The pizza will be here in 30 minutes. What do we do till then?" and the husband saying he has an idea. Then the ad cuts to another scene with the man in his bathrobe and the woman saying, "Now what do we do for the other 28 minutes?" What is the message being communicated about (especially male) sexuality?

Attitudes toward Women

One type of sexual value of particular concern involves men's attitudes toward women. One of the major criticisms of traditional pornography is that it is anti-women in an ideological sense. It is usually women, not men, who are the playthings or victims of the opposite sex. Although this concern spans the gamut of sexual content in media, it is particularly leveled at sexual violence. What are teenage boys who are first learning about sex going to think that women want when they see a picture of a jackhammer in a woman's vagina as the opening photo to a story called "How to Cure Frigidity"? When *Hustler* magazine runs a photo spread of a gang rape turning into an orgy, showing the women appearing to be aroused by the assault, what is being taught about women and their reactions to forcible sex? Can a curious boy resist the temptation to click on Internet links to see *Live Asian Sluts* or *Farm Girls: Bizarre Barnyard Sex*?

Several studies have shown effects on attitudes and values about sex as a result of exposure to nonviolent sexually explicit materials. After seeing slides and movies of beautiful female nudes engaged in sexual activity, men rated their own partners as being less physically endowed, although they reported undiminished sexual satisfaction (Weaver, Masland, & Zillmann, 1984). In another study, men reported loving their own mates less after seeing sexually explicit videos of highly attractive models (Kenrick, Gutierres, & Goldberg, 1989). Men who saw a pornographic video responded more sexually to a subsequent female interviewer than those seeing a control video, although this result only held for men holding traditional gender schemas (McKenzie-Mohr & Zanna, 1990). Yet another study (Sun, Bridges, Johnson, & Ezzell, 2016) found there was a positive correlation between the amount of sexually explicit media men watched and the likelihood they were to ask their partners to perform sex acts they had seen. There was also an association between men watching porn and them thinking about the scenes they had witnessed during sex with their partners.

The sexual material need not be explicit or graphic to affect attitudes. Bryant and Rockwell (1994) found that, compared to controls, teenagers who watched a heavy diet of highly sexual prime-time programs showed an influence on their judgments of the degree of sexual impropriety or of how much the victim had been wronged, although these effects were greatly attenuated by a clear and well-defined family value system, active critical viewing, and open discussion within the family. Some of these results mirror those of a 1980 study in which men who watched a single episode of the *Charlie's Angels* TV show rated real women as less attractive than did men in a control group who had not seen the show before making ratings (Kenrick & Gutierres, 1980). All of these studies showed significant attitude changes after a very limited exposure to sexual media.

More recent research has shed light onto the cognitive processes that may be at play. Specifically, some studies (e.g., Bernard *et al.*, 2012) have indicated that when people, particularly men, see women in the media in sexualized situations (e.g., skimpy outfits), women become objectified. On a deeper level, what may be going on here is that when women are objectified, they are perceived as less human, and indeed more of an object (Vaes, Paladino, & Puvia, 2011).This objectification can lead to assumptions about the women portrayed in media and even women in general. For example, exposure to media (e.g., magazines, television shows, sexually explicit images) that objectify women has been associated with men being more tolerant of sexual harassment (Bernard, Legrand, & Klein, 2018) and violence against women (Wright & Tokunaga, 2016). There can even be "spillover" effects. For example, a group of researchers had male college students read a newspaper page that contained a statement by the university president. In one condition, the statement appeared next to an objectifying ad. In another condition, the statement appeared next to a neutral article. Compared to other conditions, the participants who saw the statement next to an objectifying ad rated the president as less competent (Schooler, 2015).

Attitudes toward Different Sex Acts

Exposing ourselves to sexual media can also affect our perceptions of sex practices. Using a paradigm of showing participants weekly films and testing them 1 to 3 weeks later, Zillmann and Bryant (1982, 1984) found that participants watching sexually explicit films overestimated the frequency of sexual practices like fellatio, cunnilingus, anal intercourse, sadomasochism, and bestiality, relative to perceptions of a control group seeing nonsexual films. This may reflect the cognitive *heuristic of availability*, whereby we judge the frequency of occurrence of various activities by the ease with which we can generate examples (Kahneman, 2011; Taylor, 1982; Tversky & Kahneman, 1973, 1974). In line with cultivation theory, vivid media instances thus lead to an overestimation of such behavior in the real world and a perceived reality at odds with actual reality. These kinds of cognitive misperceptions may translate into our own behaviors (or behavior intentions). For example, compared to other teens, adolescents who consumed sexually explicit media were more likely to say they would engage in casual sex (van Oosten, Peter, & Vandenbosch, 2017). Similarly, gay men who had viewed a film of men having unprotected sex were more likely to say they would do the same than gay men who had watched a film that depicted sex with condoms (Jonas, Hawk, Vastenburg, & de Groot, 2014).

Behavioral and Cognitive Effects

Another large class of effects of sexual media consists of effects on behavior, or how consuming sexual media leads to changes in actual sexual behaviors. Research on some of these behavioral (and a few cognitive) effects are discussed in this section.

Teaching New Behaviors

On the one hand, sexual media may actually teach new behaviors. As part of sex therapy, a couple may buy a sex manual like *The Joy of Sex* in order to learn new sexual positions or behaviors that they had not tried before. New behaviors are not always so benign, however. One issue of *Penthouse* contained a series of photographs of Asian women bound with heavy rope, hung from trees, and sectioned into parts. Two months later an 8-year-old Chinese girl in Chapel Hill, North Carolina, was kidnapped, raped, murdered, and left hanging from a tree limb (*New York Times*, 1985, cited in Department of Justice, 1986, p. 208). In the United Kingdom, a 12-year-old boy repeatedly raped his younger sister after becoming fascinated with incest porn he accessed on the Internet (Worley, 2016). Thankfully, such cases are not commonplace, and definitively demonstrating a causal relationship between exposure to the media and acting the behavior is difficult, but the juxtaposition is nonetheless disturbing.

Disinhibition of Known Behaviors

As discussed earlier in this chapter, erotic material may also disinhibit previously learned behaviors, as when the viewing of TV's treatment of premarital sex disinhibits a viewer's inhibition against engaging in such behavior. Watching a rape scene in which a woman is portrayed as enjoying being assaulted may weaken some men's moral prohibitions against committing such a crime. This is of particular concern given some evidence suggesting that a surprisingly large number of college men reported that they might commit rape if they were sure they would not be caught (Check, 1985; Stotzer & MacCartney, 2016).

Sex Crimes

One of the main concerns about a behavioral effect of viewing sexually explicit materials is that such viewing may lead to sex crimes. There have been many studies that have looked at rates of crimes like rape, sexual assault, indecent exposure, and child sexual molestation, relative to changes in the availability of sexually explicit materials. Drawing scientifically sound general conclusions has been difficult, however. Court (1977, 1982, 1984) argued that there is in fact a correlation between availability of sexually explicit materials and certain sex crimes. Court claimed that earlier studies, especially the Kutchinsky (1973) study claiming a drop in reported sex crimes in Denmark after liberalization of pornography restrictions in the 1960s, were not really valid, due to an inappropriate lumping of rape with nonviolent acts of voyeurism, indecent exposure, and gay sex.

Most Western nations have experienced a large increase in both the availability of sexually explicit media and the rise in reported rapes in the last 50 years. However, Court (1984) presented some data from two Australian states that showed a sharp increase in rape reports in South Australia, but not Queensland, after state pornography laws were liberalized in South Australia in the early 1970s. A comparable downturn in reported rapes occurred temporarily in Hawaii between 1974 and 1976 during a temporary imposition of restraints on sexually explicit media. For an interesting apparent counterexample, see Close-up 10.5.

❖ CLOSE-UP 10.5 PORNOGRAPHY IN JAPAN

Japan is an interesting and unusual case study of a society with wide availability of sexual media, but very low rape rates (Diamond & Uchiyama, 1999). Sexual themes in art and society go back centuries to ancient religious fertility objects and wood block prints called ukiyo-e. Although some restriction and censorship occurred after the Meiji Restoration in 1868 and even more under the U.S. occupation that began in 1945, sexuality continued to be a strong theme of Japanese society and one not particularly associated with shame or guilt. Although there are specific restrictions in Japan on showing pictorial representations of pubic hair or adult genitalia, there is less compartmentalization of sexual media to certain types of magazines, bookstores, or theaters than occurs in the United States. There has even been a surge of popularity in recent years of "elder-porn," series with names like Maniac Training of Lolitas and Forbidden Elderly Care, which star actors into their 70s and have been immensely popular with the aging population of Japan ("Japan's Sex Industry," 2018; Toyama, 2008). Why, then, is the incidence of reported rapes so much lower in Japan than elsewhere (2.4 per 100,000 vs. 34.5 in the United States, 10.1 in England, and 10.7 in Germany)? Abramson and Hayashi (1984) argued that the answer may lie in cultural differences. Japanese society emphasizes order, obligation, cooperation, and virtue, and one *who violates social norms is the object of shame. Others have suggested that rape in Japan is more likely to be group instigated, perpetrated by juveniles, and greatly underreported by victims (Goldstein & Ibaraki, 1983).*

Firmly establishing a causal relationship between the availability of sexually explicit media and the frequency of rape is extremely difficult, due to the many other relevant factors that cannot be controlled, including the different varieties of sexual material, changes in social consciousness about reporting sexual assaults, and changing norms that sanction such behavior.

Although some have argued from the evidence that an increase in sex crimes follows greater availability of sexually explicit media (Court, 1984) and others have argued that there is no such demonstrated relationship (Diamond, Jozifkova, & Weiss, 2011; Kutchinsky, 1991), there has been no recent support for an explanation that greater availability of sexually explicit media decreases the rate of sex crimes. However, some experimental studies (Vega & Malamuth, 2007), surveys (Simons, Wurtele, & Durham, 2008), and reviews (Bauserman, 1996; Malamuth, Addison, & Koss, 2000) have concluded that there is an association between the heavy consumption of sexually explicit media, especially sexual violence, and the perpetration of sex crimes.

Socialization of Adolescent Behavior

Teenagers who watch a heavy diet of television with sexual content were twice as likely to engage in sexual intercourse over the following year as teens who were light viewers of sexual content, even after controlling for other possible factors (Collins, Elliott, Berry, Kanouse, & Hunter, 2003). Heavy TV viewing of sexual content was also associated with other non-coital sexual behaviors (heavy petting, deep kissing, etc.). These findings were the same regardless of whether the sexual content was explicitly shown in behavior or only discussed in dialogue. In another, longitudinal study on adolescents, a relationship was found between heavy exposure to sexual media (music, movies, TV, and magazines) at ages 12–14 and having had sexual intercourse by 14–16 (Brown *et al.*, 2006). One study even found that heavy exposure to sexual content on television predicted teen pregnancy, even when controlling for other variables like low grades and deviant behaviors (Chandra *et al.*, 2008). However, parental or mixed-sex co-viewing of media with sexual content lowered the likelihood of teens engaging in sexual intercourse (Parkes, Wight, Hunt, Henderson, & Sargent, 2013). Of course, the causative relation works both ways: more sexually active adolescents seek out more sex in the media, and those exposed to more sex in media gradually become more sexually active themselves (Bleakley, Hennessy, Fishbein, & Jordan, 2008). Also, one recent meta-analysis indicated that the overall correlation between consuming sexual media and adolescent sexual behavior may be relatively weak (Ferguson, Nielsen, & Markey, 2017).

Catharsis

Another alleged effect of media sex is catharsis, that emotional release so important to psychodynamic models of personality (e.g., Freud; Scheele & DuBois, 2006). Applied to sex, the catharsis argument says that consuming media sex relieves sexual urges, with the erotic film or magazine acting (perhaps in conjunction with masturbation) as a sort of imperfect substitute for the real thing. A catharsis argument was used some years ago by civil libertarians to support appeals for lessening restrictions on sexually explicit material (Kutchinsky, 1973). However, the research support for catharsis as a function of viewing media sex is basically nonexistent (Bushman *et al.*, 1999; U.S. Department of Justice, 1986) and is not researched much by media scholars these days. In fact, exposure to sexual media typically energizes the sex drive and leads one to do more, not less, to try to satisfy it. However, as we saw with the violence research on catharsis, the popular belief in this scientifically discredited process remains strong.

Sexting

A number of effects have been noted in the research for a newer kind of sexual communication, sexting, discussed briefly earlier in this chapter. Although usually more a form of interpersonal than mass communication, *sexting*, sending or receiving sexual words and/or images online, is increasingly easy and common (Galovan, Drouin, & McDaniel, 2018). People can send sexts via their mobile phone's text function or through social media like Snapchat. They may or may not sext with persons with whom they have a face-to-face relationship.

Of particular concern is sexting among young people (Strohmaier, Murphy, & DeMatteo, 2014). Sexting prevalence among youth has varied across studies. One review (Barrense-Dias, Berchtold, Surís, & Akre, 2017) found that depending on the definition, prevalence rates ranged from 0.9% to 60% among children and adolescents! However, among young adults, most of those who have reported sexting say they have only tried it once or do it only occasionally, and there seems to be no clear evidence whether those of different genders or sexual orientations sext more or less (Dir, Coskunpinar, Steiner, & Cyders, 2013).

Studies have also shown various effects and associations with sexting behavior. In particular, sexting among young adults has been associated with greater consumption of sexually explicit media (Galovan *et al.*, 2018), higher sensation seeking (Champion & Pedersen, 2015; Dir & Cyders, 2015), and poorer personal relationships (Galovan *et al.*, 2018). Sexting among youth has been connected with alcohol and marijuana use as well as bullying and being a victim of bullying (Woodward, Evans, & Brooks, 2017).

Many juveniles may not fully understand the possible legal ramifications of sexting (such as the images being shared widely online or the possibility of the images being considered child pornography) (Dir & Cyders, 2015; Strohmaier *et al.*, 2014). Saved sexts are sometimes a tool of aggression, such as when they are used as "revenge porn," the non-consensual sharing of nude or sexual images with the intent to harm (Bothamley & Tully, 2018; Walker & Sleath, 2017).

Interference with Cognitive Processing

Although there has been very little study of the effects of sexual media on information processing, at least one study suggests watching sexy pictures really can make young men think less clearly. See Close-up 10.6.

❖ CLOSE-UP 10.6 DOES WATCHING WOMEN IN BIKINIS REALLY MAKE MEN STUPID?

Believe it or not, three Belgian researchers (Van den Bergh, Dewitte, & Warlop, 2008) conducted several studies to examine this question. In one, young men watched either a series of landscapes or a series of pictures of women in bikinis or lingerie. In another they were given a series of either T-shirts or bras to examine and evaluate. In a third they watched a video of either a group of men or bikini-clad young women running across landscapes. Afterward, all the men were given a choice of receiving 15 euros immediately or bargaining for more over a longer period of time. In each case the men exposed to the sexual media or clothing settled for a less lucrative bet and chose not to negotiate for a better deal. Apparently the bikinis had made them more impulsive and less thoughtful, seeking more immediate gratification, rather than holding out for what would probably be a better deal.

Positive Socialization Effects

Although consuming sexual media is frequently associated with negative outcomes, sexual content in media can have positive effects like increasing knowledge and instigating information seeking. For example, after an episode of the medical drama *ER* with three minutes on emergency contraception, 51% of viewers reported talking with others about the issue, 23% sought information from another source, and 14% talked to their doctor about it (Kaiser Family Foundation, 2002). After an episode of *Friends* that portrayed a pregnancy resulting from condom failure, about two thirds of viewers aged 12 to 17 reported learning that condoms could fail, and most remembered that six months later (Collins *et al.*, 2003). After airing several episodes of a character dealing with an HIV diagnosis in 2001, the soap opera *The Bold and the Beautiful* displayed the National STD and AIDS Hotline toll-free phone number. During the time periods when those episodes aired (and immediately afterward), the number of calls to the hotline increased significantly (Kennedy, O'Leary, Beck, Pollard, & Simpson, 2004). Even racy shows may show positive sex behaviors. An analysis of the HBO show *Girls* showed that compared to other programs, *Girls* contained far more character discussion of sexual risks and responsibilities (Stevens & Garrett, 2016). For a review of how TV dramas can affect other perceptions of health, see Hoffman, Shensa, Wessel, Hoffman, and Primack (2017).

Context of Sexuality

The perceived reality of media sex and the effects of sex in media also depend on the context of the sexual images and the context in which the person sees it, all of which can make an enormous difference in the experience of consuming sexually explicit media. One of the relevant contextual variables is the degree of playfulness or seriousness of the material. For example, a documentary on rape or a tastefully done TV drama on incest may be considered perfectly acceptable, whereas a far less explicit comedy with the same theme may be highly offensive and considered too sexual. What is really the concern in such cases is not the sex as such, but rather the comedic treatment of it.

A second contextual consideration is the artistic worth and intent. We react very differently to a sexually explicit drawing by Picasso versus one in *Hustler* magazine. Shakespeare, Chaucer, the Song of Solomon in the Bible, and serious sex manuals like *The Joy of Sex* are seen to have serious literary or didactic intentions, and thus the sex therein is considered acceptable, perhaps even healthy. One interesting issue in this regard is how to respond to something of clear artistic worth that was written at a time when standards differed from what they are today. For example, should Rhett Butler's forcing his attentions on Scarlett O'Hara in *Gone with the Wind* be seen as rape or as the noncontroversial romantic moment that it appeared to be in 1939? In fact, a man continuing to press his sexual desires against a woman who has clearly stated her wish that he stop is today legally defined as rape; however, this was a common theme in films in the mid-twentieth century.

The relation and integration of sex to the overall plot and intent of the piece is another important contextual factor. A sex scene, even a mild and non-explicit one, may be offensive if it appears to be thrown in merely to spice up the story but has no intrinsic connection to the plot. Something far more explicit may find greater acceptance if it is necessary and central to the storyline. Sex scenes in a story about a prostitute may be much less gratuitous than comparable scenes in a story about a female corporate executive. Sex, of course, is not the only common gratuitous factor in media; for example, TV shows and movies frequently insert car chases and rock video-style sequences only tangentially related to the plot.

The context of the viewing also influences the experience and effect of sex in the media. Watching an erotic film may elicit different reactions, depending on whether you watch it with your parents, your grandparents, or your children, by yourself, in a group of close friends, or with your significant other. It can be seen as more or less erotic or arousing and more or less entertaining, appropriate, or offensive. For example, watching a movie that is more sexual than you had realized with a first date might be quite embarrassing, whereas it might be quite enjoyable and arousing if seen with a long-time partner. In a study asking college students to rate the degree of hypothetical discomfort from watching various types of movies with different co-viewers, by far the most uncomfortable situation was watching an R-rated sexually explicit movie with one's parents (Harris & Cook, 2011).

The cultural context is also important. Some cultures do not consider female breasts to be particularly erotic or inappropriate for public view. We recognize these cultural differences and thus, at least after the age of 14, most readers do not consider topless women from an unfamiliar culture in a documentary to be the slightest bit erotic, sexual, or inappropriate. Even in Western culture, standards have changed. For much of the nineteenth century, knees and calves were thought to be erotic, and the sight of a bare-kneed woman would be as scandalous, even as sexually arousing, as would a topless woman today. As societies go, North America overall is a bit more conservative in allowable sexual expression than many Western European or Latin American cultures but far more permissive than most Islamic and East Asian cultures.

Messages about sexuality are often, though by no means always, presented in a context of romance, especially so in song lyrics and TV and movie entertainment, much less so in the case of pornography. Romance, however, has its own media skewing. There are prevalent myths about romance which emanate from song lyrics of virtually every genre and era, as well as from love stories in TV and movies (Galician, 2004, 2007). To the extent that these drive people's search for mates and evaluation of relationships, they may be using very unrealistic, even impossible, standards. Contrary to popular belief, it is not only women who like romantic movies or are affected by romantic myths (Harris *et al.*, 2004; Taylor, 2015). See Close-up 10.7 for the 12 media myths of romance.

> ❖ **CLOSE-UP 10.7 MEDIA'S MYTHS OF ROMANCE**
>
> *Related to sexuality is romance, which is also the subject of interesting and sometimes less than helpful media messages. Galician (2004, 2007) argues that the media perpetuate 12 myths of romance which lead young viewers to expect very unrealistic outcomes from relationships. These myths are rampant in song lyrics, movie plotlines, TV shows, Internet quizzes, and self-help magazine articles.*
>
> 1. *Your perfect partner is cosmically predestined, so nothing/nobody can ultimately separate you.*
> 2. *"Love at first sight" exists and is highly desirable.*
> 3. *Your true "soul mate" should know what you're thinking or feeling without you having to tell.*
> 4. *If your partner is truly "meant for you," sex is easy and wonderful.*
> 5. *To attract and keep a man, a woman should look like a model or centerfold.*
> 6. *The man should not be shorter, weaker, younger, poorer, or less successful than the woman.*
> 7. *The love of a good and faithful true woman can change a man from a "beast" into a "prince."*
> 8. *Bickering and fighting a lot mean that a man and a woman really love each other passionately.*
> 9. *All you really need is love, so it doesn't matter if you and your partner have very different values.*
> 10. *The right mate "completes you," filling your needs and making your dreams come true.*
> 11. *In real life, actors are often like the romantic characters they portray.*
> 12. *Since mass media portrayals of romance aren't "real," they don't really affect you.*
>
> *All of these are wrong, in terms of people's real lives and what the research shows (a perusal of most social psychology textbooks will verify the falsehood of most of these myths). How many of them do you (perhaps secretly) believe and how do these affect how you look at relationships? Where did you get these ideas, anyway? Look to the media.*

Finally, the expectations we have about the appearance of media sex affect our perception. Sex is less offensive and shocking if it is expected than if it appears as a surprise. Seeing a video of an orgy on a sexually explicit website is less shocking than suddenly encountering explicit sex in a *New York Times* article. The stimulus may be similar, but the perceived experiential reality of the fact of seeing it would differ considerably in the two cases.

We now examine that potent combination of sex and violence in the media: sexual violence.

Sexual Violence

Although neither sex nor violence in the media is new, the integral combination of the two has become more prevalent in recent decades. As discussed previously, cable, digital, and Internet technology have greatly expanded the capability of privately and conveniently viewing all sorts of sexually explicit material. Whereas many people would not have been comfortable seeking out and visiting theaters that showed such films in the past, the chance to view such material safely and privately in one's own home or hotel room today makes it much more accessible. Another old familiar genre, the horror film, has evolved into showing frequent and extensive scenes of violence against women in a sexual context. These films are widely viewed by teens and preteens, in spite of their R ratings. A major concern beyond the sex or violence itself is the way the two appear together. The world constructed in the mind of the viewer of such materials can have some very serious consequences. Let us turn now to examining some of the effects of viewing sexual violence.

Erotica as Stimulator of Aggression

Links between sex and aggression have long been speculated upon, particularly in the sense of sexual arousal facilitating violent behavior. The research has been inconsistent, however, with some studies showing that erotic materials facilitate aggression (Baron, 1979; Donnerstein & Hallam, 1978; Willoughby, Carroll, Busby, & Brown, 2016) and others showing that they inhibit it (Donnerstein, Donnerstein, & Evans, 1975; White, 1979). The resolution of this issue apparently concerns the nature of the material. Sexual violence and unpleasant themes typically facilitate aggression, whereas nonviolent, more loving and pleasant soft-core explicit materials may inhibit it (Kingston, Fedoroff, Firestone, Curry, & Bradford, 2008; Sapolsky, 1984; Zillmann, Bryant, Comisky, & Medoff, 1981). Individual differences such as overall aggression levels and agreeableness also play a role in whether sexual aggression is perceived as sexually arousing (Baer, Kohut, & Fisher, 2015; Hald & Malamuth, 2015; Kingston & Malamuth, 2011) as do the kinds of aggression depicted (verbal and/or physical) (Wright, Tokunaga, & Kraus, 2016).

How the Woman Is Portrayed

Men who see films with scenes of sexual violence later show a more callous attitude toward rape and women in general, especially if the women victims were portrayed as being aroused by the assault. In terms of sexual arousal, men were aroused by the sexual violence only if the victim was shown to be aroused but not if she was not so portrayed (Malamuth, 1984). Also, when female characters in sexually violent media are portrayed as subordinate, the result tends to be more negative attitudes toward women. Interestingly, however, negative attitudes toward women don't seem to result from sexually violent media that portray female characters as empowered (Ferguson, 2012).

Individual Differences in Male Viewers

While viewing sexually violent media, convicted sex offenders tend to be aroused by both rape and consenting sex, whereas men in control groups are aroused only by the consenting sex (Abel, Barlow, Blanchard, & Guild, 1977; Harris, Lalumière, Seto, Rice, & Chaplin, 2012; Quinsey, Chapman, & Upfold, 1984; Rice, Chaplin, Harris, & Coutts, 1994). An important exception to this occurs if the victim is portrayed as enjoying the rape and coming to orgasm; in this case non-rapist U.S. and Japanese college men, though not women, were equally or more aroused by the rape than by the consenting sex (Malamuth, Heim, & Feshbach, 1980; Ohbuchi, Ikeda, & Takeuchi, 1994).

Malamuth and Check (1983) had men listen to an audiotape of a sexual encounter of either (1) consenting sex; (2) non-consenting sex in which the woman showed arousal; or (3) non-consenting sex in which she showed disgust. When the woman showed disgust, both dispositionally violent and nonviolent men were more aroused by the consenting than the nonconsenting (rape) scene. However, when the woman was portrayed as being aroused, the nonviolent men were equally aroused by both consenting and non-consenting versions, whereas the violent men actually showed more arousal to the non-consenting (rape) version. Analogous results were obtained using video stimuli (Malamuth, 1981). Using a similar design, Bushman, Bonacci, van Dijk, and Baumeister (2003) discovered that men scoring high in narcissism found a rape scene preceded by affection between the parties as more entertaining and more sexually arousing than those low in narcissism did. It has also been demonstrated that among sex offenders, arousal during sexually violent media is a good predictor for sex crime recidivism (Kingston, Seto, Firestone, & Bradford, 2010).

Some situational variables can affect arousal as well. For example, ordinary men were more aroused than usual by a rape scene if they had been previously angered by a female confederate (Yates, Barbaree, & Marshall, 1984). Also, alcohol consumption can decrease sensitivity to victim distress and thus allow greater arousal to sexual violence (Norris, George, Davis, Martell, & Leonesio, 1999). Alcohol can even affect women's judgments. Women reading an eroticized rape description while intoxicated were less likely than a sober control group to label coercive sex events as rape (Davis, Norris, George, Martell, & Heiman, 2006). In addition, Shope (2004) found that men who used sexually explicit media, especially if they also abused alcohol, were more likely than nonusers to batter their partners.

Can such effects transfer to new situations? Donnerstein and Berkowitz (1981; see also Donnerstein, 1980) showed men a sexually violent film in which a woman was attacked, stripped, tied up, and raped. In one version of the film, the woman was portrayed as enjoying the rape. Afterward, participants were given a chance to administer electric shocks to a confederate who had earlier angered them. Men who had seen the film in which the woman appeared to enjoy being raped administered more shocks to a female confederate, though not to a male. This suggests that the association of sex and violence in the film allows violent behavior to be transferred to a new situation.

Most of this research has been conducted on men, partially because women have different bodily arousal processes in response to sexual media, and results testing women's physical arousal in response to media have been mixed (Lee, Hust, Zhang, & Zhang, 2011; Suschinsky & Lalumière, 2011). However, a few studies examining women and sexually violent media have shown behavioral effects of increased aggression toward other women (Baron, 1979) and desensitization effects of trivialization of rape and acceptance of rape myths (defined in Chapter 9) and more traditional gender-role attitudes (Malamuth, Check, & Briere, 1986; Mayerson & Taylor, 1987; Schwarz & Brand, 1983; Zillmann & Bryant, 1982).

Sexual Violence: Conclusions

In a meta-analysis of studies examining the relationship of exposure to sexually explicit media and the acceptance of rape myths, researchers conclude that experimental studies show a consistent positive effect between pornography exposure and rape myth acceptance, while non-experimental studies show only a very small positive or nonexistent effect. The relationship was consistently stronger with violent than non-violent erotica, although some experimental studies obtained effects from both (Allen *et al.*, 1995). Also see the section entitled "Press Coverage of Sexually Violent Crimes" later in this chapter for further discussion of rape myths.

Several conclusions emerge from the sexual violence research. The most critical aspect of the sexually violent film is whether the woman is shown as enjoying and being aroused by the assault. Far more undesirable effects occur in men if the woman is shown as aroused than if she is seen to be terrorized. This media portrayal of women as being turned on by rape is not only a highly unrealistic and distasteful deviation from reality, but also a potentially dangerous one. For example, imagine how a sexually inexperienced young man might behave with a real woman if his primary model for sexual behavior has been sexually violent media he's found online. A second important conclusion is that sexually violent media affect men differently, depending on their propensity to use force in their own lives. Convicted rapists and other men prone to use violence in their own lives are more likely to become aroused or even incited to violence by sexually violent media, even more so if the woman is portrayed as being aroused by the assault. Also see Bridges and Anton (2013) for a review of research on sexually violent media and its effects.

Slasher Films

The studies discussed so far in this section used very sexually explicit materials that would usually be considered hard-core pornography. However, sexual violence is by no means confined to material generally considered pornographic.

Sex and Violence in Mainstream Movies

Hundreds of mainstream R-rated films are readily available to teenagers anywhere, especially on DVD and online. There are the highly successful series like *Halloween*, *Child's Play*, *Friday the Thirteenth*, *Scream*, *Nightmare on Elm Street*, *Happy Death Day*, *Saw*, and *The Texas Chainsaw Massacre*. Many are extremely violent with strong sexual overtones. This genre of film is often identified as *slasher movies*, in which victims, often female, are pursued by a violent aggressor, usually a male acting alone (Molitor & Sapolsky, 1993; Weaver, Ménard, Cabrera, & Taylor, 2015). Some have noted a trend toward stronger, less victimized female characters in some films like *Urban Legend*, *I Know What You Did Last Summer*, and *The Bride of Chucky*. Even the 1995 James Bond movie *Goldeneye* featured a villainess who seduces Bond, only to alternatively pull a gun on him or throw him against a wall and kiss or embrace him passionately. Such seduction scenes show very violent mutual battering as a sort of foreplay. In some countries, rape and other acts of violence against women are even more standard entertainment fare (see Close-up 10.8).

❖ CLOSE-UP 10.8 RAPE TO SELL, INDIAN STYLE

By far, the nation producing the largest number of movies annually is India (Cain, 2015). Some of these use rape scenes as major audience draws. The great Indian epics Mahabharata *and* Ramayana *have demure heroines who are nearly raped but are rescued just in time from their attackers by their own virtue. This theme also appears in Indian movies featuring the same type of heroine. But the women characters who are portrayed as more independent, corrupt, immoral, or even morally ambiguous must suffer their fate, which is more typically blamed on their lifestyle rather than on the attacker. One film,* Crime Time, *advertised: "See first-time underwater rapes on Indian screen." A popular Indian actor, Ranjeet, has enacted over 350 rape scenes in his career (Pratap, 1990). There also seems to be an ongoing theme in many Bollywood movies that women don't really mean it when they resist sexual advances (Brook, 2014). In addition, the rate of actual rapes in India is quite high, and the number of reported rapes of children has doubled in recent years (Biswas, 2018). Is Bollywood to blame? Indian mega movie star Shah Rukh Khan doesn't think so. "You know that's like saying 'You show violence on a film then that comes on the streets.' I haven't seen comedy come on streets because of comedy, then why do you start assuming that the treatment of women, and the commodification of women is now coming on because of Bollywood. I don't think so at all" (Brook, 2014, ¶11).*

Although most slasher films have R ratings in the United States, others are released unrated to avoid the accompanied-by-parent restriction of R-rated movies. Because few restrictions apply in stores or on the Internet, the rating is not a major issue. The viewing of such films is widespread among youth. Oliver (1993) found that punitive attitudes toward sexuality and traditional attitudes toward women's sexuality were associated with high school students' greater enjoyment of previews of slasher films.

The major concern with slasher films is the juxtaposition of erotic sex and violence. Arguably, this began when a nude Janet Leigh was stabbed to death in the 1960 Alfred Hitchcock movie *Psycho*. More recent slasher films have gotten considerably more graphic. For example, the 2007 horror hit *Hostel: Part II* is set in a mysterious Slovakian spa where rich people can pay large sums of money to experience the thrill of torturing and killing someone. Three young American women in Rome are lured eastward to become the next victims. One scene in the film shows a woman suspended upside down and naked and being tortured with a sickle. Another shows her head being sliced open with a circular saw, while a third shows two vicious dogs eating her various body parts. Other scenes in recent horror films include a naked woman strung up in a meat locker and sprayed with cold water that turns to ice (*Saw III*), the organs of a woman disemboweled by a truck and shining in the sun (*The Devil's Rejects*), and six young women spelunkers being tormented by creepy men/monsters, with one left standing in a pool of blood reaching up to her chin (*The Descent*) (Keegan, 2006). Although sex is a key element of slasher films, one content analysis (Welsh, 2010) found that compared to female characters who did not have sex, those who did were less likely to survive and more likely to have lingering death scenes. The women who do survive in slasher films, sometimes labeled "final girls," usually are not nude or seen having sex, either (Weaver et al., 2015).

Effects of Viewing Slasher Films

A series of studies starting in the 1980s examined the effects of viewing slasher films (Linz *et al.*, 1984; Linz, Donnerstein, & Adams, 1989). Male college students were initially screened to exclude those who had prior hostile tendencies or psychological problems. The remaining men in the experimental group were shown one standard

Hollywood R-rated film per day over one week. All of the films were very violent and showed multiple instances of women being killed in slow, lingering, painful deaths in situations associated with erotic content. Each day the participants completed questionnaires evaluating the film, as well as some personality measures. These ratings showed that the men became progressively less depressed, less annoyed, and less anxious in response to the films during the week. The films themselves were gradually rated over time as more enjoyable, more humorous, more socially meaningful, less violent and offensive, and less degrading to women. Over the week's time, the violent episodes in general and rape episodes in particular were remembered as occurring less and less frequently. A similar study (Krafka, Linz, Donnerstein, & Penrod, 1997) tested women and did not find the same effects on perception. Although these data provide clear evidence of desensitization in men, there is still the question of whether there is generalization from the films to other situations.

To answer this question, the same people participated in what they thought was an unrelated study (Krafka *et al.*, 1997; Linz, Turner, Hesse, & Penrod, 1984; Weisz & Earls, 1995). For these experiments, participants observed a mock rape trial at a law school and evaluated it. Compared to control groups seeing nonsexual violent or sexually explicit nonviolent films, both men and women who had seen the sexually violent films, regardless of whether a man or a woman was the rape victim, rated the female rape victim in the trial as less physically and emotionally injured. These results are consistent with those of Zillmann and Bryant (1984), who found that jurors' massive exposure to sexually explicit media, even nonviolent, resulted in shorter recommended prison sentences for a rapist. Such findings show that the world we construct in response to seeing such movies not only can be at odds with reality but also can have very serious consequences when actions are taken in response to believing that such a world is reality.

Although a majority of these studies have been done with male participants viewing women as the sex object, gender is obviously a very important variable (Clover, 1992; Grant, 1996; Pinedo, 1997), and men and women see these films quite differently. In an interesting text analysis of students' writing about the most memorable slasher film they had seen, Nolan and Ryan (2000) found that men wrote more themes with fear of strangers and rural landscapes, while women wrote more about betrayed intimacy, stalkings, and spiritual possession.

Slasher Films: Conclusions

Although the slasher movie genre may be experiencing a bit of a resurgence (Lee, 2017), arguably, the heyday of slasher movies was during the 1970s through the 1990s (Murphy, 2017). That era also saw the majority of the effects of viewing slasher films. Not surprisingly, these studies caused considerable concern in the public, as well as considerable scientific concern. Some of the major effects have not been replicated in later work (Linz & Donnerstein, 1988), and there have been some methodological (Weaver, 1991) and content (Sapolsky & Molitor, 1996) criticisms.

The sharp distinction that Donnerstein and Linz have made between the effects of violent and nonviolent sexually explicit media has been questioned by some. Zillmann and Bryant (1988c) argued that Linz and Donnerstein were too quick to cite failures to reject the null hypothesis as support for the harmlessness of nonviolent sexually explicit media. Further, Check and Guloien (1989) found that men exposed to a steady diet of rape-myth-supporting sexual violence reported a higher likelihood of committing rape themselves, compared to a no-exposure control group; however, the same result was found for a group exposed to nonviolent sexually explicit material. There is considerable controversy, both scientific and political (see Close-up 10.9), about the use and interpretation of data from particular studies. Although there is some difference of opinion about how serious the effects of nonviolent sexual media are, there is little dispute about the serious effects of sexual violence in media, especially if it shows the woman as being aroused by being attacked.

❖ CLOSE-UP 10.9 THE PORNOGRAPHY COMMISSIONS, OR WHY SCIENCE AND POLITICS DON'T MIX

A commission was established by U.S. President Lyndon Johnson in 1967 to analyze (1) pornography control laws; (2) the distribution of sexually explicit materials; (3) the effects of consuming such materials; and (4) to recommend appropriate legislative or administrative action. It funded more than 80 research studies on the topic, providing an important impetus to the scientific study of sexually explicit material. The final report three years later recommended stronger controls on distribution to minors but an abolition of all limits on access by adults. The latter recommendation was based on the majority conclusion that "there was no evidence that exposure to or use of explicit sexual materials play a significant role in the causation of social or individual harms such as crime, delinquency, sexual or nonsexual deviancy or severe emotional disturbance" (Commission on Obscenity and Pornography, 1970, p. 58). Although the composition of the commission was criticized for being overloaded with anticensorship civil libertarians, its majority conclusions were rejected anyway by the new administration of Richard Nixon, who declared, "so long as I am in the White House there will be no relaxation of the national effort to control and eliminate smut from our national life" (Eysenck & Nias, 1978, p. 94).

Fifteen years later during the Reagan administration, a second commission was formed. U.S. Attorney General Edwin Meese charged this commission to assess the nature, extent, and impact of pornography on U.S. society, and to recommend more effective ways to contain the spread of pornography, clearly stating a political position. One of the major conclusions of the commission dealt with the effect of sexual violence: "the available evidence strongly supports the hypothesis that substantial exposure to sexually violent materials bears a causal relationship to antisocial acts of sexual violence, and for some subgroups, possibly the unlawful acts of sexual violence" (Department of Justice, 1986, p. 40).

Groups like these commissions typically have both a scientific and a political agenda (Einsiedel, 1988; Paletz, 1988; Wilcox, 1987). Sometimes, even if there is relative consensus on the scientific conclusions, there is often strong disagreement about the policy ramifications. For example, Linz, Donnerstein, and Penrod (1987) took exception to some of the conclusions drawn by the 1986 commission from those researchers' own work demonstrating deleterious effects of sexual violence. Linz and colleagues (1987) argued that the commission's call for strengthening obscenity laws was not an appropriate policy change based on the research, because it ignored the strong presence of sexually violent themes in other media not covered by such laws.

Such political-scientific adventures are not unique to the United States. During the same period, the Longford (1972) and Williams (1979) commissions in Great Britain issued reports, followed a few years later by the Fraser commission in Canada (Report of the Special Committee on Pornography and Prostitution, 1985). The major conclusion of these commissions was that there is a lack of conclusiveness of the research to date. As of 2018, there has not been another wide-ranging government-sanctioned study of the effects of sexually explicit media. Do such commissions serve a useful purpose, and would one get much traction among politicians or the public today?

Press Coverage of Sexually Violent Crimes

In addition to entertainment media, the news media can have an effect on how we perceive sex and violence. The way that the press covers crimes like rape can subtly support rape myths. For example, even severe violence may sometimes be described in terms of passion or love by reporters. When a woman kills her husband's alleged mistress and then herself, the press may call it a "love triangle." When a man shoots and kills several co-workers, including a woman who refused to date him, it is called a "tragedy of spurned love." When a man kidnaps, rapes, and strangles to death his estranged wife, the press reports that he "made love to his wife, and then choked her when he became overcome with jealous passion" (Jones, 1994; Sokmensuer, 2018). Does love really have anything to do with such crimes?

Benedict (1992) identified several problems with the newspaper coverage of sex crimes. To begin with, there is often a gender bias of the writers, reporters, and editors covering such crimes. Traditionally, reporters who cover rape cases are more likely to be male than female and are usually crime and police reporters. There is also a gender bias of language, with women more likely than men to be described in terms of their physical appearance and sexuality. A content analysis of local television news (Dowler, 2006) found that compared to other crime stories, sexual crime reporting also focused on fear.

Some rape myths are subtly supported by describing rape as a crime due to unfulfilled sexual need. Less often do we encounter rape presented as an act of torture, although that perspective is more likely to be used in reporting of wartime rapes. For example, when mass rapes of Bosnian women occurred in the Bosnian civil war of the mid-1990s, they were reported as acts of war and torture, and there was no description of the victims' attractiveness or dress or flirtatious behavior.

In her content analysis studies of numerous newspaper reports of several high-profile rape cases, Benedict (1992) identified two common rape narratives, both of which distort and trivialize the crime. The most common "story" is the *vamp*, a sexy woman who incites the lust of a man, who then cannot control himself and rapes her. A second narrative is the *virgin*, the pure and innocent woman attacked by a vicious monster. Benedict identifies several factors that increase the likelihood that the press will use the vamp narrative; that is, blaming the victim. She is more likely to be described with the vamp narrative if (1) she knew the assailant; (2) no weapon was used; (3) she was young and pretty; (4) her behavior showed deviation from traditional sex roles; and (5) she was of the same or lower-status race, class, or ethnic group as the rapist. The more of these conditions that existed in a particular case, the more likely it was that the reporting would conform to the vamp narrative; the fewer of them that existed, the more likely it was that the case would be told as a virgin narrative.

Why does such bias occur? Benedict in part blames the habitual pressure of deadlines but also our heavy emphasis on victims of crimes. While this in part reflects genuine empathy for the victims, it also taps into a desire of reporters and the public to reassure themselves that such acts will not happen to them because they don't behave like that. Thus, the behaviors and attributes of the victim are highlighted. There is less emphasis on the rapist, especially in the vamp narrative, and not much examination in either narrative of the societal forces that drive some men to behave in such violent ways. Such biases can have consequences. When a Texas grand jury in 1993 refused to indict a man for rape because his quick-thinking victim had convinced him to use a condom, the public outcry forced a reconsideration of the decision.

There is some evidence that sexual violence news reporting has gotten better over the years, with more empathic reporting on victims. However, Serisier (2017) contends that coverage has mainly improved for stories of sex crime allegations brought forth by celebrities in the "Me Too" era. Unfortunately, for non-celebrities, news coverage still seems to include the narrative frames of a "dangerous stranger" (Jewkes & Wykes, 2012), victim blaming, and myths about false rape accusations (Serisier, 2017).

Conclusion

What may we conclude from the research on the perceived reality and effects from viewing sexual media? First, it is useful to make a distinction between violent and non-violent sexual media, although this distinction may not be quite as important as some have argued. Although there are some negative effects of nonviolent erotica, especially on attitudes toward women (Hald, Malamuth, & Lange, 2013; Weaver, 1991; Zillmann & Bryant, 1984, 1988a, 1988b), the research is particularly compelling in the case of sexual violence. Sexual violence is arousing to sex offenders, naturally violent men, and sometimes even to other men if the woman is portrayed as somehow enjoying the attack. For reviews and meta-analyses of results from numerous experimental studies on the effects of viewing sexually explicit media, see Gunter (2001), Harris and Barlett (2008), Malamuth and Impett (2001), Mundorf et al. (2007), Oddone-Paolucci, Genuis, and Violato (2000), and Wright et al., (2016).

We know that repeated exposure to sexual violence may lead to desensitization toward violence against women in general and greater acceptance of rape myths. Even exposure to nonsexually explicit media like "lads' mags" (e.g., Maxim, Esquire) and some crime drama shows has been shown to lead to greater acceptance of rape myths (Hust, Marett, Lei, Ren, & Ran, 2015; Romero-Sánchez, Toro-García, Horvath, & Megías, 2017). Not only does this suggest that the combination of sex and violence together is worse than either one separately, but it also matters further what the nature of the portrayal is. If the woman being assaulted is portrayed as being terrorized and brutalized, negative effects on normal male viewers are less than if she is portrayed as being aroused or achieving orgasm through being attacked. Perhaps more than any other topic discussed in this book, this is an extremely dangerous reality for the media to create and for us to accept as real. There is nothing arousing or exciting about being raped, and messages to the contrary do not help teenage boys understand the reality of how to relate to girls and women, nor do they help young girls learn what is reasonable to expect from boys.

Not all the themes of sexual aggression against women are limited to specifically sexual material or even very violent movies. These images are even found in mainstream television. As discussed in Chapter 5, many years ago a storyline of the soap opera *General Hospital* focused on the rape of one main character, Laura, by Luke. Although Laura first felt humiliated, she later fell in love with Luke and married him in a fairy-tale wedding seen by 30 million viewers in 1981 (a cultural phenomenon at the time, "Luke" and "Laura" were on the covers on *People* and *Newsweek* magazines, and the "wedding" was attended by movie superstar Elizabeth Taylor). Although Laura and Luke had been through a lot in over 30 years, including death and resurrection, extra-marital affairs, marriages to other people, and several children with serious problems, Laura was revived from a four-year catatonic state just in time to marry Luke again in a gala reunion wedding in 2006 before promptly returning to her catatonic state. The saga only ended in 2015 when the actor who played Luke decided to retire. We all know that soaps aren't realistic, but what kinds of messages are such portrayals conveying?

Sexually violent images also appear in media other than film and TV, including detective magazines (Dietz, Harry, & Hazelwood, 1986), music videos (Hansen & Hansen, 1990a; Zillmann & Mundorf, 1987), and music lyrics (Bretthauer, Zimmerman, & Banning, 2007; Christenson, 1992). The reality of some of these media is that men dominate and brutalize women. Moreover, the women are sometimes portrayed as being sexually turned on by being raped or tortured. What is the cost of this message about how men treat women, especially for those in the public who may not realize that this picture deviates so significantly from reality?

As a final thought on this emotionally charged topic, we need to be aware of our own biases and ideology that we bring to the topic. Even the scientific research can be directed, in part, by the researchers' ideology (see Close-up 10.10). Just as people believe that other people are influenced more in general by media than they are themselves, the so-called third-person effect (Gunther, 1991; Perloff, 2002), people believe that others are influenced more by sexual media than they are (Gunther, 1995). This is exactly what people believe about the effects of advertising (Gunther & Thorson, 1992) and news coverage (Gunther, 1991; Perloff, 1989). It always affects the other person but certainly not me.

❖ CLOSE-UP 10.10 NORMATIVE PORNOGRAPHY THEORIES

Two of the most prominent researchers on sexual media, Daniel Linz and Neil Malamuth (1993), have talked about how various normative theories have guided research and may be lurking behind the scientific evidence. First is the conservative-moralist theory. This position, very prominent in Anglo-American history and culture, sees public portrayals of sex as disgusting and offensive. However, they are at the same time arousing and are seen as very threatening if the sex occurs outside of monogamous relationships. There is an implicit belief that a heavy emphasis on sexual gratification and permissiveness leads to behavior that undermines other moral beliefs about women and sexuality and ultimately to the decay of family and other traditional societal structures. This position tends to encourage research on sexual arousal, what materials produce it, and how exposure to sexual materials undermines traditional attitudes and can affect later reactions.

A second normative theory is the liberal theory, which endorses the idea that sexual depictions trigger fantasies but that these fantasies are not acted out and thus no one is hurt. They may even be socially beneficial through liberating a person's excessive prud-ishness. Liberals believe that if sexual behavior (and the viewing of it) is kept private, then the government should not restrict or regulate what is best left to the marketplace of ideas, which will adjust on its own to changing social standards. The liberal theory tends to more highly value research on physical and behavioral effects of sexual media in the real world rather than in the laboratory. It would also favor media literacy education and counteracting antisocial messages with competing messages rather than through legislative restriction.

The third and most recent normative theory is feminist theory, *which views pornography as a powerful socializing agent that promotes the sexual abuse of women and the social subor-dination of women as a group. Feminist-inspired research tends to focus on the arousal, or lack thereof, of women in rape scenes. It also tends to look more at attitudes than behaviors, including differences between men with or without a propensity to rape.*

Linz and Malamuth recognize that each normative theory has inspired some useful research, but they stress that we must recognize researchers' ideological positions when we evaluate their conclusions and the contributions of their studies to the matrix of overall media effects research.

Media Applications, Chapter 10: Counteracting Negative Effects of Sexual Media

Some interesting research has emerged on ways that the harmful effects of consuming sexual media might be mitigated. A lot of it seems to deal with how people think about sexually explicit images. For example, one study (Rasmussen, Rhodes, Ortiz, & White, 2016) examined young adults' social norms about sexually explicit media use. The researchers found that the more young adults think about their peers and parents dis-approving of their use of such media, the less likely they are to view it. Also, when parents put restrictions on access to sexually explicit media during adolescence, people were less likely to report using pornography as an adult.

Education about sexually explicit media can have an effect, too. Because of the explicit nature of pornography, lessons teaching children and adolescents about its effects are probably rare. However, some schools are choosing to incorporate discussions about porn into a broader sex education curriculum (Albury, 2014). When they do, such lessons may have an effect in terms of less sexist views of women (Vandenbosch & van Oosten, 2017) and increased critical thinking about the realism of media portrayals of sex (Austin, Pinkleton, Chen, & Austin, 2015). Increasingly, there have been calls for building young adults' sexually explicit media literacy in this way, thereby encouraging them to critically evaluate the explicit images they encounter (Lamb & Randazzo, 2016; Štulhofer, Buško, & Landripet, 2010).

Mitigating the Negative Effects of Sexual Violence

There are also some lessons from the research on how we may more effectively deal with sexually violent media. With regard to the possible desensitization effects discussed earlier in this chapter, Malamuth and colleagues (1980) offered an extensive debriefing after participants had viewed a sexually violent movie. This was complete with information on the horrible reality of rape and the complete unreality of the victim enjoying it. They even included a discussion of why the myth of women enjoying rape was so prevalent in sexually violent media. Other studies included evaluations of such debriefing sessions and showed that, compared to a control group not in the experiment, debriefed people showed less acceptance of rape myths (Donnerstein & Berkowitz, 1981; Malamuth & Check, 1980). In a related study that included post-viewing debriefing about the inaccuracy of rape portrayals, (Vance, Sutter, Perrin, & Heesacker, 2015), at least some participants were more impressed with such arguments after they had felt themselves excited and aroused by the film and had seen specific examples to illustrate the point of the debriefing/mitigation information. Thus, in the context of having actually seen examples of sexually violent media, the specific points of the sensitization training had greater impact. A meta-analysis of these kinds of studies concluded that the education and debriefing included largely eradicated any harmful effects of viewing the material and in fact often left participants with less antisocial attitudes than those they held before participation (Mundorf *et al.*, 2007).

Using a different approach to mitigating the negative effects of sexually violent media, a group of researchers (Bonomi, Nichols, Carotta, Kiuchi, & Perry, 2016) had college-age women watch the film *Fifty Shades of Grey* and then asked critical thinking questions as part of a discussion of the sexual relationship depicted. The authors concluded that using a popular film in this way was an effective method for getting women to critically evaluate media sexual violence. Another study (Gilliam *et al.*, 2016) used the medium of video games to try to sensitize high school students to sexual violence. In playing the game, participants learned the backstory of a character who had been sexually assaulted by her boyfriend. Those who had played the game were found to have been likely to have a real-life discussion about sexual violence with a peer, parent, or teacher.

Some studies have developed and evaluated more extensive pre-exposure training procedures to attempt to lessen the desensitizing effects of sexual violence (Intons-Peterson & Roskos-Ewoldsen, 1989; Intons-Peterson, Roskos-Ewoldsen, Thomas, Shirley, & Blut, 1989; Linz, Donnerstein, Bross, & Chapin, 1986; Linz, Fuson, & Donnerstein, 1990). This research has typically shown mitigating effects on some measures but not on others. For example, Linz and colleagues (1990) found that men were most strongly affected by the information that women are not responsible for sexual assaults perpetrated upon them.

Viewer characteristics matter, too. Wilson, Linz, Donnerstein, and Stipp (1992) measured the effect of seeing a prosocial movie about rape. They found that, compared to a control group, people viewing the film generally showed heightened awareness and concern about rape. However, not all groups were so affected. Unlike women and young and middle-aged men, men over 50 had their preexisting attitudes reinforced and actually blamed women more for rape after seeing the film. This suggests that the attitudes and experiences of the target audience of interventions must be carefully considered with any intervention.

Taken as a whole, the research on mitigating the negative effects of sexual media, particularly sexual violence, also suggests that we should take a critical look at the nature of our media. See Oliver (2016) for a discussion of how stories from Sleeping Beauty to *Fifty Shades of Grey* may perpetuate rape myths and a sexually violent culture.

Also see Ward, Reed, Trinh, and Foust (2014) for a thorough review on sexuality and media entertainment.

Further Reading

Oliver, K. (2016). *Hunting girls: Sexual violence from The Hunger Games to campus rape.* New York: Columbia University Press.

Peter, J., & Valkenburg, P. M. (2016). Adolescents and pornography: A review of 20 years of research. *The Journal of Sex Research*, 53(4–5), 509–531. https://doi.org/10.1080/00224499.2016.1143441

Ward, L. M., Reed, L., Trinh, S. L., & Foust, M. (2014). Sexuality and entertainment media. In D. L. Tolman, L. M. Diamond, J. A. Bauermeister, W. H. George, J. G. Pfaus, & L. M. Ward (Eds.), *APA handbook of sexuality and psychology, Vol. 2: Contextual approaches* (pp. 373–423). Washington, DC: American Psychological Association. doi:10.1037/14194-012

Useful Links

Pornography Literacy:
http://sites.bu.edu/rothmanlab/research/span-sex-positive-and-abuse-negative/

"Sex is Good" TV Trope:
http://tvtropes.org/pmwiki/pmwiki.php/Main/SexIsGood

For more resources, please visit the companion website:
www.routledge.com/cw/harris

Chapter 11

Socially Positive Media

Teaching Good Things to Children (and the Rest of Us)

Q: What is the most watched educational television program of all time?

A: *Sesame Street*, on the air continuously with new episodes since 1969, and popular among children and their parents all those years.

Q: What is the "Angelina Jolie Effect"?

A: It's a term given to the influence that celebrities (in particular Angelina Jolie) can have on public health. After having been discovered to have a specific gene mutation that causes breast cancer, Jolie decided to have a pre-emptive double mastectomy to prevent breast cancer from occurring in her body. Jolie's subsequent public discussion of this led to a 285% increase in women being tested to see if their genetics put them at risk for breast cancer (Troiano, Nante, & Cozzolino, 2017).

Q: What is the purpose of an organizational called "Hollywood, Health, and Society (HH&S)"?

A: Affiliated with the Annenberg School for Communication and Journalism at the University of Southern California, HH&S works with screenwriters to insert health-related information into popular TV shows. HH&S has consulted with writers of many shows, including *Breaking Bad*, *The Young and Restless*, and *Boardwalk Empire*.

Q: How did Nicholas Johnson, a member of the Federal Communications Commission in the 1960s and 1970s, respond when asked the question, "How much TV is educational"?

A: He said, "All of it! It just depends on what it's teaching" (Liebert & Schwartzberg, 1977, p. 170).

Much of this book has focused on rather problematic perceived realities gleaned from the media: worlds of excessive violence, deception, stereotyping, sexual promiscuity, or fake news reporting. However, we must not lose sight of the fact that the power of media can also be used in very positive ways. In this chapter we examine some of this potential, when the media are intentionally used to produce or encourage socially positive ("prosocial") outcomes. We begin by looking at prosocial children's television, programming specifically designed to help kids to learn or to be better people in some way.

Next, we will look at social marketing, with a focus on public service media campaigns to teach improved health behaviors. We will then examine the use of entertainment media such as prime-time television and movies to teach explicit prosocial lessons and healthy behavior and end with a discussion of how some individuals have chosen to harness the power of media for social change.

Prosocial Children's Television

Given children's massive exposure to media, primarily television, it is inconceivable that they are not learning anything from it. In fact, throughout this book we have been examining what children learn from media. Here, however, we focus on some specific projects explicitly designed to teach kids prosocial behaviors and attitudes through television (see Close-up 11.1 for a discussion of how another popular medium among children, video games, has been used for prosocial ends).

❖ CLOSE-UP 11.1 CAN PLAYING VIDEO GAMES HAVE POSITIVE EFFECTS?

Although there is considerable evidence of the negative outcomes of playing video games (see Chapter 9), recent research suggests that not all video games are created equal. Building on previous studies investigating prosocial effects associated with music, Greitemeyer and his colleagues in Europe have discovered some positive outcomes from playing video games in which players provide help to others within the game. For example, as compared to those who played a "neutral" video game (Tetris), participants who played "prosocial" video games (Lemmings, City Crisis) in which they rescued other characters were more likely to help real people in real-life situations, including a person they believed was being harassed (Greitemeyer & Osswald, 2010). In other studies, those who had just played prosocial video games reported more prosocial thoughts (Greitemeyer & Osswald, 2011), more feelings of empathy (Harrington & O'Connell, 2016), and less schadenfreude (pleasure at others' misfortune) than those who had just played a neutral video game (Greitemeyer, Osswald, & Brauer, 2010).

Other research has indicated that playing prosocial games can increase positive affect (Harrington & O'Connell, 2016; Saleem, Anderson, & Gentile, 2012) and even reduce trait hostility (Saleem, Anderson, & Gentile, 2012) and aggression (Liu, Teng, Lan, Zhang, & Yao, 2015). When compared to the number of violent video games on the market, there are no doubt fewer with prosocial elements. However, there could be important implications from this line of research for those who design and buy video games. Also see Greitemeyer and Mügge (2014) for a meta-analysis of the benefits of prosocial video games.

Although there had been some specifically educational children's shows on the U.S. commercial networks since TV debuted (e.g., *Kukla, Fran, and Ollie*; *Romper Room*; *Captain Kangaroo*), by the mid-1960s there was increased interest in developing more children's television programming that would be commercial-free, explicitly educational, socially positive, and of high technical quality. Towards this end, in the United States, National Educational Television (NET) began in 1954, followed by the Corporation for Public Broadcasting (CPB), founded in 1967, and eventually the Public Broadcasting Service

(PBS) in 1970. The CPB was created by a 1967 act of Congress that also established National Public Radio (NPR). The artistic and technical quality of children's programming greatly improved during this period, particularly with the founding of the Children's Television Workshop (CTW, later known as Sesame Workshop) in 1968, initially supported by both public and private funds (Stewart, 1999).

Sesame Street

Sesame Street, one of the most important television shows of all time in terms of viewership and research, saw its debut in 1969. Designed from the beginning to be "hip and fast and funny," the show was a hit from the start (Stewart, 1999, p. 113). Although there would be periodic struggles with the U.S. government over funding (Davis, 2008), even President Richard Nixon was a fan of the early show, writing to CTW: "The many children and families now benefiting from '*Sesame Street*' are participants in one of the most promising experiments in the history of that medium … This administration is enthusiastically committed to opening up opportunities for every youngster, particularly during his first five years of life, and is pleased to be among the sponsors of your distinguished program" (Ferretti, 1970, p. 79).

After humming along for decades, changes came to *Sesame Street* around 2015. Sesame Workshop, receiving less funding from PBS over the years as production costs rose, increasingly relied on licensing, DVD, and toy sales to fund the show. When those revenue sources began to dwindle, the length of the episodes was cut from an hour to 30 minutes, and some longtime human characters like Bob, Gordon, and Luis were let go (Hill, 2016). Eventually, a collaboration was announced in which the new episodes would air first on premium cable channel HBO, and would appear online and on PBS months later (Steel, 2015). Although criticized by some as making *Sesame Street* a gated community in the land of pay cable, the collaboration did allow the program to continue with some enhanced graphics and a revamped style designed to appeal to tech-savvy kids who might be watching on mobile devices (Poniewozik, 2016a).

Although it was only the first of several such shows, *Sesame Street* is still by far the most successful and popular young children's show worldwide; it is seen in well over 100 countries with about 20 different adaptations, from Kuwait and Turkey to Sweden and China. As appropriate, it has been translated into many languages but is always locally produced and adapted to local culture (Fisch, 2004; Gettas, 1990; Gikow, 2009). A version has even been created targeting Syrian refugee children who are living in places like Jordan and Lebanon. The familiar characters speak in Arabic or Kurdish and focus on building trauma resilience … and learning letters and numbers (Victor, 2017b).

The original stated purpose of *Sesame Street* was to provide preschoolers with an enriched experience leading to prereading skills. With its urban, multicultural setting, the program was especially targeted at so-called disadvantaged children who often entered school less prepared for reading than were their suburban peers. However, the show would come to appeal to children across the social spectrum. Regular characters like Big Bird, Cookie Monster, Oscar the Grouch, and Bert and Ernie have become part of almost everyone's childhood.

What the Show Is Like

The technical quality of *Sesame Street* has been consistently very high throughout the years, using a combination of live action, animation, and puppetry, with much humor and lots of movement. There is a pleasing mixture of human and Muppet characters. Recognizing that commercials are familiar and appealing to young children, *Sesame Street* draws on many technical characteristics of ads (e.g., "This program has been brought to you by the letter H and the number 6"). In later years the influence of music videos became apparent with the use of that format within the show. Many segments are short, so as to not lose even the youngest viewers' interest. In fact, even some infants under 1 year old are regular watchers. Practically all people under 50 in many societies of the world have had some exposure to *Sesame Street*, and many have had very heavy exposure. In numerous markets the show is on three or more times per day on HBO, PBS affiliates, and their digital subchannels. Much more is available on DVD and online. All of this has combined to make *Sesame Street* by far one of the most watched TV shows, educational or otherwise, in history.

In addition to the attractive technical aspects, there is also wordplay and satire to amuse adults watching with their children or listening in the background. A segment called "Orange is the New Snack" features familiar characterizations from the Netflix prison show, *Orange is the New Black*. Instead of prison food, though, the Muppet characters discuss healthy options in the school cafeteria. There was also "Sharing Things," a prosocial version of another Netflix hit, *Stranger Things*. Yet another playful parody was when Elmo sang, "I'm Elmo and I Know it," a take on the pop song "I'm Sexy and I Know it." There is also spoofing of the show's own network, PBS. The segment "Monsterpiece Theater" featured a smoking jacket attired Cookie Monster ("Good evening. I'm Alastair Cookie") introducing classics about numbers and letters, including "The Old Man and the C" and "1 Flew over the Cuckoo's Nest." Popular (and sometimes unexpected) adult celebrities frequently put in guest appearances, too: Stephen Colbert, Bruno Mars, Taylor Swift, Robert De Niro, and news anchors like Anderson Cooper and Barbara Walters have all visited *Sesame Street* for a chat or a song. Even Supreme Court justice Sonia Sotomayor once stopped by to mediate a conflict between Goldilocks and one of the Three Bears. Adults who had earlier watched the show as preschoolers frequently have the feeling seeing *Sesame Street* as adults that there are a lot of nuances that they had missed earlier, unlike shows like *Barney and Friends*, *Caillou*, and *Teletubbies*, which have little intrinsic attraction for grownups. This appeal is not accidental; children get more out of *Sesame Street* if their parents watch and discuss it with them, and the producers know that. Sadly, however, there seems to be less adult-style humor woven into the more recent, shorter versions of *Sesame Street* (Harwell, 2016).

The intentional use of a multiracial, multiethnic, multiclass, and increasingly gender-balanced cast ensemble has set a valued social model for children as well; it provides far more diverse and positive multicultural modeling than most of what is offered by commercial television. Among the human characters on the show, there have always been substantial numbers of women and members of diverse ethnic groups; they go about their business of being human, not particularly identifying as members of some social group. Sometimes the teaching is more focused. For example, there is a heavy draw from various Hispanic cultures, including Spanish and bilingual English–Spanish songs, such as "Somos Hermanos/We are Brothers." On another occasion, the characters from *Sesame Street* took a trip to the Crow Reservation in Montana to learn about that particular Native American culture. There have been visits to Louisiana to learn about Cajun culture and food and zydeco music. Over the years, there have also been discussions of people with differing abilities, and in 2017 a new Muppet on the autistic spectrum, Julia, was introduced.

Effects of Watching *Sesame Street*

Besides being the most watched young children's TV show of all time, *Sesame Street* has also been the most extensively evaluated show, in terms of scientific research, generating by one estimate well over 1,000 studies (Fisch, 2004). One author described the show as "perhaps the most vigorously researched, vetted, and fretted-over program on the planet" (Davis, 2008, p. 357). We turn now to some of the effects of watching *Sesame Street* (Fisch, 2002, 2004; Fisch & Truglio, 2000; Huston *et al.*, 1990; Kearney & Levine, 2015).

As most parents know very well, children's attention and interest level while watching *Sesame Street* is typically high; preschoolers really do like the show. In terms of more substantive effects on learning, there is solid evidence for short-term effects, in the sense of vocabulary growth and the acquisition of prereading skills and positive social skills and attitudes, such as showing evidence of nonracist attitudes and behavior (D. R. Anderson, 1998; Ball & Bogatz, 1970; Huston & Wright, 1998; Rice, Huston, Truglio, & Wright, 1990). In a meta-analysis, such effects were found in the international versions of *Sesame Street* as well (Mares & Pan, 2013). In addition, it has been demonstrated that those who watched *Sesame Street* also spent more time reading and doing other educational activities and needed less remedial instruction (Fisch, Truglio, & Cole, 1999; Zill, 2001).

Longer term effects are less clear, with some early studies showing that the advantages of watching *Sesame Street*, compared to a control group not watching it, disappear after a few months or years (Bogatz & Ball, 1971). However, later longitudinal research showed that heavy viewing of *Sesame Street* in the preschool years is positively correlated with later school grades in English, math, and science, even with early language ability and parental education level taken into account (Huston, Anderson, Wright, Linebarger, & Schmitt, 2001; Huston & Wright, 1998).

A more recent, wide-ranging study (Kearney & Levine, 2015) examined the availability of *Sesame Street* when it was introduced in 1969 and its effects years later. The authors looked at demographic data of children who were preschool age in 1969 and lived near a PBS broadcast tower. They then compared those children's information against older cohorts and those who would not have had access to PBS or *Sesame Street* because of where they lived. Data tracked included grade-for-age status in 1980, likelihood of being a high school graduate by 1990, and employment rates in 2000. The authors concluded that preschoolers who had access to *Sesame Street*, particularly boys in disadvantaged areas, received definite gains in school readiness. Possible longer-term benefits of high school graduation and income were less clear.

Some interesting qualifications of these effects have been found. For example, the positive effects are stronger if combined with parental discussion and teaching (Cook *et al.*, 1975). This suggests that, among other functions, the program can serve as a good catalyst for informal media literacy education within the family. Another interesting finding is that, at least initially, *Sesame Street* helped higher socioeconomic status children more than lower socioeconomic status children, although both groups improved significantly (Ball & Bogatz, 1970). However, this result should not have been unexpected, because any kind of intervention generally most helps those who are most capable or advantaged to begin with and thus more able to take full advantage of what it has to offer.

In addition to academic gains, there have also been positive social effects. Minority children watching *Sesame Street* showed increased cultural pride, confidence, and interpersonal cooperation (Greenberg, 1982) and more prosocial free play (Zielinska & Chambers, 1995). Also, after two years of watching *Sesame Street*, White children showed more positive attitudes toward children of other races (Bogatz & Ball, 1971; Christenson & Roberts, 1983). One recent effort in this regard introduced an African American Muppet, Segi, who celebrates her natural hair with the song "I Love My Hair."

Although very widely praised, *Sesame Street* does have its critics (e.g., Healy, 1990; Oldenburg, 2006; Winn, 2002), who mostly fault its encouragement of passivity and short attention span, as well as its slighting of language skills by the necessarily highly visual nature of television. However, these criticisms are mostly general criticisms of television, with little recognition of the differential quality of programming. See Anderson (1998) for a careful discussion and refutation of specific claims of these critics and Close-up 11.2 for hypotheses about the effects of TV in general on reading.

❖ CLOSE-UP 11.2 DOES TELEVISION INTERFERE WITH READING?

A common concern of many parents is that their children watch too much television and do not read enough. Researchers in the Netherlands (Koolstra, van der Voort, & van der Kamp, 1997) identified several hypotheses about the effect of watching TV on reading and looked at the support for each of them. Facilitation hypotheses *argue that watching television facilitates or encourages reading. Not widely held, only a few small pieces of evidence support it, namely learning to read from reading subtitles on TV (onscreen reading hypothesis—see Close-up 1.5) and reading a book either reviewed on or directly based on a TV show after watching the show (Book-reading promotion hypothesis—see Close-up 11.4). Both of these, however, apply to only very restricted, specific contexts.*

More widely believed and scientifically studied is some sort of inhibition hypothesis, *with TV watching reputed to have a negative impact on reading. There are four variations of inhibition hypotheses. First, the* passivity hypothesis *argues that TV causes children to become more mentally lazy and less prepared to invest the mental effort necessary for reading. Although it is true that TV requires less mental effort than reading (Salomon, 1984, 1987; Rosenqvist, Lahti-Nuuttila, Holdnack, Kemp, & Laasonen, 2016; Shin, 2004), viewers are far from totally passive. A second variety of inhibition hypothesis is* concentration-deterioration, *which says that TV weakens a child's ability to concentrate. The* reading depreciation (antischool) hypothesis *argues that TV leads children to expect school to be as entertaining as Sesame Street or Dora the Explorer and, when it is not, they lose motivation. Finally, the* displacement hypothesis *argues that television hurts reading but only when it takes away time from reading.*

Although all the research is not entirely consistent (Koolstra & van der Voort, 1996; Koolstra et al., 1997; Mutz et al., 1993; Ritchie, Price, & Roberts, 1987), the displacement and reading depreciation hypotheses appear to have the most support. If children watch TV instead of reading, it may induce more negative attitudes about reading and diminish their reading skills (Koolstra et al., 1997). This effect may be especially pronounced if children have access to television in their bedrooms (Gentile, Berch, Choo, Khoo, & Walsh, 2017). If they watch TV in addition to reading, there probably is no detrimental effect on reading. Regarding play, watching nonviolent TV programs does not interfere with children's fantasy play, but violent shows reduce fantasy play (van der Voort & Valkenburg, 1994). Overall, TV appears to stimulate day dreaming but reduce creative imagination (van der Voort & Valkenburg, 1994). Also see Valkenburg and Calvert (2012) for a review of the research on children, television, and imagination.

Sesame Street is still going strong after 50 years. New material is continually being created, but there is also some recycling of old material, and old and new segments sometimes appear together in the same show. Preschoolers are not bothered by reruns; in fact, familiarity often makes them more attractive. Although often at the forefront of dealing with social issues (see Close-up 11.3), there are some areas about which *Sesame Street* has remained silent. For example, there generally is little treatment of mainstream religion or religious holidays, and there are no openly LGBT characters (despite rumors about Bert and Ernie's relationship[1]).

❖ CLOSE-UP 11.3 SESAME STREET DEALS WITH DIFFICULT ISSUES

One of the most remembered segments in the history of Sesame Street *is the death of Mr. Hooper in 1983. When the human actor playing Mr. Hooper passed away, the producers decided to have the character die as well. They used the segments around his death to teach three specific points they believed all viewers would accept: (1) Mr. Hooper died; (2) he is not coming back; and (3) he will be missed. In order not to offend any viewers with particular religious beliefs (or lack of them) in regard to any afterlife or reasons for the death, no mention was made of heaven or hell. Evaluation research showed that half of preschool viewers' parents reported discussing death with their child after watching the critical episode.*

A few years later the show dealt with the human characters Luis and Maria falling in love, getting married, and having a baby. Teaching goals for this sequence were for the children to understand that: (1) people can love each other even when they argue; (2) a baby grows inside its mother's body; and (3) the baby can move inside the womb. Once, Big Bird was also schooled about breast feeding while a mom nursed her baby on Sesame Street.

In the 1990s, an interracial couple explained to Telly Monster that some people don't like it when people with different skin colors are friends. In response to increased concern about children's poor eating habits, in the 2000s Cookie Monster started eating vegetables and encouraging children to do likewise, which required a major evolution in his character. In the 2010s, several of the Muppet characters discussed the challenges of having a parent who is incarcerated or deployed overseas. Provocative topics are not new to Sesame Street, *however. Reflecting the times, one early episode from 1969 even had Grover learning rules of civil disobedience (Conan, 2009).*

Sometimes the program's planned campaigns did not work. For example, a 1990s proposal to deal with divorce through Snuffy and Alice's parents divorcing was scrapped and never aired after a pilot version showed that young viewers did not understand that the parents still loved their children and that the children would continue to see their dad after the divorce (Fisch et al., 1999).

Other CTW/Sesame Workshop Projects

In the fall of 1971, CTW launched a second major program, *The Electric Company (TEC)*, which used much of the successful *Sesame Street* format but was aimed at improving the reading skills of older children (around second grade). *TEC* was heavily used in schools as well as at home. Evaluative research (Ball & Bogatz, 1973) found that viewing *TEC* led to improved scores on a reading test battery in children who had watched in school, but there was no improvement in a control group who had merely watched *TEC* at home. This suggests that the show was helpful in teaching reading, but primarily so in conjunction with the experiences offered in the classroom by the teacher and the curriculum. Never as popular as *Sesame Street*, *TEC* later operated in reruns until it was finally canceled in 1986, only to be revived in 2009 for a few seasons. There have been other CTW/Sesame Workshop projects (e.g., *Ghostwriter*, *Square One TV*), as well as independently produced prosocial programs that have shown up on PBS like *Where in the World is Carmen Sandiego? Mister Rogers' Neighborhood*, *Barney and Friends*, *Arthur*, and *Caillou*.

Many of these kinds of shows have produced demonstrable positive effects. For example, when preschoolers watch Barney, the cheery purple dinosaur that anyone over 6 loves to hate, they show better manners than a control group not watching Barney's show on manners (Singer & Singer, 1998). A more recent study (Penuel *et al.*, 2012) revealed that in comparison to a control group, preschoolers who were exposed to in-class media clips from shows like *Super Why!* showed enhanced prereading skills relating to letters and sounds. In fact, a number of studies indicate that children are quite able to pick up the intended curriculum of educational shows, whether it be related to academic or social skills (Kirkorian & Anderson, 2011). It's important to remember, however, that individual children also may have differing effects, based on things like their socioeconomic status, prior knowledge of the subject being discussed, and individual verbal and short-term memory abilities (Aladé & Nathanson, 2016; Linebarger, Moses, Garrity Liebeskind, & McMenamin, 2013; Piotrowski, 2014).

In light of increased difficulties in obtaining funding for such shows, some have criticized the newer programs, especially, for being more entertaining than educational, a situation brought about by increasing economic pressures to attract an audience as public television increasingly relies on corporate funding. However, in a move some may find ironic, television has even been used to teach children about literature and to encourage reading (see Close-up 11.4). For reviews of these educational kids' programs and their effects, see Calvert and Wilson (2011), Chen (1994), Fisch (2002), and Mares and Woodard (2001).

❖ CLOSE-UP 11.4 USING TELEVISION TO ENCOURAGE READING

Using a television show to encourage reading? Surely that is a contradiction in terms and a waste of time. The producers of a few popular PBS shows think otherwise. The children's book review show, Reading Rainbow, *ran from 1983 to 2006, and was hosted by* Roots *and* Star Trek: The Next Generation's *Levar Burton. During the show, children were read stories that were accompanied by compelling illustrations and live-action photography as well as Burton's visit to a setting described in the story. Near the end of the show other books were read or reviewed in briefer fashion. Does it matter? Sales of books featured on* Reading Rainbow *jumped 150% to 900%, and a survey of librarians found that 82% reported children asking for books featured on* Reading Rainbow *(Fisch, 2002; Wood & Duke, 1997). Years later, after a legal fight with the PBS station that originated* Reading Rainbow*, Burton brought back the program, this time as an app called* Skybrary *and a podcast entitled* Levar Burton Reads *(Martin, 2018).*

Super Why!*, a more recent animated PBS offering, follows the adventures of Whyatt and his friends who become super-hero-like "Super Readers," complete with capes and alter egos (e.g., Whyatt transforms into Super Why). After saying, "Calling all Super Readers! To the Book Club!," the Super Readers become physically immersed in the plot of a book, reading along the way to address real-life kid issues like sharing, offering help to others, or making friends. Other PBS children's shows that encourage reading such as* Martha Speaks *and* Word World *also are designed to inspire book sales and library visits.*

Can the same phenomenon happen with adults? Although acclaimed novelist Toni Morrison won a Nobel Prize in 1993, that was nothing compared to having her novel Song of Solomon *selected as the second offering of the Oprah Book Club in December 1996. Although Morrison, who seldom watches TV, had never heard of the Oprah Book Club, she quickly realized its importance. Within months, a million copies of her selected novel sold, and paperback sales of her other novels jumped about 25% (Gray, 1998)! When Oprah announced in 2002 that she would be discontinuing her book club, publishers and authors emitted a collective gasp. The first 48 selections on Oprah's Book Club all sold at least 500,000 copies after being featured, and many sold over one million (Sachs, 2002). Oprah revived her book club in 2003, although with selections offered less frequently. That version of the club ended when her daytime show closed its run in 2011. However, in 2012 Oprah again announced that the book club would be reincarnated as "Oprah's Book Club 2.0." This time, though, discussion would take place on her Oprah Winfrey Network (OWN) cable channel and via Facebook and Twitter. Those who read the book selections in electronic form on e-readers could even see "margin notes" written by Winfrey herself. After the first book selection was made for "2.0," sales of the title surged and continued to do so years afterward, indicating that Oprah had not lost her influence on reading (Berg, 2016; Minzesheimer, 2012).*

Commercial TV Contributions

The 1990 Children's Television Act, which required all broadcast stations in the United States to provide educational programming for children, was clarified by the 1996 interpretation of this law by the FCC, which required each station to provide a minimum of three hours a week of educational and informational programming for children (Kunkel, 1998; also see Close-up 6.9). At least one extensive study (Calvert & Kotler, 2003), has found many overall positive effects associated with the Children's Television Act, one of which has been a substantial increase in commercial educational programming for children. The most extensive single project has been the cable channel Nickelodeon's intensive investment in new children's programs (Anderson, 1998). The network, along with its sister channels like Nick Jr., present preschool shows that have been popular and have shown some promising evaluation research results and recommendations. *Gullah Gullah Island* featured a real human family from a little-known American culture, the

Gullah of the South Carolina Sea Islands. *Wallykazam!* is a literacy show that features trolls and goblins. *Spongebob Squarepants* is a popular animated show aimed at children but, like *Sesame Street*, has a subtext of more mature humor that appeals to teens and preteens. So do shows like The Disney Channel's *Phineas and Ferb*, which features imaginative half-brothers who concoct grand schemes like building a time machine. Nickelodeon's *The Loud House* offers stories about a boy, Lincoln Loud, with 10 sisters who lives in a diverse neighborhood, including a married same-sex couple with a son who is Lincoln's best friend.

Blue's Clues, one of the best-known Nickelodeon shows, was aimed at preschoolers and featured a human character with an animated dog (Blue) in an animated world. Every episode invited the viewers to help solve the day's mystery, for which Blue had left her paw print in three places as clues. Her human sidekick frequently "needed help" and asked the audience questions and waited for them to answer, in order to more actively involve the child viewer in creative problem solving. The same episode was shown five days in a row, in order to better empower the child to make use of all the clues; research shows that attention is maintained at a high level, at least through three episodes (82% of the time looking at the screen), after which it drops to around the average level of attention to entertainment programming (Anderson *et al.*, 2000). Research also showed that viewers of *Blue's Clues*, compared to a non-viewing control group (or sometimes in comparison to those viewing other shows), performed better on several measures of cognitive development (Anderson *et al.*, 2000; Crawley, Anderson, Wilder, Williams, & Santomero, 1999; Linebarger & Walker, 2005).

Science Shows for Children

Although science and nature shows for children are not new (*Wild Kingdom* and *Mr. Wizard* appeared in the 1950s), one of the earliest modern science shows was the CTW project, *3-2-1 Contact*, which debuted in 1980 with the goal of teaching scientific thinking to 8- to 12-year-olds. It attempted to help children experience the excitement of scientific discovery and to encourage all children, particularly girls and minorities, to feel comfortable with science as an endeavor (Mielke & Chen, 1983).

More recently, the PBS programs *Zooboomafoo*, *Kratt's Creatures*, and *Wild Kratts* featured naturalists Chris and Martin Kratt, who go romping over the world in their quest to see interesting creatures and teach young viewers how important it is to preserve these species and their habitats. In an animated series on PBS, *Sid the Science Kid* runs experiments and examines topics like the five senses or simple machines. *SciGirls* has tween girls investigating scientific discoveries; a goal of the PBS series is to increase the number of girls interested in STEM (science, technology, engineering, and mathematics) careers. A somewhat different, very high energy approach was taken by *Bill Nye, the Science Guy*, another PBS program that offered a wide variety of high-tech, high-action science demonstrations, with a generous helping of wisecracks thrown in. There is modeling of conducting experiments in many settings. The commercial offering *Beakman's World* took a similar approach. Both shows effectively counter the image of science as being difficult, stuffy, and generally uncool. Many such shows also include interactive websites where kids can run "experiments" of their own. See Fisch (2002, 2015) for excellent reviews of educational effects of children's prosocial television programs.

International Contributions

Many nations are getting in on the rush to create high-quality, commercially successful prosocial children's programs. One of the most successful, *LazyTown*, began in one of the world's smallest nations, Iceland, but is now seen in over 110 countries, including the United States. Its creator Magnus Scheving, a.k.a. "Sportacus" on the show, uses acrobatics and "sports candy," that is, fruits and vegetables, to try to save *LazyTown* from the temptations of junk food by the villain Robbie Rotten. After a 2004 healthy-eating campaign on *LazyTown*, sales of fruits and vegetables rose 22% in Iceland, so much that the country's president called the program a "brilliant tax-saving phenomenon," in spite of being one of the most expensive children's programs ever, at $800,000 per 25-minute episode. Its combination of live action, puppets, and computer graphics used state-of-the-art technology (Bates, 2008).

A hugely popular program for preschoolers in South Korea and over 80 other countries is Choi Jong Il's *Pororo the Little Penguin*, about a 3-D penguin who lives on a snowy island with six animal friends. Pororo is 4 years old and wants to fly and wears an aviator hat and goggles. He and his friends have a rich fantasy life (Veale, 2008).

With the worldwide reach of online streaming services, companies like Netflix are getting in on the international children's TV act, too (Littleton, 2017). One of the most interesting shows offered by Netflix is an animated series called *Ask the StoryBots*. StoryBots are animated creatures that live inside computers and help answer kid questions like, "Why is the sky blue?"

Channel One

One of the most controversial efforts in prosocial children's TV has been Channel One News, a service of daily news for secondary school students. Offered directly to schools at no charge since 1990, Channel One was in about 40% of all middle and high schools in the United States by 1997 (Bachen, 1998), with an audience of approximately 6 million adolescents in 8,000 schools by 2009 (About Channel One News, 2009). Channel One has been controversial since its inception, primarily because of its inclusion of two minutes of commercials, the revenues of which support the 10 minutes of news in the program. Although commercials are hardly new to teenagers, the captive audience nature of the in-school setting has caused particular concern. Evaluation research (see Bachen, 1998, for a review) suggests a small positive effect of learning about events in the news. However, some research has also shown that students report a greater desire to buy the advertised products, relative to a control group (Greenberg & Brand, 1993), and that children tended to remember advertising more than news after watching Channel One (Austin, Chen, Pinkleton, & Johnson, 2006). Interestingly, another potential but seldom expressed concern about Channel One is the possibility for abuse by some future producers who might choose to set a particular political agenda or offer a very biased view of the news to this young captive audience.

In an attempt to compete with Channel One, CNN began offering CNN Student News (now called CNN 10), a 10-minute, commercial-free online news source targeting students. Interestingly, in one content analysis comparing CNN Student News, CBS Evening News, and Channel One News, researchers concluded that Channel One had more references to commercial websites and less information about how to be a dutiful citizen (Scott, Chanslor, & Dixon, 2014).

Teen Programs

Beginning in the late 1950s and into the 1960s when the baby boom generation started entering adolescence, advertisers saw in teenagers a very lucrative new marketing opportunity. In the United States, this translated into the first TV shows aimed directly at teenagers, with sitcoms like *The Many Loves of Dobie Gillis*, *The Patty Duke Show*, *The Monkees*, and *Gidget*. In the 1970s and 1980s, an interesting television genre became popular with older children and teens. Somewhat ahead of their time, these shows took on controversial topics several times a year in the late afternoon hours. *ABC Afterschool Specials* and *CBS Schoolbreak Specials* presented dramatized stories of serious topics like racism, suicide, teen pregnancy, drug use, and sexual minorities.

Compared to decades past, the proliferation of cable channels in the new millennium has resulted in greater amounts of programming targeted at preteens ("tweens") and early adolescents. These programs, particularly prevalent on the Nickelodeon and Disney cable channels (and their various sister channels), are the most extensive attempts ever on commercial TV to develop older children's programming. Such shows as *Andi Mack*, *Girl Meets World*, *iCarly*, and *The Suite Life of Zack and Cody* are immensely popular with 11- to 15-year-olds and have launched the movie careers of several hot young actors and musicians, including Zac Efron, Miley Cyrus, Selena Gomez, and Ariana Grande. These shows model behavioral scripts of dealing with difficult situations common to that age; for example, bullying, trying to be popular, maintaining friendships, and relating to parents and siblings. They present interesting and humorous characters in amusing situations, but with a refreshing lack of bad language, sexual overtones, or violence. See Close-up 11.5 for a look at how one set of movies portrayed teen friendships.

❖ CLOSE-UP 11.5 TEEN FRIENDSHIPS IN HARRY POTTER

Some of the most popular books and movies of recent years have been J. K. Rowling's seven Harry Potter books (1997–2007), all made into highly successful movies (2001–2011). Throughout his seven years at Hogwarts school (one book per year), Harry's long-time best friends were Ron Weasley and Hermione Granger. This trio hung out together in and out of school. One interesting aspect of Harry's support system was that, of his two best friends, one was a boy, and one was a girl. Hermione was not Harry's girlfriend, though there was some periodic attraction between Hermione and Ron.

Although perhaps surprising that a teen boy would have a girl as a close friend, it is actually a relatively common configuration in TV shows, books, and movies targeted at teens and preteens. For example, Pretty in Pink *(1986) portrayed the complicated adolescent friendship of female Andie and male Duckie. The film* Big Fat Liar *(2002) showed 14-year-old Jason and Kaylee going on an adventure in Hollywood together to exact revenge on a ruthless film producer who stole Jason's script idea. Using slightly younger characters in a semi-fantasy setting,* The Bridge to Terabithia *(2007) also depicted a strong friendship bond between a boy and a girl.*

Although no doubt one reason for these cross-sex friendships is commercial, that is, to attract both the boy and girl audiences, it also may serve a useful prosocial function. This prevalent model communicates that you can have close friends of the opposite sex with no romantic or sexual component, and it is a positive social model for an age when preoccupation with coupling is strong. Indeed, some research (Sanborn, 2004) indicates that there can be considerable non-romantic, nonsexual benefits to such cross-sex friendships in childhood, adolescence, and adulthood. It is also interesting that in this world of media saturated with sex and sexual innuendo that there is this common nonsexual model of friendship, although there is also frequently speculation about whether romance may be in the works (McDonnell & Mehta, 2016). In the Harry Potter stories, we ultimately learn that Ron and Hermione become romantic partners as adults. There has been some interesting writing on the psychology of the Harry Potter stories, including some fMRI research (e.g., Crysel, Cook, Schember, & Webster, 2015; Hsu, Jacobs, Citron, & Conrad, 2015; Mulholland, 2006).

Children's Prosocial Learning from Adult Television

Although children's television is important, a large majority of what children watch is not television produced for children but rather programs produced for a general audience of primarily adults. A content analysis of programming on 18 broadcast network and cable channels found that 73% of the shows included some instance (2.92 incidents per hour) of people sharing or helping each other (Smith *et al.*, 2006). However, another content analysis (Hahn *et al.*, 2017) found more altruism displayed in shows targeted at young viewers (e.g., *Doc McStuffins, Dora the Explorer*) than those meant for older viewers (e.g., *Bob's Burgers, New Girl*). See Close-up 11.6 for a discussion of how media that we find meaningful can have positive psychological benefits.

❖ CLOSE-UP 11.6 POSITIVE PSYCHOLOGY, MEANING, AND MEDIA ELEVATION

In contrast to older areas of psychology, which have focused on human suffering and mental illness, a newer field, positive psychology, *is dedicated to studying human happiness and building psychological strengths (Lopez, Pedrotti, & Snyder, 2015). While researching happiness and well-being, positive psychologists often highlight an important distinction first proposed by Aristotle. Specifically, it's important to understand the difference between* hedonic well-being *(pleasure, fun) and* eudaimonic well-being *(satisfaction that comes in deriving deeper meaning from an experience); these concepts were briefly discussed in Chapter 2. Although both kinds of well-being are certainly positive, eudaimonic well-being is what most people think makes life worth living, and eudaimonia has received the most research attention within positive psychology.*

Increasingly, positive psychology has also been related to the study of media. In specific, some researchers have been examining what has become known as elevated responses *to media, or those eudaimonic experiences that we sometimes have while consuming media (Oliver & Bartsch, 2011). An example would be watching a touching movie that stirs deep emotions in you and makes you want to become more connected to loved ones in your life. In one study, Janicke and Oliver (2017) asked participants to name and rate either a movie they remembered being particularly meaningful or one that they remembered being pleasurable. In comparison to the pleasurable movie group, the meaningful group indicated that their films contained more portrayals of love, kindness, and interconnectedness. The meaningful movies indeed seemed to elevate people, too, and made them more likely to think about love and gratitude. Another study that demonstrated a media elevation effect had participants in one condition watch short clips of "underdogs" over a period of five days (Prestin, 2013). One example was a story about a dog born with two legs who learned to cope by walking upright. Compared to participants who had viewed clips that were humorous or about nature, the people who had watched the underdog videos reported higher motivation to pursue their own goals in life.*

There has also been some evidence that elevation effects can happen with some unexpected forms of media. For instance, during the Pokémon Go *craze of 2016, many people enjoyed playing the augmented reality video game on their mobile devices in which they "hunted" Pokémon in the real world, often outdoors and in public spaces. In a survey of* Pokémon Go *fans and non-fans, it was reported that there was an association between playing the game and increased positive affect and friendship formation (Bonus, Peebles, Mares, & Sarmiento, 2018). Even reality TV, despite its many flaws (see Close-up 11.10) has shown some elevation effects. Specifically, compared to game-show-style reality shows (e.g.,* The Amazing Race, Survivor*), lifestyle transformation reality shows (e.g.,* Supernanny, Extreme Makeover Home Edition*) were perceived as more thought-provoking and meaningful (Tsay-Vogel & Krakowiak, 2016).*

Can children learn such prosocial attitudes and behaviors from watching them on television? A few studies suggest they can. Rosenkoetter (1999) had first, third, and fifth graders watch episodes of the family sitcoms *The Cosby Show* and *Full House* and found that the large majority at all ages comprehended the lessons from the *Cosby* episode, and about half did so from the *Full House* episode. How many hours of prosocial sitcoms children watched was a moderate predictor of first graders' actual prosocial behavior, as judged by their parents, although this difference was less pronounced with older children. In a meta-analysis of 34 studies of the positive effects of prosocial TV content, Mares and Woodard (2005) found strong effects of such content on prosocial behaviors, especially altruism. Another study exposed some kids to a prosocial news segment about UNICEF. Compared to children who had not seen the news clip, the ones who had were significantly more likely to donate money and help with UNICEF in their own school (de Leeuw, Kleemans, Rozendaal, Anschütz, & Buijzen, 2015). Other studies have shown that virtual reality technology can be used to teach compassion and empathy (Gillath, McCall, Shaver, & Blascovich, 2008). For a good review of the possible prosocial effects of media, particularly with regard to children, see Mares, Palmer, and Sullivan (2011).

Now let us turn from specific programming and effects for children to the use of media more broadly to further prosocial aims. We begin by looking at the general area of social marketing.

Media Use in Social Marketing

A traditionally under-emphasized but currently booming area in the world of marketing is social marketing. Sometimes difficult to define, the general goal of *social marketing* is to use media to promote behaviors that lead to improved health or well-being (Quinn,

Ellery, Thomas, & Marshall, 2010). This can involve the "selling" of socially and personally positive actions to improve one's health or safety such as avoiding tobacco and drunk driving (Backer, Rogers, & Sopory, 1992; Brown & Walsh-Childers, 2002; Cismaru, Lavack, & Markewich, 2009; White, Durkin, Coomber, & Wakefield, 2015). Thus, many social critics, researchers, and practitioners long concerned with selling products are now turning their attention to selling healthy, safe, and socially positive lifestyles. Mass media are a major, although not the only, component of a social marketing campaign.

Although theory building in this area has not been extensive (Luca & Suggs, 2013), some researchers have offered possible theoretical foundations behind social marketing. For example, Manrai and Gardner (1992) developed a model to explain how the differences between social and product advertising predict a consumer's cognitive, social, and emotional reactions to social advertising. Hornik and Yanovitzky (2003) argued that a theory of prosocial media effects is essential in designing such campaigns. Dutta (2007) suggested some directions for including cultural variables in theory development in regard to health communication, Southwell (2005) proposed a multilevel model of memory to look at memory for health ads, and Dunlop, Wakefield, and Kashima (2008) proposed a model looking at types of emotional responses to health communication.

Obstacles to Social Marketing

Although selling good health or safety is in many ways not unlike selling products like soap or automobiles (Andreasen, 2012; Dann, 2010), there are some challenges that are particularly acute for social marketing that don't apply to the selling of products. Social and product advertising differ in several important ways, most of which lead to greater obstacles facing public health and other social advertisers, compared to those faced by commercial advertisers (Goldberg, 1995; Manrai & Gardner, 1992; Storey, Hess, & Saffitz, 2015). First, social ideas tend to have a higher degree of both shared benefits and shared responsibilities than products, whose use is most often entirely an individual choice. For example, some (perhaps most) of the benefits of recycling household waste will be to society, not to the individual. Consequently, individuals may view society, not themselves, as also having much (or most) of the responsibility for the problem. Thus, motivating (i.e., selling) the social message will be more difficult than selling a product, which has clear benefits to the individual.

Second, the benefits that do exist with social marketing tend to be delayed or intangible. Often there is a great physical, or at the very least psychological, distance between the consumer and the product. Selling cologne can stress how much sexier you will be for that big date tonight. Selling the idea of quitting smoking has a much less immediate payoff. Teen smokers think much more about looking cool with their friends today than about dying from lung cancer or emphysema in 30 or 40 years. Young, healthy adults do not typically feel much urgency to sign an organ donor card; psychologically the need is very distant. With social marketing, consumers are often not all that opposed to the message and may even support it; they simply do not feel the immediacy of it and thus are not particularly motivated to make much effort to act on the message.

Third, social marketing campaigns are often very complex, compared to what is typically involved in commercial marketing. Particularly with regard to health, the beliefs, attitudes, and motives for unhealthy practices tend to be deeply rooted and highly emotion-laden and thus rigidly resistant to change. For example, efforts to convince women to self-examine their breasts for lumps flies against their enormous fear of cancer and the potential damage to their sexual self-image by the contemplation of possible breast surgery. Convincing people to wear seatbelts when they have driven for 50 years without doing so is not easy. People are particularly resistant to change if anxieties occur in response to unrealistic but prevalent fears, such as the irrational fear of being declared dead prematurely in order for the doctors to acquire organs for transplantation (Harris, Jasper, Lee, & Miller, 1991; Nizza, Britton, & Smith, 2016; Shanteau & Harris, 1990). The complexity of the interaction of individual motives for behavior, the social context of that behavior, and the specific prosocial appeals can be very difficult to unravel in conceptual and theoretical terms (Logie-MacIver, Piacentini, & Eadie, 2012; Yanovitzky & Bennett, 1999).

Fourth, social marketing messages frequently face strong opposition, unlike product advertising. This opposition may be social, as in the adolescent peer group that encourages and glamorizes smoking and tanned bodies, or it may be organized and institutional, as when tobacco companies threaten to withdraw advertising from magazines that carry articles about the dangers of smoking. Social marketing campaigns tend to be poorly funded compared to product advertising, and they often face opposing forces that hold enormous economic and political power. For example, the Tobacco Institute, pharmaceutical industries, oil companies, and the National Rifle Association are tremendously powerful lobbies quick to oppose media messages against smoking or prescription drug abuse, or in favor of alternative energy sources or gun controls, respectively. PSAs, whether print or broadcast, tend to be poorer in technical quality and appear less frequently than commercial ads because of lower budgets. Although radio and TV stations air a certain number of unpaid PSAs, they generally do so at times when they are least able to profitably sell advertising. We see many PSAs while watching late night TV, but there are very few during the Olympics, *Monday Night Football*, or *American Idol*. Thus, specific demographic groups cannot be targeted by PSAs as well as they can by commercial advertising.

Fifth, social marketers often set unrealistically high goals, such as changing the behavior of 50% of the public. Although a commercial ad that affects 1–10% of consumers is hugely successful, social marketers often have not fully appreciated that an ad that affects even a very small percentage of a mass audience is a substantial accomplishment. Persons preparing social marketing campaigns are often less thoroughly trained in advertising, media, and marketing than are those conducting product ad campaigns. A few meta-analyses of mediated health campaigns (Cugelman, Thelwall, & Dawes, 2011; Parcell, Kwon, Miron, & Bryant, 2007; Snyder, 2007) show significant, though modest, effect sizes for such campaigns. Effect sizes also vary depending on the subject of the campaign and whether one is looking at behavioral or attitudinal/knowledge outcomes.

Finally, social marketing appeals are often aimed at the 15% or so of the population that is least likely to change. These may be the least educated, most traditional, or oldest segments of the population, precisely the people least likely to stop smoking or overeating, or to start wearing seatbelts, exercising, or requesting medical checkups. Just as political media strategists target advertising at the few undecided voters, so might social marketing best target those people most conducive to attitude and behavior change in the intended direction, rather than the group that is least likely to ever change at all.

Considering the Audience

Knowing the audience well and targeting it as specifically as possible is as helpful in selling health or safety as it is in marketing toothpaste, beer, or political candidates. Choosing a realistic audience, not those least likely to change, and setting realistic goals and targets are useful. Trying to see the issue from the audience's point of view will make a more convincing message. Frequently social marketers are fervently convinced of the rightness of their message and fail to see how anyone else could view the issue differently. Self-righteousness or telling people they *should* do something tends not to be convincing (Pentecost, Arli, & Thiele, 2017).

The attitudes, desires, motivations, and reasonable beliefs of the audience may be used to drive the character of the message. A serious consideration of what kinds of psychological appeals will be the most effective in motivating the particular target audience will be helpful. For example, when adolescents are targeted, given their strong sense of invulnerability, their possible skepticism, and their habit of looking to other people for approval and comparison, forcing them to focus on the message and elaborate its meaning more deeply can be successful in reducing risk-taking behavior (Greene, Krcmar, Rubin, Walters, & Hale, 2002; Thakor & Goneau-Lessard, 2009). If the goal of a social marketing campaign is a reduction in binge drinking in college students, there could be important differences in the motivations of "light," "medium," and "heavy" binge drinkers (Deshpande & Rundle-Thiele, 2011). To focus an appeal on the notion that some behavior is stupid when in fact it appears adaptive within the target person's world (e.g., smoking, drug use, driving recklessly) or from the framework of his or her personality (e.g., as a sensation seeker) is not likely to be convincing (Morgan, Palmgreen, Stephenson, Hoyle, & Lorch, 2003; Nell, 2002; Stephenson, 2003). In cases when the approval and influence of peers is especially critical, such as in young adults' decision to start smoking or drinking, those seeking to promote healthier alternatives must understand the complexities of how this peer influence operates (Fitzpatrick, Martinez, Polidan, & Angelis, 2016; Gunther, Bolt, Borzekowski, Liebhart, & Dillard, 2006; Paek & Gunther, 2007). Perceived realism and relevance to one's life are also important (Andsager, Austin, & Pinkleton, 2001), as is the nature of the specific language used in the appeal (Miller, Lane, Deatrick, Young, & Potts, 2007), perceived risk (Falco, Piccirelli, Girardi, Dal Corso, & De Carlo, 2013), and the personality of members of the target audience (Lang, Chung, Lee, Schwartz, & Shin, 2005).

When designing social marketing for children, the age of the child in the target group is vitally important to consider. For example, in researching obstacles to promoting sunscreen use, Paul, Tzelepis, Parfitt, and Girgis (2008) found that the social pressure of getting a tan was higher in older adolescents than in younger kids. In another example testing anti-smoking posters, Peracchio and Luna (1998) found that 7- to 8-year-olds responded best to a picture of a dirty sock labeled "gross" next to an ashtray full of cigarette butts labeled "really gross." The 9- to 10-year-olds responded best to pictures of dead insects with a message saying smoking is chemically equivalent to spraying yourself in the face with insecticide, while 11-year-olds responded best to a poster of a car's tailpipe with written copy asking why you would smoke if you wouldn't suck car exhaust. Even adolescents and college students may respond differently to the same PSAs (Lang *et al.*, 2005; Paek, 2008). Recent research has also found that targeting young people technologically can be smart in that mobile text messaging can be a very effective way to promote healthy behaviors in children and adolescents

(Militello, Kelly, & Melnyk, 2012). See Close-up 11.7 for other examples of how clever social marketers have used familiar characters and technology to encourage safe and healthy behaviors.

❖ CLOSE-UP 11.7 CAN CHANGING BEHAVIOR BE FUN? HEALTH PROMOTION VIA GAMES, COMICS, AND SUPERHEROES

Throughout this book, we have discussed video games and some of their effects. Gamification *is a twenty-first century attempt to add features of games, particularly video games, to encourage some behaviors. The idea is generally that by adding elements of achievement, reward, competition, and fun, people may become more motivated to do some tasks, particularly ones that might seem mundane. Gamification has been applied to areas like education (Mora, Riera, González, & Arnedo-Moreno, 2017), learning to drive (Fitz-Walter, Johnson, Wyeth, Tjondronegoro, & Scott-Parker, 2017), banking (Rodrigues, Oliveira, & Costa, 2016), and even parenting (Love et al., 2016).*

One of the most interesting ways that gamification has been used is for health promotion. Many mobile phone apps for weight loss, nutrition, and activity monitoring use elements of gamification like electronic badges or trophies as rewards for achieving a goal (such as walking 10,000 steps in a day or losing a few pounds). Maturo and Setiffi (2016) found that such gamification apps can be effective because they combine rational thinking through quantification (e.g., calorie intake) and emotional fun and support (e.g., virtual prizes) to keep people motivated to continue. However, another study found that while health gamification may promote short-term behavior change, it seems to do little to alter internal motivations, so lasting change may be more difficult to achieve (Mitchell, Schuster, & Drennan, 2017).

A safety campaign years ago in Central America also sought to use fun elements as a way to teach children in war-torn lands how to avoid the lethal land mines that remain dangerous long after a war has ended. A part of the Organization of American States (OAS) De-mining Assistance Program in Central America involved the distribution of over 600,000 copies of special Superman y la Mujer Maravilla *comic books in schools in Honduras, Guatemala, and Nicaragua. In this collaborative project of UNICEF, D.C. Comics, and the U.S. Army's Southern Command, Superman grabs Diego just before he steps on an antipersonnel mine, while Wonder Woman (La Mujer Maravilla) saves little Gabriela from a mine in a stream where she is washing clothes. A similar comic book had been successful at alerting children to land mines in the former Yugoslavia in 1996 (Mesmer, Baskind, & Lerdau, 1998).*

Popular but non-superhero comic book characters can also be useful in social marketing. In Zambia and several other African countries, a popular comic book and video character is 12-year-old Sara, a girl whose adventures include outwitting her greedy uncle who tries to steal her school fees, rescuing a friend who is about to be sexually molested, escaping from older women attempting genital mutilation, and making a smokeless cooking stove for her mother. The UNICEF-produced series has become very popular and provides a role model for empowering adolescent girls in societies that have not always valued education for girls (Bald, 1998).

In the United States, the organization Stomp out Bullying *teamed up with Marvel Comics for a campaign that featured comic book covers with anti-bullying scenes featuring the likes of Captain America and the Hulk ("Marvel Entertainment," 2014). The collaboration was seen as logical given that many comic book superheroes' backstories include incidences of bullying. Taking it a step further, one group of advocates (Brown, Nasiruddin, Cabral, & Soohoo, 2016) has even suggested creating comic book heroes out of historic public health figures. Imagine one day reading a comic book about how Louis Pasteur saves lives by battling food-borne illnesses or how Edward Jenner eradicates smallpox by developing a vaccine!*

Demographic factors may also affect viewers' response to a PSA. For instance, Meirick (2008) found that people would infer that the predominant gender, age, and ethnic groups present in antidrug PSAs were the predominant target of the PSA. The more of those groups the viewer belonged to, the more he or she self-identified as the intended audience.

Emphasizing specific behaviors that the audience may be able to change one small step at a time is often more useful than a general exhortation aimed at changing general attitudes. People may know very well that they should stop smoking, lose weight, or start wearing seatbelts. What they most need are more specific, realistic behaviors that can be successfully used to meet that end. Often, existing motivation may be harnessed and channeled to build confidence in taking appropriate specific actions.

Merely exhorting people to stop smoking may be of limited use. Showing a PSA of a young child smoking and talking about how cool he looks, just like Daddy, might reach the smoking parent more effectively. In one study, a workshop in which teens not only discussed and analyzed but also actually wrote and produced anti-smoking messages was more effective than a workshop in which they merely analyzed cigarette and anti-smoking ads (Banerjee & Greene, 2006). Further, if people are told that many others are also engaging in the bad behavior it may boomerang by legitimatizing the unwanted behavior (see Close-up 11.8).

❖ CLOSE-UP 11.8 CONVINCING PEOPLE NOT TO STEAL PETRIFIED WOOD FROM A NATIONAL PARK

Social psychologist Robert Cialdini and his colleagues (Cialdini, 2003; Cialdini et al., 2006) have discovered that some types of appeals are more effective than others in discouraging environmental theft. He performed a very clever field experiment in Arizona's Petrified Forest National Park, which had suffered from a loss of 14 tons of petrified wood stolen by visitors each year. Cialdini tested the relative effectiveness of two types of signs posted at entrances to visitor walking paths. The descriptive-norm appeal read, "Many visitors have removed petrified wood from the park, changing the natural state of the Petrified Forest" and was accompanied by pictures of three visitors taking wood. The injunctive-norm sign stated, "Please don't remove the petrified wood from the park, in order to preserve the natural state of the Petrified Forest" and was accompanied by a picture of one person stealing a piece of wood with a red circle and bar over his hand. Results showed that theft of specially marked pieces of petrified wood over five weeks was higher (7.9%) in the vicinity of the descriptive-norm signs than it was around the injunctive-norm signs (1.7%).

Why the difference? Cialdini argued that the descriptive-norm approach, although trying to impress on visitors the enormity of the theft problem, in fact may have legitimized it by suggesting "everybody does it." This was exactly the problem with the very popular "social norms" approach to curb binge drinking in the 1990s and 2000s; by stressing how many people are doing it, the PSAs actually legitimized the behavior they were trying to eliminate.

Positive Effects of Social Marketing

In spite of the obstacles, a spate of research has shown that social marketing media campaigns do have some clear positive effects. The first kind of effect is an altered perceived reality that includes a heightened awareness of the problem. Virtually everyone in North America is aware of the health dangers of smoking, driving drunk, and not wearing seatbelts; such was not the case 40 or 50 years ago. Unlike 30 years ago, most people today are also aware of the need to recycle and sign organ donor cards, largely due to media publicity.

A second positive effect is making the problem more salient, thereby increasing receptivity to other influences in the same direction later. Even though a particular PSA may not immediately send a person to the doctor to check a suspicious mole for possible melanoma, that person may pay more attention to a later message on that topic and perhaps be a little more careful about excessive exposure to the sun. An eventual behavioral change may actually be a cumulative effect from several influences. This, of course, makes it very difficult to scientifically measure precise effects of particular media campaigns.

A third effect is stimulating later conversation with one's family, friends, or doctor. Publicity about the dangers of smoking may encourage dinner table conversation between parents and teenagers who are being encouraged by peers to smoke. Although a decision not to smoke may result more from the personal interaction than directly from the message, the latter may have partially laid the groundwork for the discussion. Sometimes such conversation may not have the desired effect, however. For example, David, Cappella, and Fishbein (2006) found that teens discussing anti-marijuana ads actually had stronger pro-marijuana attitudes after discussing the ads in an online chat room than did teens who had not had the online chat opportunity. Also, the attitudes were not affected by the strength of the anti-marijuana arguments in the ads.

Sometimes media publicity may help create an overreaction. In the early 1990s, pediatricians were being warned against overdiagnosing Lyme disease. A high level of media publicity over the preceding few years was leading patients to ask about this illness and physicians to be quick to diagnose it. In the psychological realm, the explosion in the 1990s of the "recovery" of repressed memories relating to child sexual abuse in adults, based only on very common and nonspecific symptoms (sometimes accompanied by some widely publicized celebrity "victims"), led to huge overdiagnosis of child sexual abuse effects. This in turn resulted in highly divisive controversies in the counseling field (Loftus & Ketcham, 1994).

A fourth effect of social marketing campaigns is self-initiated information seeking in individuals (Afifi & Weiner, 2006). People may seek additional information on some topic as a result of interest being piqued by media attention to that issue. They might ask their doctor about it on their next visit; they might search the Internet for information; or they may read an online article on the topic that they would have passed by before. For instance, one study found that people exposed to online smoking cessation PSAs were more likely than those who had not to seek out additional anti-smoking information online (Kim, Duke, Hansen, & Porter, 2012). However, sometimes sick people seek additional information and sometimes they do not, and the reasons for doing so may be complex (Rains, 2008; Zhao & Cai, 2008). For example, in a study of breast cancer patients, Lee, Hwang, Hawkins, and Pingree (2008) found that negative emotion (feeling bad about one's illness) was correlated with greater health information seeking in those with high health self-efficacy, that is, those who felt in control of their situation. On the other hand, negative emotion was negatively correlated with health information seeking in those low in health self-efficacy. Thus, that bad feeling may work in opposite directions, depending on the degree of control over a given condition that the individual feels.

Finally, prosocial media campaigns can reinforce positive existing attitudes and behavior, such as encouraging the ex-smoker to try hard not to succumb or reinforcing someone's feeling that he or she really should see a doctor about some medical condition. Often people know what they should do but need a little encouragement to actually do it. For example, newspaper coverage of youth advocacy efforts against smoking contributed to a decline in smoking among those exposed to those news stories (Niederdeppe, Farrelly, Thomas, Wenter, & Weitzenkamp, 2007).

Now we examine one of the major domains of social marketing campaigns, public health.

Public Health Media Campaigns

Public health pioneer Breslow (1978) identified three methods of risk-factor intervention in public health campaigns. *Epidemiological intervention* involves identifying the characteristics correlated with increased frequency of the disease and taking steps to alter those characteristics. For example, cardiovascular risk factors like smoking, obesity, cholesterol level, physical inactivity, and hypertension are first identified, followed by screening people using blood pressure and blood chemistry tests.

Environmental intervention involves changing the environment in a healthier direction. For example, legislation restricting smoking in public places or reducing industrial emissions into the air or water, and adding fluoride to drinking water illustrate such interventions. Adding air bags to cars, substituting canola oil for coconut oil in fried foods, and selling lower fat milk also manipulate the environment. Although sometimes harder to implement politically, such changes often yield huge improvements in health over time.

The third type of intervention, *educational programming*, often involves media and is of most concern for our purposes. Such programs may aim to alter the perceived reality by providing more information or providing an impetus for changing behavior and thereby making a change in the knowledge base. Often changes in knowledge are easier to produce than changes in behavior. For example, even though most smokers are well aware that smoking is bad for their health, their own perceived reality, at least at an emotional level, is that they will not themselves develop lung cancer (the kind of cognitive dissonance discussed in Chapter 2). Sometimes the most important cognitive message of such a campaign is that treatment and cure is possible if the illness is diagnosed early enough. This is important in combating irrational fears that a diagnosis of cancer is a death sentence and thus to be avoided at all costs.

All three types of interventions must keep in mind the culture and demographics of the target population (Deshpande & Rundle-Thiele, 2011; Ilola, 1990). For example, an HIV/AIDS-prevention campaign would (or at least should) take a very different form if targeted at North American gay men, IV drug users, health care workers, or African heterosexual women without much social power to resist their partners' requests for intercourse.

Multiple Channels: Cardiac Risk Reduction Projects

One thing social marketers often consider is using multiple media forms to promote health campaigns. Social media, being one of the newer forms of communication, have been employed as one element in a number health promotion studies recently; overall, results of social media's effectiveness in this role seem unclear (Balatsoukas, Kennedy, Buchan, Powell, & Ainsworth, 2015). However, a very clear and consistent finding from studies of public health social marketing campaigns is that mass media campaigns are most successful when used in conjunction with other types of intervention (see Borland, 2014, and Solomon & Cardillo, 1985, for discussions of the components of such campaigns). A good example of such a campaign is the extensive and relatively well-controlled project conducted by some years ago by Stanford University to reduce the instance of coronary heart disease and related factors (Farquhar *et al.*, 1990; Schooler, Chaffee, Flora, & Roser, 1998; Schooler, Flora, & Farquhar, 1993; Schooler, Sundar, & Flora, 1996). This project involved three central California towns, each with a population of 12,000 to 15,000. Two of the towns received multimedia (newspaper, television, radio, direct mail) campaigns over a two-year period about the risks of coronary heart disease (CHD). One of those towns also received intensive interventions targeted at the high-risk population. These interventions involved both media messages and cooperation from the medical community. Health screenings were held, specific behavior-modification programs were set up, and people's attempts to reduce high-risk behaviors and characteristics were monitored.

Changes in both knowledge and behavior were monitored in the experimental towns and in the control town, which received no media campaign and no intervention. Results showed that media campaigns by themselves produced some increases in knowledge but only very modest, if any, changes in behavior or decreases in the overall percentage of at-risk people. Only when media campaigns were coupled with specific behavioral interventions and health monitoring were significant improvements and reduction of the numbers in the at-risk population seen. Similar results were found with other projects on cardiovascular health, such as a six-city study in Minnesota (Luepker *et al.*, 1994) and in developing countries like India and Indonesia (van de Vijver, Oti, Addo, de Graft-Aikins, & Agyemang, 2012).

Even more dramatic success came in the North Karelia project in rural Eastern Finland, which had one of the highest CHD rates in the world. Along with media campaigns and medical intervention, environmental interventions were also instituted, including restrictions on smoking, selling more low-fat dairy foods, and the substitution of mushrooms for fat in the local sausage. After four and a half years of the project, there were dramatic reductions in systolic blood pressure and stroke incidence (McAlister, Puska, & Salonen, 1982). This project had local and national government cooperation and combined what Wallack, Dorfman, Jernigan, and Themba (1993) labeled downstream and upstream marketing.

Downstream efforts have been widely researched (Truong, 2014) and involve attempts to change consumers' behavior (e.g., stopping smoking, starting to exercise, seeking medical checkups), while *upstream* efforts work at changing the conditions that produce or encourage the unhealthy behaviors (e.g., restricting tobacco sales to minors, prohibiting smoking in some places, stopping the sale of high-fat meat, raising the drinking age, forcing insurance companies to pay for mammograms). Downstream promotion, which has been the predominant approach in social marketing, is often limited in what it can accomplish without some upstream changes as well (Goldberg, 1995; Wood, 2016).

Even the riches of health information on the Internet are of limited value in isolation. For example, Gustafson and colleagues (2008) studied newly diagnosed breast cancer patients and tested the relative efficacy of a control group, an Internet-only group, and a group with Internet access plus additional support and decision and analysis tools. The group with the comprehensive resources did better than the control group or the group with Internet access only in terms of quality of life and social support, even though that included numerous high-quality medical websites. Other research has shown that the thoroughness of websites and user motivation are critical factors in the perceived source credibility of health websites (Dutta-Bergman, 2004) and that misleading health information on social media may actually be detrimental in coping with illnesses (Balatsoukas *et al.*, 2015).

HIV/AIDS Awareness Campaigns

One of the most pressing public health issues of the past 40 years has been HIV/AIDS. Worldwide, nations and organizations have taken a variety of media approaches to try to increase general awareness and knowledge and to change risky behaviors, especially in high-risk target groups like gay men having unprotected sex, IV drug users, and heterosexuals with multiple sex partners. A content analysis of AIDS-awareness PSAs in the United States televised in 1988 (during the height of the AIDS crisis in the United States) showed that most were directed at the general population, rather than at high-risk target audiences. The ads also tended to emphasize the acquisition of information rather than change of behaviors (Freimuth, Hammond, Edgar, & Monahan, 1990). A later content analysis (DeJong, Wolf, & Austin, 2001) found that most of the PSAs that aired in the United States between 1987 and the early 2000s focused on fear rather than information and skill building. A similar analysis of PSAs in 33 different countries from 1991 to 1994 found that the major emphasis was on general facts and non-behavioral content targeted at a general, poorly defined heterosexual audience (Johnson & Rimal, 1994).

Sometimes particular target groups react differently to HIV/AIDS spots than the general public does (Baggaley, 1988). Historically, prevention programs aimed at gay White men have been the most successful in changing risky behaviors (Coates, 1990; Stall, Coates, & Hoff, 1988; Witte, 1992a), whereas more general appeals and messages targeted at other groups have been less successful. For that reason, those who create PSAs more recently have tried harder to make the ads speak to particular audiences. For example, in testing the appeal of HIV/AIDS PSAs with African American college students, Keys, Morant, and Stroman (2009) found that when celebrities (like Justin Timberlake) appeared in ads, they were most likely to induce attitude change. In an attempt to be even more strategic, Solorio and colleagues (2016) tested a multimedia HIV campaign in Seattle designed for a group deemed at high risk for not getting tested for HIV (and subsequently not receiving early treatment when HIV positive). The campaign included radio PSAs, a hotline, print materials, and social media elements targeting Latino immigrant men between the ages of 18 and 30. In the marketing materials, the authors were careful to not use the label "gay" but rather "men who have sex with other men" because some men in the target audience might not have identified themselves as gay. Using such strategies, there were significant changes in the target audience's attitudes about HIV testing.

Social marketers have also learned that cultural differences are important when designing public health campaigns for different areas of the world. Especially in the developing world, changes in longstanding and deep-rooted social customs are required to slow the spread of HIV. For example, in parts of central Africa, where AIDS is spread primarily from men to women by heterosexual intercourse, polygamy and multiple sex partners for men are condoned, and women may have little social power to resist their husbands' sexual advances or to insist on condom use. Such behaviors and attitudes may be extremely resistant to change, but will have to be altered before the spread of HIV/AIDS can be contained. In recent years there is some encouraging evidence that the spread of HIV/AIDS in some areas of Africa has finally started to decline, due in part to more effective media campaigns but primarily to the greatly increased numbers of HIV-positive patients receiving anti-retroviral drugs in countries like Botswana, South Africa, and Zimbabwe (Rosenberg, 2017).

It's also interesting to note that some HIV/AIDS media health campaigns targeting specific cultural audiences have been heavily criticized. In India, for example, a campaign funded by the Gates Foundation and aimed at truck drivers was criticized as distorted through a Western lens of individualism (Dutta & Archarya, 2015). Another analysis of Indian PSAs found them to be overly focused on victim blaming and HIV being a disease of the poor (Khan, 2014).

In addition to cultural considerations, individual differences matter in how pro-social messages are received. Zhang, Zhang, and Chock (2014) tested multiple factors that might affect people's reception to HIV/AIDS PSAs. One interesting finding was that *self-efficacy*, one's own belief about his or her ability to do something, made a difference. Specifically, those who were already high in condom self-efficacy (e.g., feeling comfortable discussing them with a partner) were more likely to have a change in attitude and behavior after watching a PSA. In addition, Wang and Arpan (2008) reported that African American participants found HIV/AIDS PSAs more persuasive when the spokesperson was of the same rather than a different race.

Sometimes circumstances allow the use of a celebrity to advance the cause of some pro-health topic, as when a celebrity's public admission of dealing with a certain illness or health issue captures considerable press attention (see the discussion of the "Angelina Jolie Effect" at the beginning of this chapter). One of the most celebrated and influential cases came with basketball great Magic Johnson's announcement in 1991 that he was HIV positive. In his particular case, evaluative research has been performed on the effects of his public announcement. Casey and colleagues (2007) performed a meta-analysis of studies reporting the effects of Johnson's revelation that he was HIV positive, having contracted the illness through promiscuous heterosexual behavior. Results showed significant gains in adults' feelings of vulnerability to HIV, children's and adults' knowledge of HIV infection, more positive perception of people with AIDS, and increased numbers of people seeking HIV testing. So Magic's announcement of his condition probably did save many lives.

Although the use of PSAs and other media-based campaigns, especially if coupled with medical or environmental interventions and specific behavioral tips, can be useful in increasing knowledge and sometimes in changing behavior, the sell is a difficult one. Another very different use of media for prosocial ends comes in using entertainment media to convey these prosocial messages in the context of captivating fictional stories. We now turn to this type of media.

Entertainment-Education (E-E) Media

Entertainment media may sometimes be explicitly and intentionally used for socially positive purposes within a society. Many such *entertainment-education (E-E)* campaigns have been implemented in dozens of nations worldwide and are especially prevalent in developing countries (Riley *et al.*, 2017; Sherry, 2002; Singhal, Cody, Rogers, & Sabido, 2004; Singhal & Rogers, 1999). Some of these projects have been carefully evaluated and have shown impressive successes, especially compared to other forms of persuasive messaging (e.g, Borrayo, Rosales, & Gonzalez, 2017). Such results have contributed to their implementation throughout the world. Interestingly enough, this type of media is relatively unknown in much of North America and Europe, but even there it is starting to appear in a somewhat covert fashion.

Sample E-E Programs

In many developing countries, radio and television have long been seen as tools for development and positive social change, rather than merely vehicles for entertainment. Although there were a few early efforts in Peru and the United Kingdom, the first concerted effort in this direction began in 1975, when the giant Mexican network Televisa began to produce several series of programs, many in the very popular genre of telenovela (soap opera) (Khalid & Ahmed, 2014). These programs were explicitly designed to promote gender equality, adult literacy, sexual responsibility, and family planning (Brown, Singhal, & Rogers, 1989; Rogers & Singhal, 1990; Singhal & Rogers, 1989b), though they were first and foremost entertainment. The shows were very popular, and viewers often requested the services promoted by the programs (Lozano, 1992).

Televisa's Descendants

Televisa's model of communicating prosocial messages through entertainment was emulated elsewhere. In 1987, Kenya aired the prosocial soap opera *Tushariane* ("Let's Discuss"), designed to promote family planning; it became one of the most popular shows in the history of Kenyan TV (Brown & Singhal, 1990). The Nigerian soap opera *Cock Crow at Dawn* encouraged the adoption of modern agricultural practices (Ume-Nwagbo, 1986). Televisa's *Sangre Joven* ("Young Blood") telenovela of the early 1990s dealt with family planning, AIDS, and drug abuse. Jamaica produced a family planning radio soap opera, *Naseberry Street*, which reached 40% of the Jamaican population from 1985 to 1989 (Rogers & Singhal, 1990). Peru's *¡Bienvenida Salud!* ("Welcome, Health!") combined a radio drama with popular music, local news, contests, and listener letters and testimonials (Sypher, McKinley, Ventsam, & Valdeavellano, 2002). Created by an international branch of MTV, the soap opera *Shuga* (discussed in more detail below) deals with safe sex practices and the spread of HIV. Originated in Kenya, the show has proven so popular and influential that it spread to Nigeria, and additional versions are also planned for Egypt and India (Szalai, 2017).

Africa

The Rwandan radio drama *Musekeweya* ("New Dawn") is a sort of Romeo-and-Juliet story of Tutsi and Hutu villages on the brink of conflict but saved from it by improved communication. The program was launched in 2007 to try to lead to reconciliation and avoidance of a repeat of the calamitous 1994 Hutu–Tutsi civil war and genocide (Phillips, 2007). The Tanzanian radio soap opera *Twende na Wakati* ("Let's Go with the Times") featured a promiscuous truck driver who contracted HIV. His wife then left him to set up her own business and was "rewarded" by not contracting AIDS. This program reached 55% of the population from 1993 to 1998, with 82% of those saying they had changed their behavior to reduce the chance of HIV infection (Rogers *et al.*, 1999). A somewhat similar radio program in Botswana called *Makgabaneng* ("We Fall and We Rise") featured storylines like lovers falling in love and discussing HIV testing before marriage and couples with one HIV-positive and one HIV-negative partner. Results from one study (Pappas-DeLuca *et al.*, 2008) indicated that those who had listened to the show, particularly frequent listeners, were more willing to get tested for HIV and talk to a partner about testing.

Soul City

One of the most ambitious and successful E-E projects was the South African TV, radio, and public health campaign *Soul City* (Singhal & Rogers, 1999), which over 10 seasons dealt with a range of themes like HIV prevention, maternal and child health, domestic violence, financial literacy, and alcohol abuse. It used a multifaceted approach, with its prime-time TV segment becoming South Africa's top-rated television show and its radio drama airing daily in eight different languages. Very importantly, accompanying public health materials were widely distributed in multiple languages, along with the broadcasts. *Soul City* was very successful in generating discussion and in furthering information-seeking, and the show also led to impressive increases in reported condom use and a commitment to tell one's partner of HIV infection. Before *Soul City*, only 3% agreed that one's HIV-positive status should not be kept secret from one's partner, but afterward 75% agreed the partner should be told. The show also introduced the behavior of banging kitchen pots as a community signal that domestic violence is taking place and as a way of identifying abusers and showing support for victims (Singhal *et al.*, 2004). Since it began airing, *Soul City* has since grown into the Soul City Institute, an organization with a special dedication to women and HIV, including research into the effectiveness of media campaigns in multiple African countries (Jana, Letsela, Scheepers, & Weiner, 2015).

Shuga

Originally set in Kenya (later Nigeria), the drama *Shuga* first aired in 2009. The goal of the series' producers was to portray healthy sexual practices among young adults. A huge hit, the show featured attractive young characters struggling with relationships. Celebrity cameos were also frequent. Some criticized *Shuga* as containing too much sex, and one content analysis (Booker, Miller, & Ngure, 2016) indicated that the show did indeed contain over 10 times the sexual content of typical American TV fare. However, the sex portrayed did have frequent condom use and discussion of sexual risks (Booker *et al.*, 2016). Such portrayals appear to have been beneficial because one analysis found that compared to those who had watched a non-educational program, Nigerian viewers of *Shuga* had improved knowledge and attitudes about HIV and other sex practices (Banerjee, Ferrara, & Orozco, 2017).

India

India has been another country where E-E has taken off. One impressive commercial success was the Indian TV drama *Hum Log* ("We People"), which debuted in 1984. It became the most popular program in the history of Indian TV and also had substantial social impact (Brown & Cody, 1991; Singhal & Rogers, 1989a, 1989c). Although it was a commercial entertainment program, *Hum Log* also had the overt purpose of advancing the status of women through dealing with such issues as wife battering, the dowry system, and the political and social equality of women and men. At the end of every episode, a famous Indian film actor gave a 30- to 50-second summary of the episode and appropriate guides to action. *Hum Log* also encouraged women to work outside of the home and to make more of their own decisions.

Evaluation research (Brown & Cody, 1991) found *Hum Log*'s impact to be substantial, though complex and not always what was expected. For example, many women viewers identified with Bhagwanti, the family matriarch and traditional woman, rather than with her more independent daughters Badki and Chutki, at least in part because of concern over the difficulties that the younger women's more independent stance had brought to them. There is an interesting parallel between the effects of *Hum Log* and the 1970s U.S. sitcom *All in the Family*, in which more traditional viewers identified with the bigoted patriarch Archie Bunker and found him to be a more positive figure than the producers had envisioned (Vidmar & Rokeach, 1974). This phenomenon of some viewers identifying with the intended negative role models has been observed in several nations and has come to be known as the "Archie Bunker effect," so named after the lead character in *All in the Family* (Singhal & Rogers, 1999).

A more recent Indian program, *Jasoos Vijay*, featured a famous Indian actor as a detective who solves mysteries while trying to provide information and reduce the stigma of HIV/AIDS. Each episode ended with a cliff-hanger plot twist, followed by an epilogue by a famous actor. Viewers were encouraged to respond to these epilogues (Singhal *et al.*, 2004). Evaluation of *Jasoos Vijay* found that 16% of the audience reported changing their sexual behavior in the months following the show (Singhal *et al.*, 2004).

Beginning in 2008, another Indian show, *Kyunki ... Jeena Issi Ka Naam Hai* (Because ... That's What Life Is) was a collaboration with UNICEF. The show was somewhat unique in that it was set in a rural part of India. The main goal of the program was to educate women, mothers in particular, about raising healthy children. Topics of episodes included issues such as child marriage, immunization, sanitation, and gender equality. *Kyunki* was widely viewed, and at least one study indicated that it was effective at helping change ideas about social norms (Riley *et al.*, 2017).

Conclusions

Even if there have been some self-reporting biases with E-E research, the effects are impressive. Campaigns have shown considerable effects, if well implemented. The basic entertainment function seems to provide interesting characters with whom the public develops parasocial relationships (Papa *et al.*, 2000; Sood, 2002); see Chapter 3 for further discussion of parasocial media relationships.

The narrative form may also be an especially good format for inserting persuasive messages (Brusse, Fransen, & Smit, 2017; Slater & Rouner, 2002). A good E-E program can increase a viewer/listener's sense of self-efficacy (Bandura, 1997). These beliefs can then lead to prosocial behaviors like using condoms, seeking medical advice, or taking control over one's reproductive health. It can also contribute to a sense of *collective efficacy*, the belief in joint capabilities to forge individual self-interests into a shared agenda (Bandura, 1995). For example, after watching an E-E soap opera with characters dealing with abdominal pain and cervical cancer screenings, Thai American women indicated that they were more likely than a control group to discuss Pap tests with doctors and friends (Love, Mouttapa, & Tanjasiri, 2009). More dramatically, when viewers of a *Soul City* story on wife-battering gather in front of a neighborhood batterer's home and bang their pans in censure, a behavior seen in the series, collective efficacy is achieved (Singhal & Rogers, 2002).

In considering the effectiveness of entertainment-education media in developing countries, Rogers and Singhal (1990; see also Singhal & Rogers, 1999, 2002; Singhal *et al.*, 2004) drew several conclusions:

1. Placing an educational message in an entertainment context can draw a mass audience and earn large profits, which can then be used to support the prosocial campaign.
2. The educational message cannot be too blatant or too much of a hard sell, or the audience will reject it.
3. The effect of the media message in such programs is enhanced by supplementary specific tips about behavior change.
4. The repetition of prosocial themes in a telenovela has a greater effect than a one-shot media PSA campaign. A continuing series like *Soul City* generally will have greater impact than a one-episode story on *Law and Order*. Prosocial campaigns are most successful if the media, government, commercial sponsors, and public health organizations work together.

E-E in the United States

Although few broad-based, popular E-E campaigns have been promulgated in the United States (see the discussion of Afterschool Specials earlier in this chapter, for example), elements of E-E have appeared on American entertainment television from time to time. One of the earliest was the designated driver campaign of the late 1980s (Rosenzweig, 1999). Professor Jay Winsten of the Harvard School of Public Health worked with NBC and over 250 writers, producers, and TV executives over six months to try to incorporate what was then a new idea—the "designated driver"—into TV plotlines. By 1994, the designated driver message had appeared on 160 prime-time shows and had been the main topic of 25. Two-thirds of the public had noted the mention of designated drivers in TV shows, and just over half of young adults reported they had served as a designated driver. By the late 1990s, the drunk-driving fatality rate had fallen by one-third from 10 years earlier, in part due to greater use of designated drivers.

This concept achieved acceptance in part due to a subtle entertainment-education campaign and in part due to changing societal values about the use and abuse of alcohol (see Close-up 11.9).

❖ **CLOSE-UP 11.9 MEDIA VALUES ABOUT SUBSTANCE ABUSE**

Some very deeply held personal values center on substance use and abuse, but even these can change, albeit slowly. In regard to alcohol, the most widely abused drug, the United States has seen decreasing acceptance of alcohol abuse since the mid-1980s. Although social drinking has been modestly reduced, levels remain high, and alcoholism as a disease and a social problem is still rampant, but attitudes toward excessive drinking are somewhat less tolerant than they once were. The drunk is not so much an object of humor as of pity or disgust. Portrayals of drinking on TV have had to, at least implicitly, take note of this. There are still concerns, however, one of the biggest being binge drinking among college students. This is perhaps encouraged by, for example, university newspaper stories about people celebrating their 21st birthdays by visiting several bars until they pass out, or by ads showing a fellow passed out on the bathroom floor with "Happy 21st" written below. Is this just reporting reality or is it legitimizing dangerous antisocial behavior?

Attitudes toward smoking have changed far more dramatically. Like many early TV characters, Lucy and Ricky Ricardo smoked cigarettes regularly in the old I Love Lucy show of the 1950s, sometimes at the specific request of Philip Morris, the tobacco company sponsor. For the most part, however, regular characters on TV series have not smoked since the 1960s, clearly out of a health concern over a possible negative effect on youth seeing admired TV characters smoking (one notable exception is the throwback show Mad Men, which was set in the 1960s). Although this certainly reflects the great decline in the percentage of adult smokers since 1960, it may have also contributed to that decline. Even among teens, smoking is much less cool than it used to be, and television may be part of the reason for that. Curiously, however, the same trend is not as apparent in movies, where characters smoke more frequently; this is probably due in part to product-placement agreements with tobacco companies to feature those products (see Chapter 6).

Finally, most TV shows today are careful not to show illicit drug use by respected characters. Adults or teens may occasionally be shown using drugs, but it is nearly always presented as wrong. For instance, a storyline on the drama This is Us portrayed a main character struggling with a prescription medication addiction. The show was careful to portray the negative effects of the character's addiction, including how it affected family members.

As another example, consider when *ER* Dr. Mark Greene, concerned about overuse of antibiotics and later brutally honest as a side effect of brain surgery, walked into his hospital waiting room and told the patients there not to expect antibiotics for the flu, after which half of them left. Another episode of *ER* used a plotline about morning-after contraception; subsequent research showed that 6 million of the show's 34 million viewers had learned about morning-after contraception from watching the show (Rosenzweig, 1999).

Unbeknownst to many viewers, these plotlines (along with those in many other shows like *Law and Order* and *24*) were written by, or with the cooperation of, the Center for Disease Control and Prevention (CDC), which since 1998 has had an entertainment-education department to assist screenwriters in placing positive health messages in their entertainment scripts for popular TV shows. Viewers do find the information from such shows helpful. A Kaiser Family Foundation study found that one-third of *ER* viewers reported learning something from the show that had been helpful in making health care decisions in their own families ("Going Hollywood," 2007; Stolberg, 2001).

One of the most carefully evaluated cases (also mentioned in Chapter 10) came in the response to the 2001 HIV subplot on the daytime soap opera *The Bold and the Beautiful* (*B&B*), which reached about 4.5 million households at the time. Written in collaboration with the CDC, this week-long sequence had an attractive young man test positive for HIV. He told his doctor that he had always used condoms with recent sexual partners (all women). He also disclosed his HIV-positive status to all of his partners, including the woman he planned to marry. Moreover, he worked to overcome emotional obstacles and interpersonal issues and tried to live a full and productive life. Immediately after each episode, a toll-free phone number for the CDC's national AIDS and HIV hotline appeared on the screen. Call attempts to the HIV hotline increased dramatically just after the airing of the *B&B* episode on these days, and these were not explained by typical daily time trends in calls. For example, on one day there were fewer than 200 calls every hour until the hour just after the show, when there were 1,840 (Kennedy *et al.*, 2004)! This suggests an enormous, and in the United States largely untapped, potential pro-health role for entertainment-education programming.

An organization that the CDC often cooperates with is Hollywood, Health, and Society, which is affiliated with the University of Southern California and was mentioned at the start of this chapter. One collaboration involved spreading the word about BRCA gene mutation and the risk of breast cancer in women. Storylines were woven into two scripted dramas (*ER* and *Grey's Anatomy*) in the fall of 2005. Both stories involved characters learning they had the gene mutation and struggling with the idea of having preventative mastectomies before cancer inevitably set in. Results from one study (Hether, Huang, Beck, Murphy, & Valente, 2008) indicated that this sort of repeated exposure (multiple episodes, multiple shows) was more associated with positive outcomes (like understanding that getting a second opinion is important) than watching just one show.

A review of research done on E-E programming in the United States (Hoffman *et al.*, 2017) revealed that the most evaluated shows over the years have been *ER*, *Grey's Anatomy*, and *House*. Overall, about a third of the studies on E-E found that the programming had a positive influence, with over half having a mixed positive and negative influence. The authors recommended that future research be longitudinal and more directly assess behavioral outcomes rather than just intentions.

E-E or Social Marketing?

In examining explicit public health media campaigns, Flay and Burton (1990; see also Brown & Einsiedel, 1990; Rice & Atkin, 2013) identified seven steps for such a campaign to be maximally effective:

1. Develop and use high-quality messages, sources, and channels.
2. Disseminate effectively to the most appropriate target audience.
3. Gain and keep the attention of the audience.
4. Encourage favorable interpersonal communication about the issue after exposure to the message.
5. Work for behavior changes, as well as changes in awareness, knowledge, and attitudes.
6. Work for broader societal changes.
7. Obtain knowledge of campaign effectiveness through evaluation research.

Interestingly enough, all of these apply just as well to E-E as to traditional public health media campaigns, and in fact some may often be better met through E-E than through traditional social marketing PSA campaigns. For example, people will pay more attention to gripping entertainment media than to PSAs and will talk more about them later. The audiences are potentially huge for E-E messages. Of course, there are ethical issues of concern, particularly in the case of messages not everyone would agree with. For example, if *Modern Family* had a script strongly supporting or opposing the right to abortion, large numbers of viewers would likely be incensed. Still, the E-E path is probably one that deserves a closer look in Western countries. Indeed, one study showed that even just thinking about a popular and sympathetic gay character like Will Truman on *Will and Grace* can do a lot toward increasing that person's acceptance of LGBT people (Bonds-Raacke *et al.*, 2007). This suggests a huge potential role for entertainment media in promoting social change.

Conclusion

A recurring theme throughout this chapter, indeed throughout the entire book, is that the effects of the media depend on more than its content. A perceived reality is constructed by viewers, readers, or listeners as their minds interact with the media message. Reactions also depend on individual factors like personality and one's cultural influences. This is just as true of prosocial media as it is of any other kind of mass communication. We also know that media exhortations to treat other people better or live a healthier lifestyle are more effective if combined with behavioral interventions with specific tips on lifestyle change and support for efforts to do so.

This idea is not unlike research on how children and adults survive traumatic life experiences in general (e.g., Leavitt & Fox, 1993; McAdams & Jones, 2017). The ones who survive and grow, rather than succumb to defeat and trauma, are those who have support in the rough times, those who can talk over the troubling events and have countervailing positive influences to partially balance the strong negative ones. It is almost a truism that media may be a force for ill or good. Much writing and research has focused on the ill wind of TV or the Internet. Media are with us to stay, however; we cannot isolate our children from these influences. However, we can take steps to make that interaction a more positive, even rewarding, experience than it would be otherwise.

Do media merely reflect the state of society or do they serve as a catalyst for changing and even improving that state? Clearly, they do in some sense mirror the state of society, but they can and do serve as a catalyst for change. How this change occurs is of great importance but is far more difficult to study. The cultivation theory approach (see Chapter 2) has been particularly useful here (e.g., Morgan *et al.*, 2009). Television and other media cultivate a worldview through the interaction of the viewer and the content presented. The social reality presented in media gradually becomes the reality for the public. If that media world includes designated drivers and regular use of seatbelts, sunscreen, bike helmets, and condoms as normal, the adoption of that world by the viewers will improve their lives.

Of course, media in fact send many mixed messages on health issues, such as when PSAs stress using condoms and not smoking, on the one hand, and at the same time respected characters in movies smoke and have casual, unprotected intercourse. No wonder many young people are confused about what is normal. In the final analysis, of course, we must remember that, given the economic realities of media, whatever sells the best will be what we see the most of. For example, the relatively recent genre of the so-called "reality shows" offers a quite unrealistic, and even unhealthy, slice of life, yet they draw large numbers of viewers (see Close-up 11.10).

❖ CLOSE-UP 11.10 REALITY SHOWS SHOW THE WORST SIDE OF REALITY

MTV's notorious reality show Jackass *featured stunts like having a group of guys kick their friend in the groin for the amusement of the audience (there were disclaimers of "Don't try this at home"). Another episode featured diving into a sewage holding tank ("poo-diving").* Jackass *was so popular that it became a series of movies, starting in 2002. Along the same line,* Fear Factor *had contestants perform stunts like eating live slugs or dunking their head into a tankful of snakes.*

By 2005, out-of-control brides became common as a reality show sub-category on cable channels. Relatively tame programs like Say Yes to the Dress, *which followed brides making decisions about their wedding gowns, was supplemented by shows like* Bridezillas, *which featured self-centered, pouting, and sometimes violent brides-to-be. Perhaps the worst of this genre was* Bridalplasty, *in which brides competed for their dream gown and the perfect plastic surgery for their wedding day. Taking the wedding theme a step further,* Married at First Sight *had "relationship experts" pair two people who had never met but agreed to get married for the show. "Relationship experts" were also an element of* Sex Box, *a show in which couples had sex in a soundproof box on stage. When the couples were done, they joined the experts on stage to discuss their relationship problems.*

The Survivor-*style reality shows which gained popularity in the early 2000s centered on entertaining audiences by placing groups of people in competition with each other to survive on a desert island. Daily tallies of whom to "vote off the island" kept fans riveted for weeks. An African version of the show* Big Brother *was very popular but was condemned by government and religious leaders of several African nations for its explicit sexual content (Malawi bans* Big Brother Africa, *2003). Perhaps the pinnacle (or pit) of this genre was* Temptation Island, *where faithful couples were surrounded by beautiful opportunities to be unfaithful to their partners while the audience cheered them on. The show* Who Wants to Marry a Millionaire? *presented a handsome young man as a millionaire to be the object of several women's competing affections. The "punch line" was their reactions when the women found out he wasn't really a millionaire. A somewhat similar show called* I Wanna Marry "Harry" *aired a few years before Prince Harry of Britain married Meghan Markle in 2018. In this show, 12 women competed for the affections of a Harry lookalike, whom they were led to believe was the real prince.*

How real are reality shows, anyway? On ABC's The Dating Experiment *the producers wanted a contestant to like one of her "suitors" whom she did not, so they asked her who her favorite celebrity was. "Oh, I really love Adam Sandler," she said. Sandler's name was spliced out and replaced with the name of the suitor before it appeared on the show. On* Joe Millionaire *a contestant and his date disappeared offstage, while "lusty noises and captions" were edited in. A contestant on* The Amazing Race *appeared to be kicked out of a cab after browbeating the driver. In fact the driver had had an accident and the vehicle could not continue, but facile editing made it look like a hostile altercation (Poniewozik, 2006).*

Many have argued that the values communicated by such shows are unhealthy and distressing. In some anxious people they may even trigger anxiety attacks (McCook, 2003). They affect our views of the world, too; those who watch more reality dating shows are more likely to expect real dating to be similar (Ferris, Smith, Greenberg, & Smith, 2007). Some research (Lewis & Weaver, 2015; Marling, 2002; Scarborough & McCoy, 2016) has argued a class bias at work here: we like to watch lower-class "trailer park trash" demean themselves while we smugly sit back and watch and comfort ourselves that we would never stoop so low. Or have we already stooped that low by watching? As a contrast to the reality shows discussed here, see Close-up 5.3 for a description of a very early reality show.

Media Applications, Chapter 11: Harnessing Media Technology to Instigate Change

For all sorts of reasons discussed in this book, it is becoming increasingly difficult to know exactly where mass media stop and personal media begin or to identify the boundary between entertainment or popular culture and mass media. We have taken a broad view of what constitute media, and, as such, have considered films, video games, social media, and various computer-mediated communications as well as the traditional print and broadcast media. It seems likely that such an inclusive scope of what is considered media will continue to be useful and probably necessary in the future. In any event, the evolution of media has had a significant effect on how people use them to instigate or perpetuate social change in what has come to be called "participatory cultures" (Delwiche & Henderson, 2012).

One of the earliest major manifestations of this new communications technology integration appeared in the worldwide fax revolution of Chinese students in response to the 1989 Tiananmen Square massacre and subsequent government crackdown, in which the estimated 10,000 fax numbers in China were jammed for weeks with reports from abroad about what had really happened in Beijing (Ganley, 1992). Much of the communication among those sending the fax messages was by e-mail. Taped newscasts out of Hong Kong (not yet part of China) circulated widely on the 2 million or more VCRs in China. The democratic uprising in China was suppressed, but it would never again be possible to so totally isolate a society from the news of its own oppression, as seen, for example, in the difficulty the Chinese had in blocking news of the 2008 protests over Tibet just before the opening of the Beijing Olympics. Indeed, the technology revolution has been a major factor in the opening up of China in the last two decades. Electronic information in all its forms is not easily controlled, although the Chinese government never seems to stop trying to do so.

Skilled use of the Internet has come to be a common prerequisite for any grassroots social movement, from the Zapatista Army of National Liberation in Chiapas, Mexico (Wolfson, 2012), to the International Campaign for Justice in Bhopal, still fighting for justice for the victims of the catastrophic 1984 gas leak from the Union Carbide plant in Bhopal, India (Goddard, 2017; Pal & Dutta, 2012). As discussed earlier in this book, social media have also been given credit for everything from mobilizing governmental revolutions in the Middle East to social movements like Black Lives Matter in the United States (Chokshi, 2016; Wilson, Gosling, & Graham, 2012).

A newer online tool for social change is *crowdfunding*, in which people set up online accounts through websites like GoFundMe, Kickstarter, and Indiegogo to fund causes. Although people can (and do) make self-centered requests (like booze money) (Timpf, 2016), crowdfunding is more often used to ask for help for things like surgery costs, buying a new wheelchair, or helping animals dislocated from a natural disaster (Mac, 2015). Of course, many crowdfunding campaigns are fueled by pleas on social media. Crowdfunding can get political, too. For example, one movement in Ireland funded the Home to Vote campaign, which helped pay for Irish citizens abroad to travel home to vote on a constitutional amendment overturning abortion (Cogley, 2018). *Civic crowdfunding* is a way for citizens to help their local communities fund projects, like a community garden or saving a historic theater (Stiver, Barroca, Minocha, Richards, & Roberts, 2015). However, some have questioned whether local governments should have to rely on such avenues for funds. What makes a successful crowdfunding case? One study that analyzed Kickstarter appeals found that the more prosocial words there were in the funding description (e.g., "nonprofit," "charity," "humanitarian"), the more investors signed on (Pietraszkiewicz, Soppe, & Formanowicz, 2017).

Cell phone technology, including smartphones, may be changing more lives faster than any other invention. For example, Kenya seems to have mastered the art of bringing wired capability to the masses, with the lowest cell phone charges in Africa. Beyond that, a mobile banking platform called M-Pesa allows the majority of Kenyans to use a text message to pay rent and utilities, buy groceries, or even send money to relatives in isolated villages. M-Pesa and similar monetary technologies have exploded in other areas of the developing world, including Pakistan, India, Tanzania, and Albania ("Mobile financial services," 2018; Murray, 2012; Mutiga, 2014).

Still, however, grandiose claims about new technologies revolutionizing the lives of everyone on the planet may be somewhat premature. Although there are encouraging examples of marginalized people having voices on the Internet (e.g., Mitra, 2004), they may be more the exception than the rule for the poor majority of the planet. In fact, many believe that new communications technologies will only widen the gap between the rich and the poor. Consider, for example, Wresch's (1996) look at two Namibian men, one rich and one poor. The poor man, Negumbo, has no skills, no job, and no electricity. Newspapers cost one-tenth of his daily wage, on days that he manages to find work. Few in his neighborhood have TV, and it is all in English, a language he does not understand. His news sources are largely limited to one radio station that broadcasts in his language. He has traveled nowhere but his village in northern Namibia and the capital, Windhoek.

The rich Namibian man, Theo, is president of his own computer company, drives a BMW, speaks three languages, and is wired into the world via mobile phone, e-mail, and the Internet. He also makes at least yearly trips to Germany and the United States and has a buyer in California who sends him a weekly shipment. He can come home and watch American sitcoms, Mexican soap operas, or a variety of movies on his TV (but no Namibian movies—there aren't any). Even as the information revolution wires Theo into more and more places, his countryman Negumbo becomes more and more isolated. Developing countries like Namibia are becoming increasingly divided by information as well as income, and it is not at all clear that technology will bridge this gap anytime soon.

All of this brings us back to the question of why study the psychology, especially cognitive psychology, of the media? At heart media offer an experience that emerges from the interaction of our minds with the content of the communication. Media affect our minds: they give us ideas, change our attitudes, and show us what the world is like or what it can be like. Our mental constructions (i.e., our perceived reality) then become the framework around which we interpret the totality of experience. Thus, media consumption and effects are very much cognitive phenomena.

In one sense, media production is a creation, a fabrication. But yet, as Picasso once said, "Art is a lie through which we can see the truth." The same is often true of media. Performing in media is action, pretending, taking a role, but as Oscar Wilde once said, "I love acting; it is so much more real than life." One might say the same about media. Life imitates art, and art imitates life. After a while, it becomes hard to tell which is which.

Further Reading

Calvert, S. L. (2015). Children and digital media. In R. M. Lerner (Ed.), *Handbook of child psychology and developmental science* (pp. 1–41). Hoboken, NJ: John Wiley & Sons. https://doi.org/10.1002/9781118963418.childpsy410

Danish, S. J., & Donohue, T. R. (1996). Understanding the media's influence on the development of antisocial and prosocial behavior. In R. Hampton, P. Jenkins, & T. Gullotta (Eds.), *Preventing violence in America* (pp. 133–156). Thousand Oaks, CA: Sage.

Davis, M. (2014). *Street gang: The complete history of Sesame Street*. New York: Penguin Books.

Greitemeyer, T., & Mügge, D. O. (2014). Video games do affect social outcomes: A meta-analytic review of the effects of violent and prosocial video game play. *Personality and Social Psychology Bulletin*, 40(5), 578–589. doi:10.1177/0146167213520459

Useful Links

Centers for Disease Control and Prevention Resources for Entertainment Writers:
www.cdc.gov/healthcommunication/ToolsTemplates/EntertainmentEd/

Hollywood, Health, and Society:
https://hollywoodhealthandsociety.org/about-us/overview

Some international versions of *Sesame Street*:
http://muppet.wikia.com/wiki/International_Sesame_Street

For more resources, please visit the companion website:
www.routledge.com/cw/harris

Note

1 For years, comedians, bloggers, and others have been speculating, and joking, that the *Sesame Street* characters Bert and Ernie might be more than roommates. One independent filmmaker even made a spoof called *Ernest and Bertram* in 2002, about the two characters being outed as a gay couple in the press. Sesame Workshop did not respond kindly to the film, ordering screenings stopped under charges of copyright infringement. An official at Sesame Workshop at the time said that Bert and Ernie "do not portray a gay couple, and there are no plans for them to do so in the future. They are puppets, not humans" (Maerz, 2010, ¶14). Nevertheless, the "rumors" have continued, and Bert and Ernie were featured on an illustrated cover of *The New Yorker*, cuddling romantically after the U.S. Supreme Court decision that legalized same-sex marriage in 2015.

References

Abel, G. G., Barlow, D. H., Blanchard, E. B., & Guild, D. (1977). The components of rapists' sexual arousal. *Archives of General Psychiatry*, 34, 895–903.

Abelman, R., Atkin, D. J., & Lin, C. A. (2007). Meta-analysis of television's impact on special populations. In R. W. Preiss, B. M. Gayle, N. Burrell, M. Allen, & J. Bryant (Eds.), *Mass media effects research: Advances through meta-analysis* (pp. 119–135). Mahwah, NJ: Erlbaum.

About Channel One News (2009, December 16). Retrieved from www.channelone.com/about/faq/

Abramsky, S. (2017). *Jumping at shadows: The triumph of fear and the end of the American dream.* New York: Nation Books.

Abramson, P. R., & Hayashi, H. (1984). Pornography in Japan: Cross-cultural and theoretical considerations. In N. M. Malamuth & E. Donnerstein (Eds.), *Pornography and sexual aggression* (pp. 173–183). Orlando, FL: Academic Press.

Abril, E. P., Szczypka, G., & Emery, S. L. (2017). LMFAO! Humor as a response to fear: Decomposing fear control within the extended parallel process model. *Journal of Broadcasting & Electronic Media*, 61(1), 126–143.

Adams, R. C., Sumner, P., Vivian-Griffiths, S., Barrington, A., Williams, A., Boivin, J., … Bott, L. (2017). How readers understand causal and correlational expressions used in news headlines. *Journal of Experimental Psychology: Applied*, 23(1), 1–14.

Aday, S. (2010). Chasing the bad news: An analysis of 2005 Iraq and Afghanistan war coverage on NBC and Fox News Channel. *Journal of Communication*, 60, 144–164.

Afifi, W. A., & Weiner, J. L. (2006). Seeking information about sexual health: Applying the theory of motivated information management. *Human Communication Research*, 32(1), 35–57.

Ahn, D., Jin, S.-A. A, & Ritterfeld, U. (2012). "Sad movies don't always make me cry?" The cognitive and affective processes underpinning enjoyment of tragedy. *Journal of Media Psychology*, 24(1), 9–18.

Ahn, H.-Y., Park, J. S., & Haley, E. (2014). Consumers' optimism bias and responses to risk disclosures in direct-to-consumer (DTC) prescription drug advertising: The moderating role of subjective health literacy. *Journal of Consumer Affairs*, 48(1), 175–194.

Ahn, W. K., Brewer, W. F., & Mooney, R. J. (1992). Schema acquisition from a single example. *Journal of Experimental Psychology: Learning, Memory, and Cognition*, 18, 391–412.

Aladé, F., & Nathanson, A. I. (2016). What preschoolers bring to the show: The relation between viewer characteristics and children's learning from educational television. *Media Psychology*, 19(3), 406–430.

Alali, A. O., & Eke, K. K. (Eds.). (1991). *Media coverage of terrorism: Methods of diffusion.* Newbury Park, CA: Sage.

Albury, K. (2014). Porn and sex education, porn as sex education. *Porn Studies*, 1(1–2), 172–181.

Alia-Klein, N., Wang, G.-J., Preston-Campbell, R. N., Moeller, S. J., Parvaz, M. A., Zhu, W., … Volkow, N. D. (2014). Reactions to media violence: It's in the brain of the beholder. *PLOS ONE*, 9(9), e107260. doi: 10.1371/journal.pone.0107260

Allen, M., Emmers, T., Gebhardt, L., & Giery, M. A. (1995). Exposure to pornography and acceptance of rape myths. *Journal of Communication*, 45(1), 5–26.

Allen, M., d'Alessio, D., Emmers, T., & Gebhardt, L. (1996). The role of educational briefings in mitigating effects of experimental exposure to violent sexually explicit material: A meta-analysis. *Journal of Sex Research*, 33, 135–141.

Allen, M., Emmers-Sommer, T. M., D'Alessio, D., Timmerman, L., Hanzal, A., & Korus, J. (2007). The connection between the physiological and psychological reactions to sexually explicit materials: A literature summary using meta-analysis. *Communication Monographs*, 74(4), 541–560.

Allen, M., Herrett-Skjellum, J., Jorgenson, J., Ryan, D. J., Kramer, M. R., & Timmerman, L. (2007). Effects of music. In R. W. Preiss, B. M. Gayle, N. Burrell, M. Allen, & J. Bryant (Eds.), *Mass media effects research: Advances through meta-analysis* (pp. 263–279). Mahwah, NJ: Erlbaum.

Alperstein, N. (1991). Imaginary social relationships with celebrities appearing in television commercials. *Journal of Broadcasting and Electronic Media*, 35, 43–58.

Alsultany, E. (2016). The cultural politics of Islam in U.S. reality television. *Communication, Culture & Critique*, 9(4), 595–613.

Altman, A. (2008). Debating Iwo Jima. *Time*, June 23, p. 42.

Alwitt, L. F., Deighton, J., & Grimm, J. (1991). Reactions to political advertising depend on the nature of the voter-candidate bond. In F. Biocca (Ed.), *Television and political advertising: Psychological processes* (Vol. 1, pp. 329–350). Hillsdale, NJ: Erlbaum.

Ambrosius, J. D., & Valenzano III, J. M. (2016). "People in hell want Slurpees": The redefinition of the zombie genre through the salvific portrayal of family on AMC's *The Walking Dead*. *Communication Monographs*, 83(1), 69–93.

American Psychological Association (1993). *Violence and youth: Psychology's response*, volume 1, summary report of the American Psychological Association Commission on Violence and Youth.

An, C., & Pfau, M. (2004). The efficacy of inoculation in televised political debates. *Journal of Communication*, 54, 421–436.

Andersen, P. A., & Kibler, R. J. (1978). Candidate valence as a predictor of voter preference. *Human Communication Research*, 5, 4–14.

Anderson, B., Fagan, P., Woodnutt, T., & Chamorro-Premuzic, T. (2012). Facebook psychology: Popular questions answered by research. *Psychology of Popular Media Culture*, 1, 23–27.

Anderson, C. A., & Bushman, B. J. (2001). Effects of violent video games on aggressive behavior, aggressive cognition, aggressive affect, physiological arousal, and prosocial behavior: A meta-analytic review of the scientific literature. *Psychological Science*, 12, 353–359.

Anderson, C. A., & Bushman, B. J. (2002). Human aggression. *Annual Review of Psychology*, 53, 27–51.

Anderson, C. A., & Dill, K. E. (2000). Video games and aggressive thoughts, feelings, and behavior in the laboratory and in life. *Journal of Personality and Social Psychology*, 78, 772–790.

Anderson, C. A., & Morrow, M. (1995). Competitive aggression without interaction: Effects of competitive versus cooperative instructions on aggressive behavior in video games. *Personality and Social Psychology Bulletin*, 21(10), 1020–1030.

Anderson, C. A., Berkowitz, L., Donnerstein, E., Huesmann, L. R., Johnson, J. D., Linz, D., ... Wartella, E. (2003). The influence of media violence on youth. *Psychological Science in the Public Interest*, 4, 81–110.

Anderson, C. A., Carnagey, N. L., & Eubanks, J. (2003). Exposure to violent media: The effects of songs with violent lyrics on aggressive thoughts and feelings. *Journal of Personality and Social Psychology*, 84, 960–971.

Anderson, C. A., Carnagey, N. L., Flanagan, M., Benjamin, A. J., Eubanks, J., & Valentine, J. C. (2004). Violent video games: Specific effects of violent content on aggressive thoughts and behavior. *Advances in Experimental Social Psychology*, 36, 199–249.

Anderson, C. A., Shibuya, A., Ihori, N., Swing, E. L., Bushman, B. J., Sakamoto, A., ... Saleem, M. (2010). Violent video game effects on aggression, empathy, and prosocial behavior in Eastern and Western countries. *Psychological Bulletin*, 136, 151–173.

Anderson, C. A., Bushman, B. J., Donnerstein, E., Hummer, T. A., & Warburton, W. (2015). SPSSI research summary on media violence. *Analyses of Social Issues and Public Policy*, 15(1), 4–19.

Anderson, C. A., Suzuki, K., Swing, E. L., Groves, C. L., Gentile, D. A., Prot, S., ... Petrescu, P. (2017). Media violence and other aggression risk factors in seven nations. *Personality and Social Psychology Bulletin*, 43(7), 986–998.

Anderson, D. R. (1998). Educational television is not an oxymoron. *Annals of the American Academy of Political and Social Science*, 557, 24–38.

Anderson, D. R., & Burns, J. (1991). Paying attention to television. In J. Bryant & D. Zillmann (Eds.), *Responding to the screen: Reception and reaction processes* (pp. 3–25). Hillsdale, NJ: Erlbaum.

Anderson, D. R., & Field, D. E. (1991). Online and offline assessment of the television audience. In J. Bryant & D. Zillmann (Eds.), *Responding to the screen: Reception and reaction processes* (pp. 199–216). Hillsdale, NJ: Erlbaum.

Anderson, D. R., & Kerkorian, H. L. (2006). Attention and television. In J. Bryant & P. Vorderer (Eds.), *Psychology of entertainment* (pp. 35–54). Mahwah, NJ: Erlbaum.

Anderson, D. R., Bryant, J., Wilder, A., Santomero, A., Williams, M., & Crawley, A. M. (2000). Researching Blue's Clues: Viewing behavior and impact. *Media Psychology*, 2, 179–194.

Anderson, D. R., Fite, K. V., Petrovich, N., & Hirsh, J. (2006). Cortical activation while watching video montage: An fMRI study. *Media Psychology*, 8, 7–24.

Anderson, M., & Perrin, A. (2017). Tech adoption climbs among older adults. Retrieved from www.pewinternet.org

Anderson, M. C. (2017). Trump's appeal to myth and the 2016 presidential election. *Journal of Psychohistory*, 45, 41–45.

Andreasen, A. R. (2012). Rethinking the relationship between social/nonprofit marketing and commercial marketing. *Journal of Public Policy & Marketing*, 31(1), 36–41.

Andreasen, M. S. (1994). Patterns of family life and television consumption from 1945 to the 1990s. In D. Zillmann, J. Bryant, & A. C. Huston (Eds.), *Media, children, and the family: Social scientific, psychodynamic, and clinical perspectives* (pp. 19–36). Hillsdale, NJ: Erlbaum.

Andsager, J. L., Austin, E. W., & Pinkleton, B. E. (2001). Questioning the value of realism: Young adults' processing of messages in alcohol-related public service announcements and advertising. *Journal of Communication*, 51(1), 121–142.

Anker, E. (2005). Villains, victims, and heroes: Melodrama, media, and September 11. *Journal of Communication*, 55, 22–37.

Appel, M. (2008). Fictional narratives cultivate just-world beliefs. *Journal of Communication*, 58, 62–83.

Appel, M., & Richter, T. (2010). Transportation and need for affect in narrative persuasion: A mediated moderation model. *Media Psychology*, 13, 101–135.

Appiah, O. (2002). Black and white viewers' perception and recall of occupational characters on television. *Journal of Communication*, 52, 776–793.

Apter, M. J. (1982). *The experience of motivation: The theory of psychological reversals*. San Diego, CA: Academic Press.

Arab American Institute (2014). National demographic profile. Retrieved from www.aaiusa.org/demographics

Armstrong, E. G. (1993). The rhetoric of violence in rap and country music. *Sociological Inquiry*, 63, 64–84.

Armstrong, J. (2011). The rise and fall and rise again of Black TV. *Entertainment Weekly*, May 20, p. 21.

Arpan, L. M., & Tüzünkan, F. (2011). Photographic depiction of normative deviance and informational utility as predictors of protest news exposure, related perceptions, and story comprehension. *Mass Communication and Society*, 14(2), 178–195.

Arriaga, P., Zillmann, D., & Esteves, F. (2016). The promotion of violence by the mainstream media of communication. In J. Vala, S. Waldzus, M. M. Calheiros, J. Vala, S. Waldzus, & M. O. Calheiros (Eds.), *The social developmental construction of violence and intergroup conflict* (pp. 171–195). Cham, Switzerland: Springer International Publishing.

Arrington-Sanders, R., Harper, G. W., Morgan, A., Ogunbajo, A., Trent, M., & Fortenberry, J. D. (2015). The role of sexually explicit material in the sexual development of same-sex-attracted black adolescent males. *Archives of Sexual Behavior, 44*(3), 597–608.

Asamen, J. K., & Berry, G. L. (2003). The multicultural worldview of children through the lens of television. In E. L. Palmer & B. M. Young (Eds.), *The faces of televisual media: Teaching, violence, selling to children* (pp. 107–123). Mahwah, NJ: Erlbaum.

Atkin, C., Greenberg, B., & McDermott, S. (1983). Television and race role socialization. *Journalism Quarterly, 60*(3), 407–414.

Attardo, S. (1997). The semantic foundations of cognitive theories of humor. *Humor, 10,* 395–420.

Aubrey, J. S. (2007). Does television exposure influence college-aged women's sexual self-concept? *Media Psychology, 10,* 157–181.

Aubrey, J. S., & Harrison, K. (2004). The gender-role content of children's favorite television programs and its links to their gender-related perceptions. *Media Psychology, 6,* 111–146.

Audit Bureau of Circulations (2011). Consumer magazines. Retrieved from http://abcas3.accessabc.com/ecirc/magform.asp.

Austin, A., Barnard, J., & Hutcheon, N. (2015). Media consumption forecasts, 2015. Retrieved from www.zenithmedia.com

Austin, E. W. (1993). Exploring the effects of active parental mediation of television content. *Journal of Broadcasting & Electronic Media, 37,* 147–158.

Austin, E. W. (2001). Effects of family communication on children's interpretation of television. In J. Bryant & J. A. Bryant (Eds.), *Television and the American family.* 2nd ed. (pp. 377–395). Mahwah, NJ: Erlbaum.

Austin, E. W., Roberts, D. F., & Nass, C. I. (1990). Influences of family communication in children's television-interpretation processes. *Communication Research, 17,* 545–564.

Austin, E. W., Bolls, P., Fujioka, Y., & Engelbertson, J. (1999). How and why parents take on the tube. *Journal of Broadcasting & Electronic Media, 43,* 175–192.

Austin, E. W., Pinkleton, B. E., & Fujioka, Y. (2000). The role of interpretation processes and parental discussion in the media's effects on adolescents' use of alcohol. *Pediatrics, 105,* 343–349.

Austin, E. W., Pinkleton, B. E., Hust, S. J., & Cohen, M. (2005). Evaluation of an American legacy foundation/Washington State Department of Health media literacy pilot study. *Health Communication, 18,* 75–95.

Austin, E. W., Chen, Y., Pinkleton, B. E., & Johnson, J. Q. (2006). Benefits and costs of Channel One in a middle school setting and the role of media-literacy training. *Pediatrics, 117,* 423–433.

Austin, E. W., Pinkleton, B. E., & Funabiki, R. P. (2007). The desirability paradox in the effects of media literacy training. *Communication Research, 34,* 483–506.

Austin, E. W., Pinkleton, B. E., Chen, Y.-C., & Austin, B. W. (2015). Processing of sexual media messages improves due to media literacy effects on perceived message desirability. *Mass Communication and Society, 18*(4), 399–421.

Auter, Z. J., & Fine, J. A. (2016). Negative campaigning in the social media age: Attack advertising on Facebook. *Political Behavior, 38*(4), 999–1020.

Axthelm, P. (1989). Cover story: An innocent life, a heartbreaking death. *People, 32*(5), July 31. Retrieved from http://people.com

Bachen, C. M. (1998). Channel One and the education of American youths. *Annals of the American Academy of Political and Social Science, 557,* 132–147.

Backer, T. E., Rogers, E. M., & Sopory, P. (1992). *Designing health communication campaigns: What works?* Newbury Park, CA: Sage.

Baden, C., & Tenenboim-Weinblatt, K. (2017). Convergent news? A longitudinal study of similarity and dissimilarity in the domestic and global coverage of the Israeli–Palestinian conflict. *Journal of Communication, 67*(1), 1–25.

Baer, J. L., Kohut, T., & Fisher, W. A. (2015). Is pornography use associated with anti-woman sexual aggression? Re-examining the confluence model with third variable considerations. *Canadian Journal of Human Sexuality, 24*(2), 160–173.

Baggaley, J. P. (1988). Perceived effectiveness of interactional AIDS campaigns. *Health Education Research: Theory and Practice*, 3, 7–17.

Bailes, F. (2007). The prevalence and nature of imagined music in the everyday lives of music students. *Psychology of Music*, 35, 555–570.

Baker, K. (2004). The shriek heard round the world: When does a single gaffe sink a campaign? *American Heritage*, April/May, 34–36.

Baker, P., & Kang, C. (2017). Trump threatens NBC over nuclear weapons report. *The New York Times*, October 11. Retrieved from www.nytimes.com

Baker, T., & Chan, T. (2017). From an anchor's lips to Trump's ears to Sweden's disbelief. *The New York Times*, February 20. Retrieved from www.nytimes.com/2017/02/20/world/europe/trump-pursues-his-attack-on-sweden-with-scant-evidence.html

Balatsoukas, P., Kennedy, C. M., Buchan, I., Powell, J., & Ainsworth, J. (2015). The role of social network technologies in online health promotion: A narrative review of theoretical and empirical factors influencing intervention effectiveness. *Journal of Medical Internet Research*, 17(6). doi:10.2196/jmir.3662

Bald, M. (1998). Africa's wonderchild. *World Press Review*, 45: 22.

Ball, S., & Bogatz, G. A. (1970). *The first year of Sesame Street: An evaluation*. Princeton, NJ: Educational Testing Service.

Ball, S., & Bogatz, G. A. (1973). *Reading with television: An evaluation of The Electric Company*. Princeton, NJ: Educational Testing Service.

Ballard, M. E., & Coates, S. (1995). The immediate effects of homicidal, suicidal, and nonviolent heavy metal and rap songs on the mood of college students. *Youth & Society*, 27, 148–169.

Balmas, M., & Sheafer, T. (2010). Candidate image in election campaigns: Attribute agenda setting, affective priming, and voting intentions. *International Journal of Public Opinion Research*, 22(2), 204–229.

Balter, R. (1999). From stigmatization to patronization: The media's distorted portrayal of physical disability. In L. L. Schwartz (Ed.), *Psychology and the media: A second look* (pp. 147–171). Washington, DC: American Psychological Association.

Balteş, F. R., Avram, J., Miclea, M., & Miu, A. C. (2011). Emotions induced by operatic music: Psychophysiological effects of music, plot, and acting. *Brain and Cognition*, 76, 146–157.

Banaji, M. R. (2008). The science of satire. *The Chronicle Review*, August 1, p. B13.

Bandura, A. (1965). Influence of models' reinforcement contingencies on the acquisition of imitative responses. *Journal of Personality and Social Psychology*, 1, 585–595.

Bandura, A. (1977). *Social learning theory*. Englewood Cliffs, NJ: Prentice-Hall.

Bandura, A. (1995). Exercise of personal and collective efficacy. In A. Bandura (Ed.), *Self-efficacy in changing societies* (pp. 1–45). New York: Cambridge University Press.

Bandura, A. (1997). *Self-efficacy: The essence of control*. New York: Freeman.

Bandura, A. (2001). Social cognitive theory of mass communication. *Media Psychology*, 3, 265–299.

Bandura, A. (2002). Social cognitive theory of mass communication. In J. Bryant & D. Zillmann (Eds.), *Media effects*. 2nd ed. (pp. 121–153). Mahwah, NJ: Erlbaum.

Bandura, A. (2009). Social cognitive theory of mass communication. In J. Bryant & M. B. Oliver (Eds.), *Media effects: Advances in theory and research*. 3rd ed. (pp. 94–124). New York: Taylor & Francis.

Bandura, A., & Walters, R. H. (1963). *Social learning and personality development*. New York: Holt, Rinehart & Winston.

Bandura, A., Ross, D., & Ross, S. A. (1961). Transmission of aggression through imitation of aggressive models. *Journal of Abnormal and Social Psychology*, 63, 575–582.

Bandura, A., Ross, D., & Ross, S. A. (1963). Imitation of film-mediated aggressive models. *Journal of Abnormal and Social Psychology*, 66, 3–11.

Banerjee, A., Ferrara, E., & Orozco, V. M. (2017). The entertaining way to behavioral change. Working paper. Retrieved from https://economics.yale.edu/sites/default/files/banerjeelaferraraorozco_29sept2017.pdf

Banerjee, S., & Greene, K. (2006). Analysis versus production: Adolescent cognitive and attitudinal responses to antismoking interventions. *Journal of Communication*, 56, 773–794.

Banerjee, S., & Greene, K. (2007). Antismoking initiatives: Effects of analysis versus production media literacy interventions on smoking-related attitude, norm, and behavioral intention. *Health Communication*, 22, 37–48.

Bannon, L. (1995). Bazaar gossip: How a rumor spread about subliminal sex in Disney's *Aladdin* – schoolyards, churches buzz over supposed smut, but who started it all? Evangelical actors play role. *Wall Street Journal*, October 24.

Barber, N. (2013). Women flock to pornography. *Psychology Today*, June 7. Retrieved from www.psychologytoday.com/

Barber, N. (2015). Does Bond's product placement go too far? Retrieved from www.bbc.com/culture

Barcus, F. E. (1983). *Images of life on children's television*. New York: Praeger.

Barker, J. (2017). Ravens fans to be offered DNA test kits Sunday in unusual NFL promotion. *The Baltimore Sun*, September 14. Retrieved from www.baltimoresun.com/business/

Barlett, C. P., & Gentile, D. A. (2012). Attacking others online: The formation of cyberbullying in late adolescence. *Psychology of Popular Media Culture*, 1, 123–135.

Barlett, C. P., Smith, S. J., & Harris, R. J. (2006). The interference effect of men's handling of muscular action figures on a lexical decision task. *Body Image*, 3, 375–383.

Barlett, C. P., Harris, R. J., & Baldassaro, R. (2007). Longer you play, the more hostile you feel: Examination of first person shooter video games and aggression during video game play. *Aggressive Behavior*, 33, 486–497.

Barlett, C. P., Harris, R. J., & Bruey, C. (2008). The effect of the amount of blood in a violent video game on aggression, hostility, and arousal. *Journal of Experimental Social Psychology*, 44, 539–546.

Barlett, C. P., Rodeheffer, C. D., Baldassaro, R., Hinkin, M. P., & Harris, R. J. (2008). The effect of advances in video game technology and content on aggressive cognitions, hostility, and heart rate. *Media Psychology*, 11, 540–565.

Barnes, B. (2016). Grand Cherokee product placement becomes awkward for Fox. *The New York Times*, June 22. Retrieved from www.nytimes.com/

Baroffio-Bota, D., & Banet-Weiser, S. (2006). Women, team sports, and the WNBA: Playing like a girl. In A. A. Raney & J. Bryant (Eds.), *Handbook of sports and media* (pp. 485–500). Mahwah, NJ: Erlbaum.

Baron, R. A. (1979). Heightened sexual arousal and physical aggression: An extension to females. *Journal of Research in Personality*, 13, 91–102.

Barr, R., Zack, E., Garcia, A., & Muentener, P. (2008). Infants' attention and responsiveness to television increases with prior exposure and parental interaction. *Infancy*, 13, 30–56.

Barranco, R. E., Rader, N. E., & Smith, A. (2017). Violence at the box office: Considering ratings, ticket sales, and content of movies. *Communication Research*, 44(1), 77–95.

Barrense-Dias, Y., Berchtold, A., Surís, J., & Akre, C. (2017). Sexting and the definition issue. *Journal of Adolescent Health*, 61(5), 544–555.

Barrett, B. J., & Levin, D. S. (2015). You can't touch me, you can't touch me: Inter-gender violence and aggression in the PG era of World Wrestling Entertainment (WWE) programming. *Feminism & Psychology*, 25(4), 469–488.

Barthel, M., & Mitchell, A. (2017). Americans' attitudes about the news media deeply divided along partisan lines. Retrieved from www.journalism.org

Barthel, M., Mitchell, A., & Holcomb, J. (2016). Many Americans believe fake news is sowing confusion. Retrieved from www.journalism.org

Bartholow, B. D., & Anderson, C. A. (2002). Effects of violent video games on aggressive behavior: Potential sex differences. *Journal of Experimental Social Psychology*, 38(3), 283–290.

Bartholow, B. D., Sestir, M. A., & Davis, E. B. (2005). Correlates and consequences of exposure to video game violence: Hostile personality, empathy, and aggressive behavior. *Personality and Social Psychology Bulletin*, 31(11), 1573–1586.

Bartsch, A. (2012). As time goes by: What changes and what remains the same in entertainment experience over the life span? *Journal of Communication, 62*, 588–608.

Bartsch, A., Mares, M.-L., Scherr, S., Kloß, A., Keppeler, J., & Posthumus, L. (2016). More than shoot-em-up and torture porn: Reflective appropriation and meaning-making of violent media content. *Journal of Communication, 66*(5), 741–765.

Bartsch, R. A., Burnett, T., Diller, T. R., & Rankin-Williams, E. (2000). Gender representation in television commercials: Updating an update. *Sex Roles, 43*, 735–743.

Basil, M. D. (1994). Secondary reaction-time measures. In A. Lang (Ed.), *Measuring psychological responses to media* (pp. 85–98). Hillsdale, NJ: Erlbaum.

Basil, M., Schooler, C., & Reeves, B. (1991). Positive and negative political advertising: Effectiveness of ads and perceptions of candidates. In F. Biocca (Ed.), *Television and political advertising: Psychological processes* (Vol. 1, pp. 245–262). Hillsdale, NJ: Erlbaum.

Bateman, T. S., Sakano, T., & Fujita, M. (1992). Roger, me, and my attitude: Film propaganda and cynicism toward corporate leadership. *Journal of Applied Psychology, 77*, 768–771.

Bates, T. (2008). Hip hero. *Time*, May 26, p. 55.

Battaglio, S. (2017a). Megyn Kelly's interview with conspiracy theorist Alex Jones becomes a headache for NBC News. *Los Angeles Times*, June 13. Retrieved from www.latimes.com/

Battaglio, S. (2017b). President Trump turned cable news into must-see TV in 2017. *Los Angeles Times*, December 30. Retrieved from www.latimes.com

Battles, K., & Hilton-Morrow, W. (2002). Gay characters in conventional spaces: *Will and Grace* and the situation comedy genre. *Critical Studies in Media Communication, 19*(1), 87–106.

Baum, M. A. (2002). Sex, lies, and war: How soft news brings foreign policy to the inattentive public. *American Political Science Review, 96*, 91–109.

Baumgartner, S. E., & Wirth, W. (2012). Affective priming during the processing of news articles. *Media Psychology, 15*, 1–18.

Bauserman, R. (1996). Sexual aggression and pornography: A review of correlation research. *Basic and Applied Social Psychology, 18*, 405–427.

Baym, G. (2005). The Daily Show: Discursive integration and the reinvention of political journalism. *Political Communication, 22*, 259–276.

Bazzini, D. G., Pepper, A., Swofford, R., & Cochran, K. (2015). How healthy are health magazines? A comparative content analysis of cover captions and images of *Women's* and *Men's Health* magazine. *Sex Roles, 72*(5–6), 198–210.

Beaman, C. P., & Williams, T. I. (2010). Earworms (stuck song syndrome): Towards a natural history of intrusive thoughts. *British Journal of Psychology, 101*, 637–653.

Bech Sillesen, L. (2014). What America looks like in the media abroad. Retrieved from www.cjr.org

Becker, A. E. (2004). Television, disordered eating, and young women in Fiji: Negotiating body image and identity during rapid social change. *Culture, Medicine and Psychiatry, 28*, 533–559.

Becker-Blease, K. A., Finkelhor, D., & Turner, H. (2008). Media exposure predicts children's reactions to crime and terrorism. *Journal of Trauma & Dissociation, 9*(2), 225–248.

Beech, H. (2017). How China is remaking the global film industry. *Time*, January 26. Retrieved from http://time.com/

Beeman, W. O. (1984). The cultural role of the media in Iran: The revolution of 1978–1979 and after. In A. Anno & W. Dissayanake (Eds.), *The news media and national and international conflict* (pp. 147–165). Boulder, CO: Westview Press.

Beentjes, J. W. J., van Oordt, M. N., & van der Voort, T. H. A. (2002). How television commentary affects children's judgments on soccer fouls. *Communication Research, 29*, 31–45.

Behm-Morawitz, E., Lewallen, J., & Miller, B. (2016). Real mean girls? Reality television viewing, social aggression, and gender-related beliefs among female emerging adults. *Psychology of Popular Media Culture, 5*(4), 340–355.

Belkin, L. (2001). Primetime pushers. *Mother Jones*, March/April, 30–37.

Belson, K. (2012). Former coach testifies against Sandusky. *New York Times*, June 12. Retrieved from www.nytimes.com

Benedict, H. (1992). *Virgin or vamp: How the press covers sex crimes*. New York: Oxford University Press.

Bennett, W. L. (2016). *News: The politics of illusion*. 10th ed. Chicago: University of Chicago Press.

Benoit, W. L. (2006). Retrospective versus prospective statements and outcome of the presidential elections. *Journal of Communication*, 56, 331–345.

Benoit, W. L., & Hansen, G. J. (2004). Presidential debate watching, issue knowledge, character evaluation, and vote choice. *Human Communication Research*, 30, 121–144.

Ben-Porath, E. N., & Shaker, L. K. (2010). News images, race, and attribution in the wake of Hurricane Katrina. *Journal of Communication*, 60, 466–490.

Berelson, B. R., Lazarsfeld, P. F., & McPhee, W. N. (1954). *Voting*. Chicago: University of Chicago Press.

Berg, M. (2016). With new book club pick, Oprah's still got the golden touch. *Forbes*, August 3. Retrieved from www.forbes.com/

Berg, M. (2017). How 10 social stars use their influence for good. *Forbes*, February 2. Retrieved from www.forbes.com/

Bergen, L., Grimes, T., & Potter, D. (2005). How attention partitions itself during simultaneous message presentations. *Human Communication Research*, 31, 311–336.

Berger, C. R. (1998). Processing quantitative data about risk and threat in news reports. *Journal of Communication*, 48(3), 87–106.

Berger, C. R. (2000). Quantitative depictions of threatening phenomena in news reports. *Human Communication Research*, 26, 27–52.

Berger, J., & Milkman, K. L. (2012). What makes online content viral? *Journal of Marketing Research*, 49(2), 192–205.

Bergsma, L. J., & Carney, M. E. (2008). Effectiveness of health-promoting media literacy education: A systematic review. *Health Education Research*, 23, 522–542.

Berkowitz, L. (1965). Some aspects of observed aggression. *Journal of Personality and Social Psychology*, 2, 359–369.

Berkowitz, L. (1984). Some effects of thoughts on anti- and prosocial influences of media events: A cognitive neoassociation analysis. *Psychological Bulletin*, 95, 410–427.

Bernard, P., Gervais, S. J., Allen, J., Campomizzi, S., & Klein, O. (2012). Integrating sexual objectification with object versus person recognition: The sexualized-body-inversion hypothesis. *Psychological Science*, 23(5), 469–471.

Bernard, P., Legrand, S., & Klein, O. (2018). From bodies to blame: Exposure to sexually objectifying media increases tolerance toward sexual harassment. *Psychology of Popular Media Culture*, 7(2), 99–112.

Berry, G. L. (1980). Television and Afro-Americans: Past legacy and present portrayals. In S. B. Withey & R. P. Abeles (Eds.), *Television and social behavior* (pp. 231–247). Hillsdale, NJ: Erlbaum.

Bessenoff, G. R. (2006). Can the media affect us? Social comparison, self-discrepancy, and the thin ideal. *Psychology of Women Quarterly*, 30, 239–251.

Best, J. (1999). *Random violence: How we talk about new crimes and new victims*. Berkeley, CA: University of California Press.

Bever, T., Smith, M., Bengen, B., & Johnson, T. (1975). Young viewers' troubling responses to TV ads. *Harvard Business Review*, 53(6), 109–120.

Bezdek, M. A., & Gerrig, R. J. (2017). When narrative transportation narrows attention: Changes in attentional focus during suspenseful film viewing. *Media Psychology*, 20(1), 60–89.

Bickham, D. S., Wright, J. C., & Huston, A. C. (2001). Attention, comprehension, and the educational influences of television. In D. G. Singer & J. L. Singer (Eds.), *Handbook of children and the media* (pp. 101–119). Thousand Oaks, CA: Sage.

Bilandzic, H. (2006). The perception of distance in the cultivation process. *Communication Theory*, 16, 333–355.

Billings, A. C. (Ed.). (2011). *Sports media: Transformation, integration, and consumption.* New York: Routledge.

Billings, A. C., & Eastman, S. T. (2003). Framing identities: Gender, ethnic, and national parity in network announcing of the 2002 Winter Olympics. *Journal of Communication, 53,* 569–585.

Bilton, N. (2014). Ferguson reveals a Twitter loop. *The New York Times,* August 27. Retrieved from www.nytimes.com

Bird, S. E. (Ed.). (1996). *Dressing in feathers: The construction of the Indian in popular culture.* Boulder, CO: Westview Press.

Bird, S. E. (1999). Gendered construction of the American Indian in popular media. *Journal of Communication, 49*(3), 61–83.

Bird, S. E. (2009). True believers and atheists need not apply: Faith and mainstream television drama. In D. H. Winston (Ed.), *Small screen, big picture: Television and lived religion* (pp. 17–42). Waco, TX: Baylor University Press.

Bischoff, R. J., & Reiter, A. D. (1999). The role of gender in the presentation of mental health clinicians in the movies: Implications for clinical practice. *Psychotherapy, 36*(2), 180–189.

Bissell, K. L., & Zhou, P. (2004). Must-see TV or ESPN: Entertainment and sports media exposure and body-image distortion in college women. *Journal of Communication, 54,* 5–21.

Biswas, S. B. (2018). Why India's rape crisis shows no signs of abating. *BBC News,* April 17. Retrieved from www.bbc.com/

Bjerklie, D. (2002). Label reform. *Time,* August 12, p. 4.

Black, G. D. (1994). *Hollywood censored: Morality codes, Catholics, and the movies.* New York: Cambridge University Press.

Blackford, B. J., Gentry, J., Harrison, R. L., & Carlson, L. (2011). The prevalence and influence of the combination of humor and violence in Super Bowl commercials. *Journal of Advertising, 40*(4), 123–134.

Blain, N., Boyle, R., & O'Donnell, H. (1993). *Sport and national identity in the European media.* Leicester: Leicester University Press.

Blake, M. (2017). From dramas like *Scandal* to documentaries like *Abortion: Stories Women Tell,* the hot-button topic is evolving on TV. *Los Angeles Times,* March 31. Retrieved from www.latimes.com

Blanc, N., Kendeou, P., van den Broek, P., & Brouillet, D. (2008). Updating situation models during reading of news reports: Evidence from empirical data and simulations. *Discourse Processes, 45,* 103–121.

Blanc, N., Stiegler-Balfour, J. J., & O'Brien, E. J. (2011). Does the uncertainty of information influence the updating process? Evidence from the reading of news articles. *Discourse Processes, 48,* 387–403.

Blatt, J., Spencer, L., & Ward, S. (1972). A cognitive developmental study of children's reactions to television advertising. In E. A. Rubinstein, G. A. Comstock, & J. P. Murray (Eds.), *Television and social behavior: Television in everyday life. Patterns of use* (Vol. 4, pp. 452–467). Washington, DC: U.S. Government Printing Office.

Bleakley, A., Hennessy, M., Fishbein, M., & Jordan, A. (2008). It works both ways: The relationship between exposure to sexual content in the media and adolescent sexual behavior. *Media Psychology, 11,* 443–461.

Bleakley, A., Hennessy, M., Fishbein, M., & Jordan, A. (2009). How sources of sexual information relate to adolescents' beliefs about sex. *American Journal of Health Behavior, 33*(1), 37–48.

Bleakley, A., Romer, D., & Jamieson, P. E. (2014). Violent film characters' portrayal of alcohol, sex, and tobacco-related behaviors. *Pediatrics, 133*(1), 71–77.

Block, C. (1972). White backlash to Negro ads: Fact or fantasy? *Journalism Quarterly, 49*(2), 253–262.

Blumler, J. G., & McQuail, D. (1969). *Television in politics: Its uses and influences.* Chicago: University of Chicago Press.

Boese, A. (2006). *Hippo eats dwarf: A field guide to hoaxes and other B.S.* Orlando, FL: Harcourt.

Bogart, L. (1980). Television news as entertainment. In P. H. Tannenbaum (Ed.), *The entertainment functions of television* (pp. 209–249). Hillsdale, NJ: Erlbaum.

Bogatz, G. A., & Ball, S. (1971). *The second year of Sesame Street: A continuing evaluation.* Princeton, NJ: Educational Testing Service.

Bogle, D. (1973). *Toms, coons, mulattoes, and bucks: An interpretive history of blacks in American films.* New York: Viking Press.

Bolls, P. D., & Lang, A. (2003). I saw it on the radio: The allocation of attention to high-imagery radio advertisements. *Media Psychology, 5,* 33–55.

Bolls, P. D., Lang, A., & Potter, R. F. (2001). The effects of message valence and listener arousal on attention, memory, and facial muscular responses to radio advertisements. *Communication Research, 28,* 627–651.

Bond, B. J. (2014). Sex and sexuality in entertainment media popular with lesbian, gay, and bisexual adolescents. *Mass Communication and Society, 17*(1), 98–120.

Bond, B. J. (2015). Portrayals of sex and sexuality in gay- and lesbian-oriented media: A quantitative content analysis. *Sexuality & Culture, 19*(1), 37–56.

Bond, B. J., & Compton, B. L. (2015). Gay on-screen: The relationship between exposure to gay characters on television and heterosexual audiences' endorsement of gay equality. *Journal of Broadcasting & Electronic Media, 59*(4), 717–732.

Bonds-Raacke, J. M., & Harris, R. J. (2006). Autobiographical memories of televised sporting events watched in different social settings. *Psychological Reports, 99,* 197–208.

Bonds-Raacke, J. M., Cady, E. T., Schlegel, R., Harris, R. J., & Firebaugh, L. C. (2007). Remembering gay/lesbian media characters: Can Ellen and Will improve attitudes toward homosexuals? *Journal of Homosexuality, 53*(3), 19–34.

Bonomi, A. E., Nichols, E. M., Carotta, C. L., Kiuchi, Y., & Perry, S. (2016). Young women's perceptions of the relationship in *Fifty Shades of Grey. Journal of Women's Health, 25*(2), 139–148.

Bonus, J. A., Peebles, A., Mares, M.-L., & Sarmiento, I. G. (2018). Look on the bright side (of media effects): *Pokémon Go* as a catalyst for positive life experiences. *Media Psychology, 21*(2), 263–287.

Booker, N. A., Miller, A. N., & Ngure, P. (2016). Heavy sexual content versus safer sex content: A content analysis of the entertainment education drama *Shuga. Health Communication, 31*(12), 1437–1446.

Borah, P. (2011). Conceptual issues in framing theory: A systematic examination of a decade's literature. *Journal of Communication, 61,* 246–263.

Borah, P. (2014). The hyperlinked world: A look at how the interactions of news frames and hyperlinks influence news credibility and willingness to seek information. *Journal of Computer-Mediated Communication, 19*(3), 576–590.

Borchers, C. (2017). Trump falsely claims (again) that he coined the term "fake news." *The Washington Post,* October 26. Retrieved from www.washingtonpost.com

Bordeaux, B. R., & Lange, G. (1991). Children's reported investment of mental effort when viewing television. *Communication Research, 18,* 617–635.

Borden, S. L., & Tew, C. (2007). The role of journalist and the performance of journalism: Ethical lessons from "fake" news (seriously). *Journal of Mass Media Ethics, 22,* 300–314.

Borland, R. (2014). *Understanding hard to maintain behaviour change: A dual process approach.* Chichester: Wiley-Blackwell.

Borrayo, E. A., Rosales, M., & Gonzalez, P. (2017). Entertainment-education narrative versus nonnarrative interventions to educate and motivate Latinas to engage in mammography screening. *Health Education & Behavior, 44*(3), 394–402.

Bothamley, S., & Tully, R. J. (2018). Understanding revenge pornography: Public perceptions of revenge pornography and victim blaming. *Journal of Aggression, Conflict and Peace Research, 10*(1), 1–10.

Boucher, E. M., Hancock. J. T., & Dunham, P. J. (2008). Interpersonal sensitivity in computer-mediated and face-to-face conversations. *Media Psychology, 11,* 235–258.

Boukes, M., & Boomgaarden, H. G. (2015). Soft news with hard consequences? Introducing a nuanced measure of soft versus hard news exposure and its relationship with political cynicism. *Communication Research, 42*(5), 701–731.

Bower, A. (2002). Fast-food networks. *Time,* May 6, p. 161.

Bowerman, M. (2015). New York Daily News' cover causes outrage over graphic images of slain journalist. *USA Today*, August 27. Retrieved from www.usatoday.com/

Boydstun, A. E. (2013). *Making the news: Politics, the media, and agenda setting*. Chicago: University of Chicago Press.

Boyland, E. J., & Halford, J. C. G. (2013). Television advertising and branding: Effects on eating behaviour and food preferences in children. *Appetite*, 62 (Supplement C), 236–241.

Boyle, M. P., Schmierbach, M., Armstrong, C. L., Cho, J., McCluskey, M., McLeod, D. M., & Shah, D. V. (2006). Expressive responses to news stories about extremist groups: A framing experiment. *Journal of Communication*, 56, 271–288.

Brasel, S. A., & Gips, J. (2011). Media multitasking behavior: Concurrent television and computer usage. *Cyberpsychology, Behavior, and Social Networking*, 14(9), 527–534.

Breslow, L. (1978). Risk factor intervention for health maintenance. *Science*, 200, 908–912.

Bretthauer, B., Zimmerman, T. S., & Banning, J. H. (2007). A feminist analysis of popular music. *Journal of Feminist Family Therapy*, 18(4), 29–51.

Brewer, W. F., & Nakamura, G. V. (1984). The nature and functions of schemas. In R. S. Wyer & T. K. Srull (Eds.), *Handbook of social cognition* (pp. 119–160). Hillsdale, NJ: Erlbaum.

Bridges, A. J., & Anton, C. (2013). Pornography and violence against women. In J. A. Sigal, & F. L. Denmark (Eds.), *Violence against girls and women: International perspectives* (pp. 183–206). Santa Barbara, CA: Praeger/ABC-CLIO.

Brockmyer, J. F. (2015). Playing violent video games and desensitization to violence. *Child and Adolescent Psychiatric Clinics of North America*, 24(1), 65–77.

Brook, T. (2014). Does Bollywood incite sexual violence in India? *BBC News*, October 21. Retrieved from www.bbc.com/

Brooks, M. E., Bichard, S., & Craig, C. (2016). What's the score? A content analysis of mature adults in Super Bowl commercials. *Howard Journal of Communications*, 27(4), 347–366

Brosius, H.-B., & Kepplinger, H. M. (1990). The agenda-setting function of television news: Static and dynamic views. *Communication Research*, 17, 183–211.

Brown, A. (2017). Younger men play video games, but so do a diverse group of other Americans. Retrieved from www.pewresearch.org

Brown, A. S., & Logan, C. (Eds.). (2005). *The psychology of The Simpsons*. Dallas, TX: Benbella.

Brown, B., Nasiruddin, M., Cabral, A., & Soohoo, M. (2016). Childhood idols, shifting from superheroes to public health heroes. *Journal of Public Health*, 38(3), 625–629.

Brown, C. L., Matherne, C. E., Bulik, C. M., Howard, J. B., Ravanbakht, S. N., Skinner, A. C., ... Perrin, E. M. (2017). Influence of product placement in children's movies on children's snack choices. *Appetite*, 114 (Supplement C), 118–124.

Brown, D., & Bryant, J. (1983). Humor in the mass media. In P. E. McGhee & J. H. Goldstein (Eds.), *Handbook of humor research* (Vol. 2, pp. 143–172). New York: Springer-Verlag.

Brown, J. A. (1991). *Television "critical viewing skills" education: Major media literacy projects in the United States and selected countries*. Hillsdale, NJ: Erlbaum.

Brown, J. D., & Einsiedel, E. F. (1990). Public health campaigns: Mass media strategies. In E. B. Ray & L. Donohew (Eds.), *Communication and health: Systems and applications* (pp. 153–170). Hillsdale, NJ: Erlbaum.

Brown, J. D., & Walsh-Childers, K. (2002). Effects of media on personal and public health. In J. Bryant & D. Zillmann (Eds.), *Media effects*. 2nd ed. (pp. 453–488). Mahwah, NJ: Erlbaum.

Brown, J. D., L'Engle, K. L., Pardun, C. J., Guo, G., Kenneavy, K., & Jackson, C. (2006). Sexy media matter: Exposure to sexual content in music, movies, television, and magazines predicts Black and White adolescents' sexual behavior. *Pediatrics*, 117, 1018–1027.

Brown, N. R., & Siegler, R. S. (1992). The role of availability in the estimation of national populations. *Memory & Cognition*, 20, 406–412.

Brown, W. J., & Cody, M. J. (1991). Effects of a prosocial television soap opera in promoting women's status. *Human Communication Research*, 18, 114–142.

Brown, W. J., & Singhal, A. (1990). Ethical dilemmas of prosocial television. *Communication Quarterly*, 38, 268–280.

Brown, W. J., Singhal, A., & Rogers, E. M. (1989). Pro-development soap operas: A novel approach to development communication. *Media Development*, 36(4), 43–47.

Brown, W. J., Basil, M. D., & Bocarnea, M. C. (2003). Social influence of an international celebrity: Responses to the death of Princess Diana. *Journal of Communication*, 53, 587–605.

Bruce, S. (1990). *Pray TV: Televangelism in America*. London: Routledge.

Bruno, K. J., & Harris, R. J. (1980). The effect of repetition on the discrimination of asserted and implied claims in advertising. *Applied Psycholinguistics*, 1, 307–321.

Brusse, E. D. A., Fransen, M. L., & Smit, E. G. (2017). Framing in entertainment-education: Effects on processes of narrative persuasion. *Health Communication*, 32(12), 1501–1509.

Bryant, J., & Bryant, J. A. (2001). *Television and the American family*. 2nd ed. Mahwah, NJ: Erlbaum.

Bryant, J., & Raney, A. A. (2000). Sports on the screen. In D. Zillmann & P. Vorderer (Eds.), *Media entertainment: The psychology of its appeal* (pp. 153–174). Mahwah, NJ: Erlbaum.

Bryant, J., & Rockwell, S. C. (1994). Effects of massive exposure to sexually oriented prime-time television programming on adolescents' moral judgment. In D. Zillmann, J. Bryant, & A. C. Huston (Eds.), *Media, children, and the family: Social scientific, psychodynamic, and clinical perspectives* (pp. 183–195). Hillsdale, NJ: Erlbaum.

Bryant, J., Zillmann, D., & Raney, A. A. (1998). Violence and the enjoyment of media sports. In L. A. Wenner (Ed.), *Media Sport* (pp. 252–265). London: Routledge.

Bryant, J., Thompson, S., & Finklea, B. W. (2013). *Fundamentals of media effects*. 2nd ed. Long Grove, IL: Waveland Press.

Buckingham, D. (1993). *Children talking television: The making of television literacy*. London: Falmer.

Buckingham, D. (1998). Media education in the UK: Moving beyond protectionism. *Journal of Communication*, 48(1), 33–43.

Buckingham, D. (2003). *Media education: Literacy, learning, and contemporary culture*. Cambridge: Polity/Blackwell.

Bucy, E. P., & Grabe, M. E. (2007). Taking television seriously: A sound and image bite analysis of presidential campaign coverage, 1992–2004. *Journal of Communication*, 57, 652–675.

Bucy, E. P., Kim, S. C., & Park, M. C. (2011). Host selling in cyberspace: Product personalities and character advertising on popular children's websites. *New Media & Society*, 13(8), 1245–1264.

Buerkel-Rothfuss, N. L., & Buerkel, R. A. (2001). Family mediation. In J. Bryant & J. A. Bryant (Eds.), *Television and the American family*. 2nd ed. (pp. 355–376). Mahwah, NJ: Erlbaum.

Buerkel-Rothfuss, N. L., & Mayes, S. (1981). Soap opera viewing: The cultivation effect. *Journal of Communication*, 31, 108–115.

Buijzen, M. (2007). Reducing children's susceptibility to commercials: Mechanisms of factual and evaluative advertising interventions. *Media Psychology*, 9, 411–430.

Buijzen, M., & Valkenburg, P. M. (2004). Developing a typology of humor in audiovisual media. *Media Psychology*, 6, 147–167.

Buijzen, M., & Valkenburg, P. M. (2008). Observing purchase-related parent–child communication in retail environments. *Human Communication Research*, 34, 50–69.

Buijzen, M., Walma van der Molen, J. H., & Sondij, P. (2007). Parental mediation of children's emotional responses to a violent news event. *Communication Research*, 34, 212–230.

Bureau of Labor Statistics (2015). American time use survey. Retrieved from www.bls.gov/tus/

Burke, R. R., DeSarbo, W. S., Oliver, R. L., & Robertson, T. S. (1988). Deception by implication: An experimental investigation. *Journal of Consumer Research*, 14, 483–494.

Burt, M. R. (1980). Cultural myths and supports for rape. *Journal of Personality and Social Psychology*, 38, 217–230.

Bushman, B. J. (1998). Effects of television violence on memory of commercial messages. *Journal of Experimental Psychology: Applied*, 4, 291–307.

Bushman, B. J. (2005). Violence and sex in television programs do not sell products in advertisements. *Psychological Science*, 16, 702–708.

Bushman, B. J. (2016). Violent media and hostile appraisals: A meta-analytic review. *Aggressive Behavior*, 42(6), 605–613.

Bushman, B. J., & Anderson, C. A. (2001). Media violence and the American public: Scientific facts versus media misinformation. *American Psychologist, 56*, 477–489.

Bushman, B. J., & Anderson, C. A. (2002). Violent video games and hostile expectations: A test of the general aggression model. *Personality and Social Psychology Bulletin, 28*, 1679–1686.

Bushman, B. J., & Huesmann L. R. (2001). Effects of televised violence on aggression. In D. Singer, & J. Singer J, (Eds.), *Handbook of children and the media* (pp. 223–254). Thousand Oaks, CA: Sage.

Bushman, B. J., & Huesmann, L. R. (2014). Twenty-five years of research on violence in digital games and aggression revisited. *European Psychologist, 19*(1), 47–55.

Bushman, B. J., & Phillips, C. M. (2001). If the television program bleeds, memory for the advertisement recedes. *Current Directions in Psychological Science, 10*, 43–47.

Bushman, B. J., Baumeister, R. F., & Stack, A. D. (1999). Catharsis, aggression, and persuasive influences: Self-fulfilling or self-defeating prophecies? *Journal of Personality and Social Psychology, 76*, 367–376.

Bushman, B. J., Bonacci, A. M., van Dijk, M., & Baumeister, R. (2003). Narcissism, sexual refusal, and aggression: Testing a narcissistic reactance model of sexual coercion. *Journal of Personality and Social Psychology, 84*, 1027–1040.

Bushman, B. J., Chandler, J., & Huesmann, L. R. (2010). Do violent media numb our consciences? In W. Koops, D. Brugman, T. J. Ferguson, & A. F. Sanders (Eds.), *The development and structure of conscience* (pp. 237–251). New York: Psychology Press.

Bushman, B. J., Gollwitzer, M., & Cruz, C. (2015). There is broad consensus: Media researchers agree that violent media increase aggression in children, and pediatricians and parents concur. *Psychology of Popular Media Culture, 4*(3), 200–214.

Busselle, R. W. (2001). Television exposure, perceived realism, and exemplar accessibility in the social judgment process. *Media Psychology, 3*(1), 43–67.

Busselle, R. W., & Bilandzic, H. (2009). Measuring narrative engagement. *Media Psychology, 12*, 321–347.

Busselle, R. W., & Shrum, L. J. (2003). Media exposure and exemplar accessibility. *Media Psychology, 5*, 255–282.

Cady, E. T., Harris, R. J., & Knappenberger, J. B. (2008). Using music to cue autobiographical memories of different lifetime periods. *Psychology of Music, 36*(2), 157–177.

Cai, X., & Zhao, X. (2010). Click here kids! Online advertising practices on children's websites. *Journal of Children and Media, 4*(2), 135–154.

Cain, R. (2015). India's film industry—a $10 billion business trapped in a $2 billion body. *Forbes*, October 23. Retrieved from www.forbes.com/

Calderon, J., Ayala, G. X., Elder, J. P., Belch, G. E., Castro, I. A., Weibel, N., & Pickrel, J. (2017). What happens when parents and children go grocery shopping? An observational study of Latino dyads in Southern California, USA. *Health Education & Behavior, 44*(1), 5–12.

Calfano, B. R., Djupe, P. A., Cox, D., & Jones, R. (2016). Muslim mistrust: The resilience of negative public attitudes after complimentary information. *Journal of Media and Religion, 15*(1), 29–42.

Calvert, S. L. (1988). Television production feature effects of children's comprehension of time. *Journal of Applied Developmental Psychology, 9*, 263–273.

Calvert, S. L., & Kotler, J. A. (2003). Lessons from children's television: The impact of the Children's Television Act on children's learning. *Journal of Applied Developmental Psychology, 24*(3), 275–335.

Calvert, S. L., & Valkenburg, P. M. (2013). The influence of television, video games, and the Internet on children's creativity. In M. Taylor (Ed.), *The Oxford handbook of development and imagination* (pp. 438–450). New York: Oxford University Press.

Calvert, S. L., & Wilson, B. J. (Eds.). (2011). *The handbook of children, media, and development*. Malden, MA: Wiley-Blackwell.

Calvert, S. L., Appelbaum, M., Dodge, K. A., Graham, S., Nagayama Hall, G. C., Hamby, S., ... Hedges, L. V. (2017). The American Psychological Association Task Force assessment of violent video games: Science in the service of public interest. *American Psychologist, 72*(2), 126–143.

Cameron, G. T., & Frieske, D. A. (1994). The time needed to answer: Measurement of memory response latency. In A. Lang (Ed.), *Measuring psychological responses to media* (pp. 149–164). Hillsdale, NJ: Erlbaum.

Campbell, C., Thompson, F. M., Grimm, P. E., & Robson, K. (2017). Understanding why consumers don't skip pre-roll video ads. *Journal of Advertising*, 46(3), 411–423.

Campbell, H. A. (2010). *When religion meets new media*. New York: Routledge.

Cantor, J. (1996). Television and children's fear. In T. M. Macbeth (Ed.), *Tuning in to young viewers: Social science perspectives on television* (pp. 87–115). Thousand Oaks, CA: Sage.

Cantor, J. (1998a). Ratings for program content: The role of research findings. *Annals of the American Academy of Political and Social Science*, 557, 54–69.

Cantor, J. (1998b). *"Mommy, I'm scared": How TV and movies frighten children and what we can do to protect them*. San Diego, CA: Harcourt Brace.

Cantor, J. (2002). Fright reactions to mass media. In J. Bryant & D. Zillmann (Eds.), *Media effects* (pp. 287–306). Mahwah, NJ: Erlbaum.

Cantor, J. (2006). Why horror doesn't die: The enduring and paradoxical effects of frightening entertainment. In J. Bryant & P. Vorderer (Eds.), *Psychology of entertainment* (pp. 315–327). Mahwah, NJ: Erlbaum.

Cantor, J. (2009). Fright reactions to mass media. In J. Bryant & M. B. Oliver (Eds.), *Media effects: Advances in theory and research*. 3rd ed. (pp. 287–303). New York: Routledge.

Cantor, J. (2011). Fear reactions and the mass media. In K. Döveling, C. von Scheve, & E. A. Konijn (Eds.). *The Routledge handbook of emotions and mass media* (pp. 148–165). New York: Routledge.

Cantor, J., & Oliver, M. B. (1996). Developmental differences in responses to horror. In J. B. Weaver & R. Tamborini (Eds.), *Horror films: Current research on audience preferences and reactions* (pp. 63–80). Mahwah, NJ: Erlbaum.

Cantor, J., & Riddle, K. (2014). Media and fear in children and adolescents. In D. A. Gentile & D. A. Gentile (Eds.), *Media violence and children: A complete guide for parents and professionals* (pp. 179–207). Santa Barbara, CA: Praeger/ABC-CLIO.

Cantor, J., & Wilson, B. J. (2003). Media and violence: Intervention strategies for reducing aggression. *Media Psychology*, 5, 363–403.

Cantor, J., Wilson, B. J., & Hoffner, C. (1986). Emotional responses to a televised nuclear holocaust film. *Communication Research*, 13, 257–277.

Cantor, J., Mares, M. L., & Hyde, J. S. (2003). Autobiographical memories of exposure to sexual media content. *Media Psychology*, 5, 1–31.

Cao, X. (2010). Hearing it from Jon Stewart: The impact of the *Daily Show* on public attentiveness to politics. *International Journal of Public Opinion Research*, 22(1), 26–46.

Caplan, S. E. (2005). A social skill account of problematic Internet use. *Journal of Communication*, 55, 721–736.

Capsuto, S. (2000). *The uncensored story of gay and lesbian images on radio and television*. New York: Ballantine Books.

Carey, B. (2018). How fiction becomes fact on social media. *The New York Times*, August 9. Retrieved from www.nytimes.com

Carlson, D. (2018). How to be smarter about buying organic. *Chicago Tribune*, April 16. Retrieved from www.chicagotribune.com/

Carlsson-Paige, N. (2008). *Taking back childhood: Helping your kids thrive in a fast-paced, media-saturated, violence-filled world*. New York: Hudson Street Press.

Carlsson-Paige, N., & Levin, D. E. (1990). *Who's calling the shots? How to respond effectively to children's fascination with war play and war toys*. Philadelphia: New Society.

Carnagey, N. L., & Anderson, C. A. (2005). The effects of reward and punishment in violent video games on aggressive affect, cognition, and behavior. *Psychological Science*, 16, 882–889.

Carroll, L. (2009). Mom and Dad make scary movies even scarier: Kids who watch TV with their parents get even more freaked out. Retrieved from www.msnbc.com

Carter, O. B. J., Patterson, L. J., Donovan, R. J., Ewing, M. T., & Roberts, C. M. (2011). Children's understanding of the selling versus persuasive intent of junk food advertising: Implications for regulation. *Social Science & Medicine*, 72(6), 962–968.

Carveth, R., & Alexander, A. (1985). Soap opera viewing motivations and the cultivation process. *Journal of Broadcasting & Electronic Media*, 29, 259–273.

Casey, M. K., Allen, M., Emmers-Sommer, T., Sahlstein, E., DeGooyer, D., Winters, A. M., ... Dun, T. (2007). The impact of Earvin "Magic" Johnson's HIV-positive announcement. In R. W. Preiss, B. M. Gayle, N. Burrell, M. Allen, & J. Bryant (Eds.), *Mass media effects research: Advances through meta-analysis* (pp. 363–375). Mahwah, NJ: Erlbaum.

Cassata, M., & Irwin, B. J. (1997). Young by day: The older person on daytime serial drama. In H. S. Noor Al-deen (Ed.), *Cross-cultural communication and aging in the United States* (pp. 215–230). Mahwah, NJ: Erlbaum.

Castillo, M. (2015). Bratz says toy commercial is no longer enough. Retrieved from www.cnbc.com

CDC (2015). Smoking and tobacco use; fact sheet; adult cigarette smoking in the United States. Retrieved from www.cdc.gov/tobacco/

CDC (2016). E-cigarette use by youth is dangerous. Retrieved from www.cdc.gov

CDC (2017). Smoking and tobacco use fact sheet: Smoking in the movies. Retrieved from www.cdc.gov/tobacco

Celluloid Closet, The (1995). Written by V. Russo, R. Epstein, J. Friedman, & S. Wood. Columbia Tristar Home Video.

Center for the Study of Women in Television and Film (2012). It's a man's (celluloid) world: On-screen representations of female characters in the top 100 films of 2011. Center for the Study of Women in Television and Film. San Diego, CA. Retrieved from www.wif.org/

Centerwall, B. S. (1989). Exposure to television as a risk factor for violence. *American Journal of Epidemiology*, 129, 643–652.

Centerwall, B. S. (1992). Television and violence: The scale of the problem and where to go from here. *Journal of the American Medical Association*, 267, 3059–3063.

Chadee, D., Smith, S., & Ferguson, C. J. (2017). Murder she watched: Does watching news or fictional media cultivate fear of crime? *Psychology of Popular Media Culture*. doi: 10.1037/ppm0000158

Champion, A. R., & Pedersen, C. L. (2015). Investigating differences between sexters and non-sexters on attitudes, subjective norms, and risky sexual behaviours. *Canadian Journal of Human Sexuality*, 24(3), 205–214.

Chan, M. S., Jones, C. R., Hall Jamieson, K., & Albarracín, D. (2017). Debunking: A meta-analysis of the psychological efficacy of messages countering misinformation. *Psychological Science*, 28(11), 1531–1546.

Chandler, D. (1997). Children's understanding of what is "real" on television: A review of the literature. *Journal of Educational Media*, 23, 65–80.

Chandra, A., Martino, S. C., Collins, R. L., Elliott, M. N., Berry, S. H., Kanouse, D. E., & Miu, A. (2008). Does watching sex on television predict teen pregnancy? Findings from a national longitudinal survey of youth. *Pediatrics*, 122(5), 1047–1054.

Chang, C. (2004). Country of origin as a heuristic cue: The effects of message ambiguity and product involvement. *Media Psychology*, 6, 169–192.

Chang, H. J. J., O'Boyle, M., Anderson, R. C., & Suttikun, C. (2016). An fMRI study of advertising appeals and their relationship to product attractiveness and buying intentions. *Journal of Consumer Behaviour*, 15(6), 538–548.

Channick, R. (2016). State Farm rebrands with less disastrous message. *Chicago Tribune*, June 3. Retrieved from www.chicagotribune.com/

Chapin, A. (2016). WD-40 and microwaved tampons: Secrets of food photography revealed. *The Guardian*, January 4. Retrieved from www.theguardian.com

Chappell, C. R., & Hartz, J. (1998). The challenge of communicating science to the public. *The Chronicle of Higher Education*, 45 (March 20), B7.

Charlton, T., Gunter, B., & Hannan, A. (Eds.). (2002). *Broadcast television effects in a remote community*. Mahwah, NJ: Erlbaum.

Check, J. V. P. (1985). *The effects of violent and nonviolent pornography*. Ottawa: Department of Justice for Canada.

Check, J. V. P., & Guloien, T. H. (1989). Reported proclivity for coercive sex following repeated exposure to sexually violent pornography, nonviolent pornography, and erotica. In D. Zillmann & J. Bryant (Eds.), *Pornography: Research advances and policy considerations* (pp. 159–184). Hillsdale, NJ: Erlbaum.

Chen, L., Zhou, S., & Bryant, J. (2007). Temporal changes in mood repair through music consumption: Effects of mood, mood salience, and individual differences. *Media Psychology*, 9, 695–713.

Chen, M. (1994). *The smart parent's guide to kids' TV*. San Francisco: KQED Books.

Cheong, Y., Kim, K., & Zheng, L. (2010). Advertising appeals as a reflection of culture: A cross-cultural analysis of food advertising appeals in China and the US. *Asian Journal of Communication*, 20(1), 1–16.

Chia, S. C. (2006). How peers mediate media influence on adolescents' sexual attitudes and sexual behavior. *Journal of Communication*, 56, 585–606.

Chiang, O. J. (2009). The challenge of user-generated porn. *Forbes*, August 5. Retrieved from www.forbes.com/2009/08/04/digital-playground-video-technology-e-gang-09-ali-joone.html

Chivers, M. L., Seto, M. C., Lalumière, M. L., Laan, E., & Grimbos, T. (2010). Agreement of self-reported and genital measures of sexual arousal in men and women: A meta-analysis. *Archives of Sexual Behavior*, 39, 5–56.

Cho, J. (2005). Media, interpersonal discussion, and electoral choice. *Communication Research*, 32, 295–322.

Cho, J. (2008). Political ads and citizen communication. *Communication Research*, 35, 423–451.

Cho, J. (2011). The geography of political communication: Effects of regional variations in campaign advertising on citizen communication. *Human Communication Research*, 37, 434–462.

Chock, T. M. (2011). Is it seeing or believing? Exposure, perceived realism, and emerging adults' perceptions of their own and others' attitudes about relationships. *Media Psychology*, 14, 355–386.

Choi, Y. J. (2011). Do central processing and online processing always concur? Analysis of scene order and proportion effects in broadcast news. *Applied Cognitive Psychology*, 25, 567–575.

Chokshi, N. (2016). How #BlackLivesMatter came to define a movement. *The New York Times*, August 22. Retrieved from www.nytimes.com/

Chozik, A. (2016). Hillary Clinton blames F.B.I. director for election loss. *The New York Times*, November 12. Retrieved from www.nytimes.com/

Christ, W. G., & Potter, W. J. (1998). Media literacy, media education, and the academy. *Journal of Communication*, 48(1), 5–15.

Christensen, P. N., & Wood, W. (2007). Effects of media violence on viewers' aggression in unconstrained social interaction. In R. W. Preiss, B. M. Gayle, N. Burrell, M. Allen, & J. Bryant (Eds.), *Mass media effects research: Advances through meta-analyses* (pp. 145–168). Mahwah, NJ: Erlbaum.

Christenson, P. G. (1992). The effects of parental advisory labels on adolescent music preferences. *Journal of Communication*, 42(1), 106–113.

Christenson, P. G., & Roberts, D. F. (1983). The role of television in the formation of children's social attitudes. In M. J. A. Howe (Ed.), *Learning from television: Psychological and educational research* (pp. 79–99). London: Academic Press.

Christianson, S., & Loftus, E. F. (1987). Memory for traumatic events. *Applied Cognitive Psychology*, 1, 225–239.

Chung, J. E. (2011). Mapping international film trade: Network analysis of international film trade between 1996 and 2004. *Journal of Communication*, 61, 618–640.

Cialdini, R. B. (2003). Crafting normative messages to protect the environment. *Current Directions in Psychological Science*, 12(4), 105–109.

Cialdini, R. B. (2006). *Influence: The psychology of persuasion*. Rev. ed. New York: Collins.

Cialdini, R. B., Demaine, L. J., Sagarin, B. J., Barrett, D. W., Rhoads, K., & Winter, P. L. (2006). Managing social norms for persuasive impact. *Social Influence*, 1(1), 3–15.

Cismaru, M., Lavack, A. M., & Markewich, E. (2009). Social marketing campaigns aimed at preventing drunk driving: A review and recommendations. *International Marketing Review*, 26(3), 292–311.

Clark, C. (1969). Television and social controls: Some observation of the portrayal of ethnic minorities. *Television Quarterly*, 8(2), 18–22.

Clover, C. J. (1992). *Men, women, and chainsaws: Gender in the modern horror film.* Princeton, NJ: Princeton University Press.

Coates, T. J. (1990). Strategies for modifying sexual behavior for primary and secondary prevention of HIV disease. *Journal of Consulting and Clinical Psychology*, 58, 57–69.

Coe, K., Tewksbury, D., Bond, B. J., Drogos, K. L., Porter, R. W., Yahn, A., & Zhang, Y. (2008). Hostile news: Partisan use and perceptions of cable news programming. *Journal of Communication*, 58, 201–219.

Cogley, M. (2018). Home to vote "is biggest crowdfunding campaign." *The Times*, May 26. Retrieved from www.thetimes.co.uk/

Cohen, J. (2001). Defining identification: A theoretical look at the identification of audience with media characters. *Mass Communication and Society*, 4, 245–264.

Cohen, J. (2004). Parasocial breakup from favorite television characters: The role of attachment styles and relationship intensity. *Journal of Social and Personal Relationships*, 21, 187–202.

Cohen, J. (2006). Audience identification with media characters. In J. Bryant & P. Vorderer (Eds.), *Psychology of entertainment* (pp. 183–198). Mahwah, NJ: Erlbaum.

Cohn, N. (2017). A 2016 review: Why key state polls were wrong about Trump. *The New York Times*, May 31. Retrieved from www.nytimes.com

Cole, J. (2000). *Surveying the digital future.* Los Angeles: UCLA Center for Communication Policy.

Colfax, D., & Steinberg, S. (1972). The perpetuation of racial stereotypes: Blacks in mass circulation magazine advertisements. *Public Opinion Quarterly*, 35, 8–18.

Coll, S. (2017). Donald Trump's "fake news" tactics. *The New Yorker*, December 3. Retrieved from www.newyorker.com/

Collen, J. (2013). How much to tattoo my trademark on your body? *Forbes*, May 4. Retrieved from www.forbes.com

Collier, K. M., Coyne, S. M., Rasmussen, E. E., Hawkins, A. J., Padilla-Walker, L. M., Erickson, S. E., & Memmott-Elison, M. K. (2016). Does parental mediation of media influence child outcomes? A meta-analysis on media time, aggression, substance use, and sexual behavior. *Developmental Psychology*, 52(5), 798–812.

Collins, A. M., & Loftus, E. F. (1975). A spreading activation theory of semantic processing. *Psychological Review*, 82, 407–428.

Collins, J. (1998). Talking trash. *Time*, March 30, pp. 63–66.

Collins, R. L., Elliott, M. N., Berry, S. H., Kanouse, D. E., & Hunter, S. B. (2003). Entertainment television as a healthy sex educator: The impact of condom-efficiency information in an episode of *Friends. Pediatrics*, 112, 1115–1121.

Collins, S. (2015). Super Bowl 2015: Sunday's game a ratings winner for NBC. *Los Angeles Times*, February 3. Retrieved from www.latimes.com/

Collum, D. D. (2008). Blocking the big mouths. *Sojourners* (March), p. 38.

Comer, J. S., Furr, J. M., Beidas, R. S., Weiner, C. L., & Kendall, P. C. (2008). Children and terrorism-related news: Training parents in coping and media literacy. *Journal of Consulting and Clinical Psychology*, 76(4), 568–578.

Commission on Obscenity and Pornography (1970). *The report of the Commission on Obscenity and Pornography.* New York: Bantam.

Common Sense Media (2013). Zero to eight: Children's media use in America. Retrieved from www.commonsensemedia.org

Common Sense Media (2014). Advertising to children and teens: Current practices. Retrieved from www.commonsensemedia.org

Common Sense Media (2018). Common Sense and SurveyMonkey poll parents on YouTube and technology addiction. Retrieved from www.commonsensemedia.org

Conan, N. (2009). On *Sesame Street*, "c" is for controversy. Retrieved from www.npr.org/templates/story/story.php?storyId=120355663

Confessore, N., Dance, G. J. X., Harris, R., & Hansen. N. (2018). The Follower factory. *The New York Times*, January 27. Retrieved from www.nytimes.com/

Conklin, J. E. (2008). *Campus life in the movies: A critical survey from the silent era to the present*. Jefferson, NC: McFarland.

Conley, T. D., & Ramsey, L. R. (2011). Killing us softly? Investigating portrayals of women and men in contemporary magazine advertisements. *Psychology of Women Quarterly*, 35(3), 469–478.

Connaughton, S. L., & Jarvis, S. E. (2004). Invitations for partisan identification: Attempts to court Latino voters through televised Latino-oriented political advertisements, 1984–2000. *Journal of Communication*, 54, 38–54.

Connolly-Ahern, C., & Castells i Talens, A. (2010). The role of indigenous peoples in Guatemalan political advertisements. *Communication, Culture & Critique*, 3, 310–333.

Conrad, P. (2001). Genetic optimism: Framing genes and mental illness in the news. *Culture, Medicine and Psychiatry*, 25, 225–247.

Conroy-Krutz, J., & Moehler, D. C. (2015). Moderation from bias: A field experiment on partisan media in a new democracy. *Journal of Politics*, 77(2), 575–587.

Conway, J. C., & Rubin, A. M. (1991). Psychological predictors of television viewing motivation. *Communication Research*, 18, 443–463.

Cook, G. (1992). *Discourse of advertising*. London: Routledge.

Cook, J., Oreskes, N., Doran, P. T., Anderegg, W. R. L., Verheggen, B., Maibach, E. W., ... Rice, K. (2016). Consensus on consensus: A synthesis of consensus estimates on human-caused global warming. *Environmental Research Letters*, 11(4), 048002. doi: 10.1088/1748-9326/11/4/048002

Cook, T. D., Appleton, H., Conner, R. F., Shaffer, A., Tabkin, G., & Weber, J. S. (1975). *Sesame Street revisited*. New York: Sage.

Corcoran, F. (1986). KAL 007 and the evil empire: Mediated disaster and forms of rationalization. *Critical Studies in Mass Communication*, 3, 297–316.

Coscarelli, J. (2017). Beyoncé is pregnant with twins. *The New York Times*, February 1. Retrieved from www.nytimes.com

Cougar Hall, P., West, J. H., & Neeley, S. (2013). Alcohol, tobacco, and other drug references in lyrics of popular music from 1959 to 2009. *Addiction Research & Theory*, 21(3), 207–215.

Coulson, M., Barnett, J., Ferguson, C. J. & Gould, R. L. (2012). Real feelings for virtual people: Emotional attachments and interpersonal attraction in video games. *Psychology of Popular Media Culture*, 1, 176–184.

Coulter, R. H., & Pinto, M. B. (1995). Guilt appeals in advertising: What are their effects? *Journal of Applied Psychology*, 80(6), 697–705.

Courbet, D., Fourquet-Courbet, M.-P., Kazan, R., & Intartaglia, J. (2014). The long-term effects of e-advertising: The influence of Internet pop-ups viewed at a low level of attention in implicit memory. *Journal of Computer-Mediated Communication*, 19(2), 274–293.

Court, J. H. (1977). Pornography and sex crimes: A re-evaluation in the light of recent trends around the world. *International Journal of Criminology and Penology*, 5, 129–157.

Court, J. H. (1982). Rape trends in New South Wales: A discussion of conflicting evidence. *Australian Journal of Social Issues*, 17, 202–206.

Court, J. H. (1984). Sex and violence: A ripple effect. In N. M. Malamuth & E. Donnerstein (Eds.), *Pornography and sexual aggression* (pp. 143–172). Orlando, FL: Academic Press.

Cox, N. B. (2015). Banking on females: Bravo's commodification of the female audience. *Communication, Culture & Critique*, 8(3), 466–483.

Coyne, S. M., & Archer, J. (2004). Indirect, relational, and social aggression in the media: A content analysis of British television programs. *Aggressive Behavior*, 30, 254–271.

Coyne, S. M., & Archer, J. (2005). The relationship between indirect aggression on television and in real life. *Social Development*, 14, 324–336.

Coyne, S. M., & Whitehead, E. (2008). Indirect aggression in animated Disney films. *Journal of Communication*, 58, 382–395.

Craig, R. (2000). Expectations and elections: How television defines campaign news. *Critical Studies in Media Communication*, 17, 28–44.

Craig, R. S. (1992). Women as home caregivers: Gender portrayal in OTC drug commercials. *Journal of Drug Education*, 22(4), 303–312.

Craig, R.T. (2014). *African Americans and mass media: A case for diversity in media ownership.* Lanham, MD: Lexington Books.

Crawley, A. M., Anderson, D. R., Wilder, A., Williams, M., & Santomero, A. (1999). Effects of repeated exposures to a single episode of the television program *Blue's Clues* on the viewing behaviors and comprehension of preschool children. *Journal of Educational Psychology*, 91, 630–637.

Creedon, P. J. (Ed.). (1994). *Women, media, and sport: Challenging gender values.* Thousand Oaks, CA: Sage.

Cruea, M., & Park, S.-Y. (2012). Gender disparity in video game usage: A third-person perception-based explanation. *Media Psychology*, 15, 44–67.

Crysel, L. C., Cook, C. L., Schember, T. O., & Webster, G. D. (2015). Harry Potter and the measures of personality: Extraverted Gryffindors, agreeable Hufflepuffs, clever Ravenclaws, and manipulative Slytherins. *Personality and Individual Differences*, 83, 174–179.

Cugelman, B., Thelwall, M., & Dawes, P. (2011). Online interventions for social marketing health behavior change campaigns: A meta-analysis of psychological architectures and adherence factors. *Journal of Medical Internet Research*, 13(1), e17. doi: 10.2196/jmir.1367

Cumberbatch, G., & Negrine, R. (1991). *Images of disability on television.* London: Routledge.

Cumings, B. (1992). *War and television.* New York: Verso.

Cuperfain, R., & Clarke, T. K. (1985). A new perspective on subliminal perception. *Journal of Advertising*, 14(1), 36–41.

Cwalina, W., Falkowski, A., & Kaid, L. L. (2000). Role of advertising in forming the image of politicians: Comparative analysis of Poland, France, and Germany. *Media Psychology*, 2, 119–146.

D'Addario, D. (2016). How NBC took advantage of Olympic fans. *Time*, August 19. Retrieved from http://time.com/4459016/rio-2016-olympics-nbc/

D'Haenens, L. (2001). Old and new media: Access and ownership in the home. In S. Livingstone & M. Bovill (Eds.), *Children and their changing media environment: A European comparative study* (pp. 53–84). Mahwah, NJ: Erlbaum.

d'Ydewalle, G., & De Bruycker, W. (2007). Eye movements of children and adults while reading subtitles. *European Psychologist*, 12(3), 196–205.

d'Ydewalle, G., & Van de Poel, M. (1999). Incidental foreign-language acquisition by children watching subtitled television programs. *Journal of Psycholinguistic Research*, 28, 227–244.

d'Ydewalle, G., Praet, C., Verfaillie, K., & Van Rensbergen, J. (1991). Watching subtitled television: Automatic reading behavior. *Communication Research*, 18, 650–666.

Dahl, M. (2011). Why watching "The Office" makes us cringe. Retrieved from http://bodyodd.msnbc.com/_news/2011/04/14/6472696

Dal Cin, S., Gibson, B., Zanna, M. P., Shumate, R., & Fong, G. T. (2007). Smoking in movies, implicit associations of smoking with the self, and intentions to smoke. *Psychological Science*, 18, 559–563.

Dall, P. W. (1988). Prime-time television portrayals of older adults in the context of family life. *The Gerontologist*, 28, 700–706.

Dalton, M. A., Ahrens, M. B., Sargent, J. D., Mott, L. A., Beach, M. L., & Tickle, J. J. (2002). Relation between adolescent use of tobacco and alcohol and parental restrictions on movies. *Effective Clinical Practice*, 5, 1–10.

Danish, S. J., & Donohue, T. R. (1996). Understanding the media's influence on the development of antisocial and prosocial behavior. In R. Hampton, P. Jenkins, & T. Gullotta (Eds.), *Preventing violence in America* (pp. 133–156). Thousand Oaks, CA: Sage.

Dann, S. (2010). Redefining social marketing with contemporary commercial marketing definitions. *Journal of Business Research*, 63(2), 147–153.

Dardis, F. E., Shen, F., & Edwards, H. H. (2008). Effects of negative political advertising on individuals' cynicism and self-efficacy: The impact of ad type and message exposures. *Mass Communication and Society*, 11(1), 24–42.

Darke, P. R., & Ritchie, R. J. (2007). The defensive consumer: Advertising deception, defensive processing, and distrust. *Journal of Marketing Research, 44*(1), 114–127.

David, C., Cappella, J. N., & Fishbein, M. (2006). The social diffusion of influence among adolescents: Group interaction in a chat room environment about antidrug advertisements. *Communication Theory, 16*, 118–140.

David, C. C. (2009). Learning political information from the news: A closer look at the role of motivation. *Journal of Communication, 59*, 243–261.

David, P., Horton, B., & German, T. (2008). Dynamics of entertainment and affect in a Super Bowl audience. *Communication Research, 35*, 398–420.

Davies, M. M. (1997). *Fake, fact, and fantasy: Children's interpretations of television reality.* Mahwah, NJ: Erlbaum.

Davis, K. C., Norris, J., George, W. H., Martell, J., & Heiman, J. R. (2006). Men's likelihood of sexual aggression: The influence of alcohol, sexual arousal, and violent pornography. *Aggressive Behavior, 32*, 581–589.

Davis, M. (2008). *Street gang: The complete history of Sesame Street.* New York: Viking.

Davis, M. H., Hull, J. G., Young, R. D., & Warren, G. G. (1987). Emotional reactions to dramatic film stimuli: The influence of cognitive and emotional empathy. *Journal of Personality and Social Psychology, 52*, 126–133.

Davis, R. H., & Davis, J. A. (1985). *TV's image of the elderly.* Lexington, MA: Lexington Books/D. C. Heath.

Davis, W. (2016). Fake news or real? How to self-check the news and get the facts. Retrieved from www.npr.org

Dawson, J. (2016). NBC Universal, Olympics 2016: As broadcast costs rise, can NBC score? *Variety*, July 12. Retrieved from http://variety.com

Day, D. M., & Page, S. (1986). Portrayal of mental illness in Canadian newspapers. *Canadian Journal of Psychiatry, 31*, 813–816.

De Bruycker, W., & d'Ydewalle, G. (2003). Reading native and foreign language television subtitles in children and adults. In J. Hyönä, R. Radach, & H. Deubel (Eds.), *The mind's eye: Cognitive and applied aspects of eye movement research* (pp. 671–684). Amsterdam: Elsevier Science.

De keersmaecker, J., & Roets, A. (2017). "Fake news": Incorrect, but hard to correct: The role of cognitive ability on the impact of false information on social impressions. *Intelligence.* doi: 10.1016/j.intell.2017.10.005

De Laat, K., & Baumann, S. (2016). Caring consumption as marketing schema: Representations of motherhood in an era of hyperconsumption. *Journal of Gender Studies, 25*(2), 183–199.

De Leeuw, R. H., Kleemans, M., Rozendaal, E., Anschütz, D. J., & Buijzen, M. (2015). The impact of prosocial television news on children's prosocial behavior: An experimental study in the Netherlands. *Journal of Children and Media, 9*(4), 419–434.

De Moraes, L. (2017). Ken Burns' "The Vietnam War" averaged 6.7M viewers for PBS, reached 34M in Live+7. Retrieved from http://deadline.com/

Dearing, J., & Rogers, E. (1996). *Agenda setting.* Thousand Oaks, CA: Sage.

Deb, S. (2017). Kathy Griffin is being investigated by the Secret Service, her lawyers say. *The New York Times*, June 2. Retrieved from www.nytimes.com

DeFleur, M. L. (2010). *Mass communication theories: Explaining origins, processes, and effects.* Boston: Allyn & Bacon.

DeJong, W., Wolf, R. C., & Austin, S. B. (2001). U.S. federally funded television Public Service Announcements (PSAs) to prevent HIV/AIDS: A content analysis. *Journal of Health Communication, 6*(3), 249–263.

Delwiche, A., & Henderson, J.J. (Eds.). (2012). *The participatory cultures handbook.* New York: Routledge/Taylor & Francis.

Demorest, J. A. (2009). Corporate interests and their impact on news coverage. Retrieved from www.ohio.edu/ethics

Dempsey, P. C., Howard, B. J., Lynch, B. M., Owen, N., & Dunstan, D. W. (2014). Associations of television viewing time with adults' well-being and vitality. *Preventive Medicine, 69*, 69–74.

Department of Justice (1986). *Final report of the Attorney General's Commission on Pornography.* Nashville, TN: Rutledge Hill Press.

Dermody, J., & Scullion, R. (2001). An exploration of the advertising ambitions and strategies of the 2001 British general election. *Journal of Marketing Management*, 17, 969–987.

Derrick, J. L., Gabriel, S., & Hugenberg, K. (2009). Social surrogacy: How favored television programs provide the experience of belonging. *Journal of Experimental Social Psychology*, 45, 352–362.

Deshpande, A., Menon, A., Perri, M., & Zinkhan, G. (2004). Direct-to-consumer advertising and its utility in health care decision-making: A consumer perspective. *Journal of Health Communication*, 9, 499–514.

Deshpande, S., & Rundle-Thiele, S. (2011). Segmenting and targeting American university students to promote responsible alcohol use: A case for applying social marketing principles. *Health Marketing Quarterly*, 28(4), 287–303.

Desmond, R. (1987). Adolescents and music lyrics: Implications of a cognitive perspective. *Communication Quarterly*, 35(3), 276–284.

Desmond, R., & Carveth, R. (2007). The effects of advertising on children and adolescents: A meta-analysis. In R. W. Preiss, B. M. Gayle, N. Burrell, M. Allen, & J. Bryant (Eds.), *Mass media effects research: Advances through meta-analysis* (pp. 169–179). Mahwah, NJ: Erlbaum.

Desmond, R., Singer, J. L., & Singer, D. G. (1990). Family mediation: Parental communication patterns and the influences of television on children. In J. Bryant (Ed.), *Television and the American family* (pp. 293–309). Hillsdale, NJ: Erlbaum.

Detenber, B. H., & Reeves, B. (1996). A bio-informational theory of emotion: Motion and image size effects on viewers. *Journal of Communication*, 46(3) 66–84.

Deutsch, L., & Lee, J. (2014). No filter: Social media show raw video of #Ferguson. *USA Today*, August 14. Retrieved from www.usatoday.com

Devlin, L. P. (1987). Campaign commercials. In A. A. Berger (Ed.), *Television in society* (pp. 17–28). New Brunswick, NJ: Transaction Books.

Diamond, J. (1997). Kinship with the stars. *Discover* (May), 44–49.

Diamond, M., & Uchiyama, A. (1999). Pornography, rape, and sex crimes in Japan. *International Journal of Law and Psychiatry*, 22, 1–11.

Diamond, M., Jozifkova, E., & Weiss, P. (2011). Pornography and sex crimes in the Czech Republic. *Archives of Sexual Behavior*, 40(5), 1037–1043.

Dick, K. (2006). *This film is not yet rated.* Documentary film.

Dietz, P. E., Harry, B., & Hazelwood, R. R. (1986). Detective magazines: Pornography for the sexual sadist? *Journal of Forensic Sciences*, 31(1), 197–211.

Dillard, J. P., Weber, K. M., & Vail R. G. (2007). The relationship between the perceived and actual effectiveness of persuasive messages: A meta-analysis with implications for formative campaign research. *Journal of Communication*, 57, 613–631.

Dillman Carpentier, F. R., & Potter, R. F. (2007). Effects of music on physiological arousal: Explorations into tempo and genre. *Media Psychology*, 10, 339–363.

Dillman Carpentier, F. R., Brown, J. D., Bertocci, M., Silk, J. S., Forbes, E. E., & Dahl, R. E. (2008). Sad kids, sad media? Applying mood management theory to depressed adolescents' use of media. *Media Psychology*, 11, 143–166.

Dimitrova, D. V., & Bystrom, D. (2013). The effects of social media on political participation and candidate image evaluations in the 2012 Iowa Caucuses. *American Behavioral Scientist*, 57(11), 1568–1583.

Dimmick, J. (2003). *Media competition and coexistence: The theory of the niche.* Mahwah, NJ: Erlbaum.

Dine Young, S. (2012). *Psychology at the movies.* Chichester: Wiley-Blackwell.

Dir, A. L., & Cyders, M. A. (2015). Risks, risk factors, and outcomes associated with phone and Internet sexting among university students in the United States. *Archives of Sexual Behavior*, 44(6), 1675–1684.

Dir, A. L., Coskunpinar, A., Steiner, J. L., & Cyders, M. A. (2013). Understanding differences in sexting behaviors across gender, relationship status, and sexual identity, and the role of expectancies in sexting. *Cyberpsychology, Behavior, and Social Networking*, 16(8), 568–574.

Distefan, J. M., Gilpin, E. A., Sargent, J. D., & Pierce, J. P. (1999). Do movie stars encourage adolescents to start smoking? *Preventive Medicine*, 28, 1–11.

Dixon, T. L. (2007). Black criminals and white officers: The effect of racially misrepresenting law breakers and law defenders on television news. *Media Psychology*, 10, 270–291.

Dixon, T. L. (2008a). Crime news and racialized beliefs: Understanding the relationship between local news viewing and perceptions of African Americans and crime. *Journal of Communication*, 58, 106–125.

Dixon, T. L. (2008b). Network news and racial beliefs: Exploring the connection between national television news exposure and stereotypical perceptions of African Americans. *Journal of Communication*, 58, 321–337.

Dixon, T. L., & Linz, D. (2000). Overrepresentation and underrepresentation of African Americans and Latinos as lawbreakers on television news. *Journal of Communication*, 50(2), 131–154.

Dixon, T. L., & Williams, C. L. (2015). The changing misrepresentation of race and crime on network and cable news: Race and crime on network and cable news. *Journal of Communication*, 65(1), 24–39.

Dobrow, J. R., & Gidney, C. L. (1998). The good, the bad, and the foreign: The use of dialect in children's animated television. *Annals of the American Academy of Political and Social Science*, 557, 105–119.

Doherty, T. (1999). *Pre-code Hollywood: Sex, immorality, and insurrection in American cinema 1930–1934*. New York: Columbia University Press.

Dominick, J. R., & Rauch, G. E. (1972). The image of women in network TV commercials. *Journal of Broadcasting*, 16, 259–265.

Donnerstein, E. (1980). Aggressive erotica and violence against women. *Journal of Personality and Social Psychology*, 39, 269–277.

Donnerstein, E., & Berkowitz, L. (1981). Victim reactions in aggressive erotic films as a factor in violence against women. *Journal of Personality and Social Psychology*, 41, 710–724.

Donnerstein, E., & Hallam, J. (1978). Facilitating effects of erotica on aggression against women. *Journal of Personality and Social Psychology*, 36, 1270–1277.

Donnerstein, E., Donnerstein, M., & Evans, R. (1975). Erotic stimuli and aggression: Facilitation or inhibition? *Journal of Personality and Social Psychology*, 32, 237–244.

Donohew, L., Helm, D., & Haas, J. (1989). Drugs and (Len) Bias on the sports page. In L. A. Wenner (Ed.), *Media, sports, and society* (pp. 225–237). Newbury Park, CA: Sage.

Donvan, J., & Zucker, C. (2017). *In a different key: the story of autism*. New York: Broadway.

Doob, A. N., & Macdonald, G. E. (1979). Television viewing and fear of victimization: Is the relationship causal? *Journal of Personality and Social Psychology*, 37, 170–179.

Douglas, S. J. (1994). *Where the girls are: Growing up female with the mass media*. New York: Times Books.

Douglas, S. J. (1997). Mixed signals: The messages TV sends to girls. *TV Guide*, October 25, pp. 24–29.

Douglas, W. (2001). Subversion of the American television family. In J. Bryant & J. A. Bryant (Eds.), *Television and the American family*. 2nd ed. (pp. 229–246). Mahwah, NJ: Erlbaum.

Douglas, W. (2003). *Television families: Is something wrong in suburbia?* New York: Routledge.

Döveling, K., von Scheve, C. & Konijn, E. (Eds.). (2015). *The Routledge handbook of emotions and mass media*. London and New York: Routledge.

Dow, B. J. (2001). Ellen, television, and the politics of gay and lesbian visibility. *Critical Studies in Media Communication*, 18(2), 123–140.

Dowler, K. (2006). Sex, lies, and videotape: The presentation of sex crime in local television news. *Journal of Criminal Justice*, 34(4), 383–392.

Drabman, R. S., & Thomas, M. H. (1974). Does media violence increase children's toleration of real-life aggression? *Developmental Psychology*, 10, 418–421.

Drabman, R. S., & Thomas, M. H. (1976). Does watching violence on television cause apathy? *Pediatrics*, 57, 329–331.

Dubow, E. F., & Miller, L. S. (1996). Televised violence viewing and aggressive behavior. In T. M. Macbeth (Ed.), *Tuning in to young viewers: Social science perspectives on television* (pp. 117–147). Thousand Oaks, CA: Sage.

Dudo, A., Brossard, D., Shanahan, J., Scheufele, D. A., Morgan, M., & Signorielli, N. (2011). Science on television in the 21st century: Recent trends in portrayals and their contributions to public attitudes toward science. *Communication Research*, 38, 754–777.

Dujardin, H. (2011). *Plate to pixel: Digital food photography & styling*. Indianapolis: Wiley.

Duncan, M. C. (2006). Gender warriors in sport: Women and the media. In A. A. Raney & J. Bryant (Eds.), *Handbook of sports and media* (pp. 231–252). Mahwah, NJ: Erlbaum.

Dunlop, S., Wakefield, M., & Kashima, Y. (2008). Can you feel it? Negative emotion, risk, and narrative in health communication. *Media Psychology*, 11, 52–75.

Dunn, S. W. (2009). Candidate and media agenda setting in the 2005 Virginia gubernatorial election. *Journal of Communication*, 59, 635–652.

Duran, R. L., Yousman, B., Walsh, K. M., & Longshore, M. A. (2008). Holistic media education: An assessment of the effectiveness of a college course in media literacy. *Communication Quarterly*, 56(1), 49–68.

DuRant, R. H., Rich, M., Emans, S. J., Rome, E. S., Allred, E., & Woods, E. R. (1997). Violence and weapon carrying in music videos: A content analysis. *Archives of Pediatric & Adolescent Medicine*, 151, 443–448.

Durham, M. G. (2009). *The Lolita effect: The media sexualization of young girls and what we can do about it*. Woodstock, NY: Overlook Press.

Dutta, M. J. (2007). Communication about culture and health. *Communication Theory*, 17, 304–328.

Dutta, M. J., & Archarya, L. (2015). Power, control, and the margins in an HIV/AIDS intervention: A culture-centered interrogation of the "Avahan" campaign targeting Indian truckers. *Communication, Culture and Critique*, 8(2), 254–272.

Dutta-Bergman, M. J. (2004). The impact of completeness and web use motivation on the credibility of e-health information. *Journal of Communication*, 54, 253–269.

Easterbrook, G. (1989). *Satanic Verses* as Muslims see it. *Manhattan Mercury*, February 20, A5.

Eastin, M. S., & Griffiths, R. P. (2006). Beyond the shooter game: Examining presence and hostile outcomes among male game players. *Communication Research*, 33, 448–466.

Eastman, S. T., & Billings, A. C. (2000). Sportscasting and sports reporting: The power of gender bias. *Journal of Sport and Social Issues*, 23, 192–213.

Edelstein, A. S. (1993). Thinking about the criterion variable in agenda-setting research. *Journal of Communication*, 43(2), 85–99.

Edwards, E. B. (2016). "It's irrelevant to me!" Young black women talk back to VH1's *Love and Hip Hop New York*. *Journal of Black Studies*, 47(3), 273–292.

Edwards-Levy, A. (2017). New poll suggests "fake news" has almost no meaning anymore. Retrieved from www.huffingtonpost.com/

Edy, J. A., & Snidow, S. M. (2011). Making news necessary: How journalism resists alternative media's challenge. *Journal of Communication*, 61, 816–834.

Ehrenreich, B. (2006). *Dancing in the streets: A history of collective joy*. New York: Metropolitan Books.

Einsiedel, E. F. (1988). The British, Canadian, and U.S. pornography commissions and their use of social science research. *Journal of Communication*, 38(2), 108–121.

Eisenberg, D. (2002). It's an ad, ad, ad, ad world. *Time*, September 2, pp. 38–41.

Eisend, M. (2011). How humor in advertising works: A meta-analytic test of alternative models. *Marketing Letters*, 22(2), 115–132.

Elliott, S. (2002a). Campaign spotlight: State Farm aims for where you live. *New York Times*, April 16. Retrieved from www.ads.nyt.com/ia.ad/ia-court08/courttv2.html/4-16-02

Elliott, S. (2002b). The ad within the ad. *New York Times*, May 14. Retrieved from www.ads.nyt.com/ia.ad

Ely, M. P. (2001). *The adventures of Amos 'n' Andy: A social history of an American phenomenon*. Charlottesville, VA: University of Virginia Press.

Ember, S. (2015a). Comcast and NBCUniversal open cross-promotional ad strategy. *The New York Times*, June 21. Retrieved from www.nytimes.com

Ember, S. (2015b). X marks the spot that makes online ads so maddening. *The New York Times*, December 6. Retrieved from www.nytimes.com/

Ember, S. (2017a). Some see media bias. But "the enemy"? Not quite. *The New York Times*, February 24. Retrieved from www.nytimes.com

Ember, S. (2017b). Sinclair requires TV stations to air segments that tilt to the right. *The New York Times*, May 12. Retrieved from www.nytimes.com

Emmers-Sommer, T. M., Triplett, L., Pauley, P., Hanzal, A., & Rhea, D. (2005). The impact of film manipulation on men's and women's attitudes toward women and film editing. *Sex Roles*, 52(9–10), 683–695.

Enda, J. (2011). Retreating from the world. Retrieved from www.ajrarchive.org

Engber, D. (2014). Who made that antiperspirant? *The New York Times*, February 28. Retrieved from www.nytimes.com

Englis, B. G. (1994). The role of affect in political advertising: Voter emotional responses to the nonverbal behavior of politicians. In E. M. Clark, T. C. Brock, & D. W. Stewart (Eds.), *Attention, attitude, and affect in response to advertising* (pp. 223–247). Hillsdale, NJ: Erlbaum.

Entertainment Software Association (2017). 2017 sales, demographic, and usage data: The essential facts about the computer and video game industry. Retrieved from www.theesa.com

Entman, R. (1990). Modern racism and the images of Blacks in local television news. *Critical Studies in Mass Communication*, 7, 332–345.

Entman, R. (1991). Framing U.S. coverage of international news: Contrasts in the narratives of the KAL and Iran Air incidents. *Journal of Communication*, 42(1), 6–27.

Entman, R. (1992). Blacks in the news: Television, modern racism, and cultural change. *Journalism Quarterly*, 69, 341–361.

Entman, R. (1993). Framing: Toward clarification of a fractured paradigm. *Journal of Communication*, 43(4), 51–58.

Entman, R. (1994a). Representation and reality in the portrayal of Blacks on network television news. *Journalism Quarterly*, 71, 509–520.

Entman, R. (1994b). African Americans according to TV news. *Media Studies Journal*, 8, 29–38.

Erlanger, S. (2017). "Fake news," Trump's obsession, is now a cudgel for strongmen. *The New York Times*, December 13. Retrieved from www.nytimes.com/

Eron, L. D., & Huesmann, L. R. (1984). The control of aggressive behavior by changes in attitudes, values, and the conditions of learning. In R. J. Blanchard & D. C. Blanchard (Eds.), *Advances in the study of aggression* (pp. 139–171). Orlando, FL: Academic Press.

Eron, L. D., Huesmann, L. R., Lefkowitz, M. M., & Walder, L. O. (1972). Does television violence cause aggression? *American Psychologist*, 27, 253–263.

Esser, A., Bernal-Merino, M. Á., & Smith, I. R. (Eds.). (2016). *Media across borders: Localizing TV, film and video games*. New York: Routledge.

Esslin, M. (1982). *The age of television*. San Francisco: Freeman.

Eveland, W. P., Jr., & Dunwoody, S. (2001). User control and structural isomorphism or disorientation and cognitive load? Learning from the web versus print. *Communication Research*, 28, 48–78.

Eveland, W. P., Jr., & Dunwoody, S. (2002). An investigation of elaboration and selective scanning as mediators of learning from the Web versus print. *Journal of Broadcasting & Electronic Media*, 46, 34–53.

Eveland, W. P., Jr., Seo, M., & Marton, K. (2002). Learning from the news in campaign 2000: An experimental comparison of TV news, newspapers, and online news. *Media Psychology*, 4, 353–378.

Eveland, W. P., Jr., Cortese, J., Park, H., & Dunwoody, S. (2004). How web site organization influences free recall, factual knowledge, and knowledge structure density. *Human Communication Research*, 30, 208–233.

Everts, S. (2012). How advertisers convinced Americans they smelled bad. *Smithsonian*, August 3. Retrieved from www.smithsonianmag.com

Excerpts from psychiatric evaluation of Hinckley by the mental hospital (1982). *The New York Times*, August 10. Retrieved from www.nytimes.com/1982/08/10/us/excerpts-from-psychiatric-evaluation-of-hinckley-by-the-mental-hospital.html?pagewanted=all&mcubz=1

Eyal, K., & Cohen, J. (2006). When good Friends say goodbye: A parasocial breakup study. *Journal of Broadcasting and Electronic Media*, 50, 502–523.

Eyal, K., & Finnerty, K. (2009). The portrayal of sexual intercourse on television: How, who, and with what consequence? *Mass Communication and Society*, 12(2), 143–169.

Eysenck, H. J., & Nias, N. K. B. (1978). *Sex, violence and the media*. New York: Harper.

Fabes, R. A., & Strouse, J. S. (1984). Youth's perception of models of sexuality: Implications for sexuality education. *Journal of Sex Education and Therapy*, 10, 33–37.

Fabes, R. A., & Strouse, J. S. (1987). Perceptions of responsible and irresponsible models of sexuality: A correlational study. *Journal of Sex Research*, 23, 70–84.

Facebook (2017). Newsroom key facts, May 19. Retrieved from https://newsroom.fb.com/company-info/

Fackler, M., Barnes, B., & Sanger, D. E. (2014). Sony's international incident: Making Kim Jong-un's head explode. *The New York Times*, December 14. Retrieved from www.nytimes.com/

Fahy, T. (Ed.). (2010). *The philosophy of horror*. Lexington, KY: University of Kentucky Press.

Falco, A., Piccirelli, A., Girardi, D., Dal Corso, L., & De Carlo, N. A. (2013). Risky riding behavior on two wheels: The role of cognitive, social, and personality variables among young adolescents. *Journal of Safety Research*, 46, 47–57.

Falk, E. B., O'Donnell, M. B., Tompson, S., Gonzalez, R., Dal Cin, S., Strecher, V., ... An, L. (2016). Functional brain imaging predicts public health campaign success. *Social Cognitive and Affective Neuroscience*, 11(2), 204–214.

Fanti, K. A., Vanman, E., Henrich, C. C., & Avraamides, M. N. (2009). Desensitization to media violence over a short period of time. *Aggressive Behavior*, 35(2), 179–187.

Farhi, P. (2001). Nightly news blues. *American Journalism Review* (June), 32–37.

Farquhar, J. C., & Wasylkiw, L. (2007). Media images of men: Trends and consequences of body conceptualization. *Psychology of Men & Masculinity*, 8(3), 145–160.

Farquhar, J. W., Fortmann, S. P., Flora, J. A., Taylor, B., Haskell, W. L., Williams, P. T., ... Wood, P. D. (1990). Effects of communitywide education on cardiovascular disease risk factors: The Stanford five-city project. *Journal of the American Medical Association*, 264, 359–365.

Farrar, K. M., Krcmar, M., & Nowak, K. L. (2006). Contextual features of violent video games, mental models, and aggression. *Journal of Communication*, 56, 387–405.

Feaster, F., & Wood, B. (1999). *Forbidden fruit: The golden age of the exploitation film*. Baltimore: Midnight Marquee Press.

Fehrman, C. (2011). The incredible shrinking sound bite. *The Boston Globe*, January 2. Retrieved from http://archive.boston.com/

Feng, G. C., & Guo, S. Z. (2012). Support for censorship: A multilevel meta-analysis of the third-person effect. *Communication Reports*, 25(1), 40–50.

Ferguson, C. J. (2012). Positive female role-models eliminate negative effects of sexually violent media. *Journal of Communication*, 62(5), 888–899.

Ferguson, C. J., & Konijn, E. A. (2015). She said/he said: A peaceful debate on video game violence. *Psychology of Popular Media Culture*, 4(4), 397–411.

Ferguson, C. J., Nielsen, R. K. L., & Markey, P. M. (2017). Does sexy media promote teen sex? A meta-analytic and methodological review. *Psychiatric Quarterly*, 88(2), 349–358.

Fernandes, J. (2013). Effects of negative political advertising and message repetition on candidate evaluation. *Mass Communication and Society*, 16(2), 268–291.

Fernando, A., Suganthi, G. L., & Sivakumaran, B. (2014). If you blog, will they follow? Using online media to set the agenda for consumer concerns on "greenwashed" environmental claims. *Journal of Advertising*, 43(2), 167–80.

Ferrante, C. L., Haynes, A. M., & Kingsley, S. M. (1988). Image of women in television advertising. *Journal of Broadcasting & Electronic Media*, 32, 231–237.

Ferretti, F. (1970). *Sesame Street* plan may alter public-TV form. *The New York Times*, February 9. Retrieved from www.nytimes.com

Ferris, A. L., Smith, S. W., Greenberg, B. S., & Smith, S. L. (2007). The content of reality dating shows and viewer perceptions of dating. *Journal of Communication*, 57, 490–510.

Ferris, T. (1997). The risks and rewards of popularizing science. *The Chronicle of Higher Education*, April 4, p. 43.

Feshbach, N. D. (1988). Television and the development of empathy. In S. Oskamp (Ed.), *Television as a social issue* (pp. 261–269). Newbury Park, CA: Sage.

Feshbach, N. D., & Feshbach, S. (1997). Children's empathy and the media: Realizing the potential of television. In S. Kirschner & D. A. Kirschner (Eds.), *Perspectives on psychology and the media* (pp. 3–27). Washington, DC: American Psychological Association.

Feshbach, S. (1955). The drive-reducing function of fantasy behavior. *Journal of Abnormal and Social Psychology*, 50, 3–11.

Feshbach, S., & Singer, R. (1971). *Television and aggression.* San Francisco: Jossey-Bass.

Festinger, L. (1954). A theory of social comparison processes. *Human Relations*, 7, 117–140.

Festinger, L. (1957). *A theory of cognitive dissonance.* Stanford, CA: Stanford University Press.

Fidler, A. E., Zack, E., & Barr, R. (2010). Television viewing patterns in 6- to 18-month olds: The role of caregiver–infant interactional quality. *Infancy*, 15, 176–196.

Fikkers, K. M., Piotrowski, J. T., & Valkenburg, P. M. (2017). A matter of style? Exploring the effects of parental mediation styles on early adolescents' media violence exposure and aggression. *Computers in Human Behavior*, 70, 407–415.

Fine, C. (2010). *Delusions of gender: How our minds, society, and neurosexism create difference.* New York: W. W. Norton.

Finnegan, M. (2016). Trump says the FBI knows Clinton is guilty of crimes. *Los Angeles Times*, November 6. Retrieved from www.latimes.coml

Firger, J. (2016). For runway models, high fashion means a dangerously low—16 on average—BMI. *Newsweek*, February 10. Retrieved from www.newsweek.com.

Fisch, S. M. (2002). Vast wasteland or vast opportunity: Effects of educational television on children's academic knowledge, skills, and attitudes. In J. Bryant & D. Zillmann (Eds.), *Media effects* (pp. 397–426). Mahwah, NJ: Erlbaum.

Fisch, S. M. (2004). *Children's learning from educational television: Sesame Street and beyond.* Mahwah, NJ: Erlbaum.

Fisch, S. M. (2015). Learning from educational television. In D. Lemish (Ed.), *The Routledge international handbook of children, adolescents and media* (pp. 403–409). New York: Routledge.

Fisch, S. M., & Truglio, R. T. (Eds.). (2000). *"G" is for growing: Thirty years of research on children and "Sesame Street."* Mahwah, NJ: Erlbaum.

Fisch, S. M., Truglio, R. T., & Cole, C. F. (1999). The impact of *Sesame Street* on preschool children: A review and synthesis of 30 years' research. *Media Psychology*, 1, 165–190.

Fischer, P. M., Schwartz, M. P., Richards, J. W., Goldstein, A. O., & Rojas, T. H. (1991). Brand logo recognition by children aged 3 to 6 years. *Journal of the American Medical Association*, 266, 3145–3148.

Fischer, P., Greitemeyer, T., Kastenmuller, A., Vogrincic, C., & Sauer, A. (2011). The effects of risk-glorifying media exposure on risk-positive cognitions, emotions, and behaviors: A meta-analytic review. *Psychological Bulletin*, 137, 367–390.

Fischhoff, B., Gonzalez, R. M., Lerner, J. S., & Small, D. A. (2005). Evolving judgments of terror risk: Foresight, hindsight, and emotion. *Journal of Experimental Psychology: Applied*, 11, 124–139.

Fisher, D. A., Hill, D. L., Grube, J. W., & Gruber, E. L. (2004). Sex on American television: An analysis across program genres and network types. *Journal of Broadcasting & Electronic Media*, 48(4), 529–553.

Fitch, M., Huston, A. C., & Wright, J. C. (1993). From television forms to genre schemata: Children's perceptions of television reality. In G. L. Berry & J. K. Asamen (Eds.), *Children and television: Images in a changing sociocultural world* (pp. 38–52). Newbury Park, CA: Sage.

Fitzpatrick, B. G., Martinez, J., Polidan, E., & Angelis, E. (2016). On the effectiveness of social norms intervention in college drinking: The roles of identity verification and peer influence. *Alcoholism: Clinical and Experimental Research*, 40(1), 141–151.

Fitz-Walter, Z., Johnson, D., Wyeth, P., Tjondronegoro, D., & Scott-Parker, B. (2017). Driven to drive? Investigating the effect of gamification on learner driver behavior, perceived motivation and user experience. *Computers in Human Behavior*, 71, 586–595.

Flanagan, C. (2017) How late-night comedy fueled the rise of Trump. *The Atlantic* (May). Retrieved from www.theatlantic.com

Flay, B. R., & Burton, D. (1990). Effective mass communication strategies for health campaigns. In C. Atkin & L. Wallack (Eds.), *Mass communication and public health* (pp. 129–146). Newbury Park, CA: Sage.

Flegenheimer, M. (2017). What's a "Covfefe"? Trump Tweet unites a bewildered nation. *The New York Times*, May 31. Retrieved from www.nytimes.com

Fleming, M. J., & Rickwood, D. J. (2001). Effects of violent versus nonviolent video games on children's arousal, aggressive mood, and positive mood. *Journal of Applied Social Psychology*, 31(10), 2047–2071.

Folkenflik, D. (2009). Final words: Cronkite's Vietnam commentary. Retrieved from www.npr.org

Follman, M. (2015). Here's the disturbing new evidence on how the media inspires mass shooters. *Mother Jones*, October 6. Retrieved from www.motherjones.com/

Fonda, D. (2003). Baby, you can drive my car. *Time*, June 30, pp. 46–48.

Fonda, D. (2004). Food ads: Kill the messenger? *Time*, June 7, p. 87.

Ford, D. (2015). Ivory Coast elections: Seven things you should know. Retrieved from www.bbc.com/news

Fore, W. F. (1987). *Television and religion: The shaping of faith, values, and culture*. Minneapolis, MN: Augsburg.

Fosu, I., Wicks, J. L., Warren, R., & Wicks, R. H. (2013). What's on the menu? Disclaimers, emotional appeals and production techniques in food advertising on child-rated programs in the United States. *Journal of Children and Media*, 7(3), 334–348.

Fowler, K., & Thomas, V. (2015). A content analysis of male roles in television advertising: Do traditional roles still hold? *Journal of Marketing Communications*, 21(5), 356–371.

Fox, J. R. (2004). A signal detection analysis of audio/video redundancy effects in television news video. *Communication Research*, 31, 524–536.

Fox, J. R., Lang, A., Chung, Y., Lee, S., Schwartz, N., & Potter, D. (2004). Picture this: Effects of graphics on the processing of television news. *Journal of Broadcasting & Electronic Media*, 48, 646–674.

Fox, J. R., Angelini, J. R., & Goble, C. (2005). Hype versus substance in network television coverage of presidential election campaigns. *Journalism & Mass Communication Quarterly*, 82, 97–109.

Frank, T. (2012), It's a rich man's world: How billionaire backers pick America's candidates. *Harper's Magazine* (April), pp. 22–27.

Fraser, M., & Dutta, S. (2008). Obama's win means future elections must be fought online. *The Guardian*, November 7. Retrieved from www.theguardian.com

Freeman, W. (2014). Six of the best product placements in video games. *The Guardian*, July 13. Retrieved from www.theguardian.com/technology

Freimuth, V. S., Hammond, S. L., Edgar, T., & Monahan, J. L. (1990). Reaching those at risk: A content-analytic study of AIDS PSAs. *Communication Research*, 17, 775–791.

French, A. (2017). How to make a movie out of anything—even a mindless phone game. *The New York Times*, July 27. Retrieved from www.nytimes.com

Fried, C. B. (1996). Bad rap for rap: Bias in reactions to music lyrics. *Journal of Applied Social Psychology*, 26, 2135–2146.

Fried, C. B. (1999). Who's afraid of rap: Differential reactions to music lyrics. *Journal of Applied Social Psychology*, 29, 705–721.

Friedman, S. M., Dunwoody, S., & Rogers, C. L. (Eds.). (1999). *Communicating uncertainty: Media coverage of new and controversial science*. Mahwah, NJ: Erlbaum.

Frith, K., Shaw, P., & Cheng, H. (2005). The construction of beauty: A cross-cultural analysis of women's magazine advertising. *Journal of Communication*, 55, 56–70.

Fuchs, D. A. (1966). Election-day radio-television and Western voting. *Public Opinion Quarterly*, 30, 226–236.

Fulgoni, G. M., Lipsman, A., & Davidsen, C. (2016). The power of political advertising: Lessons for practitioners—how data analytics, social media, and creative strategies shape U.S. presidential election campaigns. *Journal of Advertising Research*, 56(3), 239–244.

Fullerton, L., & Rarey, M. (2012). Virtual materiality: Collectors and collection in the Brazilian music blogosphere. *Communication, Culture, & Critique*, 5, 1–19.

Furnham, A., Gunter, B., & Walsh, D. (1998). Effects of programme context on memory of humorous television commercials. *Applied Cognitive Psychology*, 12, 555–567.

Furnham, A., Bergland, J., & Gunter, B. (2002). Memory for television advertisements as a function of advertisement–programme congruity. *Applied Cognitive Psychology*, 16, 525–545.

Fussell, J. A. (2000). Horror show. *Kansas City Star*, September 21, E1.

Gabbard, G. O., & Gabbard, K. (1999). *Psychiatry and the cinema*. 2nd ed. New York: Psychiatric Press.

Gabler, N. (2015). The weird science of naming new products. *The New York Times*, January 15. Retrieved from www.nytimes.com

Gabrielli, J., Traore, A., Stoolmiller, M., Bergamini, E., & Sargent, J. D. (2016). Industry television ratings for violence, sex, and substance use. *Pediatrics*, 138(3), e20160487. doi: 10.1542/peds.2016-0487

Galician, M.-L. (2004). *Sex, love, and romance in the mass media: Analysis and criticism of unrealistic portrayals and their influence*. Mahwah, NJ: Erlbaum.

Galician, M.-L. (2007). "Dis-illusioning" as discovery: The research basis and media literacy applications of Dr. Fun's Mass Media Love Quiz and Dr. Galician's Prescriptions. In M.-L. Galician & D. L. Merskin (Eds.), *Critical thinking about sex, love, and romance in the mass media* (pp. 1–20). Mahwah, NJ: Erlbaum.

Galovan, A. M., Drouin, M., & McDaniel, B. T. (2018). Sexting profiles in the United States and Canada: Implications for individual and relationship well-being. *Computers in Human Behavior*, 79, 19–29.

Gamson, J. (1995). Do ask, do tell: Freak talk on TV. *The American Prospect* (Fall).

Gan, S. L., Zillmann, D., & Mitrook, M. (1997). Stereotyping effect of black women's sexual rap on white audiences. *Basic and Applied Social Psychology*, 19(3), 381–399.

Ganahl, D. J., Prinsen, T. J., & Netzley, S. B. (2003). A content analysis of prime time commercials: A contextual framework of gender representation. *Sex Roles*, 49, 545–551.

Ganley, G. D. (1992). *The exploding political power of personal media*. Norwood, NJ: Ablex.

Gantz, W., Wang, Z., & Bradley, S. D. (2006). Televised NFL games, the family, and domestic violence. In A. A. Raney & J. Bryant (Eds.), *Handbook of sports and media* (pp. 365–381). Mahwah, NJ: Erlbaum.

Gardikiotis, A. (2008). Group distinctiveness, political identification, and the third-person effect: Perceptions of a political campaign in the 2004 Greek national election. *Media Psychology*, 11, 331–354.

Gardner, D. (2008). *The science of fear: Why we fear the things we shouldn't—and put ourselves in greater danger*. New York: Dutton.

Gardner, D. M., & Leonard, N. H. (1990). Research in deceptive and corrective advertising: Progress to date and impact on public policy. *Current Issues and Research in Advertising*, 12, 275–309.

Gardner, M. P., & Houston, M. J. (1986). The effects of verbal and visual components of retail communications. *Journal of Retailing*, 62, 64–78.

Garramone, G. M. (1984). Voter responses to negative political ads. *Journalism Quarterly*, 61(2), 250–259.

Garramone, G. M. (1985). Effects of negative political advertising: The role of sponsor and rebuttal. *Journal of Broadcasting and Electronic Media*, 29(2), 147–159.

Garramone, G. M., Atkin, C. K., Pinkleton, B. E., & Cole, R. T. (1990). Effects of negative political advertising on the political process. *Journal of Broadcasting and Electronic Media*, 34, 299–311.

Garramone, G. M., Steele, M. E., & Pinkleton, B. (1991). The role of cognitive schemata in determining candidate characteristic effects. In F. Biocca (Ed.), *Television and political advertising: Psychological processes* (Vol. 1, pp. 311–328). Hillsdale, NJ: Erlbaum.

Garry, M., Strange, D., Bernstein, D. M., & Kinzett, T. (2007). Photographs can distort memory for the news. *Applied Cognitive Psychology*, 21, 995–1004.

Gearan, A. (2015). Hillary Clinton apologizes for e-mail system: "I take responsibility." *The Washington Post*, September 8. Retrieved from www.washingtonpost.com

Geen, R. G., & Quanty, M. B. (1977). The catharsis of aggression: An evaluation of a hypothesis. In L. Berkowitz (Ed.), *Advances in experimental social psychology* (Vol. 10, pp. 1–37). New York: Academic Press.

Geena Davis Institute on Gender in Media (2016). The reel truth: women aren't seen or heard: An automated analysis on gender representation in popular film. Retrieved from http://seejane.org

Geer, J. G. (2006). *In defense of negativity: Attack ads in Presidential campaigns.* Chicago: University of Chicago Press.

Gehrau, V., Brüggemann, T., & Handrup, J. (2016). Media and occupational aspirations: The effect of television on career aspirations of adolescents. *Journal of Broadcasting & Electronic Media*, 60(3), 465–483.

Geiger, S., & Reeves, B. (1993a). The effects of scene changes and semantic relatedness on attention to television. *Communication Research*, 20, 155–175.

Geiger, S., & Reeves, B. (1993b). We interrupt this program ... Attention for television sequences. *Human Communication Research*, 19, 368–387.

Geiogamah, H., & Pavel, D. M. (1993). Developing television for American Indian and Alaska native children in the late 20th century. In G. L. Berry & J. K. Asamen (Eds.), *Children and television: Images in a changing sociocultural world* (pp. 191–204). Newbury Park, CA: Sage.

Gentile, D. A., Coyne, S., & Walsh, D. A. (2011). Media violence, physical aggression, and relational aggression in school age children: a short-term longitudinal study. *Aggressive Behavior*, 37(2), 193–206.

Gentile, D. A., Nathanson, A. I., Rasmussen, E. E., Reimer, R. A., & Walsh, D. A. (2012). Do you see what I see? Parent and child reports of parental monitoring of media. *Family Relations: An Interdisciplinary Journal of Applied Family Studies*, 61(3), 470–487.

Gentile, D. A., Swing, E. L., Anderson, C. A., Rinker, D., & Thomas, K. M. (2016). Differential neural recruitment during violent video game play in violent- and nonviolent-game players. *Psychology of Popular Media Culture*, 5(1), 39–51.

Gentile, D. A., Bender, P. K., & Anderson, C. A. (2017). Violent video game effects on salivary cortisol, arousal, and aggressive thoughts in children. *Computers in Human Behavior*, 70, 39–43.

Gentile, D. A., Berch, O. N., Choo, H., Khoo, A., & Walsh, D. A. (2017). Bedroom media: One risk factor for development. *Developmental Psychology*, 53(12), 2340–2355.

Genzlinger, N. (2017). John Oliver hatches a plan to reach Trump where he watches. *The New York Times*, February. 13. Retrieved from www.nytimes.com

Gerbner, G. (1997). Gender and age in prime-time television. In S. Kirschner & D. A. Kirschner (Eds.), *Perspectives on psychology and the media* (pp. 69–94). Washington, DC: American Psychological Association.

Gerbner, G., & Signorielli, N. (1979). *Women and minorities in television drama (1969–1978).* Philadelphia: Annenberg School of Communication, University of Pennsylvania.

Gerbner, G., Gross, L., Morgan, M., & Signorielli, N. (1981). Health and medicine on television. *New England Journal of Medicine*, 305(15), 901–904.

Gerbner, G., Gross, L., Morgan, M., & Signorielli, N. (1982). Charting the mainstream: Television's contributions to political orientations. *Journal of Communication*, 32(2), 100–127.

Gerbner, G., Gross, L., Morgan, M., & Signorielli, N. (1984). Political correlates of television viewing. *Public Opinion Quarterly*, 48, 283–300.

Gerbner, G., Gross, L., Signorielli, N., & Morgan, M. (1986). *Television's mean world: Violence profile No. 14–15.* Philadelphia: Annenberg School of Communication, University of Pennsylvania.

Gerbner, G., Gross, L., Morgan, M., Signorielli, N., & Shanahan, J. (2002). Growing up with television: Cultivation processes. In J. Bryant & D. Zillmann (Eds.), *Media effects: Advances in theory and research*. 2nd ed. (pp. 43–67). Mahwah, NJ: Erlbaum.

Gerding, A., & Signorielli, N. (2014). Gender roles in tween television programming: A content analysis of two genres. *Sex Roles*, 70(1–2), 43–56.

Gettas, G. J. (1990). The globalization of *Sesame Street*: A producer's perspective. *Educational Technology Research and Development*, 38(4), 55–63.

Gibbons, J. A., Lukowski, A. F., & Walker, W. R. (2005). Exposure increases the believability of unbelievable news headlines via elaborate cognitive processing. *Media Psychology*, 7, 273–300.

Gibbons, J. A., Taylor, C., & Phillips, J. (2005). Gender and racial stereotypes in the mass media. In W. R. Walker & D. J. Herrmann (Eds.), *Cognitive technology: Essays on the transformation of thought and society* (pp. 149–171). Jefferson, NC: McFarland.

Gibbs, S. (2015). Facebook and Twitter users complain over Virginia shooting videos autoplay. *The Guardian*, August 27. Retrieved from www.theguardian.com/us

Gibson, B., Redker, C., & Zimmerman, I. (2014). Conscious and nonconscious effects of product placement: Brand recall and active persuasion knowledge affect brand attitudes and brand self-identification differently. *Psychology of Popular Media Culture*, 3(1), 19–37.

Gibson, R., & Zillmann, D. (1994). Exaggerated versus representative exemplification in news reports: Perception of issues and personal consequences. *Communication Research*, 21, 603–624.

Gibson, R., Callison, C., & Zillmann, D. (2011). Quantitative literacy and affective reactivity in processing statistical information and case histories in the news. *Media Psychology*, 14, 96–120.

Gikow, L. A. (2009). *Sesame Street: A celebration—40 years of life on the street*. New York: Black Dog & Leventhal.

Gil de Zúñiga, H., Molyneux, L., & Zheng, P. (2014). Social media, political expression, and political participation: Panel analysis of lagged and concurrent relationships. *Journal of Communication*, 64(4), 612–634.

Gil de Zúñiga, H., Garcia-Perdomo, V., & McGregor, S. C. (2015). What is second screening? Exploring motivations of second screen use and its effect on online political participation. *Journal of Communication*, 65(5), 793–815.

Gil de Zúñiga, H., Weeks, B., & Ardèvol-Abreu, A. (2017). Effects of the news-finds-me perception in communication: Social media use implications for news seeking and learning about politics. *Journal of Computer-Mediated Communication*, 22(3), 105–123.

Gilboa, E. (2002). Global communication and foreign policy. *Journal of Communication*, 52, 731–748.

Giles, D. (2002). Parasocial interaction: A review of the literature and a model for future research. *Media Psychology*, 4, 279–305.

Gillath, O., McCall, C., Shaver, P. R., & Blascovich, J. (2008). What can virtual reality teach us about prosocial tendencies in real and virtual environments? *Media Psychology*, 11, 259–282.

Gillespie, B., & Joireman, J. (2016). The role of consumer narrative enjoyment and persuasion awareness in product placement advertising. *American Behavioral Scientist*, 60(12), 1510–1528.

Gilliam, M., Jagoda, P., Jaworski, E., Hebert, L. E., Lyman, P., & Wilson, M. C. (2016). "Because if we don't talk about it, how are we going to prevent it?" Lucidity, a narrative-based digital game about sexual violence. *Sex Education*, 16(4), 391–404.

Gillig, T. K., Rosenthal, E. L., Murphy, S. T., & Folb, K. L. (2018). More than a media moment: The influence of televised storylines on viewers' attitudes toward transgender people and policies. *Sex Roles*, 78, 515–527.

Gilly, M. C. (1988). Sex roles in advertising: A comparison of television advertisements in Australia, Mexico, and the United States. *Journal of Marketing*, 52, 75–85.

Giobbi, M. (2014). *Media psychology*. New York: Atropos.

Givens, S. M. B., & Monahan, J. L. (2005). Priming mammies, jezebels, and other controlling images: An examination of the influence of mediated stereotypes on perceptions of an African American woman. *Media Psychology*, 7, 87–106.

GLAAD (2016). Where we are on TV report. Retrieved from www.glaad.org/

Glackin, E., & Gray, S. A. O. (2016). Violence in context: Embracing an ecological approach to violent media exposure. *Analyses of Social Issues and Public Policy*, 16(1), 425–428.

Glantz, S. A., Mitchell, S., Titus, K., Polansky, J. R., Kaufmann, R. B., & Bauer, U. E. (2011). Smoking in top-grossing movies—United States, 2010. *Morbidity and Mortality Weekly Report*, 60 (July 13), 909–913. Retrieved from www.cdc.gov/mmwr

Glascock, J. (2014). Contribution of demographics, sociological factors, and media usage to verbal aggressiveness. *Journal of Media Psychology*, 26(2), 92–102.

Glassner, B. (1999). *The culture of fear: Why Americans are afraid of the wrong things.* New York: Basic Books.

Glassner, B. (2010). Still fearful after all these years. *The Chronicle Review*, January 22, B11–B12.

Goddard, E. (2017). Bhopal disaster victims may never get compensation following Dow-DuPont merger, fears UN official. Retrieved from www.independent.co.uk/

Going Hollywood: CDC keeps medical TV real (2007). Associated Press, April 20. Retrieved from www.msnbc.msn.com

Gold, J., & Gold, I. (2012). The "Truman Show" delusion: Psychosis in the global village. *Cognitive Neuropsychiatry*, 17(6), 455–472.

Goldberg, B. (2002). *A CBS insider exposes how the media distort the news.* Washington, DC: Regnery.

Goldberg, M. (1988). Take two doses for Kildare and Casey and don't call me in the morning. *TV Guide*, February 20, pp. 12–13.

Goldberg, M. E. (1995). Social marketing: Are we fiddling while Rome burns? *Journal of Consumer Psychology*, 4, 347–370.

Goldberg, R. (2018). 2018 Super Bowl commercials: grading the best and worst ads. Retrieved from http://bleacherreport.com/

Golde, J. A., Strassberg, D. S., & Turner, C. M. (2000). Psychophysiologic assessment of erectile response and its suppression as a function of stimulus media and previous experience with plethysmography. *Journal of Sex Research*, 37(1), 53–59.

Goldman, A. (2016). The Comet Ping Pong gunman answers our reporter's questions. *The New York Times*, December 7. Retrieved from www.nytimes.com/2016/12/07/us/edgar-welch-comet-pizza-fake-news.html

Goldstein, J. H. (1998). Why we watch. In J. H. Goldstein (Ed.), *Why we watch: The attractions of violent entertainment* (pp. 212–226). New York: Oxford University Press.

Goldstein, K., & Freedman, P. (2002). Campaign advertising and voter turnout: New evidence for a stimulation effect. *Journal of Politics*, 64, 721–740.

Goldstein, S., & Ibaraki, T. (1983). Japan: Aggression and aggression control in Japanese society. In A. Goldstein & M. Segall (Eds.), *Aggression in global perspective.* New York: Pergamon Press.

Goldstein, W. (1998). Bad history is bad for a culture. *The Chronicle of Higher Education*, 44 (April 10), A64.

Gonzales, A. L., & Hancock, J. T. (2008). Identity shifts in computer-mediated environments. *Media Psychology*, 11, 167–185.

González-Bailón, S., Banchs, R. E., & Kaltenbrunner, A. (2012). Emotions, public opinion, and U.S. presidential approval rates. *Human Communication Research*, 38, 121–143.

Goodall, C. E., & Reed, P. (2013). Threat and efficacy uncertainty in news coverage about bed bugs as unique predictors of information seeking and avoidance: An extension of the EPPM. *Health Communication*, 28(1), 63–71.

Goodin, S. M., Van Denburg, A., Murnen, S. K., & Smolak, L. (2011). "Putting on" sexiness: A content analysis of the presence of sexualizing characteristics in girls' clothing. *Sex Roles*, 65, 1–12.

Goodman, E. (1999). Our culture can make any woman anywhere feel insecure. *Manhattan Mercury*, June 1, A5.

Gorn, G. I., Goldberg, M. E., & Kanungo, R. N. (1976). The role of educational television in changing intergroup attitudes of children. *Child Development*, 47, 277–280.

Gornstein, L. (1997). Advertising finding its way into movies. *Manhattan Mercury*, April 13, C5.

Gottfried, J., & Shearer, E. (2016). News use across social media platforms 2016. Retrieved from www.journalism.org

Gottfried, J., Barthel, M., Shearer, E., & Mitchell, A. (2016). The 2016 presidential campaign—a news event that's hard to miss. Retrieved from www.journalism.org

Grabe, M. E., Lombard, M., Reich, R. D., Bracken, C. C., & Ditton, T. B. (1999). The role of screen size in viewer experiences of media content. *Visual Communication Quarterly*, 6(2), 4–9.

Graber, D. A. (1990). Seeing is remembering: How visuals contribute to learning from television news. *Journal of Communication*, 40(3), 134–155.

Graber, D. A., & Dunaway, J. (2018). *Mass media and American politics*. 10th ed. Thousand Oaks, CA: CQ Press.

Grainger, A., Newman, J. I., & Andrews, D. L. (2006). Sport, the media, and the construction of race. In A. A. Raney & J. Bryant (Eds.), *Handbook of sports and media* (pp. 447–467). Mahwah, NJ: Erlbaum.

Gram, M. (2007). Children as co-decision makers in the family? The case of family holidays. *Young Consumers*, 8(1), 19–28.

Gramlich, J. (2017). Five facts about crime in the U.S. Retrieved from www.pewresearch.org/

Grant, B. K. (Ed.). (1996). *The dread of difference: Gender and the horror film*. Austin, TX: University of Texas Press.

Granville, K. (2018). Facebook and Cambridge Analytica: What you need to know as fallout widens. *The New York Times*, March 19. Retrieved from www.nytimes.com

Grau, S. L., & Zotos, Y. C. (2016). Gender stereotypes in advertising: A review of current research. *International Journal of Advertising*, 35(5), 761–770.

Graves, S. B. (1996). Diversity on television. In T. M. Macbeth (Ed.), *Tuning in to young viewers: Social science perspectives on television* (pp. 61–86). Thousand Oaks, CA: Sage.

Gray, P. (1998). Paradise found. *Time*, January 19, pp. 63–68.

Green, M. C., & Brock, T. C. (2000). The role of transportation in the persuasiveness of public narratives. *Journal of Personality and Social Psychology*, 79, 701–721.

Green, M. C., & Brock, T. C. (2002). In the mind's eye: Transportation-imagery model of narrative persuasion. In M. C. Green, J. J. Strange, & T. C. Brock (Eds.), *Narrative impact: Social and cognitive foundations* (pp. 315–341). Mahwah, NJ: Erlbaum.

Green, M. C., & Clark, J. L. (2013). Transportation into narrative worlds: Implications for entertainment media influences on tobacco use. *Addiction*, 108(3), 477–484.

Green, M. C., Brock. T. C., & Kaufman, G. F. (2004). Understanding media enjoyment: The role of transportation into narrative worlds. *Communication Theory*, 14, 311–327.

Green, M. C., Hilken, J., Friedmann, H., Grossman, K., Gasiewski, J., Adler, R., & Sabini, J. (2005). Communication via instant messenger: Short- and long-term effects. *Journal of Applied Social Psychology*, 35, 445–462.

Green, M. C., Kass, S., Carrey, J., Herzig, B., Feeney, R., & Sabini, J. (2008). Transportation across media: Repeated exposure to print and media. *Media Psychology*, 11, 512–539.

Greenberg, B. S. (1982). Television and role socialization. In D. Pearl, L. Bouthilet, & J. Lazar (Eds.), *Television and behavior: Ten years of scientific progress and implications for the eighties: Vol. 2. Technical reviews* (pp. 179–190). Rockville, MD: National Institute of Mental Health.

Greenberg, B. S. (1988). Some uncommon television images and the Drench Hypothesis. In S. Oskamp (Ed.), *Television as a social issue* (pp. 88–102). Newbury Park, CA: Sage.

Greenberg, B. S., & Brand, J. E. (1993). Television news and advertising in schools: The Channel One controversy. *Journal of Communication*, 43(1), 143–151.

Greenberg, B. S., & Brand, J. E. (1994). Minorities and the mass media: 1970s to 1990s. In J. Bryant & D. Zillmann (Eds.), *Media effects: Advances in theory and research* (pp. 273–314). Hillsdale, NJ: Erlbaum.

Greenberg, B. S., & Gantz, W. (Eds.). (1993). *Desert Storm and the mass media*. Cresskill, NJ: Hampton Press.

Greenberg, B. S., & Hofschire, L. (2000). Sex on entertainment television. In D. Zillmann & P. Vorderer (Eds.), *Media entertainment: The psychology of its appeal* (pp. 93–111). Mahwah, NJ: Erlbaum.

Greenberg, B. S., & Woods, M. G. (1999). The soaps: Their sex, gratifications, and outcomes. *Journal of Sex Research*, 36(3), 250–257.

Greenberg, B. S., Neuendorf, K., Buerkel-Rothfuss, N., & Henderson, L. (1982). The soaps: What's on and who cares? *Journal of Broadcasting*, 26(2), 519–535.

Greenberg, B. S., Ku, L., & Li, H. (1992). Parental mediation of children's mass media behaviors in China, Japan, Korea, Taiwan, and the United States. In F. Korzenny & S. Ting-Toomey (Eds.), *Mass media effects across cultures* (pp. 150–172). Newbury Park, CA: Sage.

Greenberg, B. S., Mastro, D., & Brand, J. E. (2002). Minorities and the mass media: Television into the 21st century. In J. Bryant & D. Zillmann (Eds.), *Media effects: Advances in theory and research*. 2nd ed. (pp. 333–351). Mahwah, NJ: Erlbaum.

Greene, K., Krcmar, M., Rubin, D. L., Walters, L. H., & Hale, J. L. (2002). Elaboration in processing adolescent health messages: The impact of egocentrism and sensation seeking on message processing. *Journal of Communication*, 52, 812–831.

Greenfield, P. M. (1984). *Mind and media*. Cambridge, MA: Harvard University Press.

Greenfield, P. M., Bruzzone, L., Koyamatsu, K., Satuloff, W., Nixon, K., Brodie, M., & Kingsdale, D. (1987). What is rock music doing to the minds of our youth? A first experimental look at the effects of rock music lyrics and music videos. *Journal of Early Adolescence*, 7, 315–330.

Greenfield, P. M., Yut, E., Chung, M., Land, D., Kreider, H., Pantoja, M., & Horsley, K. (1993). The program-length commercial: A study of the effects of television/toy tie-ins on imaginative play. In G. L. Berry & J. K. Asamen (Eds.), *Children and television: Images in a changing sociocultural world* (pp. 53–72). Newbury Park, CA: Sage.

Greenwald, A. G., Spangenberg, E. R., Pratkanis, A. R., & Eskenazi, J. (1991). Double-blind tests of subliminal self-help audiotapes. *Psychological Science*, 2, 119–122.

Greitemeyer, T. (2009a). Effects of songs with prosocial lyrics on prosocial thoughts, affect, and behavior. *Journal of Experimental Social Psychology*, 45, 186–190.

Greitemeyer, T. (2009b). Effects of songs with prosocial lyrics on prosocial behavior: Further evidence and a mediating mechanism. *Personality and Social Psychology Bulletin*, 35, 1500–1511.

Greitemeyer, T. (2011a). Exposure to music with prosocial lyrics reduces aggression: First evidence and test of the underlying mechanism. *Journal of Experimental Social Psychology*, 47, 28–36.

Greitemeyer, T. (2011b). Effects of prosocial media on social behavior: When and why does media exposure affect helping and aggression? *Current Directions in Psychological Science*, 20, 251–255.

Greitemeyer, T., & Mügge, D. O. (2014). Video games do affect social outcomes: A meta-analytic review of the effects of violent and prosocial video game play. *Personality and Social Psychology Bulletin*, 40(5), 578–589.

Greitemeyer, T., & Osswald, S. (2010). Effects of prosocial videogames on prosocial behavior. *Journal of Personality and Social Psychology*, 98(2), 211–221.

Greitemeyer, T., & Osswald, S. (2011). Playing prosocial video games increases the accessibility of prosocial thoughts. *Journal of Social Psychology*, 151(2), 121–128.

Greitemeyer, T., Osswald, S., & Brauer, M. (2010). Playing prosocial video games increases empathy and decreases schadenfreude. *Emotion*, 10(2), 796–802.

Grimes, T. (1990). Audio-video correspondence and its role in attention and memory. *Educational Technology, Research, and Development*, 38, 15–25.

Grimes, T. (1991). Mild auditory-visual dissonance in television news may exceed viewer attentional capacity. *Human Communication Research*, 17, 268–298.

Grimes, T., Anderson, J. A., & Bergen., L. (2008). *Media violence and aggression: Science and ideology*. Thousand Oaks CA: Sage.

Grold, J. (1968). Mother's Day. *American Journal of Psychiatry*, 124, 1456–1458.

Gross, K., Brewer, P.R., & Aday, S. (2009). Confidence in government and emotional responses to terrorism after September 11, 2001. *American Politics Research*, 37, 107–128.

Gross, L. (1984). The cultivation of intolerance: Television, blacks, and gays. In G. Melischek, K. E. Rosengren, & J. Stappers (Eds.), *Cultural indicators: An international symposium* (pp. 345–364). Vienna: Austrian Academy of Sciences.

Grossman, D. (1996). *On killing: The psychological cost of learning to kill in war and society.* New York: Little, Brown.

Grossman, D. (2018). Whatever happened to the V-Chip? Retrieved from www.popularmechanics.com/

Grossman, D., & DeGaetano, G. (1999). *Stop teaching our kids to kill.* New York: Crown.

Grossman, D., & DeGaetano, G. (2014). *Stop teaching our kids to kill: A call to action against TV, movie, and video game violence.* Rev. ed. New York: Harmony Books.

Gruszczynski, M., & Wagner, M. W. (2017). Information flow in the 21st century: The dynamics of agenda-uptake. *Mass Communication and Society*, 20(3), 378–402.

Grynbaum, M. M. (2017a). Trump calls the news media the "enemy of the American people." *The New York Times*, February 17. Retrieved from www.nytimes.com

Grynbaum, M. M. (2017b). "Wow": Stunned TV hosts reacted in real time to Trump. *The New York Times*, August 16. Retrieved from www.nytimes.com

Grynbaum, M. M., & Ember, S. (2016a). Trump summons TV figures for private meeting, and lets them have it. *The New York Times*, November 21. Retrieved from www.nytimes.com

Grynbaum, M. M., & Ember, S. (2016b). If Trump Tweets it, is it news? A quandary for the news media. *The New York Times*, November 29. Retrieved from www.nytimes.com

Grynbaum, M. M., & Koblin, J. (2017). For solace and solidarity in the Trump age, liberals turn the TV back on. *The New York Times*, March 12. Retrieved from www.nytimes.com

Gubash, C. (2002). U.S. woos Arabs with pop music. Retrieved from www.msnbc.com/news/784495.asp

Guess, A., Nyhan, B., & Reifler, J. (2018). Selective exposure to misinformation: Evidence from the consumption of fake news during the 2016 U.S. presidential campaign. Retrieved from www.dartmouth.edu

Gunter, B. (2001). *Media sex: What are the issues?* Mahwah, NJ: Erlbaum.

Gunter, B. (2003). *News and the net.* Mahwah, NJ: Erlbaum.

Gunter, B. (2006). Sport, violence, and the media. In A. A. Raney & J. Bryant (Eds.), *Handbook of sports and media* (pp. 383–395). Mahwah, NJ: Erlbaum.

Gunter, B., Furnham, A., & Griffiths, S. (2000). Children's memory for news: A comparison of three presentation media. *Media Psychology*, 2, 119–146.

Gunter, B., Furnham, A., & Pappa, E. (2005). Effects of television violence on memory for violent and nonviolent advertising. *Journal of Applied Social Psychology*, 35, 1680–1697.

Gunther, A. C. (1991). What we think others think: Cause and consequence in the third-person effect. *Communication Research*, 18, 355–372.

Gunther, A. C. (1995). Overrating the X-rating: The third-person perception and support for censorship of pornography. *Journal of Communication*, 45(1), 27–38.

Gunther, A. C., & Storey, J. D. (2003). The influence of presumed influence. *Journal of Communication*, 53, 199–215.

Gunther, A. C., & Thorson, E. (1992). Perceived persuasive effects of product commercials and public-service announcements: Third-person effects in new domains. *Communication Research*, 19, 574–596.

Gunther, A. C., Bolt, D., Borzekowski, D. L. G., Liebhart, J. L., & Dillard, J. P. (2006). Presumed influence on peer norms: How mass media indirectly affect adolescent smoking. *Journal of Communication*, 56, 52–68.

Gustafson, D. H., Hawkins, R., McTavish, F., Pingree, S., Chen, W. C., Volrathongchai, K., … Serlin, R. C. (2008). Internet-based interactive support for cancer patients: Are integrated systems better? *Journal of Communication*, 58, 238–257.

Gustin, S. (2012). The $100 billion question. *Time*, May 21, p. 14.

Guttmann, A. (1998). The appeal of violent sports. In J. H. Goldstein (Ed.), *Why we watch: The attractions of violent entertainment* (pp. 1–26). New York: Oxford University Press.

Haberstroh, J. (1994). *Ice cube sex: The truth about subliminal advertising.* Notre Dame, IN: Cross Cultural.

Haddock, C. K., Hoffman, K., Taylor, J. E., Schwab, L., Poston, W. S. C., & Lando, H. A. (2008). An analysis of messages about tobacco in the *Military Times* magazine. *Nicotine & Tobacco Research,* 10(7), 1191–1197.

Hafner, K., & Lyon, M. (2006). *Where wizards stay up late: The origins of the Internet.* New York: Simon & Schuster.

Hahn, L., Tamborini, R., Prabhu, S., Klebig, B., Grall, C., & Pei, D. (2017). The importance of altruistic versus egoistic motivations: A content analysis of conflicted motivations in children's television programming. *Communication Reports,* 30(2), 67–79.

Haines, E. (2011). Budget targets leisure travelers with car ad deals. Retrieved from www.nbcnews.com

Hajjar, W. J. (1997). The image of aging in television commercials: An update for the 1990s. In H. S. Noor Al-deen (Ed.), *Cross-cultural communication and aging in the United States* (pp. 231–244). Mahwah, NJ: Erlbaum.

Hald, G. M., & Malamuth, N. N. (2015). Experimental effects of exposure to pornography: The moderating effect of personality and mediating effect of sexual arousal. *Archives of Sexual Behavior,* 44(1), 99–109.

Hald, G. M., Malamuth, N. N., & Lange, T. (2013). Pornography and sexist attitudes among heterosexuals. *Journal of Communication,* 63(4), 638–660.

Halim, S., & Meyers, M. (2010). News coverage of violence against Muslim women: A view from the Arabian Gulf. *Communication, Culture & Critique,* 3, 85–104.

Hallin, D. C. (1992). Sound bite news: Television coverage of elections, 1968–1988. *Journal of Communication,* 42, 5–24.

Ham, C.-D. (2017). Exploring how consumers cope with online behavioral advertising. *International Journal of Advertising,* 36(4), 632–658.

Hamdy, N., & Gomaa, E. H. (2012). Framing the Egyptian uprising in Arabic language newspapers and social media. *Journal of Communication,* 62, 195–211.

Hamilton, J. T. (1998). *Channeling violence: The economic market for violent television programming.* Princeton, NJ: Princeton University Press.

Hancock, K. A., & Haldeman, D. C. (2017). Between the lines: Media coverage of Orlando and beyond. *Psychology of Sexual Orientation and Gender Diversity,* 4(2), 152–159.

Hansen, C. H., & Hansen, R. D. (1990a). The influence of sex and violence on the appeal of rock music videos. *Communication Research,* 17, 212–234.

Hansen, C. H., & Hansen, R. D. (1990b). Rock music videos and antisocial behavior. *Basic and Applied Social Psychology,* 11(4), 357–369.

Hansen, C. H., & Hansen, R. D. (2000). Music and music videos. In P. Vorderer & D. Zillmann (Eds.), *Media entertainment: The psychology of its appeal* (pp. 175–196). Mahwah, NJ: Erlbaum.

Happ, C., & Melzer, A. (2014). *Empathy and violent video games: Aggression and prosocial behavior.* New York: Palgrave Macmillan.

Happer, C., & Philo, G. (2016). New approaches to understanding the role of the news media in the formation of public attitudes and behaviours on climate change. *European Journal of Communication,* 31(2), 136–151.

Haridakis, P. M. (2002). Viewer characteristics, exposure to television violence, and aggression. *Media Psychology,* 4, 323–352.

Harp, D., Loke, J., & Bachmann, I. (2010). First impressions of Sarah Palin: Pit bulls, politics, gender performance, and a discursive media (re)contextualization. *Communication, Culture & Critique,* 3, 291–309.

Harrington, B., & O'Connell, M. (2016). Video games as virtual teachers: Prosocial video game use by children and adolescents from different socioeconomic groups is associated with increased empathy and prosocial behaviour. *Computers in Human Behavior,* 63, 650–658.

Harris, B. D., Morgan, C. V., & Gibbs, B. G. (2014). Evidence of political moderation over time: Utah's immigration debate online. *New Media & Society,* 16(8), 1309–1331.

Harris, G. T., Lalumière, M. L., Seto, M. C., Rice, M. E., & Chaplin, T. C. (2012). Explaining the erectile responses of rapists to rape stories: The contributions of sexual activity, non-consent, and violence with injury. *Archives of Sexual Behavior*, 41(1), 221–229.

Harris, R. J. (1981). Inferences in information processing. In G. H. Bower (Ed.), *The psychology of learning and motivation* (Vol. 15, pp. 82–128). New York: Academic Press.

Harris, R. J., & Barlett, C. P. (2008). Effects of sex in the media. In J. Bryant & M. B. Oliver (Eds.), *Media effects: Advances in theory and research*. 3rd ed. (pp. 304–24). Mahwah, NJ: Erlbaum.

Harris, R. J., & Cook. L.G. (2011). How content and co-viewers elicit emotional discomfort in moviegoing experiences: Where does the discomfort come from and how is it handled? *Applied Cognitive Psychology*, 25, 850–861.

Harris, R. J., & Karafa, J. A. (1999). A cultivation theory perspective of worldwide national impressions of the United States. In Y. Kamalipour (Ed.), *Images of the U.S. around the world: A multicultural perspective* (pp. 3–17). Albany, NY: SUNY Press.

Harris, R. J., Dubitsky, T. M., & Bruno, K. J. (1983). Psycholinguistic studies of misleading advertising. In R. J. Harris (Ed.), *Information processing research in advertising* (pp. 241–262). Hillsdale, NJ: Erlbaum.

Harris, R. J., Sturm, R. E., Klassen, M. L., & Bechtold, J. I. (1986). Language in advertising: A psycholinguistic approach. *Current Issues and Research in Advertising*, 9, 1–26.

Harris, R. J., Trusty, M. L., Bechtold, J. I., & Wasinger, L. (1989). Memory for implied versus directly asserted advertising claims. *Psychology & Marketing*, 6, 87–96.

Harris, R. J., Jasper, J. D., Lee, B. J., & Miller, K. E. (1991). Consenting to donate organs: Whose wishes carry the most weight? *Journal of Applied Social Psychology*, 21, 3–14.

Harris, R. J., Schoen, L. M., & Hensley, D. (1992). A cross-cultural study of story memory. *Journal of Cross-Cultural Psychology*, 23, 133–147.

Harris, R. J., Pounds, J. C., Maiorelle, M. J., & Mermis, M. M. (1993). The effect of type of claim, gender, and buying history on the drawing of pragmatic inferences from advertising claims. *Journal of Consumer Psychology*, 2, 83–95.

Harris, R. J., Garner-Earl, B., Sprick, S. J., & Carroll, C. (1994). Effects of foreign product names and country-of-origin attributions on advertisement evaluations. *Psychology & Marketing*, 11, 129–144.

Harris, R. J., Hoekstra, S. J., Scott, C. L., Sanborn, F. W., Karafa, J. A., & Brandenburg, J. D. (2000). Young men's and women's different autobiographical memories of the experience of seeing frightening movies on a date. *Media Psychology*, 2, 245–268.

Harris, R. J., Hoekstra, S. J., Sanborn, F. W., Scott, C. L., Dodds, L., & Brandenburg, J. D. (2004). Autobiographical memories for seeing romantic movies on a date: Romance is not just for women. *Media Psychology*, 6, 257–284.

Harris, R. J., Cady, E. T., & Tran, T. Q. (2006). Comprehension and memory. In J. Bryant & P. Vorderer (Eds.), *Psychology of entertainment* (pp. 71–84). Mahwah, NJ: Erlbaum.

Harris, R. J., Borror, S. W., Koblitz, K. R., Pearn, M., & Rohrer, T. C. (2017). Memory for emotional content from entertainment film: The role of subtitles, sex, and empathy. *Media Psychology*, 20(1), 28–59.

Harrison, K. (1997). Does interpersonal attraction to thin media personalities promote eating disorders? *Journal of Broadcasting & Electronic Media*, 41, 478–500.

Harrison, K., & Cantor, J. (1999). Tales from the screen: Enduring fright reactions to scary media. *Media Psychology*, 1, 97–116.

Harrison, K., & Fredrickson, B. L. (2003). Women's sports media, self-objectification, and mental health in black and white adolescent females. *Journal of Communication*, 53, 216–232.

Harrison, K., & Hefner, V. (2014). Virtually perfect: Image retouching and adolescent body image. *Media Psychology*, 17(2), 134–153.

Harrison, K., Taylor, L. D., & Marske, A. L. (2006). Women's and men's eating behavior following exposure to ideal-body images and text. *Communication Research*, 33, 507–529.

Hart, R. P. (1994). *Seducing America: How television charms the modern voter*. New York: Oxford University Press.

Hart, R. P., & Jarvis, S. E. (1997). Political debate: Forms, styles, and media. *American Behavioral Scientist*, 40, 1095–1122.

Hartmann, D. P. (1969). Influence of symbolically modelled instrumental aggression and pain cues on aggressive behavior. *Journal of Personality and Social Psychology*, 11, 280–288.

Hartmann, E., & Basile, R. (2003). Dream imagery becomes more intense after 9/11/01. *Dreaming*, 13, 61–66.

Hartmann, T. (2017). Parasocial interaction, parasocial relationships, and well-being. In L. Reineke & M. B. Oliver (Eds.), *The Routledge handbook of media use and well-being* (pp. 131–144). New York: Routledge.

Hartmann, T., & Goldhoorn, C. (2011). Horton and Wohl revisited: Exploring viewers' experience of parasocial interaction. *Journal of Communication*, 61, 1104–1121.

Hartmann, T., & Vorderer, P. (2010). It's okay to shoot a character: Moral disengagement in violent video games. *Journal of Communication*, 60(1), 94–119.

Hartmann, T., Toz, E., & Brandon, M. (2010). Just a game? Unjustified virtual violence produces guilt in empathetic players. *Media Psychology*, 13(4), 339–363.

Haruko Smith, S. (2012). The history of sanitizing wipes: How hand sanitizer dominated the market. Retrieved from https://hubpages.com/health/

Harwell, D. (2016). "Sesame Street," revamped for HBO, aims for toddlers of the Internet age. *Washington Post*, January 12. Retrieved from www.washingtonpost.com/

Harwood, J., & Giles, H. (1992). "Don't make me laugh": Age representations in a humorous context. *Discourse & Society*, 3, 403–436.

Hasan, Y., Bègue, L., & Bushman, B. J. (2012). Viewing the world through "blood-red tinted glasses": The hostile expectation bias mediates the link between violent video game exposure and aggression. *Journal of Experimental Social Psychology*, 48(4), 953–956.

Hasan, Y., Bègue, L., & Bushman, B. J. (2018). Viewing the world through "blood-red tinted glasses": The hostile expectation bias mediates the link between violent video game exposure and aggression—Corrigendum. *Journal of Experimental Social Psychology*, 74, 329.

Hasell, A., & Weeks, B. E. (2016). Partisan provocation: The role of partisan news use and emotional responses in political information sharing in social media. *Human Communication Research*, 42(4), 641–661.

Hastak, M., & Mazis, M. B. (2011). Deception by implication: A typology of truthful but misleading advertising and labeling claims. *Journal of Public Policy & Marketing*, 30(2), 157–167.

Hatfield, E., Cacioppo, J. T., & Rapson, R. L. (1992). Primitive emotional contagion. In M. S. Clark (Ed.), *Review of personality and social psychology: Vol. 14. Emotions and social behavior* (pp. 151–177). Newbury Park, CA: Sage.

Hatfield, E., Cacioppo, J. T., & Rapson, R. L. (1993). Emotional contagion. *Current Directions in Psychological Science*, 2, 96–99.

Hatzithomas, L., Boutsouki, C., & Ziamou, P. (2016). A longitudinal analysis of the changing roles of gender in advertising: A content analysis of Super Bowl commercials. *International Journal of Advertising*, 35(5), 888–906.

Hausknecht, D., & Moore, D. L. (1986). The effects of time compressed advertising of brand attitude judgments. *Advances in Consumer Research*, 13, 105–110.

Hawkins, I., & Scherr, K. (2017). Engaging the CSI effect: The influences of experience-taking, type of evidence, and viewing frequency on juror decision-making. *Journal of Criminal Justice*, 49, 45–52.

Hawkins, R. P., & Pingree, S. (1981). Uniform messages and habitual viewing: Unnecessary assumptions in social reality effects. *Human Communication Research*, 7, 291–301.

Hawkins, R. P., & Pingree, S. (1990). Divergent psychological processes in constructing social reality from mass media content. In N. Signorielli & M. Morgan (Eds.), *Cultivation analysis* (pp. 35–50). Newbury Park, CA: Sage.

Hawkins, R. P., Pingree, S., & Adler, I. (1987). Searching for cognitive processes in the cultivation effect: Adult and adolescent samples in the United States and Australia. *Human Communication Research*, 13, 553–577.

Hawkins, R. P., Kim, Y. H., & Pingree, S. (1991). The ups and downs of attention to television. *Communication Research*, 18, 53–76.

Hawkins, R. P., Pingree, S., Hitchon, J., Radler, B., Gorham, B. W., Kahlor, L., … Kolbeins, G. H. (2005). What produces television attention and attention style? Genre, situation, and individual differences as predictors? *Human Communication Research*, 31, 162–187.

Haynes, E., & Rich, N. (2002). Obsessed fans! *YM* [Your Magazine], 50 (April), 196–199.

Hazlett, R. L., & Hazlett, S. Y. (1999). Emotional response to television commercials: Facial EMG vs. self-report. *Journal of Advertising Research*, 39(2), 7–23.

Healy, J. (1990). *Endangered minds: Why our children don't think—and what we can do about it.* New York: Simon & Schuster.

Hearold, S. (1986). A synthesis of 1043 effects of television on social behavior. In G. Comstock (Ed.), *Public communication and behavior* (Vol. 1, pp. 65–133). Orlando, FL: Academic Press.

Heath, R. L., & Bryant, J. (1992). *Human communication theory and research: Concepts, contexts, and challenges.* Hillsdale, NJ: Erlbaum.

Heath, T. B., Mothersbaugh, D. L., & McCarthy, M. S. (1993). Spokesperson effects in high involvement markets. *Advances in Consumer Research*, 20, 704–707.

Hefner, V., Woodward, K., Figge, L., Bevan, J. L., Santora, N., & Baloch, S. (2014). The influence of television and film viewing on midlife women's body image, disordered eating, and food choice. *Media Psychology*, 17(2), 185–207.

Heider, D. (2000). *White news: Why local news programs don't cover people of color.* Mahwah, NJ: Erlbaum.

Heintz-Knowles, K. E. (2001). Balancing acts: Work–family issues on prime-time TV. In J. Bryant & J. A. Bryant (Eds.), *Television and the American family.* 2nd ed. (pp. 177–206). Mahwah, NJ: Erlbaum.

Hellman, M., & Wagnsson, C. (2015). New media and the war in Afghanistan: The significance of blogging for the Swedish strategic narrative. *New Media & Society*, 17(1), 6–23.

Henson, L., & Parameswaran, R. E. (2008). Getting real with "tell it like it is" talk therapy: Hegemonic masculinity and the Dr. Phil show. *Communication, Culture, & Critique*, 1, 287–310.

Herman, E. S., & Chomsky, N. (1988). *Manufacturing consent: The political economy of the mass media.* New York: Pantheon.

Herman, E. S., & O'Sullivan, G. (1989). *The terrorism industry: The experts and institutions that shape our view of terror.* New York: Pantheon.

Herrett-Skjellum, J., & Allen, M. (1996). Television programming and sex-stereotyping: A meta-analysis. In B. R. Burleson (Ed.), *Communication yearbook* (Vol. 19, pp. 157–185). Thousand Oaks, CA: Sage.

Hether, H. J., Huang, G. C., Beck, V., Murphy, S. T., & Valente, T. W. (2008). Entertainment-education in a media-saturated environment: Examining the impact of single and multiple exposures to breast cancer storylines on two popular medical dramas. *Journal of Health Communication*, 13(8), 808–823.

Hetsroni, A. (2007). Three decades of sexual content on prime-time network programming: A longitudinal meta-analytic review. *Journal of Communication*, 57, 318–348.

Hetsroni, A., & Tukachinsky, R. H. (2006). Television-world estimates, real-world estimates, and television viewing. *Journal of Communication*, 56, 133–156.

Hicks, D. J. (1965). Imitation and retention of film-mediated aggressive peer and adult models. *Journal of Personality and Social Psychology*, 2, 97–100.

Higgins, A., McIntire, M., & Dance, G. J. (2016). Inside a fake news sausage factory: "This is all about income." *The New York Times*, December 22. Retrieved from www.nytimes.com/

Hill, L. (2016). "Sesame Street" says goodbye to Bob, Luis and Gordon as cast members are let go. *Los Angeles Times*, July 28. Retrieved from www.latimes.com

Hilt, M. L., & Lipschultz, J. H. (2004). Elderly Americans and the Internet: E-mail, TV news, information and entertainment websites. *Educational Gerontology*, 30(1), 57–72.

Hinck, E. A. (1992). *Enacting the presidency: Political argument, presidential debates, and presidential character.* Westport, CT: Praeger.

Hinshaw, S. (2007). *The mark of shame: Stigma of mental illness and an agenda for change.* New York: Oxford University Press.

Hirsch, P. M. (1980). The scary world of the nonviewer and other anomalies: A reanalysis of Gerbner et al.'s findings on cultivation analysis, part I. *Communication Research*, 7, 403–456.

Hirschberg, M. S. (1993). *Perpetuating patriotic perceptions: The cognitive function of the Cold War*. Westport, CT: Greenwood.

Ho, E. A., Sanbonmatsu, D. M., & Akimoto, S. A. (2002). The effects of comparative status on social stereotypes: How the perceived success of some persons affects the stereotypes of others. *Social Cognition*, 20, 36–57.

Hodgetts, D., Cullen, A., & Radley, A. (2005). Television characterizations of homeless people in the United Kingdom. *Analyses of Social Issues and Public Policy (ASAP)*, 5(1), 29–48.

Hoechsmann, M., & Poyntz, S. (2012). *Media literacies: A critical introduction*. Chichester: Wiley-Blackwell.

Hoekstra, S. J. (1998). Docudrama as psychobiography: A case study of HBO's "Stalin." *The Psychohistory Review*, 26, 253–264.

Hoekstra, S. J., Harris, R. J., & Helmick, A. L. (1999). Autobiographical memories about the experience of seeing frightening movies in childhood. *Media Psychology*, 1, 117–140.

Hoerl, K. E. (2002). Monstrous youth in suburbia: Disruption and recovery of the American dream. *Southern Communication Journal*, 67, 259–275.

Hoerl, K. E., Cloud, D. L., & Jarvis, S. E. (2009). Deranged loners and demented outsiders? Therapeutic news frames of presidential assassination attempts, 1973–2001. *Communication, Culture & Critique*, 2, 83–109.

Hoewe, J. (2014). Memory of an outgroup. *Journal of Media Psychology*, 26(4), 161–175.

Hoewe, J., & Hatemi, P. K. (2017). Brand loyalty is influenced by the activation of political orientations. *Media Psychology*, 20(3), 428–449.

Hoffman, B. L., Shensa, A., Wessel, C., Hoffman, R., & Primack, B. A. (2017). Exposure to fictional medical television and health: A systematic review. *Health Education Research*, 32(2), 107–123.

Hoffner, C., & Buchanan, M. (2002). Parents' responses to television violence: The third-person effect, parental mediation, and support for censorship. *Media Psychology*, 4, 231–252.

Hoffner, C., & Buchanan, M. (2005). Young adults' wishful identification with television characters: The role of perceived similarity and character attributes. *Media Psychology*, 7, 325–351.

Hoffner, C. A., & Levine, K. J. (2005). Enjoyment of mediated fright and violence: A meta-analysis. *Media Psychology*, 7(2), 207–237.

Hoffner, C. A., & Levine, K. J. (2007). Enjoyment of mediated fright and violence: A meta-analysis. In R. W. Preiss, B. M. Gayle, N. Burrell, M. Allen, & J. Bryant (Eds.), *Mass media effects research: Advances through meta-analysis* (pp. 215–244). Mahwah, NJ: Erlbaum.

Hoffner, C. A., & Rehkoff, R. A. (2011). Young voters' responses to the 2004 U.S. presidential election: Social identity, perceived media influence, and behavioral outcomes. *Journal of Communication*, 61, 732–757.

Hoffner, C. A., Plotkin, R. S., Buchanan, M., Anderson, J. D., Kamigaki, S. K., Hubbs, L. A., … Pastorek, A. (2001). The third-person effect in perceptions of the influence of television violence. *Journal of Communication*, 51(2), 283–299.

Holbert, R. L., & Hansen, G. J. (2006). Fahrenheit 9/11, need for closure and the priming of affective ambivalence: An assessment of intra-affective structures by party identification. *Human Communication Research*, 32, 109–129.

Holbert, R. L., & Hansen, G. J. (2008). Stepping beyond message specificity in the study of emotion as mediator and inter-emotion associations across attitude objects: Fahrenheit 9/11, anger, and debate superiority. *Media Psychology*, 11, 98–118.

Holbert, R. L., Pillion, O., Tschida, D. A., Armfield, G. G., Kinder, K., Cherry, K. L., & Daulton, A. R. (2003). *The West Wing* as endorsement of the U.S. presidency: Expanding the bounds of priming in political communication. *Journal of Communication*, 53(3), 427–443.

Holbert, R. L., Hansen, G. J., Caplan, S. E., & Mortensen, S. (2007). Presidential debate viewing and Michael Moore's *Fahrenheit 9/11*: A study of affect-as-transfer and passionate reasoning. *Media Psychology*, 9, 673–694.

Holbert, R. L., LaMarre, H. L., & Landreville, K. D. (2009). Fanning the flames of a partisan divide: Debate viewing, vote choice, and perceptions of vote count accuracy. *Communication Research*, 36, 155–177.

Holden, S. (2008). John Lennon's death revisited through the words of his killer. *The New York Times*, January 2. Retrieved from www.nytimes.com

Holz Ivory, A., Gibson, R., & Ivory, J. D. (2009). Gendered relationships on television: Portrayals of same-sex and heterosexual couples. *Mass Communication and Society*, 12(2), 170–192.

Hong, S. C. (2015). Do cultural values matter? A cross-cultural study of the third-person effect and support for the regulation of violent video games. *Journal of Cross-Cultural Psychology*, 46(7), 964–976.

Hong, S. T., & Wyer, R. S., Jr. (1989). Effects of country-of-origin and product-attribute information on product evaluation: An information-processing experiment. *Journal of Consumer Research*, 16, 175–187.

Hong, S. T., & Wyer, R. S., Jr. (1990). Determinants of product evaluation: Effects of the time interval between knowledge about a product's country of origin and information about its specific attributes. *Journal of Consumer Research*, 17, 277–288.

Hooton, C. (2016). What actors are actually snorting and smoking in movies. Retrieved from www.independent.co.uk

Hoover, S. M. (1988). *Mass media religion*. Newbury Park, CA: Sage.

Hoover, S. M. (1998). *Religion in the news: Faith and journalism in American public discourse*. Thousand Oaks, CA: Sage.

Hoover, S. M. (2006). *Religion in the media age*. New York: Routledge.

Hopf, W. H., Huber, G. L., & Weiß, R. H. (2008). Media violence and youth violence: A 2-year longitudinal study. *Journal of Media Psychology: Theories, Methods, and Applications*, 20(3), 79–96.

Hopkins, R., & Fletcher, J. E. (1994). Electrodermal measurement: Particularly effective for forecasting message influence on sales appeal. In A. Lang (Ed.), *Measuring psychological responses to media* (pp. 113–132). Hillsdale, NJ: Erlbaum.

Hopmann, D. N., de Vreese, C. H., & Albaek, E. (2011). Incumbency bonus in election news coverage explained: The logics of political power and the media market. *Journal of Communication*, 61, 264–282.

Hopwood, T. L., & Schutte, N. S. (2017). Psychological outcomes in reaction to media exposure to disasters and large-scale violence: A meta-analysis. *Psychology of Violence*, 7(2), 316–327.

Hornik, J., Ofir, C., & Rachamim, M. (2016). Quantitative evaluation of persuasive appeals using comparative meta-analysis. *The Communication Review*, 19(3), 192–222.

Hornik, R., & Yanovitzky, I. (2003). Using theory to design evaluations of communication campaigns: The case of the National Youth Anti-Drug Media Campaign. *Communication Theory*, 13, 204–224.

Horowitz, B., & Appleby, J. (2017). Prescription drug costs are up; so are TV ads promoting them. *USA Today*, March 16. Retrieved from www.usatoday.com

Horowitz, J. (2017). In Italian schools, reading, writing, and recognizing fake news. *The New York Times*, October 18. Retrieved from www.nytimes.com

Horowitz, J. (2018). For Pope Francis, fake news goes back to the Garden of Eden. *The New York Times*, January 24. Retrieved from www.nytimes.com

Horrigan, J. B., & Duggan, M. (2015). One-in-seven Americans are television "cord cutters." Retrieved from www.pewinternet.org

Hot type (1998). *The Chronicle of Higher Education*, 44 (February 20), A22.

Houck, M. M. (2006). CSI: Reality. *Scientific American*, 295(1), 85–89.

Houston, J. B., Spialek, M. L., & Perreault, M. F. (2016). Coverage of posttraumatic stress disorder in the *New York Times*, 1950–2012. *Journal of Health Communication*, 21(2), 240–248.

Howard, T. (2009). Push is on to end prescription drug ads targeting consumers. *USA Today*, August 10. Retrieved from www.usatoday.com

Howden, L. M., & Meyer, J. A. (2011). Age and sex composition: 2010. 2010 census briefs. Retrieved from http://2010.census.gov/2010census/data/

Hoy, M. G., Young, C. E., & Mowen, J. C. (1986). Animated host-selling advertisements: Their impact on young children's recognition, attitudes, and behavior. *Journal of Public Policy and Marketing*, 5, 171–184.

Hsu, C., Jacobs, A. M., Citron, F. M., & Conrad, M. (2015). The emotion potential of words and passages in reading Harry Potter: An fMRI study. *Brain and Language*, 142, 96–114.

Hubbard, B. (2015). Young Saudis, bound by conservative strictures, find freedom on their phones. *The New York Times*, May 22. Retrieved from www.nytimes.com

Huddy, L., Feldman, S., & Cassese, E, (2007). On the distinct political effects of anxiety and anger. In A. Crigler, M. MacKuen, G. E. Marcus, & W. R. Neuman (Eds.), *The affect effect: The dynamics of emotion in political thinking and behavior* (pp. 202–230). Chicago: University of Chicago Press.

Huesmann, L. R. (2007). The impact of electronic media violence: Scientific theory and research. *Journal of Adolescent Health*, 41(6 Suppl 1), S6–S13.

Huesmann, L. R. (2010). Nailing the coffin shut on doubts that violent video games stimulate aggression: Comment on Anderson et al. (2010). *Psychological Bulletin*, 136, 179–181.

Huesmann, L. R. (2013). Cross-national communalities in the learning of aggression from media violence. In L. R. Huesmann & L. D. Eron (Eds.), *Television and the aggressive child: A cross-national comparison* (pp. 239–257). New York: Routledge.

Huesmann, L. R., & Eron, L. D. (Eds.). (1986). *Television and the aggressive child*. Hillsdale, NJ: Erlbaum.

Huesmann, L. R., Eron, L. D., Klein, R., Brice, P., & Fischer, P. (1983). Mitigating the imitation of aggressive behaviors by changing children's attitudes about media violence. *Journal of Personality and Social Psychology*, 44, 899–910.

Huesmann, L. R., Eron, L. D., Lefkowitz, M. M., & Walder, L. O. (1984). Stability of aggression over time and generations. *Developmental Psychology*, 20, 1120–1134.

Huesmann, L. R., Lagerspetz, K., & Eron, L. D. (1984). Intervening variables in the TV violence–aggression relation: Evidence from two countries. *Developmental Psychology*, 20, 746–775.

Huesmann, L. R., Moise-Titus, J., Podolski, C. L., & Eron, L. D. (2003). Longitudinal relations between children's exposure to TV violence and their aggressive and violent behavior in young adulthood: 1977–1992. *Developmental Psychology*, 39, 201–221.

Huesmann, L. R., Dubow, E. F., & Yang, G. (2013). Why it is hard to believe that media violence causes aggression? In K. E. Dill (Ed.), *The Oxford handbook of media psychology* (pp. 159–171). New York: Oxford University Press.

Huh, J., & Langteau, R. (2007). Presumed influence of DTC prescription drug advertising. *Communication Research*, 34, 25–52.

Hui, C. Y. T., & Lo, T. W. (2017). Examination of the "CSI Effect" on perceptions of scientific and testimonial evidence in a Hong Kong Chinese sample. *International Journal of Offender Therapy and Comparative Criminology*, 61(7), 819–833.

Hull, J. D. (1995). The state of the union. *Time*, January 30, pp. 53–75.

Humes, K. R., Jones, N. A., & Ramirez, R. R. (2011). Overview of race and Hispanic origin: 2010. Retrieved from http://2010.census.gov/2010census/data/

Hummer, T. A., Wang, Y., Kronenberger, W. G., Mosier, K. M., Kalnin, A. J., Dunn, D. W., & Mathews, V. P. (2010). Short-term violent video game play by adolescents alters prefrontal activity during cognitive inhibition. *Media Psychology*, 13(2), 136–154.

Hummer, T. A., Kronenberger, W. G., Wang, Y., & Mathews, V. P. (2017). Decreased prefrontal activity during a cognitive inhibition task following violent video game play: A multi-week randomized trial. *Psychology of Popular Media Culture*. doi: 10.1037/ppm0000141

Hurley, R. J., Jensen, J. J., Weaver, A., & Dixon, T. (2015). Viewer ethnicity matters: Black crime in TV news and its impact on decisions regarding public policy—ethnicity, crime news, and policy decisions. *Journal of Social Issues*, 71(1), 155–170.

Hurst, L. (1998). History repeats itself—again. *World Press Review* (April), 28–29.

Husson, W., Stephen, T., Harrison, T. M., & Fehr, B. J. (1988). An interpersonal communication perspective on images of political candidates. *Human Communication Research*, 14, 397–421.

Hust, S. T., Marett, E. G., Lei, M., Ren, C., & Ran, W. (2015). Law & Order, CSI, and NCIS: The association between exposure to crime drama franchises, rape myth acceptance, and sexual consent negotiation among college students. *Journal of Health Communication*, 20(12), 1369–1381.

Huston, A. C., & Wright, J. C. (1998). Television and the informational and educational needs of children. *Annals of the American Academy of Political and Social Science*, 557, 9–23.

Huston, A. C., Wright, J. C., Rice, M. L., Kerkman, D., & St. Peters, M. (1990). The development of television viewing patterns in early childhood: A longitudinal investigation. *Developmental Psychology*, 26, 409–420.

Huston, A. C., Anderson, D. R., Wright, J. C., Linebarger, D. L., & Schmitt, K. L. (2001). *Sesame Street* viewers as adolescents: The recontact study. In S. M. Fisch & R. T. Truglio (Eds.), *"G" is for growing: Thirty years of research on children and Sesame Street* (pp. 131–144). Mahwah, NJ: Erlbaum.

Hutcheon, D. (2002). Mixing up the world's beat. *Mother Jones* (July/August), 74–75.

Huus, K. (2005). Hair-raising TV spot shunned by broadcasters. Retrieved from www.msnbc.cm/id/7351263/print/1/displaymode/1098

Hwang, Y., & Southwell, B. G. (2009). Science TV news exposure predicts science beliefs: Real world effects among a national sample. *Communication Research*, 36, 724–742.

Hyler, S. E. (1988). DSM-III at the cinema: Madness in the movies. *Comprehensive Psychiatry*, 29, 195–206.

Hyler, S. E., Gabbard, G. O., & Schneider, I. (1991). Homicidal maniacs and narcissistic parasites: Stigmatization of mentally ill persons in the movies. *Hospital and Community Psychiatry*, 42, 1044–1048.

Igartua, J.-J., & Barrios, I. (2012). Changing real-world beliefs with controversial movies: Processes and mechanisms of narrative persuasion. *Journal of Communication*, 62, 514–531.

Igartua, J.-J., & Cheng, L. (2009). Moderating effect of a group cue while processing news on immigration: Is the framing effect a heuristic process? *Journal of Communication*, 59, 726–749.

Ignatius, D. (2010). The dangers of embedded journalism, in war and politics. *The Washington Post*, May 2. Retrieved from www.washingtonpost.com

Iiyama, P., & Kitano, H. H. L. (1982). Asian-Americans and the media. In G. L. Berry & C. Mitchell-Kernan (Eds.), *Television and the socialization of the minority child* (pp. 151–186). New York: Academic Press.

Ilola, L. M. (1990). Culture and health. In R. W. Brislin (Ed.), *Applied cross-cultural psychology* (pp. 278–301). Newbury Park, CA: Sage.

IMDB (2012). Judge Judy. Retrieved from www.imdb.com/title/tt0115227/quotes

Infinite Dial 2017—Edison Research (2017). Retrieved from www.edisonresearch.com/infinite-dial-2017/

Ingraham, C. (2015). There's never been a safer time to be a kid in America. *Washington Post*, April 14. Retrieved from www.washingtonpost.com

Intons-Peterson, M. J., & Roskos-Ewoldsen, B. (1989). Mitigating the effects of violent pornography. In S. Gubar & J. Hoff-Wilson (Eds.), *For adult users only*. Bloomington, IN: Indiana University Press.

Intons-Peterson, M. J., Roskos-Ewoldsen, B., Thomas, L., Shirley, M., & Blut, D. (1989). Will educational materials reduce negative effects of exposure to sexual violence? *Journal of Social and Clinical Psychology*, 8, 256–275.

Intravia, J., Wolff, K. T., Paez, R., & Gibbs, B. R. (2017). Investigating the relationship between social media consumption and fear of crime: A partial analysis of mostly young adults. *Computers in Human Behavior*, 77, 158–168.

Isaac, M., & Eddy, M. (2017). Facebook responds to Trump and positions itself as election-ready. *The New York Times*, September 27. Retrieved from www.nytimes.com

Isin, F. B., & Alkibay, S. (2011). Influence of children on purchasing decisions of well-to-do families. *Young Consumers*, 12(1), 39–52.

Itzkoff, D. (2018). Trump slings Twitter insults with Alec Baldwin, his "S.N.L." impersonator. *The New York Times*, March 2. Retrieved from www.nytimes.com

Ivory, J. D., & Kalyanaraman, S. (2007). The effects of technological advancement and violent content in video games on players' feelings of presence, involvement physiological arousal, and aggression. *Journal of Communication*, 57, 532–555.

Iyengar, S., & Hahn, K. S. (2009). Red media, blue media: Evidence of ideological selectivity in media use. *Journal of Communication*, 59(1), 19–39.

Iyengar, S., & Simon, A. (1993). News coverage of the Gulf Crisis and public opinion. *Communication Research*, 20, 365–383.

Iyer, E., & Banerjee, B. (1993). Anatomy of green advertising. *Advances in Consumer Research*, 20, 494–501.

Jackson, D. Z. (1989). Calling the plays in black and white. *The Boston Globe*, January 22, A30–A33.

Jacob, C., Guéguen, N., & Boulbry, G. (2010). Effects of songs with prosocial lyrics on tipping behavior in a restaurant. *International Journal of Hospitality Management*, 29, 761–763.

Jacobson, J. (2001). In brochures, what you see isn't necessarily what you get. *The Chronicle of Higher Education*, 47 (March 16), A41–A42.

Jacques, W. W., & Ratzan, S. C. (1997). The Internet's World Wide Web and political accountability: New media coverage of the 1996 presidential debates. *American Behavioral Scientist*, 40, 1226–1237.

Jago, R., Sebire, S. J., Gorely, T., Cillero, I., & Biddle, S. J. (2011). "I'm on it 24/7 at the moment": A qualitative examination of multi-screen viewing behaviours among UK 10–11 year olds. *International Journal of Behavioral Nutrition and Physical Activity*, 8(1), 85.

Jakes, J. (1985). What? A successful media campaign without TV spots and Phil Donohue? *TV Guide*, November 2, pp. 12–15.

James, G. (2014). Twenty epic fails in global branding. Retrieved from www.inc.com

Jamieson, K. H. (1992). *Packaging the presidency: A history and criticism of presidential campaign advertising*. 2nd ed. New York: Oxford University Press.

Jamieson, K. H., & Campbell, K. K. (2006). *The interplay of influence: News, advertising, politics, and the mass media*. 6th ed. Belmont, CA: Wadsworth.

Jamieson, K. H., & Waldman, P. (1997). Mapping campaign discourse: An introduction. *American Behavioral Scientist*, 40, 1133–1138.

Jamieson, K. H., & Waldman, P. (2003). *The press effect: Politicians, journalists, and the stories that shape the political world*. New York: Oxford University Press.

Jamieson, P. E., More, E., Lee, S. S., Busse, P., & Romer, D. (2008). It matters what young people watch: Health-risk behaviors in top-grossing movies since 1950. In P. E. Jamieson & D. Romer (Eds.), *The changing portrayal of adolescents in the media since 1950* (pp. 105–131). New York: Oxford University Press.

Jana, M., Letsela, L., Scheepers, E., & Weiner, R. (2015). Understanding the role of the OneLove campaign in facilitating drivers of social and behavioral change in Southern Africa: A qualitative evaluation. *Journal of Health Communication*, 20(3), 252–258.

Janicke, S. H., & Oliver, M. B. (2017). The relationship between elevation, connectedness, and compassionate love in meaningful films. *Psychology of Popular Media Culture*, 6(3), 274–289.

Janicke, S. H., & Raney, A. A. (2017). Modeling the antihero narrative enjoyment process. *Psychology of Popular Media Culture*. doi: 10.1037/ppm0000152

Japan's sex industry is becoming less sexual, more smutty than slutty (2018). *The Economist*, April 5. Retrieved from www.economist.com

Jenkins, P. (2001). *Beyond tolerance: Child pornography on the Internet*. New York: New York University Press.

Jensen, J. D., Weaver, A. J., Ivic, R., & Imboden, K. (2011). Developing a brief sensation seeking scale for children: Establishing concurrent validity with video game use and rule-breaking behavior. *Media Psychology*, 14(1), 71–95.

Jeong, E. J., Biocca, F. A., & Bohil, C. J. (2012). Sensory realism and mediated aggression in video games. *Computers in Human Behavior*, 28(5), 1840–1848.

Jeong, S.-H., & Fishbein, M. (2007). Predictors of multitasking with media: Media factors and audience factors. *Media Psychology*, 10, 364–384.

Jeong, S.-H., Cho, H., & Hwang, Y. (2012). Media literacy interventions: A meta-analytic review. *Journal of Communication*, 62, 454–472.

Jewkes, Y., & Wykes, M. (2012). Reconstructing the sexual abuse of children: "Cyber-paeds," panic and power. *Sexualities*, 15(8), 934–952.

Jhally, S., & Lewis, J. (1992). *Enlightened racism: The Cosby Show, audiences, and the myth of the American dream.* Boulder, CO: Westview Press.

Johnson, D., & Rimal, R. N. (1994). Analysis of HIV/AIDS television public service announcements around the world. Paper presented at International Communication Association meeting, July, Sydney, Australia.

Johnson, G. (2006). Internet use and cognitive development: A theoretical framework. *E-Learning and Digital Media*, 3(4), 565–573.

Johnson, J. D., Adams, M. S., Ashburn, L., & Reed, W. (1995). Differential gender effects of exposure to rap music on African American adolescents' acceptance of teen dating violence. *Sex Roles*, 33, 597–606.

Johnson, J. D., Jackson, L. A., & Gatto, L. (1995). Violent attitudes and deferred academic aspirations: Deleterious effects of exposure to rap music. *Basic and Applied Social Psychology*, 16, 27–41.

Johnson, J. G., Cohen, P., Smailes, E. M., Kasen, S., & Brook, J. S. (2002). Television viewing and aggressive behavior during adolescence and adulthood. *Science*, 295, 2468–2471.

Johnson, K. A., Dolan, M. K., & Sonnett, J. (2011). Speaking of looting: An analysis of racial propaganda in national television coverage of Hurricane Katrina. *Howard Journal of Communications*, 22(3), 302–318.

Johnson, M. K. (2007). Reality monitoring and the media. *Applied Cognitive Psychology*, 21, 981–993.

Johnson, T. (2016). VidAngel defends $1-per-film streaming service after studios' copyright suit. *Variety*, June 17. Retrieved from http://variety.com

Johnson, T. (2017). Smart billboards are checking you out—and making judgments. *McClatchy Washington Bureau*, September 20. Retrieved from www.mcclatchydc.com/news/

Jonas, K. J., Hawk, S. T., Vastenburg, D., & de Groot, P. (2014). "Bareback" pornography consumption and safe-sex intentions of men having sex with men. *Archives of Sexual Behavior*, 43(4), 745–753.

Jones, A. (1994). Crimes against women: Media part of problem for masking violence in the language of love. *USA Today*, March 10.

Jones, D. A. (2016). *U.S. media and elections in flux: Dynamics and strategies.* New York: Routledge.

Jones, K. (1997). Are rap videos more violent? Style differences and the prevalence of sex and violence in the age of MTV. *Howard Journal of Communication*, 8, 343–356.

Jones, M. (2018). What teenagers are learning from online porn. *The New York Times Magazine*, February 7. Retrieved from www.nytimes.com

Jordan, A. B. (2001). Public policy and private practice. In D. G. Singer & J. L. Singer (Eds.), *Handbook of children and the media* (pp. 651–662). Thousand Oaks, CA: Sage

Joy, L. A., Kimball, M. M., & Zabrack, M. L. (1986). Television and children's aggressive behavior. In T. M. Williams (Ed.), *The impact of television: A natural experiment in three communities* (pp. 303–360). Orlando, FL: Academic Press.

Jungherr, A. (2014). The logic of political coverage on Twitter: Temporal dynamics and content. *Journal of Communication*, 64(2), 239–259.

Jurgensen, J. (2012). Binge viewing: TV's lost weekends. *The Wall Street Journal*, July 12. Retrieved from http://online.wsj.com

Just, M., Crigler, A., & Wallach, L. (1990). Thirty seconds or thirty minutes: What viewers learn from spot advertisements and candidate debates. *Journal of Communication*, 40(3), 120–133.

Kahle, L. R., & Homer, P. M. (1985). Physical attractiveness of the celebrity endorsers: A social adaptation perspective. *Journal of Consumer Research*, 11, 954–961.

Kahneman, D. (2011). *Thinking, fast and slow*. New York: Farrar, Straus & Giroux.

Kaid, L. L., & Boydston, J. (1987). An experimental study of the effectiveness of negative political advertisements. *Communication Quarterly*, 35, 193–201.

Kaid, L. L., & Johnston, A. (1991). Negative versus positive television advertising in U.S. presidential campaigns, 1960–1988. *Journal of Communication*, 41(3), 53–64.

Kaiser Family Foundation (2002). *The impact of TV's health content: A case study of ER viewers*. Menlo Park, CA: Kaiser Family Foundation.

Kaiser Family Foundation (2005). *Sex on TV 4*. Retrieved from www.kff.org/entmedia/upload/Sex-on-TV-4-Full-Report.pdf

Kaiser Family Foundation (2007). *Food for thought: Television food advertising to children in the United States*. Retrieved from www.kff.org/entmedia/upload/7618.pdf

Kaiser Family Foundation (2010). *Generation M2: Media in the lives of 8- to 18-year-olds*. Retrieved from www.kff.org/entmedia/

Kamalipour, Y. (Ed.). (1999). *Images of the U.S. around the world: A multicultural perspective*. Albany, NY: SUNY Press.

Kane, M. J. (1996). Media coverage of the post Title IX female athlete. *Duke Journal of Gender Law & Policy*, 3, 95–127.

Kang, C., & Goldman, A. (2016). In Washington pizzeria attack, fake news brought real guns. *The New York Times*, December 5. Retrieved from www.nytimes.com

Kaplan, T. (2017). Trump feuds with Democrats ahead of a possible government shutdown. *The New York Times*, November 28. Retrieved from www.nytimes.com

Kassarjian, H. (1969). The Negro and American advertising: 1946–1965. *Journal of Marketing Research*, 6, 29–39.

Katz, A. J. (2016a). The presidential debates set ratings records in 2016. Retrieved from http://adweek.com

Katz, A. J. (2016b). 2016 election forecast: Who will be president? *The New York Times*, November 8. Retrieved from www.nytimes.com

Kaveney, R. (2006). *Teen dreams: Reading teen film and television from Heathers to Veronica Mars*. New York: I. B. Tauris.

Kay, A., & Furnham, A. (2013). Age and sex stereotypes in British television advertisements. *Psychology of Popular Media Culture*, 2(3), 171–186.

Kaye, K. (2017). Data-driven targeting creates huge 2016 political ad shift: Broadcast TV down 20%, cable and digital way up. Retrieved from http://adage.com

Kazakova, S., Cauberghe, V., Pandelaere, M., & De Pelsmacker, P. (2015). Can't see the forest for the trees? The effect of media multitasking on cognitive processing style. *Media Psychology*, 18(4), 425–450.

Kearney, M., & Levine, P. (2015). *Early childhood education by MOOC: Lessons from Sesame Street*. Cambridge, MA: National Bureau of Economic Research.

Keegan, R. W. (2006). The splat pack. *Time*, October 30, pp. 66–70.

Kehr, D. (2011). Goodbye, DVD, hello future. *The New York Times*, March 4. Retrieved from www.nytimes.com.

Kellaris, J. J., & Cline, T. W. (2007). Humor and ad memorability: On the contributions of humor expectancy, relevancy, and need for humor. *Psychology and Marketing*, 24(6), 497–509.

Kelly, H. (1981). Reasoning about realities: Children's evaluations of television and books. In H. Kelly & H. Gardner (Eds.), Viewing children through television (pp. 59–72). San Francisco: Jossey-Bass.

Kennedy, M. G., O'Leary, A., Beck, V., Pollard, K., & Simpson, P. (2004). Increases in calls to the CDC national STD and AIDS hotline following AIDS-related episodes in a soap opera. *Journal of Communication*, 54, 287–301.

Kenrick, D. T., & Gutieres, S. E. (1980). Contrast effects and judgments of physical attractiveness: When beauty becomes a social problem. *Journal of Personality and Social Psychology*, 38, 131–140.

Kenrick, D. T., Gutierres, S. E., & Goldberg, L. L. (1989). Influence of popular erotica on judgments of strangers and mates. *Journal of Experimental Social Psychology*, 25, 159–167.

Kern-Foxworth, M. (1994). *Aunt Jemima, Uncle Ben, and Rastus: Blacks in advertising, yesterday, today, and tomorrow*. Westport, CT: Praeger.

Keum, H., Hillback, E. D., Rojas, H., De Zuniga, H. G., Shah, D. V., & McLeod, D. M. (2005). Personifying the radical: How news framing polarizes security concerns and tolerance judgments. *Human Communication Research*, 31, 337–364.

Key, W. B. (1976). *Media sexploitation*. New York: Signet.

Key, W. B. (1981). *The clam-plate orgy*. New York: Signet.

Key, W. B. (1989). *The age of manipulation*. New York: Henry Holt.

Keys, J. (2016). *Doc McStuffins* and *Dora the Explorer*: Representations of gender, race, and class in US animation. *Journal of Children and Media*, 10(3), 355–368.

Keys, T. R., Morant, K. M., & Stroman, C. A. (2009). Black youth's personal involvement in the HIV/AIDS issue: Does the Public Service Announcement still work? *Journal of Health Communication*, 14(2), 189–202.

Khalid, M. Z. & Ahmed, A. (2014). Entertainment-education media strategies for social change: Opportunities and emerging trends. *Review of Journalism & Mass Communication*, 2, 69–89.

Khan, S. (2014). Manufacturing consent? Media messages in the mobilization against HIV/AIDS in India and lessons for health communication. *Health Communication*, 29(3), 288–298.

Kiang, L., Huynh, V. W., Cheah, C. S. L., Wang, Y., & Yoshikawa, H. (2017). Moving beyond the model minority. *Asian American Journal of Psychology*, 8(1), 1–6.

Kilbourne, J. (1995). *Slim hopes: Advertising and the obsession with thinness* [Video]. Northampton, MA: Media Education Foundation.

Kilbourne, J. (2010). *Killing us softly 4: Advertising's image of women*. Northampton, MA: Media Education Foundation.

Kilbourne, W. E., Painton, S., & Ridley, D. (1985). The effect of sexual embedding on responses to magazine advertisements. *Journal of Advertising*, 14(2), 48–56.

Kim, A. E., Duke, J. C., Hansen, H., & Porter, L. (2012). Using Web Panels to understand whether online ad exposure influences information-seeking behavior. *Social Marketing Quarterly*, 18(4), 281–292.

Kim, M. (2015). Partisans and controversial news online: Comparing perceptions of bias and credibility in news content from blogs and mainstream media. *Mass Communication and Society*, 18(1), 17–36.

King, C. M. (2000). Effects of humorous heroes and villains in violent action films. *Journal of Communication*, 50(1), 5–24.

King, C. M., & Hourani, N. (2007). Don't tease me: Effects of ending type on horror film enjoyment. *Media Psychology*, 9, 473–492.

King, K. W., & Reid, L. N. (1990). Fear arousing anti-drinking and driving PSAs: Do physical injury threats influence young people? *Current Issues and Research in Advertising*, 12, 155–175.

Kingston, D. A., & Malamuth, N. M. (2011). Problems with aggregate data and the importance of individual differences in the study of pornography and sexual aggression: Comment on Diamond, Jozifkova, and Weiss (2010). *Archives of Sexual Behavior*, 40, 1045–1048.

Kingston, D. A., Fedoroff, P., Firestone, P., Curry, S., & Bradford, J. M. (2008). Pornography use and sexual aggression: The impact of frequency and type of pornography use on recidivism among sexual offenders. *Aggressive Behavior*, 34(4), 341–351.

Kingston, D. A., Seto, M. C., Firestone, P., & Bradford, J. M. (2010). Comparing indicators of sexual sadism as predictors of recidivism among adult male sexual offenders. *Journal of Consulting and Clinical Psychology*, 78(4), 574–584.

Kintsch, W. (1977). On comprehending stories. In P. Carpenter & M. Just (Eds.), *Cognitive processes in comprehension* (pp. 33–61). Hillsdale, NJ: Erlbaum.

Kiousis, S., & McDevitt, M. (2008). Agenda setting in civic development. *Communication Research*, 35, 481–502.

Kiousis, S., McDevitt, M., & Wu, X. (2005). The genesis of civic awareness: Agenda setting in political socialization. *Journal of Communication*, 55, 756–774.

Kirk, C., & Wade, C. (2015). Can you tell if your favorite TV show is secretly sped up? Take our quiz. *Slate*, March 4. Retrieved from www.slate.com

Kirkorian, H. L., & Anderson, D. R. (2011). Learning from educational media. In S. L. Calvert & B. J. Wilson (Eds.), *The handbook of children, media, and development* (pp. 188–213). Malden, MA: Wiley-Blackwell.

Kirsch, A. C., & Murnen, S. K. (2015). "Hot" girls and "cool dudes": Examining the prevalence of the heterosexual script in American children's television media. *Psychology of Popular Media Culture*, 4(1), 18–30.

Kirsh, S. J. (1998). Seeing the world through Mortal Kombat-colored glasses: Violent video games and the development of a short-term hostile attribution bias. *Childhood: Global Journal of Childhood Research*, 5(2), 177–184.

Kirsh, S. J. (2006). *Children, adolescents, and media violence: A critical look at the research.* Thousand Oaks, CA: Sage.

Kirsh, S. J., Olczak, P. V., & Mounts, J. R. W. (2005). Violent video games induce an affect processing bias. *Media Psychology*, 7, 239–250.

Kirzinger, A. E., Weber, C., & Johnson, M. (2012). Genetic and environmental influences on media use and communication behaviors. *Human Communication Research*, 38, 144–171.

Kitchen, P., Kerr, G. E., Schultz, D., McColl, R., & Pals, H. (2014). The elaboration likelihood model: Review, critique and research agenda. *European Journal of Marketing*, 48(11/12), 2033–2050.

Kivel, B. D., & Johnson, C. W. (2009). Consuming media, making men: Using collective memory work to understand leisure and the construction of masculinity. *Journal of Leisure Research*, 41(1), 109–133.

Kiviat, B. (2005). Ten questions for Andrea Mitchell. *Time*, August 22. Retrieved from http://content.time.com

Klein, J. G., & Ahluwalia, R. (2005). Negativity in the evaluation of political candidates. *Journal of Marketing*, 69, 131–142.

Kleiner, C. (2001). Disney makes nice to Japan. *U.S. News & World Report*, June 4, 46–47.

Klimmt, C., Hartmann, T., & Schramm, H. (2006). Parasocial interactions and relationships. In J. Bryant & P. Vorderer (Eds.), *Psychology of entertainment* (pp. 291–313). Mahwah, NJ: Erlbaum.

Kline, S. (1992). *Out of the garden: Toys, TV, and children's culture in the age of marketing.* New York: Verso.

Knill, B. J., Pesch, M., Pursey, G., Gilpin, P., & Perloff, R. M. (1981). Still typecast after all these years? Sex role portrayals in television advertising. *International Journal of Women's Studies*, 4, 497–506.

Knobloch, S. (2003). Mood adjustment via mass communication. *Journal of Communication*, 53, 233–250.

Knobloch, S., & Zillmann, D. (2002). Mood management via the digital jukebox. *Journal of Communication*, 52, 351–366.

Knobloch, S., Callison, C., Chen, L., Fritzsche, A., & Zillmann, D. (2005). Children's sex-stereotyped self-socialization through selective exposure to entertainment: Cross-cultural experiments in Germany, China, and the United States. *Journal of Communication*, 55, 122–138.

Knobloch-Westerwick, S. (2006). Mood management: Theory, evidence, and advancements. In J. Bryant & P. Vorderer (Eds.), *Psychology of entertainment* (pp. 239–254). Mahwah, NJ: Erlbaum.

Knobloch-Westerwick, S., & Alter, S. (2006). Mood adjustment to social situations through mass media use: How men ruminate and women dissipate angry moods. *Human Communication Research*, 32, 58–73.

Knobloch-Westerwick, S., & Alter, S. (2007). The gender news use divide: Americans' sex-typed selective exposure to online news topics. *Journal of Communication*, 57, 739–758.

Knobloch-Westerwick, S., & Meng, J. (2011). Reinforcement of the political self through selective exposure to political messages. *Journal of Communication*, 61, 349–368.

Knobloch-Westerwick, S., Appiah, O., & Alter, S. (2008). News selection patterns as a function of race: The discerning minority and the indiscriminating majority. *Media Psychology*, 11, 400–417.

Knobloch-Westerwick, S., David, P., Eastin, M. S., Tamborini, R., & Greenwood, D. (2009). Sports spectators' suspense: Affect and uncertainty in sports entertainment. *Journal of Communication*, 59, 750–767.

Koblin, J. (2017). A sharp decline for Jimmy Fallon's "Tonight Show." *The New York Times*, November 28. Retrieved from www.nytimes.com

Kolbe, R. H., & Muehling, D. D. (1992). A content analysis of the fine print in television advertising. *Journal of Current Issues and Research in Advertising*, 14(2), 47–61.

Konijn, E. A. (2013). The role of emotion in media use and effects. In K. Dill (Ed.), *The Oxford handbook of media psychology* (pp. 186–211). New York: Oxford University Press.

Koolstra, C. M., & Beentjes, J. W. J. (1999). Children's vocabulary acquisition in a foreign language through watching subtitled television programs at home. *Education Technology, Research, and Development*, 47, 51–60.

Koolstra, C. M., & van der Voort, T. H. A. (1996). Longitudinal effects of television on leisure-time reading. *Human Communication Research*, 23, 4–35.

Koolstra, C. M., van der Voort, T. H. A., & Van der Kamp, L. J. T. (1997). Television's impact on children's reading comprehension and decoding skills: A 3-year panel study. *Reading Research Quarterly*, 32, 128–152.

Korzenny, F., & Ting-Toomey, S. (Eds.). (1992). *Mass media effects across cultures*. Newbury Park, CA: Sage.

Kosicki, G. M. (1993). Problems and opportunities in agenda-setting research. *Journal of Communication*, 43(2), 100–127.

Kotler, J. A., Wright, J. C., & Huston, A. C. (2001). Television use in families with children. In J. Bryant & J. A. Bryant (Eds.), *Television and the American family*. 2nd ed. (pp. 33–48). Mahwah, NJ: Erlbaum.

Kottak, C. P. (2009). *Prime-time society: An anthropological analysis of television and culture*. New York: Taylor & Francis.

Krahé, B. (2014). Media violence use as a risk factor for aggressive behaviour in adolescence. *European Review of Social Psychology*, 25(1), 71–106.

Krahé, B., & Möller, I. (2010). Longitudinal effects of media violence on aggression and empathy among German adolescents. *Journal of Applied Developmental Psychology*, 31(5), 401–409.

Krahé, B., & Möller, I. (2011). Links between self-reported media violence exposure and teacher ratings of aggression and prosocial behavior among German adolescents. *Journal of Adolescence*, 34(2), 279–287.

Krahé, B., Möller, I., Huesmann, L. R., Kirwil, L., Felber, J., & Berger, A. (2011). Desensitization to media violence: Links with habitual media violence exposure, aggressive cognitions, and aggressive behavior. *Journal of Personality and Social Psychology*, 100(4), 630–646.

Krahé, B., Busching, R., & Möller, I. (2012). Media violence use and aggression among German adolescents: Associations and trajectories of change in a three-wave longitudinal study. *Psychology of Popular Media Culture*, 1(3), 152–166.

Krafka, C. L., Linz, D., Donnerstein, E., & Penrod, S. (1997). Women's reactions to sexually aggressive mass media depictions. *Violence against Women*, 3(2), 148–181.

Kraft, R. N., Cantor, P., & Gottdiener, C. (1991). The coherence of visual narratives. *Communication Research*, 18, 601–616.

Krakowiak, K. M. & Oliver, M. B. (2012). When good characters do bad things. *Journal of Communication*, 62, 117–135.

Krantz, A., Shukla, V., Knox, M., & Schrouder, K. (2017). Violent video games exposed: A blow by blow account of senseless violence in games. *Journal of Psychology*, 151(1), 76–87.

Kraus, S. (1988). *Televised presidential debates and public policy*. Hillsdale, NJ: Erlbaum.

Kraus, S. (1996). Winners of the first 1960 televised presidential debate between Kennedy and Nixon. *Journal of Communication*, 46(4), 78–96.

Kraut, R., Patterson M., Lundmark, V., Kiesler, S., Mukopadhyay, T., & Scherlis, W. (1998). Internet paradox: A social technology that reduces social involvement and psychological well-being? *American Psychologist*, 53, 1017–1031.

Krcmar, M., & Cooke, M. C. (2001). Children's moral reasoning and their perceptions of television violence. *Journal of Communication*, 51(2), 300–316.

Krcmar, M., & Curtis, S. (2003). Mental models: Understanding the impact of fantasy violence on children's moral reasoning. *Journal of Communication*, 53(3), 460–478.

Krcmar, M., & Greene, K. (1999). Predicting exposure to and uses of television violence. *Journal of Communication*, 49(3), 24–45.

Krcmar, M., & Kean, L. G. (2005). Uses and gratifications of media violence: Personality correlates of viewing and liking violent genres. *Media Psychology*, 7, 399–420.

Krcmar, M., Farrar, K. M., Jalette, G., & McGloin, R. (2015). Appetitive and defensive arousal in violent video games: Explaining individual differences in attraction to and effects of video games. *Media Psychology*, 18(4), 527–550.

Krishnan, H. S., & Chakravarti, D. (2003). A process analysis of the effects of humorous advertising executions on brand claims memory. *Journal of Consumer Psychology*, 13(3), 230–245.

Krohn, F. B., & Suazo, F. L. (1995). Contemporary urban music: Controversial messages in hip-hop and rap lyrics. *ETC: A Review of General Semantics*, 52, 139–155.

Kroon, A. C., van Selm, M., ter Hoeven, C. L., & Vliegenthart, R. (2016). Poles apart: The processing and consequences of mixed media stereotypes of older workers. *Journal of Communication*, 66(5), 811–833.

Krosnick, J. A. & MacInnis, B. (2015). Fox and not-Fox television news impact on opinions on global warming: Selective exposure, not motivated reasoning. In J. P., Forgas, K. Fiedler, & W. D. Crano (Eds.). *Social psychology and politics* (pp. 75–90). New York: Psychology Press.

Kruglanski, A. W., Crenshaw, M., Post, J. M., & Victoroff, J. (2007). What should this fight be called? Metaphors of counterterrorism and their implications. *Psychological Science in the Public Interest*, 8, 97–133.

Kruse, M., & Gee, T. (2016). The 37 fatal gaffes that didn't kill Donald Trump. Retrieved from www.politico.com

Kubey, R. (1986). Television use in everyday life: Coping with unstructured time. *Journal of Communication*, 36, 108–123.

Kukkonen, T. M., Binik, Y. M., Amsel, R., & Carrier, S. (2007). Thermography as a physiological measure of sexual arousal in both men and women. *Journal of Sexual Medicine*, 4(1), 93–105.

Kunkel, D. (1988). Children and host-selling television commercials. *Communication Research*, 15(1), 71–92.

Kunkel, D. (1998). Policy battles over defining children's educational television. *Annals of the American Academy of Political and Social Science*, 557, 39–53.

Kunkel, D., & Gantz, W. (1992). Children's television advertising in the multichannel environment. *Journal of Communication*, 42(3), 134–152.

Kunkel, D., & McIlrath, M. (2003). Message content in advertising to children. In E. L. Palmer & B. M. Young (Eds.), *The faces of televisual media: Teaching, violence, and selling to children* (pp. 301–325). Mahwah, NJ: Erlbaum.

Kunkel, D., Farinola, W. J. M., Farrar, K., Donnerstein, E., Biely, E., & Zwarun, L. (2002). Deciphering the V-chip: An examination of the television industry's program rating judgments. *Journal of Communication*, 52, 112–138.

Kunkel, D., Eyal, K., Donnerstein, E., Farrar, K. M., Biely, E., & Rideout, V. (2007). Sexual socialization messages on entertainment television: Comparison content trends 1997–2002. *Media Psychology*, 9, 595–622.

Kurtz, H. (2013). Media's failure on Iraq still stings. Retrieved from www.cnn.com

Kushner, H. W. (2001). *Terrorism in the 21st century*. Newbury Park CA: Sage.

Kutchinsky, B. (1973). The effect of easy availability of pornography on the incidence of sex crimes: The Danish experience. *Journal of Social Issues*, 29(3), 163–181.

Kutchinsky, B. (1991). Pornography and rape: Theory and practice? *International Journal of Law and Psychiatry*, 14, 47–64.

Kwong, J. (2017). Why Clinton lost: What Russia did to control the American mind and put Trump in the White House. *Newsweek*, November 18. Retrieved from www.newsweek.com

Labi, N. (1999). Classrooms for sale. *Time*, April 19, pp. 44–45.

Labre, M. P. (2005). Burn fat, build muscle: A content analysis of *Men's Health* and *Men's Fitness*. *International Journal of Men's Health*, 4, 187–200.

Lacayo, R. (2003). Heart of glass. *Time*, May 19, p. 57.

Lagus, K. A., Bernat, D. H., Bearinger, L. H., Resnick, M. D., & Eisenberg, M. E. (2011). Parental perspectives on sources of sex information for young people. *Journal of Adolescent Health*, 49(1), 87–89.

Lakoff, G. (2009). *The political mind: A cognitive scientist's guide to your brain and its politics*. New York: Penguin.

Lamb, S., & Randazzo, R. (2016). Obstacles to teaching ethics in sexuality education. In J. J. Ponzetti (Ed.), *Evidence-based approaches to sexuality education: A global perspective* (pp. 113–127). New York: Routledge.

Lambert, W. E., & Klineberg, O. (1967). *Children's views of foreign peoples: A cross-national study*. New York: Appleton-Century-Crofts.

Landry, S., Goncalves, M. K., & Kukkonen, T. M. (2016). Assessing differences in physiologic subjective response toward male and female orientated sexually explicit videos in heterosexual individuals. *Canadian Journal of Human Sexuality*, 25(3), 208–215.

Lang, A. (1990). Involuntary attention and physiological arousal evoked by structural features and emotional content in TV commercials. *Communication Research*, 17, 275–299.

Lang, A. (1991). Emotion, formal features, and memory for televised political advertisements. In F. Biocca (Ed.), *Television and political advertising: Psychological processes* (Vol. 1, pp. 221–243). Hillsdale, NJ: Erlbaum.

Lang, A. (1994). What can the heart tell us about thinking? In A. Lang (Ed.), *Measuring psychological responses to media* (pp. 99–112). Hillsdale, NJ: Erlbaum.

Lang, A. (2000). The limited capacity model of mediated message processing. *Journal of Communication*, 50, 46–70.

Lang, A., Geiger, S., Strickwerda, M., & Sumner, J. (1993). The effects of related and unrelated cuts on television viewers' attention, processing capacity, and memory. *Communication Research*, 20, 4–29.

Lang, A., Chung, Y., Lee, S., Schwartz, N., & Shin, M. (2005). It's an arousing, fast-paced kind of world: The effects of age and sensation seeking on the information processing of substance-abuse PSAs. *Media Psychology*, 7, 421–454.

Lang, A., Shin, M., Bradley, S. D., Wang, Z., Lee, S., & Potter, D. (2005). Wait! Don't turn that dial! More excitement to come! The effect of story length and production pacing in local television news on channel changing behavior and information processing in a free choice environment. *Journal of Broadcasting and Electronic Media*, 49, 3–22.

Lang, A., Potter, R. F., & Bolls, P. (2009). Where psychophysiology meets the media: Taking the effects out of mass media research. In J. Bryant and M. B. Oliver (Eds.), *Media effects: Advances in theory and research*. 3rd ed. (pp. 185–206). New York: Taylor & Francis.

Lang, G. E., & Lang, K. (1984). *Politics and television reviewed*. Beverly Hills, CA: Sage.

Lang, K., & Lang, G. E. (1968). *Politics and television*. Chicago: Quadrangle Books.

Larson, J. F. (1986). Television and U.S. foreign policy: The case of the Iran hostage crisis. *Journal of Communication*, 36(4), 108–130.

Larson, J. F., McAnany, E. G., & Storey, J. D. (1986). News of Latin America on network television, 1972–1981: A northern perspective on the southern hemisphere. *Critical Studies in Mass Communication*, 3, 169–183.

Larson, M. S. (2001a). Sibling interaction in situation comedies over the years. In J. Bryant & J. A. Bryant (Eds.), *Television and the American family*. 2nd ed. (pp. 163–176). Mahwah, NJ: Erlbaum.

Larson, M. S. (2001b). Interactions, activities, and gender in children's television commercials: A content analysis. *Journal of Broadcasting & Electronic Media*, 45, 41–56.

Lasisi, M. J., & Onyehalu, A. S. (1992). Cultural influences of a reading text on the concept formation of second-language learners of two Nigerian ethnic groups. In R. J. Harris (Ed.), *Cognitive processing in bilinguals* (pp. 459–471). Amsterdam: Elsevier/ North Holland.

LaTour, K. A., & LaTour, M. S. (2009). Positive mood and susceptibility to false advertising. *Journal of Advertising*, 38(3), 127–142.

Lau, R. R. (1986). Political schemata, candidate evaluations, and voting behavior. In R. R. Lau & D. O. Sears (Eds.), *Political cognition* (pp. 95–126). Hillsdale, NJ: Erlbaum.

Lau, R. R., Sigelman, L., Heldman, C., & Babbitt, P. (1999). The effects of negative political advertisements: A meta-analytic assessment. *American Political Science Review*, 93, 851–875.

Lavaur, J.-M., & Bairstow, D. (2011). Languages on the screen: Is film comprehension related to the viewers' fluency level and to the language in the subtitles? *International Journal of Psychology*, 46, 455–462.

Lawlor, M.-A., Dunne, Á., & Rowley, J. (2016). Young consumers' brand communications literacy in a social networking site context. *European Journal of Marketing*, 50(11), 2018–2040.

Lawson, V. Z., & Strange, D. (2015). News as (hazardous) entertainment: Exaggerated reporting leads to more memory distortion for news stories. *Psychology of Popular Media Culture*, 4(2), 188–198.

Lazarsfeld, P. F., Berelson, B., & Gaudet, H. (1948). *The people's choice*. New York: Columbia University Press.

Leaper, C., Breed, L., Hoffman, L., & Perlman, C. A. (2002). Variations in the gender-stereotyped content of children's television cartoons across genres. *Journal of Applied Social Psychology*, 32, 1653–1662.

Leavitt, J. D., & Christenfeld, N. J. S. (2011). Story spoilers don't spoil stories. *Psychological Science*, 22, 1152–1154.

Leavitt, L. A., & Fox, N. A. (Eds.). (1993). *The psychological effects of war and violence on children*. Hillsdale, NJ: Erlbaum.

Leavitt, P. A., Covarrubias, R., Perez, Y. A., & Fryberg, S. A. (2015). "Frozen in Time": The impact of Native American media representations on identity and self-understanding. *Journal of Social Issues*, 71(1), 39–53.

Lecheler, S., & de Vreese, C. H. (2011). Getting real: The duration of framing effects. *Journal of Communication*, 61, 959–983.

Lee, B. (2017). Back from the dead: Is the slasher movie set to make a killing? *The Guardian*, October 17. Retrieved from www.theguardian.com

Lee, B., & Tamborini, R. (2005). Third-person effect and internet pornography: The influence of collectivism and internet self-efficacy. *Journal of Communication*, 55, 292–310.

Lee, C.-J., & Niederdeppe, J. (2011). Genre-specific cultivation effects: Lagged associations between overall TV viewing, local TV news viewing, and fatalistic beliefs about cancer prevention. *Communication Research*, 38, 731–753.

Lee, E.-J. (2007). Wired for gender: Experientiality and gender-stereotyping in computer-mediated communication. *Media Psychology*, 10, 182–210.

Lee, E.-J., & Oh, S. Y. (2012). To personalize or depersonalize? When and how politicians' personalized Tweets affect the public's reactions. *Journal of Communication*, 62(6), 932–949.

Lee, E.-J., & Shin, S. Y. (2014). When the medium is the message: How transportability moderates the effects of politicians' Twitter communication. *Communication Research*, 41(8), 1088–1110.

Lee, H. (2000). Reggae power. *World Press Review* (June), 37.

Lee, H., & Park, S. A. (2016). Third-person effect and pandemic flu: The role of severity, self-efficacy method mentions, and message source. *Journal of Health Communication*, 21(12), 1244–1250.

Lee, K. M., & Peng, W. (2006). What do we know about social and psychological effects of computer games? A comprehensive review of the current literature. In P. Vorderer & J. Bryant (Eds.), *Playing video games: Motives, responses, and consequences* (pp. 327–345). Mahwah, NJ: Erlbaum.

Lee, M. A., & Solomon, N. (1991). *Unreliable sources: A guide to detecting bias in news media.* New York: Carol.

Lee, M. J., Hust, S., Zhang, L., & Zhang, Y. (2011). Effects of violence against women in popular crime dramas on viewers' attitudes related to sexual violence. *Mass Communication and Society,* 14(1), 25–44.

Lee, M. Y. H. (2015). Analysis: Donald Trump's false comments connecting Mexican immigrants and crime. *Washington Post,* July 8. Retrieved from www.washingtonpost.com

Lee, S. J. (1996). *Unraveling the "model minority" stereotype: Listening to Asian American youth.* New York: Teachers College Press.

Lee, S. Y., Hwang, H., Hawkins, R., & Pingree, S. (2008). Interplay of negative emotion and health self-efficacy on the use of health information and its outcomes. *Communication Research,* 35, 358–381.

Lefevere, J., de Swert, K., & Walgrave, S. (2012). Effects of popular exemplars in television news. *Communication Research,* 39, 103–119.

Lefkowitz, M. M., Eron, L. D., Walder, L. O., & Huesmann, L. R. (1977). *Growing up to be violent: A longitudinal study of the development of aggression.* New York: Pergamon.

Legrain, P. (2003). Cultural globalization is not Americanization. *The Chronicle of Higher Education,* 49 (May 9), B7–B10.

Leka, J., McClelland, A., & Furnham, A. (2013). Memory for sexual and nonsexual television commercials as a function of viewing context and viewer gender. *Applied Cognitive Psychology,* 27(5), 584–592.

Lemert, J. B., Wanta, W., & Lee, T. T. (1999). Party identification and negative advertising in a U.S. Senate election. *Journal of Communication,* 49(2), 123–134.

Lenhart, A. (2015). Video games are key elements in friendships for many boys. Retrieved www.pewinternet.org

Leonard, R. (2006). *Movies that matter: Reading film through the eyes of faith.* Chicago: Loyola Press.

Leone, R. (2002). Contemplating ratings: An examination of what the MPAA considers "too far for R" and why. *Journal of Communication,* 52, 938–954.

Leone, R., Peek, W. C., & Bissell, K. L. (2006). Reality television and third-person perception. *Journal of Broadcasting & Electronic Media,* 50(2), 253–269.

Leonhardt, D. (2017). What I was wrong about this year. *The New York Times,* December 24. Retrieved from www.nytimes.com

Levendusky, M. (2013). *How partisan media polarize America.* Chicago: University of Chicago Press.

Levenson, E. (2017). Why does Las Vegas shooter's motive matter? Retrieved from www.cnn.com

Levin, A. (2011). Media cling to stigmatizing portrayals of mental illness. *Psychiatric News.* Retrieved from http://psychnews.psychiatryonline.org

Levin, D. E., & Kilbourne, J. (2009). *So sexy so soon: The new sexualized childhood and what parents can do to protect their kids.* New York: Ballantine Books.

Levin, D. T. (2010). Spatial representations of the sets of familiar and unfamiliar television programs. *Media Psychology,* 13, 54–76.

Levin, G. (2017). We break down top TV series among racial and ethnic groups. *USA Today,* June 27. Retrieved from www.usatoday.com/

Levin, I. P., & Gaeth, G. J. (1988). How consumers are affected by the framing of attribute information before and after consuming the product. *Journal of Consumer Research,* 15, 374–378.

LeVine, M. (2008). *Heavy metal Islam: Rock, resistance, and the struggle for the soul of Islam.* New York: Three Rivers Press.

Levinson, P. (2016). *Fake news in real context.* Connected Editions, Inc.

Levitin, D. J. (2006). *This is your brain on music: The science of a human obsession.* New York: Penguin.

Levitin, D. (2017). *Weaponized lies: How to think critically in the post-truth era.* Toronto: Penguin.

Levy, M. R. (1982). Watching TV news as para-social interaction. In G. Gumpert & R. Cathcart (Eds.), *Inter/media*. 2nd ed. (pp. 177–187). New York: Oxford University Press.

Levy, M. R., & Windahl, S. (1984). Audience activity and gratifications: A conceptual clarification and exploration. *Communication Research*, 11, 51–78.

Lewis, N., & Weaver, A. J. (2015). Emotional responses to social comparisons in reality television programming. *Journal of Media Psychology*, 28(2), 65–77.

Lewy, G. (1978). Vietnam: New light on the question of American guilt. *Commentary*, 65, 29–49.

Leyens, J., Camino, L., Parke, R., & Berkowitz, L. (1975). The effects of movie violence on aggression in a field setting as a function of group dominance and cohesion. *Journal of Personality and Social Psychology*, 32, 346–360.

Li, X. (2008). Third-person effect, optimistic bias, and sufficiency resource in Internet use. *Journal of Communication*, 58, 568–587.

Liasson, M. (2012). Do political ads actually work? Retrieved from www.npr.org/

Lichter, S. R. (2001). A plague on both parties: Substance and fairness in TV election news. *Harvard Journal of Press/Politics*, 6(3), 8–30.

Lieberman, T. (2000). You can't report what you don't pursue. *Columbia Journalism Review* (May/June), 44–49.

Liebert, R., & Schwartzberg, N. (1977). Effects of mass media. *Annual Review of Psychology*, 28, 141–174.

Liebert, R. M., & Sprafkin, J. (1988). *The early window: Effects of television on children and youth*. 3rd ed. New York: Pergamon.

Lightdale, J. R., & Prentice, D. A. (1994). Rethinking sex differences in aggression: Aggressive behavior in the absence of social roles. *Personality and Social Psychology Bulletin*, 20(1), 34–44.

Liikkanen, L. A. (2008). Music in everymind: Commonality of involuntary music imagery. In K. Miyazaki, Y. Hiragi, M. Adachi, Y. Nakajima, & M. Tsuzaki (Eds.), *Proceedings of the 10th International Conference on Music Perception and Cognition* (pp. 408–412). Sapporo, Japan.

Lim, M. (2012). Clicks, cabs, and coffee houses: Social media and oppositional movements in Egypt 2004–2011. *Journal of Communication*, 62, 231–248.

Lindstrom, M. (2011). *Brandwashed: Tricks companies use to manipulate our minds and persuade us to buy*. New York: Crown Business.

Linebarger, D. L., & Walker, D. (2005). Infants' and toddlers' television viewing and language outcomes. *American Behavioral Scientist*, 48(5), 624–645.

Linebarger, D. L., Moses, A., Garrity Liebeskind, K., & McMenamin, K. (2013). Learning vocabulary from television: Does onscreen print have a role? *Journal of Educational Psychology*, 105(3), 609–621.

Linz, D., & Donnerstein, E. (1988). The methods and merits of pornography research. *Journal of Communication*, 38(2), 180–184.

Linz, D., & Malamuth, N. (1993). *Pornography*. Newbury Park, CA: Sage.

Linz, D., Donnerstein, E., & Penrod, S. (1984). The effects of multiple exposures to filmed violence against women. *Journal of Communication*, 34(3), 130–147.

Linz, D., Turner, C. W., Hesse, B. W., & Penrod, S. D. (1984). Bases of liability for injuries produced by media portrayals of violent pornography. In N. M. Malamuth & E. Donnerstein (Eds.), *Pornography and sexual aggression* (pp. 277–304). Orlando, FL: Academic Press.

Linz, D., Donnerstein, E., Bross, M., & Chapin, M. (1986). Mitigating the influence of violence on television and sexual violence in the media. In R. Blanchard (Ed.), *Advances in the study of aggression* (Vol. 2, pp. 165–194). Orlando, FL: Academic Press.

Linz, D., Donnerstein, E., & Penrod, S. (1987). The findings and recommendations of the Attorney General's Commission on Pornography: Do the psychological "facts" fit the political fury? *American Psychologist*, 42, 946–953.

Linz, D., & Donnerstein, E., & Adams, S. M. (1989). Physiological desensitization and judgments about female victims of violence. *Human Communication Research*, 15, 509–522.

Linz, D., Fuson, I. A., & Donnerstein, E. (1990). Mitigating the negative effects of sexually violent mass communications through preexposure briefings. *Communication Research*, 17, 641–674.

Littleton, C. (2017). Netflix to boost international kids' content as viewership spikes. *Variety*, October 15. Retrieved from http://variety.com

Liu, F. C. S. (2017). Declining news media viewership and the survival of political disagreement. *International Journal of Public Opinion Research*, 29(2), 240–268.

Liu, X., & Lo, V.-H. (2014). Media exposure, perceived personal impact, and third-person effect. *Media Psychology*, 17(4), 378–396.

Liu, Y., Teng, Z., Lan, H., Zhang, X., & Yao, D. (2015). Short-term effects of prosocial video games on aggression: An event-related potential study. *Frontiers in Behavioral Neuroscience*, 9.

Livingstone, S., & Helsper, E. J. (2006). Does advertising literacy mediate the effects of advertising on children? *Journal of Communication*, 56, 560–584.

Lo, N. C., & Hotez, P. J. (2017). Public health and economic consequences of vaccine hesitancy for measles in the United States. *JAMA Pediatrics*, 171(9), 887–892.

Loftus, E. F., & Burns, T. E. (1982). Mental shock can produce retrograde amnesia. *Memory & Cognition*, 10, 318–323.

Loftus, E. F., & Ketcham, K. (1994). *The myth of repressed memory*. New York: St. Martin's Press.

Logie-MacIver, L., Piacentini, M., & Eadie, D. (2012). Using qualitative methodologies to understand behaviour change. *Qualitative Market Research: An International Journal*, 15(1), 70–86.

Lohr, B. A., Adams, H. E., & Davis, M. J. (1997). Sexual arousal to erotic and aggressive stimuli in sexually coercive and noncoercive men. *Journal of Abnormal Psychology*, 106, 230–242.

Lombard, M., Reich, R. D., Grabe, M. E., Bracken, C. C., & Ditton, T. B. (2000). Presence and television: The role of screen size. *Human Communication Research*, 26, 75–98.

Lombard, M., Snyder-Duch, J., & Bracken, C. C. (2002). Content analysis in mass communication: Assessment and reporting of intercoder reliability. *Human Communication Research*, 28, 587–604.

Longford, Lord (Ed.). (1972). *Pornography: The Longford report*. London: Coronet.

Longmore, P. K. (1985). Screening stereotypes: Images of disabled people. *Social Policy* (Summer), 31–37.

Lopez, S., Pedrotti, J., & Snyder, C. (2015). *Positive psychology: the scientific and practical explorations of human strengths*. Thousand Oaks, CA: Sage.

Loth, R. (2012). What's black and white and re-tweeted all over? *The Chronicle Review of Higher Education*, February 5. Retrieved from: http://www.chronicle.com

Love, G. D., Mouttapa, M., & Tanjasiri, S. P. (2009). Everybody's talking: Using entertainment-education video to reduce barriers to discussion of cervical cancer screening among Thai women. *Health Education Research*, 24(5), 829–838.

Love, S. M., Sanders, M. R., Turner, K. M. T., Maurange, M., Knott, T., Prinz, R., ... Ainsworth, A. T. (2016). Social media and gamification: Engaging vulnerable parents in an online evidence-based parenting program. *Child Abuse & Neglect*, 53, 95–107.

Lowry, D. T., Nio, T. C. J., & Leitner, D. W. (2003). Setting the public fear agenda: A longitudinal analysis of network TV crime reporting, public perceptions of crime, and FBI crime statistics. *Journal of Communication*, 53(1), 61–73.

Lozano, E. (1992). The force of myth on popular narratives: The case of melodramatic serials. *Communication Theory*, 2, 207–220.

Luca, N. R., & Suggs, L. S. (2013). Theory and model use in social marketing health interventions. *Journal of Health Communication*, 18(1), 20–40.

Luepker, R. V. Murray, D. M., Jacobs, D. R., Mittelmark, M. B., Bracht, N., Carlaw, R., ... Folsom, A. R. (1994). Community education for cardiovascular disease prevention: Risk factor changes in the Minnesota Heart Health Program. *American Journal of Public Health*, 84, 1383–1393.

Luke, C. (1987). Television discourse and schema theory: Toward a cognitive model of information processing. In M. E. Manley-Casimir & C. Luke (Eds.), *Children and television: A challenge for education* (pp. 76–107). New York: Praeger.

Lull, R. B., & Bushman, B. J. (2015). Do sex and violence sell? A meta-analytic review of the effects of sexual and violent media and ad content on memory, attitudes, and buying intentions. *Psychological Bulletin*, 141(5), 1022–1048.

Lull, R. B., Gibson, B., Cruz, C., & Bushman, B. J. (2018). Killing characters in video games kills memory for in-game ads. *Psychology of Popular Media Culture*, 7(1), 87–97.

Luscombe, B. (2000). Laugh track. *Time*, October 9, p. 102.

Luyt, R. (2011). Representation of gender in South African television advertising: A content analysis. *Sex Roles*, 65, 356–370.

Lyman, R. (2002). Hollywood balks at hightech sanitizers. *New York Times*, September 19. Retrieved from www.nytimes.com/2002/09/19/movies/19CLEA.html

Lynch, T., Tompkins, J. E., van Driel, I. I., & Fritz, N. (2016). Sexy, strong, and secondary: A content analysis of female characters in video games across 31 years. *Journal of Communication*, 66(4), 564–584.

Mac, R. (2015). How anti-Kickstarter GoFundMe became the crowdfunding king with causes not projects. *Forbes*, September 24. Retrieved from www.forbes.com

McAdams, D. P., & Jones, B. K. (2017). Making meaning in the wake of trauma: Resilience and redemption. In E. M. Altmaier (Ed.), *Reconstructing meaning after trauma: Theory, research, and practice* (pp. 3–16). San Diego, CA: Elsevier Academic Press.

McAlister, A. L., Puska, P., & Salonen, J. T. (1982). Theory and action for health promotion: Illustrations from the North Karelia project. *American Journal of Public Health*, 72, 43–50.

McAlister, A. R., & Cornwell, T. B. (2009). Preschool children's persuasion knowledge: The contribution of theory of mind. *Journal of Public Policy & Marketing*, 28(2), 175–185.

McAnany, E. G. (1983). Television and crisis: Ten years of network news coverage of Central America, 1972–1981. *Media, Culture and Society*, 5(2), 199–212.

Macbeth, T. M. (1996). Indirect effects of television: Creativity, persistence, school achievement, and participation in other activities. In T. M. Macbeth (Ed.), *Tuning in to young viewers: Social science perspectives on television* (pp. 149–219). Thousand Oaks, CA: Sage.

McCauley, C. (1998). When screen violence is not attractive. In J. H. Goldstein (Ed.), *Why we watch: The attractions of violent entertainment* (pp. 144–162). New York: Oxford University Press.

McCombs, M. E. (1994). News influence on our pictures of the world. In J. Bryant & D. Zillmann (Eds.), *Media effects: Advances in theory and research* (pp. 1–16). Hillsdale, NJ: Erlbaum.

McCombs, M. E., & Ghanem, S. (2001). The convergence of agenda setting and framing. In S. D. Reese, O. Gandy, & A. Grant (Eds.), *Framing in the new media landscape* (pp. 67–94). Mahwah, NJ: Erlbaum.

McCombs, M. E., & Reynolds, A. (2002). News influence on our pictures of the world. In J. Bryant & D. Zillmann (Eds.), *Media effects: Advances in theory and research*. 2nd ed. (pp. 1–18). Mahwah, NJ: Erlbaum.

McCombs, M. E., & Reynolds, A. (2009). How the news shapes our civic agenda. In J. Bryant & M. B. Oliver (Eds.), *Media effects: Advances in theory and research*. 3rd ed. (pp. 1–16). New York: Taylor & Francis.

McCombs, M. E., & Shaw, D. L. (1993). The evolution of agenda-setting research: Twenty-five years in the marketplace of ideas. *Journal of Communication*, 43(2), 58–67.

McCombs, M. E., Shaw, D. L., & Weaver, D. (Eds.). (1997). *Communication and democracy: Exploring the intellectual frontiers in agenda-setting theory*. Mahwah, NJ: Erlbaum.

McCook, A. (2003). "Fear Factor" TV show may be too scary for some. Reuters, April 17. Health on the Web. Retrieved from www.reuters.com

McCool, J. P., Cameron, L. D., & Petrie, K. J. (2001). Adolescent perceptions of smoking imagery in film. *Social Science & Medicine*, 52, 1577–1587.

McCoy, T. (2016). For "the new yellow journalists," it's about clicks and bucks: Lucrative site stokes alt-right, plays fast and loose with facts. *The Washington Post*, November 21. Retrieved from www.thewashingtonpost.com

McCutcheon, L. E., Ashe, D. D., Houran, J., & Maltby, J. (2003). A cognitive profile of individuals who tend to worship celebrities. *Journal of Psychology*, 137, 309–322.

McDermott, S., & Greenberg, B. (1985). Parents, peers, and television as determinants of black children's esteem. In R. Bostrom (Ed.), *Communication yearbook 8*. Beverly Hills, CA: Sage.

McDonald, D. N., Wantz, R. A., & Firmin, M. W. (2014). Sources informing undergraduate college student perceptions of psychologists. *The Psychological Record*, 64(3), 537–542.

McDonnell, A., & Mehta, C. M. (2016). We could never be friends: Representing cross-sex friendship on celebrity gossip web sites. *Psychology of Popular Media Culture*, 5(1), 74–84.

McDonnell, J. (1992). Rap music: Its role as an agent of change. *Popular Music and Society*, 16, 89–108.

MacFarquhar, N. & Rossback, A. (2017). Anatomy of fake news Russian propaganda. *The New York Times*, June 7. Retrieved from www.nytimes.com

McGinty, E. E., Webster, D. W., Jarlenski, M., & Barry, C. L. (2014). News media framing of serious mental illness and gun violence in the United States, 1997–2012. *American Journal of Public Health*, 104(3), 406–413.

McGinty, E. E., Kennedy-Hendricks, A., Choksy, S., & Barry, C. L. (2016). Trends in news media coverage of mental illness in the United States: 1995–2014. *Health Affairs*, 35(6), 1121–1129.

McGloin, R., Farrar, K., & Krcmar, M. (2013). Video games, immersion, and cognitive aggression: Does the controller matter? *Media Psychology*, 16(1), 65–87.

McGloin, R., Farrar, K. M., & Fishlock, J. (2015). Triple whammy! Violent games and violent controllers: Investigating the use of realistic gun controllers on perceptions of realism, immersion, and outcome aggression. *Journal of Communication*, 65(2), 280–299.

McGloin, R., Farrar, K. M., Krcmar, M., Park, S., & Fishlock, J. (2016). Modeling outcomes of violent video game play: Applying mental models and model matching to explain the relationship between user differences, game characteristics, enjoyment, and aggressive intentions. *Computers in Human Behavior*, 62, 442–451.

McGregor, S. C., & Mourão, R. R. (2017). Second screening Donald Trump: Conditional indirect effects on political participation. *Journal of Broadcasting & Electronic Media*, 61(2), 264–290.

McKenna, K. Y. A., & Bargh, J. A. (1999). Causes and consequences of social interaction on the Internet: A conceptual framework. *Media Psychology*, 1, 249–269.

McKenna, K. Y. A., & Seidman, G. (2005). Social identity and the self: Getting connected online. In W. R. Walker & D. J. Herrmann (Eds.), *Cognitive technology: Essays on the transformation of thought and society* (pp. 89–110). Jefferson, NC: McFarland.

McKenzie-Mohr, D., & Zanna, M. P. (1990). Treating women as sexual objects: Look to the (gender schematic) male who has viewed pornography. *Personality and Social Psychology Bulletin*, 16, 296–308.

McLeod, D. M., & Shah, D. V. (2014). *News frames and national security: Covering Big Brother*. New York: Cambridge University Press.

McNeal, J. U. (1999). *The kids' market: Myths and realities*. Ithaca, NY: Paramount Market.

Madden, N. (2010). China had 174 million cable TV subscribers in 2009. *Advertising Age*, January 27. Retrieved from http://adage.com

Madrigal, R., Bee, C., Chen, J., & LaBarge, M. (2011). The effect of suspense on enjoyment following a desirable outcome: The mediating role of relief. *Media Psychology*, 14, 259–288.

Maerz, M. (2010). Some *Sesame Street* viewers sense a gay-friendly vibe. *Los Angeles Times*, October 24. Retrieved from www.latimes.com/

Maheshwari, S. (2016). How fake news goes viral: A case study. *The New York Times*, November 20. Retrieved from www.nytimes.com

Maheshwari, S. (2017a). For marketers, TV sets are an invaluable pair of eyes. *The New York Times*, February 25. Retrieved from www.nytimes.com

Maheshwari, S. (2017b). Networks offer taste of TV's ad future. Marketers are hungry for more. *The New York Times*, May 21. Retrieved from www.nytimes.com

Maheshwari, S. (2017c). Six-second commercials are coming to N.F.L. games on Fox. *The New York Times*, August 30. Retrieved from www.nytimes.com/

Maheshwari, S. (2017d). With Bill O'Reilly gone from Fox News, will advertisers return? *The New York Times*, April 20. Retrieved from www.nytimes.com

Maier, J. A., Gentile, D. A., Vogel, D. L., & Kaplan, S. A. (2014). Media influences on self-stigma of seeking psychological services: The importance of media portrayals and person perception. *Psychology of Popular Media Culture*, 3(4), 239–256.

Malamuth, N. M. (1981). Rape fantasies as a function of exposure to violent sexual stimuli. *Archives of Sexual Behavior*, 10, 33–47.

Malamuth, N. M. (1984). Aggression against women: Cultural and individual causes. In N. M. Malamuth & E. Donnerstein (Eds.), *Pornography and sexual aggression* (pp. 19–52). Orlando, FL: Academic Press.

Malamuth, N. M. (1996). Sexually explicit media, gender differences, and evolutionary theory. *Journal of Communication*, 46(3), 8–31.

Malamuth, N. M., & Check, J. V. P. (1980). Sexual arousal to rape and consenting depictions: The importance of the woman's arousal. *Journal of Abnormal Psychology*, 89, 763–766.

Malamuth, N. M., & Check, J. V. P. (1983). Sexual arousal to rape depictions: Individual differences. *Journal of Abnormal Psychology*, 92, 55–67.

Malamuth, N. M., & Impett, E. A. (2001). Research on sex in the media: What do we know about effects on children and adolescents? In D. Singer & J. Singer (Eds.), *Handbook of children and the media* (pp. 269–287). Newbury Park, CA: Sage.

Malamuth, N. M., Heim, M., & Feshbach, S. (1980). Sexual responsiveness of college students to rape depictions: Inhibitory and disinhibitory effects. *Journal of Personality and Social Psychology*, 38, 399–408.

Malamuth, N. M., Check, J. V. P., & Briere, J. (1986). Sexual arousal in response to aggression: Ideological, aggressive, and sexual correlates. *Journal of Personality and Social Psychology*, 50, 330–340.

Malamuth, N. M., Addison, T., & Koss, M. (2000). Pornography and sexual aggression: Are there reliable effects and can we understand them? *Annual Review of Sex Research*, 11, 26–91.

Malawi bans *Big Brother Africa* (2003). BBC News, August 6. Retrieved from www.news.bbc.co.uk

Maloney, E. K., Lapinski, M. K., & Witte, K. (2011). Fear appeals and persuasion: A review and update of the extended parallel process model. *Social and Personality Psychology Compass*, 5(4), 206–219.

Malsin, J. (2014). Why it's getting harder to report on Syria. *Columbia Journalism Review*, September 22. Retrieved from https://archives.cjr.org

Manrai, L. A., & Gardner, M. P. (1992). Consumer processing of social ideas advertising: A conceptual model. *Advances in Consumer Research*, 19, 15–20.

Manusov, V., & Harvey, J. (2011). Bumps and tears on the road to the presidency: Media framing of key nonverbal events in the 2008 Democratic election. *Western Journal of Communication*, 75(3), 282–303.

Manyika, J., Lund, S., Singer, M., White, O., & Berry, S. (2016). Digital finance for all: Powering inclusive growth in emerging economies. Retrieved from www.mckinsey.com

Mar, R. A., Oatley, K., Hirsh, J., dela Paz, J., & Peterson, J. B. (2006). Bookworms versus nerds: Exposure to fiction versus non-fiction, divergent associations with social ability, and the simulation of fictional social worlds. *Journal of Research in Personality*, 40(5), 694–712.

Marcin, T. (2017). Donald Trump again slammed election polls, but the national surveys weren't that far off results. *Newsweek*, April 24. Retrieved from www.newsweek.com

Mares, M.-L., & Pan, Z. (2013). Effects of *Sesame Street*: A meta-analysis of children's learning in 15 countries. *Journal of Applied Developmental Psychology*, 34(3), 140–151.

Mares, M. L., & Woodard, E. H. (2001). Prosocial effects on children's social interactions. In D. G. Singer & J. L. Singer (Eds.), *Handbook of children and the media* (pp. 183–205). Thousand Oaks, CA: Sage.

Mares, M. L., & Woodard, E. H. (2005). Positive effects of television on children's social interactions: A meta-analysis. *Media Psychology*, 7, 301–322.

Mares, M. L., Palmer, E., & Sullivan, T. (2011). Prosocial effects of media exposure. In S. L. Calvert & B. J. Wilson (Eds.). *The handbook of children, media, and development* (pp. 268–289). Malden, MA: Wiley-Blackwell

Markey, C. N., & Markey, P. M. (2012). Emerging adults' responses to a media presentation of idealized female beauty: An examination of cosmetic surgery in reality television. *Psychology of Popular Media Culture*, 1(4), 209–219.

Marling, K. A. (2002). They want their mean TV. *The New York Times*, May 28. Retrieved from www.nytimes.com/2002/05/26/arts/television/26MARL.html

Marshall, R. D., Bryant, R. A., Amsel, L., Suh, E. J., Cook, J. M., & Neria, Y. (2007). The psychology of ongoing threat: Relative risk appraisal, the September 11 attacks, and terrorism-related fears. *American Psychologist*, 62, 304–316.

Martellozzo, E., Monaghan, A., Adler, J. R., Davidson, J., Leyva, R., & Horvath, M. A. H. (2017). "I wasn't sure it was normal to watch it" (Version 4). figshare. doi: 10.6084/m9.figshare.3382393.v4

Martin, B. (2018). LeVar Burton would like to read you a story. *Los Angeles Magazine*, April 6. Retrieved from www.lamag.com/

Martin, J. (2014). In this election, Obama's party benches him. *The New York Times*, October 7. Retrieved from www.nytimes.com/

Martin, J. & Chozik, A. (2016). Hillary Clinton's doctor says pneumonia led to abrupt exit from 9/11 event. *The New York Times*, September 11. Retrieved from www.nytimes.com

Martin, J. C. (2015). Making money off miracles: The gospel of televangelists. Retrieved from http://gawker.com/

Martin, M. C. (1997). Children's understanding of the intent of advertising: A meta-analysis. *Journal of Public Policy and Marketing*, 16, 205–216.

Martins, N., & Wilson, B.J. (2012). Social aggression on television and its relationship to children's aggression in the classroom. *Human Communication Research*, 38, 48–71.

Martins, N., Weaver, A. J., Yeshua-Katz, D., Lewis, N. H., Tyree, N. E., & Jensen, J. D. (2013). A content analysis of print news coverage of media violence and aggression research. *Journal of Communication*, 63(6), 1070–1087.

Martz, L. (1998). Defending the most basic freedom. *World Press Review*, 45 (May), 14–16.

Marvel Entertainment and Stomp Out Bullying™ Team Up (2014). Retrieved from www.stompoutbullying.org/media/press-relea/marvel-entertainment-and-stomp-out-bullying-team

Mastro, D. E., & Behm-Morawitz, E. (2005). Latino representations on primetime television. *Journalism & Mass Communication Quarterly*, 82, 110–130.

Mastro, D. E., & Greenberg, B. S. (2000). The portrayal of racial minorities on prime-time television. *Journal of Broadcasting & Electronic Media*, 44, 690–703.

Mastro, D. E., Behm-Morawitz, E., & Ortiz, M. (2007). The cultivation of social perceptions of Latinos: A mental models approach. *Media Psychology*, 9, 347–365.

Mastro, D. E., Behm-Morawitz, E., & Kopacz, M. A. (2008). Exposure to television portrayals of Latinos: The implications of aversive racism and social identity theory. *Human Communication Research*, 34, 1–27.

Matabane, P. W., & Merritt, B. D. (2014). Media use, gender, and African American college attendance: The Cosby effect. *Howard Journal of Communications*, 25(4), 452–471.

Matas, M., Guebaly, N., Harper, D., Green, M., & Peterkin, A. (1986). Mental illness and the media: Part II. Content analysis of press coverage of mental health topics. *Canadian Journal of Psychiatry*, 31, 431–433.

Matthes, J., & Naderer, B. (2015). Children's consumption behavior in response to food product placements in movies. *Journal of Consumer Behaviour*, 14(2), 127–136.

Matthes, J., Prieler, M., & Adam, K. (2016). Gender-role portrayals in television advertising across the globe. *Sex Roles*, 75(7–8), 314–327.

Maturo, A., & Setiffi, F. (2016). The gamification of risk: How health apps foster self-confidence and why this is not enough. *Health, Risk & Society*, 17(7–8), 477–494.

Maurer, M., & Reinemann, C. (2006). Learning versus knowing: Effects of misinformation in televised debates. *Communication Research*, 33, 489–506.

Mayer, J. (2000). Bad news: What's behind the recent gaffes at ABC? *The New Yorker*, August 14, pp. 30–36.

Mayerson, S. E., & Taylor, D. A. (1987). The effects of rape myth pornography on women's attitudes and the mediating role of sex role stereotyping. *Sex Roles*, 17, 321–338.

Mead, M. (1973). As significant as the invention of drama or the novel. A famed anthropologist takes a careful look at "An American Family." *TV Guide*, 21, 21–23.

Meadowcroft, J. M., & Reeves, B. (1989). Influence of story schema development on children's attention to television. *Communication Research*, 16, 352–374.

Media deconstruction as an essential learning skill (2012). *Connections*, 39 (May), 2–3.

Médioni, G. (2002). Stand up, Africa! *World Press Review* (July), 34–35.

Meeter, M., Murre, J. M. J., & Janssen, S. M. J. (2005). Remembering the news: Modeling retention data from a study with 14,000 participants. *Memory & Cognition*, 33, 793–810.

Meffert, M. F., Chung, S., Joiner, A. J., Waks, L., & Garst, J. (2006). The effects of negativity and motivated information processing during a political campaign. *Journal of Communication*, 56, 27–51.

Mehari, K. R., & Farrell, A. D. (2018). Where does cyberbullying fit? A comparison of competing models of adolescent aggression. *Psychology of Violence*, 8(1), 31–42.

Meirick, P. C. (2008). Targeted audiences in anti-drug ads: Message cues, perceived exposure, perceived effects, and support for funding. *Media Psychology*, 11, 283–309.

Meirick, P. C., & Dunn, S. S. (2015). Obama as exemplar: Debate exposure and implicit and explicit racial affect. *Howard Journal of Communications*, 26(1), 57–73.

Meirick, P. C., & Nisbett, G. S. (2011). I approve this message: Effects of sponsorship, ad tone, and reactance in 2008 presidential advertising. *Mass Communication and Society*, 14(5), 666–689.

Mele, C. (2017). Montana Republican Greg Gianforte is sentenced in assault on reporter. *The New York Times*, June 13. Retrieved from www.nytimes.com

Mendelsohn, H. A. (1966). Election-day broadcasts and terminal voting decisions. *Public Opinion Quarterly*, 30, 212–225.

Mercer, A., Deane, C., & McGeeney, K. (2016). Why 2016 election polls missed their mark. Retrieved from www.pewresearch.org/

Merikle, P. M. (1988). Subliminal auditory messages: An evaluation. *Psychology & Marketing*, 5, 355–372.

Merikle, P. M., & Cheesman, J. (1987). Current status of research on subliminal advertising. *Advances in Consumer Research*, 14, 298–302.

Merikle, P. M., & Skanes, H. E. (1992). Subliminal self-help audiotapes: A search for placebo effects. *Journal of Applied Psychology*, 77, 772–776.

Merskin, D. (1998). Sending up signals: A survey of Native American media use and representation in the mass media. *Howard Journal of Communication*, 9, 333–345.

Mesmer, T., Baskind, I., & Lerdau, E. (1998). Reflecting on an alliance. *Americas*, 50(5), 52–55.

Messaris, P. (1994). *Visual literacy: Image, mind, and reality*. Boulder, CO: Westview Press.

Messaris, P. (1997). *Visual persuasion: The role of images in advertising*. Thousand Oaks, CA: Sage.

Messaris, P. (1998). Visual aspects of media literacy. *Journal of Communication*, 48(1), 70–80.

Messing, S. (2018). Use of election forecasts in campaign coverage can confuse voters and may lower turnout. Retrieved from www.pewresearch.org

Meyer, P. (1990). News media responsiveness to public health. In C. Atkin & L. Wallack (Eds.), *Mass communication and public health: Complexities and conflicts* (pp. 52–57). Newbury Park, CA: Sage.

Meyers, M. (2013). *African American women in the news: Gender, race, and class in journalism*. New York: Routledge.

Meyrowitz, J. (1985). *No sense of place: The impact of electronic media on social behavior*. New York: Oxford University Press.

Meyrowitz, J. (1998). Multiple media literacies. *Journal of Communication*, 48(1), 96–108.

Michel, E., & Roebers, C. M. (2008). Children's knowledge acquisition through film: Influence of programme characteristics. *Applied Cognitive Psychology*, 22, 1228–1244.

Mielke, K. W., & Chen, M. (1983). Formative research for 3-2-1 Contact: Methods and insights. In M. J. A. Howe (Ed.), *Learning from television: Psychological and educational research* (pp. 31–55). London: Academic Press.

Militello, L. K., Kelly, S. A., & Melnyk, B. M. (2012). Systematic review of text-messaging interventions to promote healthy behaviors in pediatric and adolescent populations: Implications for clinical practice and research. *Worldviews on Evidence-Based Nursing*, 9(2), 66–77.

Miller, C. H., Lane, L. T., Deatrick, L. M., Young, A. M., & Potts, K. A. (2007). Psychological reactance and promotional health messages: The effects of controlling language, lexical correctness, and the restoration of freedom. *Human Communication Research*, 33, 219–240.

Miller, M., & Pearlstein, E. (Producers) (2004). *TV revolution* [Television documentary series]. Hollywood: Bravo.

Mills, J. (1993). The appeal of tragedy: An attitude interpretation. *Basic and Applied Social Psychology*, 14, 255–271.

Mills, J. S., Polivy, J., Herman, C. P., & Tiggemann, M. (2002). Effects of exposure to thin media images: Evidence of self-enhancement among restrained eaters. *Personality and Social Psychology Bulletin*, 28, 1687–1699.

Minow, N. N., LaMay, C. L., & Gregorian, V. (2008). *Inside the presidential debates: Their improbable past and promising future*. Chicago: University of Chicago Press.

Minzesheimer, B. (2012). Oprah's Book Club 2.0 goes digital to study Cheryl Strayed's "Wild". *Chicago Sun Times*, July 19. Retrieved from www.suntimes.com

Mitchell, A., Gottfried, J., Barthel, M., & Shearer, E. (2016). Pathways to news. Retrieved from www.journalism.org

Mitchell, A., Gottfried, J., Stocking, G., Matsa, K. E., & Grieco, E. (2017). Covering President Trump in a polarized media environment. Retrieved from www.journalism.org

Mitchell, J. (2012). *Promoting peace, inciting violence: The role of religion and media*. New York: Routledge.

Mitchell, R., Schuster, L., & Drennan, J. (2017). Understanding how gamification influences behaviour in social marketing. *Australasian Marketing Journal*, 25(1), 12–19.

Mitra, A. (2004). Voices of the marginalized on the Internet: Examples from a website for women of South Asia. *Journal of Communication*, 54, 492–510.

Mobile financial services are cornering the market (2018). *The Economist*, May 3. Retrieved from www.economist.com/

Mößle, T., Kliem, S., & Rehbein, F. (2014). Longitudinal effects of violent media usage on aggressive behavior: The significance of empathy. *Societies*, 4(1), 105–124.

Moisy, C. (1997). Myths of the global information village. *Foreign Policy* (Summer), 78–87.

Mok, T. (1998). Getting the message: Media images and stereotypes and their effect on Asian Americans. *Culture Diversity and Mental Health*, 4, 185–202.

Mölders, C., Quaquebeke, N. V., & Paladino, M. P. (2017). Consequences of politicians' disrespectful communication depend on social judgment dimensions and voters' moral identity. *Political Psychology*, 38(1), 119–135.

Molitor, F., & Sapolsky, B. S. (1993). Sex, violence, and victimization in slasher films. *Journal of Broadcasting & Electronic Media*, 37(2), 233–242.

Mongeau, P. A. (2013). Fear appeals. In J. P. Dillard & L. Shen (Eds). *The SAGE handbook of persuasion: Developments in theory and practice* (pp. 184–199) New York: Sage.

Moniz, D. (2003). Secrecy, precautions minimized risk. *USA Today*, November 27. Retrieved from https://usatoday30.usatoday.com

Monk-Turner, E., Heiserman, M., Johnson, C., Cotton, V., & Jackson, M. (2010). The portrayal of racial minorities on prime time television: A replication of the Mastro and Greenberg study a decade later. *Studies in Popular Culture*, 32, 101–114.

Montero, D. (2017). The trick play that Nevada used to whisk O.J. Simpson out of prison. *Los Angeles Times*, October 1. Retrieved from www.latimes.com

Mooney, C., & Kirshenbaum. S. (2009). *Unscientific America: How scientific illiteracy threatens our future*. New York: Basic Books.

Moore, D. L., Hausknecht, D., & Thamodaran, K. (1986). Time compression, response opportunity, and persuasion. *Journal of Consumer Research, 13*, 85–99.

Moore, S. R., & Cockerton, T. (1996). Viewers' ratings of violence presented in justified and unjustified contexts. *Psychological Reports, 79*(3), 931–935.

Moore, T. E. (1982). What you see is what you get. *Journal of Marketing, 46*(2), 38–47.

Moore, T. E. (1988). The case against subliminal manipulation. *Psychology & Marketing, 5,* 297–316.

Moore, T. E. (2008). Subliminal perception: Facts and fallacies. In S. O. Lilienfeld, J. Ruscio, J., & S. J. Lynn (Eds.), *Navigating the mindfield: A guide to separating science from pseudoscience in mental health* (pp. 589–601). Amherst, NY: Prometheus Books.

Moorti, S. (2017). Brown girls who don't need saving: Social media and the role of "possessive investment" in *The Mindy Project* and *The Good Wife*. In R. Moseley, H. Wheatley, & H. Wood (Eds.), *Television for women: New directions* (pp. 90–109). New York: Routledge.

Mora, A., Riera, D., González, C., & Arnedo-Moreno, J. (2017). Gamification: A systematic review of design frameworks. *Journal of Computing in Higher Education, 29*(3), 516–548.

Morgan, F. W., & Stoltman, J. J. (2002). Television advertising disclosures: An empirical assessment. *Journal of Business and Psychology, 16,* 515–535.

Morgan, M. (1982). Television and adolescents' sex-role stereotypes: A longitudinal study. *Journal of Personality and Social Psychology, 43*(5), 947–955.

Morgan, M. (1990). International cultivation analysis. In N. Signorielli & M. Morgan (Eds.), *Cultivation analysis: New directions in media effects research* (pp. 225–247). Newbury Park, CA: Sage.

Morgan, M., & Shanahan, J. (1991). Television and the cultivation of political attitudes in Argentina. *Journal of Communication, 41*(1), 88–103.

Morgan, M., & Shanahan, J. (1992). Comparative cultivation analysis: Television and adolescents in Argentina and Taiwan. In F. Korzenny & S. Ting-Toomey (Eds.), *Mass media effects across cultures* (pp. 173–197). Newbury Park, CA: Sage.

Morgan, M., & Shanahan, J. (1995). *Democracy tango: Television, adolescents, and authoritarian tensions in Argentina.* Cresskill, NJ: Hampton Press.

Morgan, M., Shanahan, J., & Signorielli, N. (2009). Growing up with television: Cultivation processes. In J. Bryant and M. B. Oliver (Eds.), *Media effects: Advances in theory and research.* 3rd ed. (pp. 34–49). New York: Taylor & Francis.

Morgan, M., Shanahan, J., & Signorielli, N. (2015). Yesterday's new cultivation, tomorrow. *Mass Communication and Society, 18*(5), 674–699.

Morgan, S. E., Palmgreen, P., Stephenson, M. T., Hoyle, R. H., & Lorch, E. P. (2003). Associations between message features and subjective evaluations of the sensation value of antidrug public service announcements. *Journal of Communication, 53*(3), 512–526.

Moriarty, C. M., & Harrison, K. (2008). Television exposure and disordered eating among children: A longitudinal panel study. *Journal of Communication, 58*(2), 361–381.

Moritz, M. J. (1995). The gay agenda: Marketing hate speech to the mainstream media. In R. K. Whillock & D. Slayden (Eds.), *Hate speech* (pp. 55–79). Thousand Oaks, CA: Sage.

Morrison, M. A., Krugman, D. M., & Park, P. (2008). Under the radar: Smokeless tobacco advertising in magazines with substantial youth readership. *American Journal of Public Health, 98*(3), 543–548.

Moscowitz, L. (2010). Gay marriage in television news: Voice and visual representation in the same-sex marriage debate. *Journal of Broadcasting & Electronic Media, 54,* 24–39.

Mosher, D. L., & Maclan, P. (1994). College men and women respond to X-rated videos intended for male or female audiences: Gender and sexual scripts. *Journal of Sex Research, 31,* 99–113.

Moskalenko, S., & Heine, S. J. (2003). Watching your troubles away: Television viewing as a stimulus for subjective self-awareness. *Personality and Social Psychology Bulletin, 29,* 76–85.

Motro, J., & Vanneman, R. (2015). The 1990s shift in the media portrayal of working mothers. *Sociological Forum, 30*(4), 1017–1037.

Mowlana, H. (1984). The role of the media in the U.S.–Iranian conflict. In A. Arno & W. Dissayanake (Eds.), *The news media in national and international conflict* (pp. 71–99). Boulder, CO: Westview Press.

Mowlana, H., Gerbner, G., & Schiller, H. (Eds.). (1993). *Triumph of the image: The media's war in the Persian Gulf—a global perspective.* Boulder, CO: Westview Press.

Mozur, P., & Scott, M. (2016). Fake news in U.S. election? Elsewhere, that's nothing new. *The New York Times,* November 17. Retrieved from www.nytimes.com

Mrug, S., Madan, A., Cook, E. W., & Wright, R. A. (2015). Emotional and physiological desensitization to real-life and movie violence. *Journal of Youth and Adolescence,* 44(5), 1092–1108.

Muehling, D. D., & Kolbe, R. H. (1999). A comparison of children's and prime-time fine-print advertising disclosure practices. In M. C. Macklin & L. Carlson (Eds.), *Advertising to children: Concepts and controversies* (pp. 143–164). Thousand Oaks, CA: Sage.

Muk, A., Chung, C., & Chang, E.-C. (2017). The effects of comparative advertising on young consumers' perceptions: Cross-cultural comparison between the United States and Taiwan. *Journal of Promotion Management,* 23(1), 100–122.

Mulholland, N. (Ed.). (2006). *The psychology of Harry Potter.* Dallas, TX: Benbella Books.

Mundorf, N., & Laird, K. R. (2002). Social and psychological effects of information technologies and other interactive media. In J. Bryant & D. Zillmann (Eds.), *Media effects.* 2nd ed. (pp. 583–602). Mahwah, NJ: Erlbaum.

Mundorf, N., & Mundorf, J. (2003). Gender socialization of horror. In J. Bryant, D. Roskos-Ewoldsen, & J. Cantor (Eds.), *Communication and emotion: Essays in honor of Dolf Zillmann* (pp. 155–178). Mahwah, NJ: Erlbaum.

Mundorf, N., Weaver, J., & Zillmann, D. (1989). Effects of gender roles and self-perceptions on affective reactions to horror films. *Sex Roles,* 20, 655–673.

Mundorf, N., Drew, D., Zillmann, D., & Weaver, J. (1990). Effects of disturbing news on recall of subsequently presented news. *Communication Research,* 17, 601–615.

Mundorf, N., Allen, M., D'Alessio, D., & Emmers-Sommer, T. (2007). Effects of sexually explicit media. In R. W. Preiss, B. M. Gayle, N. Burrell, M. Allen, & J. Bryant (Eds.), *Mass media effects research: Advances through meta-analysis* (pp. 181–198). Mahwah, NJ: Erlbaum.

Münzer, S., & Borg, A. (2008). Computer-mediated communication: Synchronicity and compensatory effort. *Applied Cognitive Psychology,* 22, 663–683.

Murnen, S. K., & Stockton, M. (1997). Gender and self-reported sexual arousal in response to sexual stimuli: A meta-analytic review. *Sex Roles,* 37, 135–153.

Murphy, M. (2017). 2017: The biggest year in horror history. *The New York Times,* October 26. Retrieved from www.nytimes.com

Murphy, S. T. (1998). The impact of factual versus fictional media portrayals on cultural stereotypes. *Annals of the American Academy of Political and Social Science,* 560, 165–178.

Murray, E., Lo, B., Pollack, L, Donelan, K., & Lee, K. (2003). Direct-to-consumer advertising: Public perceptions of its effects on health behaviors, health care, and the doctor–patient relationship. *Journal of the American Board of Family Practice,* 16, 513–524.

Murray, J. P. (1999). Studying television violence: A research agenda for the 21st century. In J. K. Asamen & G. L. Berry (Eds.), *Research paradigms, television, and social behavior* (pp. 369–410). Thousand Oaks, CA: Sage.

Murray, J. P. (2008). Media violence: The effects are both real and strong. *American Behavioral Scientist,* 51(8), 1212–1230.

Murray, J. P., Liotti, M., Ingmundson, P. T., Mayberg, H. S., Pu, Y., Zamarripa, F., ... Fox, P. T. (2006). Children's brain activations while watching televised violence revealed by fMRI. *Media Psychology,* 8, 25–37.

Murray, M. (2012). Kenyans use cell phones for everything from buying groceries to paying rent. NBCNews.com. Retrieved from http://worldnews.nbcnews.com/_news/2012/07/24/12909129-kenyans-use-cell-phones-for-everything-from-buying-groceries-to-paying-rent

Musto, M., Cooky, C., & Messner, M. A. (2017). "From Fizzle to Sizzle!" Televised sports news and the production of gender-bland sexism. *Gender & Society,* 31(5), 573–596.

Mutiga, M. (2014). Kenya's banking revolution lights a fire. *The New York Times,* January 20. Retrieved from www.nytimes.com/

Mutz, D. C., Roberts, D. F., & van Vuuren, D. P. (1993). Reconsidering the displacement hypothesis. *Communication Research,* 20, 51–75.

Myers, P. N., Jr., & Biocca, F. A. (1992). The elastic body image: The effect of television advertising and programming on body image distortions in young women. *Journal of Communication*, 42(3), 108–133.

Nabi, R. L., & Clark, S. (2008). Exploring the limits of social cognitive theory: Why negatively reinforced behaviors on TV may be modeled anyway. *Journal of Communication*, 58, 407–427.

Nacos, B. L., & Torres-Reyna, O. (2007). *Fueling our fears: Stereotyping, media coverage, and public opinion of Muslim Americans.* New York: Rowman & Littlefield.

Nathanson, A. I. (1999). Identifying and explaining the relationship between parental mediation and children's aggression. *Communication Research*, 26, 124–143.

Nathanson, A. I. (2004). Factual and evaluative approaches to modifying children's responses to violent television. *Journal of Communication*, 54, 321–336.

Nathanson, A. I., & Yang, M. S. (2003). The effects of mediation content and form on children's response to violent television. *Human Communication Research*, 29, 111–134.

Nathanson, A. I., & Rasmussen, E. E. (2011). TV viewing compared to book reading and toy playing reduces responsive maternal communication with toddlers and preschoolers. *Human Communication Research*, 37, 465–487.

National Television Violence Study (1997). Vols. 1–2. Thousand Oaks, CA: Sage.

Naveh, C. (2002). The role of the media in foreign policy decision-making: A theoretical framework. *Conflict & Communication Online*, 1(2), 1–14.

Neeley, S. M., & Schumann, D. W. (2004). Using animated spokes-characters in advertising to young children. *Journal of Advertising*, 33(3), 7–23.

Neely, B. (2016). Trump doesn't own most of the products he pitched last night. Retrieved from www.npr.org

Nell, V. (2002). Why young men drive dangerously: Implications for injury prevention. *Current Directions in Psychological Science*, 11, 75–79.

Nelson, J. P., Gelfand, D. M., & Hartmann, D. P. (1969). Children's aggression following competition and exposure to an aggressive model. *Child Development*, 40, 1085–1097.

Nelson, M. R. (2002). Recall of brand placements in computer/video games. *Journal of Advertising Research*, 42, 80–92.

Neria, Y., & Sullivan, G. M. (2011). Understanding the mental health effects of indirect exposure to mass trauma through the media. *Journal of the American Medical Association*, 306(12), 1374–1375.

Nettelhorst, S. C., & Brannon, L. A. (2012). The effect of advertisement choice on attention. *Computers in Human Behavior*, 28, 683–687.

Neuendorf, K. A. (2002). *The content analysis guidebook.* Thousand Oaks, CA: Sage.

Newell, B. R., & Shanks, D. R. (2014). Unconscious influences on decision making: A critical review. *Behavioral and Brain Sciences*, 37(1), 1–19.

Newhagen, J. E., & Reeves, B. (1991). Emotion and memory responses for negative political advertising: A study of television commercials used in the 1988 presidential election. In F. Biocca (Ed.), *Television and political advertising: Psychological processes* (Vol. 1, pp. 197–220). Hillsdale, NJ: Erlbaum.

Newport, F. (2016). Five key findings on religion in the U.S. Retrieved from www.gallup.com

Newport, F., & Carroll, C. (2005). Iraq versus Vietnam: A comparison of public opinion. Retrieved from http://news.gallup.com

Newton, J. D., Wong, J., & Newton, F. J. (2015). The social status of health message endorsers influences the health intentions of the powerless. *Journal of Advertising*, 44(2), 151–160.

Niederdeppe, J., Farrelly, M. C., Thomas, K. Y., Wenter, D., & Weitzenkamp, D. (2007). Newspaper coverage as indirect effects of a health communication intervention. *Communication Research*, 34, 382–406.

Nielsen Company (2010a). Television audience report 2009. Retrieved from www.nielsen.com

Nielson Company (2010b). What Americans do online. Retrieved from http://blog.nielsen.com/nielsenwire/online_mobile/what-americans-do-online-social-media-and-games-dominate-activity/

Nielsen Company (2011). The cross platform report, Quarter 1, 2011. Retrieved from www.nielsen.com

Neilsen Company (2016). Nielsen total audience report: Q1 2016. Retrieved from www.nielsen.com

Nielsen Company (2017). The Nielsen total audience report: Q1 2017. Retrieved from www.nielsen.com

Niemiec, R. M., & Wedding, D. (2008). *Positive psychology at the movies: Using films to build virtues and character strengths.* Cambridge, MA: Hogrefe.

Niemiec, R. M., & Wedding, D. (2014). *Positive psychology at the movies: Using films to build character strengths and well-being.* 2nd ed. Boston: Hogrefe.

Niesen, M. (2015). From Gray Panther to National Nanny: The kidvid crusade and the eclipse of the U.S. Federal Trade Commission, 1977–1980. *Communication, Culture & Critique,* 8(4), 576–593.

Nightingale, S. J., Wade, K. A., & Watson, D. G. (2017). Can people identify original and manipulated photos of real-world scenes? *Cognitive Research: Principles and Implications,* 2, 30. doi: 10.1186/s41235-017-0067-2

Nimmo, D., & Savage, R. L. (1976). *Candidates and their images.* Pacific Palisades, CA: Goodyear.

Nisbet, E. C., Stoycheff, E., & Pearce, K. E. (2012). Internet use and democratic demands: A multinational, multilevel model of Internet use and citizen attitudes about democracy. *Journal of Communication,* 62, 249–265.

Nisbett, R. E. (2003). *The geography of thought: How Asians and Westerners think differently … and why.* New York: Free Press.

Nizza, I. E., Britton, H. P., & Smith, J. A. (2016). "You have to die first": Exploring the thoughts and feelings on organ donation of British women who have not signed up to be donors. *Journal of Health Psychology,* 21(5), 650–660.

Noe, D. (1995). Parallel worlds: The surprising similarities (and differences) of country-and-western and rap. *The Humanist,* 55, 20–23.

Noice, H., & Noice, T. (2006). What studies of actors and acting can tell us about memory and cognitive functioning. *Current Directions in Psychological Science,* 15, 14–18.

Noice, T., & Noice, N. (1997). *The nature of expertise in professional acting: A cognitive view.* Mahwah, NJ: Erlbaum.

Nolan, J. M., & Ryan, G. W. (2000). Fear and loathing at the Cineplex: Gender differences in descriptions and perceptions of slasher films. *Sex Roles,* 42, 39–56.

Norris, J., George, W. H., Davis, K. C., Martell, J., & Leonesio, R. J. (1999). Alcohol and hypermasculinity as determinants of men's empathic responses to violent pornography. *Journal of Interpersonal Violence,* 14, 683–700.

North Korean movies' propaganda role (2003). BBC News online, August 18. Retrieved from www.news.bbc.co.uk

Numbers (1999). *Time,* May 31, p. 29.

Oates, J. (2012). Learning from watching. In N. Brace & J. Byford (Eds.), *Investigating psychology: Key concepts, key studies, key approaches* (pp. 100–138). New York: Oxford University Press.

O'Connell, M. (2017). TV ratings: "SNL" and Alec Baldwin make strong return after record election year. Retrieved from www.hollywoodreporter.com/

Oddone-Paolucci, E., Genuis, M., & Violato, C. (2000). A meta-analysis of the published research on the effects of pornography. In C. Violato, E. Oddone-Paolucci, & M. Genuis (Eds.), *The changing family and child development* (pp. 48–59). Aldershot: Ashgate.

O'Donnell, C. (2011). *New study quantifies use of social media in Arab Spring.* Retrieved from www.washington.edu

Offit, P. A. (2011). *Deadly choices: How the anti-vaccine movement threatens us all.* New York: Basic Books.

Ohbuchi, K., Ikeda, T., & Takeuchi, G. (1994). Effects of violent pornography upon viewers' rape myth beliefs: A study of Japanese males. *Psychology, Crime, & Law,* 1, 71–81.

Oldenburg, D. (2006). Experts rip "Sesame" TV aimed at tiniest tots. *The Washington Post,* March 21. Retrieved from www.washingtonpost.com/

Oliver, K. (2016). *Hunting girls: Sexual violence from The Hunger Games to campus rape.* New York: Columbia University Press.

Oliver, M. B. (1993). Adolescents' enjoyment of graphic horror. *Communication Research, 20,* 30–50.

Oliver, M. B. (1994). Portrayals of crime, race, and aggression in "reality-based" police shows: A content analysis. *Journal of Broadcasting and Electronic Media, 38,* 179–192.

Oliver, M. B., & Bartsch, A. (2010). Appreciation as audience response: Exploring entertainment gratification beyond hedonism. *Human Communication Research, 36,* 53–81.

Oliver, M. B., & Bartsch, A. (2011). Appreciation of entertainment: The importance of meaningfulness via virtue and wisdom. *Journal of Media Psychology, 23*(1), 29–33.

Oliver, M. B., & Fonash, D. (2002). Race and crime in the news: Whites' identification and misidentification of violent and nonviolent criminal suspects. *Media Psychology, 4,* 137–156.

Oliver, M. B., & Raney, A. A. (2011). Entertainment as pleasurable and meaningful: Identifying hedonic and eudaimonic motivations for entertainment consumption. *Journal of Communication, 61,* 984–1004.

Oliver, M. B., Jackson, R. L., Moses, N., & Dangerfield, C. L. (2004). The face of crime: Viewers' memory of race-related facial features of individuals pictured in the news. *Journal of Communication, 54,* 88–104.

Olson, D. R. (1994). *The world on paper.* New York: Cambridge University Press.

Onishi, N. (2001). Maradi journal: On the scale of beauty in Niger, weight weighs heavily. *The New York Times,* February 12. Retrieved from www.nytimes.com

Oppliger, P. A. (2007). Effects of gender stereotyping on socialization. In R. W. Preiss, B. M. Gayle, N. Burrell, M. Allen, & J. Bryant (Eds.), *Mass media effects research: Advances through meta-analysis* (pp. 199–214). Mahwah, NJ: Erlbaum.

Orgad, S., & Meng, B. (2017). The maternal in the city: Outdoor advertising representations in Shanghai and London. *Communication, Culture & Critique, 10*(3), 460–478.

Orman, J. (1992). Conclusion: The impact of popular music in society. In K. J. Bindas (Ed.), *America's musical pulse: Popular music in twentieth-century society* (pp. 281–287). Westport, CT: Praeger.

Orue, I., Bushman, B. J., Calvete, E., Thomaes, S., de Castro, B. O., & Hutteman, R. (2011). Monkey see, monkey do, monkey hurt: Longitudinal effects of exposure to violence on children's aggressive behavior. *Social Psychological and Personality Science, 2*(4), 432–437.

Osborn, J. L. (2012). When TV and marriage meet: A social exchange analysis of the impact of television viewing on marital satisfaction and commitment. *Mass Communication and Society, 15*(5), 739–757.

Otgaar, H., Candel, I., Merckelbach, H., & Wade, K. A. (2009). Abducted by a UFO: Prevalence information affects young children's false memories for an implausible event. *Applied Cognitive Psychology, 23,* 115–125.

Otterson, J. (2017). Cable news ratings: MSNBC posts big percentage gains, Fox News stays number one, CNN sets records. Retrieved from http://variety.com/

Paavonen, E. J., Roine, M., Pennonen, M., & Lahikainen, A. R. (2009). Do parental co-viewing and discussions mitigate TV-induced fears in young children? *Child: Care, Health and Development, 35,* 773–780.

Paek, H.-J. (2008). Mechanisms through which adolescents attend and respond to anti-smoking media campaigns. *Journal of Communication, 58,* 84–105.

Paek, H.-J., & Gunther, A. C. (2007). How peer proximity moderates indirect media influence on adolescent smoking. *Communication Research, 34,* 407–432.

Paek, H.-J., Nelson, M. R., & Vilela, A. M. (2011). Examination of gender-role portrayals in television advertising across seven countries. *Sex Roles, 64,* 192–207.

Page, J. T., & Duffy, M. E. (2009). A battle of visions: Dueling images of morality in U.S. political campaign UV ads. *Communication, Culture & Critique, 2,* 110–135.

Pal, M., & Dutta, M. J. (2012). Organizing resistance on the Internet: The case of the International Campaign for Justice in Bhopal. *Communication, Culture & Critique, 5,* 230–251.

Paletz, D. L. (1988). Pornography, politics, and the press: The U.S. attorney general's commission on pornography. *Journal of Communication*, 38(2), 122–136.

Paletz, D. L., & Schmid, A. P. (Eds.). (1992). *Terrorism and the media*. Newbury Park, CA: Sage.

Paley Center for Media (2010). I want my gay TV: The LGBT history of television. Retrieved from www.paleycenter.org/i-want-my-gay-tv

Palmgreen, P. (1984). Uses and gratifications: A theoretical perspective. In R. N. Bostrom (Ed.), *Communication Yearbook 8* (pp. 20–55). Newbury Park, CA: Sage.

Panee, C. D., & Ballard, M. E. (2002). High versus low aggressive priming during video game training: Effects of violent action during game play, hostility, heart rate, and blood pressure. *Journal of Applied Social Psychology*, 32, 2458–2474.

Papa, M. J., Singhal, A., Law, S., Pant, S., Sood, S., Rogers, E. M., & Shefner-Rogers, C. L. (2000). Entertainment-education and social change: An analysis of parasocial interaction, social learning, collective efficacy, and paradoxical communication. *Journal of Communication*, 50(4), 31–55.

Pappas-DeLuca, K. A., Kraft, J., Galavotti, C., Warner, G., Mooki, M., Hastings, P., & ... Kilmarx, P. H. (2008). Entertainment-education radio serial drama and outcomes related to HIV testing in Botswana. *AIDS Education and Prevention*, 20(6), 486–503.

Papper, B. (2016). Newsroom research project. Retrieved from www.rtdna.org

Parcell, L. M., Kwon, J., Miron, D., & Bryant, J. (2007). An analysis of media health campaigns for children and adolescents: Do they work? In R. W. Preiss, B. M. Gayle, N. Burrell, M. Allen, & J. Bryant (Eds.), *Mass media effects research: Advances through meta-analysis* (pp. 345–361). Mahwah, NJ: Erlbaum.

Pariera, K. L., Hether, H. J., Murphy, S. T., de Castro Buffington, S., & Baezconde-Garbanati, L. (2014). Portrayals of reproductive and sexual health on prime-time television. *Health Communication*, 29(7), 698–706.

Park, J. H., Gabbadon, N. G., & Chernin, A. R. (2006). Neutralizing racial differences through comedy: Asian, black, and white views on racial stereotypes in *Rush Hour 2*. *Journal of Communication*, 56, 157–177.

Parker, A. (2017). Trump defends Arpaio pardon, assumed "ratings would be far higher" by announcing during hurricane. *The Washington Post*, August 28. Retrieved from www.washingtonpost.com

Parker, E., & Furnham, A. (2007). Does sex sell? The effect of sexual programme content on the recall of sexual and non-sexual advertisements. *Applied Cognitive Psychology*, 21, 1217–1228.

Parkes, A., Wight, D., Hunt, K., Henderson, M., & Sargent, J. (2013). Are sexual media exposure, parental restrictions on media use and co-viewing TV and DVDs with parents and friends associated with teenagers' early sexual behaviour? *Journal of Adolescence*, 36(6), 1121–1133.

Parkin, K. J. (2006). *Food is love: Advertising and gender roles in modern America*. Philadelphia: University of Pennsylvania Press.

Parks, M. R. (1996). Making friends in cyberspace. *Journal of Communication*, 46(1), 80–97.

Parrott, S., & Parrott, C. T. (2015a). Law & disorder: The portrayal of mental illness in U.S. crime dramas. *Journal of Broadcasting & Electronic Media*, 59(4), 640–657.

Parrott, S., & Parrott, C. T. (2015b). U.S. television's "mean world" for White women: The portrayal of gender and race on fictional crime dramas. *Sex Roles*, 73(1–2), 70–82.

Patihis, L., & Loftus, E. F. (2016). Crashing Memory 2.0: False memories in adults for an upsetting childhood event. *Applied Cognitive Psychology*, 30(1), 41–50.

Paul, B., & Linz, D. (2008). The effects of exposure to virtual child pornography on viewer cognitions and attitudes toward deviant sexual behavior. *Communication Research*, 35, 3–38.

Paul, B., Salwen, M. B., & Dupagne, M. (2007). The third-person effect: A meta-analysis of the perceptual hypothesis. In R. W. Preiss, B. M. Gayle, N. Burrell, M. Allen, & J. Bryant (Eds.), *Mass media effect research: Advances through meta-analysis* (pp. 81–102). Mahwah, NJ: Erlbaum.

Paul, C., Tzelepis, F., Parfitt, N., & Girgis, A. (2008). How to improve adolescents' sun protection behavior? Age and gender issues. *American Journal of Health Behavior*, 32(4), 387–398.

Payne, D. (2003). In your face. *The Chronicle of Higher Education*, 49 (February 21), A6–A8.

Peck, J. (1992). *The gods of televangelism: The crisis of meaning and the appeal of religious television*. Cresskill, NJ: Hampton Press.

Pecora, N. O. (1997). *The business of children's entertainment*. New York: Guilford.

Pellegrinelli, L. (2009). Scholarly discord: The politics of music in the war on terrorism. *The Chronicle Review* (May 8), B7–B9.

Penney, J. (2017). Social media and citizen participation in "official" and "unofficial" electoral promotion: A structural analysis of the 2016 Bernie Sanders digital campaign. *Journal of Communication*, 67(3), 402–423.

Pentecost, R., Arli, D., & Thiele, S. (2017). It's my choice! Investigating barriers to pro-social blood donating behaviour. *Marketing Intelligence & Planning*, 35(2), 243–258.

Penuel, W. R., Bates, L., Gallagher, L. P., Pasnik, S., Llorente, C., Townsend, E., ... VanderBorght, M. (2012). Supplementing literacy instruction with a media-rich intervention: Results of a randomized controlled trial. *Early Childhood Research Quarterly*, 27(1), 115–127.

Peracchio, L. A., & Luna, D. (1998). The development of an advertising campaign to discourage smoking initiation among children and youth. *Journal of Advertising*, 27(3), 49–56.

Percy, L., & Lautman, M. R. (1994). Advertising, weight loss, and eating disorders. In E. M. Clark, T. C. Brock, & D. W. Stewart (Eds.), *Attention, attitude, and affect in response to advertising* (pp. 301–311). Hillsdale, NJ: Erlbaum.

Perego, E., del Missier, F., Porta, M., & Mosconi, M. (2010). The cognitive effectiveness of subtitle processing. *Media Psychology*, 13, 243–272.

Perlman, D. C., & Jordan, A. E. (2017). To neither target, capture, surveille, nor wage war: Ongoing need for attention to metaphor theory in care and prevention for people who use drugs. *Journal of Addictive Diseases*, 36(1), 1–4.

Perlmutter, D. D. (2000). Tracing the origin of humor. *Humor*, 13, 457–468.

Perloff, R. M. (1989). Ego-involvement and the third person effect of television news coverage. *Communication Research*, 16, 236–262.

Perloff, R. M. (2002). The third-person effect. In J. Bryant & D. Zillmann (Eds.), *Media effects: Advances in theory and research*. 2nd ed. (pp. 489–506). Mahwah, NJ: Erlbaum.

Perloff, R. M. (2009). Mass media, social perception, and the third-person effect. In J. Bryant & M. B. Oliver (Eds.), *Media effects: Advances in theory and research*. 3rd ed. (pp. 252–268). New York: Taylor & Francis.

Perloff, R. M. (2015a). Mass communication research at the crossroads: Definitional issues and theoretical directions for mass and political communication scholarship in an age of online media. *Mass Communication and Society*, 18(5), 531–556.

Perloff, R. M. (2015b). A three-decade retrospective on the hostile media effect. *Mass Communication and Society*, 18(6), 701–729.

Perrin, A. (2015). Social media usage: 2005–2015. Retrieved from www.pewinternet.org

Perry, S. D. (2008). Keeping our research up to date: Is the election cycle too fast for scholarship? *Mass Communication and Society*, 11(2), 113–114.

Perse, E. M. (1986). Soap opera viewing patterns of college students and cultivation. *Journal of Broadcasting & Electronic Media*, 30, 175–193.

Perse, E. M. (2001). *Media effects and society*. Mahwah, NJ: Erlbaum.

Perse, E. M. (2007). Meta-analysis: Demonstrating the power of mass communication. In R. W. Preiss, B. M. Gayle, N. Burrell, M. Allen, & J. Bryant (Eds.), *Mass media effects research: Advances through meta-analysis* (pp. 467–488). Mahwah, NJ: Erlbaum.

Perse, E. M., & Lambe, J. (2017). *Media effects and society*. 2nd ed. New York: Routledge.

Perse, E. M., & Rubin, R. B. (1989). Attribution in social and parasocial relationships. *Communication Research*, 16, 59–77.

Peter, J., & Valkenburg, P. M. (2016). Adolescents and pornography: A review of 20 years of research. *Journal of Sex Research*, 53(4–5), 509–531.

Peters, S., & Leshner, G. (2013). Get in the game: The effects of game-product congruity and product placement proximity on game players' processing of brands embedded in advergames. *Journal of Advertising*, 42(2–3), 113–130.

Petty, R. E., Priester, J. R., & Briñol, P. (2002). Mass media attitude change: Implications of the elaboration likelihood model of persuasion. In J. Bryant & D. Zillmann (Eds.), *Media effects*. 2nd ed. (pp. 155–198). Mahwah, NJ: Erlbaum.

Petty, R. E., Briñol, P., & Priester, J. R. (2009). Media attitude change: Implications of the elaboration-likelihood model of persuasion. In J. Bryant & M. B. Oliver (Eds.), *Media effects: Advances in theory and research*. 3rd ed. (pp. 125–164). New York: Taylor & Francis.

Pew Research Center (2011). Pew Research Center's Project for Excellence in Journalism: The state of the news media 2011, an annual report on American journalism. Retrieved from http://stateofthemedia.org/

Pew Research Center (2012). Video length. Retrieved from www.journalism.org

Pew Research Center (2013). The rise of Asian Americans. Retrieved from www.pewsocialtrends.org

Pew Research Center (2015). Teens, social media, and technology overview, 2015. Retrieved from http://pewinternet.org/

Pew Research Center (2016). Pew Research Center's Project for Excellence in Journalism: The state of the news media 2016, an annual report on American journalism. Retrieved from http://stateofthemedia.org/

Pew Research Center (2017). Internet/broadband fact sheet. Retrieved from www.pewinternet.org

Pezdek, K., Lehrer, A., & Simon, S. (1984). The relationship between reading and cognitive processing of television and radio. *Child Development*, 55, 2072–2082.

Pfau, M., Mullen, L. J., Deidrich, T., & Garrow, K. (1995). Television viewing and the public perception of attorneys. *Human Communication Research*, 21, 307–330.

Phillips, J. M., Urbany, J. E., & Reynolds, T. J. (2008). Confirmation and the effects of valenced political advertising: A field experiment. *Journal of Consumer Research*, 34, 794–806.

Phillips, K. (2007). Rwandan radio soap opera might help end violence. *Kansas State Collegian*, September 27, 4.

Piaget, J. (1972). The intellectual evolution from adolescence to adulthood. *Human Development*, 15, 1–12.

Picard, R. G. (1993). *Media portrayals of terrorism: Functions and meaning of news coverage*. Ames, IA: Iowa State University Press.

Pierce, M. C., & Harris, R. J. (1993). The effect of provocation, race, and injury description on men's and women's perception of a wife-battering incident. *Journal of Applied Social Psychology*, 23, 767–790.

Pietraszkiewicz, A., Soppe, B., & Formanowicz, M. (2017). Go pro bono: Prosocial language as a success factor in crowdfunding. *Social Psychology*, 48(5), 265–278.

Pinedo, I. C. (1997). *Recreational terror: Women and the pleasures of horror film viewing*. Albany NY: SUNY Press.

Pingree, R. J., Scholl, R. M., & Quenette, A. M. (2012). Effects of postdebate coverage on spontaneous policy reasoning. *Journal of Communication*, 62(4), 643–658.

Pinker, S. (2018). The media exaggerates negative news: This distortion has consequences. *The Guardian*, February 17. Retrieved from www.theguardian.com/

Pinkleton, B. E. (1998). Effects of print comparative political advertising on political decision-making and participation. *Journal of Communication*, 48(4), 24–36.

Pinsker, J. (2016). The hidden economics of porn. *The Atlantic*, April 4. Retrieved from www.theatlantic.com/

Pinsky, M. I. (2007). *The gospel according to the Simpsons: Bigger and possibly even better edition*. Louisville, KY: Westminster John Knox Press.

Piotrowski, J. T. (2014). Participatory cues and program familiarity predict young children's learning from educational television. *Media Psychology*, 17(3), 311–331.

Pitkanen-Pulkkinen, L. (1981). Concurrent and predictive validity of self-reported aggressiveness. *Aggressive Behavior*, 7, 97–110.

Plissner, M. (2003). The most trusted man in America. Retrieved from www.cbsnews.com/news/the-most-trusted-man-in-america/

Ponce De Leon, C. L. (2015). "Perilously close to propaganda": How Fox News shilled for Iraq War, and Jon Stewart returned sanity. Retrieved from www.salon.com

Poniewozik. J. (2006). How reality TV fakes it. *Time*, February 6, pp. 60–62.

Poniewozik, J. (2016a). Review: HBO's "Sesame Street," fancy but not free. *The New York Times*, January 13. Retrieved from www.nytimes.com

Poniewozik, J. (2016b). Two astonishing views of O.J. Simpson and his trial. *The New York Times*, June 20. Retrieved from www.nytimes.com/

Pope, H. G., Jr., Olivardia, R., Gruber, A., & Borowiecki, J. (1999). Evolving ideals of male body image as seen through action toys. *International Journal of Eating Disorders*, 26, 65–72.

Pope, H. G., Jr., Phillips, K. A., & Olivardia, R. (2000). *The Adonis complex: The secret crisis of male body obsession*. New York: Free Press.

Postman, N. (1982). *The disappearance of childhood*. New York: Delacorte.

Postman, N. (1985). *Amusing ourselves to death*. New York: Viking Penguin.

Potter, W. J. (1986). Perceived reality and the cultivation hypothesis. *Journal of Broadcasting & Electronic Media*, 30, 159–174.

Potter, W. J. (1988). Perceived reality in television effects research. *Journal of Broadcasting & Electronic Media*, 32, 23–41.

Potter, W. J. (1989). Three strategies for elaborating the cultivation hypothesis. *Journalism Quarterly*, 65, 930–939.

Potter, W. J. (1991a). Examining cultivation from a psychological perspective: Component subprocesses. *Communication Research*, 18, 77–102.

Potter, W. J. (1991b). The relationships between first- and second-order measures of cultivation. *Human Communication Research*, 18, 92–113.

Potter, W. J. (1993). Cultivation theory and research: A conceptual critique. *Human Communication Research*, 19, 564–601.

Potter, W. J. (1999). *On media violence*. Thousand Oaks CA: Sage.

Potter, W. J. (2001). *Media literacy*. 2nd ed. Thousand Oaks, CA: Sage.

Potter, W. J. (2004). *Theory of media literacy: A cognitive approach*. Thousand Oaks, CA: Sage.

Potter, W. J. (2011). Conceptualizing mass media effect. *Journal of Communication*, 61, 896–915.

Potter, W. J. (2014). A critical analysis of cultivation theory. *Journal of Communication*, 64(6), 1015–1036.

Potter, W. J. (2016). *Media literacy*. 8th ed. Los Angeles, CA: Sage.

Potter, W. J., & Tomasello, T. K. (2003). Building upon the experimental design in media violence research: The importance of including receiver interpretations. *Journal of Communication*, 53, 315–329.

Potts, R., & Martinez, I. (1994). Television viewing and children's beliefs about scientists. *Journal of Applied Developmental Psychology*, 15, 287–300.

Potts, R., & Sanchez, D. (1994). Television viewing and depression: No news is good news. *Journal of Broadcasting & Electronic Media*, 38, 79–90.

Potts, R., & Swisher, L. (1998). Effects of televised safety models on children's risk taking and hazard identification. *Journal of Pediatric Psychology*, 23, 157–163.

Potts, R., Doppler, M., & Hernandez, M. (1994). Effects of television content on physical risk-taking in children. *Journal of Experimental Child Psychology*, 58, 321–331.

Pouliot, L., & Cowen, P. S. (2007). Does perceived reality really matter in media effects? *Media Psychology*, 9, 241–259.

Pratap, A. (1990). Romance and a little rape. *Time*, August 13, p. 69.

Pratkanis, A. R. (1992). The cargo-cult science of subliminal persuasion. *Skeptical Inquirer*, 16, 260–272.

Pratkanis, A. R., & Greenwald, A. G. (1988). Recent perspectives on unconscious processing: Still no marketing applications. *Psychology & Marketing*, 5, 339–355.

Prestin, A. (2013). The pursuit of hopefulness: Operationalizing hope in entertainment media narratives. *Media Psychology*, 16(3), 318–346.

Preston, E. H. (1990). Pornography and the construction of gender. In N. Signorielli & M. Morgan (Eds.), *Cultivation analysis* (pp. 107–122). Newbury Park, CA: Sage.

Preston, I. L. (1975). *The great American blow-up: Puffery in advertising and selling*. Madison, WI: University of Wisconsin Press.

Preston, I. L. (1994). *The tangled web they weave: Truth, falsity, & advertisers*. Madison, WI: University of Wisconsin Press.

Preston, I. L., & Richards, J. I. (1986). Consumer miscomprehension as a challenge to FTC prosecutions of deceptive advertising. *The John Marshall Law Review*, 19, 605–635.

Price, M. E. (Ed.). (1998). *The V-chip debate: Content filtering from television to the Internet*. Mahwah, NJ: Erlbaum.

Price, M. E. (2009). End of television and foreign policy. *Annals of the American Academy of Political and Social Science*, 625(1), 196–204.

Primack, B. A., Dalton, M. A., Carroll, M. V., Agarwal, A. A., & Fine, M. J. (2008). Content analysis of tobacco, alcohol, and other drugs in popular music. *Archives of Pediatrics and Adolescent Medicine*, 162, 169–175.

Pritchard, D., & Hughes, K. D. (1997). Patterns of deviance in crime news. *Journal of Communication*, 47(3), 49–67.

Propper, R. E., Stickgold, R., Keeley, R., & Christman, S. D. (2007). Is television traumatic? Dreams, stress, and media exposure in the aftermath of September 11, 2001. *Psychological Science*, 18, 334–340.

Pullido, M. L. (2014). Child pornography: Basic facts about a horrific crime. Retrieved from www.huffingtonpost.com/

Quackenbush, D. M., Strassberg, D. S., & Turner, C. W. (1995). Gender effects of romantic themes in erotica. *Archives of Sexual Behavior*, 24, 21–35.

Quan-Haase, A., & Young, A. L. (2010). Uses and gratifications of social media: A comparison of Facebook and instant messaging. *Bulletin of Science, Technology & Society*, 30, 350–361.

Quealy, K. (2017). We avoid the news we don't like: Some Trump-era evidence. *The New York Times*, February 21. Retrieved from www.nytimes.com

Quinn, G. P., Ellery, J., Thomas, K. B., & Marshall, R. (2010). Developing a common language for using social marketing: An analysis of public health literature. *Health Marketing Quarterly*, 27(4), 334–353.

Quinsey, V. L., Chapman, T. C., & Upfold, D. (1984). Sexual arousal to nonsexual violence and sadomasochistic themes among rapists and non-sex offenders. *Journal of Consulting and Clinical Psychology*, 52, 651–657.

Quintero Johnson, J. M., & Riles, J. (2016). "He acted like a crazy person": Exploring the influence of college students' recall of stereotypic media representations of mental illness. *Psychology of Popular Media Culture*. doi: 10.1037/ppm0000121

Rabinovitch, M. S., McLean, M. S., Markham, J. W., & Talbott, A. D. (1972). Children's violence perception as a function of television violence. In G. A. Comstock, E. A. Rubinstein, & J. P. Murray (Eds.), *Television and social behavior: Vol. 5. Television's effects: Further explorations*. Washington, DC: U.S. Government Printing Office.

Rader, B. G. (1984). *In its own image: How television has transformed sports*. New York: Free Press.

Rains, S. A. (2008). Health at high speed: Broadband Internet access, health communication, and the digital divide. *Communication Research*, 35, 283–297.

Raju, P. S., & Lonial, S. C. (1990). Advertising to children: Findings and implications. *Current Issues and Research in Advertising*, 12, 231–274.

Ramasubramanian, S. (2015). Using celebrity news stories to effectively reduce racial/ethnic prejudice: Celebrity news and prejudice reduction. *Journal of Social Issues*, 71(1), 123–138.

Ramasubramanian, S., & Oliver, M. B. (2007). Activating and suppressing hostile and benevolent racism: Evidence for comparative media stereotyping. *Media Psychology*, 9, 623–646.

Ramirez, A., Jr., Dimmick, J., Feaster, J., & Lin, S.-F. (2008). Revisiting interpersonal media competition: The gratification niches of instant messaging, e-mail, and the telephone. *Communication Research*, 35, 529–547.

Ramirez Berg, C. (1990). Stereotyping in films in general and of the Hispanic in particular. *Howard Journal of Communication*, 2, 286–300.

Ramirez Berg, C. (2002). *Latino images in film: Stereotypes, subversions, and resistance.* Austin, TX: University of Texas Press.

Raney, A. A. (2002). Moral judgment as a predictor of enjoyment of crime drama. *Media Psychology*, 4, 305–322.

Raney, A. A., & Bryant, J. (2002). Moral judgment and crime drama: An integrated theory of enjoyment. *Journal of Communication*, 52(2), 402–415.

Raney, A. A. & Bryant, J. (Eds.) (2006). *Handbook of sports and media.* Mahwah, NJ: Erlbaum.

Rappeport, A. & Sanger-Katz. M. (2016). Hillary Clinton takes a step to the left on health care. *The New York Times*, May 10. Retrieved from www.nytimes.com

Rasmussen, E. E., Rhodes, N., Ortiz, R. R., & White, S. R. (2016). The relation between norm accessibility, pornography use, and parental mediation among emerging adults. *Media Psychology*, 19(3), 431–454.

Rasmussen, E. E., Keene, J. R., Berke, C. K., Densley, R. L., & Loof, T. (2017). Explaining parental coviewing: The role of social facilitation and arousal. *Communication Monographs*, 84(3), 365–384.

Ravaja, N. (2004). Contributions of psychophysiology to media research: Review and recommendations. *Media Psychology*, 6, 193–235.

Rawson, H. (2003). The road to freedom fries. *American Heritage* (June/July), 12.

Rayner, K., Miller, B., & Rotello, C. M. (2008). Eye movements when looking at print advertisements: The goal of the viewer matters. *Applied Cognitive Psychology*, 22, 697–707.

Reams, J. C. P. (2016). Twenty-first century advertising and the plight of the elderly consumer. *Willamette Law Review*, 52, 325–352.

Reese-Weber, M., & McBride, D. M. (2015). The effects of sexually explicit literature on sexual behaviors and desires of women. *Psychology of Popular Media Culture*, 4(3), 251–257.

Reeve, D. K., & Aggleton, J. P. (1998). On the specificity of expert knowledge about a soap opera: An everyday story of farming folk. *Applied Cognitive Psychology*, 12, 35–42.

Reeves, B., & Nass, C. (1996). *The media equation: How people treat computer, television, and the new media like real people and places.* New York: Cambridge University Press.

Reeves, B., Thorson, E., Rothschild, M., McDonald, D., Hirsch, J., & Goldstein, R. (1985). Attention to television: Intrastimulus effects of movement and scene changes on alpha variation over time. *International Journal of Neuroscience*, 25, 241–255.

Reid, S. A. (2012). A self-categorization explanation for the hostile media effect. *Journal of Communication*, 62, 381–399.

Reid, S. A., & Hogg, M. A. (2005). A self-categorization explanation for the third-person effect. *Human Communication Research*, 31, 129–161.

Reilly, K. (2016). Hillary Clinton's response to criticism has changed. *Time*, April 29. Retrieved from http://time.com/

Reinecke, L., Tamborini, R., Grizzard, M., Lewis, R., Eden, A., & Bowman, N. D. (2012). Characterizing mood management as need satisfaction: The effects of intrinsic needs on selective exposure and mood repair. *Journal of Communication*, 62, 437–453.

Reinemann, C., & Maurer, M. (2005). Unifying or polarizing? Short-term effects of postdebate consequences of different rhetorical strategies in televised debates. *Journal of Communication*, 55, 775–794.

Reinhardt, J. D., Pennycott, A., & Fellinghauer, B. A. G. (2014). Impact of a film portrayal of a police officer with spinal cord injury on attitudes towards disability: A media effects experiment. *Disability and Rehabilitation*, 36(4), 289–294.

Rice, M. E., Chaplin, T. C., Harris, G. T., & Coutts, J. (1994). Empathy for the victim and sexual arousal among rapists and nonrapists. *Journal of Interpersonal Violence*, 9(4), 435–449.

Rice, M. L., Huston, A. C., & Wright, J. C. (1986). Replays as repetitions: Young children's interpretation of television forms. *Journal of Applied Developmental Psychology*, 7, 61–76.

Rice, M. L., Huston, A. C., Truglio, R., & Wright, J. C. (1990). Words from *Sesame Street*: Learning vocabulary skills while viewing. *Developmental Psychology*, 26, 421–428.

Rice, R. & Atkin, C. (2013). *Public communication campaigns.* Thousand Oaks, CA: Sage.

Rich, F. (1997). Mental illness still needs a spokesman. *Manhattan Mercury*, December 26, A7.

Richards, J. I. (1990). *Deceptive advertising*. Hillsdale, NJ: Erlbaum.

Richardson, G. W., Jr. (2001). Looking for meaning in all the wrong places: Why negative advertising is a suspect category. *Journal of Communication*, 51(4), 775–800.

Richardson, S. M., Paxton, S. J., & Thomson, J. S. (2009). Is BodyThink an efficacious body image and self-esteem program? A controlled revaluation with adolescents. *Body Image*, 6, 75–82.

Richter, W. (2017). Google, Facebook earn most online ad revenues. Retrieved from www.businessinsider.com

Riddle, K. (2012). Young adults' autobiographical memories of frightening news stories seen during childhood. *Communication Research*, 39(6), 738–756.

Riddle, K. (2014). A theory of vivid media violence. *Communication Theory*, 24(3), 291–310.

Riddle, K. (2018). Men's and women's situation models for violent movies and television programs. *Psychology of Popular Media Culture*, 7(1), 72–86.

Riddle, K., Potter, W. J., Metzger, M. J., Nabi, R. L., & Linz, D. G. (2011). Beyond cultivation: Exploring the effects of frequency, recency, and vivid autobiographical memories for violent media. *Media Psychology*, 14, 168–191.

Rideout, V., Foehr, U. G., & Roberts, D. F. (2010). *Generation M2: Media in the lives of 8- to 18-year-olds*. Menlo Park, CA: Kaiser Family Foundation.

Riffe, D., & Freitag, A. A. (1997). A content analysis of content analyses: Twenty-five years of *Journalism Quarterly*. *Journalism and Mass Communication Quarterly*, 74, 873–882.

Riffe, D., Lacy, S., & Fico, F. G. (1998). *Analyzing media messages: Using quantitative content analysis in research*. Mahwah, NJ: Erlbaum.

Riggle, E. D. B., Ellis, A. L., & Crawford, A. M. (1996). The impact of "media contact" on attitudes toward gay men. *Journal of Homosexuality*, 31(3), 55–69.

Riggs, M. (1992). *Color adjustment* [documentary, June 15]. New York: PBS.

Riley, A. H., Sood, S., Mazumdar, P. D., Choudary, N. N., Malhotra, A., & Sahba, N. (2017). Encoded exposure and social norms in entertainment-education. *Journal of Health Communication*, 22(1), 66–74.

Rimmer, L. (2002). Brand-new day. *World Press Review* (October), 36–37.

Rinallo, D., & Basuroy, S. (2009). Does advertising spending influence media coverage of the advertiser? *Journal of Marketing*, 73(6), 33–46.

Risley, F. (2008). *Abolition and the press: The moral struggle against slavery*. Evanston, IL: Northwestern University Press.

Ritchie, D., Price, V., & Roberts, D. F. (1987). Reading and television: A longitudinal investigation of the displacement hypothesis. *Communication Research*, 14, 292–315.

Rivadeneyra, R., Ward, L. M., & Gordon, M. (2007). Distorted reflections: Media exposure and Latino adolescents' conceptions of self. *Media Psychology*, 9, 261–290.

Roarty, A. (2017). Americans blame Facebook for fake news, new poll finds. Retrieved from www.mcclatchydc.com

Roberts, D. F. (2000). Media and youth: Access, exposure, and privatization. *Journal of Adolescent Health*, 27(2), 8–14.

Roberts, D. F., & Christenson, P. G. (2001). Popular music in childhood and adolescence. In D. G. Singer & J. L. Singer (Eds.), *Handbook of children and the media* (pp. 395–413). Thousand Oaks, CA: Sage.

Roberts, D. F., Henriksen, L., & Christenson, P. G. (1999). *Substance use in popular movies and music*. Washington, DC: Office of National Drug Control Policy.

Robinson, A. R., Hohmann, K. B., Rifkin, J. I., Topp, D., Gilroy, C. M., & Pickard, J. A. (2004). Direct-to-consumer pharmaceutical advertising: Physician and public opinion and potential effects on the physician-patient relationship. *Archives of Internal Medicine*, 164, 427–432.

Robinson, J. D. (1989). Mass media and the elderly: A uses and dependency interpretation. In J. F. Nussbaum (Ed.), *Lifespan communication* (pp. 319–337). Hillsdale, NJ: Erlbaum.

Robinson, J. D., & Skill, T. (2001). Five decades of families on television: From the 1950s through the 1990s. In J. Bryant & J. A. Bryant (Eds.), *Television and the American family*. 2nd ed. (pp. 139–162). Mahwah, NJ: Erlbaum.

Robinson, M. J., & Sheehan, M. A. (1983). *Over the wire and on TV: CBS and UPI in Campaign 80.* New York: Sage.

Robinson, P., Goddard, P., Parry, K., & Murray, C. (2009). Testing models of media performance in wartime: U.K. TV news and the 2003 invasion of Iraq. *Journal of Communication*, 59, 534–563.

Robinson, T. N., Saphir, M. N., Kraemer, H. C., Varady, A., & Haydel, K. F. (2001). Effects of reducing television viewing on children's request for toys: A randomized control trial. *Journal of Developmental and Behavioral Pediatrics*, 22, 179–184.

Robinson, T. N., Wilde, M. L., Navracruz, L. C., Haydel, F., & Varady, A. (2001). Effects of reducing children's television and video game use on aggressive behavior. *Archives of Pediatric and Adolescent Medicine*, 155, 17–23.

Roche, S. P., Pickett, J. T., & Gertz, M. (2016). The scary world of online news? Internet news exposure and public attitudes toward crime and justice. *Journal of Quantitative Criminology*, 32(2), 215–236.

Rodan, D., Ellis, K., & Lebek, P. (2014). *Disability, obesity, and ageing: Popular media identification.* Farnham: Ashgate Publishing.

Rodgers, K. B., & Hust, S. J. T. (2017). Sexual objectification in music videos and acceptance of potentially offensive sexual behaviors. *Psychology of Popular Media Culture*. doi: 10.1037/ppm0000142

Rodrigues, L. F., Oliveira, A., & Costa, C. J. (2016). Playing seriously: How gamification and social cues influence bank customers to use gamified e-business applications. *Computers in Human Behavior*, 63, 392–407.

Rogers, E. M., & Singhal, A. (1990). The academic perspective. In C. Atkin & L. Wallack (Eds.), *Mass communication and public health* (pp. 176–181). Newbury Park, CA: Sage.

Rogers, E. M., Vaughan, P. W., Swalehe, R. M. A., Rao, N., Svenkerud, P., & Sood, S. (1999). Effects of an entertainment-education radio soap opera on family planning behavior in Tanzania. *Studies in Family Planning*, 30(3), 193–211.

Rojahn, K., & Pettigrew, T. F. (1992). Memory for schema-relevant information: A meta-analytic resolution. *British Journal of Social Psychology*, 31, 81–109.

Rolandelli, D. R., Wright, J. C., Huston, A. C., & Eakins, D. (1991). Children's auditory and visual processing of narrated and nonnarrated television programming. *Journal of Experimental Child Psychology*, 51, 90–122.

Romer, D., Jamieson, K. H., & Aday, S. (2003). Television news and the cultivation of fear of crime. *Journal of Communication*, 53, 88–104.

Romer, D., Jamieson, P. E., & Jamieson, K. H. (2017). The continuing rise of gun violence in PG-13 movies, 1985 to 2015. *Pediatrics*, 139, 2–4.

Romero, S. (2000). A cell phone surge among world's poor in Haiti. *The New York Times*, December 19. Retrieved from www.nytimes.com/2000/12/19/technology/19CELL.html

Romero-Sánchez, M., Toro-García, V., Horvath, M. H., & Megías, J. L. (2017). More than a magazine: Exploring the links between lads' mags, rape myth acceptance, and rape proclivity. *Journal of Interpersonal Violence*, 32(4), 515–534.

Rosen, R. J. (2011). So, was Facebook responsible for the Arab Spring after all? *The Atlantic*, September 3. Retrieved from www.theatlantic.com

Rosenbaum, J., & Prinsky, L. (1987). Sex, violence, and rock 'n' roll: Youth's perception of popular music. *Popular Music and Society*, 11, 79–90.

Rosenberg, R., & Golding, B. (2016). Anthony Weiner sexted busty brunette while his son was in bed with him. *The New York Post*, August 29. Retrieved from https://nypost.com

Rosenberg, T. (2003). In Colombia, muckrakers have become scarce. *The New York Times*, July 3. Retrieved from www.nytimes.com

Rosenberg, T. (2017). In Africa, a glimpse of hope for beating H.I.V. *The New York Times*, September 19. Retrieved from www.nytimes.com/

Rosencrans, M. A., & Hartup, W. W. (1967). Imitative influences of consistent and inconsistent response consequences to a model on aggressive behavior in children. *Journal of Personality and Social Psychology*, 7, 429–434.

Rosengren, K. E., Wenner, L. A., & Palmgreen, P. (Eds.). (1985). *Media gratifications research: Current perspectives.* Newbury Park, CA: Sage.

Rosenkoetter, L. I. (1999). The television situation comedy and children's prosocial behavior. *Journal of Applied Social Psychology*, 29, 979–993.

Rosenqvist, J., Lahti-Nuuttila, P., Holdnack, J., Kemp, S. L., & Laasonen, M. (2016). Relationship of TV watching, computer use, and reading to children's neurocognitive functions. *Journal of Applied Developmental Psychology*, 46 11–21.

Rosenzweig, J. (1999). Can TV improve us? *The American Prospect*, 45, 58–63.

Ross, A. (2016). When music is violence. *The New Yorker*, July 4. Retrieved from www.newyorker.com/magazine/2016/07/04/when-music-is-violence

Rotfeld, H. J. (1988). Fear appeals and persuasion: Assumptions and errors in advertising research. *Current Issues and Research in Advertising*, 11, 21–40.

Rotunno, T. (2012). Armstrong loses eight sponsors in a day. Retrieved from www.cnbc.com

Rowling, C. M., Jones, T. M., & Sheets, P. (2011). Some dared call it torture: Cultural resonance, Abu Ghraib, and a selectively echoing press. *Journal of Communication*, 61, 1043–1061.

Roy, A., & Harwood, J. (1997). Underrepresented, positively portrayed: Older adults in television commercials. *Journal of Applied Communication Research*, 25, 39–56.

Rubin, A. M. (2002). The uses-and-gratifications perspective of media effects. In J. Bryant & D. Zillmann (Eds.), *Media effects: Advances in theory and research*. 2nd ed. (pp. 525–548). Mahwah, NJ: Erlbaum.

Rubin, A. M. (2009). Uses-and-gratifications perspective on media effects. In J. Bryant and M. B. Oliver (Eds.), *Media effects: Advances in theory and research*. 3rd ed. (pp. 165–184). New York: Taylor & Francis.

Rubin, A. M., & Perse, E. M. (1988). Audience activity and soap opera involvement. *Human Communication Research*, 14, 246–268.

Rubin, A. M., Perse, E. M., & Powell, R. A. (1985). Loneliness, parasocial interaction, and local television news viewing. *Human Communication Research*, 12, 155–180.

Rubin, A. M., Perse, E. M., & Taylor, D. S. (1988). A methodological examination of cultivation. *Communication Research*, 15, 107–134.

Rubin, D. C. (1995). *Memory in oral traditions: The cognitive psychology of epic, ballads, and counting-out rhymes*. New York: Oxford University Press.

Rubin, R. B., & McHugh, M. P. (1987). Development of parasocial interaction relationships. *Journal of Broadcasting & Electronic Media*, 31, 279–292.

Ruiter, R. A. C., Kessels, L. T. E., Peters, G.-J. Y., & Kok, G. (2014). Sixty years of fear appeal research: Current state of the evidence. *International Journal of Psychology*, 49(2), 63–70.

Rumelhart, D. E. (1980). Schemata: Building blocks of cognition. In R. J. Spiro, B. C. Bruce, & W. F. Brewer (Eds.), *Theoretical issues in reading comprehension* (pp. 33–58). Hillsdale, NJ: Erlbaum.

Ruoff, J. (2002). *An American family: A televised life*. Minneapolis: University of Minnesota Press.

Russell, C. A., Swasy, J. L., Russell, D. W., & Engel, L. (2017). Eye-tracking evidence that happy faces impair verbal message comprehension: The case of health warnings in direct-to-consumer pharmaceutical television commercials. *International Journal of Advertising*, 36(1), 82–106.

Russell, J. A., & Barrett, L. F. (1999). Core affect, prototypical emotional episodes, and other things called emotion: Dissecting the elephant. *Journal of Personality and Social Psychology*, 76(5), 805–819.

Russo, J. E., Metcalf, B. L., & Stephens, D. (1981). Identifying misleading advertising. *Journal of Consumer Research*, 8, 119–131.

Russo, V. (1981). *The celluloid closet: Homosexuality in the movies*. New York: Harper & Row.

Russonello, G. (2017). Jimmy Kimmel accuses Bill Cassidy, G.O.P. Senator behind health bill, of lying. *The New York Times*, September 20. Retrieved from www.nytimes.com

Rutenberg, J. (2017a). As Trump berates news media, a new strategy is needed to cover him. *The New York Times*, January 11. Retrieved from www.nytimes.com

Rutenberg, J. (2017b). Colbert, Kimmel and the politics of late night. *The New York Times*, September 24. Retrieved from www.nytimes.com

Ruva, C. L., & Guenther, C. C. (2015). From the shadows into the light: How pretrial publicity and deliberation affect mock jurors' decisions, impressions, and memory. *Law and Human Behavior*, 39(3), 294–310.

Ruva, C., McEvoy, C., & Bryant, J. B. (2007). Effects of pre-trial publicity and jury deliberation on juror bias and source memory errors. *Applied Cognitive Psychology*, 21(1), 45–67.

Ryalls, E. (2012). Demonizing "mean girls" in the news: Was Phoebe Prince "bullied to death?" *Communication, Culture & Critique*, 5(3), 463–481.

Ryzik, M. (2016). Can television be fair to Muslims? *The New York Times*, November 30. Retrieved from www.nytimes.com/

Sacchi, D. L. M., Agnoli, F., & Loftus, E. F. (2007). Changing history: Doctored photographs affect memory for past public events. *Applied Cognitive Psychology*, 21, 1005–1022

Sachs, A. (2002). Oprah turns the page. *Time*, April 15, p. 63.

Sagarin, B., Britt, M. A., Heider, J. D., Wood, S. E., & Lynch, J. E. (2005). Intrusive technology: Bartering and stealing consumer attention. In W. R. Walker & D. J. Herrmann (Eds.), *Cognitive technology: Essays on the transformation of thought and society* (pp. 69–88). Jefferson, NC: McFarland.

St. John Kelly, E. (1998). Springer's harvest. *The New York Times*, April 27. Retrieved from www. nytimes.com

Saito, S. (2007). Television and the cultivation of gender-role attitudes in Japan: Does television contribute to the maintenance of the status quo? *Journal of Communication*, 57(3), 511–531.

Saleem, M., Anderson, C. A., & Gentile, D. A. (2012). Effects of prosocial, neutral, and violent video games on college students' affect. *Aggressive Behavior*, 38(4), 263–271.

Salomon, G. (1984). Television is "easy" and print is "tough": The differential investment of mental effort in learning as a function of perceptions and attributions. *Journal of Educational Psychology*, 76, 647–658.

Salomon, G. (1987). Television and reading: The roles of orientations and reciprocal relations. In M. E. Manley-Casimir & C. Luke (Eds.), *Children and television* (pp. 15–33). New York: Praeger.

Samson, L., & Potter, R. F. (2016). Empathizing and systemizing (un)justified mediated violence: Psychophysiological indicators of emotional response. *Media Psychology*, 19(1), 156–180.

Sanborn, F. W. (2004). Cross-sex friendships: A cross-sectional exploration (Unpublished doctoral dissertation). Kansas State University, Manhattan, KS.

Sanders, M. S., & Ramasubramanian, S. (2012). An examination of African Americans' stereotyped perceptions of fictional media characters. *Howard Journal of Communications*, 23(1), 17–39.

Sapolsky, B. S. (1984). Arousal, affect, and the aggression-moderating effect of erotica. In N. M. Malamuth & E. Donnerstein (Eds.), *Pornography and sexual aggression* (pp. 85–113). Orlando, FL: Academic Press.

Sapolsky, B. S., & Molitor, F. (1996). Content trends in contemporary horror films. In J. B. Weaver & R. Tamborini (Eds.), *Horror films: Current research on audience preferences and reactions* (pp. 33–48). Mahwah, NJ: Erlbaum.

Sargent, J. D., Beach, M. L., Dalton, M. A., Mott, L. A., Tickle, J. J., Ahrens, M. B., & Heatherton, T. F. (2001). Effect of seeing tobacco use in films on trying smoking among adolescents: Cross sectional study. *British Medical Journal*, 323, 1394–1397.

Sauer, J. D., Drummond, A., & Nova, N. (2015). Violent video games: The effects of narrative context and reward structure on in-game and postgame aggression. *Journal of Experimental Psychology: Applied*, 21(3), 205–214.

Saux, G., Britt, A., Le Bigot, L., Vibert, N., Burin, D., & Rouet, J. (2017). Conflicting but close: Readers' integration of information sources as a function of their disagreement. *Memory & Cognition*, 45(1), 151–167.

Scarborough, R. C., & McCoy, C. A. (2016). Moral reactions to reality TV: Television viewers' endogenous and exogenous loci of morality. *Journal of Consumer Culture*, 16(1), 164–191.

Schachter, S., & Singer, J. E. (1962). Cognitive, social, and physiological determinants of emotional state. *Psychological Review*, 69, 379–399.

Schacter, D. L. (1996). *Searching for memory*. New York: Basic Books.

Scharrer, E. (2001). From wise to foolish: The portrayal of the sitcom father, 1950s–1990s. *Journal of Broadcasting & Electronic Media*, 45(1), 23–40.

Scharrer, E. (2005). Hypermasculinity, aggression, and television violence: An experiment. *Media Psychology*, 7, 353–376.

Scharrer, E. (2006). "I noticed more violence": The effects of a media literacy program on critical attitudes toward media violence. *Journal of Mass Media Ethics*, 21(1), 69–86.

Scharrer, E., & Ramasubramanian, S. (2015). Intervening in the media's influence on stereotypes of race and ethnicity: The role of media literacy education. *Journal of Social Issues*, 71(1), 171–185.

Schaub, M. (2017). Trump's claim to have come up with the term "fake news" is fake news, Merriam-Webster dictionary says. *Los Angeles Times*, October 9. Retrieved from www.latimes.com

Scheele, B., & DuBois, F. (2006). Catharsis as a moral form of entertainment. In J. Bryant & P. Vorderer (Eds.), *Psychology of entertainment* (pp. 405–422). Mahwah, NJ: Erlbaum.

Scheiber, N. (2017). Facebook's ad-targeting problem, captured in a literal shade of gray. *The New York Times*, September 28. Retrieved from www.nytimes.com

Schemer, C. (2012). Reinforcing spirals of negative affects and selective attention to advertising in a political campaign. *Communication Research*, 39(3), 413–434.

Schenk-Hamlin, W. J., Procter, D. E., & Rumsey, D. J. (2000). The influence of negative advertising frames on political cynicism and politician accountability. *Human Communication Research*, 26, 53–74.

Scheufele, D. A., & Tewksbury, D. (2007). Framing, agenda-setting, and priming. *Journal of Communication*, 57, 9–20.

Schiappa, E., Allen, M., & Gregg, P. B. (2007). Parasocial relationships and television: A meta-analysis of the effects. In R. W. Preiss, B. M. Gayle, N. Burrell, M. Allen, & J. Bryant (Eds.), *Mass media effects research: Advances through meta-analysis* (pp. 301–314). Mahwah, NJ: Erlbaum.

Schill, D., & Kirk, R. (2014). Courting the swing voter: "Real Time" insights into the 2008 and 2012 US presidential debates. *American Behavioral Scientist*, 58(4), 536–555.

Schill, D., & Kirk, R. (2017). Angry, passionate, and divided: Undecided voters and the 2016 presidential election. *American Behavioral Scientist*, 61(9), 1056–1076.

Schlenger, W. E., Caddell, J. M., Ebert, L., Jordan, B. K., Rourke, K. M., & Wilson, D. (2002). Psychological reactions to terrorist attacks: Findings from the national study of Americans' reactions to September 11. *Journal of the American Medical Association*, 288, 581–588.

Schleuder, J., McCombs, M. E., & Wanta, W. (1991). Inside the agenda-setting process: How political advertising and TV news prime viewers to think about issues and candidates. In F. Biocca (Ed.), *Television and political advertising: Psychological processes* (Vol. 1, pp. 265–309). Hillsdale, NJ: Erlbaum.

Schmader, T., Block, K., & Lickel, B. (2015). Social identity threat in response to stereotypic film portrayals: Effects on self-conscious emotion and implicit ingroup attitudes. *Journal of Social Issues*, 71(1), 54–72.

Schmitt, K. L., Anderson, D. R., & Collins, P. A. (1999). Form and content: Looking at visual features of television. *Developmental Psychology*, 35, 1156–1167.

Schmitt, K. L., Woolf, K. D., & Anderson, D. R. (2003). Viewing the viewers: Viewing behaviors by children and adults during television programs and commercials. *Journal of Communication*, 53, 265–281.

Schmitt, K. M., Gunther, A. C., & Liebhart, J. L. (2004). Why partisans see mass media as biased. *Communication Research*, 31, 623–641.

Schmitz, R. M. (2016). Constructing men as fathers: A content analysis of formulations of fatherhood in parenting magazines. *Journal of Men's Studies*, 24(1), 3–23.

Schneider, A. (1998). Advising Spielberg: A career studying the Amistad rebellion. *The Chronicle of Higher Education*, 44 (January 9), A12.

Schneider, J. A. (1987). Networks hold the line. In A. A. Berger (Ed.), *Television in society* (pp. 163–172). New Brunswick, NJ: Transaction Books.

Schneider, S. L., & Laurion, S. K. (1993). Do we know what we've learned from listening to the news? *Memory & Cognition*, 21, 198–209.

Scholfield, J., & Pavelchak, M. (1985). The day after: The impact of a media event. *American Psychologist*, 40, 542–548.

Schooler, C., Flora, J. A., & Farquhar, J. W. (1993). Moving toward synergy: Media supplementation in the Stanford five-city project. *Communication Research*, 20, 587–610.

Schooler, C., Sundar, S. S., & Flora, J. (1996). Effects of the Stanford five-city project media advocacy program. *Health Education Quarterly*, 23(3), 346–364.

Schooler, C., Chaffee, S. H., Flora, J. A., & Roser, C. (1998). Health campaign channels: Tradeoffs among reach, specificity, and impact. *Human Communication Research*, 24, 410–432.

Schooler, D. (2015). The woman next to me: Pairing powerful and objectifying representations of women. *Analyses of Social Issues and Public Policy*, 15(1), 198–212.

Schouten, A. P., Valkenburg, P. M., & Peter, J. (2007). Precursors and underlying processes of adolescents' online self-disclosure: Developing and testing an "internet-attribute-perception" model. *Media Psychology*, 10, 292–315.

Schulkind, M. D., Hennis, L. K., & Rubin, D. C. (1999). Music, emotion, and autobiographical memory: They're playing your song. *Memory & Cognition*, 27, 948–955.

Schwan, S., & Ildirar, S. (2010). Watching film for the first time: How adult viewers interpret perceptual discontinuities in film. *Psychological Science*, 21, 970–976.

Schwarz, N., & Brand, J. F. (1983). Effects of salience of rape on sex role attitudes, trust, and self-esteem in non-raped women. *European Journal of Social Psychology*, 13, 71–76.

Scott, D. K., Chanslor, M., & Dixon, J. (2014). Analysis of televised adolescent classroom news in the United States. *Journal of Children and Media*, 8(4), 457–473.

Scott, M. (2017). Facebook aims to tackle fake news ahead of U.K. election. *The New York Times*, May 8. Retrieved from www.nytimes.com

Scott, M., & Eddy, M. (2017). Europe combats a new foe of political stability: Fake news. *The New York Times*, February 20. Retrieved from www.nytimes.com

Segal, D. (2014). The great unwatched. *The New York Times*, May 3. Retrieved from www.nytimes.com

Segev, S., Fernandes, J., & Hong, C. (2016). Is your product really green? A content analysis reassessing green advertising. *Journal of Advertising*, 45(1), 85–93.

Seggar, J. F., Hafen, J., & Hannonen-Gladden, H. (1981). Television's portrayal of minorities and women in drama and comedy drama, 1971–1980. *Journal of Broadcasting*, 25(3), 277–288.

Seiter, J. S., & Gass, R. H. (2005). The effect of patriotic messages on restaurant tipping. *Journal of Applied Social Psychology*, 35, 1197–1205.

Selnow, G. W. (1997). *Electronic whistle-stops: The impact of the Internet on American politics*. New York: Praeger.

Senn, C. Y., & Desmarais, S. (2004). Impact of interaction with a partner or friend on the exposure effects of pornography and erotica. *Violence and Victims*, 19, 645–658.

Serisier, T. (2017). Sex crimes and the media. *Oxford Research Encyclopedia of Criminology*. Retrieved from http://criminology.oxfordre.com

Shaheen, J. G. (1984). *The TV Arab*. Bowling Green, OH: Bowling Green State University Popular Press.

Shaheen, J. G. (2008). *Guilty: Hollywood's verdicts on Arabs after 9/11*. Northampton, MA: Olive Branch Press.

Shaheen, J. G. (2014). *Reel bad Arabs: How Hollywood vilifies a people*. New York: Olive Branch Press.

Shain, R., & Phillips, J. (1991). The stigma of mental illness: Labeling and stereotyping in the news. In L. Wilkins & P. Patterson (Eds.), *Risky business: Communicating issues of science, risk, and public policy* (pp. 61–74). Westport, CT: Greenwood Press.

Shales, T. (2009). Remembering legendary CBS News anchor Walter Cronkite. *The Washington Post*, July 18. Retrieved from www.washingtonpost.com

Shane, S. (2018). The fake Americans Russia created to influence the election. *The New York Times*, January 20. Retrieved from www.nytimes.com

Shankman, A. (1978). Black pride and protest: The Amos 'n' Andy crusade. *Journal of Popular Culture*, 12, 236–252.

Shanteau, J., & Harris, R. J. (Eds.). (1990). *Organ donation and transplantation: Psychological and behavioral factors*. Washington, DC: American Psychological Association.

Shapiro, M. A. (1991). Memory and decision processes in the construction of social reality. *Communication Research*, 18, 3–24.

Shapiro, M. A., & Chock, T. M. (2003). Psychological processes in perceiving reality. *Media Psychology*, 5, 163–198.

Shapiro, M. A., & Kim, H. K. (2012). Realism judgment and mental resources: A cue processing model of media narrative realism. *Media Psychology*, 15, 93–119.

Shapiro, M. A., Barriga, C. A., & Beren, J. (2010). Causal attribution and perceived realism of stories. *Media Psychology*, 13, 273–300.

Shaw, M. (2017). Photos reveal media's softer tone on opioid crisis. *Columbia Journalism Review*, July 6. Retrieved from www.cjr.org

Sheafer, T., & Weimann, G. (2005). Agenda building, agenda setting, priming, individual voting intentions, and the aggregate results: An analysis of four Israeli elections. *Journal of Communication*, 55, 347–365.

Sheikh, A. A., Prasad, V. K., & Rao, T. R. (1974). Children's TV commercials: A review of research. *Journal of Communication*, 24(4), 126–136.

Sheldon, K. M., Abad, N., & Hinsch, C. (2011). A two-process view of Facebook use and relatedness need-satisfaction: Disconnection drives use, and connection rewards it. *Psychology of Popular Media Culture*, 1, 2–15.

Shen, F., & Eveland, W. P. (2010). Testing the intramedia interaction hypothesis: The contingent effects of news. *Journal of Communication*, 60, 364–387.

Sherman, E. (2017). Harley-Davidson pulls off marketing stunt ride with an entire town. Retrieved from www.inc.com

Shermer, M. (2015). Why climate skeptics are wrong. *Scientific American*, 313, 81.

Sherry, J. L. (2001). The effects of violent video games on aggression: A meta-analysis. *Human Communication Research*, 27, 409–431.

Sherry, J. L. (2002). Media saturation and entertainment-education. *Communication Theory*, 12, 206–224.

Sherry, J. L. (2007). Violent video games and aggression: Why can't we find effects? In R. W. Preiss, B. M. Gayle, N. Burrell, M. Allen, & J. Bryant (Eds.), *Mass media effects research: Advances through meta-analyses* (pp. 245–262). Mahwah, NJ: Erlbaum.

Shim, H., Oh, P., Song, H., & Lee, Y. (2015). An exploration of motivations for two screen viewing, social interaction behaviors, and factors that influence viewing intentions. *Cyberpsychology, Behavior, and Social Networking*, 18(3), 158–164.

Shimp, T. A., & Gresham, L. G. (1983). An information-processing perspective on recent advertising literature. *Current Issues and Research in Advertising*, 5, 39–75.

Shin, N. (2004). Exploring pathways from television viewing to academic achievement in school age children. *Journal of Genetic Psychology*, 165(4), 367–382.

Shniderman, A. B. (2014). Ripped from the headlines: Juror perceptions in the *Law and Order* era. *Law and Psychology Review*, 38, 97–133.

Shoemaker, P. J., Chang, T., & Brendlinger, N. (1987). Deviance as a predictor of news-worthiness: Coverage of international events in U.S. media. *Communication Yearbook*, 10, 348–365.

Shoemaker, P. J., Danielian, L. H., & Brendlinger, N. (1987). Deviant acts, risky business, and U.S. interests: The newsworthiness of world events. *Journalism Quarterly*, 68, 781–795.

Shoop, T. J. (2010). From professionals to potential first ladies: How newspapers told the stories of Cindy McCain and Michelle Obama. *Sex Roles*, 63, 807–819.

Shope, J. H. (2004). When words are not enough: The search for the effect of pornography on abused women. *Violence against Women*, 10, 56–72.

Shrum, L. J. (2001). Processing strategy moderates the cultivation effect. *Human Communication Research, 27*, 94–120.

Shrum, L. J. (2002). Media consumption and perceptions of social reality: Effects and underlying processes. In J. Bryant & D. Zillmann (Eds.), *Media effects: Advances in theory and research.* 2nd ed. (pp. 69–95). Mahwah, NJ: Erlbaum.

Shrum, L. J. (2009). Media consumption and perceptions of social reality: Effects and underlying processes. In J. Bryant & M. B. Oliver (Eds.), *Media effects: Advances in theory and research.* 3rd ed. (pp. 50–73). New York: Taylor & Francis.

Shrum, L. J., & Bischak, V. D. (2001). Mainstreaming, resonance, and impersonal impact: Testing moderators of the cultivation effect for estimates of crime risk. *Human Communication Research, 27*, 187–215.

Shrum, L. J., Lee, J., Burroughs, J. E., & Rindfleisch, A. (2011). An online processing model of second-order cultivation effects: How television cultivates materialism and its consequences for life satisfaction. *Human Communication Research, 37*, 34–57.

Siegel, A. N. (1956). Film-mediated fantasy aggression and strength of aggressive drive. *Child Development, 27*, 365–378.

Sigesmund, B. J. (2003). XXX-ceptable. Retrieved from www.msnbc.com/m/pt/printthismain. asp?storyID-934252

Signorielli, N. (1989). The stigma of mental illness on television. *Journal of Broadcasting and Electronic Media, 33*, 325–331.

Signorielli, N. (1990). Television's mean and dangerous world: A continuation of the Cultural Indicators perspective. In N. Signorielli & M. Morgan (Eds.), *Cultivation analysis: New directions in media effects research* (pp. 85–106). Newbury Park, CA: Sage.

Signorielli, N. (1993). Television, the portrayal of women, and children's attitudes. In G. L. Berry & J. K. Asamen (Eds.), *Children and television: Images in a changing sociocultural world* (pp. 229–242). Newbury Park, CA: Sage.

Signorielli, N. (2001). Television's gender role images and contribution to stereotyping. In D. G. Singer & J. L. Singer (Eds.), *Handbook of children and the media* (pp. 341–358). Thousand Oaks, CA: Sage.

Silva, D. (2017). Trump tweets video of himself body-slamming "CNN." Retrieved from www. nbcnews.com

Silver, R. C., Holman, E. A., McIntosh, D. M., Poulin, M., & Gil-Rivas, V. (2002). Nationwide longitudinal study of psychological responses to September 11. *Journal of the American Medical Association, 288*, 1235–1244.

Simmons, R. (2002). *Odd girl out: The hidden culture of aggression in girls.* New York: Harcourt.

Simon, L., & Daneback, K. (2013). Adolescents' use of the internet for sex education: A thematic and critical review of the literature. *International Journal of Sexual Health, 25*(4), 305–319.

Simons, D. A., Wurtele, S. K., & Durham, R. L. (2008). Developmental experiences of child sexual abusers and rapists. *Child Abuse & Neglect, 32*(5), 549–560.

Simons, D. J., & Ambinder, M. S. (2005). Change blindness: Theory and consequences. *Current Directions in Psychological Science, 14*, 44–48.

Simons, D. J., & Chabris C. F. (1999). Gorillas in our midst: Sustained inattentional blindness for dynamic events. *Perception, 28*, 1059–1074.

Simons, D. J., & Levin, D. T. (1997). Change blindness. *Trends in Cognitive Sciences, 8*, 261–267.

Simons, D. J., & Levin, D. T. (1998). Failure to detect changes to people in a real-world interaction. *Psychonomic Bulletin & Review, 5*, 644–649.

Simons, R. F., Detenber, B. H., Cuthbert, B. N., Schwartz, D. D., & Reiss, J. E. (2003). Attention to television: Alpha power and its relationship to image motion and emotional content. *Media Psychology, 5*, 283–301.

Singer, D. G., & Singer, J. L. (1983). Learning how to be intelligent consumers of television. In M. J. A. Howe (Ed.), *Learning from television: Psychological and educational research* (pp. 203–222). London: Academic Press.

Singer, D. G., Zuckerman, D. M., & Singer, J. L. (1980). Helping elementary school children learn about TV. *Journal of Communication, 30*(3), 84–93.

Singer, D. G., Singer, J. L., & Zuckerman, D. M. (1981). *Getting the most out of TV*. Santa Monica, CA: Goodyear.

Singer, J. L., & Singer, D. G. (1976). Can TV stimulate imaginative play? *Journal of Communication*, 26, 74–80.

Singer, J. L., & Singer, D. G. (1981). *Television, imagination, and aggression: A study of preschoolers*. Hillsdale, NJ: Erlbaum.

Singer, J. L., & Singer, D. G. (1998). Barney & Friends as entertainment and education. In J. K. Asamen & G. Berry (Eds.), *Research paradigms, television, and social behavior* (pp. 305–367). Thousand Oaks, CA: Sage.

Singer, M. I., Slovak, K., Frierson, T., & York, P. (1998). Viewing preferences, symptoms of psychological trauma, and violent behaviors among children who watch television. *Journal of the American Academy of Child and Adolescent Psychiatry*, 37(10), 1041–1048.

Singer, N. (2017). Silicon Valley courts brand-name teachers, raising ethics issues. *The New York Times*, September 2. Retrieved from www.nytimes.com

Singhal, A., & Rogers, E. M. (1989a). Prosocial television for development in India. In R. E. Rice & C. Atkin (Eds.), *Public communication campaigns*. 2nd ed. (pp. 331–350). Newbury Park, CA: Sage.

Singhal, A., & Rogers, E. M. (1989b). Entertainment-education strategies for family planning. *Populi*, 16(2), 38–47.

Singhal, A., & Rogers, E. M. (1989c). *India's information revolution*. New Delhi: Sage.

Singhal, A., & Rogers, E. M. (1999). *Entertainment-education: A communication strategy for social change*. Mahwah, NJ: Erlbaum.

Singhal, A., & Rogers, E. M. (2002). A theoretical agenda for entertainment-education. *Communication Theory*, 12, 117–135.

Singhal, A., Cody, M., Rogers, E., & Sabido, M. (Eds.). (2004). *Entertainment-education and social change: History, research, and practice*. Mahwah, NJ: Erlbaum.

Sinha, I., & Smith, M. F. (2000). Consumers' perceptions of promotional framing of price. *Psychology and Marketing*, 17(3), 257–275.

Sink, A., & Mastro, D. (2017). Depictions of gender on primetime television: A quantitative content analysis. *Mass Communication and Society*, 20(1), 3–22.

Sisario, B. (2013). Beyonce rejects tradition for social media's power. *The New York Times*, December 15. Retrieved from www.nytimes.com

Sivulka, J. (1998). *Soap, sex, and cigarettes: A cultural history of American advertising*. New York: Wadsworth.

Sivulka, J. (2001). *Stronger than dirt: A cultural history of advertising personal hygiene in American, 1875 to 1940*. New York: Humanity Books.

Skal, D. (1993). *The monster show: A cultural history of horror*. New York: Faber & Faber.

Skeggs, B., & Wood, H. (2012). *Reacting to reality television: Performance, audience, and value*. New York: Routledge.

Slater, D., & Elliott, W. R. (1982). Television's influence on social reality. *Quarterly Journal of Speech*, 68, 69–79.

Slater, M. D. (1990). Processing social information in messages: Social group familiarity, fiction versus nonfiction, and subsequent beliefs. *Communication Research*, 17, 327–343.

Slater, M. D. (2003). Alienation, aggression, and sensation seeking as predictor of adolescent use of violent film, computer, and website content. *Journal of Communication*, 53(1), 105–121.

Slater, M. D., & Rasinski, K. A. (2005). Media exposure and attention as mediating variables influencing social risk judgments. *Journal of Communication*, 55, 810–827.

Slater, M. D., & Rouner, D. (2002). Entertainment-education and elaboration likelihood: Understanding the process of narrative persuasion. *Communication Theory*, 12, 173–191.

Slater, M. D., Henry, K. L., Swaim, R. C., & Cardador, J. M. (2004). Vulnerable teens, vulnerable times: How sensation seeking, alienation, and victimization moderate the violent media content-aggressiveness relation. *Communication Research*, 31, 642–668.

Slater, M. D., Hayes, A. F., & Ford, V. L. (2007). Examining the moderating and mediating roles of news exposure and attention on adolescent judgments of alcohol-related risks. *Communication Research*, 34, 355–381.

Slovic, P., Finucane, M. L., Peters, E., & MacGregor, D. G. (2004). Risks as analysis and risk as feelings: Some thoughts about affect, reason, risk, and rationality. *Risk Analysis*, 24, 311–321.

Smith, A. (2016). Fifteen percent of American adults have used online dating sites or mobile dating apps. Retrieved from www.pewinternet.org/

Smith, C. (2007). Pornography for women, or what they don't show you in Cosmo! *Journalism Studies*, 8(4), 529–538.

Smith, M. (2013). Youth viewing sexually explicit material online: Addressing the elephant on the screen. *Sexuality Research and Social Policy*, 10(1), 62–75.

Smith, M. E., & Gevins, A. (2004). Attention and brain activity while watching television: Components of viewer engagement. *Media Psychology*, 6, 285–305.

Smith, S. L., & Atkin, C. (2003). Television advertising and children: Examining the intended and unintended effects. In E. L. Palmer & B. M. Young (Eds.), *The faces of televisual media: Teaching, violence, and selling to children* (pp. 327–346). Mahwah, NJ: Erlbaum.

Smith, S. L., & Choueiti, M. (2010). Gender disparity on screen and behind the camera in family films: The executive report. Retrieved from www.seejane.org

Smith, S. L., & Cook, C. A. (2008). Gender stereotypes: An analysis of popular films and TV. Retrieved from www.seejane.org

Smith, S. L., Nathanson, A. I., & Wilson, B. J. (2002). Prime-time television: Assessing violence during the most popular viewing hours. *Journal of Communication*, 52, 84–111.

Smith, S. L., Choueiti, M., Prescott, K., & Pieper, K. (2013). Gender roles and occupations: A look at character attributes and job aspirations in film and television. Retrieved from www.seejane.org

Smith, S. L., Choueiti, M., & Pieper, K. (2014). Gender bias without borders. Retrieved from www.seejane.org

Smith, S. L., Choueiti, M., & Pieper, K. (2016a). Inclusion or invisibility? Comprehensive Annenberg report on diversity in entertainment. Retrieved from http://annenberg.usc.edu

Smith, S. L., Choueiti, M., & Pieper, K. (2016b). Inequality in 800 popular films: Examining portrayals of gender, race/ethnicity, LGBT, and disability from 2007–2015. Retrieved from http://annenberg.usc.edu

Smith, S. L., Pieper, K., & Choueiti, M. (2016). The rare and ridiculed: Senior citizens in the top 100 films of 2015. Retrieved from http://annenberg.usc.edu

Smith, S. L., Choueiti, M., & Pieper, K. (2017). Over sixty, underestimated: A look at aging on the "silver" screen in best picture nominated films. Retrieved from http://annenberg.usc.edu

Smith, S. W., Smith, S. L., Pieper, K. M., Yoo, J. H., Ferris, A. L., Downs, E., & Bowden, B. (2006). Altruism on American television: Examining the amount of, and context surrounding, acts of helping and sharing. *Journal of Communication*, 56, 707–727.

Smith, T. J., & Martin-Portugues Santacreu, J. Y. (2017). Match-action: The role of motion and audio in creating global change blindness in film. *Media Psychology*, 20(2), 317–348.

Smith, T. J., Levin, D., & Cutting, J. E. (2012). A window on reality: Perceiving edited moving images. *Current Directions in Psychological Science*, 21, 104–113.

Smith, T. M. (1998). *The myth of green marketing: Tending our goats at the edge of apocalypse.* Toronto: University of Toronto Press.

Snider, M. (2017). *Playboy* brings nudity back to magazine. *USA Today*, February 13. Retrieved from www.usatoday.com

Snyder, L. B. (2007). Meta-analyses of mediated health campaigns. In R. W. Preiss, B. M. Gayle, N. Burrell, M. Allen, & J. Bryant (Eds.), *Mass media effects research: Advances through meta-analysis* (pp. 327–344). Mahwah, NJ: Erlbaum.

Sokmensuer, H. (2018). Love triangle murder-suicide: Woman fatally shoots husband's alleged mistress before killing self. *People*, April 25. Retrieved from http://people.com/

Soley, L. (1983). The effect of black models on magazine ad readership. *Journalism Quarterly,* 60(4), 686–690.

Solomon, D. S., & Cardillo, B. A. (1985). The elements and process of communication campaigns. In T. A. van Dijk (Ed.), *Discourse and communication* (pp. 60–68). Berlin: de Gruyter.

Solomon, N. (2009). Cronkite and Vietnam: Beyond the hype. Retrieved from www. huffingtonpost.com

Solorio, R., Norton-Shelpuk, P., Forehand, M., Montaño, D., Stern, J., Aguirre, J., & Martinez, M. (2016). Tu amigo pepe: Evaluation of a multi-media marketing campaign that targets young Latino immigrant MSM with HIV testing messages. *AIDS and Behavior,* 20(9), 1973–1988.

Somaiya, R. (2015). As Playboy and Penthouse fade, newer magazines tilt artistic. *The New York Times,* January 18. Retrieved from www.nytimes.com

Sommerfeld, J. (2002). Most weight-loss ads too good to be true, report shows. MSNBC online news, September 17.

Sommers-Flanagan, R., Sommers-Flanagan, J., & Davis, B. (1993). What's happening on music television? *Sex Roles,* 28, 745–753.

Sonnett, J., Johnson, K. A., & Dolan, M. K. (2015). Priming implicit racism in television news: Visual and verbal limitations on diversity. *Sociological Forum,* 30(2), 328–347.

Sood, S. (2002). Audience involvement and entertainment-education. *Communication Theory,* 12, 153–172.

Soriano, C. R. R., Lim, S. S., & Rivera-Sanchez, M. (2015). The Virgin Mary with a mobile phone: Ideologies of mothering and technology consumption in Philippine television advertisements. *Communication, Culture & Critique,* 8(1), 1–19.

Southwell, B. G. (2005). Between messages and people: A multilevel model of memory for television content. *Communication Research,* 32, 112–140.

Southwell, B. G., & Torres, A. (2006). Connecting interpersonal and mass communication: Science news exposure, perceived ability to understand science, and conversation. *Communication Monographs,* 73, 334–350.

Spangler, L. C. (1989). A historical overview of female friendships in prime-time television. *Journal of Popular Culture,* 22(4), 13–23.

Spangler, L. C. (1992). Buddies and pals: A history of male friendships on prime-time television. In S. Craig (Ed.), *Men, masculinity, and the media* (pp. 93–110). Newbury Park, CA: Sage.

Sparks, G. G. (2016). *Media effects research: A basic overview.* 5th ed. Boston, MA: Cengage.

Sparks, G. G., & Sparks, C. W. (2000). Violence, mayhem, and horror. In D. Zillmann & P. Vorderer (Eds.), *Media entertainment: The psychology of its appeal* (pp. 73–91). Mahwah, NJ: Erlbaum.

Sparks, G. G., & Sparks, C. W. (2002). Effects of media violence. In J. Bryant & D. Zillmann (Eds.), *Media effects* (pp. 269–285). Mahwah, NJ: Erlbaum.

Sparks, G. G., Pellechia, M., & Irvine, C. (1999). The repressive coping style and fright reactions to mass media. *Communication Research,* 26, 176–192.

Sparks, G. G., Sparks, C. W., & Sparks, E. A. (2009). Media violence. In J. Bryant & M.B. Oliver (Eds.), *Media effects: Advances in theory and research.* 3rd ed. (pp. 269–286). New York: Taylor & Francis.

Special Committee on Pornography and Prostitution (1985). *Report* (Vol. 1). Ottawa: Minister of Supply.

Speers, S., Harris, J., & Schwartz, M. (2011). Child and adolescent exposure to food and beverage brand appearances during prime-time television programming. *American Journal of Preventive Medicine,* 41(3), 291–296.

Sperber, M. (2001). *Beer and circus: How big-time college sports is crippling undergraduate education.* New York: Henry Holt.

Spezio, M. L., Loesch, L., Gosselin, F., Mattes, K., & Alvarez, R. M. (2012). Thin-slice decisions do not need faces to be predictive of election outcomes. *Political Psychology,* 33(3), 331–341.

Sprafkin, J. N., Gadow, K. D., & Abelman, R. (1992). *Television and the exceptional child: A forgotten audience.* Hillsdale, NJ: Erlbaum.

Squires, N. (2008). Prince Harry: magazine "unaware" of embargo. *The Daily Telegraph*, February 29. Retrieved from www.telegraph.co.uk

Srinivasan, S., Rutz, O. J., & Pauwels, K. (2016). Paths to and off purchase: Quantifying the impact of traditional marketing and online consumer activity. *Journal of the Academy of Marketing Science*, 44(4), 440–453.

Stall, R. D., Coates, T. J., & Hoff, C. (1988). Behavioral risk reduction for HIV infection among gay and bisexual men. *American Psychologist*, 43, 878–885.

Stanley, A. (2000). Rome journal. *The New York Times*, September 14.

Stayman, D. M., & Kardes, F. R. (1992). Spontaneous inference processes in advertising: Effects of need for cognition and self-monitoring on inference generation and utilization. *Journal of Consumer Psychology*, 1, 125–142.

Steel, E. (2015). "Sesame Street" to air first on HBO for next 5 seasons. *The New York Times*, August 13. Retrieved from www.nytimes.com/

Steel, E. (2016). Nielsen plays catch-up as streaming era wreaks havoc on TV Raters. *The New York Times*, February 2. Retrieved from www.nytimes.com/

Steinberg , B. (2016). TV ad prices: Football hikes, "Walking Dead" stumbles, "Chicago Fire," "Goldbergs" on the rise. Retrieved from http://variety.com/

Steinem, G. (1990). Sex, lies, and advertising. *Ms* (July/August), pp. 18–28.

Steinhauer, J. (2014). In U.S., fear of Ebola closes schools and shapes politics. *The New York Times*, October 19. Retrieved from www.nytimes.com

Stelter, B. (2008). TV networks rewrite the definition of a news bureau. *The New York Times*, August 12. Retrieved from www.nytimes.com

Stelter, B. (2016). How ABC covered the awful news involving its parent Disney. Retrieved from www.cnn.com

Stephens, N., & Stutts, M. A. (1982). Preschoolers' ability to distinguish between television programming and commercials. *Journal of Advertising*, 11, 16–26.

Stephenson, M. T. (2003). Examining adolescents' responses to antimarijuana PSAs. *Human Communication Research*, 29, 343–369.

Stermer, S. P., & Burkley, M. (2015). SeX-Box: Exposure to sexist video games predicts benevolent sexism. *Psychology of Popular Media Culture*, 4(1), 47–55.

Stern, S. R., & Mastro, D. E. (2004). Gender portrayals across the lifespan: A content analytic look at broadcast commercials. *Mass Communication and Society*, 7, 215–236.

Sternberg, R. J. & Sternberg, K. (2016). *Cognitive psychology*. 7th ed. Boston, MA: Cengage.

Stevens, E. M., & Garrett, K. P. (2016). Girls and sex: A content analysis of sexual health depictions in HBO's Girls. *Sexuality & Culture*, 20(4), 923–935.

Stewart, D. (1999). *The PBS companion: A history of public television*. New York: TV Books.

Stewart, D. W., Pavlou, P., & Ward, S. (2002). Media influences on marketing communications. In J. Bryant & D. Zillmann (Eds.), *Media effects*. 2nd ed. (pp. 353–396). Mahwah, NJ: Erlbaum.

Steyer, J. P. (2002). *The other parent: The inside story of media's effect on our children*. New York: Atria Books.

Stitt, C., & Kunkel, D. (2008). Food advertising during children's television programming on broadcast and cable channels. *Health Communication*, 23, 573–584.

Stiver, A., Barroca, L., Minocha, S., Richards, M., & Roberts, D. (2015). Civic crowdfunding research: Challenges, opportunities, and future agenda. *New Media & Society*, 17(2), 249–271.

Stolberg, S. G. (2001). C.D.C. injects dramas with health messages. Retrieved from www.nytimes.com/2001/06/26/health/26CDC.html

Stonehill, B. (1995). Hearts, smarts, and sparkle. *Los Angeles Times*, February 20.

Storey, J. D., Hess, R., & Saffitz, G. (2015). Social marketing. In K. Glanz, B. K. Rimer, & K. Viswanath (Eds.), *Health behavior: Theory, research, and practice* (pp. 411–438). San Francisco: Jossey-Bass.

Stotzer, R. L., & MacCartney, D. (2016). The role of institutional factors on on-campus reported rape prevalence. *Journal of Interpersonal Violence*, 31(16), 2687–2707.

Stout, D. A. (2012). *Media and religion: Foundations of an emerging field*. New York: Routledge.

Stransky, D. (2011). New product placement hits old sitcom reruns. *Entertainment Weekly*, July 22, p. 20.

Strasburger, V. C. (1995). *Adolescents and the media: Medical and psychological impact*. Thousand Oaks, CA: Sage.

Strasburger, V. C., & Donnerstein, E. (1999). Children, adolescents, and the media: Issues and solutions. *Pediatrics*, 103, 129–139.

Strasburger, V. C., & Wilson, B. J. (2002). *Children, adolescents, and the media*. Thousand Oaks, CA: Sage.

Strasburger, V. C., Wilson, B. J., & Jordan, A. B. (2014). *Children, adolescents, and the media*. 3rd ed. Thousand Oaks, CA: Sage.

Straubhaar, J. D. (2007). *World television: From global to local*. Thousand Oaks, CA: Sage.

Strause, J. (2017). Mike Huckabee says "SNL" parody of his daughter was "sexist." Retrieved from www.hollywoodreporter.com

Strayer, D., Drews., F. A., Crouch, D. J., & Johnston, W. A. (2005). Why do cell phone conversations interfere with driving? In W. R. Walker & D. J. Herrmann (Eds.), *Cognitive technology: Essays on the transformation of thought and society* (pp. 51–68). Jefferson, NC: McFarland.

Strick, M., Holland, R. W., van Baaren, R. B., van Knippenberg, A., & Dijksterhuis, A. (2013). Humour in advertising: An associative processing model. *European Review of Social Psychology*, 24(1), 32–69.

Strick, M., de Bruin, H. L., de Ruiter, L. C., & Jonkers, W. (2015). Striking the right chord: Moving music increases psychological transportation and behavioral intentions. *Journal of Experimental Psychology: Applied*, 21(1), 57–72.

Strobel, W. P. (1997). *Late-breaking foreign policy: The news media's influence on peace operations*. Washington, DC: Institute of Peace Press.

Strohmaier, H., Murphy, M., & DeMatteo, D. (2014). Youth sexting: Prevalence rates, driving motivations, and the deterrent effect of legal consequences. *Sexuality Research and Social Policy*, 11(3), 245–255.

Strouse, J. A., & Fabes, R. A. (1985). Formal vs. informal sources of sex education: Competing forces in the sexual socialization process. *Adolescence*, 78, 251–263.

Štulhofer, A., Buško, V., & Landripet, I. (2010). Pornography, sexual socialization, and satisfaction among young men. In S. R. Harper & F. I. Harris (Eds.), *College men and masculinities: Theory, research, and implications for practice* (pp. 191–211). San Francisco: Jossey-Bass.

Stutts, M. A., & Hunnicutt, G. G. (1987). Can young children understand disclaimers in television commercials? *Journal of Advertising*, 16(1), 41–46.

Stutts, M. A., Vance, D., & Hudelson, S. (1981). Program-commercial separators in children's television: Do they help a child tell the difference between Bugs Bunny and The Quik Rabbit? *Journal of Advertising*, 10(2), 16–48.

Suleiman, M. W. (1988). *The Arabs in the mind of America*. Brattleboro, VT: Amana Books.

Sullivan, D. B. (2006). Broadcast television and the game of packaging sports. In A. A. Raney & J. Bryant (Eds.), *Handbook of sports and media* (pp. 131–145). Mahwah, NJ: Erlbaum.

Sullivan, S. (2014). Republican Jolly wins Florida special election. *The Washington Post*, March 11. Retrieved from www.washingtonpost.com

Sun, C., Bridges, A., Johnson, J. A., & Ezzell, M. B. (2016). Pornography and the male sexual script: An analysis of consumption and sexual relations. *Archives of Sexual Behavior*, 45(4), 983–994.

Sun, Y., Pan, Z., & Shen, L. (2008). Understanding the third-person perception: Evidence from a meta-analysis. *Journal of Communication*, 58, 280–300.

Surette, R. (2015). *Media, crime, and criminal justice: Images, realities, and policies*. 5th ed. Stamford, CT: Cengage Learning.

Suschinsky, K. D., & Lalumière, M. L. (2011). Prepared for anything? An investigation of female genital arousal in response to rape cues. *Psychological Science*, 22(2), 159–165.

Sutton, M. J., Brown, J. D., Wilson, K. M., & Klein, J. D. (2002). Shaking the tree of knowledge for forbidden fruit: Where adolescents learn about sexuality and contraception. In J. D. Brown,

J. R. Steele, & K. Walsh-Childers (Eds.), *Sexual teens, sexual media* (pp. 25–55). Mahwah, NJ: Erlbaum.

Swant, M. (2017). Facebook raked in $9.16 billion in ad revenue in the second quarter of 2017. Retrieved from www.adweek.com

Sweeney, D. (2017). News anchor's water broke on-air. She finished her report, then had a baby boy. *The Miami Herald*, September 29. Retrieved from www.miamiherald.com

Swift, A. (2016). Americans' trust in mass media sinks to new low. *Gallup*, September 14. Retrieved from https://news.gallup.com

Swing, E. L., & Anderson, C. A. (2014). The role of attention problems and impulsiveness in media violence effects on aggression. *Aggressive Behavior*, 40(3), 197–203.

Sypher, B. D., McKinley, M., Ventsam, S., & Valdeavellano, E. E. (2002). Fostering reproductive health through entertainment-education in the Peruvian Amazon: The social construction of Bienvenida Salud! *Communication Theory*, 12, 192–205.

Szalai, G. (2017). African drama *MTV Shuga* to get Indian version. *Hollywood Reporter*, July 11. Retrieved from www.hollywoodreporter.com/

Tackett, M. (2017). In Virginia governor's race, immigrants' turnout may be key. *The New York Times*, October 28. Retrieved from www.nytimes.com

Tai, Z. (2009). The structure of knowledge and dynamic of scholarly communication in agenda setting research, 1996–2005. *Journal of Communication*, 59, 481–513.

Tal-Or, N., & Tsfati, Y. (2007). On the substitutability of the third-person perception. *Media Psychology*, 10, 231–249.

Tal-Or, N., Cohen, J., Tsfati, Y., & Gunther, A.C. (2010). Testing causal direction in the influence of presumed media influence. *Communication Research*, 37, 801–824.

Tamborini, R. (1996). A model of empathy and emotional reactions to horror. In J. B. Weaver, III & R. Tamborini (Eds.), *Horror films: Current research on audience preferences and reactions* (pp. 103–123). Mahwah, NJ: Erlbaum.

Tamborini, R., & Choi, J. (1990). The role of cultural diversity in cultivation research. In N. Signorielli & M. Morgan (Eds.), *Cultivation analysis: New directions in media effects research* (pp. 157–180). Newbury Park, CA: Sage.

Tamborini, R., & Stiff, J. (1987). Predictors of horror film attendance and appeal: An analysis of the audience for frightening films. *Communication Research*, 14, 415–436.

Tamborini, R., Stiff, J., & Zillmann, D. (1987). Preference for graphic horror featuring male versus female victimization: Individual differences associated with personality characteristics and past film viewing experiences. *Human Communication Research*, 13, 529–552.

Tamborini, R., Stiff, J., & Heidel, C. (1990). Reacting to graphic horror: A model of empathy and emotional behavior. *Communication Research*, 17, 616–640.

Tamborini, R., Grizzard, M., Bowman, N. D., Reinecke, L., Lewis, R. J., & Eden, A. (2011). Media enjoyment as need satisfaction: The contribution of hedonic and nonhedonic needs. *Journal of Communication*, 61, 1025–1042.

Tannen, D. (1990). *You just don't understand: Women and men in conversation.* New York: Ballantine Books.

Tannen, D. (1998). *The argument culture: Stopping America's war of words.* New York: Ballantine Books.

Tannenbaum, P. H. (1971). *Emotional arousal as a mediator of communication effects* (Technical reports of the Commission on Obscenity and Pornography, Vol. 8). Washington, DC: U.S. Government Printing Office.

Tannenbaum, P. H. (1980). Entertainment as vicarious emotional experience. In P. H. Tannenbaum (Ed.), *The entertainment functions of television* (pp. 107–131). Hillsdale, NJ: Erlbaum.

Tapper, J. (1995). The ecology of cultivation: A conceptual model for cultivation research. *Communication Theory*, 5, 36–57.

Taruskin, R. (2001). Music's dangers and the case for control. *The New York Times*, December 10. Retrieved from www.nytimes.com/2001/12/09/arts/music.09TARU.html

Tavernise, S. (2016). Safer to puff, e-cigarettes can't shake their reputation as a menace. *The New York Times*, November 1. Retrieved from www.nytimes.com/

Tavris, C. (1986). How to publicize science: A case study. In J. H. Goldstein (Ed.), *Reporting science: The case of aggression* (pp. 23–32). Hillsdale, NJ: Erlbaum.

Taylor, C. R., Lee, J. Y., & Stern, B. B. (1995). Portrayals of African, Hispanic, and Asian Americans in magazine advertising. *American Behavioral Scientist*, 38, 608–621.

Taylor, L. D. (2015). Men's sexual selectivity, romantic confidence, and gender ratios in the media. *Journal of Men's Studies*, 23(1), 107–113.

Taylor, S. (1982). The availability bias in social perception and interaction. In D. Kahneman, P. Slovic, & A. Tversky (Eds.), *Judgment under uncertainty: Heuristics and biases* (pp. 190–200). Cambridge: Cambridge University Press.

Taylor, T. (2005). Advertisers growing fond of dead celebrities. *Manhattan Mercury*, May 13, p. A6.

Te'eni-Harari, T., & Eyal, K. (2015). Liking them thin: Adolescents' favorite television characters and body image. *Journal of Health Communication*, 20(5), 607–615.

Teeny, J. Briñol, P., & Petty, R. E. (2017). The elaboration likelihood model: Understanding consumer attitude change. In C. V. Jansson-Boyd & M. J. Zawisza (Eds.). *Routledge international handbook of consumer psychology*. London: Routledge.

Teplin, L. A. (1985). The criminality of the mentally ill: A dangerous misconception. *American Journal of Psychiatry*, 142, 593–599.

Terry, C. P., & Terry, D. L. (2016). Distracted driving among college students: Perceived risk versus reality. *Current Psychology*, 35(1), 115–120.

Tewksbury, D. (1999). Differences in how we watch the news. *Communication Research*, 26, 4–29.

Tewksbury, D., & Rittenberg, J. (2012). *News on the internet: Information and citizenship in the 21st century*. New York: Oxford University Press.

Tewksbury, D., & Scheufele, D. A. (2009). News framing theory and research. In J. Bryant & M. B. Oliver (Eds.), *Media effects: Advances in theory and research*. 3rd ed. (pp. 17–33). New York: Taylor & Francis.

Tewksbury, D., Jensen, J., & Coe, K. (2011). Video news releases and the public: The impact of source labeling on the perceived credibility of television news. *Journal of Communication*, 61, 328–348.

Thakor, M. V., & Goneau-Lessard, K. (2009). Development of a scale to measure skepticism of social advertising among adolescents. *Journal of Business Research*, 62(12), 1342–1349.

Thaler, P. (1994). *The watchful eye: American justice in the age of the television trial*. New York: Praeger.

The Faustian bargain (1997, Sept. 6). *The Economist*, September 6.

The size of the World Wide Web (2017). Retrieved from www.worldwidewebsize.com/

Thomas, B. (2003). What the world's poor watch on TV. *World Press Review* (March), 30–33.

Thomas, S. (1986). Gender and social-class coding in popular photographic erotica. *Communication Quarterly*, 34(2), 103–114.

Thompson, D. (2016). Why do Americans distrust the media? Donald Trump, anti-elite sentiment, and the dark side of media abundance. *The Atlantic*, September 16. Retrieved from www.theatlantic.com

Thompson, R. A., & Nelson, C. A. (2001). Developmental science and the media: Early brain development. *American Psychologist*, 56, 5–15.

Thompson, T. L., & Zerbinos, E. (1995). Gender roles in animated cartoons: Has the picture changed in 20 years? *Sex Roles*, 32, 651–673.

Thompson, T. L., Kiang, L., & Witkow, M. R. (2016). "You're Asian; you're supposed to be smart": Adolescents' experiences with the Model Minority Stereotype and longitudinal links with identity. *Asian American Journal of Psychology*, 7(2), 108–119.

Thorson, E. (1990). Consumer processing of advertising. *Current Issues and Research in Advertising*, 12, 197–230.

Thorson, E., Christ, W. G., & Caywood, C. (1991). Selling candidates like tubes of toothpaste: Is the comparison apt? In F. Biocca (Ed.), *Television and political advertising: Psychological processes* (Vol. 1, pp. 145–172). Hillsdale, NJ: Erlbaum.

Tian, Q., & Hoffner, C. A. (2010). Parasocial interaction with liked, neutral, and disliked characters on a popular TV series. *Mass Communication and Society*, 13(3), 250–269.

Tickle, J. J., Sargent, J. D., Dalton, M. A., Beach, M. L., & Heatherton, T. F. (2001). Favourite movie stars, their tobacco use in contemporary movies, and its association with adolescent smoking. *Tobacco Control*, 10, 16–22.

Tiggemann, M. (2014). The status of media effects on body image research: Commentary on articles in the themed issue on body image and media. *Media Psychology*, 17(2), 127–133.

Timberg, C. (2016). Russian propaganda effort helped spread "fake news" during election experts say. *The Washington Post*, November 24. Retrieved from www.washingtonpost.com

Timmer, J. (2013). Television violence and industry self-regulation: The V-Chip, television program ratings, and the TV Parental Guidelines Oversight Monitoring Board. *Communication Law and Policy*, 18(3), 265–307.

Timmermans, E., & van den Bulck, J. (2018). Casual sexual scripts on the screen: A quantitative content analysis. *Archives of Sexual Behavior*, 47(5), 1481–1496.

Timpf, K. (2016). Top 18 dumbest GoFundMe pages that don't deserve your money. *National Review*, August 26. Retrieved from www.nationalreview.com/

Tinic, S. (1997). United Colors and untied meanings: Benetton and the commodification of social issues. *Journal of Communication*, 47(3), 3–25.

Tinsley, H. E. A., & Weiss, D. J. (2000). Interrater reliability and agreement. In H. E. A. Tinsley & S. D. Brown (Eds.), *Handbook of applied multivariate statistics and mathematical modeling* (pp. 95–124). San Diego, CA: Academic Press.

Toepfl, F. (2011). Managing public outrage: Power, scandal, and new media in contemporary Russia. *New Media & Society*, 13(8), 1301–1319.

Toney, G. T., & Weaver, J. B. (1994). Effects of gender and gender role self-perceptions on affective reactions to rock music videos. *Sex Roles*, 30, 567–583.

Toobin, J. (2017). The *National Enquirer*'s fervor for Trump. *The New Yorker*, June 26. Retrieved from www.newyorker.com

Took, K. J., & Weiss, D. S. (1994). The relationship between heavy metal and rap music and adolescent turmoil: Real or artifact? *Adolescence*, 29, 613–621.

Toplin, R. B. (1995). *History by Hollywood: The use and abuse of the American past*. Urbana: University of Illinois Press.

Torabi, M. R., & Seo, D. C. (2004). National study of behavior and life changes since September 11. *Health Education Behavior*, 31, 179–192.

Tower, R. B., Singer, D. G., & Singer, J. L. (1979). Differential effects of television programming on preschoolers' cognition, imagination, and social play. *American Journal of Orthopsychiatry*, 49, 265–281.

Toyama, M. (2008). Where older dogs are learning new tricks. *Time*, July 7, p. 4.

Trier, J. (2008a). The *Daily Show* with Jon Stewart: Part 1. *Journal of Adolescent and Adult Literacy*, 51(5), 424–428.

Trier, J. (2008b). The *Daily Show* with Jon Stewart: Part 2. *Journal of Adolescent and Adult Literacy*, 51(7), 600–606.

Troiano, G., Nante, N., & Cozzolino, M. (2017). The Angelina Jolie effect—impact on breast and ovarian cancer prevention: A systematic review of effects after the public announcement in May 2013. *Health Education Journal*, 76(6), 707–715.

Troilo, J. (2017). Stay tuned: Portrayals of fatherhood to come. *Psychology of Popular Media Culture*, 6(1), 82–94.

Truong, V. D. (2014). Social marketing: A systematic review of research 1998–2012. *Social Marketing Quarterly*, 20(1), 15–34.

Tryon, C. (2016). *Political TV*. New York: Routledge.

Tsay, M., & Bodine, B. M. (2012). Exploring parasocial interaction in college students as a multidimensional construct: Do personality, interpersonal need, and television motive predict their relationships with media characters? *Psychology of Popular Media Culture*, 1, 185–200.

Tsay-Vogel, M., & Krakowiak, K. M. (2016). Inspirational reality TV: The prosocial effects of lifestyle transforming reality programs on elevation and altruism. *Journal of Broadcasting & Electronic Media*, 60(4), 567–586.

Tsfati, T. (2007). Hostile media perceptions presumed media influence, and minority alienation. *Journal of Communication*, 57, 632–651.

Tsfati, Y., & Cappella, J. N. (2005). Why do people watch news they do not trust? The need for cognition as a mediator in the association between news media skepticism and exposure. *Media Psychology, 7*, 251–271.

Tsiantar, D. (2006). Getting on board. *Time*, April 10, A1–A4.

Tuchman, S., & Coffin, T. E. (1971). The influence of election nights television broadcasts in a close election. *Public Opinion Quarterly, 35*, 315–326.

Tukachinsky, R., Mastro, D., & Yarchi, M. (2015). Documenting portrayals of race/ethnicity on primetime television over a 20-year span and their association with national-level racial/ ethnic attitudes. *Journal of Social Issues, 71*(1), 17–38.

Tunstall, J. (2007). *The media were American: U.S. mass media in decline.* New York: Oxford University Press.

Turkle, S. (2011). *Alone together: Why we expect more from technology and less from each other.* New York: Basic Books.

Tversky, A., & Kahneman, D. (1973). Availability: A heuristic for judging frequency and probability. *Cognitive Psychology, 5*, 207–232.

Tversky, A., & Kahneman, D. (1974). Judgment under uncertainty: Heuristics and biases. *Science, 185*, 1124–1131.

Twitter (2017). Twitter counter, June 5. Retrieved from https://twittercounter.com/pages/100

Tyler, T. R. (2006). Viewing CSI and the threshold of guilt: Managing truth and justice in reality and fiction. *Yale Law Journal, 115*, 1050–1085.

Tynan, M. A., Polansky, J. R., Titus, K., Atayeva, R., & Glantz, S. A. (2017). Tobacco use in top-grossing movies: United States, 2010–2016. *MMWR. Morbidity and Mortality Weekly Report, 66*(26), 681–686.

Ume-Nwagbo, E. N. E. (1986). "Cock Crow at Dawn": A Nigerian experiment with television drama in development communication. *Gazette, 37*(4), 155–167.

U.S. Census Bureau (2016). Hispanic Heritage Month 2016. Retrieved from www.census.gov

U.S. Census Bureau (2017). Women's History Month: March 2017. Retrieved from www.census.gov

U.S. Energy Information Administration (2017). Average number of televisions in U.S. homes declining: Today in energy. Retrieved from www.eia.gov

Vaala, S. E., Bleakley, A., Castonguay, J., & Jordan, A. B. (2017). Parents' use of the V-Chip and perceptions of television ratings: The role of family characteristics and the home media environment. *Journal of Broadcasting & Electronic Media, 61*(3), 518–537.

Vaccari, C., Chadwick, A., & O'Loughlin, B. (2015). Dual screening the political: Media events, social media, and citizen engagement. *Journal of Communication, 65*(6), 1041–1061.

Vaes, J., Paladino, P., & Puvia, E. (2011). Are sexualized women complete human beings? Why men and women dehumanize sexually objectified women. *European Journal of Social Psychology, 41*(6), 774–785.

Vaid, J. (1999). The evolution of humor: Do those who laugh last? In D. H. Rosen & M. C. Luebbert (Eds.), *Evolution of the psyche: Human evolution, behavior, and intelligence* (pp. 123–138). Westport, CT: Praeger.

Valentino, N. A., Hutchings, V. L., & Williams, D. (2004). The impact of political advertising on knowledge, Internet information seeking, and candidate preference. *Journal of Communication, 54*, 337–354.

Vales, V., Pollock, J. C., Scarfone, V., Koziol, C., Wilson, A., & Flanagan, P. (2014). Nationwide newspaper coverage of same-sex marriage: A community structure approach. *Atlantic Journal of Communication, 22*(3–4).

Valiente, C., & Rasmusson, X. (2015). Bucking the stereotypes: *My Little Pony* and challenges to traditional gender roles. *Journal of Psychological Issues in Organizational Culture, 5*(4), 88–97.

Valkenburg, P. M. (2001). Television and the child's developing imagination. In D. G. & J. L. Singer (Eds.), *Handbook of children and the media* (pp. 121–134). Thousand Oaks, CA: Sage.

Valkenburg, P. M. (2004). *Children's responses to the screen: A media psychological approach.* Mahwah, NJ: Erlbaum.

Valkenburg, P. M., & Beentjes, J. W. J. (1997). Children's creative imagination in response to radio and television stories. *Journal of Communication, 47*(2), 21–38.

Valkenburg, P. M., & Buijzen, M. (2005). Identifying determinants of young children's brand awareness: Television, parents, and peers. *Journal of Applied Developmental Psychology, 26,* 454–468.

Valkenburg, P. M., & Calvert, S. L. (2012). Media and the child's developing imagination. In D. G. Singer & J. L. Singer (Eds.), *Handbook of children and the media* (pp. 157–170). Thousand Oaks, CA: Sage.

Valkenburg, P. M., & Cantor, J. (2001). The development of a child into a consumer. *Journal of Applied Developmental Psychology, 22,* 61–72.

Valkenburg, P. M., & Peter, J. (2006). Fantasy and imagination. In J. Bryant & P. Vorderer (Eds.), *Psychology of entertainment* (pp. 105–117). Mahwah, NJ: Erlbaum.

Valkenburg, P. M., & Piotrowski, J. T. (2017). *Plugged in: How media attract and affect youth.* New Haven, CT: Yale University Press.

Valkenburg, P. M., & van der Voort, T. H. A. (1994). Influence of TV on daydreaming and creative imagination: A review of research. *Psychological Bulletin, 116,* 316–339.

Valkenburg, P. M., Peter, J., & Schouten, A. (2006). Friend networking sites and their relationship to adolescents' well-being and social self-esteem. *Cyber Psychology & Behavior, 9,* 584–590.

Vance, K., Sutter, M., Perrin, P. B., & Heesacker, M. (2015). The media's sexual objectification of women, rape myth acceptance, and interpersonal violence. *Journal of Aggression, Maltreatment & Trauma, 24*(5), 569–587.

Van de Vijver, S., Oti, S., Addo, J., de Graft-Aikins, A., & Agyemang, C. (2012). Review of community-based interventions for prevention of cardiovascular diseases in low- and middle-income countries. *Ethnicity & Health, 17*(6), 651–676.

Vandeberg, L., Murre, J. M. J., Voorveld, H. A. M., & Smit, E. G. (2015). Dissociating explicit and implicit effects of cross-media advertising. *International Journal of Advertising, 34*(5), 744–764.

Van den Bergh, B., Dewitte, S., & Warlop, L. (2008). Bikinis instigate generalized impatience in intertemporal choice. *Journal of Consumer Research, 35,* 85–97.

Vandenbosch, L., & van Oosten, J. F. (2017). The relationship between online pornography and the sexual objectification of women: The attenuating role of porn literacy education. *Journal of Communication.* doi:10.1111/jcom.12341

Van der Meij, L., Almela, M., Hidalgo,V., Villada, C., Ijzerman, H., van Lange, P. A. M., & Salvador, A. (2012). Testosterone and cortisol release among Spanish soccer fans watching the 2010 World Cup final. *PLOS ONE, 7*(4), 1–7.

Van Oosten, J. M. F., Peter, J., & Vandenbosch, L. (2017). Adolescents' sexual media use and willingness to engage in casual sex: Differential relations and underlying processes. *Human Communication Research, 43*(1), 127–147.

Van Steenburg, E. (2015). Areas of research in political advertising: A review and research agenda. *International Journal of Advertising, 34*(2), 195–231.

Veale, J. (2008), Dreamer. *Time,* May 26, p. 59.

Vega, V., & Malamuth, N. M. (2007). Predicting sexual aggression: The role of pornography in the context of general and specific risk factors. *Aggressive Behavior, 33,* 104–117.

Veldhuis, J., Konijn, E. A., & Seidell, J. C. (2014). Counteracting media's thin-body ideal for adolescent girls: Informing is more effective than warning. *Media Psychology, 17*(2), 154–184.

Velki, T., & Kuterovac Jagodić, G., (2017). Testing the moderating role of social context on media violence effect in the case of peer aggression among adolescents. *Studia Psychologica, 59*(1), 34–49.

Vergeer, M., Lubbers, M., & Scheepers, P. (2000). Exposure to newspapers and attitudes toward ethnic minorities: A longitudinal analysis. *Howard Journal of Communications, 11*(2), 127–143.

Verhellen, Y., Dens, N., & de Pelsmacker, P. (2016). A longitudinal content analysis of gender role portrayal in Belgian television advertising. *Journal of Marketing Communications, 22*(2), 170–188.

Verser, R., & Wicks, R. H. (2006). Managing voter impressions: The use of images on presidential candidate websites during the 2000 campaign. *Journal of Communication*, 56, 178–197.

Vettehen, P. H., Nuijten, K., & Peeters, A. (2008). Explaining effects of sensationalism on liking of television news stories: The role of emotional arousal. *Communication Research*, 35, 319–338.

Victor, D. (2017a). Pepsi pulls ad accused of trivializing Black Lives Matter. *The New York Times*, April 5. Retrieved from www.nytimes.com

Victor, D. (2017b). MacArthur grant will create "Sesame Street" for Syrian refugees. *The New York Times*, December 21. Retrieved from www.nytimes.com

Victor, D., & McPhate, M. (2016). Critics of police welcome Facebook Live and other tools to stream video. *The New York Times*, July 7. Retrieved from www.nytimes.com

Vidal, M. Á., Clemente, M., & Espinosa, P. (2003). Types of media violence and degree of acceptance in under-18s. *Aggressive Behavior*, 29(5), 381–392.

Vidmar, N., & Rokeach, M. (1974). Archie Bunker's bigotry: A study in selective perception and exposure. *Journal of Communication*, 24(1), 35–47.

Vincent, R. C., Davis, D. K., & Boruszkowski, L. A. (1987). Sexism on MTV: The portrayal of women in rock videos. *Journalism Quarterly*, 64(4), 750–755.

Vittrup, B., & Holden, G. W. (2011). Exploring the impact of educational television and parent–child discussions on children's racial attitudes. *Analyses of Social Issues and Public Policy*, 11(1), 82–104.

Vokey, J. R., & Read, J. D. (1985). Subliminal messages: Between the devil and the media. *American Psychologist*, 40, 1231–1239.

Vollaro, D. R. (2009). Lincoln, Stowe, and the "Little Woman/Great War" story: The making, and breaking, of a great American anecdote. *Journal of the Abraham Lincoln Association*, 30, 18–34.

van der Voort, T. H. A. (1986). *Television violence: A child's eye view*. Amsterdam: North-Holland.

van der Voort, T. H. A., & Valkenburg, P. M. (1994). Television's impact on fantasy play: A review of research. *Developmental Review*, 14, 27–51.

Voorveld, H. A. M., & Viswanathan, V. (2015). An observational study on how situational factors influence media multitasking with TV: The role of genres, dayparts, and social viewing. *Media Psychology*, 18(4), 499–526.

Vorderer, P., & Knobloch, S. (2000). Conflict and suspense in drama. In D. Zillmann & P. Vorderer (Eds.), *Media entertainment: The psychology of its appeal* (pp. 59–72). Mahwah, NJ: Erlbaum.

Vorderer, P., Wulff, H. J., & Friedrichsen, M. (Eds.). (1996). *Suspense: Conceptualizations, theoretical analyses, and empirical explorations*. Mahwah, NJ: Erlbaum.

Vossen, H. G. M., Piotrowski, J. T., & Valkenburg, P. M. (2017). The longitudinal relationship between media violence and empathy: Was it sympathy all along? *Media Psychology*, 20(2), 175–193.

Vraga, E. K., Edgerly, S., Wang, B. M., & Shah, D. V. (2011). Who taught me that? Repurposed news, blog structure, and source identification. *Journal of Communication*, 61, 795–815.

Vraga, E. K., Edgerly, S., Bode, L., Carr, D. J., Bard, M., Johnson, C. N., ... Shah, D. V. (2012). The correspondent, the comic, and the combatant: The consequences of host style in political talk shows. *Journalism and Mass Communication Quarterly*, 89, 5–22.

Wachs, S., Wright, M. F., & Wolf, K. D. (2017). Psychological correlates of teen sexting in three countries: Direct and indirect associations between self-control, self-esteem, and sexting. *International Journal of Developmental Science*, 11(3/4), 109–120.

Waddell, T. F., Bailey, E., & Davis, S. E. (2017). Does elevation reduce viewers' enjoyment of media violence? *Journal of Media Psychology*. doi: 10.1027/1864-1105/a000214

Wahl, O. F. (1995). *Media madness: Public images of mental illness*. New Brunswick, NJ: Rutgers University Press.

Wakabayashi, D., & Qiu, L. (2017). Google serves fake news ads in an unlikely place: Fact-checking sites. *The New York Times*, October 17. Retrieved from www.nytimes.com

Waldman, P. (2013). Just how bad is television news? *The American Prospect*, March 8. Retrieved from http://prospect.org

Walgrave, S., Sevenans, J., Camp, K. V., & Loewen, P. (2017). What draws politicians' attention? An experimental study of issue framing and its effect on individual political elites. *Political Behavior.* doi: 10.1007/s11109-017-9413-9

Walker, K., & Sleath, E. (2017). A systematic review of the current knowledge regarding revenge pornography and non-consensual sharing of sexually explicit media. *Aggression and Violent Behavior*, 36, 9–24.

Walker, M., Langemeyer, L., & Langemeyer, D. (1992). Celebrity endorsers: Do you get what you pay for? *Journal of Consumer Marketing*, 9, 69–76.

Wallace, A. (1998). 'Ryan' ends vets' years of silence. *Los Angeles Times*, August 6. Available at http://articles.latimes.com

Wallace, C. (2018). Why *Black Panther* is a defining moment for Black America. *The New York Times*, February 12. Retrieved from www.nytimes.com/

Wallace, G. (2016). Negative ads dominate in campaign's final days. Retrieved from www.cnn. com/

Wallack, L., Dorfman, L., Jernigan, D., & Themba, M. (1993). *Media advocacy and public health.* Newbury Park, CA: Sage.

Wallis, C. (2011). Performing gender: A content analysis of gender display in music videos. *Sex Roles*, 64(3–4), 160–172.

Walters, R. H., & Willows, D. C. (1968). Imitative behavior of disturbed and nondisturbed children following exposure to aggressive and nonaggressive models. *Child Development*, 39, 79–89.

Walther, J. B., & Bunz, U. (2005). The rules of virtual groups: Trust, liking, and performance in computer-mediated communication. *Journal of Communication*, 55, 828–846.

Walther, J. B., Gay, G., & Hancock, J. T. (2005). How do communication and technology researchers study the Internet? *Journal of Communication*, 55, 632–657.

Walther, J. B., Van de Heide, B., Kim, S.-Y., Westerman, D., & Tong, S. T. (2008). The role of friends' appearance and behavior on evaluations of individuals on Facebook: Are we known by the company we keep? *Human Communication Research*, 34, 28–49.

Walton, J. L. (2009). *Watch this! The ethics and aesthetics of black televangelism.* New York: New York University Press.

Wang, X., & Arpan, L. M. (2008). Effects of race and ethnic identity on audience evaluation of HIV public service announcements. *Howard Journal of Communications*, 19(1), 44–63.

Wang, Y., Mathews, V. P., Kalnin, A. J., Mosier, K. M., Dunn, D. W., Saykin, A. J., & Kronenberger, W. G. (2009). Short term exposure to a violent video game induces changes in frontolimbic circuitry in adolescents. *Brain Imaging and Behavior*, 3, 38–50.

Wang, Z., & Lang, A. (2012). Reconceptualizing excitation transfer as motivational activation changes and a test of the television program context effects. *Media Psychology*, 15, 68–92.

Wang, Z., & Tchernev, J. M. (2012). The "myth" of media multitasking: Reciprocal dynamics of media multitasking, personal needs, and gratifications. *Journal of Communication*, 62(3), 493–513.

Wann, D. L., Melnick, M. J., Russell, G. W., & Pease, D. G. (2001). *Sports fans: The psychology and social impact of spectators.* New York: Routledge.

Wanta, W. (1997). *The public and the national agenda: How people learn about important issues.* Mahwah, NJ: Erlbaum.

Wanta, W., & Ghanem, S. (2007). Effects of agenda-setting. In R. W. Preiss, B. M. Gayle, N. Burrell, M. Allen, & J. Bryant (Eds.), *Mass media effects research: Advances through meta-analysis* (pp. 37–51). Mahwah, NJ: Erlbaum.

Ward, L. M., Reed, L., Trinh, S. L., & Foust, M. (2014). Sexuality and entertainment media. In D. L. Tolman, L. M. Diamond, J. A. Bauermeister, W. H. George, J. G. Pfaus, & L. M. Ward (Eds.), *APA handbook of sexuality and psychology, Vol. 2: Contextual approaches* (pp. 373–423). Washington, DC: American Psychological Association.

Ward, L. M., Seabrook, R. C., Grower, P., Giaccardi, S., & Lippman, J. R. (2018). Sexual object or sexual subject? Media use, self-sexualization, and sexual agency among undergraduate women. *Psychology of Women Quarterly*, 42(1), 29–43.

Ward, S., Wackman, D., & Wartella, E. (1977). *How children learn to buy: The development of consumer information-processing skills*. Beverly Hills, CA: Sage.

Warren, R. (2005). Parental mediation of children's television viewing in low-income families. *Journal of Communication*, 55, 847–863.

Wartella, E., & Jennings, N. (2001). Hazards and possibilities of commercial TV in the schools. In D. G. Singer & J. L. Singer (Eds.), *Handbook of children and the media* (pp. 557–570). Thousand Oaks, CA: Sage.

Wasike, B. (2017). Persuasion in 140 characters: Testing issue framing, persuasion and credibility via Twitter and online news articles in the gun control debate. *Computers in Human Behavior*, 66 (Supplement C), 179–190.

Watson, J. M., & Strayer, D. L. (2010). Supertaskers: Profiles in extraordinary multitasking ability. *Psychonomic Bulletin and Review*, 17, 479–485.

Weaver, A. D., Ménard, A. D., Cabrera, C., & Taylor, A. (2015). Embodying the moral code? Thirty years of Final Girls in slasher films. *Psychology of Popular Media Culture*, 4(1), 31–46.

Weaver, J. (2003a). A hot "Hispanicized" consumer market. Retrieved from www.msnbc.com/news/912895.asp?0cv=CB20

Weaver, J. (2003b). Teens tune out TV, log on instead. Retrieved July 25, 2003, from www.msnbc.com.

Weaver, J. B., III. (1991). Responding to erotica: Perceptual processes and dispositional implications. In J. Bryant & D. Zillmann (Eds.), *Responding to the screen* (pp. 329–354). Hillsdale, NJ: Erlbaum.

Weaver, J. B., III, & Wakshlag, J. (1986). Perceived vulnerability to crime, criminal victimization experience, and television viewing. *Journal of Broadcasting & Electronic Media*, 30, 141–158.

Weaver, J. B., III, Masland, J. L., & Zillmann, D. (1984). Effects of erotica on young men's aesthetic perception of their female sexual partners. *Perceptual and Motor Skills*, 58, 929–930.

Webb, T., Martin, K., Afifi, A. A., & Kraus, J. (2010). Media literacy as a violence-prevention strategy: A pilot evaluation. *Health Promotion Practice*, 11(5), 714–722.

Webel, A. R., Okonsky, J., Trompeta, J., & Holzemer, W. L. (2010). A systematic review of the effectiveness of peer-based interventions on health-related behavior in adults. *American Journal of Public Health*, 100, 247–253.

Weber, J. D., & Carini, R. M. (2013). Where are the female athletes in *Sports Illustrated*? A content analysis of covers (2000–2011). *International Review for the Sociology of Sport*, 48(2), 196–203.

Weber, M., Quiring, O., & Daschmann, G. (2012). Peers, parents and pornography: Exploring adolescents' exposure to sexually explicit material and its developmental correlates. *Sexuality & Culture*, 16(4), 408–427.

Weber, R., Ritterfeld, U., & Kostygina, A. (2006). Aggression and violence as effects of playing violent video games? In P. Vorderer & J. Bryant (Eds.), *Playing video games: Motives, responses, and consequences* (pp. 347–361). Mahwah, NJ: Erlbaum.

Weber, R., Ritterfeld, U., & Mathiak, K. (2006). Does playing violent video games induce aggression? Empirical evidence of a functional magnetic resonance imaging study. *Media Psychology*, 8, 39–60.

Wedding, D., & Niemiec, R. M. (2014). *Movies and mental illness: Using films to understand psychopathology*. 4th ed. Boston, MA: Hogrefe.

Wei, R., & Lo, V.-H. (2007). The third-person effects of political attack ads in the 2004 U.S. presidential elections. *Media Psychology*, 9, 367–388.

Weigel, R. H., Loomis, J., & Soja, M. (1980). Race relations on prime time television. *Journal of Personality and Social Psychology*, 39(5), 884–893.

Weinmann, C. (2017). Feeling political interest while being entertained? Explaining the emotional experience of interest in politics in the context of political entertainment programs. *Psychology of Popular Media Culture*, 6(2), 123–141.

Weimann, G., & Brosius, H.-B. (1991). The newsworthiness of international terrorism. *Communication Research*, 18, 333–354.

Weisbuch, M., & Mackie, D. (2009). False fame, perceptual clarity, or persuasion? Flexible fluency attribution in spokesperson familiarity effects. *Journal of Consumer Psychology*, 19(1), 62–72.

Weiss, A. J., & Wilson, B. J. (1998). Children's cognitive and emotional responses to the portrayal of negative emotions in family-formatted situation comedies. *Human Communication Research*, 24, 584–609.

Weisz, M. G., & Earls, C. M. (1995). The effects of exposure to filmed sexual violence on attitudes toward rape. *Journal of Interpersonal Violence*, 10, 71–84.

Welsh, A. (2010). On the perils of living dangerously in the slasher horror film: Gender differences in the association between sexual activity and survival. *Sex Roles*, 62(11–12), 762–773.

Wenner, L. A., & Gantz, W. (1998). Watching sports on television: Audience experience, gender, fanship, and marriage. In L. A. Wenner (Ed.), *Media Sport* (pp. 233–251). New York: Routledge.

Wernick, R. (1996). Let's hear it for the lowly sound bite! *Smithsonian*, 27(5), 62–65.

West, D. M. (2005). *Air wars: Television advertising in election campaigns, 1952–2004*. 4th ed. Washington DC: Congressional Quarterly.

Weston, M. A. (1996). *Native Americans in the news: Images of Indians in the twentieth century press*. Westport, CT: Greenwood.

Weymouth, L. (1981). Walter Cronkite remembers. *Washington Journalism Review* (January–February), 23.

What's so funny? (1997). *The Economist*, December 20.

What's up, doc? (1995). *Manhattan Mercury*, February 5, p. A7.

Wheeler, D. L. (2001). Embracing technology and spirituality, at the top of the world. *The Chronicle of Higher Education*, 47 (January 5), A64.

Wheeler, T. H. (2002). *Phototruth or photofiction? Ethics and media imagery in the digital age*. Mahwah, NJ: Erlbaum.

Whillock, R. K. (1997). Cyber-politics: The on-line strategies of '96. *American Behavioral Scientist*, 40, 1208–1225.

White, D. (2015). Here's why Gallup won't poll the 2016 election. Retrieved from www.time.com

White, L. A. (1979). Erotica and aggression: The influence of sexual arousal, positive affect, and negative affect on aggressive behavior. *Journal of Personality and Social Psychology*, 37, 591–601.

White, V. M., Durkin, S. J., Coomber, K., & Wakefield, M. A. (2015). What is the role of tobacco control advertising intensity and duration in reducing adolescent smoking prevalence? Findings from 16 years of tobacco control mass media advertising in Australia. *Tobacco Control*, 24(2), 198–204.

Whiteside, E., & Hardin, M. (2011). Women (not) watching women: Leisure time, television, and implications for televised coverage of women's sports. *Communication, Culture & Cognition*, 4, 122–143.

Wicks, R. H. (2001). *Understanding audiences: Learning to use the media constructively*. Mahwah, NJ: Erlbaum.

Wike, R., Stokes, B., Poushter, J., & Fetterolf, J. (2017). U.S. image suffers as publics around world question Trump's leadership. Retrieved from www.pewinternet.org

Wilcox, B. L. (1987). Pornography, social science, and politics: When research and ideology collide. *American Psychologist*, 42, 941–943.

Wilkes, M. S., Bell, R. A., & Kravitz, R. L. (2000). Direct-to-consumer prescription drug advertising: Trends, impact, and implications. *Health Affairs*, 19(2), 110–128.

Wilksch, S. M., & Wade, T. D. (2009). Reduction of shape and weight concern in young adolescents: A 30-month controlled evaluation of a media literacy program. *Journal of the American Academy of Child & Adolescent Psychiatry, 48*, 652–661.

Will, E. (1987). Women in media. *The Other Side, 23*(4), 44–46.

Williams, B. (1979). *Report of the Departmental Committee on Obscenity and Film Censorship*. London: Her Majesty's Stationery Office. Command 7772.

Williams, T. M. (Ed.). (1986). *The impact of television*. Orlando, FL: Academic Press.

Williamson, V. J., Jilka, S. R., Fry, J., Finkel, S., Mullensiefen, D., & Stewart, L. (2011). How do "earworms" start? Classifying the everyday circumstances of involuntary musical imagery. *Psychology of Music, 39*, 1–26.

Willman, C. (2005). *Rednecks and bluenecks: The politics of country music*. New York: New Press.

Willoughby, B. J., Carroll, J. S., Busby, D. M., & Brown, C. C. (2016). Differences in pornography use among couples: Associations with satisfaction, stability, and relationship processes. *Archives of Sexual Behavior, 45*(1), 145–158.

Willoughby, T., Adachi, P. J. C., & Good, M. (2012). A longitudinal study of the association between violent video game play and aggression among adolescents. *Developmental Psychology, 48*(4), 1044–1057.

Wilson, B. J. (1991). Children's reactions to dreams conveyed in mass media programming. *Communication Research, 18*, 283–305.

Wilson, B. J., & Weiss, A. J. (1992). Developmental differences in children's reactions to a toy advertisement linked to a toy-based cartoon. *Journal of Broadcasting & Electronic Media, 36*, 371–394.

Wilson, B. J., Linz, D., Donnerstein, E., & Stipp, H. (1992). The impact of social issue television programming on attitudes toward rape. *Human Communication Research, 19*, 179–208.

Wilson, B. J., Colvin, C. M., & Smith, S. L. (2002). Engaging in violence on American television: A comparison of child, teen, and adult perpetrators. *Journal of Communication, 52*(1), 36–60.

Wilson, B. J., Smith, S. L., Potter, W. J., Kunkel, D., Linz, D., Colvin, C. M., & Donnerstein, E. (2002). Violence in children's television programming: Assessing the risks. *Journal of Communication, 52*(1), 5–35.

Wilson, J. R., & Wilson, S. L. R. (1998). *Mass media/mass culture*. 4th ed. New York: McGraw-Hill.

Wilson, J. W. (2013). Lance Armstrong's doping drugs. Retrieved from www.cnn.com

Wilson, R. E., Gosling, S. D., & Graham, L. T. (2012). A review of Facebook research in the social sciences. *Perspectives on Psychological Science, 7*, 203–220.

Wilson, W. (1999). *The psychopath in film*. Washington, DC: University Press of America.

Winfrey, K. L., Warner, B. R., & Banwart, M. C. (2014). Gender identification and young voters: Predicting candidate evaluations and message effectiveness. *American Behavioral Scientist, 58*(6), 794–809.

Winn, M. (1987). *Unplugging the plug-in drug*. New York: Penguin Books.

Winn, M. (2002). *The plug-in drug: Television, computers, and family life*. New York: Penguin [replaces Winn, 1987].

Winston, D. H. (Ed.). (2009). *Small screen, big picture: Television and lived religion*. Waco, TX: Baylor University Press.

Wisser, J. (2016) "The Daily Show (The Book)" offers candid history of Jon Stewart's fake newscast. *Chicago Tribune*, December 8. Retrieved from www.chicagotribune.com

Witte, K. (1992a). Preventing AIDS through persuasive communications. In F. Korzenny & S. Ting-Toomey (Eds.), *Mass media effects across cultures* (pp. 67–86). Newbury Park, CA: Sage.

Witte, K. (1992b). Putting the fear back into fear appeals: The extended parallel process model. *Communication Monographs, 59*(4), 329–349.

Wittebols, J. H. (1991). The politics and coverage of terrorism: From media images to public consciousness. *Communication Theory, 1*, 253–266.

Wober, J. M. (1986). The lens of television and the prism of personality. In J. Bryant & D. Zillmann (Eds.), *Perspectives on media effects* (pp. 205–231). Hillsdale, NJ: Erlbaum.

Wojcieszak, M. E., & Mutz, D. C. (2009). Online groups and political discourse: Do online discussion spaces facilitate exposure to political disagreement? *Journal of Communication*, 59, 40–56.

Wojcik, N. (2017). Shares of *New York Times* surge after subscriber growth. Retrieved www.cnbc.com

Wojdynski, B. W. (2016). The deceptiveness of sponsored news articles: How readers recognize and perceive native advertising. *American Behavioral Scientist*, 60(12), 1475–1491.

Wolfson, T. (2012). From the Zapatistas to Indymedia: Dialectics and orthodoxy in contemporary social movements. *Communication, Culture, & Critique*, 5, 149–170.

Women's Media Center (2017). The status of women in the U.S. media 2017. Retrieved from www.womensmediacenter.com

Wood, J. M., & Duke, N. K. (1997). Inside Reading Rainbow: A spectrum of strategies for promoting literacy. *Language Arts*, 74, 95–106.

Wood, M. (2016). Social marketing for social change. *Social Marketing Quarterly*, 22(2), 107–118.

Woodburn, D., & Kopić, K. (2016). The Ruderman White Paper on the employment of actors with disabilities in television. Retrieved from www.rudermanfoundation.org/

Woodward, V. H., Evans, M., & Brooks, M. (2017). Social and psychological factors of rural youth sexting: An examination of gender-specific models. *Deviant Behavior*, 38(4), 461–476.

Worden, N. (2011). Web advertising eclipsed newspapers in 2010. *The Wall Street Journal*, April 14. Retrieved from http://online.wsj.com.

Worley, W. (2016). A 12-year-old repeatedly raped his little sister after watching incest porn. Retrieved from www.independent.co.uk/

Worth, K. A., Chambers, J. G., Nassau, D. H., Rakhra, B. K., & Sargent, J. D. (2008). Exposure of US adolescents to extremely violent movies. *Pediatrics*, 122(2), 306–312.

Worthen, B., & Tuna, C. (2011). Web running out of addresses: Internet sites, carriers are laying the groundwork for a new routing system. *The Wall Street Journal*, February 1. Retrieved from http://online.wsj.com.

Wresch, W. (1996). *Disconnected: Haves and have-nots in the information age*. New Brunswick, NJ: Rutgers University Press.

Wright, C. R. (1986). *Mass communication: A sociological perspective*. 3rd ed. New York: Random House.

Wright, J. C., Kunkel, D., Pinon, M., & Huston, A. C. (1989). How children reacted to televised coverage of the space shuttle disaster. *Journal of Communication*, 39(2), 27–45.

Wright, J. C., St. Peters, M., & Huston, A. C. (1990). Family television use and its relation to children's cognitive skills and social behavior. In J. Bryant (Ed.), *Television and the American family* (pp. 227–251). Hillsdale, NJ: Erlbaum.

Wright, J. C., Huston, A. C., Reitz, A. L., & Piemyat, S. (1994). Young children's perceptions of television reality: Determinants and developmental differences. *Developmental Psychology*, 30, 229–239.

Wright, J. C., Huston, A. C., Truglio, R., Fitch, M., Smith, E., & Piemyat, S. (1995). Occupational portrayals on television: Children's role schemata, career aspirations, and perceptions of reality. *Child Development*, 66(6), 1706–1718.

Wright, P. J. (2015). Americans' attitudes toward premarital sex and pornography consumption: A national panel analysis. *Archives of Sexual Behavior*, 44(1), 89–97.

Wright, P. J., & Tokunaga, R. S. (2016). Men's objectifying media consumption, objectification of women, and attitudes supportive of violence against women. *Archives of Sexual Behavior*, 45(4), 955–964.

Wright, P. J., Tokunaga, R. S., & Bae, S. (2014). More than a dalliance? Pornography consumption and extramarital sex attitudes among married U.S. adults. *Psychology of Popular Media Culture*, 3(2), 97–109.

Wright, P. J., Tokunaga, R. S., & Kraus, A. (2016). A meta-analysis of pornography consumption and actual acts of sexual aggression in general population studies. *Journal of Communication*, 66(1), 183–205.

Wroblewski, R., & Huston, A. C. (1987). Televised occupational stereotypes and their effects on early adolescence: Are they changing? *Journal of Early Adolescence*, 7, 283–297.

Wu, F. H. (2002). *Yellow: Race in America beyond Black and White*. New York: Basic Books.

Wyatt, E. (2014). Fictional disaster, made to sound real, draws F.C.C. fine. *The New York Times*, March 3. Retrieved from www.nytimes.com/2014/03/04/business/media/fictional-disaster-made-to-sound-real-draws-fcc-fine.html

Wyer, R. S., & Collins, J. E. (1992). A theory of humor elicitation. *Psychological Review*, 99, 663–688.

Wyer, R. S., & Shrum, L. J. (2015). The role of comprehension processes in communication and persuasion. *Media Psychology*, 18(2), 163–195.

Wyer, R. S., Jiang, Y., & Hung, I. (2008). Visual and verbal information processing in a consumer context: Further considerations. *Journal of Consumer Psychology*, 18(4), 276–280.

Xenos, M., & Moy, P. (2007). Direct and differential effects of the Internet on political and civic engagement. *Journal of Communication*, 57, 704–718.

Xie, G. X. (2016). Deceptive advertising and third-person perception: The interplay of generalized and specific suspicion. *Journal of Marketing Communications*, 22(5), 494–512.

Xie, G.-X., & Lee, M. J. (2008). Anticipated violence, arousal, and enjoyment of movies: Viewers' reactions to violent previews based on arousal-seeking tendency. *Journal of Social Psychology*, 148(3), 277–292.

Xu, B. & Albert, E. (2017). Media censorship in China. Retrieved from www.cfr.org

Yalch, R. F. (1991). Memory in a jingle jungle: Music as a mnemonic device in communicating advertising slogans. *Journal of Applied Psychology*, 76, 268–275.

Yamamiya, Y., Cash, T. F., Melnyk, S. E., Posavec, H. D., & Posavec, S. S. (2005). Women's exposure to thin-and-beautiful media images: Body image effects of media-ideal internalization and impact-reduction interventions. *Body Image*, 2, 74–80.

Yang, M., & Roskos-Ewoldson, D. R. (2007). The effectiveness of brand placements in the movies: Levels of placements, explicit and implicit memory, and brand-choice behavior. *Journal of Communication*, 57, 469–489.

Yanovitzky, I., & Bennett, C. (1999). Media attention, institutional response, and health behavior change: The case of drunk driving, 1978–1996. *Communication Research*, 26, 429–453.

Yates, E., Barbaree, H. E., & Marshall, W. L. (1984). Anger and deviant sexual arousal. *Behavior Therapy*, 15, 287–294.

Yeu, M., Yoon, H.-S., Taylor, C. R., & Lee, D.-H. (2013). Are banner advertisements in online games effective? *Journal of Advertising*, 42(2–3), 241–250.

Yoo, J. J., & Lee, W.N. (2016). Calling it out: The impact of national identity on consumer response to ads with a patriotic theme. *Journal of Advertising*, 45(2), 244–255.

Young, B. (2011). Media and advertising effects. In S. L. Calvert & B. J. Wilson (Eds.), *The handbook of children, media, and development* (pp. 407–431). Malden, MA: Wiley-Blackwell.

Young, S. D., Boester, A, Whitt, M. T., & Stevens, M. (2008). Character motivations in the representation of mental health professionals in popular film. *Mass Communication and Society*, 11, 82–99.

Yukawa, S., Endo, K., & Yoshida, F. (2001). The effects of media violence on aggression: Focus on the role of anger evoked by provocation. *Japanese Journal of Psychology*, 72(1), 1–9.

Yun, G. W., Park, S.-Y., Holody, K., Yoon, K. S., & Xie, S. (2013). Selective moderation, selective responding, and Balkanization of the blogosphere: A field experiment. *Media Psychology*, 16(3), 295–317.

Zelizer, B. (1992). CNN, the Gulf War, and journalistic practice. *Journal of Communication*, 42(1), 66–81.

Zhang, J., Zhang, D., & Chock, T. M. (2014). Effects of HIV/AIDS public service announcements on attitude and behavior: Interplay of perceived threat and self-efficacy. *Social Behavior and Personality: An International Journal*, 42(5), 799–809.

Zhao, X., & Cai, X. (2008). The role of ambivalence in college nonsmokers' information seeking and information processing. *Communication Research*, 35, 298–318.

Zhao, X., Leiserowitz, A. A., Maibach, E. W., & Roser-Renouf, C. (2011). Attention to science/environmental news positively predicts and attention to political news negatively predicts global warming risk perceptions and policy support. *Journal of Communication*, 61, 713–731.

Zielinska, I. E., & Chambers, B. (1995). Using group viewing of television to teach preschool children social skills. *Journal of Educational Television*, 21, 85–99.

Zill, N. (2001). Does *Sesame Street* enhance school readiness? Evidence from a national survey of children. In S. M. Fisch & R. Truglio (Eds.), *"G" is for "growing": Thirty years of research on children and Sesame Street* (pp. 115–130). Mahwah, NJ: Erlbaum.

Zillmann, D. (1978). Attribution and mis-attribution of excitatory reactions. In J. H. Harvey, W. J. Ickes, & R. F. Kidd (Eds.), *New directions in attribution research* (Vol. 2). Hillsdale, NJ: Erlbaum.

Zillmann, D. (1996). The psychology of suspense in dramatic exposition. In P. Vorderer, H. J. Wulff, & M. Friedrichsen (Eds.), *Suspense: Conceptualizations, theoretical analyses, and empirical explorations* (pp. 199–231). Mahwah, NJ: Erlbaum.

Zillmann, D. (2000). Humor and comedy. In D. Zillmann & P. Vorderer (Eds.), *Media entertainment* (pp. 37–57). Mahwah, NJ: Erlbaum.

Zillmann, D. (2006a). Empathy: Affective reactivity to others' emotional experiences. In J. Bryant & P. Vorderer (Eds.), *Psychology of entertainment* (pp. 151–182). Mahwah, NJ: Erlbaum.

Zillmann, D. (2006b). Dramaturgy for emotions from fictional narration. In J. Bryant & P. Vorderer (Eds.), *Psychology of entertainment* (pp. 215–238). Mahwah, NJ: Erlbaum.

Zillmann, D., & Bryant, J. (1982). Pornography, sexual callousness, and the trivialization of rape. *Journal of Communication*, 32(4), 10–21.

Zillmann, D., & Bryant, J. (1984). Effects of massive exposure to pornography. In N. M. Malamuth & E. Donnerstein (Eds.), *Pornography and sexual aggression* (pp. 115–141). Orlando, FL: Academic Press.

Zillmann, D., & Bryant, J. (1988a). Pornography's impact on sexual satisfaction. *Journal of Applied Social Psychology*, 18, 438–453.

Zillmann, D., & Bryant, J. (1988b). Effects of prolonged consumption of pornography on family values. *Journal of Family Issues*, 9, 518–544.

Zillmann, D., & Bryant, J. (1988c). A response to Linz and Donnerstein. *Journal of Communication*, 38(2), 185–192.

Zillmann, D., & Mundorf, N. (1987). Image effects in the appreciation of video rock. *Communication Research*, 14, 316–334.

Zillmann, D., & Weaver, J. B., III (1996). Gender-socialization theory of reactions to horror. In J. B. Weaver & R. Tamborini (Eds.), *Horror films: Current research on audience preferences and reactions* (pp. 81–101). Mahwah, NJ: Erlbaum.

Zillmann, D., & Weaver, J. B., III (1997). Psychoticism in the effect of prolonged exposure to gratuitous media violence on the acceptance of violence as a preferred means of conflict resolution. *Personality and Individual Differences*, 22, 613–627.

Zillmann, D., & Weaver, J. B., III (1999). Effects of prolonged exposure to gratuitous media violence on provoked and unprovoked hostile behavior. *Journal of Applied Social Psychology*, 29, 145–165.

Zillmann, D., Bryant, J., & Sapolsky, B. S. (1979). The enjoyment of watching sport contests. In J. H. Goldstein (Ed.), *Sports, games, and play: Social and psychological viewpoints* (pp. 297–355). Hillsdale, NJ: Erlbaum.

Zillmann, D., Bryant, J., Comisky, P. W., & Medoff, N. J. (1981). Excitation and hedonic valence in the effect of erotica on motivated intermale aggression. *European Journal of Social Psychology*, 11, 233–252.

Zillmann, D., Weaver, J. B., Mundorf, N., & Aust, C. F. (1986). Effects of opposite-gender companion's affect to horror on distress, delight, and attraction. *Journal of Personality and Social Psychology*, 51, 586–594.

Zillmann, D., Callison, C., & Gibson, R. (2009). Quantitative media literacy: Individual differences in dealing with numbers in the news. *Media Psychology*, 12, 394–416.

Zimmermann, L. K. (2017). Preschoolers' perceptions of gendered toy commercials in the US. *Journal of Children and Media*, 11(2), 119–131.

REFERENCES

Zuckerman, M. (1994). *Behavioral expressions and psychobiological bases of sensation seeking.* New York: Cambridge University Press.

Zuckerman, M. (1996). Sensation seeking and the taste for vicarious horror. In J. B. Weaver & R. Tamborini (Eds.), *Horror films: Current research on audience preferences and reactions* (pp. 147–160). Mahwah, NJ: Erlbaum.

Zuckerman, M. (2006). Sensation seeking in entertainment. In J. Bryant & P. Vorderer (Eds.), *Psychology of entertainment* (p. 367–387). Mahwah, NJ: Erlbaum.

Zwarun, L., & Hall, A. (2012). Narrative persuasion, transportation, and the role of need for cognition in online viewing of fantastical films. *Media Psychology*, 15(3), 327–355.

Index

ABC (American Broadcasting Company) 5, 14, 52, 80, 243, 266, 310; and advertising 174, 175; and group portrayals 119, 123, 124; and news 203, 207, 209, 211; and socially positive media 350, 371

abolitionist media campaigns 232–233

Abrahamic faiths *see* Christianity; Islam; Judaism

access, blocking 205–206

active experiencing 54

active mediation 303, 304

administrative research 25

adolescents 311–312, 322

advertising 3–4, 7, 12, 20, 21, 22, 25, 32; and achievement appeals 152–153; African Americans in 111–112, 113; and Arab culture 122; attack 22; boycotts of 181–182; to children 167–174; classical conditioning in 29, 164; and classrooms 177–178; and cognition 156–159; and college football 82; controversial 152; cross-media 47; deceptive 159–163, 304; and differentiation from programming 169; disclaimers 169–170; and elaboration likelihood model (ELM) 155–156; embedded 174–177; and emotional appeals 147–151; ethics of 154–155; and fear appeals 151–152; and good will 145–146; green 163; and hero status 86; on high-tech billboards 174; history of 143–145; and humor 288; and humorous appeals 153; and image building 145–146; and information processing 156–159; and informational appeals 146–147; in-game 175, 283; and Islam 122; memory for 158–159; men in 103, 105; native 162; negative 22, 259–262; online 155, 178–180, 200–201, 263; and patriotic appeals 151; of personal hygiene products 144–145; and physical appearance 96–98; political 22, 38, 146, 255–263; and power appeals 152–153; pre-roll 179, 180; prescription drug 126, 180–181; processing stages of 157–158; and product endorsements 86, 153–154; and product placements 174–177; and psychological appeals 146–156; and public service announcements (PSAs) *see* public service announcements (PSAs); and the reflection myth 54, 55; revenue from 186, 200–201, 206; and schools 177–178; and self-censorship 207;

and sex 163–164, 308; social 353, 354; as social statement 156; and stereotypes 99–100, 102, 117, 121, 125, 128, 136, 137; subliminal 27, 164–166, 227; and success appeals 152–153; and the superwoman myth 107–108; and testimonials 86, 153–154; and third-person effect 335; tobacco 171–174; and toymakers 170–171; true-but-deceptive 161–162; types of 145–146; and unclear appeals 156; and United Colors of Benetton 156; and violence 283, 288; women in 99–100, 102, 103, 107–108

affect 63–64, 340, 352

Afghanistan, war in 75, 195, 208, 215, 223, 225, 237, 280

Africa: pop music 74; socially positive media 364–365

African Americans 15, 21; advertising 152; emotions 70, 90; music 73, 75, 77, 79; news 193, 200, 212, 223; politics 252, 258; portrayals of 93, 106, 110, 111–115, 120, 121, 138, 344; as readers and viewers 116, *116*, 214; socially positive media 362; stereotypes of 110, 112, 115, 217, 232, 246, 258; violence in the media 269

agenda setting 21–22, 30, 37–38, 55, 85; news 185, 190, 197; politics 247, 256–257

aggression 33, 34, 43, 78, 101, 302, 304, 323, 340; peer 302–303; sexual 323, 327, 328, 329, 334–335; *see also* violence

AIDS/HIV 38, 78, 123; news 193, 196, 219; sex 318, 324; socially positive media 360, 361–363, 364, 365, 368

American Broadcasting Company (ABC) *see* ABC (American Broadcasting Company)

American Civil Rights Movement 113

American Civil War 121, 232

Amistad 213

amnesia, and violence 283

Amos 'n' Andy 70, 110, 112, 113

antischool hypothesis 344

antisociality 6, 31, 128, 304, 367; emotions 65, 77, 79; sex 332, 336, 337

appeals 21, 22, 143; achievement 152–153; to beauty 144; emotional 82, 147–151, 156, 170; environmental 163, 357–358; to families 258;

to fears 97, 144, 151–152, 156; to guilt 100; to health concerns 144; humorous 153, 156, 157; informational 146–147; multiple 156; to nutritional consciousness 163; patriotic 144, 151, 156; pious 101; in political advertising 258–259; power 152–153, 156; and product endorsements 153–154; prosocial 354; psychological 21, 143, 146–154; rational 157; self-sacrificial 101; to sex 143, 144, 156, 157, 163–164; social marketing 354, 355, 357–358, 361, 372; to social responsibility 163; success 152–153; and testimonials 153–154; unethical 154–155

Arab Americans 120–122

Arabs 77–78; news 186, 200, 214; politics 264–265; portrayals of 93, 110, 120–122, 138; socially positive media 341; see also Saudi Arabia

Asian Americans 21, *116*, 119–120, 151

asynchronous communication 16

attention 26, 30, 33, 41–42, 48–49, 52, 157, 344; to changes 49–51; children's 168, 343, 348; and earworms 80; and elaboration likelihood model 155; and humor 153, 157, 176; and Internet advertising 179, 180; and peripheral cues 157; and sex appeal 157; to subtitles 13; to visual content 13; see also exposure; second screening

attitudes 2, 20, 21, 22, 29; and advertising 146; to African Americans 112; antisocial 337; and belief component of 146; and cognitive dissonance 300; to disability 127; and emotional component of 147; and feminist-inspired research 336; and fictional portrayals 138–139; gender-role 77, 105, 328; to homosexuality 36, 124; to mental illness 128–130; to "others" 31; political 246, 247, 248, 256, 260, 262, 264–265; and product placement 176; and prosocial adult television 353–354, 355, 357, 359, 361, 362, 365; and prosocial children's television 340, 343, 344, 352; to race 115; sexual 105, 106, 124, 312, 314–320, 327, 330, 335; sexual violence 334, 337; and social marketing 353–354, 355, 357, 359, 361, 362, 365; and substance abuse 367; to (non-sexual) violence 275, 282, 291–292, 297–298, 302; see also cultivation theory

attributions, effects of news on 217–218

audience, mass 11, 14, 298, 354, 366

backmasking 166, 183

Bandura, Albert 28, 33, 34, 55, 276, 284, 295, 366

BBC (British Broadcasting Corporation) 1, 4, 39, 145, 174, 209

behavior 28–29, 165–166, 336; see antisocial behavior; political behavior, on the Internet; promiscuous sexual behavior

behavioral research 16, 227, 301

bikinis, women in 323–324

billboards, high-tech 174

"binge viewing" 10

birth control, and sexually transmitted infection (STI) education 318

black Americans see African Americans

Black Lives Matter 115, 152, 193, 223, 372

blocking access 205–206

blogging 14, 17, 18, 74, 139, 189, 225, 265

Bobo doll studies 276

body image 20, 38, 98–99, 104, 139

book-reading promotion hypothesis 344

boycotts 155, 181–182, 310

boys 8, 71, 77, 89–90, 171, 343; portrayal of 98, 100, 102, 103, 106, 108; and sex 315, 319, 334; and violence 269, 287, 290, 291, 292, 293

British Broadcasting Corporation (BBC) 1, 4, 39, 145, 174, 209

broadcast media 14, 15, 16, 226, 232, 371; see also radio, television

broadcast networks 10, 14; advertising 175; group portrayal 114, 131; news 187, 194; sex 309, 310; socially positive media 351

brutalization 294

buffoon portrayal, of fathers 108

Bush, President George H. W. 198, 207, 247, 251, 258

Bush, President George W. 244, 251, 253, 259, 265: and Abu Ghraib Iraq prison scandal 208; effect of Fahrenheit 9/11 documentary on 262; and framing candidates 38, 249–250; and framing electoral uncertainty 254, 255; and "freedom fries" 149; and marital fidelity 241; and news coverage of war 225; and "war" metaphors 185–186

Cable News Network (CNN) see CNN (Cable News Network)

cable technology 2

captive marketing 178

cardiac risk reduction 360–361

casual sex 38, 316–317, 320

catharsis 22, 69–70, 84, 86–87, 288–289, 322–323

causal influence 32, 161, 217, 297

CBS 14, 52, 174, 278, 310; and group portrayals 106, 112, 119, 122–123; and news 188, 197, 198, 207, 209, 210, 211, 214, 219, 224, 225; and politics 245, 266; and socially positive media 349, 350

censorship 5, 32; direct 204–205, 206; government 224, 225, 310; indirect 206; local 223; media 207–208, 225, 311; military 224, 225; movie 309–310; self- 207–208

change blindness 49

Channel One 177, 349

child sexual abuse 315, 318, 358

children: advertising to 167–174; distinctive use of the media by 45–47; educational and informational programming for 347; prosocial learning 351–352; prosocial television for 339, 340–349; science shows for 348; and sexual media 19, 311–312; television for 173–174

Children's Television Act (1990) 173–174, 347

Christianity: emotions 75, 76; group portrayal 120, 121, 131, 132, 133; news 213, 215

Citizens United vs. Federal Election Commission 255

classical conditioning 29, 164, 165, 181, *281*, 281, 314

classrooms, and advertising 177–178

Clinton, President Bill 197, 265, 315–316; and extramarital affair allegations 240, 241, 242, 251; as a television politician 233, 245, 252

Clinton, Hillary 2, 37; and agenda setting 247, 256; and debates with Donald Trump 246, 261; and Democratic primaries 241; and e-mail server issue 252; and framing 248–249; and hostile media effect 244; and name recognition 256; and negative advertising 260; in the news 190, 194, 198, 201, 202, 204; and political polling 238, 239

CMC (computer-mediated communication) 2, 14–18, 19, 20, 37, 371

CNN (Cable News Network) 150, 177, 278, 349; and news 187, 199, 209, 211; and politics 231, 236, 239, 243, 244, 250, 266

cognition 2–3, 29, 48–54; and advertising 146, 156–159, 180; aggressive 78, 296; media 48–54; and news 218; and violence 269–270, 286–287

cognitive consistency/cognitive dissonance 299–300, 359

cognitive distraction 50–51

cognitive effects 30, 320–324

cognitive empathy 67

cognitive psychology 51, 53–54, 373

Colbert, Stephen 71, 188, 210, 211, 342

collateral instruction 38

college students 7, 24, 51, 58; advertising 178; emotions 62, 69, 79, 80; group portrayal 105–106, 114, 133, 134, 137, 138; politics 244; sex 312, 315, 317, 320, 325, 330; socially positive media 355, 361, 367; violence 272, 279, 282

comedic sex, versus serious sex 318

comedy shows 198, 210–211

commercial breaks 81, 158

communication: computer-mediated 2, 14–18, 19, 20, 37, 371; interpersonal 3, 4, 15, 369

comparative media research 13

compelling images 205, 221, 223

complaints, as media influencers 139–140, 152

complication, in stories 40–41, 56–57

computer-mediated communication (CMC) 2, 14–18, 19, 20, 37, 371

concentration-deterioration hypothesis 344

conditional effects model 26, 28, 283–284

conditioned response (CR) 164, 274

conflict, and drama 191–192

conservative-moralist theory 335

consolidation, of news media organizations 8, 208–210

construction, of reality 34, 36, 55, 56, 60, 159, 197–198, 373

content analysis 26; advertising 150, 163, 169–170; African Americans 114; emotions 77, 88, 90; families 106, 108; men 103, 108; Native Americans 118; older adults 126; politics 248; psychological disorders 128; sex 311, 330, 333; sexual minorities 125; socially positive media 349, 351, 361, 364; violence 299; women 94, 95, 96, 98

content ratings, television 302

controversial advertising 152

Cosby Show, The 111, 113–114, 352

counter-stereotypes 115, 137

courtroom shows 134–135, 221

co-viewing 272, 303, 304, 317, 322

CR (conditioned response) 164, 274

creative play 46–47, 171

credibility 56, 137; advertising 163; crosscutting sources 265; health websites 361; news 193–194, 199, 218, 227

crime 64; distortion of 218–220; the docudrama 211; fear of 217, 220–222; framing of 191; and media liabilities 274–275; perception of 226, 269, 282–283; sexually violent 314–316, 321–322, 328, 333–334; stereotypes 114, 115, 122; effect of television on 276

critical research 25

cross-cultural media research 13

crosscutting media 265–266

cross-media advertising 47

cross-sex friendships 350–351

crowdfunding 372

cultivation 22, 29, 34–36, 37, 42, 55, 56; Latinos 117–118; lawyers 135; news 217, 221; politics 234, 264; sex 320; sexist commercials 105; soap operas 317; socially positive media 370; violence 217, 269, 270, 282–283

cultural anthropology 11, 106

cumulative effects model 28, 34, 35, 291, 292, 358

cyber-bullying 16, 17

dangers 218–219, 221–222

Day After, The (TDA) 52

deceptive advertising 21, 143, 159–163, 173, 304

decision making 157, 187, 214, 217–218, 296

delusional beliefs 35

democracy 74, 202, 204, 223, 225, 235, 237

desensitization 22; emotions 79; group portrayals 102; sex 317, 328, 331, 334, 336; violence 279, 280–282, *281*, 283–284, 286, 294, 296, 297, 299, 300; *see also* sensitization
developing countries 1, 10, 12, 22, 155, 192, 202; socially positive media 360, 363, 366, 373
developmental psychology 59–61
deviance, and novelty 192
dialogue, learning 53–54
diplomacy, and pop music 77–78
direct censorship 204–205
direct effects model 27
direct parental mediation 60
disbelief 51–52, 260, 299
disclaimers 157, 162, 169–170, 370
disinhibition 275, 320–321
disordered eating 98, 99
disorders 28, 58, 63, 78; advertising 181; group portrayals 92, 98, 99, 104, 127–130; news 222–223, 228; violence 280, 291, 298
displacement hypothesis 344
distinctiveness theory 115
distraction effects 50–51
docudramas 211–213
domestic roles, and men 104–105
downward social comparison 98
drama, and conflict 191–192
dread risk 222
drench hypothesis 35–36
driving risks 50–51
dual-screen viewing 214, 235
"Dumbo" 249–250

"earworms" 80
economic pressures 5, 346
educational programming 174, 347, 359
E-E (entertainment-education) media 363–365, 366–367, 368; *see also* prosocial media
effect sizes 31–32, 167, 270, 296, 354
effects, of exposure to media 28, 30, 34; group portrayals 106, 139; sex 319; socially positive media 340; violence 277, 282, 290, 292–293, 298, 300
effects, types of: attitudinal 29; behavioral 22, 28–29, 165–166, 176, 270, 321, 328, 336; cognitive 30; of music 78–80; physiological 30; strength of 31–32, 167, 270, 296, 354; third-person 31, 61, 78, 159, 179, 181, 261, 300, 335
elaboration likelihood model (ELM) 155
election results 145, 239–240, 253, 254
electoral uncertainty, framing 254–255
Electric Company, The (TEC) 346
electronic media 2, 7, 14, 19, 35, 76, 112, 234, 309
elliptical comparative 161
ELM (elaboration likelihood model) 155

e-mail 14, 16, 18, 139; Hillary Clinton 37, 249, 252; North Korean cyber attacks 55; Tiananmen Square massacre 371
embedded advertising 21, 167, 172, 174–178, 367
embedded journalists 206
embedded messages 166, 183
emotional appeals, in product/service advertising 82, 147–151, 156, 170
emotional manipulation 66
emotions 52, 65–72, 102–103; *see also* music; sports
empathy 36, 65, 67–68, 334, 340, 352; and violence 277, 282, 290, 296, 298
encoding, of information 33, 36, 41–42, 158, 159
entertainment 8–9, 14, 22, 36–37; filmed 50; and negative emotions 66; news as 190, 191, 210–212, 226; religion in 130–131, 133; sex/sexuality in 316, 318, 325; television 51, 52, 98, 105, 119, 226, 250; and trials 135; violent 158, 289, 297, 299, 301; and women 102, 329–330; *see also* stereotypes/stereotyping
entertainment media 38, 41, 72, 118, 277
entertainment-education (E-E) media 363–365, 366–367, 368; *see also* prosocial media
environment/environmental intervention 163, 236, 357–358, 359, 360, 363
epidemiological intervention 359
EPPM (extended parallel process model) 221–222
erotica, and aggression 327, 329, 334
ethics, of appeals 154–155
ethnic minorities *see* African Americans; Arab Americans; Arabs; Asian Americans; Latinos; Native Americans
eudaimonic motivation 37, 351
evangelism, television 132–133
explicit memory 158, 176
exposition: issue 258; in stories 40–41, 56–57
exposure, to media 26
extended parallel process model (EPPM) 221–222
extramarital sex 64, 240, 242, 251, 310, 317, 318, 335; American Presidents 241, 242

fabrication 198
Facebook 1, 2, 15, 16, 17, 18, 26, 54; advertising 142, 143, 179; group portrayals 92; news 184, 200, 201–202, 203, 205; politics 235, 259; socially positive media 347
face-to-face (FTF) interaction 4, 16, 17–18, 323
facilitation hypotheses 344
fact-checking websites 202–203, 230
Fahrenheit 9/11 262
faith, people of *see* Christianity; Islam; Judaism
fake news 2, 15, 16, 19, 55, 56, 184; advertising 179; news 198–204, 226, 230; politics 235–236, 244; *see also* photographs, digital alteration of

fake websites 203
families 7, 10, 60–61, 84, 89; African American media 113–114; Arab American media 122; and disabilities 127, 220; media portrayals of 99, 100–101, 104, 105, 106–110; and religion 130–131; and sexual minorities 123; stereotypes 101, 104, 105, 106–110; television reality shows/sitcoms 60, 106–107, 113–114, 117, 122
family life, media influence on 110
family values 122, 139, 270, 317, 319
farmers, and rural life 136
FCC (Federal Communications Commission) 1, 23, 146, 173–174, 339
fear: and advertising 97, 144, 151–152, 156, 258; control of 222; counteracting 221–222; of crime 217, 218–221, 258, 333; irrational 354, 359; and media violence 7, 32, 61, 270–273, 277, 286, 290, 300, 331; and mental illness 128–129; politics 258
Federal Communications Commission (FCC) 1, 23, 146, 173–174, 339
Federal Election Commission 255
Federal Government regulation 173–174
Federal Trade Commission (FTC) 159, 173–174, 183
females *see* women
feminist theory 336
film censorship 309–310
film sanitizers 314
films: rape in Indian 329–330; scary 272–273; slasher 329–332
fMRI (functional magnetic resonance imaging) 30, 67, 157, 273, 295–296, 351
food stylists 160
forensic science shows, and jury verdicts 134
Fox 14, 180, 182, 231, 243, 264, 266, 310; and news 187, 201, 209, 219, 225
"Frail Criminal", the 248–249
framing 38, 147, 156, 162, 191, 192, 214; politics 232, 246–247, 248–250, 254–255
Frasier 51, 135, 136
friendships: male 104; online 18; teenager 350–351
FTC Federal Trade Commission) 159, 173–174, 183
FTF (face-to-face) interaction 4, 16, 17–18, 323
functional magnetic resonance imaging (fMRI) 30, 67, 157, 273, 295–296, 351
future market, for children 167, 168

gamification 356–357
gender 21, 24, 31, 44; advertising 170–171; emotions 77, 88–90; sex 328, 331, 333; socially positive media 342; violence 281, 287, 290
gender equality 363, 365
gender portrayals 93–105

gender stereotyping 65, 105–106, 114, 124, 137, 312, 319
General Aggression Model 290, 291
genetic optimism 228
girls 8, 24, 34, 171, 334, 348, 356; and disordered eating 98; and emotions 65, 71, 77, 89, 90; and feminism 108; portrayal of 92, 95, 103, 138, 139–140; role models for 100; sexualizing 96; and stereotypes 100, 114; and violence 269, 287, 290, 292, 293
Gore, Vice-President Al 38, 241, 249–250, 253–255
government policy 223
graphic violence, and sensitization 277–280
gratifications theory 36–37
green advertising 163
grievance terrorism 226
group portrayals 92–141

hard news 188, 189, 190, 192–193, 210
Harry Potter, teen friendships in 350–351
Hays Code 309–310
health promotion 20, 356–357, 360
hedonic motivation 36–37, 351
hedge words 161
helping professions 135–136
heroes 21, 85–86
high-tech billboards 174
Hispanic Americans 111, 116–118, *116*, 138, 150–151, 259
HIV/AIDS 38, 78, 123; news 193, 196, 219; sex 318, 324; socially positive media 360, 361–363, 364, 365, 368
hostility 78, 120, 291, 295, 340
host-selling 169
Hum Log 365
human interest stories 189, 210
humor 62, 64, 66, 69–72, 82, 87; advertising 176; group portrayals 108, 126, 128, 135, 136; politics 244; sex 310, 317, 331; socially positive media 341–342, 348, 350, 352, 367; violence 286, 287–288
humorous appeals 153, 156, 157
hypertextuality 16, 20
hypodermic model 27

IAMs (Involuntary Musical Imagery) 80
identification 53–54, 115
IGA (in-game advertising) 175, 283
image 22, 145, 241, 257–258
imagination/imaginative play 46–47, 171, 344
implicit memory 47, 158
implied slur 161
inattentional blindness 49–50, 61
incest 40
incongruity (humor model) 69

India: film rape scenes 329–330; socially positive media 363, 364–365
indirect censorship 206
influence market, for children 167
influence of presumed influence model 31
information processing 33, 38–39, 41, 42, 47, 77, 323; and advertising 157–158, 161
informational appeals 146–147
informational programming, for children 174, 347
in-game advertising (IGA) 175, 283
inhibition hypotheses 344
inoffensiveness 193
Instagram 2, 4, 17, 140
instant messaging 14, 16, 17–18
institutional terrorism 226
international product names, choosing 148–149
Internet: and advertising 142–143, 157, 178–179, 180; characteristics of 14, 15, 16, 20, 50, 156–157; children's use of 46; effects of 2–3, 14, 369; and health information 361; and international media boundaries 93; and music 74; origins of 14; and politics 235–236, 263; and religion 132; and sex 306, 307–308, 309, 319, 320; and social movements 372; use of 2, 7, 17, 18, 31, 47, 179, 235–236, 263
Internet news 8, 36, 47, 85, 187, 189, 210, 232
interpersonal communication 3, 4, 15, 16, 369
interrater reliability 26
intimidation 205
Involuntary Musical Imagery (IAMs) 80
Iran hostage crisis 195
Iraq, wars in 15, 76, 121, 149; news 195, 206, 208, 211, 212, 215, 223, 225; politics 237, 248, 252; violence 278, 280
Islam: emotions 74, 75; groups 92, 119, 120–122, 130; news 184, 186, 193, 195, 215–216, 226; politics 249, 260–261; sex 325; violence 278

Japan, pornography in 321–322
Judaism 93, 121, 124, 131, 132, 156, 214, 215
Judeo-Christian faith 120
juror verdicts 134, 218, 331
juxtaposition of two imperatives technique 161

Kennedy, President John F. 187, 224, 233, 242, 245

Latinos 111, 116–118, *116*, 138, 150–151, 259
Law and Order 111, 135, 366, 368
LC4MP (limited capacity model) 41–42, 56
leisure 2, 72
lesbian, gay, bisexual, transgender (LGBT) 122, 124, 306–307, 310–311, 345, 369
Levitin, Daniel 199
LGBT (lesbian, gay, bisexual, transgender) 122, 124, 306–307, 310–311, 345, 369

liberal theory 335–336
limited capacity model (LC4MP) 41–42, 56
linearity 32
lines, learning 53–54
linguistic constructions 161
literacy 9, 46; adult 363; children's 273, 348; financial 364; media *see* media literacy; and pornography 338; quantitative 221; scientific 229; visual 20
local hook 194–197
loneliness 17, 18, 75
longitudinal studies, of media violence 291–293
lyrics, music 76, 78, 79, 311, 335

magazines 7, 8, 97, 103, 108; and advertising 142, 144, 172, 186, 207, 354; and news as entertainment 190, 210; and personalization 190; and satire 260–261; and sex 308
mainstream movies, sex and violence in 329–330
mainstreaming 34–35
majority world 1, 10, 12, 22, 155, 192, 202; socially positive media 360, 363, 366, 373
male friendships 104
males 53, 77, 94–95, 102–106, 108, 114
manipulation 66, 100; of news 204–208
many-to-many asynchronous communication 16
marijuana use 27
marketing 11, 25, 90, 101; and advertising 143; and boycotts 182; captive 178; to children 167; and complaints 139–140; and docudramas 212; and emotional appeals 149, 150; and fear appeals 152; to Latinos 150; of personal hygiene products 144–145; and product endorsements 154; and product placements 176; and schools 177–178; social 352–365, 368–369; and stereotypes 137, 139; and television viewership research 180; and testimonials 154; and tobacco 172; of toys 170–171
marketing creations 144–145
mass communication: definition of 3–7; media of 7–18; prevalence of 2–3; theories of 33–42
media: and body image 20, 38, 98–99, 104, 139; broadcast *see* broadcast media; crime coverage in *see* crime; crosscutting 265–266; electronic 2, 7, 14, 19, 35, 76, 112, 234, 309; and emotional expression 65–72; entertainment 38, 41, 72, 118, 277; and family life 110; and government policy 223; mass 3, 4, 26, 39–40, 143, 326, 353, 360, 371; nonlinear 16, 20; personal 14, 371; polarized 264–266; print *see* print media; prosocial *see* prosocial media; sexual *see* sexual media; and social marketing *see* social marketing; socially positive *see* socially positive media; traditional 4, 8, 197–198, 236; as vicarious emotional experience 64–65

media attention 85, 220, 223, 237, 242, 247, 249, 358–359
media campaigns 154–155, 232, 257–258, 318, 340, 358; public health 359–363, 364, 368–369
media cognition 48–54
media consumption 6–7, 30, 64, 264, 265, 373; sexual 313; sports 84–87, 89; violent 277, 291
media content 5, 19
media education 19
media experience 34, 37, 48–54, 59, 87–88, 291
media grammar literacy 19
media literacy 19–20, 23, 43; and children 167, 173, 302–304, 343; and consumer education 162; and pornography 336; and the school curriculum 42, 43
media memories, fearful 272–273
media modalities 47, 95, 155
media news *see* news media
media ratings 6, 23, 302, 309–310
media relationships, parasocial 57–59, 188, 366
media research 13, 25–32, 42–43, 228–229
media self-censorship 207–208
media sensationalism 219, 220–223
media sex/media sexual content *see* sexual media
media stereotypes 55, 92–141
media values, and substance abuse 367
media violence 22, 25, 31, 55, 65, 227, 268–305; and amnesia 283; attraction to 289–291; brain correlates of 273; and catharsis 288–289; and children 301–302; criminal liability for 274–275; cultivation effects of 282–283; desensitization to 280–282; effects of 270–273; longitudinal studies of 291–293; and modeling 273–277; moderating variables for 283–288; public perception versus research 298–300; sensitization to 277–280
mediated communication 4; *see also* computer-mediated communication (CMC)
mediation: and media literacy training 302–304; parental 6, 60, 298
memory 15, 34, 36; and active experiencing 54; for advertisements 153, 157, 158–159; and construction 159; and elaboration likelihood model 155; explicit 158, 176; and humor 153; and identification 53; implicit 47; and information extraction 47; and information processing model 157–158; and modeling 274; multilevel model of 353; and music 79–80; for the news 216–217; and product placements 176; for public events 15; and retrograde amnesia 283; and schemas/scripts 38, 40, 41; and true-but-deceptive advertisements 161
memory-based cognitive processing 234
men 53, 77, 94–95, 102–106, 108, 114
mental effort, and social interaction 46

mental illness 28, 58, 63, 78; advertising 181; group portrayals 92, 98, 99, 104, 127–130; news 222–223, 228; stereotypes 128–130; violence 280, 291, 298
mental schemas 38, 161
metaphors, "war" 185–186
Mexican Americans 111, 116–118, *116*, 138, 150–151, 259
"Militant Black Couple", the 249
minorities, ethnic 11; African Americans *see* African Americans; Arab Americans and Arabs 120–122; Asian Americans 21, *116*, 119–120, 151; Latinos 111, 116–118, *116*, 138, 150–151, 259; Native Americans 118
minorities, sexual 122–125
minority portrayal, four stages of 110–111
model minority 119–120
modeling 33–34, 42, 97, 105, 221, 317, 342, 348; violence 273–277, 284, 285, 286, 287, 288–289, 297
moderation effect 264–266
Modern Family 36, 369; group portrayals 102–103, 108, 109, 117, 123, 130–131, 136
mood 53, 158, 162, 217; emotions 62, 63–64, 67, 72, 75, 78
moral assessment 70
motherhood/mothers 99, 100–101, 107–108, 147, 178
motion picture associations (MPAA and MPPDA) 6, 23, 309–310
movie censorship 309–310
movie sanitizers 314
movies, scary 272–273
MPAA and MPPDA (motion picture associations) 6, 23, 309–310
MSNBC 187, 210, 231, 243, 264, 266
MTV (Music Television) 73, 318, 363–364, 370
multimedia 15, 133, 360, 361–362
multitasking 48–49, 50–51, 157, 235
music 8–9, 21, 27, 64, 65, 72–80, 87–88, 147; and backmasking 166, 183; embedded messages in 166, 183; as threat 75–76; as torture 76
music lyrics 76, 78, 79, 311, 335
Music Television (MTV) 73, 318, 363–364, 370
music videos 73, 76, 77, 95, 269, 335, 342
Muslims *see* Islam

name recognition 149, 251, 256
Namibia, radio in 9
narrative 40–41, 52, 56–57, 189
National Broadcasting Company (NBC) *see* NBC (National Broadcasting Company)
native advertising 162
Native Americans 118
NBC (National Broadcasting Company) 1, 5, 14, 69, 83, 275, 310, 366; and advertising 150, 152,

175, 182; and group portrayals 122, 126; and news 188, 198, 199, 206, 207, 209, 211, 225, 228–229; and politics 236, 244, 261, 266
negative advertising 22, 259–262
negative emotions 66, 277, 295
Netflix 36, 106, 124, 126, 305, 342, 349
new media 4, 7, 233–234; *see also* fake news; magazines; newspapers; radio; television
news 184–230; and advertising 5; and African Americans 114–115; and comedy shows 210–211; and elections 231, 236–263; fake *see* fake news; as entertainment 4; hard 188, 189–197, 210; and human interest stories 189, 210; Internet 8, 36, 47, 85, 187, 189, 210, 232; manipulation of 204–213; memory for 47, 216–217; and Native Americans 118; and parental mediation 304; and perceived reality/reality 21–22, 197–198; and political campaigns/politics 231, 236–263; and reality/perceived reality 21–22, 197–198; and religion 131–133; and sexual matters 314–316, 334; and sexual minorities 124–125; and social media 15; soft 189, 210; television 125, 187–188, 216, 217, 221, 223, 240, 304, 333; and Donald Trump presidency 93; and violence 274, 277–279, 281–282, 286, 298; and women 95, 101–102
news anchors 89, 95, 188, 342
news embargoes 208
news images, extremely violent 277–279
news media *see* news
news media organizations, consolidation of 8, 208–210
news reporters, as newsmakers 197–198
newspapers 3–4, 7–8, 142, 144, 182, 194, 209
newsworthy events 189–197, 227, 232–233
Nielsen ratings 25
Nixon, President Richard 191, 193, 207, 208, 332, 341; and politics 234, 245, 247
non-hedonic motivation 37, 351
nonlinear media 16, 20
nonsexual media 307
nonviolent sexual material 308
normative deviance 192
normative theories, of pornography 335–336
North Korean cinema 54–55
novelty, and deviance 192
nuclear war drama 52

objectification 103, 105–106, 319–320
observational learning 33–34, 42, 97, 105, 221, 317, 342, 348; violence 273–277, 284, 285, 286, 287, 288–289, 297
occupations, stereotyping of 119, 133–137
O. J. Simpson 154, 196–197, 211
older adults 17, 37, 79, 293; stereotyping of 125–127

Olympics 69, 80, 82–84, 88–89, 90, 152, 354, 372
on-demand cable services 14
one-to-one asynchronous communication 16
ongoing themes, of hard news 192–193
online advertising 155, 178–180, 200–201, 263
online cognitive processing 234
online friendships/online relationships 18
online streaming 2, 9, 12, 14, 36, 75, 180, 349; and group portrayals 94, 116, 120, 129; and sex 309, 314; and violence 301, 302, 305
onscreen reading hypothesis 13, 344
operant conditioning 284, 294
operational definitions, and content analysis 26, 268

packet switching 16
parasocial interaction 57, 58, 59, 67, 188, 230; *see also* social interaction
parasocial media relationships 57–59, 67, 188, 230, 366
Parent teacher Association (PTA), national 182
parental mediation 6, 60, 298
passivity hypothesis 46–47, 344
patriotic appeals 144, 151, 156
Pavlov, Ivan 164
PBS (Public Broadcasting Service) *see* Public Broadcasting Service (PBS)
perceived reality 21, 36, 45, 54–57, 59; and advertising 143, 159, 164, 165, 181; and emotions 80, 81, 85, 88; and group portrayals 93, 120, 133, 138; and news 185, 187, 197–213, 223, 226–227; and politics 256, 263, 264; and sex 306, 312, 317, 320, 324, 334; and socially positive media 358, 359, 369, 373; and violence 270, 277, 282, 285–286, 304
personal hygiene products 144–145
personal media 14, 371
personality development 303; *see also* social learning
personalization 190–191
persuasion 21, 144, 152, 153–154, 155, 182, 259; subliminal 164, 165; *see also* advertising
photographs, digital alteration of 15; *see also* fake news
physical appearance 18, 95–99, 103–104, 333
physical barriers 127
physical disabilities 127
physiological effects 30
Piaget, Jean 59–60, 271
piecemeal comparison 162
"Pinocchio" 249–250
plagiarism 198
polarized media 264–266
political advertising 22, 38, 146, 234, 255–263
political attitudes 214, 247–248, 262, 264–266

political behavior, on the Internet 235–236
political candidate debates 245–247
political candidates 22, 35, 47, 231, 235, 245–255;
    psychological distance from voters 233–234;
    see also Presidential elections, 2016; Presidential
    elections, other
political media, cognitive processing of 234–235
political opponents, attacks from 251–253
political participation 214, 235
politics 231–266
popular culture 19, 61, 93, 133, 153,
    213, 371; and emotions 63, 65, 71, 73;
    internationalization of 39
popular music 21, 72–80, 88, 363; African 74
pornography 306–308, 312, 319, 323, 325,
    328–329, 338; and changing media landscape
    6, 16, 22; child 16, 32, 96, 152, 193, 308, 323;
    group portrayals 102; Internet 31, 307, 309; in
    Japan 321–322; and the news 227; normative
    theories of 335–336; and psychology of mass
    communication 54; and research and theory
    in mass communication 30, 31, 32, 37; and
    violence 275
pornography commissions 332–333
positive psychology 351–352
power appeals 152–153, 156
prejudices 29, 79, 196, 260–261; and group
    portrayals 112, 114, 115, 120, 122, 124, 127, 129
premarital sex 310, 316, 317, 318, 320–321
pre-roll advertising 179
prescription drug advertising 21, 126, 180–181
Presidential elections (2016): and cable news
    ratings 187; and candidates 47, 231, 248–249;
    and fake news 2, 184, 198, 200–201, 202; and
    the Internet 235; and name recognition 256;
    partisan coverage of 190; and patriotic appeals
    151; and polling 238, 239; and talk shows 188,
    210–211; and trust in news media 199
Presidential elections (others) 38, 45, 145, 194, 249,
    253–255, 263
press interpretation 241–245
prime-time programs 268, 319
print media 38, 46, 128, 231, 240, 278, 299, 309;
    changing media landscape 2, 7, 8, 9, 20
product endorsement 86, 153–154, 259, 363
product names, choosing international 148–149
product placements 21, 167, 172, 174–178, 367
prosocial media 57, 339–373; see also
    entertainment-education (E-E) media
prosocial television 22, 340–352
PSAs (public service announcements) see public
    service announcements (PSAs)
pseudo-events, created for political purposes 251
psychiatrists 135–136
psychological appeals 21, 143, 146–154

psychological disabilities/disorders see mental
    illness
psychologists 135–136
PTA (Parent teacher Association), national 182
Public Broadcasting Service (PBS) 4, 39, 106–107,
    224; socially positive media 340–341, 342, 343,
    346–347, 348
public health media campaigns 359–363, 368
public opinion polling, and election results
    239–240
public service announcements (PSAs) 5, 22, 30; as
    advertising 146, 153; and emotions 78; and news
    221, 222; socially positive media 354, 355,
    357–358, 359, 361–362, 363, 366, 369, 370

racial bias/racism 71, 79, 90, 193, 204, 270, 350;
    and group portrayals 113, 114, 124
radio 8–9, 47, 216, 264, 266, 311; and advertising
    145, 153, 165; in Namibia 9
Radio Sawa 77–78, 91
rape: in Indian films 329–330; myths of 282,
    328–329, 331–332, 333, 334, 337
ratings 5, 6, 25, 136, 174, 186, 309–310; and news
    211, 226; and violence 302, 305
reading, and television 344, 346–347
reading depreciation hypothesis 344
Reagan, President Ronald 29, 45, 58, 173, 195, 208,
    332; and politics 233, 239, 245, 247, 256, 259
reality: controlling 54–55; perceived see perceived
    reality
reality shows 35, 99, 106–107, 114, 352, 370–371
reception approach, to studying suspense 68
Reefer Madness 27
reflection myth 54–55
regulation (of industries) 16, 146, 155, 173–174,
    300, 309, 336
regulation (minority portrayal stage) 111
reinforcement, and justification of violence
    284–285
relationships, online 18
relative risk appraisal 222
religion/religious programming 38, 71, 130–133,
    141, 345; see also Christianity; Islam; Judaism
research: administrative 25; behavioral 16, 227,
    301; comparative media 13; critical 25;
    cross-cultural media 13; in mass communication
    11, 13, 15, 24–32, 42–43; social-psychological
    152, 153–154, 276–277, 357; see also content
    analysis; effect sizes; interrater reliability;
    longitudinal studies, of media violence
research methodologies 15, 20–21
resolution (humor model) 69
resolution (of stories) 40–41, 56–57
restrictive mediation 303, 304
retrieval, of information 41, 79, 157, 158, 159

retrograde amnesia 283
revenge porn 323
rock music, satanic messages in 166
role modeling 100, 107, 114, 115, 171–174, 270, 356, 365
romance 8, 62, 110, 123, 228–229, 325–326, 351
Roots 113
rural life 136

same-sex marriage 125, 348, 374n1
satanic messages, in rock music 166
Saturday Night Live 94, 188, 237, 261
scary movies 272–273
schema/script theory 56, 77, 138, 257–258, 287, 319; and advertising 159, 161, 181; research and theory 38–41, 42
schools 42–43, 177–178
science shows, for children 348
script/schema theory *see* schema/script theory
scripts, narrative 40–41, 56–57
second screening 214, 235
self-censorship, media 207–208
self-disclosure, on social media 17, 18
seniors 17, 37, 79, 293; stereotyping of 125–127
sensation seeking 49, 291, 298, 303, 312, 323
sensationalism/sensationalized reporting 219, 222–223
sensitization 277–280, *281*, 289, 337; *see also* desensitization
serious sex, versus comedic sex 318
Sesame Street 22, 46, 71, 171, 174, 374n1; and group portrayals 94, 115, 121; and socially positive media 339, 341–346, 348, 373
setup (humor model) 69
sex 7, 11, 22, 62, 306–338; and advertising 164, 182; casual 38; and catharsis 70, 288; and college students 137; comedic 318; extramarital 64, 240, 242, 251, 310, 317, 318, 335; and food 97; and media literacy 19, 20; and older adults 125, 126; and popular music 73, 76, 77; and professional boundaries 135; and ratings 6, 302; and seniors 125; serious 318; and *Shuga* 364–365; and subliminal advertising 163–164, 165; and violence 6, 32, 113–114, 301; and weight loss 97
sex crimes 321–322, 333
sex scandals 113, 154, 194, 241, 315
sexes, portrayals of the 105–106; men 102–105; women 77, 93–102, 108, 117, 138–139
"sexting" 306, 315, 323
sexual appeals 143, 144, 156, 157, 163–164
sexual arousal 30, 164
sexual assault 113, 218, 234, 321, 322, 337
sexual behavior, promiscuous 34
sexual content, in the media 309–310, 313
sexual harassment 137, 182, 194, 198, 234

sexual humor 70, 71
sexual media: and adolescents and children 311–312; and advertising 313; behavioral and cognitive effects of 319, 320–324; definition of 307–308; history of 308–310; and movie censorship 309–310; negative effects of 336–338; positive effects of 324
sexual minorities 122–125, 350
sexual pervert stereotype 120–121
sexual self-concepts 105
sexual violence 29, 40, 275, 282, 287, 301; and male viewers 327–328; negative effects of 336–338
sexuality 40, 89
sexualization 8, 95–99, 140
sexually transmitted infection (STI) 27, 270, 318, 361–363, 364
sexually violent crimes, press coverage of 314–316, 333–334
Shuga 363–364, 364–365
Simpson, O. J. 154, 196–197, 211
Simpsons, The 102–103, 108, 109, 123, 131, 133, 154
Skype 16
slasher films 329–332
slavery 113, 121, 232
slogans 148–149
Snapchat 17, 323
soap operas 9, 38, 39, 40, 41, 51, 56, 57, 64; and group portrayals 113, 127; and sex 317, 324, 335; as socially positive media 363–364, 366, 368, 373
social change 192, 371–373
social cognitive theory 28, 33–34, 42, 44, 55–56, 300
social interaction 4, 15, 46; *see also* parasocial interaction
social isolation 17, 18, 75
social learning 33–34, 42, 97, 105, 221, 317, 342, 348; violence 273–277, 284, 285, 286, 287, 288–289, 297
social learning theory 33, 295
social marketing 22, 340, 352–363, 368–369
social media 1, 2, 4, 14, 16, 17, 19, 30, 37, 46, 140, 278, 323; and advertising 142, 144, 167, 169, 179; and news 184, 188, 189, 192, 194, 200, 201–202, 203, 204, 214, 217, 221; and politics 231, 232, 233, 234, 235–236, 248, 255, 257, 263; socially positive 360, 361, 362, 371, 372
social networking 14, 17, 18
social psychology: and appeals 357; and media violence 276; and persuasion 152, 153–154; and political advertising 262; and romance 326; and satire 260–261; and social comparison theory 98; and social learning theory 33; and third-person effect 31
social realism 56, 57

social science 13, 24, 227, 228
social statement, advertising as 156
socialization 8, 21, 322; of adolescent behavior 322; gender 90, 281, 290; political 37; positive effects of 324; and sexuality 22; into subcultures 75; into television use 40
socially positive media 57, 339–373; *see also* entertainment education
soft news 189, 210
Soul City 364, 366
sound bites 132, 194
South Park 94, 123, 131
spoilers 68–69
sports 80–91
sports violence 21, 85
statistical deviance 192
stereotypes/stereotyping: African American 110, 112, 115, 217, 232, 246, 258; Arab American and Arab 120–122; Asian American 119–120; crime 114, 115, 122; family 101, 104, 105, 106–110; gender 65, 105–106, 114, 124, 137, 312, 319; Native American 118; of occupations 119, 133–137; older adult 125–127; physical disability 127; psychological disorder 128–130; of seniors 125–127; sexual minority 122; sexual pervert 120–121
STI (sexually transmitted infection) 27, 270, 318, 361–363, 364
storage, of information 36, 41
subliminal activity 21, 27, 143, 163–164, 164–166, 227
subliminal television intoxication 274
substance abuse, and media values 367
subtitles 13
supercrip image 127
superheroes, and health promotion 356–357
supermarket tabloids 190
superwoman myth 105, 107–108
suspending disbelief 52
suspense 36, 52, 53, 66, 68–69, 72, 82, 87–88
synchronicity 16, 65–66

talk shows 9, 66, 132, 176, 244, 250, 263; and the news 188, 207, 210
TDA (The Day After) 52
TEC (The Electric Company) 346
teenagers 350–351
Telecommunications Act (1996) 301
telegenic factor, the 81
telenovelas *see* soap operas
televangelism 132–133
Televisa, and its descendants 39, 363–364
television 2, 3, 6–7, 10–12, 14, 62, 92, 142, 184; and advertising (non-political) 4, 5, 12, 142, 155, 168–169, 180; and African Americans 111,

112, 113, 116; and aggression 297–298, 300; and Arabs 120, 121; and Asian Americans 119, 120; and cartoons 114; and children 45–46, 168–169, 286, 292, 297–298; and college students 137; and creativity 46–47; and criminal behavior 292; and cultivation theory 34, 35, 36, 234, 240–241, 282–283; and disclaimers 170; and drench hypothesis 35–36; and emotions 67–68, 86–87; and families 107, 109; and farmers 136; and image building 257; and imaginative play 46–47; and information extraction 47; Internet 12; and Latinos 117, 118; and minorities 110; moderation effect of 264–265; and mothers 107; and multitasking 48–49; and music videos 73; and Native Americans 118; and news *see* television news; and occupations 133–134; and older adults 125, 126; and the Olympics 69, 80, 82–84; physiological effects of 30; and political advertising 257, 263; and politics 233, 234, 245–247, 264; prosocial 339–352; psychological effects of 24–25, 59–61, 271; and psychotherapy 136; and racism 115; and reading 344, 346–347; and religion 130, 131, 132–133; and school curricula 42–43; and sex 138, 306, 309, 322; and sexual minorities 122–125; social reality of 57, 370; and socially positive media 339–352; societal interaction with 11; and sports 80–84, 88–90; and subtitling 13; and suspension of disbelief 51–52; and toys 170, 171; and trials 135; and values 24; and the "V-chip" 301; and violent content 268–269, 274–275, 276, 278–279, 297–298, 300; and women 94, 95, 96, 102; and the workplace 109
television content ratings 302, 305
television news 125, 216, 217, 221, 223, 240, 304, 333; history and trends 187–188
television programming 10, 25, 39, 111, 132, 173, 339, 340–341
television viewing 10, 11–12, 17, 58, 264
terrorism 1, 15, 64, 130, 151, 197, 225–226; and anxiety disorder symptoms 222–223; and disturbed dreaming 216–217; grievance 226; and group portrayals 120, 121–122; institutional 226; memories of 216; and politics 236, 247, 249, 250, 255, 260–261; and post-traumatic stress disorder symptoms 222–223; and public relations risk 212; radical Islamist 192, 193, 215; and sensationalized reporting 220; and victimization risk 221; and violence 271, 277, 278, 294; and "war" metaphors 185–186
testimonials 86, 153–154, 259, 363
texting 16, 17, 18, 50
The Electric Company (TEC) 346
third world 1, 10, 12, 22, 155, 192, 202; socially positive media 360, 363, 366, 373

third-person effect 31
time compression 158
time shifting 11
tobacco advertising 155, 171–173
Tonight Show, The 188, 211, 250
toymakers 170–171
traditional media 4, 8, 197–198, 236
trait fantasy empathy 67
trait hostility 78, 120, 291, 295, 340
transportation 52–53, 144, 172, 219
"trial balloon" 207
true-but-deceptive advertising 161–162
Truman Show, The 35
Trump, President Donald 4, 71, 117, 316; and news 190, 192, 194, 197, 198, 201, 204, 210; and his electoral campaigning 237, 238, 241, 243–244, 245, 247, 248–249, 256; and his electoral victory 235; and his extramarital affairs 242; media framing of 248–249; and pseudo-events 251; and public-private barrier 234; and his use of social media and television 233; *see also* tweeting/ Twitter
tweeting/Twitter 1, 2, 4, 7, 15, 16, 17, 18, 194; and advertising 143; and the Arab Spring 200; and censorship 205; and fake news 201–202, 203, 235–236; and political candidates 47; and Saudi Arabia 92; and "sexting" 315; and Donald Trump 194, 199, 231, 233, 235–236, 243, 244, 261; and unfiltered news 200

unconditioned response/unconditioned stimulus (UCR and UCS) 29, 164
uniform effects, theory of 27, 99, 286
United Colors of Benetton 156
unknown risks 222
"Unstable Rebel", the 248–249
upward social comparison 98
uses and gratifications 36–37, 74–76

values: aggressive 297; and alcohol abuse 367; antisocial 304; consumerist 156; family 60, 122, 139, 270; media transmission of 155; negative 31, 139; positive 24; and reality shows 371; and romance 326; sexual 22, 312, 314–320; social 88; societal 54, 55, 367; and substance abuse 367; traditional 109; and use of violence 285
"V-chip" 300, 301
VCR (videocassette recorder) 10, 12, 14, 371
vicarious emotional experience, media as 64–65
video cassette recorder (VCR) 10, 12, 14, 371
video games 32, 53, 65, 95, 105, 182, 273; and advertising 158, 167, 171, 175; behavioral effects of 340, 356–357; elevation effects of 352; and sexual violence 337; and violence *see* violent video games

video news releases (VNRs) 209–210
Vietnam War, media coverage of 1, 205, 206, 224–225, 278, 279–280
viewer characteristics 286–287
violence/violent media: and ratings 6; and women 139, 273, 282, 288, 290, 292, 293, 317; *see also* media violence; sexual violence; violent video games
violent news images, extremely 278–279
violent video games 22, 30, 270, 286, 287, 293–296, 299; and advertisements 283; played as anti-hero character 285; and behavioral research 301; and empathy 290; and fMRI studies of 273; and hostility 291; and 'justified' violence 285; and lawsuits 275; played in presence of parents or peers 302–303; sensation seeking 291; and shooting 276, 298; and third-person effect 300; played as violent hero 285
VNRs (video news releases) 209–210
voters, psychological distance from political candidates 233–234

war 294–295; *see also* Vietnam War, media coverage of
"war" metaphors 185–186
watchdogs 173, 182
Weaponized Lies: How to Think Critically in the Post-Truth Era 199
"Weeping Woman", the 249
weight loss 97, 159–160, 356
well-being 17, 149, 188, 219, 351, 352–353
White Americans 116, *116*, 122, 151, 276
Wikipedia 14, 205
Will and Grace 36, 117, 123, 124, 226, 369
women: Arab 121; and advertising 50, 71, 144, 147, 152, 313, 318; in bikinis 323–324; and "earworms" 80; and emotional appeals 147; and friendships 18, 104; and identification 53; in India 365; effects of media on 28, 34; and music videos 76; older adult 126; portrayal of 94–102, 304, 333; and sexual media 312, 313–314, 319–320; and sexual violence 216, 218, 244, 317, 319, 327–332, 334–335, 336, 337; stereotyping of 21, 77, 137, 138–139; as superwoman 107–108; and violence 139, 273, 282, 288, 290, 292, 293, 317
women's bodies, and advertising 97, 98–99
women's magazines 5, 8
women's sports 83, 88–89, 90
working memory 283
workplace solidarity 109
World Wide Web 1, 14

YouTube 14, 74, 140, 167, 179; and news 201, 205; parental controls 301, 305; and politics 233, 241; and pornography 307

1st

2 EX

3